HENRY I

The first biography to offer a fully rounded treatment of the life of Henry I, the youngest son of William the Conqueror, this book presents a major new interpretation of the man and his methods. Judith Green argues that although Henry's primary concern was defence of his inheritance this did not preclude expansion where circumstances were propitious, notably into Welsh territory. His skilful dealings with the Scots permitted consolidation of Norman rule in the northern counties of England, while in Normandy every sinew was strained to defend frontiers through political alliances and stone castles. Green argues that although Henry's own outlook was essentially traditional, the legacy of this fascinating but ruthless personality included some significant developments in governance. The book also offers a fresh perspective of Henry's court, which, it is suggested, made an important contribution to the flowering of court culture throughout twelfth-century Europe.

JUDITH A. GREEN is Professor of Medieval History at the University of Edinburgh. She is the author of *The Government of England under Henry I* (1986) and *The Aristocracy of Norman England* (1997) and a Fellow of the Royal Historical Society.

Frontispiece. The visions seen by King Henry I in a dream in Normandy, 1130. *Worcester Chronicle*, twelfth century. Corpus Christi College, Oxford/The Bridgeman Art Library.

HENRY I

King of England and Duke of Normandy

JUDITH A. GREEN

CAMBRIDGE
UNIVERSITY PRESS

CAMBRIDGE UNIVERSITY PRESS
Cambridge, New York, Melbourne, Madrid, Cape Town, Singapore, São Paulo

Cambridge University Press
The Edinburgh Building, Cambridge CB2 8RU, UK

Published in the United States of America by Cambridge University Press, New York

www.cambridge.org
Information on this title: www.cambridge.org/9780521591317

© Judith Green 2006

This publication is in copyright. Subject to statutory exception
and to the provisions of relevant collective licensing agreements,
no reproduction of any part may take place without
the written permission of Cambridge University Press.

First published 2006
Reprinted 2007

Printed in the United Kingdom at the University Press, Cambridge

A catalogue record for this publication is available from the British Library

ISBN 978-0-521-59131-7 hardback

Cambridge University Press has no responsibility for the persistence or accuracy of URLs for external or third-party internet websites referred to in this book, and does not guarantee that any content on such websites is, or will remain, accurate or appropriate.

Contents

Preface		*page* vii
List of abbreviations		ix
	Introduction: A surfeit of lampreys	1
1	'Born in the purple'	20
2	'By the grace of God, king of the English'	42
3	Testing times, 1101–1103	60
4	The conquest of Normandy, 1104–1107	78
5	Reform and reconstruction, 1107–1108	96
6	Defence of his dominions, 1108–1115	118
7	Triumph and disaster, 1116–1120	138
8	Surviving the wreck, 1120–1124	168
9	Matilda and the succession, 1125–1128	190
10	Rescuing the marriage, 1129–1135	206
11	The ruler	224
12	'Guardian of the church'	254
13	Court and court culture	284
	Conclusion: 'Once the peace and glory of the world'	307
	Appendix I: Inheritances and family trees	322
	1. The family of Henry I	322
	2. The illegitimate children of Henry I	323
	3. The family of Queen Matilda	324

4.	Claimants to the honour of Breteuil	325
5.	The counts of Evreux	326
6.	Claims to the county of Flanders in 1128	327
7.	The Capetian kings	328
8.	The dynasty of Powys	329
9.	Robert de Bellême and his family	330

Appendix II: Maps 331

1.	Normandy in the early twelfth century	331
2.	Western Normandy	332
3.	The southern marches of Normandy	333
4.	Evreux and the valley of the river Eure	334
5.	The Vexin	335
6.	Barfleur	336
7.	The midlands and southern England	337
8.	Northern England and southern Scotland	338
9.	Wales in the early twelfth century	339

Bibliography 340
Index 372

Preface

It is a great pleasure to be able to express in some small way my gratitude to those who have in different ways rendered assistance during the years that this book has been in preparation. Many have advised on particular problems, from sailing at Barfleur to lampreys, or sent copies of their own work, often at short notice and sometimes in advance of publication, and to all I am most grateful, especially Mathieu Arnoux, Robert Babcock, David Bates, Marjorie Chibnall, David Crouch, Elizabeth Danbury, Alistair Fair, Jim Holt, Peter Jupp, Katherine Keats-Rohan, Edmund King, Andrew McDonald, Evelyn Mullally, Bruce O'Brien, Daniel Power, Richard Sharpe, Keith Stringer, Kathleen Thompson and Liesbeth Van Houts. The late Warren Hollister, with characteristic generosity, shared his deep knowledge of Henry I with me on several memorable occasions.

Particular thanks are owed to staff at Queen's University Belfast, especially the Inter-Library Loans librarian Florence Gray, and Computing Services, especially James Jackson. At Caen M. Claude Lorren, Director of the Centre de Recherches Archéologiques et Historiques Médiévales, Université de Caen Basse Normandie, and his colleagues, made my visit in December 2001 especially productive. Without the assistance and continuing friendship of Pierre Bauduin and Véronique Gazeau my knowledge of ducal Normandy and its archives would have been materially impoverished. Likewise thanks to members of faculty at Boston College, in particular Robin Fleming and her students, during an exchange visit in fall 2000; to Lindy Grant at the Conway Library, Courtauld Institute, University of London, for help and advice over architectural matters; to M. Emmanuel Poulle at the Ecole des Chartes, Paris, for a helpful discussion of the abbey of Savigny and its records; to Ivan Nelson, who, first as an undergraduate and then more recently, has advised me from first-hand experience of the hazards of sailing round the coasts near Barfleur; to Steve Flanders, for many invigorating discussions about early twelfth-century politics, and for his help with the genealogical tables; to Richard Sharpe and his colleagues at the Anglo-Norman Acta Project at the University of Oxford for sharing information about the writs and charters of Henry I; to Bill Davies, Simon Whitmore, Rosemary Williams and their colleagues at Cambridge University Press for keeping faith in the project; and to the two readers for the Press, one of whom subsequently identified himself as Nicholas Vincent, and both of whom commented fully and constructively on the text.

To those learned societies and organisers of conferences where I have had the opportunity to present papers on Henry I, at Battle, Queen's University Belfast, Boston, Caen, Cambridge, Dublin, Poitiers, the Haskins Society and the International Medieval Congress at Leeds, I express my thanks. I should like to thank, too, Queen's University Belfast for granting two periods of study leave, 1997–8 and 2001–2, and for funding replacement teaching for parts of those years; also the Leverhulme Trust, for a Research Fellowship in 1998, and the AHRB, for a grant under its Research Leave scheme in 2002.

Above all, I should like to express my gratitude to Ian Green, for his support, encouragement and the generosity with which he has given his time in devoting hours to reading and discussing drafts of the book, and for companionship on field expeditions to many places associated with Henry I. The latter included a memorable afternoon at Gatteville in Normandy watching the tide ebb from the rocks outside the harbour of Barfleur. Without Ian, this book would not have been finished.

Abbreviations

ANS	*Anglo-Norman Studies*
ASC	*The Anglo-Saxon Chronicle, a Revised Translation*, ed. D. Whitelock, D. C. Douglas and S. I. Tucker (London, 1961)
Anselm, *Letters*	Cited by number from *Anselmi Opera Omnia*, ed. F. S. Schmitt, 6 vols. (Seckau, Edinburgh, 1938–61)
Bates, *Regesta*	*Regesta Regum Anglo-Normannorum. The Acta of William I (1066–1087)*, ed. D. Bates (Oxford, 1998)
Brut (Peniarth)	*Brut y Tywysogyon or the Chronicle of the Princes. Peniarth MS 20 Version*, trans. T. Jones (Cardiff, 1952)
Brut (RBH)	*Brut y Tywysogyon or the Chronicle of the Princes. Red Book of Hergest Version*, ed. and trans. T. Jones (Cardiff, 1955)
Complete Peerage	*Complete Peerage*, by G. E. C., revised edn V. Gibbs, H. A. Doubleday, G. H. White, 13 vols. in 12 (London, 1910–59)
DB	*Domesday Book, seu liber censualis Willelmi primi regis Angliae inter archivos regni in domo capitulari Westmonasterii asservatus. Jubente Regi Augustissimo Georgio Tertio praelo mandatus typis*, ed. A. Farley, 2 vols. (London, 1783)
Dugdale, *Mon. Ang.*	W. Dugdale, *Monasticon Anglicanum*, new edn, 6 vols. in 8 (London, 1817–30)
Eadmer, *Historia Novorum*	Eadmer, *Historia Novorum*, ed. M. Rule, Rolls Series (London, 1884)
EHR	*English Historical Review*

List of abbreviations

GND	The Gesta Normannorum Ducum of William of Jumièges, Orderic Vitalis and Robert of Torigni, ed. E. M. C. Van Houts, 2 vols. (Oxford, 1992, 1995)
Green, GOE	J. A. Green, The Government of England under Henry I, Cambridge Studies in Medieval Life and Thought, 4th series, 2 (Cambridge, 1986)
Hermann of Tournai	Hermann of Tournai, The Restoration of the Monastery of Saint Martin of Tournai, translated with an introduction and notes by L. H. Nelson (Washington, 1996)
HH	Henry of Huntingdon, Historia Anglorum, ed. D. Greenway (Oxford, 1996)
Hollister, MMI	C. Warren Hollister, Monarchy, Magnates and Institutions in the Anglo-Norman World (London, 1986). Details of the original versions of the essays in this volume are listed in the bibliography. Page references in the text, however, are to Monarchy, Magnates and Institutions.
Hugh the Chanter	Hugh the Chanter, The History of the Church of York 1066–1127, ed. C. Johnson, revised edn by M. Brett, C. N. L. Brooke and M. Winterbottom (Oxford, 1990)
JW	The Chronicle of John of Worcester, vol. ii, ed. R. R. Darlington, and vol. iii, ed. P. McGurk (Oxford, 1995, 1998)
Migne, Patrologia Latina	Patrologia Latina, ed. J.-P. Migne, 221 vols. (Paris, 1844–64)
Newburgh	William of Newburgh, Historia Rerum Anglicarum, Chronicles of the Reigns of Stephen, Henry II and Richard I, ed. R. Howlett, 4 vols., RS (London, 1884–9), i, 1–408; ii, 1–385.
OV	The Ecclesiastical History of Orderic Vitalis, ed. M. Chibnall, 6 vols. (Oxford, 1969–80)
Oxford DNB	Oxford Dictionary of National Biography: from the Earliest Times to the Year 2000, ed. H. C. G. Matthew and B. Harrison, 60 vols. (Oxford, 2004)
PR	Pipe Roll

Robert of Torigny, *Chronicle*	*Chronicles of the Reigns of Stephen, Henry II and Richard I*, ed. R. Howlett, 4 vols., RS (London, 1884–9), iv, 81–315
Robert of Torigny, *Chronique*	*Chronique, suivi de divers opuscules historiques de cet auteur*, ed. L. Delisle, 2 vols., Société de l'Histoire de Normandie (Rouen, 1872–3)
Round, *C. D. F.*	*Calendar of Documents preserved in France, Illustrative of the History of Great Britain and Ireland*, I, *A. D. 918–1216*, ed. J. H. Round (London, 1899)
RRAN	*Regesta Regum Anglo-Normannorum 1066–1154*, 4 vols., i, ed. H. W. C. Davis, ii, ed. C. Johnson and H. A. Cronne, iii and iv, ed. H. A. Cronne and R. H. C. Davis (Oxford, 1913–1969)
RS	Rolls Series
SD	Symeon of Durham
VCH	*Victoria History of the Counties of England*
WM	William of Malmesbury
WM, *GRA*	*Gesta Regum Anglorum*, i, ed. R. A. B. Mynors, R. M. Thomson and M. Winterbottom; vol. ii, General Introduction and Commentary by R. M. Thomson (Oxford, 1998, 1999)

Introduction: A surfeit of lampreys

In late November 1135 Henry I, the youngest son of William the Conqueror, was staying at a hunting lodge at Lyons-la-Forêt in Normandy. At around sixty-eight years of age, he was still in sufficiently good health to be planning to go hunting on the following day when, contrary to his doctor's orders it was said, he dined on lampreys and became ill during the night.[1] Within a few short days he was dead, and the peace that had been a hallmark of his regime in Normandy and England was thrown into jeopardy. What kind of man had been able to assert his claim to the English throne over that of his eldest brother Robert, and subsequently had wrested from him their father's duchy of Normandy? He had been able to command support, fear and, ultimately, respect, in a world that was competitive and at times brutal. He himself had been involved in the summary death of a rebel in 1090, and had lived through the deaths of his first wife, brothers and sisters, and, above all, through the tragic deaths of his heir and two other children in the wreck of the White Ship in 1120. The world changed around him, in some ways permitting a greater degree of material comfort, in other respects posing new challenges, notably in the jurisdictional claims advanced by churchmen which forced him to defend traditional royal rights. A long and eventful life at the heart of this political world is of intrinsic interest, and it gains significance from Henry's achievements as king and as duke, in the fields of administration, law and justice, and also as the centre of a flourishing court culture. The central question with which this book is concerned is: what can be learned of the man behind his recorded actions and achievements?

The biographer of Henry I is not short of source material: the narrative writing is abundant, varied in perspective, and frequently of high quality. It may be supplemented by increasing numbers of documents issued in the king's name, and a record in the form of the earliest surviving pipe roll of

---

[1] HH, p. 490.

royal finance in 1130. Finally, many of the buildings Henry built or altered survive to the present day. Both the written sources and the buildings reveal most about his career and his actions, in other words his exterior life; and, as we shall see, those authors who do comment on his temperament and personality must be treated with extreme caution. The nature of the sources, and what may be deduced about character and personality, are therefore discussed here first.

The authors of the most important narrative sources which have most to say of an explicitly biographical nature about Henry present the greatest challenges, simply because the authors' agenda was very different from that of modern biographers.[2] They held views on the appropriate conduct for men to whom God had given great power. Their comments are worked into discourses about the nature of good and evil, and God's power to intervene in the affairs of men. The three most important in this context are William of Malmesbury, Orderic Vitalis and Henry of Huntingdon.

William of Malmesbury's *History of the Kings of the English* was initiated at the behest of Queen Matilda, Henry's first wife. It includes a memorable pen portrait of the king.[3] The *History* begins with the arrival of the Angles and Saxons in 449 AD. It continues in two books down to the Norman Conquest, and three further books are devoted to each of the three Norman kings. William describes Henry as of medium height, stocky (and fat in later life), and having hair that was dark and, until his hairline receded, flopped over his forehead; his dark eyes had a kindly expression. This description is very different from that of Rufus, with his 'window-pane' hairstyle – hair parted in the centre so that his forehead was bare – his ruddy complexion, eyes with flecks in them, and stammering speech.[4] William's pen portraits of William Rufus (book four) and Henry I (book five) in particular form a diptych, from which the reader is to draw a moral about the necessity as well as the virtue of self-discipline and moderation. Rufus had had the potential for self-discipline when guided by Archbishop Lanfranc, but this was lost after Lanfranc's death. The king then became extravagant and exploitative, pressing the church for money with which to pay his knights, until he died, unshriven and unrepentant. The author ended his portrait in the Suetonian manner by listing Rufus' public works. There was only one: the building of the great hall at Westminster, probably the largest of its kind in Europe.

---

[2] For a recent discussion see A. Cooper, '"The Feet of Those that Bark Shall Be Cut Off": Timorous Historians and the Personality of Henry I', *ANS*, 23 (2000), 47–67.
[3] WM, *GRA*, i, 709–801.
[4] For an explanation of this hairstyle see F. Barlow, *William Rufus* (London, 1983), p. 99 and Barlow, 'William II (c. 1060–1100)', *Oxford DNB* .

By contrast, in William of Malmesbury's account, Henry was responsible for building several religious houses, most notably Reading abbey. He had been given an education in the classics, and was thus equipped to handle the experiences life threw at him. He was severe to wrongdoers, generous to his friends, and above all consistent. Even Henry's sexual conduct, which the author could scarcely ignore, was fitted into this theme: the king did not waste his seed but used it for the procreation of children. William's portrait was thus a collection of *topoi*, a disquisition on the need for self-discipline, as well as the picture of an individual. It cleverly avoided praise or condemnation of Henry while writing either at the queen's behest, or, after her death, for another patron.

In Normandy the outstanding author was Orderic Vitalis, a monk of Saint-Evroult. Like William of Malmesbury, Orderic was of mixed French and English parentage. He had been born in Shropshire, was sent by his father at the age of ten to enter the Norman monastery of Saint-Evroult, and spent the rest of his life as a monk there. His first literary effort was an updating of what had become the classic account of the Normans' history, *The Deeds of the Dukes of the Normans*, itself a rewriting of an earlier history.[5] Inspired by this, he embarked on a much bigger project, an *Ecclesiastical History*, in which he sought to follow in the footsteps of historians of the early church. He was almost certainly present when Henry visited Saint-Evroult early in 1113,[6] and the king's interest in the abbey was doubtless one of the reasons why the abbot set Orderic to work on his *History*.

Orderic's avowed purpose was not to write a history of kings or of peoples but a history of Christians. It grew, as he himself explained, from his work on the history of his abbey which included material on 'the good or evil leaders of this wretched age', and his purpose was 'to speak truthfully about ecclesiastical affairs as a simple son of the church'. He was aware that his life as a monk restricted the scope of his narrative, but felt he could explain 'truthfully and straightforwardly' the things which he had seen in his own times.[7] Truth for such an author was more than an issue of strict accuracy and impartial reporting: truth had a moral dimension. For a monk the temporal splendours of kingship were evanescent, and would soon be swept aside by death; what really mattered was what followed – life everlasting.

Orderic is a brilliant narrator of events, particularly of the history of Normandy with which writers based in England were naturally less concerned. He believed that it took a strong ruler to keep the aggressive

---

[5] *GND*.   [6] As M. Chibnall pointed out: OV, i, 43n.   [7] OV, i, 130–2.

characteristics of the Norman people in check. The Norman dukes had been strong until the time of Robert II (Curthose), who had failed in his task and had been found wanting by God. His youngest brother Henry had laid claim to their father's inheritance, and it had been adjudged to him in battle in 1106. He alone could provide peace for the Norman church and people, a peace which Orderic saw evaporating after 1135. Orderic's view was conditioned by personal experience of life in a community situated in the turbulent southern marches of the duchy, where Robert de Bellême, a vigorous and aggressive lord, was a feared neighbour of the monks. Henry destroyed the power of Robert de Bellême, and the protection he accorded the monks won Henry golden opinions. Orderic was notably unsympathetic towards the problems faced by Duke Robert, who did not have the English resources of his brothers on which to call for the maintenance of peace in Normandy, and he was deeply hostile towards those who disturbed the peace like Robert de Bellême.

Although naturally in favour of peace, Orderic nevertheless adopted an ambivalent tone when he came to review the personality and rule of Henry I. The king, he wrote, was a man of tremendous energy, and acquisitive in the pursuit of worldly wealth. He loved hunting, but claimed hunting rights for himself over all England. He was mean in granting hunting privileges to others; he even restricted hunting by his nobles in woods on their own lands, and he ordered the feet of dogs kept near the forests to be mutilated. He wanted to know everything about everyone, and knew so much about the affairs of his servants that he knew everything that was done secretly, hardly a heroic trait. Although Orderic's obituary of Henry was highly laudatory ('lover of peace' etc), this passage – the only one where he writes of the king's personality – is remarkable for both its content and tone.

It was Henry of Huntingdon, however, who wrote most damningly about Henry I; at least, he did until the accession of Henry FitzEmpress was in prospect, when he toned down the remarks he had made in the earliest version of his *History of the English*. In the first version of the beginning of book ten, 'On the present time', he wrote that Henry I had had three virtues: wisdom; military success in beating the king of the French; and riches, in which he far surpassed his predecessors. These qualities, which were in any case dependent on the participation of others, were counterbalanced by three vices: greed in his desire for tribute and taxes, in the pursuit of which he trapped the poor by use of informers; cruelty, in blinding his kinsman, the count of Mortain; and debauchery. Cruelty and debauchery unsurprisingly were removed from the later, toned-down version,[8] and the author added that in the dreadful time that followed Henry's death, whatever he had done, whether *tyrannice* or *regie* (in the manner of a tyrant or a king), seemed excellent. That the word *tyrannice* should have been used at all, shortly before or after the accession of Henry FitzEmpress, was striking.

Each of these authors wrote what might be called history with a capital 'H': their intention was to produce a more sophisticated work than a simple recital of events. They wrote within a framework of ideas about peoples and their rulers, about good kings and bad kings.[9] These drew on accounts of kings in the Old Testament, powerful, stern figures who meted out justice and punished evildoers, and on classical authors. William of Malmesbury's discussion of the Norman kings, for instance, was clearly influenced by Suetonius' *Lives of the Twelve Caesars*;[10] and he was also very impressed by the ideal of self-restraint. These authors conceived the purpose of historical writing as essentially didactic: history was meant chiefly to inspire good behaviour and to warn against evil. Old Testament examples and views about the purpose of history meant that their portrayal of kings was not, nor was it expected to be, rounded, in the sense of exploring their subjects' emotional or spiritual lives, unless these bore on their actions. Instead they tried to show their subjects as fitting into the image of what they thought kings ought to be and how they ought to behave.[11]

It is not always easy to see where authors are borrowing and adapting literary motifs. For instance William of Malmesbury provides details of Henry's menagerie of exotic animals housed at Woodstock. He lists some of them, including a porcupine, which he describes in a way that suggests he had seen it.[12] Henry may well have had a particular interest in the zoo, given that he chose to keep the animals and to house them at one of his favoured residences; but the gift of exotic animals to rulers, as a sign of their prestige, was far older: Charlemagne, for instance, received such gifts.[13] William of Malmesbury also tells us that Henry I snored. He may well have done,

---

[8] HH, pp. 698–700.
[9] In general see R. Morse, *Truth and Invention in the Middle Ages* (Cambridge, 1991), chapter 3.
[10] For this author's ideas of kingship see J. G. Haahr, 'The Concept of Kingship in William of Malmesbury's *Gesta Regum* and *Historia Novella*', *Medieval Studies*, 38 (1976), 351–71.
[11] J. Blacker, *The Faces of Time. Portrayal of the Past in Old French and Latin Historical Narrative of the Anglo-Norman Regnum* (Austin, Texas, 1994), chapter 2.
[12] WM, *GRA*, i, 740.
[13] Einhard and Notker the Stammerer, *Two Lives of Charlemagne*, translated L. Thorpe (Harmondsworth, 1969), p. 70.

but Karl Leyser has pointed out that this might have been a little joke against the idea that kings never rested.[14] One of the best-known anecdotes about Henry is about his death from eating lampreys, against the advice of his doctors. Henry of Huntingdon is one of the few contemporary or near-contemporary chroniclers who mentions the lampreys, but the detail, perhaps inserted to sustain the reader's interest, may have been accurate.[15] The anecdote could have come from the monks of Bec, because the old king's heart and entrails were removed from his body at Rouen and buried at Bec's priory of Notre-Dame-du-Pré.[16] Henry visited the abbey in 1139, and Stephen of Rouen, another author who mentions the lampreys, was probably a young monk at Bec at the time.[17] Another example is the account by Orderic of the grief experienced by Henry when told of the death of his only legitimate son and two of his other children, plus many of his knights and servants, in the wreck of the White Ship in November 1120 (see below, p. 167). In the graphic description provided by Orderic Vitalis, however, the king lamented particularly (*maximeque*) for his knights, and told of their feats of bravery.[18] It seems on the face of it unlikely that Henry would rate the loss of his captains higher than that of his children; Orderic may be echoing the story of Charlemagne's grief in *The Song of Roland* after the battle of Roncesvalles.[19] Despite being grief-stricken, it is surely not without significance that Henry married again on 6 January 1121. In this case, therefore, Orderic's account of Henry's reaction to the White Ship cannot be read with absolute literalness.

Although these three authors have the most to say directly about Henry's personality, there are others writing in the early twelfth century with whom they may be usefully compared. Eadmer, a monk at Christ Church Canterbury, provides a lively if partial account of Henry's difficulties with Archbishop Anselm.[20] Hugh the Chanter, precentor of York, supplies a northern view of the dispute over primacy with Canterbury which led to a protracted struggle between successive archbishops of Canterbury and York,

---

[14] K. Leyser, 'Some Reflections on Twelfth-Century Kings and Kingship', in *Medieval Germany and Its Neighbours 900–1250* (London, 1982), 264.
[15] HH, p. 490.   [16] WM, *Historia Novella*, ed. E. King and trans. K. R. Potter (Oxford, 1998), p. 26.
[17] Stephen of Rouen, 'Draco Normannicus', *Chronicles of the Reigns of Stephen, Henry II and Richard I*, ed. R. Howlett, 4 vols., RS (London, 1894–9), ii, 659; Richard of Hexham, a third source, may well have known the work of Henry of Huntingdon: 'De Gestis Regis Stephani et de Bello Standardii', *Chronicles of the Reigns of Stephen, Henry II and Richard I*, iii, 39; A. Gransden, *Historical Writing in England c. 550–c. 1307* (London, 1974), p. 216.
[18] OV, vi, 300–2.
[19] *The Song of Roland*, translated by Dorothy L. Sayers (Harmondsworth, 1957), p. 147.
[20] Eadmer, *Historia Novorum*.

and the exile of Archbishop Thurstan of York.[21] Other monastic chronicles, such as those composed at Worcester, Durham and Peterborough, provide additional details and regional perspectives.[22] The chronicle of Hyde Abbey, for instance, has valuable details about Henry's affairs in Normandy after 1106.[23] The cartulary-chronicle of Abingdon Abbey is illuminating about Henry's early life, and about the favour shown to the abbey by the king and Queen Matilda in the time of Abbot Faritius, a royal physician.[24] Details about the queen are also provided by the chronicle of Holy Trinity Aldgate.[25] By the 1130s there appeared the earliest surviving history of the English in French. Gaimar's *Lestoire des Engleis* ends in 1100, but is valuable for providing a perspective on court life more sympathetic towards lay values than that of monastic writers.[26] Geoffrey of Monmouth, a canon at Oxford, was writing his *History of the Kings of Britain* at roughly the same time as Gaimar. His portrayal of King Arthur's kingly qualities, and the code of values to which he ascribed, is thought to have been an evocation of the courtly world of early twelfth-century England.[27] In Normandy, too, Orderic's work may be supplemented by his additions to William of Jumièges's *Gesta Normannorum Ducum*, later re-revised by Robert of Torigny, who then went on to more ambitious historical works.[28]

Writers based outside England and Normandy offer a different perspective. The principal source for Welsh history, the *Brut*, is thought to record twelfth-century traditions, though the surviving recensions are later.[29] From the *Brut* comes the image of a king who was feared by the Welsh more than any other down to Edward I's reign.[30] The *Life* of King Louis VI of France

---

[21] Hugh the Chanter.
[22] JW; SD, *Historia Regum*, *Opera Omnia*, ed. T. Arnold, 2 vols., RS (London, 1882–5); *ASC*.
[23] *Liber Monasterii de Hyda*, ed. E. Edwards, RS (London, 1866). A new edition by Dr E. M. C. Van Houts for the Oxford Medieval Texts series is in preparation. She has suggested that the chronicle should be dated to the 1140s or 1150s: 'The Warenne View of the Past', *ANS*, 26 (2003), 111.
[24] *Historia Ecclesie Abbendonensis. The History of the Church of Abingdon*, ii, ed. and trans. John Hudson (Oxford, 2002).
[25] The chronicle was printed as an appendix to *Cartulary of Holy Trinity Aldgate*, ed. G. A. J. Hodgett, London Record Society, 10 (1970).
[26] Gaimar, *Lestoire des Engleis*, ed. A. Bell (Oxford, 1960); J. Gillingham, 'Kingship, Chivalry and Love. Political and Cultural Values in the Earliest History Written in French: Geoffrey Gaimar's *Estoire des Engleis*', in *Anglo-Norman Political Culture and the Twelfth-Century Renaissance*, ed. C. Warren Hollister (Woodbridge, 1997), pp. 33–58.
[27] Geoffrey of Monmouth, *The History of the Kings of Britain*, trans. L. Thorpe (Harmondsworth, 1966).
[28] *GND*, ii, 196–288; Robert of Torigny, *Chronique* (ed. Delisle).   [29] *Brut (RBH)*; *Brut (Peniarth)*.
[30] For a discussion of the portrayal of Henry I in the different versions of the *Brut*, see K. L. Maund, 'Owain ap Cadwgan: a Rebel Revisited', *Haskins Society Journal*, 13 (1999), 73.

by Abbot Suger has much to say about Henry.[31] Suger was particularly well placed to comment on Louis's great adversary: as he himself says, he was the principal emissary between the two for more than twenty years.[32] Galbert of Bruges's *The Murder of Charles the Good* is concerned with the murder of Count Charles of Flanders in 1127 and the ensuing civil war. Although Henry himself had a claim to the county through his mother, his main priority was to frustrate the claim of his nephew William, who was created count by King Louis VI.[33] Had William been able to pacify the county, he could have used its wealth to assert his claim, as Duke Robert's son, to the duchy of Normandy and thereafter to the kingdom of England. 'The Deeds of the Counts of Anjou' and the 'History of Duke Geoffrey' by John of Marmoutier, though composed later in the twelfth century, help to illuminate relations between Henry and the counts of Anjou.[34]

Narratives from the later twelfth century are not without value, either for points of detail or because they reflect different points of view. In the 1160s a canon of Bayeux cathedral, Wace, composed a verse history of the Normans, the *Roman de Rou*. This incorporated local and oral traditions about Norman history, and is particularly useful and detailed about Henry's struggles with his brothers between 1087 and 1100, and about his campaigns in Normandy in 1105 when Bayeux was sacked and burned.[35] As time passed, the likelihood of additional credible material obviously diminished. Stories about the fate of Duke Robert after his capture in battle in 1106 were elaborated. The French chronicler Geoffrey of Vigeois suggested that Robert Curthose had been released on parole and had attempted to raise an army against his brother.[36] This was a story developed further by Roger of

---

[31] *Vie de Louis VI le Gros*, ed. H. Waquet (Paris, 1929); trans. R. C. Cusimano and J. Moorhead, *The Deeds of Louis the Fat* (Washington, 1992).

[32] A. Lecoy de la Marche, *Œuvres complètes de Suger, recueillies, annotées et publiées d'après les manuscrits* (Paris, 1865), p. 265.

[33] Galbert of Bruges, *The Murder of Charles the Good*, ed. and trans. J. B. Ross, Harper Torchbook edition (New York, 1967).

[34] *Chroniques des Comtes d'Anjou et des Seigneurs d'Amboise*, ed. L. Halphen and R. Poupardin (Paris, 1913).

[35] *Le Roman de Rou de Wace*, ed. A. J. Holden, 3 vols., Société des Anciens Textes Français (Paris, 1970–3); for an English translation: Wace, *The Roman de Rou*, G. S. Burgess, Société Jersiaise (2002), revised and reprinted (Woodbridge, 2004); and for a discussion of its value for the late eleventh and early twelfth centuries, see E. M. C. Van Houts, 'Wace as Historian', in *Family Trees and the Roots of Politics*, ed. K. S. B. Keats-Rohan (Woodbridge, 1997), pp. 103–32; see also Blacker, *Faces of Time*, pp. 114–17; P. Damian-Grint, *The New Historians of the Twelfth Century* (Woodbridge, 1999).

[36] *Recueil des Historiens des Gaules et de la France*, ed. M. Bouquet and others, 24 vols. (Paris, 1738–1904), xii, 432; for discussion see C. W. David, *Robert Curthose Duke of Normandy* (Cambridge, Mass., 1920), p. 201.

Wendover and Matthew Paris, who believed that after recapture the duke was more strictly imprisoned.[37] Walter Map's *Courtiers' Trifles* is a mix of information and stories, some of which purport to relate to Henry's court. These may have some basis in fact, though they smack of a retrospective look at the 'good old days', comparing the decorum of the elder Henry's court with the scrambling way of life at his grandson's.[38]

Documentary sources present different challenges for the historian. The most important in their different ways are the documents or 'acts' issued in Henry's name, the 1130 pipe roll and legal literature. The documents are of different kinds, including solemn charters or diplomas, writs and writ-charters, notices (*notitiae*), agreements (*conventiones*), reports of lawsuits and letters.[39] Royal and ducal acts provide invaluable evidence about royal grants of lands and privileges; their place of issue casts light on the king's travels, and address clauses and witness lists provide information about individuals, especially members of his court. Historians have to rely at present on an incomplete and unsatisfactory calendar of these, rather than a full edition.[40] A full scholarly edition under the direction of Professor Richard Sharpe is under way and this will provide the basis for detailed study of the diplomatic of the texts, and an understanding of how and why they were produced.[41] They include, as well as writs and charters, letters issued in the king's name. These were formal compositions rather than private documents.

Survival of documents, royal *acta*, is uneven: naturally enough, far more survived for ecclesiastics because of the continuity of their archives than those issued for the benefit of laymen whose archives were subject to the accidents of family history, and documents of only short-term importance obviously tend not to survive. Many more survive for Henry's reign than

---

[37] *Flores Historiarum*, ed. H. O. Coxe, 4 vols. (London, 1841–4), ii, 212–13; Matthew Paris, *Chronica Majora*, ed. H. R. Luard, 7 vols., RS (London, 1872–83), iv, 63.

[38] Walter Map, *De Nugis Curialium. Courtiers' Trifles*, ed. and trans. M. R. James, rev. edn by C. N. L. Brooke and R. A. B. Mynors (Oxford, 1983), pp. xxxv–xlv.

[39] G. Constable, *Letters and Letter Collections*, Typologie des Sources du Moyen Age Occidental, fasc. 17 (Turnhout, 1976).

[40] *RRAN*, ii. The editors did not make use of the unpublished thesis of Henri Chanteux, 'Recueil des actes d'Henri Beauclerc, duc de Normandie', thèse inédite de l'Ecole des Chartes, 1932. An interim list of errata and corrigenda was published in *University of Birmingham Historical Journal*, 6/2 (1958), 176–96; for comment by recent historians see S. Mooers Christelow, 'A Moveable Feast? Itinerance and the Centralization of Government under Henry I', *Albion*, 28 (1996), 188–9; and C. Warren Hollister, *Henry I*, edited and completed by A. Clark Frost (New Haven and London, 2001), pp. 25–6.

[41] For some very pertinent remarks see D. Bates, 'The Earliest Norman Writs', *EHR*, 100 (1985), 266–84; Bates, *Reordering the Past and Negotiating the Present in Stenton's First Century*, Stenton Lecture 1999 (Reading, 2000); R. Sharpe, 'The Use of Writs in the Eleventh Century', *Anglo-Saxon England*, 32 (2003), 247–61.

for his father's or brother's reigns,[42] but these are only the tip of an iceberg. It has been pointed out that almost three hundred are referred to in the pipe roll but have not survived,[43] and a further estimate is that the total of three hundred could be multiplied ten or twenty times to give an idea of the total issued in a single year, or about ten per day.[44] Moreover, many more survive for certain periods than for others. Very few documents at all can be securely dated to the year 1118 and as a result it is very difficult to trace Henry's movements in that year with any certainty. By contrast, after his return to England in 1120, having been absent for more than four years, he was naturally in demand for charters of grant or confirmation.

In the past historians tended to quarry royal *acta* for information without perhaps making enough allowance for the context in which they were produced.[45] The idea that documents are 'objective', in a way that chroniclers are not, does not fully reflect the motives and circumstances of those who requested documents, which are reflected in the texts. For instance, address clauses of writs and writ-charters are more informative in the first half of the reign, when they were addressed to named individuals ('to X the bishop and Y the sheriff of Zshire'), than in the later years, when writ-charters with general address clauses ('to all my barons etc.') were becoming more common.[46] As a result, information about sheriffs for the first half of the reign comes chiefly from writs and writ-charters, whereas we are less well informed in general about the later years, with the exception of the years covered by the 1130 pipe roll.

The information from witness lists also has to be treated with a degree of caution. Solemn diplomas did include long lists of witnesses, but writs might be witnessed by only a single individual, whilst writ-charters might have a few, but presumably only a selection of those present. We cannot be certain that those named were physically present on the day in question: their names may have been recorded because it was deemed appropriate that they should be there. At one level it may be reasonably concluded that

---

[42] David Bates has edited some 355 for the period 1066–1087: Bates, *Regesta*, p. 3. This edition supersedes *RRAN*, i (1066–1100), ed. H. W. C. Davis (Oxford, 1913). This figure may be compared with the texts issued or attested by the Conqueror before 1066: see *Recueil des actes des ducs de Normandie de 911 à 1066*, ed. M. Fauroux (Caen, 1961) and K. Thompson, 'Une confirmation supposée de Guillaume le Bâtard', *Annales de Normandie*, 34 (1984), 411–12. Until the publication of R. Sharpe's edition of the acts of William Rufus, historians must rely on the calendar of some 198 acts listed in *RRAN*, i (1066–1100), plus 45 in 'Errata and Addenda to Regesta i', *RRAN*, ii (1100–35) .

[43] T. A. M. Bishop, *Scriptores Regis* (Oxford, 1961), p. 32.

[44] M. T. Clanchy, *From Memory to Written Record* (London, 1979), p. 42.   [45] Bates, *Regesta*, p. 5.

[46] On this subject see R. Sharpe, 'Address and Delivery in Anglo-Norman Royal Charters', *Charters and Charter Scholarship in Britain and Ireland*, ed. M. T. Flanagan and J. A. Green (Houndmills, 2005), pp. 32–52.

A surfeit of lampreys

witness lists give an indication of those alive and at court on a particular occasion, but an overly statistical approach to witness lists can be misleading. Some years ago, for instance, Warren Hollister argued, partly on the basis of witness lists, that a gulf between *curiales* (courtiers) on the one hand and magnates on the other developed under William Rufus, and that it was healed by Henry I.[47] Straightforward numerical calculation of attestations, taking no account of the changing number and form of documents, is misleading about an alleged split between magnates and *curiales*, even simply as corroborative evidence.[48]

The rapidly rising number of surviving documents was in part a reflection of both a desire and a need for documentation, as those who wished to prove their right to land, property and privileges scrambled to obtain documentary proof, or if necessary, to forge it. There is therefore a seeming paradox that the more importance was attached to documentary evidence, the more ecclesiastical communities resorted to forgery to make good the deficiencies in their archives.[49] A great deal of basic work remains to be done on some of the key archives, such as the abbeys of Westminster, Battle and Gloucester and the cathedral priories at Canterbury and Durham, so that pre- and post-Conquest documents can be studied as a group. The first issue for the historian is thus to establish the authenticity of surviving texts, though this is often less straightforward than it seems. Authentic grants might be recorded in fabricated or 'improved' texts; authentic impressions of the royal seal were sometimes attached to forged texts.[50]

Surviving wax impressions of the royal seals provide clues about the image Henry wished to convey. Henry had three or four seals, the earliest of which followed the pattern established by his father, with the king seated in majesty on one side, and mounted and armed as a knight on the other, with the legend on both sides 'Henry by the grace of God king of the English'. On the last, however, the legend on the equestrian side reads 'Henry, duke of the Normans'. The date when this last seal was introduced thus provides

---

[47] Warren Hollister used attestations in part to demonstrate allegiances in 1088 and 1101: see especially his essays 'The Anglo-Norman Civil War: 1101' and 'Magnates and "Curiales" in Early Norman England', in Hollister, *MMI*, pp. 77–115, and the appendix to *Henry I*.

[48] For a more sceptical view, see Barlow, *William Rufus*, pp. 210–13; D. Bates, 'The Prosopographical Study of Anglo-Norman Royal Charters', in *Family Trees and the Roots of Politics. The Prosopography of Britain and France from the Tenth to the Twelfth Century*, ed. K. S. B. Keats-Rohan (Woodbridge, 1997), pp. 89–102. For a reconsideration of Hollister's views about 1101 see N. Strevett, 'The Anglo-Norman Civil War of 1101', *ANS*, 26 (2003), 159–71.

[49] See most recently B. O'Brien, 'Forgery and the Literacy of the Early Common Law', *Albion*, 27 (1995), 1–18.

[50] P. Chaplais, 'The Seals and Original Charters of Henry I', *EHR*, 75 (1960), 260–75.

a clue as to the king's perception of his authority in Normandy.[51] This biography is entitled 'Henry king of England and duke of Normandy', but it is a moot point precisely when Henry began to regard himself as duke (see below, pp. 96–7).

Turning back to documents, we also have a pipe roll – the second oldest public record in the UK, Domesday Book being the oldest. This pipe roll provides unique information about the sources of English (and some Welsh) royal revenue and the personnel of Henry's regime at a particular point in time. It is undated, but its first editor, Joseph Hunter, demonstrated that the year of audit was that which ended at Michaelmas 1130.[52] Again its evidence has to be handled with care. As a solitary survival it is obviously very difficult to be certain whether the picture it reveals is that of what might be regarded as a 'typical' financial year, or a year of heavy demand: in all probability it survived because this was the last year danegeld was collected (see below, pp. 211–12). Moreover the roll deals only with revenues passing under the eyes of the exchequer, and it is not concerned with Normandy.[53] Hunter's edition of 1833 was corrected and republished by the Pipe Roll Society in 1929, but the text still lacks a study of the palaeography and construction of the roll, and a historical introduction to its contents. A new edition for the Pipe Roll Society is in preparation by the present author.

A text which is invaluable in helping to identify the officials of the domestic household is *The Constitution of the King's Household* (*Constitutio Domus Regis*), a list of the leading officials of each department of the domestic household, together with their pay and allowances. It probably originated at the time of the reform of the household in 1108, and was apparently revised at the time of Henry's death.[54] Useful as it is, the *Constitution* deals only with certain departments of the household. It does not include the military contingents attached to the household, the king's companions, the women, the specialists like physicians and astrologers or the numerous minor servants.[55]

Henry's rule in England and Normandy was particularly crucial for the administration of justice and for the development of law. Evidence on this

---

[51] Ibid.
[52] Record Commission (London, 1833), hereafter cited as *PR 31 Henry I*. Detailed arguments confirming the dating of the year of audit to Michaelmas 1129–Michaelmas 1130 will be advanced in my projected new edition.
[53] Green, *GOE*, pp. 91–4.
[54] For the text see *Dialogus de Scaccario. The Course of the Exchequer by Richard FitzNigel and Constitutio Domus Regis. The Establishment of the Royal Household*, ed. and trans. C. Johnson with corrections by F. E. L. Carter and D. E. Greenway (Oxford, 1983). A new edition in the Oxford Medieval Texts series is forthcoming.
[55] See below, chapter 13.

subject derives partly from royal writs and charters, and from reports of lawsuits, usually drawn up at the behest of the winning party. It is not easy to compare the impact of Henry's rule in England with that in Normandy, however, and here the different kinds of evidence available for England have a part to play. The pipe roll, for instance, supplies incidental evidence about the operation of royal justice. In England, there was also an upsurge in legal literature. The commitment of the Norman kings to the laws of King Edward (the Confessor) stimulated a desire amongst churchmen, in tandem with their concern with the law of the church, to ascertain exactly what the laws of the English kings were, and to write these down. The great collection called *Quadripartitus* was a compendium of Anglo-Saxon laws continued to the Norman period. *The Laws of Henry I*, possibly by the same author, represents a brave effort to discuss jurisdiction, or soke, rather than law as practised in the courts, or procedure.[56] Difficult to use, the treatise is nevertheless indicative of contemporary concern about law and justice in England.

The biographer of Henry I thus cannot complain about a dearth of evidence. His task is rather to compare and to evaluate the sources. The narratives are particularly difficult to handle because often what seems like a credible anecdote might well have been borrowed from elsewhere and adapted to suit the circumstances. Sometimes the silences are as interesting as the statements. One example of such a silence relates to the king's personal piety, to which chroniclers allude only in passing, though they have much to praise about his generous religious patronage.[57] Sir Richard Southern suggested that during two periods of his life Henry was driven to generosity by a sense of spiritual crisis, that he was 'oppressed by the weight of his sins', first after the death of his son in 1120 and secondly when his daughter's second marriage collapsed in 1129, throwing Henry's plans for the succession to England and Normandy into jeopardy once again (see below, pp. 206, 209–12).[58] In fact the timing, scale and direction of his patronage were

---

[56] *Leges Henrici Primi*, ed. L. J. Downer (Oxford, 1972), and for discussion see especially P. Wormald, *The Making of English Law. King Alfred to the Twelfth Century. Legislation and its Limits* (Oxford, 1999) and Wormald, 'Quadripartitus', in *Law and Government in Medieval England and Normandy. Essays in Honour of Sir James Holt*, ed. G. Garnett and J. Hudson (Cambridge, 1994), pp. 111–48. For a guide to the development of law and justice see J. Hudson, *The Formation of the English Common Law. Law and Society in England from the Norman Conquest to Magna Carta* (London, 1966), chapters 1–4.

[57] On this subject see J. A. Green, 'The Piety and Patronage of Henry I', *Haskins Society Journal*, 10 (2001), 1–16 and below, pp. 277–82.

[58] R. W. Southern, 'The Place of Henry I in English History', *Proceedings of the British Academy*, 48 (1962), 127–69, reprinted in *Medieval Humanism and Other Studies* (Oxford, 1970), pp. 206–33. References here are to the later version, unless otherwise stated.

affected by a mix of factors, secular as well as spiritual, though fear of hell may have played a part in the latter (see below, pp. 277, 283). It has been suggested recently that both he and Queen Matilda participated in the currently fashionable practice of penance.[59] Henry also evidently liked to acquire relics, and is thought to have been behind the arrival of some of the more unusual items known to have been at Reading abbey by the late twelfth century.[60] Yet the relative silence of the chroniclers, by comparison with the very positive comments made about the piety of his first wife and her brother King David, suggests that Henry's piety was regarded as unexceptional. Ultimately, therefore, each piece of evidence has to be weighed against a range of other sources and judged on its basic credibility.

Modern writing about Henry essentially began in 1962 with Southern's Raleigh Lecture to the British Academy, 'The Place of Henry I in English History', and in the following four decades there has been a plethora of publications on different specific aspects of his life and career. Much the greatest volume of work has concentrated on his reign in England. There have been studies of the church,[61] finance,[62] coinage,[63] law and justice,[64] patronage,[65] the new men,[66] the nobility,[67] his first wife,[68] his many illegitimate children,[69] and his chief minister, Roger, bishop of Salisbury.[70] There

---

[59] D. Crouch, 'The Troubled Deathbeds of Henry I's Servants: Death, Confession, and Secular Conduct in the Twelfth Century', *Albion*, 34 (2002), 31.

[60] D. Bethell, 'The Making of a Twelfth-Century Relic Collection', *Popular Belief and Practice, Studies in Church History*, 8 (1971), 69.

[61] M. Brett, *The English Church under Henry I* (Oxford, 1975); see also F. Barlow, *The English Church 1066–1154* (London, 1979).

[62] Green, *GOE*.

[63] M. Blackburn, 'Coinage and Currency under Henry I: A Review', *ANS*, 13 (1990), 49–81.

[64] See above n. 59.

[65] S. Mooers Christelow, 'Patronage in the Pipe Roll of 1130', *Speculum*, 59 (1984), 284–307; Christelow, 'Familial Clout and Financial Gain in Henry I's Later Reign', *Albion*, 14 (1982), 267–92.

[66] See for instance, D. Crouch, 'Geoffrey de Clinton and Roger Earl of Warwick: New Men and Magnates in the Reign of Henry I', *[Bulletin of the Institute of] Historical Research*, 55 (1982), 113–24; E. Mason, 'The King, the Chamberlain, and Southwick Priory', *Historical Research*, 53 (1980), 1–10; for Wigan the Marshal, K. S. B. Keats-Rohan, 'Two Studies in North French Prosopography', *Journal of Medieval History*, 20 (1994), 25–57; P. Dalton, 'Eustace FitzJohn and the Politics of Anglo-Norman England: the Rise and Survival of a Twelfth-Century Royal Servant', *Speculum*, 71 (1996), 358–83.

[67] Several important papers on Henry's dealings with the magnates collectively and individually were published by Warren Hollister and reprinted in *MMI*, and see also his *Henry I*, chapter 8; D. Crouch, *The Beaumont Twins*, Cambridge Studies in Medieval Life and Thought, 4th ser. i (Cambridge, 1986); J. A. Green, *The Aristocracy of Norman England* (Cambridge, 1997); K. S. B. Keats-Rohan, *Domesday Descendants. A Prosopography of Persons Occurring in English Documents 1066–1166*, vol. II (Woodbridge, 2002), pp. 8–38.

[68] L. L. Huneycutt, *Matilda of Scotland. A Study in Medieval Queenship* (Woodbridge, 2003).

[69] K. Thompson, 'Affairs of State: The Illegitimate Children of Henry I', *Journal of Medieval History*, 29 (2003), 129–51.

[70] E. J. Kealey, *Roger of Salisbury. Viceroy of England* (Berkeley, Los Angeles and London, 1972).

is only one modern biography, Warren Hollister's volume in the English Monarchs Series, completed after his death by one of his former pupils, Amanda Clark Frost, and published posthumously in 2001.[71]

Assessments of Henry as an individual and a ruler have varied sharply. Most have tended to see him as unpleasant but effective. Southern, for example, pointed to the ferocity with which he punished opponents.[72] Warren Hollister argued, however, that Henry was not exceptionally cruel by the standards of the day, that he loved peace and was generous to the magnates, and was more successful in his handling of them than Rufus had been.[73]

The appearance of an exchequer, the proliferation of writs and the work of royal justices have been seen as key developments in the rise of the state, in a form that was increasingly centralised and systematised. Hollister and Baldwin coined the phrase 'administrative kingship' to sum up the characteristics of kingship in this era.[74] Not all historians have agreed with this interpretation. Southern argued that the importance of the reign lay not in the development of structures, but in the use of new men, whom Henry allowed to enrich themselves through officeholding.[75] T. N. Bisson has argued that what counted was royal power rather than administration,[76] and D. Matthew concurs.[77] J. Campbell[78] and W. L. Warren set Henry's reign in a longer context of the history of royal administration and of the state, and argued that by the early twelfth century Anglo-Saxon structures were coming under increasing pressure, and then fractured under Stephen, to be fundamentally reshaped under Henry II.[79] Work on particular regions

---

[71] *Henry I*; see also Hollister's entry on Henry I in *Oxford DNB*.
[72] Southern, 'Place of Henry I', p. 231; cf. the view of A. L. Poole, *From Domesday Book to Magna Carta*, 2nd edn (Oxford, 1955), p. 130, that Henry's was a reign of 'calculated terror'.
[73] 'Royal Acts of Mutilation: The Case against Henry I', *Albion*, 10 (1978), 330–40.
[74] C. Warren Hollister with J. W. Baldwin, 'The Rise of Administrative Kingship: Henry I and Philip Augustus', *American Historical Review*, 83 (1978), 867–905; the section on Henry I was reprinted in Hollister, *MMI*, pp. 223–45. See also his 'Henry I and the Invisible Transformation of Medieval England', in *Studies in Medieval History Presented to R. H. C. Davis*, ed. H. Mayr-Harting and R. I. Moore (London, 1985), pp. 303–16, reprinted in *MMI*; Hollister, 'The Vice-Regal Court of Henry I', in *Law, Custom, and the Social Fabric. Essays in Honour of Bryce Lyon*, ed. B. S. Bachrach and D. Nicholas (Kalamazoo, 1990), pp. 131–44.
[75] 'Place of Henry I'.
[76] 'The "Feudal Revolution"', *Past and Present*, 142 (1994), 36–42; 'Introduction', in *Cultures of Power. Lordship, Status and Process in Twelfth-Century Europe*, ed. T. N. Bisson (Philadelphia, 1995), p. 2.
[77] D. Matthew, *King Stephen* (London, 2002), chapter 3.
[78] J. Campbell, 'Observations on English Government from the Tenth to the Twelfth Century', *Transactions of the Royal Historical Society*, 5th ser. 25 (1975), 39–54, reprinted in *Essays in Anglo-Saxon History* (London, 1986), pp. 165–70; *idem*, 'The Late Anglo-Saxon State: a Maximum View', *Proceedings of the British Academy*, 87 (1994), 39–65.
[79] W. L. Warren, 'The Myth of Norman Administrative Efficiency', *Transactions of the Royal Historical Society*, 5th ser. 34 (1984), 113–32.

and families has led to a greater awareness of the varying strength of royal administration in southern and northern England, for instance.[80] Studies of northern England in particular have demonstrated the small numbers of Normans in much of the north, and how an alliance between the sons of Malcolm III of Scots, William Rufus and Henry I created a situation where Norman settlement could take shape, though it formed only a thin veneer over northern society.[81]

The social context of governance has also been differently assessed. Detailed study of the operation of royal patronage has led some to stress its role in weaving a network of loyalty which included not only the great men but a host of lesser ones too.[82] Dr Keats-Rohan has argued that through the use of patronage contemporary perceptions of noble status shifted over time: instead of the term 'noble' being confined to those of illustrious descent, it widened to give due recognition to those who provided important forms of royal service.[83] Historians have come to different conclusions on how relations between Normans and English were affected by Henry's rule. The issue of assimilation and identity after 1066 has been discussed many times, and Henry's first marriage to a woman descended from the pre-Conquest kings, liaisons with women of native stock, and his commitment to the law of King Edward have pointed some historians to the view that Normans were beginning to assimilate with the English by the early twelfth century. In the nineteenth century Stubbs argued that Henry sought to ally with the native English against the feudal nobility,[84] and Freeman went even further and saw the reign as a time when the Normans began to take root in English society.[85] Recently the idea that Henry was an Anglophile has been suggested by D. Crouch.[86] However, in a careful analysis of ideas about ethnicity and interaction between Normans and English, H. M. Thomas

---

[80] See H. M. Jewell, *The North–South Divide: The Origins of Northern Consciousness in England* (Manchester, 1984); *Government, Religion and Society in Northern England 1000–1700*, ed. J. C. Appleby and P. Dalton (Stroud, 1997).

[81] W. E. Kapelle, *The Norman Conquest of the North* (London, 1979); G. W. S. Barrow, 'The Pattern of Lordship and Feudal Settlement in Cumbria', *Journal of Medieval History*, 1 (1975), 117–38; P. Dalton, *Conquest, Anarchy and Lordship. Yorkshire 1066–1154*, Cambridge Studies in Medieval Life and Thought, 4th ser. 27 (Cambridge, 1994); W. Aird, *St Cuthbert and the Normans. The Church of Durham, 1071–1153* (Woodbridge, 1998); J. A. Green, 'Aristocratic Loyalties on the Northern Frontier of England, c. 1100–1174', in *England in the Twelfth Century* (Woodbridge, 1990), pp. 83–100; Green, 'David I and Henry I', *Scottish Historical Review*, 75 (1996), 1–19; see also the essays by P. Dalton, W. Aird and K. Stringer in *Government, Religion and Society in Northern England 1000–1700* (ed. Appleby and Dalton).

[82] Christelow, 'Familial Clout and Financial Gain in Henry I's Later Reign'.

[83] *Domesday Descendants*, p. 31.

[84] W. Stubbs, *Constitutional History of Medieval England*, 3 vols., i, 6th edn (Oxford, 1897), para. 110.

[85] E. A. Freeman, *The History of the Norman Conquest of England: Its Causes and Results*, 6 vols. (Oxford, 1867–79), v, 148–67.

[86] D. Crouch, *The Normans. The History of a Dynasty* (London, 2002), pp. 159–160.

A surfeit of lampreys 17

has argued that the process of assimilating the minority Normans into the majority population was by no means straightforward. He has suggested that the immigrants and their descendants should perhaps be thought of as having a choice of identities. Norman identity remained strong well into Henry I's reign, but despite predisposition towards the former, some of continental origin were beginning to adopt at least partially English identities.[87] A further question, which lies outside Thomas's remit, is how Henry I and members of his court, many of whom like him had been born in England and some of whom had relations of native stock, were regarded by the Normans of Normandy?

In contrast with the plethora of studies on early twelfth-century England, most of those on early twelfth-century Normandy have appeared in the form of specialised or thematic works.[88] However, thanks to the work of David Crouch on the Beaumont twins,[89] Pierre Bauduin and Daniel Power on the frontiers,[90] Véronique Gazeau on the Benedictine abbeys[91]

---

[87] H. M. Thomas, *The English and the Normans. Ethnic Hostility, Assimilation, and Identity 1066–c. 1220* (Oxford, 2003), pp. 77–8.

[88] Meanwhile see F. Neveux, *La Normandie des ducs aux rois Xe–XIIe siècle* (Rennes, 1998), chapter 20; J. A. Green, 'Le gouvernement d'Henri Ier Beauclerc en Normandie', in *La Normandie et l'Angleterre au moyen âge*, ed. P. Bouet and V. Gazeau, Colloque de Cerisy-la-Salle (Caen, 2003), pp. 61–73; Green, 'Lords of the Norman Vexin,' in *War and Government in the Middle Ages. Studies in Honour of J. O. Prestwich*, ed. J. Gillingham and J. C. Holt (Woodbridge, 1984), pp. 47–61; K. Thompson, 'Robert de Bellême', *ANS*, 13 (1990), 263–86; Thompson, 'William Talvas, Count of Ponthieu, and the Politics of the Anglo-Norman Realm', in *England and Normandy in the Middle Ages*, ed. D. Bates and A. Curry (London, 1994), pp. 169–84; Thompson, 'The Lords of Laigle: Ambition and Insecurity on the Borders of Normandy', *ANS*, 18 (1995), 177–99; Thompson, *Power and Border Lordship in Medieval France. The County of the Perche, 1000–1226* (Woodbridge, 2002); P. Bauduin, 'Une famille châtelaine sur les confins normanno-manceaux: les Géré (xe–xiiie siècles)', *Archéologie Médiévale*, 22 (1992), 309–56; Bauduin, 'Le baron, le château et la motte: baronnage et maîtrise du territoire châtelain dans la seigneurie de Breteuil (xie–xiie siècles), 'Autour du château médiéval' (Rencontres historiques et archéologiques de l'Orne), *Société Historique et Archéologique de l'Orne, Mémoires et documents*, 1 (1998), 37–53. For the church see D. S. Spear, 'The Norman Episcopate under Henry I, King of England and duke of Normandy (1106–35)', unpublished Ph.D. thesis, University of California, Santa Barbara, 1982; *idem*, 'Geoffrey Brito, Archbishop of Rouen (1111–28)', *Haskins Society Journal*, 2 (1990), 123–37; *idem*, 'Les doyens de Rouen au cours de la période ducale', *Annales de Normandie*, 33 (1983), 91–119; *idem*, 'Les archidiacres de Rouen au cours de la période ducale', *loc. cit.*, 34 (1984), 15–50; *idem*, 'Les dignitaires de la cathédrale de Rouen pendant la période ducale', *loc. cit.*, 37 (1987), 121–47; *idem*, 'Les chanoines de la cathédrale de Rouen pendant la période ducale', *loc. cit.*, 41 (1991), 135–76; T. G. Waldman, 'Hugh "of Amiens", Archbishop of Rouen (1130–64)', Oxford Unversity D. Phil. thesis (1970).

[89] See above, n. 67.

[90] P. Bauduin, *La première Normandie (Xe–XIe siècles). Sur les frontières de la haute Normandie: identité et construction d'une principauté* (Caen, 2004); D. Power, *The Norman Frontier in the Twelfth and Early Thirteenth Centuries*, Cambridge Studies in Medieval Life and Thought, 4th ser., lxii (Cambridge, 2004).

[91] V. Gazeau, 'Recherches sur l'histoire de la principauté normande (911–1204). I. Les abbés bénédictins de la principauté normande. II. Prosopographie des abbés bénédictins (911–1204)', dossier d'habilitation, Université de Paris, I – Paris-Sorbonne (2002).

and Mathieu Arnoux's edited volume on the Augustinians,[92] pieces of the jigsaw are falling into place, and more are likely to do so soon. But until we understand Norman society and, a key topic, the operation of law and custom, we cannot fully understand the nature of Henry's rule there.

It is, however, Henry's dealings with principalities outside England and Normandy which have attracted some of the most sharply opposed views. John Le Patourel rightly suggested that the whole complex of lands and claims held by the Normans had to be treated as one, and he investigated key themes, such as colonisation and imperialism, and explored the effects on England and Normandy of a lengthy period of rule by Henry I.[93] However, the application of the term 'colonisation' in this context has been queried,[94] and some doubt has been expressed about the strength of centripetal tendencies.[95] Some have argued that Henry was content with his inheritance, and fought essentially in its defence;[96] others have argued that he was much more aggressive towards his neighbours in the British Isles than this allows.[97]

This book was well under way by the time that Warren Hollister's *Henry I* appeared. Readers will find that it differs from Hollister's in both its balance and interpretation. It is briefer, and yet, relatively speaking, more attention is given here to the years after 1120, to the court and court culture, and to Normandy, which may not have been regarded as central to the brief for the 'English Monarchs' series. It is, however, in interpretation of Henry's character and career that the most striking differences are to be found. Hollister's Henry is not the cruel and even sinister figure portrayed by Henry of Huntingdon: the king sought only to defend his father's legacy, not to expand its frontiers; he healed the rifts in the Anglo-Norman baronage and created political harmony which underpinned peace in England; he possessed a constructive approach to rule and, if not directly involved in administration, he may be credited with increasing centralisation and systematisation. By contrast it is argued here (chapter 11) that Henry was just as concerned as his predecessors with expanding his realms when

---

[92] *Des clercs au service de la réforme. Etudes et documents sur les chanoins réguliers de la province de Rouen*, ed. M. Arnoux, Bibliotheca Victorina, xi (Turnhout, 2000).

[93] *The Norman Empire* (Oxford, 1976), chapters 8 and 9.

[94] F. J. West, 'The Colonial History of the Norman Conquest?' *History*, 84 (1999), 219–36.

[95] J. A. Green, 'Unity and Disunity in the Anglo-Norman State', *Historical Research*, 62 (1989), 114–34. See further below, p. 253.

[96] C. Warren Hollister and T. K. Keefe, 'The Making of the Angevin Empire', *Journal of British Studies*, 12 (1973), 1–25, Hollister, *MMI*; K. J. Stringer, *The Reign of Stephen. Kingship, Warfare and Government in Twelfth-Century England* (London, 1993), p. 10.

[97] R. R. Davies, *The First English Empire. Power and Identities in the British Isles 1093–1343* (Oxford, 2000), chapter 1.

and where he could; that his dealings with the magnates (in Normandy as well as England) achieved a measure of equilibrium but were partial and sometimes coercive; and, in agreement with other historians, that too much weight has been placed on administrative process as opposed to the exercise of power. It is suggested here that too little attention has been given to understanding the social context of Henry's rule, especially in discussions of law and justice, which have been viewed very much from a top-down perspective; and that more attention needs to be given to different local and regional factors in England and Normandy, and to the importance of towns and trade. The first ten chapters of this new biography are chronologically arranged, and are followed by thematic chapters on Henry the ruler (chapter 11), Henry as guardian of the church (chapter 12), and court and court culture (chapter 13). In the conclusion I return to the issues of personality and character in the light of all the available evidence.

CHAPTER I

'Born in the purple'[1]

Henry's supporters could make much of the fact that he alone of the sons of William the Conqueror and Matilda had been born after his parents' royal coronations. So indeed he was, but it says much about the precarious position of younger sons in princely families that we do not know precisely when and where Henry was born, other than it was somewhere in England,[2] and probably in the last weeks of 1068. In later times visitors to Selby abbey in Yorkshire were told that a painted chamber there was reputedly the future king's birthplace but, as an eighteenth-century antiquary pointed out, the room in question was not apparently built before the early sixteenth century.[3] The king's father was in Yorkshire in the latter part of 1068. Whilst it is not absolutely out of the question that the queen was with him, it is much likelier that she was in the south, perhaps at Winchester within easy reach of the coast.[4] She was evidently there at Easter 1069, when the presence of another of her sons, Richard, is noted.[5] By that time Henry might have been a few months old, for, probably in the autumn of 1122, he was said to have celebrated his birthday at York, when he renewed a gift

---

[1] OV, iv, 120; *The Brevis Relatio de Guillelmo Nobilissimo Comite Normannorum Written by a Monk of Battle Abbey*, edited with an historical commentary by E. M. C. Van Houts, in *Chronology, Conquest and Conflict in Medieval England*, Camden Miscellany XXXIV, Camden Miscellany, 5th series x (1997), 37; *Newburgh*, i, 26.
[2] WM, *GRA*, i, 710; *Brevis Relatio*, p. 37; *GND*, ii, 216.
[3] J. Burton, *Monasticon Eboracense* (York, 1758), p. 387.
[4] The tradition preserved at Selby may have drawn on a tradition of the abbey that she had been involved in its early history, for a charter alleged to have been granted by Gilbert Tison, attested by Archbishop Ealdred who died in 1069, stated that he was making his gift 'at the instance of Matilda, the noble queen of England': *Coucher Book of Selby*, ii, ed. C. C. Hodges, Yorkshire Archaeological Society, Record Series, xiii (1893), 258, 279. Selby was founded around 1069 by a monk of Saint-Germain d'Auxerre with the help of the then sheriff, Hugh FitzBaldric, and although there would have been no accommodation suitable for the queen at that time, she could have given some support to the project: *Coucher Book of Selby*, i, ed. J. T. Fowler, Yorkshire Archaeological Society, Record Series, x (1892), i, 18.
[5] Bates, *Regesta*, nos. 138, 232, 254.

to the hospital of St Leonard's.[6] Such uncertainty about Henry's birthday, and the fact that he was not given a Norman ducal name but was instead named after his maternal great-uncle, King Henry I of France, underscores the fact that his arrival in the world was of importance primarily within his own family.

Henry may have spent his earliest years with his mother in Normandy.[7] As the youngest son, and possibly the youngest child, he may have had only intermittent contact with his brothers and sisters. Robert Curthose, who was born about 1051, was an adult; Richard, his next brother, died in the New Forest in about 1075; William Rufus, born about 1060, would soon have progressed beyond the nursery to an apprenticeship in arms. The girls – and here again a cloud of unknowing descends over the precise number and birthdays of the daughters – soon left their mother to become wives or, in the case of Cecilia, a child entrant into the nunnery of La Trinité at Caen.[8] Adela who, like Henry, was born after 1066, was the sister who figured largest in his life. She was powerful as the wife of Stephen count of Blois-Chartres and as mother of Count Theobald. Her role would prove to be valuable in maintaining the pro-Norman stance of the counts, and in brokering a peace between Henry and Archbishop Anselm (see below, p. 85).

We know nothing about Henry's childhood other than one incident at l'Aigle reported by Orderic Vitalis, and this may have been fictitious.[9] As Robert grew to manhood, he was increasingly irked by his dependence on his father. Although Robert had been recognised as his father's successor as duke of Normandy even before the campaign of 1066, William had failed to hand over power. Egged on by his comrades, Robert had urged his father to transfer authority over both Normandy and Maine, but William had refused. On one occasion when the Conqueror was preparing a military expedition and was lodging in the frontier town of l'Aigle, his three sons were present. Henry and William Rufus, who were on good terms with

---

[6] The story is mentioned in a *Life* of Archbishop Thurstan. If this records an authentic tradition the likeliest date is 1122, in the autumn: *The Historians of the Church of York and its Archbishops*, ed. J. Raine, 3 vols., RS (London, 1879–94), ii, 266.
[7] Bates, *Regesta*, no. 261. 'William' and 'Henry' occur without further designation, but it is obviously unlikely that they are anyone other than William's sons: nos. 45, 48, 49, 50, 53.
[8] Barlow, *William Rufus*, Appendix, pp. 441–5. Barlow corrects D. C. Douglas, *William the Conqueror. The Norman Impact upon England* (London, 1964), pp. 393–5. Constance, Adelaide and Matilda were all mentioned in the mortuary roll of Matilda, abbess of Holy Trinity Caen, and thus were evidently dead by 1113: *Rouleaux des Morts du IXe au XVe siècle*, ed. L. Delisle, Société de l'Histoire de France (1866), no. 36, 181–2. For Agatha, see OV, ii, 224.
[9] OV, ii, 356–8; David, *Robert Curthose*, chapter 2.

their father, were playing dice in an upper gallery, and poured water down on the heads of Robert and his companions. In a great rage Robert went upstairs to deal with his brothers, and the commotion brought the king from his lodging. Robert was placated, but only briefly, and on the following night he and his companions left for Rouen, where they made an abortive attempt to capture the citadel.

The quarrel between the Conqueror and his eldest son darkened the last years of the Conqueror's life. Although peace was restored for a while, father and son quarrelled again. The queen was said to be much distressed, and incurred her husband's anger by sending Robert money.[10] The Conqueror was unwilling to make any grant of land to his heir, nor were arrangements made for his marriage or those of his younger brothers. All children of royal and noble families had to face uncertainties about their future prospects, when sudden death might transform their prospects at a stroke, but for William and Henry the quarrel between their father and elder brother was an added complication.

William the Conqueror and Matilda seem to have taken particular care over the education of their children.[11] William Rufus was said to have received his education at the hands of Archbishop Lanfranc,[12] and Henry may have spent some time in the household of Bishop Osmund of Salisbury. The evidence is circumstantial: Henry was certainly in the bishop's company in 1084 when he spent Easter at Abingdon abbey, and it has been pointed out that when Henry occurs as a witness to royal acts between 1080 and 1086 it is often in the bishop's company.[13] Henry may have been originally destined for the church, hence the fact that he was taught his (Latin) letters.[14] Orderic mentioned how the king, 'who was literate', was able to read a letter sent to him. William of Malmesbury, too, commented on Henry's early education in the liberal arts, which was never wholly eradicated, though he read little openly. This author thought that such learning was a good thing, quoting Plato: 'happy would be the commonwealth if

---

[10] OV, iii, 96–112.
[11] Robert had tutors who included Tetboldus *grammaticus*: David, *Robert Curthose*, p. 6; for his sister Adela, see the letter of Hildebert of Lavardin which implies that she could read: Migne, *Patrologia Latina*, clxxi, book 1 no. 6, col. 151.
[12] WM, *GRA*, i, 542.
[13] *Historia Ecclesie Abbendonensis*, ii, 16–18; Bates, *Regesta*, nos. 39, 146, 175(1), 176, 193, 194, 253; Hollister, *Henry I*, pp. 36–7.
[14] OV, ii, 214; iii, 120. For Henry see C. W. David, 'The Claim of King Henry I to Be Called Learned', in *Anniversary Essays in Medieval History by Students of Charles Homer Haskins*, ed. C. H. Taylor and J. L. LaMonte (Boston and New York, 1929), pp. 45–56; J. W. Thompson, *The Literacy of the Laity in Norman and Angevin England* (New York, 1960), p. 168; and more recently M. T. Clanchy, *Abelard* (Oxford, 1997), chapter 3.

philosophers governed, or kings were philosophers'.[15] From such comments grew the idea of Henry's education. By the late thirteenth century he was termed 'clerc', and by the early fourteenth century this had evolved into 'Beauclerc'.[16] He could probably read Latin, but there is no information that he was able to write or, *pace* William of Malmesbury, that intellectual interests either inspired his kingship or materially assisted the practice of governance.

In 1083 his mother, Queen Matilda, died; again we do not know how keenly at a personal level Henry felt this loss. It did, however, open up the possibility that he might inherit her very substantial lands in England, for a mother's lands were often used to endow younger sons. No quick action was taken, and the lands were still in the king's hands at the time of the Domesday Inquest in 1086. In 1084 we have a fleeting glimpse of the young prince in England, possibly for the first time since his birth. The Abingdon Chronicle recorded that at the king's order Henry (who was then fifteen) spent Easter at Abingdon, and that Osmund, bishop of Salisbury, and Miles Crispin, lord of Wallingford, were 'attached' to him (*coherentibus*). This phrase presumably means that the two were in attendance. Robert d'Oilly, the king's castellan of Oxford, was also there, and supervised the household, which was provisioned with royal resources.[17]

This brief glimpse of Henry at Abingdon in 1084 suggests that his father was now planning a career in the world for him.[18] Henry would have been assigned to an instructor in the arts of war. He is known to have had a teacher (*magister*) named Robert Achard to whom he gave valuable estates in Berkshire and who could have been his instructor.[19] At Whitsuntide 1086 Henry was knighted by his father at Westminster, Archbishop Lanfranc participating.[20] This was a very public indication of his entry into adult life and status. He was some eighteen years of age.

---

[15] WM, *GRA*, i, 710.
[16] Annals of Oseney and the chronicle of Thomas Wykes: *Annales Monastici*, ed. H. R. Luard, 5 vols., RS (London, 1864–9), iv, 11; for the reference to the soubriquet Beauclerc in the Anglo-Norman *Brut*, see M. D. Legge, 'L'influence littéraire de la Cour d'Henri Beauclerc', in *Mélanges offerts à Rita Lejeune*, ed. F. Dethier, 2 vols. (Gembloux, 1969), i, 681.
[17] *Historia Ecclesie Abbendonensis*, ii, 16–18.
[18] One possibility was that Henry would become lord of Wallingford, whose lord, Toki, brother-in-law of Robert d'Oilly, had been killed at the battle of Gerberoy in 1079. For the honour see K. S. B. Keats-Rohan, 'The Devolution of the Honour of Wallingford, 1066–1148', *Oxoniensia*, 54 (1989), 311–18.
[19] K. J. Stringer, 'Some Documents concerning a Berkshire Family and Monk Sherborne Priory, Hampshire', *Berkshire Archaeological Journal*, 63 (1967), 23–37. The steward of Robert de Bellême who handed the city of Domfront over to Henry in about 1092 was named Achard: see below, p. 32.
[20] *ASC* E 1086; WM, *GRA*, i, 710.

At this time King William was proposing to take an army into the French Vexin, that part of the Vexin between the eastern border of Normandy and the French royal demesne. The old *pagus* or territory of the Vexin had been divided by the coming of the Normans, with the part between the rivers Epte and Andelle in Norman hands, and that between the Epte and Oise in French hands.[21] The last count of the Vexin, Simon, had been brought up at the court of the Conqueror. He had retired into a monastery without sons in 1077, whereupon King Philip of France had taken the French Vexin into his own hands.[22] King William believed he had a claim to the whole Vexin, and he may have thought of it as a future endowment for Henry.[23] In 1087 the men of Mantes in the French Vexin raided across the Norman border into the Evrécin, and the Conqueror decided to retaliate. He proceeded to attack Mantes and sack the town, but, whilst riding through the burning streets, he injured himself by falling against the pommel of his saddle. He became seriously ill, and it was clear that his life was in danger.

He was taken from the city of Rouen to the small church of Saint-Gervais to escape the noise and heat, and there his younger sons, the great magnates and ecclesiastics gathered around his bedside.[24] Robert however was not there. The king made his confession and received absolution; he arranged for money to be distributed to the poor; and requested that special provision should be made for the clergy of Mantes. He exhorted those about him to ensure the maintenance of justice and the preservation of the faith, and freed those who languished in his prisons. Initially he refused to free his half-brother, Bishop Odo of Bayeux, but was persuaded to do so by Robert of Mortain. What, however, of the disposition of his realms? Still bitter towards his eldest son, he was nevertheless persuaded by the Norman magnates to recognise Robert's claim to Normandy; England, however, was left to God, but in the hope that God would grant it to William Rufus, to whom he gave his sword, sceptre and crown.[25] Rufus

---

[21] Bauduin, *La première Normandie (Xe–XIe siècles). Sur les frontières de la Haute Normandie: identité et construction d'une principauté*, pp. 247–83.

[22] P. Feuchère, 'Une tentative manquée de concentration territoriale entre Somme et Seine. La principauté d'Amiens-Valois au XIe siècle', *Le Moyen Age*, 60 (1954), 1–37. D. C. Douglas pointed out that Philip may have benefited from the fact that the Conqueror was besieging Dol: *William the Conqueror*, p. 234.

[23] Henry as king always took any threat to the Norman Vexin seriously, as did Louis VI who had himself been designated count of the Vexin by his father. The region was of great strategic importance because of its proximity to Rouen and Paris, and the situation there would always have been closely monitored by the two kings.

[24] OV, iv, 78–100.   [25] 'De Obitu Willelmi', *GND*, ii, 186.

accordingly left for England bearing a letter from his father to Archbishop Lanfranc.[26]

There was thus no prospect of land for his youngest son, who received instead a large cash legacy, variously reported as between £2,000 and £5,000,[27] certainly sufficient to enable him to acquire land. However, according to Orderic, the weeping son is said to have asked his father what was to become of him, with treasure but no place to call home. The Conqueror, counselling patience, assured Henry that he would one day succeed to all his father's lands.[28] The story seems to hint that Henry was weeping more for himself than for the loss of his father, but the fact is that we have no clue about relations between father and son, except that clearly they were not as difficult as those between the Conqueror and his eldest son, Robert. Henry was still young, and the fact that he was knighted by his father possibly suggests that he was favoured. As soon as the bequest was made, Henry immediately left the court and made haste to ensure that the money assigned to him was weighed out and stored in a strong treasure house. Speed was perhaps necessary, before his brothers took over the treasure, but his action is an early indication of a man who for much of his adult life would have plenty of cash.

As soon as King William had died on 9 September, decorum departed from the court. The nobles left to protect their property, and the king's servants stripped his household of its furnishings, leaving his body virtually naked on the floor. Finally the clergy made their way from Rouen to Saint-Gervais, where prayers were said, and the archbishop of Rouen decreed that the body be taken for burial to the church of Saint-Etienne at Caen. As none of William's family or servants were by then present, it was left to a knight called Herluin to pay for the funeral arrangements out of his own pocket. At Caen the abbot and his monks processed from the town to greet the bier, but then a fire broke out and panic ensued.[29]

By this time Henry had arrived at Caen, and so it was that he alone of the Conqueror's sons attended their father's funeral, in the company of all the bishops and abbots of Normandy.[30] These proceedings, too, were marred

---

[26] For the argument that William had little choice but to do so and was following contemporary convention, see E. Zack Tabuteau, 'The Role of Law in the Succession to Normandy', *Haskins Society Journal*, 3 (1991), 141–69; cf. B. English, 'William the Conqueror and the Anglo-Norman Succession', *Historical Research*, 64 (1991), 221–36.

[27] 3,000 marks of silver, i.e. £2,000: WM, *GRA*, i, 710–12; £5,000: OV, iv, 94; Wace, *Roman de Rou* (ed. Holden), lines 9, 155–6; for the detail that this was English money see *Brevis Relatio*, p.35; *GND*, ii, 204.

[28] OV, iv, 94–6.   [29] Ibid., 100–4.   [30] Ibid., 104–8; WM, *GRA*, i, 510.

by unseemly incidents. The first occurred when the bishop of Lisieux gave a eulogy praising the duke for bringing greatness to his people, maintaining justice, punishing thieves and robbers and protecting clergy and people. The bishop asked those present to pray for the dead man and to forgive him for any wrongs he might have done, only to find himself confronted by a man named Ascelin son of Arthur, who claimed that when the Conqueror had founded Saint-Etienne he had forcibly taken away Ascelin's father's house. Ascelin had to be bought off, but this was not the last disruption. When the Conqueror's corpse was lowered into the sarcophagus, it did not fit, because the coffin was too short and narrow. The king's bowels ruptured, the stench filling the church.[31]

For the next thirteen years, Henry's fortunes were precarious. Moving between the courts of his brothers, he had to make the best terms he could. His father's bequest meant that he had money, but without backing he was unlikely to be able to win lands or a wife. Delayed marriage was not uncommon amongst younger sons of royal or noble birth, nor were liaisons which sometimes led to the birth of illegitimate children. Henry was to be famous or notorious for the number of illegitimate children – at least nine sons and thirteen daughters – whose paternity he acknowledged (see appendix I, no. 2).[32]

His known liaisons go back at least to Rufus' reign, when he was associated with a widow named Ansfrida, whose husband had been a tenant of Abingdon abbey.[33] According to the Abingdon chronicle the affair began after Ansfrida was widowed. Her husband had been thrown into prison by Rufus and died there, leaving her to try to recover his lands. She began to visit Henry 'for help in her troubles', an interesting insight into how one woman came to the notice of the young prince. Their relationship developed from there; she bore him a son, Richard,[34] and possibly other children, for it is very hard to assign Henry's many children to his known mistresses.

---

[31] OV, iv, 102–6.
[32] G. H. White, 'Henry I's Illegitimate Children', in *Complete Peerage*, xi, Appendix D; for comment and revisions see Thompson, 'Affairs of State: The Illegitimate Children of Henry I'.
[33] For the suggestion that Robert of Gloucester's mother also came from this region, see D. Crouch, 'Robert of Gloucester's Mother and Sexual Politics in Norman Oxfordshire', *Historical Research*, 72 (1999), 323–33. As Crouch shows, Earl Robert was evidently related to Philip Gay, who describes the earl as his *cognatus*, but Crouch's arguments that *cognatus* means first cousin in this context, that the earl's mother was a sister of Robert and Stephen Gay, and that their family was of English extraction, though possible, even probable, cannot be said to have been established beyond question. There is, too, the question of the date of Robert of Gloucester's birth. If he was born between 1090 and 1092, it is more likely he was conceived in Normandy, because Henry is not known to have visited England in those years.
[34] *Historia Ecclesie Abbendonensis*, ii, 52–3.

The liaison clearly mattered to Henry, because when Ansfrida died she was buried in the cloister of the abbey, before the door into the church used by the monks. This was a privilege that was not likely to have been accorded to a woman of little account,[35] and might well have displeased the monks.[36]

Henry's mistresses were not drawn from any single social group or nationality. On the whole they did not come from the ranks of the high nobility, though even here there is one exception: Isabel, daughter of his close friend Robert, count of Meulan.[37] They included two women from native families: Ede, daughter of Forne son of Sigulf;[38] and Edith, mother of the countess of Perche.[39] They also famously included a Welsh princess, Nest, wife of Gerald of Windsor.[40] These women may have been the tip of the iceberg, the ones whose families could not be ignored and whose children had to be recognised. There may have been countless other women of lower status and equally diverse origins, whose offspring were not recognised. Yet some of the known liaisons, like that with Ansfrida, were clearly more than passing fancies, and it has been suggested that Henry stationed his more important mistresses near his principal residences in Oxfordshire, or near Domfront or Caen.[41]

We cannot know what Henry *felt* about these women, but the fact that he made provision for them and their children is suggestive. They were not discarded, and Henry was happy to recognise his children and, as we shall see (below, pp. 74, 174, 309) they were provided for through marriage. His daughters particularly were provided for in marriage to high-status partners with whom Henry wished to cement relations.

From Henry's point of view, which of his brothers was likely to be the more generous? Robert was more easygoing, but loyalty to Robert might involve conflict with William Rufus, who was richer and better able to carry out his promises. Robert was probably better disposed to Henry, who must have seemed no threat to his own position, whereas William seemed already to have been uneasy about his younger brother.[42] What Henry did not need was his two brothers to ally against him, as they were to do in 1091.

---

[35] Ibid., ii, 182–6.
[36] Compare the later resistance of the nuns of Godstow to receiving the body of Henry II's mistress into their church: Roger of Howden, *Chronica*, ed. W. Stubbs, 4 vols., RS (London, 1868–71), iii, 167–8.
[37] *GND*, ii, 250; for discussion, Thompson, 'Affairs of State', 133.
[38] *Complete Peerage*, xi, Appendix D, p. 108; Thompson, 'Affairs of State', 132.
[39] *PR 31 Henry I*, p. 155; Thompson, 'Affairs of State', 132.
[40] Gerald of Wales, *Opera*, 8 vols., i–iv ed. J. S. Brewer, v–vii ed. J. F. Dimock and viii, ed. G. F. Warner, RS (London, 1861–91), i, 130; for discussion, Thompson, 'Affairs of State', 131.
[41] Ibid., 137.   [42] WM, *GRA*, i, 542.

Within a few months of their father's death Henry had offered his legacy to his elder brother in return for a grant of rights over the Cotentin and the Avranchin, including overlordship over the lands of Earl Hugh of Chester, and of the great abbey of Mont-Saint-Michel.[43] He was probably granted the title of count (of the Cotentin),[44] and he performed homage to Robert.[45] The west of Normandy was probably chosen because it had been intended as an appanage for their brother Richard; it was also further from the principal centres of ducal power. It could therefore be carved off from the rest of the duchy without jeopardising Robert's own position too much, though it gave Rufus a grievance, in that Henry had supplied Robert with the funds with which to wage war against him.[46] Henry proceeded to assert overlordship over the great lords of the area, like Earl Hugh, *vicomte* of Avranches, Richard de Redvers of Néhou[47] and Nigel of Saint-Sauveur.[48]

In 1088 a coalition of great lords headed by Odo bishop of Bayeux was aiming to put Duke Robert on the English throne instead of his brother. The threat to William Rufus was very serious, because those involved were amongst the most powerful members of the elite. The duke was himself gathering forces in Normandy, and naturally expected support from Henry.[49] The revolt collapsed before Robert had set sail, but this at least meant that Henry could remain on good terms with Rufus. Accordingly Henry crossed to England and formally requested the grant of his mother's lands, to which Rufus is said to have agreed.[50] If so, Rufus evidently had second thoughts. Henry's next problem was that when he sought land from William, his loyalty to Robert came under suspicion. When he returned to Normandy in the company of Robert de Bellême, a great cross-Channel lord who had charted a careful course during the events of 1088, the two were arrested, and imprisoned by the duke, on the advice of his uncle and

---

[43] OV, iv, 118–20; WM, *GRA*, i, 710–12; *GND*, ii, 204.
[44] OV, iv, 148; J. Le Patourel, 'Henri Beauclerc, Comte du Cotentin, 1088', *Revue Historique de Droit Français et Etranger*, 4th series 53 (1975), 167–8. The reference there to 'Count Henry' in a charter of Nigel of Saint-Sauveur is presumably the attestation to one of the gifts entered into Nigel's pancarte which Delisle dated to about 1090: L. Delisle, *Histoire du château et des sires de Saint-Sauveur-le-Vicomte* (Paris, Caen, 1867), pièces justificatives, no. 45. There no evidence to throw light on Henry's relations with the local bishops, Geoffrey of Coutances, who died in 1093, and Ralph of Avranches, who died in 1110.
[45] For the reference to homage see OV, v, 318; Robert of Torigny, however, suggested that this was a mortgage: *GND*, ii, 204.
[46] Wace, *Roman de Rou* (ed. Holden), lines 9, 452–8.   [47] See below, p. 33.   [48] See above, n. 44.
[49] Robert dated a charter issued on 7 July 1088 'when I should have crossed to England': C. H. Haskins, *Norman Institutions* (Cambridge, Mass., 1918), pp. 288–9.
[50] OV, iii, 148.

chief supporter, Odo of Bayeux.[51] Henry had well and truly fallen between two stools, and was to remain in prison for about six months whilst Robert marched south to reassert Norman authority over Maine.

The politics of Maine were turbulent: the count, local lords, the bishop and citizens of Le Mans, the count of Anjou and the Conqueror had all been embroiled.[52] The Angevins and the Normans in particular vied for overlordship over the county. Robert's claim had been bolstered by his betrothal to Margaret of Maine, and although she had died he may have felt an added personal motive to bring the county under Norman influence.[53] He began promisingly by successfully besieging a castle held by Robert de Bellême's men, but did not push on to destroy Robert de Bellême himself, as Orderic thought he should have done.[54] As Robert's estates stretched along the southern borders of Normandy and Maine, and included fiefs held directly of the king of France, he was probably too powerful for the duke to destroy outright, but this consideration did not weigh with Orderic, whose community at Saint-Evroult suffered from its proximity to the lord of Bellême. The duke therefore pushed on to Le Mans, before returning to Normandy and releasing his brother from prison.

Henry not surprisingly now turned away from Robert towards William, but his approaches were rebuffed. Rufus fobbed him off with empty promises for more than a year, so that, when Robert sent for him once more, Henry crossed back to Normandy, only to find Robert still suspicious and inclined to keep him in custody. All we have is a bare record of Henry's shuttling between his brothers. The precise details are not spelled out, but the message was clear enough: Henry was trusted by neither. He managed to escape from Robert's clutches, and fortified his castles in the west.[55]

By 1090 the duke was experiencing difficulties at Rouen. Here two factions had developed amongst the burgesses, one of which was led by a man called Conan son of Pilatus. He had used his wealth to hire knights and had been persuaded by William Rufus to rise against the duke.[56] The plan was for Conan's faction, the *Pilatenses*, to rise on 3 November, when the rebels were to be reinforced by the king's men from Gournay

---

[51] Ibid., iv, 148, where it was suggested that one was kept under guard at Bayeux, the other at Neuilly-l'Evêque. The version reported by William of Malmesbury is different: Henry, having garrisoned the castle at Rouen as Robert's faithful vassal, was placed under open arrest there (WM, GRA, i, 712).
[52] On Maine see now R. E. Barton, *Lordship in the County of Maine c. 890–1160* (Woodbridge, 2004).
[53] GND, ii, 202–3.   [54] OV, iv, 154–8.   [55] WM, GRA, i, 712.
[56] OV, iv, 120–8. L. Musset, 'Une aristocratie d'affaires anglo-normande après la conquête', *Etudes Normandes*, 35 (1986), 9–10. For purposes of comparison see W. Scott Jessee, 'Urban Violence and the *Coup d'Etat* of Fulk le Réchin in Angers, 1067', *Haskins Society Journal*, 7 (1995), 75–82.

and neighbouring fortresses. Hearing of the conspiracy late in the day, Robert sent messages to loyal lords, making treaties of friendship with those who, like Henry, had broken with him. Henry was in the city on 3 November, and as Gilbert de l'Aigle rode in from the south to support the duke, Reginald de Warenne with a force of three hundred men loyal to Rufus attacked the west gate. Duke Robert and Henry meanwhile attacked the rebels inside the city; Robert was advised to withdraw, and retreated to the priory of Notre-Dame-du-Pré across the river, leaving Henry and Gilbert to crush the revolt with a great deal of bloodshed, capturing Conan and other leading rebels.[57] The duke returned, intending to imprison Conan but to be merciful to the other rebels. His supporters had other ideas. William son of Ansger, one of the richest captives, was held to ransom by William of Breteuil for three thousand pounds. Moreover Henry took Conan to the top of the tower at Rouen, and had him thrown to his death.

This was one of the most dramatic incidents of Henry's life. It is described by both William of Malmesbury and Orderic, who adds that the place was still known as Conan's Leap.[58] Orderic paints a vivid picture, doubtless intended to evoke Christ's temptation by the Devil. Henry led his prisoner through the rooms of the tower, pointing out the beauty of the country Conan had tried to conquer. On one side was the hunting region to the south, wooded and well stocked with beasts of the forest. On the other was the populous city, enriched with ramparts, churches and town buildings. Conan 'grew pale with dread as he heard Henry's ironical mockery' and begged for mercy, promising all his gold and silver and faithful service. Henry replied that there would be no ransom for a traitor, and, denying Conan the opportunity to confess his sins, threw him off the tower. He was was said to have died even before his body, fractured in the fall, hit the ground; his corpse was tied to a horse's tail and dragged through the streets.

Henry's action, swift and without a formal trial, was not quickly forgotten.[59] It is possible that Conan suffered a summary death because he was not a noble but a townsman.[60] Conan's treachery to his lord, the duke,

---

[57] For discussion of Rouen in the later twelfth century see B. Gauthiez, 'Paris, un Rouen capétien? (Développements comparés de Rouen et Paris sous les règnes de Henri II et Philippe-Auguste)', *ANS*, 16 (1993), 117–36.
[58] OV, iv, 220–6; WM, *GRA*, i, 712–14.
[59] For a different interpretation of the incident see C. Warren Hollister, 'The Rouen Riot and Conan's Leap', *Peritia*, 10 (1996), 341–50.
[60] M. Strickland, *War and Chivalry. The Conduct and Perception of War in England and Normandy, 1066–1217* (Cambridge, 1996), p. 242.

was manifest, and this may have made him liable to a speedy punishment, as William of Malmesbury commented.[61] Nevertheless on the whole the dukes of Normandy did not use capital punishment against rebels, and that the duke's young brother should do so would have alerted the Normans to a ruthless streak lacking in their duke. If he was hoping to win his brother's approval, however, he miscalculated, because according to William of Malmesbury, Robert soon drove Henry out of the city.[62]

In the months that followed, Henry's fortunes continued to decline. As the year 1091 opened, the tension between his two brothers continued, and he was caught in the middle. William Rufus had been undermining Robert's position by winning over lords in eastern Normandy, and by sending help to a baron called Ralph de Tosny, who was in arms against William count of Evreux and had land in England as well as Normandy.[63] According to the Worcester chronicler, in January 1091 Rufus crossed to Normandy with the intention of seizing Normandy.[64] However, the brothers soon made peace, and this, by excluding Henry, was a personal disaster. Robert made significant territorial concessions to Rufus: the county of Eu in the north (with the abbey of Fécamp), and the port of Cherbourg in the west. The Worcester chronicler stated that the abbey of Mont-Saint-Michel was also ceded, possibly because this was where Henry made his last stand.[65] Robert's men were to remain unmolested in other castles they had taken; Rufus for his part undertook to subdue Maine for Robert, to bring to obedience those who held castles against the duke, to restore to the duke's supporters their estates in England, and to grant him such land in England as had already been agreed. The treaty was ratified by twelve barons on each side.[66] Rufus had used his superior resources to extract concessions. Henry had been sidelined.[67]

Henry did what he could. He raised a force of Bretons and Normans and put his castles, including Avranches and Coutances, in a state of defence.[68] The local magnates, thinking that his prospects of success were not good, surrendered their castles to William Rufus.[69] Counselled by Earl Hugh, it was said, Henry took refuge at Mont-Saint-Michel, where he was admitted

---

[61] WM, *GRA*, i, 712–14.   [62] Ibid., 714.
[63] OV, iv, 214.   [64] JW, iii, 56; cf. OV, iv, 250.
[65] *ASC* E 1091; JW, iii, 58.   [66] Ibid.   [67] WM, *GRA*, i, 714.
[68] In the process Henry exacted castle work from men belonging to the abbey of Holy Trinity, Caen, at Quettehou and the whole Cotentin 'and made the men of that vill and district work at the castles of his barons': *Charters and Custumals of the Abbey of Holy Trinity Caen. Part 2, The French Estates*, ed. J. Walmsley, British Academy Records of Social and Economic History, new series, xxii (London, 1994), p.127.
[69] OV, iv, 250.

by some of the monks, and was besieged by his brothers. He soon ran short of water and appealed for supplies. His elder brother consented, angering Rufus, who said enemies should be denied food and drink, to bring them to submission. Robert replied that it would be wrong to allow their brother to die of thirst.[70] Nevertheless, after fifteen days Henry had had enough and asked for a safe conduct to leave.

Henry's movements in the next few months are uncertain. He paid off his knights and, according to Wace, followed the duke to Rouen, where he was imprisoned and then released, after which he travelled to the French court.[71] Orderic believed he travelled via Brittany, and then spent nearly two years in the Vexin with a knight, a clerk and three armed attendants.[72] Both Orderic and William of Malmesbury thought that Henry's experiences in this period were character-forming: the former because Henry when king could show mercy to the poor, and the latter because poverty taught Henry prudence.[73] It is not impossible that Henry spent part of this time in the Vexin, possibly hoping to be granted land in the French Vexin.

However, his fortunes were shortly to change when the fortress of Domfront in the Passais was handed over to him by its townspeople. He was later believed to have been at Paris when a man named by Wace as 'Haschier' arrived in disguise from Domfront and sought him out.[74] Wace's Haschier seems to have been the same man as Achard, a rich local man mentioned by Orderic. Achard was possibly the steward of Robert de Bellême and keeper of the castle,[75] but he had apparently grown tired of the continuous fighting and attacks on himself and his neighbours.[76] As lord of Domfront Henry had a base of great strategic importance. It was situated at an important crossing of routes from west to east and north to south, from Normandy to Maine along the valley of the river Varenne, and it was located where the borders of Maine, Brittany and Normandy met.[77] His position there was an affront to Robert de Bellême and may well have sparked off what seems to have been a personal animosity between the two

---

[70] WM, *GRA*, i, 552. Wace elaborates the incident: Henry asked his brother for wine not water; Robert sent a tun of the best and established a truce so that Henry could take water daily, to the annoyance of William Rufus: *Roman de Rou* (ed. Holden), lines 9, 579–9, 606.
[71] Ibid., lines 9, 635–40. [72] OV, iv, 252. [73] WM, *GRA*, i, 714.
[74] Wace, *Roman de Rou* (ed. Holden), lines 9, 635–9, 644.
[75] OV, iv, 258n; *GND*, ii, 206–7; *Brevis Relatio*, p. 36. The name Achard recalls that of Robert Achard, mentioned above (p. 32) as Henry's *magister*.
[76] OV, iv, 258; for the background see Thompson, 'Robert of Bellême Reconsidered', 271–3.
[77] G. Louise, *La Seigneurie de Bellême Xe–XIIe siècles*, 2 vols., *Le Pays Bas-Normand*, 101, 102 (1990, 1991), ii, 93–4.

men: certainly Henry was later to be unrelenting over the confiscation of Robert's English estates (see below, pp. 71–2). Henry never surrendered the castle, and may have been responsible for major building works there.[78] From Domfront Henry was able to conquer the Passais. He took everything away from the inhabitants of Bellême, though their lord Robert counter-attacked.[79]

Henry's acquisition of Domfront was followed by the recovery of influence in western Normandy over lords such as Richard de Redvers, Roger de Mandeville and Earl Hugh. The earl was granted custody of the border town of Saint-James-de-Beuvron.[80] It was also during these years that Henry established the network of supporters who would prove so important to his early success in England, men like Hasculf of Saint-James (-de-Beuvron), Rualon of Avranches[81] and Robert de Brus, from Brix near Valognes.[82] Earl Hugh already had vast estates in England, and others who were very evidently in Henry's favour after 1100 may already have been established in the Cotentin before that year as members of a 'court-in-waiting'.[83]

A key member of Henry's personal following at this time was Roger, a poor priest of Avranches, later bishop of Salisbury and Henry's leading minister. He was said to have won Henry's confidence by the management of his domestic affairs and by checking the luxury of his household.[84] The later chronicler William of Newburgh provided a more highly coloured and probably fictional story: Henry passed by a church where Roger was saying mass and, impressed by the speed with which he rattled through

---

[78] For a summary account with bibliography see *Palais Médiévaux (France–Belgique)*, ed. Annie Renoux, Publications de l'Université du Maine (1994), pp. 41–2.

[79] Wace, *Roman de Rou* (ed. Holden), lines 9, 645–8.   [80] *GND*, ii, 209.

[81] Hasculf witnessed a charter issued in 1101 or 1102: *RRAN*, ii, no. 533. He acquired land in Northamptonshire (*VCH Northamptonshire*, i, 362); for his family and possible kinship to Rualon d'Avranches, see K. S. B. Keats-Rohan, 'Le rôle des Bretons dans la politique de colonisation normande de l'Angleterre (vers 1042–1135)', *Mémoires de la Société d'Histoire et d'Archéologie de Bretagne*, 74 (1996), 199 and appendix 2. Rualon had been granted the manor of Stanton Harcourt in Oxfordshire by 1101: *RRAN*, ii, no. 528.

[82] It is not precisely clear when and how Robert arrived in England. He appears before 1100 as a witness to a charter of Earl Hugh granting the church of Flamborough to Whitby Abbey. This grant did not take effect, and the authenticity of the charter has been queried: *The Charters of the Anglo-Norman Earls of Chester, c. 1071–1237*, ed. G. Barraclough, Record Society of Lancashire and Cheshire, cxxvi (1988), no. 5. Robert had acquired land in England by 1103: see *RRAN*, ii, no. 648 and for analysis, *Early Yorkshire Charters*, i–iii, ed. W. Farrer (Edinburgh, 1914–16), ii, 16–19. For his place of origin, G. W. S. Barrow, 'Scotland's "Norman" Families', in *The Kingdom of the Scots* (London, 1973), p. 322.

[83] I propose to develop this point in a future article.

[84] WM, *GRA*, i, 736–8; *Historia Novella*, pp. 64–70. Roger described himself as a poor priest of Avranches in the profession he made to Archbishop Anselm: *Canterbury Professions*, ed. M. Richter, Canterbury and York Society, lxvii (1973), p.115.

the service, decided that this was the kind of man suitable to be an army chaplain and took him into his service.[85]

Meanwhile the fragile rapprochement between William and Robert had begun to deteriorate, and once again Henry found himself caught in the middle. Robert for his part had assisted his brother: late in 1091 he had accompanied Rufus north to Durham and on into Lothian where the brothers met King Malcolm, and Robert had negotiated a renewal of the submission which King Malcolm of Scots had made to the Conqueror. For his part, however, William Rufus refused to accompany Robert back across the Channel to help restore order in Normandy and Maine. Rufus was still concerned about northern affairs. He advanced north-west in 1092 and established a castle at Carlisle, driving out the local ruler, Dolfin.[86] In the following year Malcolm came south to request fulfilment of the terms promised in 1091 but a row broke out; Malcolm retreated in anger, but when he returned with an army both he and his eldest son Edward were killed by Robert de Mowbray, earl of Northumbria. A succession crisis ensued during which Duncan, a son of Malcolm who was in Rufus' service at the time, moved quickly north with an army of Scots and Normans, and managed to establish himself for a time.[87]

Duke Robert became increasingly exasperated with his brother's reluctance to help him, and at Christmas 1093 he sent messengers to William's court at Gloucester, saying that he would renounce the peace between them if the king would not perform his side of the treaty. He called Rufus perjured and faithless, demanding that he keep his agreements or go to the place where the agreement had been made and there clear himself of the charges.[88] William crossed to Normandy to confer with his brother in the presence of the nobles who had pledged their support to the earlier treaty. The latter laid the responsibility for the breakdown squarely upon Rufus, an allegation which the king angrily rejected.[89]

---

[85] Newburgh, i, 36. Very little is known of other members of Henry's household in these years. A charter of Duke Robert for Holy Trinity Caen issued with Henry's consent was witnessed on Henry's part by Rannulf FitzUlger and Odo, Henry's chamberlain. Little can be discovered about either of these men. Between 1108 and 1118 a man named Ralph FitzOlger witnessed an agreement which the abbot of St Stephen's Caen made to restore land to William son of Ernucio: *Charters and Custumals of the Abbey of Holy Trinity, Caen. Part 2, The French Estates*, no. 13, pp. 123–4.

[86] *ASC* E 1092; JW, iii, 62.   [87] JW, iii, 68. For the Scottish royal family, see appendix I, no. 3.

[88] *ASC* E 1093; JW, iii, 66.

[89] JW, iii, 68 locates this meeting at the *Campus Martis* (sic) at Rouen, allegedly the site of the victory of William Longsword in 934: Dudo of St Quentin, *De Moribus et Actis Primorum Normanniae Ducum Auctore Dudone Sancti Quintine Decano*, ed. J. Lair (Caen, 1865); *History of the Normans*, translated by E. Christiansen (Woodbridge, 1998), p. 68 and map p. 231; *ASC* E 1094; David, *Robert Curthose*, pp. 84–5. David pointed out that Philip might have been present at this plea: there is a reference in a letter of Ivo, bishop of Chartres, to Philip's presence at an (undated) plea between the king of the English and the duke of the Normans.

William began to hire mercenaries; by using bribes he persuaded Norman lords to transfer to his allegiance, and filled their castles with his own men.[90] He besieged and captured the castle of Bures-en-Bray, whilst Robert appealed to King Philip for help, and the pair began to make some headway. King Philip besieged Argentan, which had obviously fallen out of the duke's control, and which surrendered on the first day. The duke himself captured a castle called 'Houlme' and its commander, William Peverel.[91] Rufus responded by escalating his efforts, ordering 'twenty thousand Englishmen' to be summoned. However, when the troops were assembled at Hastings they were relieved of their support money and dismissed. Philip and Robert were now advancing on William's headquarters at Eu, but at Longueville Philip was persuaded to turn back.[92] At this juncture Rufus was in considerable difficulties, for his prospects in Normandy were uncertain, and back across the Channel the Welsh had risen against the Norman invaders. Attacks were made on Norman castles in west Wales, Cheshire, Shropshire and Herefordshire, and the Welsh regained control of Anglesey. Rufus himself is said to have led an army there after Christmas 1094 and to have lost many men and horses.[93] In Scotland Duncan was killed and replaced by his uncle Domnall Bán.[94]

Rufus by this time was in such difficulty that he asked his youngest brother for help. An immediate difficulty was that Duke Robert was so powerful that Henry could not reach Rufus at Eu overland. Instead he crossed to England, and spent Christmas 1094 in London. In Lent 1095 he returned to Normandy with fresh supplies of treasure and waged war against Robert on Rufus' behalf.[95] This left Rufus free to lead another expedition into Wales;[96] he then marched north to deal with a rebellion there, and then returned to lead another army to Wales in the autumn.[97]

At this juncture, in November 1095, Pope Urban II preached the first crusade at the council of Clermont. This was attended by, amongst others, the bishops of Bayeux, Evreux and Sées, though there were no bishops present from England.[98] Duke Robert, in common with many other counts and nobles from northern France, decided to join the crusade. Orderic claimed that Robert took the cross because he had lost almost all his support at home, but this is ungenerous. What is surprising is not that Robert should have decided to go, but that his youngest brother, unmarried and young,

---

[90] JW, iii, 70.
[91] Barlow thought this castle was Briouze (*William Rufus*, p. 333); cf. Thompson, 'Robert of Bellême Reconsidered', 273 for the suggestion that it was Château-Gontier.
[92] JW, iii, 70–2; *ASC* E 1094.   [93] JW, ii, 72–3 and n.   [94] *ASC* E 1095.   [95] Ibid.
[96] JW, iii, 72 is the only chronicler to mention an expedition in 1094.
[97] Ibid., 74–8.   [98] OV, v, 18–24.

did not.[99] William, though a great warrior, was not prepared to go, and as a monarch had a duty to defend his realm. There seems to have been little encouragement for his English vassals to join, either, and those who did so tended to be those with links to Duke Robert. Perhaps the king prevented Henry from taking the cross, or perhaps Henry simply did not wish to participate.

Before Robert could leave, he had to make peace with his brother. The pope dispatched the abbot of Saint-Bénigne in Dijon as an intermediary, and he met Rufus in England at Easter 1096.[100] A treaty was arranged by which William advanced the sum of 10,000 silver marks in return for custody of the duchy, probably for three years.[101] William paid over the money at Rouen, and Robert left for the East in the autumn of 1096.

The departure of his eldest brother now cleared the way for Henry to attach himself to William Rufus more firmly. The king recognised his authority not only over the Cotentin but also, apparently, over the Bessin, excluding the towns of Bayeux and Caen.[102] If this is correctly reported, then Henry had actually benefited from the duke's departure and, if a deal had been struck beforehand, it offers a possible explanation for Henry's not going on crusade. For the next four years Henry's activities are largely unreported. Rufus himself was occupied with war. In 1097 there were two expeditions to Wales to reinforce his authority there,[103] and he also sent an army to Scotland with Edgar Aetheling and Edgar of Scots, another son of Malcolm and Margaret. Domnall Bán was defeated, and Edgar was established on the Scottish throne on terms that emphasised the debt he owed to Rufus.[104]

Rufus was prepared to take seriously his commitment to recover all the lands and rights of the Conqueror, and in 1097 he, together with Henry,

---

[99] It has been suggested that the round church of the Holy Sepulchre in Northampton was founded by Henry to excuse the fact that he had not participated in this great adventure: C. N. L. Brooke, 'Princes and Kings as Patrons of Monasteries', in *Il monachesimo e la riforma ecclesiastica (1049–1122). Atti della quarta settimana internazionale di studio. Mendola, 1968.* Miscellanea del Centro di studi medioevali, 6 (Milan, 1971), 139.

[100] Hugh of Flavigny, *Chronicon*, Migne, *Patrologia Latina*, cliv, col. 353.

[101] Ibid., col. 354; Eadmer, *Historia Novorum*, p.74. According to Orderic the term was five years (OV, v, 26, 208); according to Robert of Torigny, the money was advanced without any time limit (*GND*, ii, 210).

[102] *GND*, ii, 210–12; *Brevis Relatio*, p. 36.   [103] *ASC* E 1097.

[104] JW, iii, 84. This understanding of the precise nature of Edgar's relationship with William depends in part on accepting the validity of Edgar's purported charter to Durham, with its reference to his holding of Lothian and the kingdom of Scotland being held by the 'grant of my lord King William'. The authenticity of this charter has, however, been much disputed: see A. A. M. Duncan, 'The Earliest Scottish Charters', *Scottish Historical Review*, 37 (1958), 103–35; J. Donnelly, 'The Earliest Scottish Charters?', *Scottish Historical Review*, 68 (1989), 1–22; and A. A. M. Duncan, 'Yes, the Earliest Scottish Charters', *Scottish Historical Review*, 78 (1999), 1–38.

attacked the French Vexin.[105] This was business left unfinished since their father's death, and it had become more pressing because Duke Robert had ceded Gisors to the French.[106] King Philip had also created Prince Louis count of the Vexin, a title which gave Louis every incentive to assert his lordship over the Norman Vexin.[107]

William and Henry led an army to the Vexin and took control of Gisors, where Robert de Bellême was responsible for the building of an impressive castle.[108] William was greatly assisted by staunch support from Robert, count of Meulan, whose French county abutted the Vexin, and by Guy lord of La Roche-Guyon.[109] Rufus accordingly was able to advance into the French Vexin as far as Pontoise, and he attacked Chaumont, meeting little resistance. However, in February 1098 Rufus was diverted by an urgent need to reassert Norman authority in Maine, and he left the Vexin.[110]

The situation in Maine had altered once again with the rise to power as count of Helias, lord of La Flèche.[111] Helias had come into conflict with Robert de Bellême, who had lands and castles in Maine, and when Robert captured Helias, he handed him over to Rufus. Rufus (perhaps with Henry, we do not know) marched on Le Mans, which had been occupied by Fulk of Anjou, and, to cut a complicated story short, Fulk agreed that Le Mans and all the castles which had been occupied by the Conqueror should be handed over.

Rufus was therefore free to return to unfinished business in the Vexin, and in the autumn of 1098 he led an army across the frontier from Conches. He ravaged as far as Pontoise and laid siege to Chaumont, but then returned to Normandy.[112] By Easter 1099 he was back in England, and at Whitsun Henry was with him.[113] He may have still been in Rufus' company when the latter departed in a whirlwind to deal with Count Helias, who had reoccupied Le Mans only to retreat again before Rufus' advance, in July 1099.[114]

---

[105] OV, v, 214.
[106] *Gallia Christiana in Provincias Ecclesiasticas Distributa*, ed. P. Piolin, 16 vols. (Paris, 1715–1865), xi, *Instrumenta*, col. 18; OV, vi, xxxiv.
[107] Ibid., iv, 264.   [108] Ibid., v, 214.
[109] The castle of La Roche-Guyon is on the right bank of the Seine, not far from its junction with the river Epte. Either this or a later Guy was assassinated by a relative by marriage a few years later: Suger, *Vie de Louis VI* (ed. Waquet), pp. 115–19.
[110] OV, v, 212–8; Suger, *Vie de Louis VI* (ed. Waquet), pp. 4–10.
[111] OV, v, 246–50; cf. WM, *GRA*, i, 566; Gaimar, *Lestoire des Engleis*, lines 5925–5946; Wace, *Roman de Rou* (ed. Holden), lines 9, 977–10, 1036.
[112] OV, vi, 216–18; for a discussion of Suger's omission of the second campaign, see Barlow, *William Rufus*, p. 393.
[113] *RRAN*, ii, no. 414a.   [114] OV, v, 252–60.

On 15 July, meanwhile, the crusaders had captured Jerusalem, and by the autumn Robert was on his way back to Normandy, covered in glory. It would have been obvious that the duke's next step was to marry, and this he did. His bride was Sibyl, daughter of Count Geoffrey of Conversano, and from his father-in-law and his other friends Robert obtained sufficient money to redeem the mortgage on Normandy.[115] Rufus thus faced the prospect of losing Normandy, and both he and Henry also faced the prospect that Robert would father sons to whom the duchy of Normandy would pass. Yet on 2 August 1100, Henry's future changed forever.

On that day 'King William was shot by an arrow by one of his own men' as the *Anglo-Saxon Chronicle* stated succinctly. The possibility that he would die in this way was very remote, and it made a profound impression on contemporaries. Chroniclers of course reported portents and visions, but nowhere was it suggested that his death was anything other than an accident. According to William of Malmesbury, the Devil had appeared to men in woods and byways, and a few weeks before the king's death a spring at Finchampstead had run red, as if with blood.[116] On the night of the king's death, the abbot of Cluny dreamed that the king appeared before the throne of God, was found guilty, and condemned to death. The abbot proceeded to relate his dream to Archbishop Anselm, who was then in exile in France.[117] The king himself was said to have had a nightmare the night before he died.[118] Most sinister of all, however, was the dream of an unnamed monk: Rufus had entered a church, looked round scornfully at the congregation as usual, and then seized the Crucifix in his teeth. Eventually the figure on the cross gave Rufus such a tremendous kick that he fell over backwards with flames coming from his mouth. The monk reported his dream to Robert FitzHaimon, one of the king's closest friends. Robert went straight to the king and told him the dream, and although Rufus roared with laughter, he did hesitate about his plan to go hunting.[119]

Orderic Vitalis's account differs on details but is similarly full of foreboding. When the king was putting on his boots, a blacksmith arrived with six arrows. The king kept four for himself and gave two to Walter Tirel. A monk arrived from Gloucester with a letter from Abbot Serlo warning of a monk's vision of the king's death, which the king ridiculed: 'Does he take

---

[115] OV, v, 278–80. [116] WM, *GRA*, i, 570–4.
[117] Eadmer, *The Life of St Anselm Archbishop of Canterbury*, ed. and trans. Sir Richard Southern (Oxford, 1979), pp. 123–4.
[118] WM, *GRA*, i, 572.
[119] Ibid., 572–4. FitzHaimon was the father-in-law of Robert earl of Gloucester, one of the patrons of William of Malmesbury: *GRA*, i, 10–12.

me for an Englishman? Let them put off their journeys and business because some old woman has sneezed or had a dream! Not me!' Orderic's account thus reveals that belief in omens was widespread, especially amongst the English.

The king delayed his start until after dinner when, having drunk more heavily than was usual, he set out into the forest. He and his friend Walter Tirel were separated from their companions as they waited for the deer to be driven towards them.[120] According to William of Malmesbury, the king shot and wounded a stag, and then Walter aimed at a second stag; by mistake his arrow hit the king in the chest. Rufus broke off the shaft of the arrow, fell on the wound, and died. When Walter ran up he found the king senseless and speechless, and instantly took flight.[121]

Not all accounts agree on details. Suger, abbot of Saint-Denis near Paris, wrote later that he had often heard Tirel swear that he had not been in the same part of the wood where the king was, or even caught sight of him.[122] John of Salisbury, who in the middle of the twelfth century revised Eadmer's *Life of Anselm*, reported that Walter on his deathbed had not only proclaimed his own innocence of the shooting, but asserted that the king himself was in some way responsible.[123] Many believed this version. John of Salisbury believed that whoever was responsible was acting on the orders of God.[124] Walter took flight for France, for fear of reprisals,[125] but he did not disappear into oblivion. He was at Pontoise in 1102 as the host of Prince Louis, and in 1113 he was at the latter's court when a confirmation was issued for Cluny. In 1118 he founded a priory at Poix dedicated to Saint Denis, and in 1122 was mentioned as a knight of Count Charles of Flanders.[126]

Historians have sometimes suggested that Rufus' death was premeditated.[127] If the suggestion of a ritual killing can be discounted, that of murder has been taken more seriously.[128] The chief beneficiary, and hence the chief suspect, was Henry. The fact that there were no contemporary

---

[120] OV, v, 288–90. For Walter see J. H. Round, 'Walter Tirel and His Wife', in *Feudal England* (London, 1964 edn), pp. 355–63.
[121] WM, *GRA*, i, 572–4. [122] Suger, *Vie de Louis VI* (ed. Waquet), p. 12. [123] OV, v, 294.
[124] 'Vita S. Anselmi', Migne, *Patrologia Latina*, cxix, col. 1031. [125] OV, v, 288–94.
[126] *Cartulaire de Saint-Martin de Pontoise*, ed. J. Depoin, Publications de la Société Historique du Vexin (1909), appendix, pp. 453–4.
[127] For discussions see E. A. Freeman, *The Reign of William Rufus*, 2 vols. (Oxford, 1882), ii, 310–43, appendix SS; M. Murray, *God of the Witches* (London, 1933); H. Ross Williamson, *The Arrow and the Sword: An Essay in Detection*, 2nd edn (London, 1955); W. L. Warren, 'The Death of William Rufus', *History*, 9 (1959), 22–9; C. N. L. Brooke, *The Saxon and Norman Kings* (London, 1967), pp. 160–8; C. Warren Hollister, 'The Strange Death of William Rufus', *Speculum*, xlviii (1973), 637–53, reprinted in *MMI*, pp. 59–75; E. Mason, 'William Rufus and the Historians', *Medieval History*, 1 (1991), 6–22.
[128] See above, n. 127.

references to murder does not necessarily exonerate Henry, for it could simply mean that a successful 'accident' had been engineered. There is also some circumstantial evidence to support the idea of murder: Henry was at hand, though not, apparently, part of the king's own party; the prospect of his eldest brother's return, as a married man likely to produce heirs, would reduce his own prospects of succeeding Rufus. If Henry was behind his brother's death, he evidently had assistance. Why should Walter Tirel have been involved? Though not a Norman by birth, he was related by marriage to the powerful Clare family,[129] of whom Gilbert FitzRichard and his brother Roger were both present in the New Forest on that August afternoon; they and their family were to prosper under Henry.[130] A conspiracy to murder Rufus involving Henry, Walter Tirel and the Clares is thus not out of the question.

A further possibility has been raised, however, that these conspirators were in league with King Philip and Prince Louis.[131] The French might well have wished for Rufus' removal from the scene. His recent activities in the Vexin had showed that he was determined to reassert his father's claims there. Moreover, it was reported that Prince Louis visited Henry I's court at Christmas 1100.[132] Orderic reported that the prince came as an envoy from his father with a sealed letter containing instructions from his stepmother that he should be arrested and imprisoned.[133] Whether or not there is any truth in this story, the status of the Vexin was a matter of mutual concern for Louis and Henry. The prince may have wished particularly to secure guarantees about the future of the castle of Gisors: this was certainly to be an issue in 1108 (see below, p. 119). It is hard to see, however, why Philip and Louis would have engineered a murder, as Rufus was going to have to relinquish Normandy to his brother, and the return of Duke Robert would surely mean a less aggressive regime in Normandy. If foul play, or even fratricide, was suspected, surely there would have been some hint in the contemporary sources? Contemporaries, who clearly saw the king's death as God's judgement on his oppression of the church, nowhere speak of murder or foul play, yet if murder had been suspected, rumours would

---

[129] Round, 'Walter Tirel and His Wife', in *Feudal England*, pp. 357–8.
[130] For the presence of Gilbert FitzRichard and Roger, see Gaimar, *L'Estoire des Engleis* (ed. Bell), lines 6345–6. It has been pointed out, however, that the Clare family did not receive marks of royal favour immediately on Henry's accession, and that when these did materialise, it may have been to foster loyalty rather than to recognise past service: J. Ward, 'Royal Service and Reward: the Clare Family and the Crown, 1066–1154', *ANS*, II (1988), 267–8.
[131] Mason, 'William Rufus and the Historians', 17–20.
[132] OV, vi, 50; SD, *Opera Omnia*, ii, 232.   [133] OV, vi, 50–4.

have circulated.[134] On balance it seems most likely that Rufus died because of an accident.

The king's body, like that of his father, suffered indignities before being buried. In Rufus' case it was left to a handful of the country people to place the corpse on a cart, in which it was transported to Winchester, dripping blood all the way.[135] As those in attendance reached the outskirts of the city, they were met by the clergy and monks with some of the (poorer) citizens, and the body was buried in the cathedral on the following day, Friday, 3 August.[136] Henry is not known to have been close to his brother, but, more to the point, he was now much too busy to mourn.

---

[134] For reports about the death of Alfred, Edward the Confessor's brother, see *ASC* C 1036; JW, ii, 522–4; *Encomium Emmae*, ed. A. Campbell, Camden Society 3rd series, lxxii (reprinted 1998), pp. 41–7, says that Godwin diverted Alfred to Guildford where his companions were handed over to Harold for execution, and that Alfred was dead when handed over to the monks at Ely; cf. *The Life of King Edward Who Rests at Westminster*, ed. F. Barlow, 2nd edn (Oxford, 1992), pp. 32–4. William of Poitiers and William of Jumièges both attributed the arrest to Godwin and the blinding to Harold's orders: *The Gesta Guillelmi of William of Poitiers*, ed. and trans. R. H. C. Davis and M. Chibnall (Oxford, 1998), pp. 4–7; *GND*, ii, 106.

[135] WM, *GRA*, i, 574.   [136] OV, v, 292.

CHAPTER 2

'By the grace of God, king of the English'

By any stretch of the imagination, the year 1100 was the most dramatic of Henry's life. At Christmas 1099 he had been a younger brother whose prospects of a place in the sun had largely depended on Robert and William. Twelve months later he was a king, married to a bride of royal birth. His brother's death had almost certainly been accidental, but it was Henry who had taken advantage of his good fortune and worked to establish himself in power as quickly as he could before the inevitable challenge from Robert and his supporters.

As soon as Henry learned of Rufus' unexpected death, he went straight to the royal castle at Winchester and demanded that the royal treasure stored there be handed over.[1] Winchester was one of the principal centres of royal authority, and after 1066 it proved to have added convenience as a point of transit to lower Normandy. It is likely, therefore, that the amount of treasure being stored there was considerable. It is not certain who was in charge: the bishopric was vacant, and the sheriff was possibly, but not certainly, Henry de Port, the principal lay magnate in the county. He occurs as a witness to the Charter of Liberties, so he was presumably with Henry in London three days later.[2]

Events in Winchester did not progress smoothly, for William of Breteuil, one of the leading Norman magnates, spoke up on behalf of the absent Duke Robert. He reminded Henry that they both had obligations of homage and fealty to the duke, that Robert had served God for years as a crusader, and by God's will had been restored to his own duchy and his father's crown. Orderic alone mentions the presence of William of Breteuil in England. He had inherited the Norman estates of his father, William FitzOsbern, but perhaps he hoped that, if the duke succeeded to the throne, he would recover his father's English earldom. FitzOsbern had been the Conqueror's steward

---

[1] OV, v, 290. [2] *RRAN*, ii, nos. 488, 638, 687.

42

and possibly custodian of Winchester,[3] so Orderic may have instinctively ascribed to William the role of representative for the absent duke. Robert had been the Conqueror's eldest son, and had covered himself with glory on the crusade. On the other hand, Henry's claim rested on the fact already noted above (p. 20) that he, unlike his brothers, had been born to a crowned king and queen. Moreover, Robert had been passed over once already, in 1087.[4] Henry may also have spread rumours to the effect that Robert would never return, a charge laid against him by a later historian of the crusade, William of Tyre.[5] Moreover it was not unheard of for younger brothers to succeed even during their elder brother's lifetime. In 1067 in Anjou, for instance, Count Geoffrey the Bearded had been imprisoned by his younger brother Fulk, who ruled in his place.[6]

According to Orderic a quarrel broke out and Henry angrily drew his sword, but, thanks to the persuasions of Henry de Beaumont, earl of Warwick, wiser counsels prevailed, and the castle and the treasure it contained were handed over to Henry.[7] Earl Henry was the younger brother of Robert count of Meulan, and the two were amongst the few magnates to commit themselves openly to Henry from the start. Each had great estates in England and Normandy, and Robert in addition held the French county of Meulan. Robert had become an important figure in the preceding reign (see above, p. 37), and he seems to have passed between the courts of Duke Robert and King William, until he opted to support Rufus. As an elder statesman in 1100 his advice was particularly valuable to Henry,[8] and he accompanied Henry to London.

On 5 August Henry was crowned king in Westminster abbey by Maurice bishop of London, possibly with the assistance of Gerard, bishop of Hereford.[9] It was not essential for the coronation to take place so quickly but, as Henry himself explained to Archbishop Anselm of Canterbury, 'enemies were intending to rise up against me and the people who are mine to govern, and therefore my barons and the people did not want to delay it any

---

[3] OV, ii, 194–6.
[4] ASC E 1100; Anselm, Letters, no. 212; A. Williams, 'Some Notes and Considerations on Problems Connected with the English Royal Succession, 860–1066', ANS, 1 (1978), 144–67, discusses the various elements in king-making.
[5] Chronicon, ed. R. B. C. Huygens, Corpus Christianorum, Continuatio Mediaevalis, 2 vols. (Turnhout, 1986), 63, 63A, book ix. For a translation into English, see A History of Deeds Done Beyond the Sea by William Archbishop of Tyre, trans. E. A. Babcock and A. C. Krey, 2 vols. (New York, 1943, 1976), i, 398.
[6] OV, ii, 104; vi, 74.   [7] WM, GRA, i, 714.   [8] OV, v, 298.
[9] Walter Map, De Nugis Curialium, stated that Gerard crowned Henry and, as a reward, Henry promised him the first vacant archbishopric.

longer'.[10] Neither archbishop was able to be present: Anselm was at Lyon, and although the archbishop of York set off for London as soon as he heard the news of William's death, he arrived too late.[11]

Coronation had developed as a ceremony in which churchmen and kings cooperated. Churchmen demonstrated through anointing and coronation how God had sanctified the king and made him a holy person. Kings for their part swore publicly to keep the peace, to forbid all evils and to maintain justice and mercy.[12] The ritual was potent, even intoxicating.[13] It was held in the great abbey church, lit with many candles, glittering with gold, silver and precious stones, and resounding with the chanting of monks. After an opening chant, the king prostrated himself, and after the reading of a litany he made three promises: to maintain peace for the church and all Christian people, to root out all robberies and iniquities, and to uphold justice and mercy in all his judgements.[14] Only after the oath did those present formally consent to the coronation in the words 'Volumus et concedimus'. The king was then anointed on his head, breast, shoulders and elbows.[15] He was seated on a throne, and then received in turn a sword, to symbolise his duty to destroy the enemies of religion (*christiani nominis hostes*) and to help widows and children; a crown, through which, it was believed, God crowned the king with glory, justice, honour and valour (*opere fortitudinis*); a ring, through which the king would rule as the head and prince of the realm and people; a sceptre, the symbol of royal power; and a rod, a sign of virtue and equity to soothe the pious and cast fear into the reprobate.[16] The crowned king was kissed by the bishops and conducted to the royal throne whilst the choir sang the *Te Deum*, after which the prayer

---

[10] Anselm, *Letters*, no. 212. Ivo of Chartres wrote in a similar vein to explain the speedy coronation of Louis VI in 1108: *Letters*, no. clxxxix, Migne, *Patrologia Latina*, clxi, cols. 193–6.

[11] Hugh the Chanter, p. 1; cf. William of Malmesbury, *Gesta Pontificum*, ed. N. E. S. A. Hamilton, RS (London, 1870), p. 258, and *Liber Eliensis*, ed. E. O. Blake, Camden Society, 3rd ser., xcii (1962), p. 224 for the statement that the archbishop of York crowned the king.

[12] R. Foreville, 'Le sacre des rois anglo-normands et angevins et le serment du sacre (xie–xiie siècles)', *ANS*, 1 (1978), 205; F. Kern, *Kingship and Law in the Middle Ages* (Oxford, 1939), part 1.

[13] It is not precisely certain which form of the service was used. For the most recent discussion of the manuscripts, see G. Garnett, 'The Third Recension of the English Coronation *Ordo*: the Manuscripts', *Haskins Society Journal*, 11 (1998), 43–71; L. G. Wickham Legg, *English Coronation Records* (London, 1901), pp. 30–42; J. Brückmann, 'The Ordines of the Third Recension of the Medieval English Coronation Order', in *Essays in Medieval History Presented to Bertie Wilkinson*, ed. T. A. Sandquist and M. R. Powicke (Toronto, 1969), pp. 99–115.

[14] Wormald, 'Quadripartitus', p. 140.

[15] P. L. Ward, 'The Coronation Ceremony in Medieval England', *Speculum*, 14 (1939), 176.

[16] For the regalia see English, 'William the Conqueror and the Anglo-Norman Succession', 234. At some stage kings received spurs during the coronation service, but these are not mentioned until the coronation of Richard I: J. H. Round, *The King's Serjeants and Officers of State* (London, 1911), pp. 347–8.

'Sta et retine' was said beginning with the words 'Hold and retain the place which in succession to your father by hereditary right, delegated through the authority of Almighty Omnipotent God, [is] handed over through us present.' After mass had been celebrated, the king took homage from those present.

At some stage Henry gave orders for his coronation promises to be written down, authenticated with his seal and distributed throughout the country.[17] The resulting charter was said to have been 'given' on the day of his coronation, though this does not mean that it was literally drawn up on that day, and copies were apparently sent out to every shire and possibly to major abbeys.[18] The charter was important in its own day as a statement both of the principles by which Henry intended to rule, and of specific grievances he intended to remedy, and it achieved lasting fame as the basis for a first draft of the grievances presented to King John by the barons in 1215. Its subject matter is technical, but crucially important to understanding the basis on which Henry proposed to rule.

The text begins with a statement that the coronation had taken place, and that the realm had been oppressed by unjust exactions. The king promised 'freedom' for the church and then went on to make more specific promises. On the question of vacancies, he promised that churches would be neither 'sold' (presumably a reference to simony) nor 'let out to farm', that is, rented out during periods of vacancy; nor would he take anything from churches' demesne lands and properties. These pledges are revealing for both what is said and what is left unsaid. Henry was explicitly rejecting that fiscal exploitation of vacant churches which had attracted criticism under Rufus and Ranulf Flambard, who was soon arrested, but no reference was made to the length or number of vacancies.[19] The references to freedom and the rejection of selling churches may have been a nod towards reforming ideals, to which Rufus seems to have been indifferent.

The charter continued with a pledge to abolish certain evil customs, which were then spelled out. Such promises were traditional and, as Pauline Stafford argued some years ago, there are clear parallels between the charter and clauses 69 to 83 of Cnut's lawcode, the last great codification of English law before the Norman Conquest.[20] These may in turn represent

---

[17] Eadmer, *Historia Novorum*, p. 119.
[18] J. A. Green, '"A Lasting Memorial": The Charter of Liberties of Henry I', in *Charters and Charter Scholarship in Britain and Ireland*, ed. M. T. Flanagan and J. A. Green (Houndmills, 2005), pp. 53–69.
[19] *ASC* E 1100; L. H. Jared, 'English Ecclesiastical Vacancies during the Reigns of William II and Henry I', *Journal of Ecclesiastical History*, 42 (1991), 362–93.
[20] 'The Laws of Cnut and the History of Anglo-Saxon Royal Promises', *Anglo-Saxon England*, 10 (1981), 173–90.

the substance of concessions made by Aethelred in 1014, which were subsequently confirmed by Cnut when he accepted the submission of the English at Southampton.[21] What is significant is the way that ongoing concerns – over the transmission of land and inheritance, the hasty remarriage of widows, the exactions of royal officials, the need to avoid intestacy and protection of the king's rights – were being refashioned and updated to take account of the recent past.

Clauses two, three and four dealt with the transmission of land through inheritance and marriage. At the head of the list came the succession payments made when an heir took up his inheritance. These were not called heriots, as in Cnut's code, nor were they defined in terms of equipment graded according to status. In 1100 in clause two the king promised only that 'reliefs' would be 'reasonable', and his men (*homines*) were instructed to deal likewise with *their* men. In the following clause, three, the question of marriage was raised. Whilst it is hard to believe that earlier English kings had not kept a close watch on marriage alliances, a ruling that the king's permission had to be sought for the marriages of female relatives of his men seems to have been new. Moreover, the idea of a daughter as the heir (*haeres*), whose marriage was to be disposed of with the consent of the barons, seems also to have been new. Concern about over-hasty arrangements for widows (clause four) may be found in Cnut's code, where it was laid down that they were not to be compelled to become nuns,[22] but the provision in 1100 that they were to have their marriage portions and dowries as long as they did not have a child outside marriage may have been novel. In the case of wills, there were earlier precedents for concern lest men die intestate. Norman custom, though not English, ruled out the possibility of bequeathing land by will.[23] In clause seven of Henry's charter, permission was granted for the dying to dispose of their property, and, in the case of those who died intestate, for their relatives or their men to divide the property.

Clauses five and six of the 1100 charter dealt with exactions, and again they were a mix of old and new. In Cnut's code there was a concern about

---

[21] JW, ii, 484 and ii, 504 for an agreement at Oxford between the Danes and the English about the observance of King Edgar's laws.
[22] II Cnut, 73a.
[23] For earlier concern about intestacy, II Cnut, 70; for wills see F. Pollock and F. W. Maitland, *The History of English Law*, 2 vols., 2nd edn (Cambridge, 1968), ii, 314–63; J. Hudson, *Land, Law and Lordship in Anglo-Norman England* (Oxford, 1994), pp. 120, 122; J. C. Holt, 'Feudal Society and the Family in Early Medieval England: II. Notions of Patrimony', *Transactions of the Royal Historical Society*, 5th series, 33 (1982), 197–8; for the post-obit gift in pre-Conquest Normandy see E. Zack Tabuteau, *Transfers of Property in Eleventh-Century Norman Law* (Chapel Hill and London, 1988), pp. 24–7.

the unjust exactions of reeves,[24] and this is echoed in 1100 by a reference in clause six to the king's rightful farms and agreements. Over and above these, debts owed to Rufus were to be pardoned, a concession which may have reflected the idea that Christians when dying should confess their sins and make restitution, though Rufus had died unshriven.[25] Those who had incurred forfeitures or fines were not to be forced to hand over their property as security, but were to make amends as in the days of King Edward (clause eight). The point here seems to be the balance between the amount of security demanded (which, if too great, would remove all a man's lands until the fine had been agreed) and the nature of the offence. The shift away from fixed fines to what in effect were arbitrated damages may have begun before 1066, but the charter reflects a sense that too much was being exacted by way of security. The only exceptions made in 1100 were for those convicted of treachery or (serious) crime, *scelus*.

English kings made considerable profit from their monopoly over the coinage, which was made by moneyers situated in boroughs widely scattered up and down the country. Although the Conqueror did not alter the organisation of the coinage, he did stabilise the weight of the silver penny, and he also imposed a new tax called *monetagium*, possibly in recompense for stabilising the weight of the silver coinage.[26] In clause five Henry promised to abandon this levy, but he nevertheless pledged to punish those caught with counterfeit money.

The origins of the murder fine (clause nine) are thought to have been rooted in an old idea that it was the king's responsibility to protect strangers, those without kin, but the Conqueror's act in extending it to all Frenchmen (*Franci*) who had come with him seems to have been new.[27] Severe fines

---

[24] II Cnut, 69.
[25] Just before his own death, Henry revoked all sentences of forfeiture: OV, vi, 448.
[26] For a discussion of this tax see T. N. Bisson, *Conservation of Coinage. Monetary Exploitation and its Restraint in France, Catalonia, and Aragon c. 1000–1225 A. D.* (Oxford, 1979), chapter 2; D. M. Metcalf, 'The Taxation of Moneyers under Edward the Confessor and in 1086', in *Domesday Studies*, ed. J. C. Holt (Woodbridge, 1986), pp. 279–83; P. Nightingale, 'Some London Moneyers, and Reflections on the Organization of English Mints in the Eleventh and Twelfth Centuries', *Numismatic Chronicle*, 142 (1982), 34–50; and M. Blackburn, 'Coinage and Currency under Henry I: A Review', *ANS*, 13 (1990), 49–81.
[27] For recent discussion of the subject see G. Garnett, '*Franci et Angli*: the Legal Distinction between Peoples after the Conquest', *ANS*, 8 (1985), 116–20; and B. O'Brien, 'From *Mordor* to *Murdrum*: the Pre-Conquest Origin and Norman Revival of the Murder Fine', *Speculum*, 71 (1996), 74–110. The attribution of the murder fine specifically to Cnut has been challenged by A. Cooper, 'The Rise and Fall of the Anglo-Saxon Law of the Highway', *Haskins Society Journal*, 12 (2002), 55–8. The syntax of the clause in the text known as 'Hic intimatur' suggests that responsibility rested with the lord of the murdered man for bringing the accused man before the justices, but Cooper suggests that the thrust of the legislation was to make lords responsible for the activities of their men (i.e. that the lords in question were the lords of the murderers not of the murdered).

were imposed on local lords, and if they defaulted, on communities where corpses were found, but only where the dead men were not English. Already by 1100 there was a recognition that the new regulations were causing problems, and Henry promised that murders committed after his coronation were to be dealt with as they had been in the days of King Edward.

The final two specific issues raised in 1100 (in clauses ten and eleven) were the forests and military service, both of which had been raised in Cnut's secular code. Cnut had granted freedom of hunting to individuals on their own land whilst protecting his own forests.[28] The Conqueror had brought deer and wild boar under his protection, and had created the New Forest in Hampshire.[29] In 1100 no mention was made of the protection of the 'beasts of the chase', but in clause ten Henry simply stated that he retained the forests in his own hands by the common consent of the barons, as his father had held them. Finally, there was the issue of military service. Clauses 77 to 79 of Cnut's code were concerned with desertion, death in battle and performance of services. In 1100 service was linked specifically with geld (a form of land tax): clause eleven the manorial demesne of serving knights was to be quit of all geld and labour service, so that they would be better prepared and ready for the king's service and the defence of the realm. It appears that what was going on here was a promise that traditional exemptions, which had been ignored in the great four-shilling levy of 1096 taken to raise money for the First Crusade, were to be restored.[30]

At the core of the charter were thus a number of pledges to redress grievances on specific issues, but in the last three clauses (twelve to fourteen) there was a return to general statements. In clause twelve the king declared his 'firm peace', a pledge which may relate to the eight-day peace declared at a coronation, or, as has been suggested, to a promise of more profound significance.[31] The king also promised (clause thirteen) to restore the law of King Edward, with such emendations as his father had made, and the charter ended with an amnesty clause (fourteen) for those who had taken anything from royal property since his brother's death, provided it was returned.

Henry's charter thus represented a written statement of his coronation promises, combined with pledges on specific grievances, some old, others

---

[28] II Cnut, 80.
[29] *ASC* E 1087; for the New Forest, see F. H. Baring, 'The Making of the New Forest', *EHR*, 16 (1901), 427–38.
[30] *Leges Edwardi Confessoris*, c. 11, 2, in *Die Gesetze der Angelsachsen*, ed. F. Liebermann, 3 vols. (Halle, 1903–16); B. O'Brien, *God's Peace and King's Peace. The Laws of Edward the Confessor* (Philadelphia, 1999), pp. 168–9.
[31] Hudson, *Formation of the English Common Law*, p. 82.

reflecting the more recent past. It may not have been the first of its kind. Rufus issued written promises in 1088 and in 1093 when he believed he was dying, and these too were widely disseminated.[32] On the second occasion it seems that he ignored his promises as soon as he recovered, which may help to explain why no copies survive.[33] Henry was thus not breaking new ground in promising to redress grievances. Those which needed to be redressed most urgently would have been obvious enough, so there is no need to assume that the charter was drafted for him by others, even if he took advice on the precise wording. What was different in 1100 was the way Henry's coronation charter was widely disseminated and soon copied into compilations of law. Its survival was thus assisted by contemporary interest in legal literature, both past and present, and it survived to become a first draft for the complaints of the opposition barons in 1215.

The witnesses of the Charter of Liberties included Simon de Senlis, earl of Northampton, who had been established in England in the preceding reign. Without land in Normandy he had little option but to support Henry. Another witness was Walter Giffard, who had considerable estates in England, and was lord of Longueville in Normandy. In some versions of the witness lists he was styled earl,[34] a title conferred on him by either Rufus or Henry. He is thought to have been a kinsman of William Giffard, Rufus' chancellor, the new bishop-elect of Winchester.[35] Eudo the steward, Roger Bigod,[36] Robert de Montfort the constable[37] and Robert Malet, soon if not already a chamberlain,[38] also attested the coronation charter.

It was imperative for those who had estates and offices to hurry to court to do homage to the new king. The coronation charter was a general confirmation of liberties, but behind the scenes individual deals were being done. Henry was expected to be generous, as Orderic pointed out,[39] and he needed to be, to build up as much support as possible. The hasty coronation precluded a great assembly in August, but as the news of Rufus' death spread, others arrived at court in the hope of basking in the new king's favour. Earl Hugh of Chester had already accepted Henry's overlordship for his estates in Normandy. One of the earl's illegitimate sons, Robert, a monk of Saint-Evroult, was nominated to the wealthy abbacy of Bury St Edmunds.[40]

---

[32] For 1088, *ASC* E 1088; WM, *GRA*, i, 546; for 1093, Eadmer, *Historia Novorum*, p. 32.
[33] Eadmer, *Historia Novorum*, p. 38.   [34] *RRAN*, ii, no. 488 (d).
[35] Keats-Rohan, *Domesday Descendants*, p. 840, for the statement that he was a son of Walter I Giffard.
[36] *RRAN*, ii, no. 544.   [37] OV, vi, 100.
[38] C. Warren Hollister, 'Henry I and Robert Malet', *Viator*, 8 (1977), 63–81; reprinted in *MMI*, pp. 129–36, here, pp. 130–1.
[39] OV, v, 296.
[40] *Ungedruckte Anglo-Normannische Geschichtsquellen*, ed. F. Liebermann (Strassburg, 1879), pp. 130–1.

The brothers Robert FitzHaimon and Haimo, a royal steward, threw in their lot with the new king.[41] Robert de Bellême, his brother Roger the Poitevin and the king's cousin, William count of Mortain, also appeared at court.[42] Their English estates were too large to put at risk by staying away altogether, but their fathers had each supported Duke Robert in 1088 and there was always the prospect that they would back any effort by the duke to take the throne from his brother.[43]

The Clares were another very powerful and influential family with lands in both England and Normandy. They are not mentioned as being in attendance at Henry's court in 1100, though they appeared subsequently, and were to rise further in royal favour.[44] Gilbert FitzRichard, lord of Clare in Suffolk and Tonbridge in Kent, was connected by marriage with Walter Tirel, the man who shot the arrow which killed William Rufus. If Rufus had been murdered by Tirel, were his Clare kinsmen to receive a quick reward? Gilbert's brother Richard was soon nominated to the abbey of Ely,[45] but Gilbert himself is not mentioned as present at Henry's court before 1101. In March of that year he acted as a surety for the king in the treaty with the count of Flanders (below p. 62). His cousins Robert and Richard FitzBaldwin, sons of Baldwin FitzGilbert, are known to have been at court with him at Christmas 1101.[46]

Henry had his own inner circle on which he could rely, and whose members could now be promoted. Roger d'Avranches, who had run his household before 1100, was appointed to the chancellorship by Easter 1101.[47] William d'Aubigny, another west Norman, who had been a member of Rufus' court, was appointed as butler, an office he held throughout the reign.[48] William de Courcy, from the English branch of the family, was soon appointed as one of the royal stewards.[49] In general Henry had to take steps to ensure that castles and shrievalties were in safe hands. One conspicuous casualty was Ranulf Flambard, bishop of Durham. For churchmen he stood

---

[41] *RRAN*, ii, no. 492. Engenulf de Ferrers, Winebald de Ballon and Hamelin his brother also appear as witnesses to this document.
[42] *RRAN*, ii, no. 497.
[43] Robert de Bellême, like Earl Hugh, was in Normandy when Rufus was killed: OV, v, 296. He and his brother witnessed a royal charter for Tewkesbury abbey: *RRAN*, ii, no. 497. For Robert's family, see appendix I, no. 9.
[44] Ward, 'Royal Service and Reward', 267–8.   [45] *Liber Eliensis*, p. 225.   [46] *RRAN*, ii, no. 552.
[47] According to the editors of *RRAN*, ii, p. ix, William Giffard was replaced by Roger at about Easter 1101.
[48] William attested the treaty with the count of Flanders as butler in 1101: *RRAN*, ii, no. 515. He was a son of Roger d'Aubigny and brother of Nigel. For his family see Keats-Rohan, *Domesday Descendants*, p. 273.
[49] William attested as steward in 1101: *RRAN*, ii, no. 544.

as a symbol of fiscal oppression of the church under Rufus, and soon after the coronation he was arrested and thrown into the Tower.[50]

Another notable absentee from the scene was Archbishop Anselm, who heard of William Rufus' death while at the monastery of La Chaise-Dieu in the Auvergne.[51] Anselm and William had never managed to achieve a harmonious relationship. According to Eadmer, Anselm had fiercely resisted being appointed to Canterbury. Once consecrated, he found Rufus' rough-and-ready use of his father's 'customs' over the church difficult to deal with. There were several clashes, the most serious of which was over recognition of the pope, especially when there were disputed papal elections. Rufus shared his father's belief that the king was to determine who was to be recognised as pope in England. This placed the new archbishop, who had recognised Pope Urban II when he was abbot of Bec, in a very difficult situation. Anselm later summarised his quarrels with Rufus in a letter to Pope Paschal II: Rufus did not want appeals to go to Rome without his permission, nor did he wish Anselm to send or receive papal letters, or to obey the pope's commands. He had refused to allow Anselm to hold a council, and had given church lands to his own men.[52] When Anselm's request to visit the pope to discuss his difficulties was refused, he had finally left the country, but at Dover he was humiliated when his belongings were searched by a royal chaplain, William Warelwast. Moreover, Rufus had confiscated the archiepiscopal lands.[53]

Henry wanted the archbishop to return from exile for a variety of reasons. He wanted to demonstrate his credentials as a good son of the church; also the new bishops and abbots he had chosen needed consecration, and, although this is nowhere stated in the sources, he doubtless wanted Anselm to officiate at his own marriage. The archbishop was also one of the king's most important tenants-in-chief and his lands were thickly concentrated in the south-east. Henry therefore wrote explaining why he had not postponed his coronation until Anselm returned, begged him to return to the 'storm-tossed and desolate' mother church of Canterbury, and declared that he entrusted his kingdom to Anselm's counsel.[54] Letters were also sent from the monks at Canterbury, and from the barons.[55]

---

[50] JW, iii, 92–4; SD, *Opera Omnia*, ii, 332; for the bishop's career see R. W. Southern, 'Ranulf Flambard and Early Anglo-Norman Financial Administration', *Transactions of the Royal Historical Society*, 4th series, 16 (1933), 95–128, reprinted in *Medieval Humanism and Other Studies* (Oxford, 1970), pp. 183–205; H. S. Offler, 'Ranulf Flambard as Bishop of Durham (1099–1128)', *Durham University Journal*, 64; new series, note 33 (1971–2), 14–25.
[51] Eadmer, *Historia Novorum*, p. 118.   [52] Anselm, *Letters*, no. 210.
[53] Eadmer, *Historia Novorum*, p. 88.   [54] Anselm, *Letters*, no. 212.
[55] Eadmer, *Vita Anselmi*, p. 126.

Anselm seems to have decided to return even before the king's letter arrived.[56] His biographer, Sir Richard Southern, thought that the archbishop made a tactical error by not securing any specific commitments beforehand from the king,[57] but Anselm evidently believed that Henry would be a king with whom he could do business. Henry might have given verbal undertakings not to restrict Anselm's contacts with Rome, or have indicated that he would allow Anselm to hold reforming councils. Anselm also had to consider the consequences of prolonging his absence, for the whole English church as well as for the see of Canterbury.[58] Henry had advised Anselm to travel to Dover from Wissant, a port held by the count of Boulogne, and not to travel through Normandy, as the 'whole world round the kingdom of England had been shaken' by news of Rufus' death.[59] More to the point, the duke's return to Normandy was by then imminent. Robert arrived in September, and with his duchess he went in thanksgiving to the great abbey of Mont-Saint-Michel.[60] There was always the possibility that Robert or men loyal to him would seek to detain the archbishop, and even dissuade him from accepting Henry's coronation. There was enmity between the two brothers from the start. According to the Anglo-Saxon Chronicle the duke was received with joy in Normandy except for resistance from castles garrisoned by King Henry's men, presumably in the Cotentin. Robert faced many battles against them, and he complained to the pope about his brother's behaviour.[61]

Anselm meanwhile landed at Dover on 23 September and six days later he met the king at Salisbury. The king asked him to renew the homage he had paid to Rufus and when Anselm refused, he was stunned, 'disturbed and troubled beyond measure', as well he might be. Furthermore Anselm warned the king that if he invested bishops or abbots, he, Anselm, would have nothing to do either with them or with the king.[62] Anselm himself had apparently been invested with the ring and staff at the hands of William Rufus. According to Eadmer, 'Anselm was inducted after the manner and precedent of his predecessor and for the tenure of his land was made the

---

[56] Ibid., p. 127.
[57] R. W. Southern, *Saint Anselm. A Portrait in a Landscape* (Cambridge, 1990), pp. 291–2.
[58] B. Golding, '"Tribulationes Ecclesiae Christi": The Disruption Caused at Canterbury by Royal Confiscations in the Time of St. Anselm', *Spicilegium Beccense*, 2 (1984), 125–45.
[59] From this may be inferred that relations between Henry and Count Eustace III of Boulogne were easing. The count hoped to recover the English estates he had lost because he supported Duke Robert in 1088: *ASC* E 1088. He did not achieve a reconciliation with Henry, however, until after the Treaty of Alton: see below, p. 64.
[60] *ASC* E 1100.   [61] Anselm, *Letters*, no. 213.   [62] Eadmer, *Vita Anselmi*, p. 127.

king's man'.[63] Henry might well have anticipated that Anselm would refuse to countenance lay investiture, but what clearly came as an unwelcome shock was Anselm's refusal to perform homage. Homage was the bond between a lord and his vassal, a recognition of submission and service on the one side and protection on the other. Churchmen held vast tracts of land in England for which military service was owed, and, as Henry is reported to have said, he would lose half his kingdom if they did not recognise that obligation. In his condemnation of 1095 Pope Urban II had raised the stakes when he proscribed both homage by churchmen and lay investiture, but the condemnation of homage was a highly contentious matter.[64]

Anselm further said that if the king could not accept the pope's decrees, he would leave the country once again. This additional threat put Henry in a very difficult situation: he could not afford to surrender homage and investiture, nor could he countenance Anselm's departure. If Anselm left England, Henry's credentials as a reformer would be thrown into doubt, and there was always the possibility that an approach would be made by Duke Robert's party. If an accord could be worked out between duke and archbishop, Anselm, who had not been involved in Henry's coronation, might then make Robert king. The only practicable way forward for Henry was to refer the matter to Rome to see if the pope could be persuaded to relax his decrees on investiture and homage. Anselm was unwilling to arouse suspicions about his loyalty, and agreed to this, although he did not believe that the pope would change his mind.

Marriage and a son were high on Henry's agenda in 1100. He could have taken time to negotiate a bride from France or Germany, but he had clearly made up his mind to marry. Edith, elder daughter of King Malcolm of Scots and Queen Margaret, was his chosen bride.[65] She had probably been born in 1080 – Duke Robert, who visited the Scottish court in that year, was her godfather.[66] Her name, like those of her brothers Edward, Edmund and Edgar, underlined her mother's descent from pre-Conquest English kings. At some point during her childhood she was sent south of the border, possibly to ensure that she received a convent education. She was placed in the care of her aunt, Christina, who had had become a nun in England at Romsey in Hampshire.[67] This community, like that

---

[63] Eadmer, *Historia Novorum*, p. 41.
[64] S. Vaughn, *Anselm of Bec and Robert of Meulan. The Innocence of the Dove and the Wisdom of the Serpent* (Berkeley, Los Angeles and London, 1987), p. 25.
[65] Huneycutt, *Matilda of Scotland*, pp. 27–30; *Oxford DNB*. For Matilda's family, see appendix I, no. 3.
[66] OV, vi, 188; WM, *GRA*, i, 704.   [67] *ASC* E 1085, *recte* 1086.

at Wilton where Edith later took up residence, had close associations with pre-Conquest princesses, and thus was particularly appropriate for a girl of royal birth.[68]

In 1093 Edith had emerged briefly into the spotlight. The chronicles offer only a brief account of the incident, and it is difficult to work out what was going on. It seems that her father, King Malcolm, intended to remove her from the nunnery in order for her to be married, possibly to Count Alan, lord of Richmond. Rufus himself may have entertained some idea of marrying her, because on the way to meet her father he visited the nunnery of Wilton, where she was then living,[69] but retreated when he saw her wearing a veil. The meeting between Rufus and Malcolm did not, as we have seen (above, p. 34), take place, and after Malcolm left the court, he too visited Wilton. When he found his daughter wearing a veil, he tore it from her head and left taking her with him.[70] She herself was later to claim that she was not a professed nun, but that her aunt had made her wear the veil to protect her from the lust of the Normans.[71] Her father's action indicates that she was intended for marriage, rather than the cloister.

What happened to Edith next is uncertain. Her father and her eldest brother were killed during an attack on the North (see above, p. 34), and Queen Margaret survived her husband by only three days. Edith's brother Edgar with Rufus' support asserted his claim to succeed his father; he initially succeeded, then lost the throne, but was restored with Rufus' help. The likelihood is that meanwhile Edith continued to live in southern England, probably in the company of her sister Mary. The ancestry of both girls made them highly desirable brides. The great magnate William de Warenne was reported to have been a suitor of Edith,[72] and Henry is said to have been acquainted with her, for according to William of Malmesbury his affection for her was of long standing in 1100.[73]

As the chronicler pointed out, Edith was a descendant of English kings as well as a daughter of the king of Scots. She was thus descended from

---

[68] For an important review of links between the Scots and Anglo-Saxon aristocracy after 1066, see S. Marritt, 'Coincidences of Names, Anglo-Scottish Connections and Anglo-Saxon Society in the Late Eleventh-Century West Country', *Scottish Historical Review*, 83 (2004), 159–60.

[69] There are different accounts of Edith's whereabouts: OV, iv, 272 (Romsey); William of Malmesbury, *GRA*, i, 744 (Romsey and Wilton); Eadmer, *Historia Novorum*, p. 123 (Wilton). In 1094 Anselm addressed a letter to the bishop of Salisbury which suggests that at that time Edith was then at Wilton in the diocese of Salisbury: Anselm, *Letters*, no. 177. The simplest explanation is that she went south to England with her aunt to Romsey, and moved to Wilton in 1093.

[70] Hermann of Tournai, *The Restoration of the Monastery of Saint Martin of Tournai*, translated with an introduction and notes by L. H. Nelson (Washington, 1996), pp. 31–2.

[71] Eadmer, *Historia Novorum*, p. 122.

[72] OV, iv, 272.   [73] WM, *GRA*, i, 714–16.

two ancient and illustrious lines of kings, and, like her husband, born in the purple.[74] Any children born to the marriage would unite the past and present reigning royal houses of England, a fact which contemporary commentators were not slow to mention.[75] At a more mundane level, the marriage had the added advantage of further consolidating the alliance between the Norman kings on the one hand and the sons of Malcolm and Margaret on the other which had been initiated by William Rufus.

However, the accomplishment of the marriage was not without difficulty. The issue of Edith's freedom to marry had to be clarified and, even if this was successful, it might well be revived by their enemies to cast a shadow over the legitimacy of her children. Years later, in 1139, Edith's daughter the empress found that the emissaries of her rival King Stephen were claiming at Rome that she was the daughter of a nun.[76] Moreover Edith's descent from pre-Conquest kings was a double-edged sword. Memories of the past were not dead yet. Apart from the Anglo-Saxon prince Edgar Aetheling, the children of Malcolm and Margaret had the most credible claim to the English throne. The older sons had English royal names, and perhaps their parents nursed hopes that one day they might have prospects in England. Yet their problems in establishing their claim to succeed their father threw them into alliance with Rufus and Henry, and as the years went on the possibility of overturning Norman rule in England must have seemed increasingly remote. Edith however took no chances and gave up her English name in favour of Matilda, by which she was known henceforth.[77]

Before a marriage could take place, an investigation into her status was held, in which Archbishop Anselm played a crucial role. In fact, it was so important that his biographer, Eadmer, well aware that the archbishop was criticised because he performed the marriage,[78] felt it incumbent to explain the circumstances. Matilda came to the archbishop and asked for his advice, explaining how her aunt had made her wear a little black hood which she took off and trampled on as soon as the abbess was out of sight, and she denied categorically that she was a nun.[79] Hermann of Tournai,

---

[74] Ibid., 714–16, 754; cf. Hermann of Tournai, *Restoration*, p. 31.
[75] Eadmer, *Historia Novorum*, p. 121; OV, v, 300.
[76] Arnulf, later bishop of Lisieux, was said to have laid the charge against the empress that her birth was not legitimate: *The Letters and Charters of Gilbert Foliot*, ed. A. Morey and C. N. L. Brooke (Cambridge, 1967), p. 65; *The Historia Pontificalis of John of Salisbury*, ed. and trans. M. Chibnall (Oxford, 1986), p. 83.
[77] In the Winchcombe annals she was called both Edith and Matilda when her death was recorded: R. R. Darlington, 'Winchcombe Annals 1049–1181', in *A Medieval Miscellany for Doris Mary Stenton*, ed. P. M. Barnes and C. F. Slade, Pipe Roll Society, new series, xxxvi (1960), p. 118. In one manuscript, 'T', the name Eadgytha is interlined, possibly by the twelfth-century scribe; cf. OV, vi, 188.
[78] Eadmer, *Historia Novorum*, pp. 121–2.   [79] Ibid., p. 122.

writing decades later, offered a different version of events but one which demonstrates that there was still a belief that Matilda had been a nun: Anselm had advised against the marriage because he had been reliably informed that she had worn the veil, whereupon Henry had replied that he had promised to marry her and had even sworn an oath to her father to that effect.[80]

Anselm decided that the matter should be heard before a council, which was summoned to meet at Lambeth on the south bank of the river Thames. Witnesses spoke up in support of the girl's story, and two archdeacons who had been sent to Wilton reported that they had heard nothing there to contradict Edith's testimony. Anselm withdrew from the assembly, which then debated the issue, and found that Matilda was free to dispose of her person as she wished. Reference was made to Archbishop Lanfranc's pronouncement, that those who had taken refuge in nunneries after the Conquest could not be forced to take the veil except by their own free will.[81]

Matilda herself came into the assembly and offered to prove her story by oath or by any other method. According to Hermann, Anselm was still not keen to perform the marriage, pointing out that no one denied that Edith had worn a veil, and that the king could find a more suitable match amongst the daughters of kings and counts. Writing with the benefit of hindsight, Hermann prophesied that the country would not long rejoice 'because of a child that might be born of her'.[82] However reluctant he felt, Anselm nevertheless agreed to officiate. In front of the doors of Westminster abbey, raised above the crowd, he explained how the girl's case had been investigated, asked anyone who believed there was an impediment to the marriage to speak out, and when the crowd replied that there was no obstacle, duly performed the wedding ceremony.[83] That it should have been prefaced by a public statement of this kind cannot have been very agreeable to either party, but shows how much importance was attached to establishing the validity of the match.

Matilda was crowned by the archbishop immediately after the wedding. The queen prostrated herself, and was anointed, given a ring, and then crowned. The set prayers recalled appropriate images from the Old Testament, of Judith, who delivered her people from a cruel enemy; Sarah,

---

[80] Hermann of Tournai, *Restoration*, p. 31.
[81] Eadmer, *Historia Novorum*, p. 124; *Letters of Lanfranc*, ed. H. Clover and M. Gibson (Oxford, 1979), no. 53.
[82] Hermann of Tournai, *Restoration*, pp. 32–3.
[83] Eadmer, *Historia Novorum*, pp. 121–5. Gerard, bishop of Hereford, conducted the service: OV, v, 300; cf. JW, iii, 96, *ASC* E for the statement that the celebrant was Archbishop Anselm.

Rebecca and Rachel, whose fecundity merited honour; and Esther, who interceded for her people with King Ahasuerus.[84] The rite for the queen was thus broadly similar to that for the king, but the prayers emphasized her role as saviour of her people, mother and intercessor. As queen she had her own household, including a chancellor and chamberlains who attested her charters.[85] She was soon assigned land and property in dower.[86] For a time she had some authority over Malmesbury abbey,[87] and over at least two houses for women, Barking and Romsey.[88]

What did Matilda look like? There are references to her beauty, but these are probably conventional.[89] William of Malmesbury, who perhaps had the strongest motive for praising her looks, merely described her as 'not bad looking' ('non usquequaque despicabilis formae').[90] Marbod, bishop of Rennes, who wrote to her when she was queen, praised her for not painting her face or binding her breasts to make herself seem slimmer like other women.[91] From these sources we might infer that she was no great beauty, and did not seek to pretend that she was. Her education at Romsey and Wilton had provided her with at least the rudiments of literacy, for according to William of Malmesbury she had 'exercised her intelligence through literature'.[92]

While it is difficult to gain any impression of her personality, her actions in 1100 suggest that she was determined, even assertive. Eadmer's account may have been intended to paint the archbishop in the best possible light, but even so Matilda was prepared to speak up for herself, and was intent on marriage rather than the cloister. She fulfilled contemporary expectations

---

[84] *English Coronation Records* (ed. Wickham Legg), pp. 37–9.
[85] Reinhelm (for whom see *RRAN*, ii, nos. 544, 571, 613) was nominated to the see of Hereford in 1102: Eadmer, *Historia Novorum*, pp. 144–5, 187, 208. Bernard, his successor as chancellor, became bishop of St David's in 1115: JW iii, 136–8; for Aldwin the chamberlain see *RRAN*, ii, nos. 675, 906 (also attested by Bernard, the queen's chancellor), 971 (ditto), 1090, 1108, 1109; Alberic the chamberlain occurs in Henry's charter for Montebourg: *Charters of the Redvers Family and the Earldom of Devon 1090–1217*, ed. R. Bearman, Devon and Cornwall Record Society, new series, xxxvii (1994), pp. 58–9.
[86] Huneycutt, *Matilda of Scotland*, chapter 2.
[87] It is not clear exactly what the queen's relationship with Malmesbury abbey was, and William of Malmesbury is reticent on the subject. Eadwulf, sacrist of Winchester, was elected abbot in 1106: Winchester annals, *Annales Monastici*, ed. Luard, ii, 42. Matilda was said to have transferred the temporalities to him, and he seems to have stayed in possession until 1118. Anselm refused to confirm him because of the gift of a goblet which might have been misconstrued as simony: Anselm, *Letters*, nos. 384, 385. Bishop Roger of Salisbury deposed him in 1118, presumably after the queen's death: *Annales Monastici*, ii, 45.
[88] *RRAN*, iii, no. 31. The link with Romsey may have gone back before 1100, when Matilda was under the protection of her aunt Christina. Henry issued several documents from Romsey in 1105, and granted a fair to Romsey and to the queen: *RRAN*, ii, nos. 682–6, 802.
[89] HH, pp. 462–3; Hildebert of Lavardin, *Carmina Minora*, ed. A. B. Scott (Leipzig, 1969), no. 35.
[90] WM, *GRA*, i, 756.
[91] Marbod of Rennes, *Letters*, Migne, *Patrologia Latina*, clxxi, col. 1660.   [92] *GRA*, i, 754.

of a queen by bearing children, one of whom was a healthy son, William, born in 1103 (see below, p. 75). She would later use her great wealth to give generously to churchmen and to religious communities both in England and overseas.[93] There is a solitary reference to her help being sought as an intercessor, the traditional queenly role. Eadmer relates how in 1105 when the king had taken punitive action against married priests, a sad procession of priests besought her intervention. She wept and claimed to fear the king's anger.[94] Examples of her letters to Archbishop Anselm survive in his correspondence. The language is stilted, but the letters show that she looked on him as a spiritual adviser.[95] It was on his advice that she undertook her major religious foundation, an Augustinian priory just outside the city wall of London.[96]

Of Henry's feelings towards his queen, or hers for him, the sources remain silent. As far as we can see from witness lists, husband and wife were very much in each other's company until Henry's departure for Normandy in 1104. In that time at least two, possibly three, live children were born, who were probably quickly handed over to wet-nurses.[97] Matilda joined her husband in Normandy after the battle of Tinchebray in 1106, and possibly went with him again in 1111.[98] After 1103 she did not bear any more children, a fact which, according to William of Malmesbury, she bore with equanimity.[99]

After his marriage, Henry is known to have been at Newnham on the river Severn near the forest of Dean,[100] but the Christmas court was held at Westminster. There Henry could review his achievements with some satisfaction. He had built up a basis of support amongst the lay magnates. Anselm had returned, and there was a new archbishop at York. Most of the bishops and magnates had appeared at court, even those whose loyalties were most likely to lie with the duke, such as Robert de Bellême, his brother

---

[93] For a list of those who wrote about the queen, see E. M. C. Van Houts, 'Latin Poetry and the Anglo-Norman Court 1066–1135: The *Carmen de Hastingae Proelio*', *Journal of Medieval History*, 15 (1989), 50–1.
[94] Eadmer, *Historia Novorum*, p. 173.
[95] Anselm, *Letters*, nos. 242, 317, 320, 384, 395, 400.
[96] 'Historia Fundationis', *Cartulary of Holy Trinity Aldgate*, p. 224.
[97] The two children who survived infancy were the empress and William (see below, pp. 67, 75). According to Gervase of Canterbury there was another son, Richard: *Historical Works*, ed. W. Stubbs, 2 vols., RS (London, 1879–80), i, 91–2. According to the very late source, Boece, there was a daughter, Clarice: *The Chronicles of Scotland compiled by Hector Boece*, 2 vols., Scottish Text Society, 3rd series, x, i.e. vol. i (1938 for 1936), ed. R. W. Chambers and E. C. Batho; xv, i.e. volume ii (1941), ed. E. C. Batho and H. W. Husbands, ii, 180. Matilda was said to have been in childbed in Winchester in July 1101; see below, p. 28.
[98] She was apparently at Waltham 'in transitu' in 1111: *RRAN*, ii, no. 988.
[99] WM, *GRA*, i, 754–6.   [100] *RRAN*, ii, no. 500.

Roger the Poitevin, and William count of Mortain.[101] By Christmas Robert of Meulan had arrived, perhaps having been sent to Normandy to scout out the situation there.[102] He may have come in the company of Prince Louis of France, whose visit has already been noted.[103] There was one large cloud on the horizon, however. Henry knew only too well that there would be a challenge to his position from his brother Robert, and he would need all his intelligence and wealth in the months ahead.

---

[101] See above, n. 43.
[102] *RRAN*, ii, nos. 501, 506 cf. 495, 498 for possible earlier occurrences at court.
[103] SD, *Opera Omnia*, ii, 232.

CHAPTER 3

Testing times, 1101–1103

Henry's accession had catapulted him from the precarious position of a younger son to that of ruler of an old and wealthy kingdom. We have seen how many leading magnates appeared as witnesses of royal documents soon after the coronation, indicating that they had been prepared to offer the new king their homage. He had to be sure of the loyalty of his sheriffs and castellans, and the security of the Channel ports where his brother was most likely to land. Apart from that, he could only wait for the duke to show his hand, and ensure that his relations with Archbishop Anselm, which had got off to an inauspicious beginning over the issues of homage and investiture, remained amicable, and did not break down at a critical moment. Both the duke and the archbishop had the power to jeopardise everything that Henry had won, and strong nerves as well as political acumen were needed to survive these challenges.

The new year did not begin well for Henry when, in early February, Ranulf Flambard, bishop of Durham, made a dramatic escape from the Tower of London. The resourceful bishop had a rope smuggled into his room in a flagon containing wine (according to Orderic) or water (according to William of Malmesbury). Flambard escaped down the rope, burning his hands in the process and falling heavily. He then met his waiting friends and embarked for Normandy. His mother, reputedly a one-eyed sorceress who conversed with the Devil, crossed in another boat with Ranulf's treasure, but her boat was attacked by pirates, and when she reached Normandy she was naked. Her son, however, reached Duke Robert's court safely, and was soon urging the duke to make a fight for the kingdom.[1]

The escape of such an enterprising character was bad news for Henry. Moreover, a man of Flambard's undoubted abilities as a fundraiser would be a great asset to the hard-up duke.[2] Custody of the Tower is thought to have

---

[1] OV, v, 310–14; WM, *GRA*, i, 716.
[2] C. Warren Hollister, 'The Anglo-Norman Civil War: 1101', *EHR*, 88 (1973), 315–34; *MMI*, p. 85.

been in the hands of William de Mandeville, who might have colluded with Flambard in his escape.[3] Tension at Henry's court increased as the weeks wore on. Only a few, like Robert of Meulan and his brother Henry earl of Warwick, together with Robert FitzHaimon, Roger Bigod and Richard de Redvers, were prepared openly to declare their support.[4] Earl Hugh, who had been quick to support Henry in 1100, suffered a long illness and died in July 1101.[5] Many others were in secret negotiations with Robert, and took little trouble to conceal their contempt for the king. According to William of Malmesbury they called Henry 'Godric' and his wife 'Godiva'. Henry heard these jokes and pretended to laugh at them, but bided his time, ready to strike back when the time came.[6] English names in this context were obviously intended to insult, and presumably emanated from the duke's circle. Henry had no option but to dissemble and to try to keep the great men on his side. Robert of Meulan, his chief lay counsellor at this crucial time, advised him to promise men whatever they asked for, London or York if necessary.[7] Henry also had the unwavering support of Archbishop Anselm who, despite his stance on homage and investitures, did not want to see the brothers at war.

In March, Henry concluded a treaty with Robert count of Flanders, a sensible move since he needed to counteract any possibility that the count would intervene on behalf of Duke Robert, his companion in arms on the crusade, and also the count could provide knights.[8] The terms may well have been based on an earlier treaty between William the Conqueror and Baldwin V.[9] The count promised to supply 1,000 knights for service in England or Normandy, or 500 for service in Maine, within forty days of being summoned by King Henry, and to meet the costs of their travel, although Henry was to provide the ships for transport. The conditions of service were carefully specified, making clear in each case that they were not to bind Count Eustace of Boulogne, who was evidently someone with obligations to both parties. Eustace was mentioned as one of those whose transport costs were to be met by the count, but he was omitted from other clauses, indicating that a separate treaty was to be made with him.

---

[3] Hollister, 'The Misfortunes of the Mandevilles', *History*, 58 (1973), 315–33; *MMI*, pp. 118–19. There is no clear evidence of collusion, and the large debt which William is known to have owed the king might have been a relief payment on the death of his father, Geoffrey I de Mandeville.
[4] WM, *GRA*, i, 716. Urse d'Abetot and Eudo the steward also occur as witnesses to documents issued before and during the invasion: *RRAN*, ii, nos. 531, 536–8, 538.
[5] OV, v, 312–14.   [6] WM, *GRA*, i, 716.   [7] OV, v, 316.
[8] *Diplomatic Documents Preserved in the Public Record Office*, i, *1101–1272*, ed. P. Chaplais (London, 1972), pp. 1–4; E. M. C. Van Houts, 'The Anglo-Flemish Treaty of 1101', *ANS*, 21 (1998), 169–174; R. Nip, 'The Political Relations between England and Flanders (1066–1128)', *ANS*, 21 (1998), 145–67.
[9] WM, *GRA*, i, 728.

Careful provision was made for Count Robert to fulfil his obligations to his overlord, the king of France: if King Philip wished to invade England, the count was to seek to dissuade him, failing which he was to supply Philip with no more than twenty knights. He promised not to shelter Henry's enemies or to help them, and Henry could ask for his aid in Normandy and Maine unless King Philip decided to forbid it.[10] If Philip invaded Normandy against Henry, the count was to act in the same way as for an invasion of England.

The treaty was supplied both with witnesses and with a separate list of sureties, and the latter in particular provide a useful index of those prepared to stand surety for the king: Robert FitzHaimon (who stood surety for two hundred marks, double the amount pledged by the others), Stephen count of Brittany, Gilbert FitzRichard of Clare, Roger de Nonant, Hugh Maminot, Manasser Arsic, Haimo the steward, William de Courcy, Miles Crispin, Arnulf of Montgomery and Hugh de Beauchamp. Most occur for the first time in documents issued in Henry's name.[11] Count Stephen rarely appears in English documents, but it is likely he made an appearance at the start of the reign to perform homage. Gilbert FitzRichard's appearance indicates that he had by now openly sided with the king. Manasser Arsic and Hugh Maminot held lordships in Kent. William de Courcy, from the branch of the Courcys who had settled in England, was a royal steward, as noted above (p. 50).[12] Finally, the appearance on the king's behalf of Arnulf of Montgomery, lord of Pembroke and Holderness and younger brother of Robert de Bellême, is significant because his elder brother was very prominent amongst the duke's supporters.[13] The witnesses for the king were Archbishop Gerard, Robert bishop of Chester and Robert Bloet of Lincoln, the current chancellor; the count of Meulan, Robert FitzHaimon, Haimo and Eudo the stewards, and the butler, William d'Aubigny.

By Whitsuntide, when Henry was at St Albans, rumours of Robert's imminent arrival were spreading. The king and his magnates grew mutually suspicious, he that they would desert him, they that he would introduce harsh laws once peace had been established. Anselm was chosen as a mediator. The king publicly placed his hand in Anselm's, promising to uphold good laws as long as he lived.[14] Letters were sent out confirming the laws and customs granted the previous year at the coronation, and instructing

---

[10] The reference to service in Normandy and Maine seems to have come from the earlier treaty.
[11] Barlow suggested that these may have been sureties for an earlier treaty between William Rufus and the count: *William Rufus*, p. 325n.
[12] W. Farrer, *Honors and Knights' Fees*, 3 vols. (London and Manchester, 1923–5), i, 103.
[13] *Liber Monasterii de Hyda*, pp. 304–5.   [14] Eadmer, *Historia Novorum*, p. 126.

bishops and sheriffs to take oaths of allegiance from the king's demesne tenants, while his barons were to take the same oath from their men.[15] Henry did not count only on the personal retinues of loyal magnates, but summoned an army from all parts of the country.[16] This assembled near the south coast, in the vicinity of Hastings and Pevensey.[17] Henry presumably expected his brother to land near there, perhaps because the lord of Hastings was the count of Eu, who seems to have been an ally of the duke in that Robert's fleet set sail from the count's port of Le Tréport.[18] As the English troops arrived at Hastings, they had to be instructed in the way to counter a cavalry charge. Henry himself went through the ranks demonstrating how shields were to be used for this purpose.[19]

In the event the duke landed safely. Henry had sent English sailors to intercept the duke, but, having been bribed by Ranulf Flambard, they guided the duke's fleet to Portsmouth, where he disembarked on 20 July.[20] He came with two hundred ships and a large force of horsemen, archers and footsoldiers, and advanced to the neighbourhood of Winchester.[21] Here he halted, waiting for men to come and pay homage to him, and to see if he could gain access to the city.[22] The contemporary sources are silent about who came with him, nor is it easy to disentangle precisely which of the magnates already in England were prepared to come out openly against the king.[23] Three ringleaders were named by the Hyde Chronicler: Robert de Bellême, William count of Mortain and William de Warenne.[24] All three had great estates, many castles and powerful kinsmen. William count of Mortain was said to have been jealous of his cousin the king since youth;[25] Robert too may have resented Henry's takeover of Domfront, which had belonged to his family, but William de Warenne is not known to have had any personal grievance against Henry, nor are his precise whereabouts known.[26]

---

[15] W. H. Stevenson, 'An Inedited Charter of Henry I', *EHR*, 21 (1906), 505–9; *RRAN*, ii, no. 531.
[16] Eadmer, *Historia Novorum*, p. 126.
[17] *Historia Ecclesiae Abbendonensis*, ii, 186; JW, iii, 96–8.
[18] JW, iii, 96. Hollister points out that the lord of Pevensey was William count of Mortain, whose loyalty may already have been suspect. He suggests that Henry's army may have been stationed at Wartling: *Henry I*, p. 137.
[19] WM, *GRA*, i, 716.
[20] OV, v, 314; Hollister, 'Anglo-Norman Civil War', *MMI*, pp. 87–8.
[21] *Annales Monastici*, ii, 41; JW, iii, 96.   [22] JW, iii, 98.
[23] Cf. Hollister, 'Anglo-Norman Civil War', *MMI*, pp. 79–80.
[24] *Liber Monasterii de Hyda*, pp. 304–5; cf. Wace, *Roman de Rou* (ed. Holden), lines 10,397–10,440.
[25] WM, *GRA*, i, 720.
[26] For a royal charter for Lewes priory granted at the request of William de Warenne, which, if authentic in its present form, must date from the autumn of 1100, see *RRAN*, ii, no. 510. In August 1101 Roger Bigod sheriff of Norfolk was ordered to take action against William's men: ibid., no. 542.

At this stage, as magnates prepared to desert his cause, Henry began to fear for his life as well as his kingdom. Anselm, according to Eadmer, was one of the few whom the king could trust, and Henry took doubters to him for pep talks. He also made solemn commitments to the archbishop that he would leave him to administer the church in England and would always obey papal decrees. It now looked as though Anselm, by backing Henry in the hour of his need, had won exactly those concessions he wanted. The archbishop assembled the magnates and told them to face up to the prospect of death rather than betray their king.[27]

Robert did not try force his way into Winchester, according to Wace because the queen was awaiting the birth of her first child.[28] The two armies met nearby at Alton; each, it was said, feared to meet the other in Alton wood.[29] Henry sent messengers to demand why Robert had entered England with an armed force. Robert replied through his envoys that he had entered his father's kingdom with his magnates, and he demanded the right due to him as the eldest son.[30] Negotiations now began in earnest, with those who held land of both brothers acting as intermediaries: Robert de Bellême, William count of Mortain and Robert FitzHaimon are mentioned by Wace.[31] Orderic was sceptical about their good faith, suggesting that they were actually more interested in conflict than peacemaking, and that it was only when the brothers met face to face that a deal was worked out. After only a few words, the brothers embraced and exchanged kisses.[32]

In the resulting Treaty of Alton, Henry promised to surrender all his land in Normandy except Domfront and to pay Robert a large pension, variously reported as £2,000 or £3,000.[33] Robert did not have to contemplate the concessions of Norman land he had made to Rufus in 1091; indeed, he was to receive a pension of 'as much land in England as was laid down in their treaty'.[34] In return Duke Robert recognised Henry as king and freed him from the homage he had performed for his land in Normandy: significantly

---

[27] Eadmer, *Historia Novorum*, pp. 127–8.
[28] Wace, *Roman de Rou* (ed. Holden), lines 10,335–40; for comment see M. Chibnall, *The Empress Matilda, Queen Consort, Mother and Lady of the English* (Oxford, 1941), p. 9. For other instances of Wace's portrayal of the duke's honourable behaviour, see J. A. Green, 'Robert Curthose Reassessed', *ANS*, 22 (1999), 99–100.
[29] Hollister, 'Anglo-Norman Civil War', *MMI*, p. 90. Alton is mentioned in one version of Symeon of Durham and some manuscripts of Wace: OV, v, 318 and n.
[30] OV, v, 316–18.
[31] Wace, *Roman de Rou* (ed. Holden), lines 10,397–10,404.   [32] OV, v, 318.
[33] OV, v, 318 has £3000, but the other sources (JW, iii, 98; *ASC* E 1101; HH, p. 450; Wace, *Roman de Rou*, ed. Holden, line 10,454) say 3,000 marks, i.e. £2,000.
[34] *ASC* E 1091.

Henry did not explicitly renounce his claim to the duchy. Secondly (as in 1091), they agreed to help each other recover the lost domains of their father, possibly Maine and the Vexin. Thirdly, there was to be an amnesty for those who had supported either side in 1101.[35] The Anglo-Saxon Chronicle also mentions a specific proviso that Count Eustace of Boulogne was to recover his English estates, which his father had lost in 1088 for supporting Robert.[36] This rapprochement was subsequently sealed by a marriage between Eustace and the king's sister-in-law, Mary, indicating the high value set on securing Eustace's support.[37] Fourthly and finally, each was to be the other's heir in the event that either died without a son. This, since Henry's wife was pregnant but Robert's not, favoured the king as things stood, though neither can seriously have contemplated the idea that they would not have sons.[38] Twelve magnates on each side acted as guarantors of the treaty.

As events proved, Robert had passed up his best chance of gaining the crown, but this is of course the judgement of hindsight. Robert would have had to fight on his brother's territory, and it is not clear that his army had been reinforced by defectors from Henry. Anselm's pep talks may have been crucial in this respect: Robert's men certainly muttered afterwards that but for Anselm Robert would have had the kingdom.[39] Secondly, Henry was offering generous terms, at least as good as those Robert had accepted from Rufus in 1091. These may have been as much as contemporaries would have thought reasonable in dividing up the inheritance of William the Conqueror, and there were those who would have preferred a negotiated settlement.

However, there were difficulties in the way of peace, as there had been in 1091. For a start, each had to trust the other's good intentions. More problematic was policing the activities of the magnates. An amnesty for past actions was one thing; much more difficult was dealing with future misdeeds. Orderic reported that it was agreed that those who stirred up discord were to be punished.[40] The amnesty was presumably intended to apply to 1101 (not earlier or later), whereas the provision for punishment of traitors was to apply to future conduct. Who was going to decide who was to be punished? There was also the question whether Henry would

---

[35] In 1091 the corresponding clause had been that those who in England had lost land in the duke's cause were to be reinstated: JW, iii, 98; *ASC* E 1091.
[36] *ASC* E 1101.   [37] JW, iii, 102–3.
[38] *ASC* E 1101; HH, p. 450. For the birth of William Clito see below, p. 73.
[39] Eadmer, *Historia Novorum*, p. 131.
[40] OV, v, 318–20; Hollister, 'Anglo-Norman Civil War', *MMI*, p. 93.

ever pay the promised pension. With the benefit of hindsight, William of Malmesbury obviously thought Robert was foolish to think it would materialise.[41] On more than one occasion in the future, Henry was to reproach his brother for failing to keep the terms of the treaty, but of the two brothers it is hard to avoid the conclusion that Robert's intentions were the more honourable. It is also clear from his later moves against Robert de Bellême and William de Warenne that Henry had already made up his mind on who deserved to be punished for stirring up trouble in 1101, and he used the terms of the treaty to justify his own interventions in Normandy.

Meanwhile, the king's army was disbanded, whilst Robert stayed on in England at his brother's court, with his men reportedly causing damage wherever they went.[42] By early September the court was at Windsor, and here the king and the duke each issued confirmations of the grant of the city of Bath to the bishop. The double confirmation provides us with an interesting insight into the brothers' perception of Robert's position in England. Robert accepted his brother as king, and yet he was still thought to have some authority in England.[43]

It was believed too that Archbishop Anselm, who attended this court, would now receive a reward for his loyal support by a concession from the king on investitures. When the pope's reply to the king's request for dispensation from the decrees on homage and investiture was read out, the king was urged to give up 'this practice', i.e. investiture, and told that if he did, 'anything you ask of us . . . we shall gladly grant'.[44] In other words, whilst the pope was not going to back down on investiture, he made no specific reference to homage, indicating that already there was a recognition that homage could not realistically be surrendered by kings. The shape of the eventual settlement, in which Henry surrendered investiture but not homage, was thus already in view. Perhaps the king should have foreseen that the pope would not reconsider his position on investiture, but he was unlikely to accept easily the surrender of a right enjoyed by his father, part of the royal 'customs' over the English church. Curthose practised investiture in Normandy and, according to Eadmer, he and his men advised the king to hold out.[45] Moreover the king was in a much stronger position than he had been when he had been trying to persuade Anselm to return to

---

[41] WM, *GRA*, i, 704.   [42] *ASC* E 1101.
[43] D. Bates, 'A Neglected English Charter of Robert Curthose, Duke of Normandy', *Historical Research*, 59 (1986), 121–4.
[44] Eadmer, *Historia Novorum*, pp. 128–32; Anselm, *Letters*, no. 216.
[45] Eadmer, *Historia Novorum*, p. 131.

England. Anselm had proved invaluable during the invasion crisis, but that time was now past.

Henry therefore took a hard line. Clearly he thought he was within his rights to require Anselm both to perform homage and to consecrate those to whom the king had said he would give bishoprics or abbeys, or else leave the kingdom forthwith. Anselm refused to do either, saying he could not transgress the decrees on investiture without imperilling his soul. The king replied, 'What is that to me? The usages of my predecessors I am not willing to lose, nor to tolerate anyone in my kingdom who is not my man.' Anselm simply retreated to his estates to await further developments.[46] There for the time being matters rested: Henry clearly did not want to push the archbishop back into exile, and Anselm clearly did not want to go.

In early February 1102 a daughter was born to Henry and Matilda, and named Matilda.[47] The place of her birth is not recorded: Sutton Courtenay in Berkshire has been suggested, as it is not far from Abingdon abbey, whose abbot, Faritius, was the queen's physician.[48] Later in the twelfth century William FitzStephen, the biographer of Thomas Becket, believed that the future empress, like Becket, was born in London.[49] The birth of a daughter was of course a disappointment in contemporary eyes, but the marriage had resulted in one live birth, hopefully the first of many.

The Easter court met at Winchester, where Anselm appeared by invitation to hear new proposals from the king about investitures. This amounted to the dispatch of another mission to Rome including two representatives sent by Anselm, whose members were to explain to the pope the consequences of failing to lift the prohibition on investitures: Anselm and his men would be driven out of England and the pope would not receive the annual tribute called Peter's Pence. The king's emissaries were Gerard, now archbishop of York, who wanted to obtain his pallium; Herbert bishop of Thetford, who was trying to end the exemption from episcopal authority of the abbey of Bury St Edmunds; and Robert bishop of Chester, who wanted papal permission to transfer his see to the Benedictine abbey at Coventry.[50] The pope would prove reasonably conciliatory on these matters. Gerard

---

[46] This may also have been the occasion when Henry granted the manor of Burton Bradstock to the abbey of St Stephen's Caen for the recovery of the regalia which his father had bequeathed to the abbey on his deathbed. It is possible that Henry wanted to retrieve this set to prevent them falling into Robert's hands: *RRAN*, ii, no. 601.
[47] Winchester annals, *Annales Monastici*, ii, 43.   [48] Chibnall, *Empress Matilda*, p. 9.
[49] *Materials for the History of Thomas Becket*, 7 vols., i–vi ed. J. C. Robertson, vii ed. J. C. Robertson and J. B. Sheppard, RS (London, 1875–85), iii, 13.
[50] Eadmer, *Historia Novorum*, pp. 132–3.

obtained his pallium and Bishop Robert permission to transfer his see, a move which Archbishop Lanfranc had earlier opposed.[51] Bishop Herbert did not recover his jurisdiction over St Edmunds, because the abbey had previously been granted immunity by Pope Alexander II, but he was granted a confirmation of the transfer of the East Anglian see from Thetford to Norwich.[52] On the big issue, however, there was a period of delay, during which Anselm wrote four times asking why there had been no reply to his request to the pope for advice about the king's refusal to obey the papal decrees.[53] The pope's replies were dated 15 April 1102. One letter, addressed to Anselm urged him to remain constant in his obedience to the papal decrees, and the other, addressed to the king, urged him to refrain from investiture.[54]

Meanwhile Henry was proceeding to carry out what he saw as his obligations under the Treaty of Alton. Ranulf Flambard was restored to the temporalities of Durham by the king, though the charges against him as a bishop were not so easily sidestepped.[55] William de Warenne's lands were confiscated, indicating that the king believed him to have been a traitor in 1101. Ivo de Grandmesnil was fined heavily for waging war upon his neighbours by burning their crops. Unable to clear himself, and believing that he would never be able to assuage the king's wrath, he turned for help to Robert count of Meulan. The count promised to intercede with the king, and lent Ivo a large sum for fifteen years with the Grandmesnil lands as pledge. Ivo thereupon went on crusade and died en route.[56]

In 1102 Henry moved against Robert de Bellême and his brothers, Arnulf and Roger 'the Poitevin', and by the end of the year they had all left England. Henry apparently employed agents to watch Robert for almost a year, and then summoned him and Arnulf to court to answer forty-five charges, including the unauthorised fortification of castles at Bridgnorth in

---

[51] Anselm, *Letters*, nos. 220, 221; P. Jaffé, *Regesta Pontificum Romanorum*, 2nd edn by S. Loewenfeld, F. Kalterbrunner and P. Ewald, 2 vols. (Leipzig, 1885–8), i, no. 5912; *Letters of Lanfranc*, ed. Clover and Gibson, no. 27.
[52] J. W. Alexander, 'Herbert of Norwich, 1091–1119: Studies in the History of Norman England', *Studies in Medieval and Renaissance History*, 6 (1969), 158–60.
[53] Anselm, *Letters*, nos. 217–20. [54] Ibid., nos. 222–24.
[55] SD, *Opera Omnia*, i, 138; *RRAN*, ii, nos. 546, 547; but for the view that Ranulf was still deprived of his see in 1102 see *Annales Monastici*, ii, and OV, v, 320–2 and nn. For proceedings against Ranulf see Anselm, *Letters*, no. 214.
[56] OV, vi, 18. Ivo's sons were on the White Ship in 1120, returning to receive their father's estates, so working backwards fifteen years, Ivo could have left in 1105: OV, vi, 304. On the other hand, he did not witness charters for Henry, so it is possible that his tenure of his English estates was brief. Henry did confirm a gift of land by Ivo to Bermondsey: *RRAN*, ii, nos. 620, 1990. The punitive fine imposed upon William de Mandeville may also date from this period: see above, p. 61.

Shropshire and Carreghwfa in Wales.[57] Underlying these specific charges, however, was the issue of their loyalty during the summer of 1101. Henry's decision to summon Robert and Arnulf to court was nevertheless a risk because of the extent and location of their lands in England and Wales, their many vassals, and their allies.

Much less is heard about the western regions of Henry's kingdom than the south or even the north, because of the preoccupations of the most important narrative accounts, but these were regions of both opportunity and danger for the Norman kings. Wales was a patchwork of native principalities and lordships established by Normans since 1066, over which English kings wished to assert an effective overkingship, whether by acts of submission, by encouraging the transformation of the Welsh church, or by recognising the expansion of Norman settlement. Along the Irish littoral there were settlers of Scandinavian descent, trading across the Irish sea, and powerful figures like the Norwegian king Magnus Barelegs descended on the region from time to time.[58] In 1098 he had landed in the island of Anglesey, where Earl Hugh of Shrewsbury (Robert de Bellême's elder brother) and Robert lord of Rhuddlan had died fighting against him.[59] Ireland, more distant but nevertheless linked by political, ecclesiastical and commercial ties, could not safely be ignored, either. Harold Godwinson had gone to Ireland in 1051 in flight from the court of King Edward to recruit allies, and his sons went there after 1066, returning in 1067 with a naval force to ravage the region round the river Avon.[60]

Robert de Bellême had succeeded his brother to the Montgomery estates in Shropshire and Wales, and Arnulf was lord of Pembroke, so that they were in a powerful position to harass Henry's kingdom from the west. They ravaged Staffordshire and carried off cattle and horses into Wales.[61] Arnulf married a daughter of the powerful king of Leinster, Muirchertach Uí Briain, who was in a position to supply the brothers with men and ships.[62]

Robert attended the king's court to answer the charges against him, and asked if he could consult with his men. Realising he could not possibly clear himself, he fled, putting his castles in a state of defence and gathering his forces, which included both Normans and, significantly, Welshmen. The

---

[57] OV, vi, 20.
[58] C. Downham, 'England and the Irish-Sea Zone in the Eleventh Century', *ANS*, 26 (2003), 55–73.
[59] Ibid., v, 218–24; and see below, p. 227.   [60] *ASC* C 1051, D 1067 (*recte* 1068).
[61] *Brut (RBH)*, pp. 44–6; *Brut (Peniarth)*, pp. 22–5.
[62] For Arnulf's career see K. Thompson, 'Note de recherche. Arnoul de Montgomery', *Annales de Normandie*, 45 (1995), 49–53; V. Chandler, 'The Last of the Montgomerys: Roger the Poitevin and Arnulf', *Historical Research*, 62 (1989), 1–14.

king then assembled an army, 'the army of England' as Orderic described it, and undertook the siege of Robert's castle of Arundel in Sussex.[63] With the king's permission the garrison sent messengers for help to Robert at Bridgnorth, but when he realised he could do nothing for them, he gave his permission for them to surrender. Tickhill in south Yorkshire was also besieged by royalist forces, and soon surrendered.[64]

It looks as though Henry was justifying taking action under the terms of the treaty of 1101, because according to Orderic he sent word to the duke, advising him that Robert de Bellême had incurred forfeiture to both of them and had fled secretly from his court. He further reminded his brother of their commitment to punish traitors. The duke then summoned 'the army of Normandy' and besieged the castle of Vignats not far from Caen, held for Robert de Bellême at the time by a man named Gerard de Saint-Hilaire.[65] The garrison was hoping to surrender honourably to the duke, but the plan went awry because of the duke's failure to keep his own forces united. One party, led by Robert de Montfort, set fire to their tents, creating so much confusion that many of the besiegers fled,[66] and the duke had to retreat, suffering the insults of the garrison. In the aftermath Robert de Bellême's men went from strength to strength. Based at the castles of Château-Gontier, Fourches and Argentan, they plundered the peasants and burned their homes. Local lords like Robert de Grandmesnil, Hugh of Montpinçon and Robert II de Courcy had to defend their own lands as best they could.

Meanwhile Henry summoned the 'legions of all England' as Orderic described them on this occasion. In the autumn he marched to Bridgnorth, which was held by Robert's men, Roger son of Corbet, Robert of Neuville and Ulger the huntsman, whilst Robert himself held Shrewsbury.[67] William Pantulf, one of Robert's leading vassals, went over to Henry's side and was put in command of Stafford castle. The king meanwhile debated with his companions what to do about Robert de Bellême. The magnates wanted him to be lenient, afraid that if Robert were defeated and disinherited they would be next on the list, trampled 'like helpless slave girls', and hoping that by reconciling the king and the earl they might profit. On the other

---

[63] OV, vi, 20–2.
[64] JW, iii, 101. Orderic thought that the army was commanded by the king: OV, vi, 22. Chibnall pointed out that the speed of the surrender suggests that Robert may have held the castle as the king's castellan, not in fee.
[65] Ibid., 20–2. Orderic's use of terminology such as 'the army of England' and 'the army of Normandy' is language intended to emphasise the legitimacy of the brothers' action against one who had been condemned as a public enemy.
[66] OV, vi, 22–4. [67] Ibid., 24.

hand, some three thousand men described as 'country soldiers', presumably the shire levies who had answered the king's summons, urged the king to disregard the magnates and to pursue Robert until he was captured, dead or alive.[68] Whether they were Norman or English is not clear, but they were men who took an old-style view of the punishment to be meted out to rebels.[69]

Henry therefore withdrew and, using William Pantulf as an intermediary, set out to detach the Welsh leaders from supporting Robert. He was helped by the rivalry between the sons of Bleddyn ap Cynfyn, ruler of Powys or mid-Wales. The politics of Powys were particularly bloodthirsty in this period as individuals fought and killed to establish themselves over other members of their kin group. Henry sent messengers to Iowerth, Bleddyn's son, offering him his share of his family's land, namely, Powys, Ceredigion and half Dyfed, to hold for life but 'without rent and without tribute', in other words, on terms better than he would otherwise have had.[70] This alliance of mutual self-interest was soon shattered, but it lasted long enough to enable Henry to expel Robert.

Meanwhile Henry sent for the three men in charge of Bridgnorth and gave them three days to surrender, after which time he said he would hang all those whom he captured. Willliam Pantulf again acted as a mediator, and offered them on the king's behalf lands worth a hundred pounds. The garrison then accepted Henry's terms, but Robert's mercenaries were incensed at the surrender, because they were thereby dishonoured. They had to be penned up whilst the handover was carried out, and were allowed by Henry to march out with their horses and arms. Henry then advanced to besiege Shrewsbury, and Orderic tells us that the army widened the road to make it safer as he went. Robert decided he had little option but to surrender. Henry confiscated all his lands and those of his vassals who remained loyal. Arnulf was given a choice, either to leave the kingdom and to go with his brother, 'or else to come to [the king's] will'. When Arnulf heard that, he chose to leave with his brother. He surrendered his castle to the king, and the king placed a garrison there.[71] The third brother, Roger the Poitevin, also chose to leave.

Henry had taken a considerable risk in challenging the power of this family, but he had succeeded in driving them out. If the duke had been

---

[68] Ibid., 26.
[69] C. Warren Hollister, *The Military Organization of Norman England* (Oxford, 1965), p. 228; cf. the review by J. O. Prestwich, *EHR*, 81 (1966), 166–7; for comment see M. Chibnall, *OV*, vi, 26–7.
[70] *Brut (RBH)*, p. 45; *Brut (Peniarth)*, p. 24. For this family, see appendix 1, no. 8.
[71] *Brut (RBH)*, p. 47; *Brut (Peniarth)*, p. 25.

quick, he could have intervened to save Robert de Bellême, but he did not. The net result of the brothers' expulsion was to increase the duke's difficulties in Normandy, because Robert de Bellême and Arnulf returned to their continental estates, where their aggression against each other and against their neighbours caused major disturbances (see below, p. 72). By contrast the third brother, Roger the Poitevin, did not cause a problem because he retreated to his wife's lordship of La Marche in Poitou. Henry had profited by a very large windfall of land, some of which he retained, the rest, granted out. He restored Stephen count of Aumale to the honour of Holderness, for example, which had been confiscated and granted to Arnulf. The king had once again mobilised an army, and had seen three garrisons surrender. Above all, the fall of Robert de Bellême had demonstrated that not even the greatest magnates could act against him with impunity.

At Michaelmas 1102 Anselm was permitted to hold his long-wished-for council for the reform of the English church.[72] He had tried but failed to persuade Rufus of the urgent need for such a council[73] and, although nowhere spelled out in the sources, his decision to return to England in 1100 may have been in the correct belief that Henry would be more accommodating. Accordingly in 1102 a great council of bishops and abbots met, together with lay magnates, allegedly present at Anselm's request so that they could formally consent to the proceedings.[74]

The council was remarkable for two reasons: the number of abbots or abbots-elect who were deposed (nine), and the wide-ranging decrees on moral reform, the most comprehensive in England since the Conquest. The new king was evidently in sympathy with the desire to root out clerical marriage and simony (in theory at least), but not reforms which diminished his own powers over the church. In this he followed in his father's footsteps.[75] Moreover, once royal authority had been put behind reforming decrees, the king had a personal incentive for seeing that they were obeyed.[76] Nevertheless Anselm was still at odds with the king over investiture. Henry, urged on by the bishops and magnates, renewed his demand that Anselm should perform homage and consecrate those to whom bishoprics had been promised. Anselm, hearing that the king intended to proceed with investitures, could only respond by saying once again that he needed to consult the

---

[72] *Councils and Synods with Other Documents Relating to the English Church*, i, part ii, *1066–1154*, ed. D. Whitelock, M. Brett and C. N. L. Brooke (Oxford, 1981), 669–88.
[73] Eadmer, *Historia Novorum*, pp. 48–9, 78.   [74] Ibid., pp. 141–4.
[75] Barlow, *The English Church 1066–1154*, p. 123.
[76] For the introduction of the Augustinian rule as (in part) a means of reforming communities of secular clerks, see below, p. 278.

pope and that if the king did go ahead, he would not excommunicate him until the messengers had returned. The king, 'encouraged and triumphant', thereupon proceeded to invest two bishops, and put pressure on Anselm to consecrate them. Anselm agreed to consecrate William Giffard, who had been nominated at Henry's accession and thus before his own return from exile. The king however refused to allow one candidate to be consecrated without the others, and he persuaded the archbishop of York to act in place of Anselm. The scheme came to nothing because William Giffard got cold feet at the last minute, and when he backed out from being consecrated by the archbishop of York, he was driven out of England by the king and his property was sequestrated.[77] In the closing weeks of the year, it was hard to see how the views of the king and his archbishop could be reconciled. Henry was also faced by the fact that his brother was now the father of a baby boy, named William, born in October 1102.[78] It was to be some months before Henry was in the same happy situation.

The new year opened with the death of William of Breteuil, who, as the son of William FitzOsbern, was one of the most powerful of the Norman magnates. Because William had no sons of legitimate birth, the issue of his successor was not clear-cut, and a struggle broke out between different claimants.[79] This was serious because Breteuil was a key piece in the defences of the frontier region of south-east Normandy where dukes traditionally had needed extra vigilance to maintain their authority. That there was a struggle of this sort in such a sensitive area was also an indication of the way power was slipping into the hands of local castellans and away from the great lords.

William, lord of Gael in Brittany, had a good claim to the honour as the nephew of William of Breteuil, but he too soon died. Another external claimant was Reginald of Grancey in Burgundy. He gained the support of other Norman lords including William count of Evreux, Amaury de Montfort, Ascelin Goel lord of Ivry and Ralph de Tosny. An outsider could not win the support of the barons of the honour, however, some of whom came out in support of Eustace, an illegitimate son of the old count, and they were powerful enough to prevent a peaceful transition of power.

Duke Robert proved unable to restore order, which was achieved only by the intervention of Henry and Robert count of Meulan. The latter had inherited the Beaumont estates in central Normandy and thus had a direct

---

[77] Eadmer, *Historia Novorum*, pp. 144–6.
[78] For discussion of the date see Hollister, 'Anglo-Norman Civil War', 1101', *MMI*, p. 92. The duke's wife died soon after giving birth.
[79] OV, vi, 40–7. For the principal claimants see appendix 1, no. 4.

interest in peace in the region, and he managed to broker a peace deal. First, a marriage was arranged between Eustace of Breteuil and Juliana, an illegitimate daughter of Henry I, which meant that the 'internal candidate' for the Breteuil succession now had very strong backing. Secondly, Ralph de Tosny crossed to England, performed homage for his father's estates there, and was married to one of the daughters and co-heiresses of Count Waltheof.[80] Count Robert, who became even more directly involved when a rich burgess of Meulan was captured, made peace with the count of Evreux, and arranged a marriage between his daughter and Amaury de Montfort. The whole episode was a demonstration of how, if the duke could not arbitrate the quarrels of the Normans, others could.

The king went to Canterbury in mid-Lent 1103, ostensibly to negotiate with the count of Flanders. Whilst there he continued to put pressure on the archbishop, threatening to punish Anselm for resisting his will over the customs of the church. Anselm reported that he had received a letter from the pope, and he now asked that the contents be disclosed. The king refused, saying that he was no longer prepared to put up with prevarications, that the pope had no jurisdiction over matters which were his, and that anyone who sought to take his rights away was an enemy. The atmosphere was now becoming so fraught that the king begged Anselm to go himself to Rome to see if he could persuade the pope to allow the king his customs. After consultation with those at the king's Easter court, Anselm agreed to go, leaving the pope's letter unopened because he was afraid its contents would close off further discussions. He left England and travelled to Rome, but when he arrived, he found that the king's messengers had already arrived. Anselm departed, but William Warelwast, the king's envoy, stayed on, and obtained a letter from the pope to Henry which was relatively conciliatory in tone.[81] William Warelwast caught up with Anselm; he showed him the pope's letter, and made it clear that the king did not want Anselm back in England unless he was prepared to do homage and to consecrate those whom the king had already invested.[82] As Anselm would not agree, he stayed at Lyon with his friend Archbishop Hugh, and the exasperated king seized the temporalities of his see.[83] Anselm was once again in self-imposed exile.

---

[80] Ibid., 54.
[81] Eadmer, *Historia Novorum*, pp. 146–57; Anselm, *Letters*, no. 305; for comment see Southern, *St Anselm*, pp. 297–8.
[82] Anselm, *Letters*, no. 315.   [83] Eadmer, *Historia Novorum*, pp. 158–9.

At some point between June and August the queen gave birth to a son. Like his cousin he was named William; he was baptised by Bishop Gundulf of Rochester, who stood godfather to the prince.[84] The birth was an occasion of great joy, and also of great relief, to the parents. Henry's position on the throne was made much more secure. As contemporaries recognised, here was a child whose lineage united the old royal line and the new. For William of Malmesbury the birth represented the fulfilment of a prophecy thought to have been made by Edward the Confessor of a green tree: 'the hopes of England, like a tree cut down would, through this youth, again blossom and bring forth fruit'.[85] Henry, like Robert, had an heir, and Matilda gained prestige and security as queen as the mother of a son. The pair must have hoped for more, and one chronicler, Gervase of Canterbury, refers to a second son, Richard, who did not live very long.[86] For the time being, however, the pressing need for an heir had been met.

Towards the end of the year Duke Robert arrived in England, unheralded and without a safe conduct.[87] That he did so is perhaps an indication of his trust in his brother's goodwill, but also of his own need, because his position in Normandy, far from improving, was deteriorating. With the death of William of Breteuil he had lost a key supporter, and the eventual settlement of the disputed succession had done more to strengthen Henry's hand than his own. In the south Duke Robert had granted the town of Argentan, the forest of Gouffern, and rights over the bishopric of Sées to Robert de Bellême.[88] The latter had kept all his parents' lands for himself so that his youngest brother Arnulf was goaded into seizing Almenêches and handing it over to the duke. Robert de Bellême counter-attacked by burning the nunnery at Almenêches, even though his sister was the abbess. The duke and his allies appeared at Exmes, but somewhere in the vicinity Robert de Bellême put him to flight, took several castles, including Exmes, and retook Château-Gontier. The situation deteriorated to such a state

---

[84] *The Life of Gundulf, Bishop of Rochester*, ed. R. Thomson (Toronto, 1977), p. 71.
[85] WM, *GRA*, i, 415, 758; *Life of King Edward Who Rests at Westminster*, pp. 116–23, and pp. 131–2 for a comparison of the various versions of the prophecy.
[86] Gervase of Canterbury, *Historical Works*, i, 91.
[87] ASC E 1103; JW, iii, 104; WM, *GRA*, i, 716–8; Wace, *Roman de Rou* (ed. Holden), lines 10,653–10, 10,706. Orderic dated the visit to 1102: OV, vi, 12–14.
[88] Ibid., iv, 296–7 and nn. Orderic's statement does not make it clear exactly what rights the duke was conceding, nor at this point does he provide any context. The lords of Bellême had helped to restore the bishopric in the early eleventh century, and the family was also instrumental in restoring the abbey of Saint-Martin at Sées. Robert de Bellême's exactions from Bishop Serlo and Abbot Ralph d'Escures may thus have had their roots in family claims: Louise, *La Seigneurie de Bellême*, i, 154.

that both the bishop and the abbot of Sées took refuge at Henry's court in England. This could only add to the image Henry was building up of himself as protector of the church in Normandy.

The duke's visit to England may also have been made with a view to securing the reinstatement of William de Warenne. William's sense of grievance is an example of the difficulties inherent in the treaty of 1101, as he seems to have lost his lands without any formal trial. As lord of Bellencombre in upper Normandy, his continuing support was important to the duke. There may have been other matters to discuss, too. Robert must have been extremely short of money, and the pension pledged by his brother may not have materialised. Robert was also by this time a widower, and although he did not remarry, Henry must have been interested to know his brother's plans.

When the brothers met, Henry went on to the offensive. He was angry that the duke had arrived without permission, which could have been regarded as a prelude to raising revolt. According to Orderic, Henry alleged that the duke had failed to carry out his treaty obligations. Though Henry had expelled Robert de Bellême from England, the duke had welcomed him into Normandy, confirmed him in his father's possessions, and had been instrumental in securing the succession to the county of Ponthieu for him. The duke was said to have been alarmed by these charges and promised to make amends.[89] When the situation of William de Warenne was raised, Henry was prepared to restore his English lands in return for the duke's renunciation of the annual pension. This restoration was said to have been made at the queen's request.[90] Robert may have had little option but to agree, and may in any case have calculated by now that he was unlikely ever to receive the pension.[91]

Henry had displayed little sympathy for his brother's problems and had indeed exploited them, as Curthose's biographer pointed out.[92] Yet the duke had secured the restoration of a key supporter, who did not witness any documents for Henry and thus may be presumed to have stayed loyal to Robert until shortly before the battle of Tinchebray in 1106. He did on that occasion fight on Henry's side, but this may have been specifically because his brother Reginald de Warenne, who also had supported the duke and had been captured by Henry's forces, was released by Henry shortly before

---

[89] OV, vi, 12–14. However, Orderic dated the visit to 1102, before his discussion of Henry's move against Robert de Bellême.
[90] OV, vi, 14; WM, *GRA*, i, 704; Wace, *Roman de Rou* (ed. Holden), lines 10, 653–10, 726; David, *Robert Curthose*, p. 148.
[91] WM, *GRA*, i, 704.   [92] David, *Robert Curthose*, pp. 148–9.

the battle.[93] It was not easy for Robert to keep the Norman magnates loyal, and giving up the rights to a pension he might never have received may have seemed a price worth paying. Nevertheless he had received no help from his brother, who had already benefited from disorder in south-eastern Normandy, and had been angered by Robert's visit to England. The balance of power between the brothers was tilting even more in Henry's favour.

---

[93] OV, vi, 60, 80–2, 88; C. Warren Hollister, 'The Taming of a Turbulent Earl: Henry I and William de Warenne', *Réflexions Historiques*, 3 (1976), 83–91, reprinted in *MMI*, pp. 137–44, at pp. 141–2.

CHAPTER 4

The conquest of Normandy, 1104–1107

Henry may have dreamed of taking Normandy from his brother for years, but it was not until 1104 that the endgame began. The trigger, according to the Anglo-Saxon Chronicle, was an alliance between Duke Robert and Robert de Bellême, some time after Whitsuntide, 'and through their agreement the king of England and the count of Normandy were set at enmity'.[1] Henry argued that this agreement breached the treaty of 1101, because Robert had thus become reconciled with an enemy of the king.[2] We learn of the king's actions again from the Anglo-Saxon Chronicle: he sent his people to Normandy, 'and the chief men in that country received them and, to the betrayal of their liege lord the count, introduced them into their castles, from which they did many injuries to the count, in ravaging and burning'. The Chronicle is not specific, but it looks as though what happened was that detachments of knights of the royal household were sent to Normandy and stationed in the castles of those lords already acknowledging allegiance to Henry. Then Count William of Mortain, probably because Henry had demanded the return of 'certain illegal gains', left England for Normandy, where he made common cause with the duke and Robert de Bellême, and was able to attack the lands and castles belonging to the king and Earl Richard.[3] As count he possessed castles at Mortain, Tilleul, Tinchebray and possibly Ger.[4]

Henry was determined to show that his authority was not to be challenged, and preparations for an armed intervention were set in hand. There is much omitted or concealed in this bare recital of events. Duke Robert had little option but to come to terms with Robert de Bellême, a powerful ally but an even more dangerous enemy. Henry's action in sending his own

---

[1] *ASC* E 1104.   [2] OV, vi, 56.
[3] This may also be inferred from the account in Wace, *Roman de Rou* (ed. Holden), lines 10,735–10,814.
[4] J. Pouëssel, 'Les structures militaires du Comté de Mortain (xie et xiie siècles)', *Revue de l'Avranchin*, 58 (1981), 33–43.

agents to Normandy was provocative, even if justifiable, and he may have deliberately provoked the rupture with Count William, who had already been disappointed by his treatment at Henry's hands. Henry resolved on a show of strength, but he must already have been calculating the possibility of pushing through to a final resolution in which he would take over the duchy. His own position was much stronger than in 1101: he had expelled his most powerful opponents from England, given lands to his own supporters, and was now the father of a healthy son. Robert's position was probably stronger than might appear from the doleful stories recounted by Orderic: he was the rightful duke, a successful crusader, and he had the support of churchmen and leading counts and magnates, as well as having the ducal castles in the hands of his own men. He was almost certainly hard up (and a spendthrift), but that did not mean his situation was irretrievably lost.

A major financial effort was needed for Henry's expedition. The Anglo-Saxon Chronicle complained of 'taxes that never ceased or diminished', one of which may have been a levy of geld (the traditional land tax).[5] The king also had windfall revenue from confiscated lands and the revenues of vacant churches including those of Canterbury;[6] and there may have been a new issue of coinage from which the king was able to profit.[7] During the king's absence, the queen remained in England and was able to act as his deputy, assisted by an inner group of advisers, including Bishop Robert Bloet of Lincoln and Roger the bishop-elect of Salisbury.[8]

---

[5] *ASC* E 1104; *Westminster Abbey Charters 1066–c. 1214*, ed. E. Mason with J. Bray, London Record Society, xxv (1988), no. 65, calendared *RRAN*, ii, no. 851: a writ directing that land belonging to Westminster Abbey should be exempt from the new geld and other gelds. This text was issued between about 1104 and 1107. Hollister suggested that an aid may have been levied in 1104 on the basis of *RRAN*, ii, no. 670: 'Henry I and Robert Malet', *MMI*, p. 131n. This was issued at Easter at Winchester whilst Waldric was chancellor, which means that it must have been issued either at Easter 1103 or Easter 1104. In 1110 Henry took an aid collected in part through a levy of three shillings on the hide: see below p. 79.

[6] Brett, *The English Church under Henry I*, p. 103n. for calculations of the wealth of archbishoprics and bishoprics, and D. Knowles, *The Monastic Order in England*, 2nd edn (London, 1966), pp. 702–3 for monasteries. The most detailed survey of vacancies is Jared, 'English Ecclesiastical Vacancies'; according to her table on pp. 368–9 there were vacancies in 1104 at Ely, Bury, St Augustine's Canterbury, Peterborough, Battle, Cerne, Gloucester, Shrewsbury and Muchelney. See also C. Warren Hollister, 'William II, Henry I and the Church: Difference in Style or Change in Substance?', *Peritia*, 6–7 (1987–8), 119–40, reprinted with revisions in *The Culture of Christendom: Essays in Medieval History in Memory of Denis L. T. Bethell*, ed. M. A. Meyer (London, 1993), pp. 183–205. However, the king could not simply pocket all assets during vacancies because provision had to be made for monks and canons.

[7] Blackburn, 'Coinage and Currency under Henry I'.

[8] F. J. West, *The Justiciarship in England 1066–1232* (Cambridge, 1966), pp. 10–13; Huneycutt, *Matilda of Scotland*, pp. 78–85; for Matilda in action see *Historia Ecclesie Abbendonensis*, ii, 142–6.

Henry crossed the Channel in August 1104, and visited Domfront and other castles under his control. Orderic wrote that the king was received with enthusiasm by many magnates with estates in England, including Robert of Meulan, Richard earl of Chester, Stephen count of Aumale, Henry count of Eu, and Rotrou count of Perche.[9] The Perche was a relatively small county sandwiched between Normandy, Maine, the Dunois and the Ile-de-France;[10] Rotrou had participated in the first crusade, but any natural inclination to support Duke Robert was counterbalanced by a longstanding dispute with Robert de Bellême over the Bellême inheritance. Thus it was not surprising that he responded to overtures from King Henry, who around this time gave Rotrou his illegitimate daughter Matilda in marriage.[11] Her marriage portion consisted of two valuable manors in England.[12]

When Henry met his brother, he was in the company of his 'resident parasites' (in Orderic's phrase). Henry accused him of breaking their treaty by failing to consult him before making peace with Robert de Bellême. He also laid more serious charges against his brother, which show him preparing the ground for more radical action. He claimed that the duke had abandoned Normandy to thieves and robbers, thus neglecting one of the most important duties of a ruler. He went on to say that Robert held the office of prince and pastor in vain because he did not use the office of ruler for the good of church or people, but had abandoned them to their persecutors. It looks very much as if Robert had expected an informal meeting and instead found himself facing a tribunal. Henry is said to have pressed charges which the duke found himself unable to answer. The duke, entangled by the complexities of the charges, took counsel with his men, whom Robert condemned as lightweights, and he offered to hand over to Henry the homage of Count William of Evreux with all his dependants. According to Orderic Vitalis, Robert feared that he might be subjected to public examination and be forced either to surrender the duchy, or face his brother in war until he was utterly ruined.[13]

Orderic may of course be using hindsight in suggesting that Robert already feared that he would be forced to hand over the duchy; nevertheless the king was already making it very obvious that he was holding Robert responsible for disorder, and, in effect saying that Robert was ruler in name but not in fact, using the argument that he who could not carry out the responsibilities of office would lose it. Robert's response – to offer to transfer to his brother the homage of the count of Evreux – is also instructive, both

---

[9] OV, vi, 56.　[10] Thompson, *Power and Border Lordship in Medieval France*, chapter 1.
[11] OV, iv, 160.　[12] Thompson, *Power and Border Lordship*, pp. 185–6.　[13] OV, vi, 56–8.

of the duke's calculation of the price that would need to be paid, and his right to transfer the count's homage. Orderic reflected on the significance of this act from the point of view of the count, who had served one lord faithfully only to find that his homage was handed over to another. Orderic composed a speech for the count in which his fidelity was stressed and his objection to being handed over like a horse or an ox: as he could not serve two masters he would give his homage to only one. Robert then placed the count's hand in Henry's, peace was made between the brothers, and the king returned to England. It is true that dual and potentially conflicting allegiances and the transfer of homage from one lord to another were matters of great concern at this time, but the reality was that Robert probably had little influence over the count anyway. Henry had shown in the previous year that he had very considerable influence in south-east Normandy, and the transfer of the count's homage supplied another piece of the jigsaw. Henry's unlooked-for arrival in Normandy might well have prompted the kind of hostile response that he had accorded his brother in the previous year, but once again it was Henry who was on the offensive. He had demonstrated that his interests there could not be attacked with impunity; he had also obtained a major territorial concession, been openly critical of his brother's perfomance as duke, and been well received by some of the leading magnates. As an exercise in testing the water, his visit had gone well, and preparations for a more serious attempt to secure the duchy could be made.

The only dark cloud was Anselm's continuing obduracy over investitures.[14] In December the pope fired a warning shot across Henry's bows: he wished the king 'health, honour and victory'; he invited him to send envoys to the Lenten synod in Rome to answer Anselm's charges against him, but added a warning: 'those who do not wish to have the grace of Christ may feel the sword of Christ'.[15] In March 1105 Robert of Meulan and other royal counsellors were excommunicated at the synod for persuading the king not to surrender investitures.[16] Matters were now getting serious, because the king's own excommunication was obviously going to be next on the list. For the time being the pope was prepared to hold off, at least until the king's envoys arrived at Rome.[17]

Meanwhile the disorder in Normandy had continued after Henry's departure. Attacks were made on the king's men by Robert de Bellême and William of Mortain.[18] Henry complained to his brother about the

---

[14] Anselm, *Letters*, nos. 338, 339, 350.   [15] Ibid., no. 348.
[16] Ibid., nos. 353, 361.   [17] Ibid., no. 353.   [18] OV, vi, 58–60.

seizure of revenues in the Cotentin and Domfront, and the duke's response was that he was the ruler of both, and would not let Henry have possession.[19] A messenger from the duke put Robert's case for him: that Henry should have England and Robert Normandy, but that the duke would not give up to Henry the Cotentin and Domfront. In fact, the messenger continued, Robert as the elder had been entitled to the whole of their father's inheritance. Henry's response was to refuse a truce and he said he would never make peace. When the messengers duly reported to the duke, Robert sent out orders that all his vassals should remain in Normandy and offer him their service.[20]

The immediate trigger for Henry's return to Normandy in 1105 was said by Orderic to have been the capture of Robert FitzHaimon, lord of Torigny and Creully.[21] There may have been more to Henry's intervention than chivalry, however, because FitzHaimon had been harrying the countryside with a detachment of knights of the royal household, and Henry's aim may have been to lure the duke or his forces to military action by providing FitzHaimon with a force of royal knights. FitzHaimon was cut off in the village of Secqueville by Gontier d'Aunay, the duke's commander at Bayeux; he took refuge in the church tower, but this was burned down. He was captured and taken to Bayeux, where his betrayal of the duke attracted such hatred that his life was in danger.[22] Henry gathered men and a great deal of money, and crossed to Barfleur early in 1105. According to Wace, he lavished money on winning the support of castellans. He summoned men from Maine, Anjou and Brittany, who came willingly at the prospect of gain. The duke by contrast had little money. He strengthened his fortifications, especially at Caen, where he had a defensive trench dug, and was so desperate to pay his mercenaries that he put a price on the head of wealthy burgesses, who had to pay substantial sums to his mercenaries for their freedom. Some fled to the abbeys and handed over their possessions to the religious so that they would not fall into the duke's hands.[23]

Henry crossed the river Vire, and arrived at Carentan, where he spent Easter. The Easter services had already begun, and the bishop of Sées, returning from exile with Henry, put on his vestments and waited with the king for the people and the knights of the household to assemble. The king had taken his seat at the end of the church amongst chests belonging to the peasants. The bishop deplored the current state of Normandy: the people of the Cotentin had been uprooted, and the church was now so crammed

[19] Wace, *Roman de Rou* (ed. Holden), lines 10,727–10,756.
[20] Ibid., lines 10757–838.   [21] OV, vi, 58–60.
[22] Wace, *Roman de Rou* (ed. Holden), lines 11, 101–2.   [23] Ibid., lines 10,839–10,918.

with their possessions that there was no room to kneel before the altar. Although the church had become a refuge, it was not entirely safe: in that very year Robert de Bellême had destroyed the church of Tournai-sur-Dive and forty-five men and women had burned to death inside it. The bishop urged the king to rise up, to win the heritage of his fathers, and rescue it from the worst of men. He condemned the duke, repeating the argument heard in the previous year that Robert did not truly possess Normandy, but instead stayed in bed until noon for lack of bread, and could not rise or attend church because his breeches, socks and shoes, had been stolen by the jesters and whores who kept him company. Normandy since the days of Rollo had been ruled by active dukes, until the time of this 'defective', so Henry should take up arms, not in the pursuit of earthly power but for the defence of the fatherland. Henry is reported to have taken counsel from his companions, who included Robert of Meulan, and they urged him to action.

Before a captive audience of more knights than he usually saw in his congregation, Bishop Serlo resumed his sermon by taking the opportunity to preach against the evils of long hair, which contemporary churchmen believed made men look effeminate: real men wore their hair short. Long hair, said the bishop, made men look like women and lose their strength. Long beards made them look like billy goats, more like Saracens than Christians. The king was urged to set a good example to his subjects by having his hair cut. The bishop immediately whipped out a pair of scissors, and cut the king's hair and that of the other magnates.[24] In a dramatic, if staged, ceremony, the king and his men were now ritually prepared to do battle in a just cause. After the Easter festival Henry sent messengers to King Philip, and he summoned Geoffrey Martel, count of Anjou, to his aid.

In April Henry advanced towards Bayeux in the company of Helias count of Maine, Bretons, Angevins, and English as well as Norman troops.[25] The duke's castellan, Gontier d'Aunay, handed over Robert FitzHaimon in the hope of buying off the king, but rejected the king's demand to surrender the town.[26] Wace embellished his account of the siege with a dramatic episode: a knight of Henry's named Brun issued a challenge to all comers.

---

[24] OV, vi, 60–8; for a discussion of clerical attitudes to long hair, see R. Bartlett, 'Symbolic Meanings of Hair in the Middle Ages', *Transactions of the Royal Historical Society*, 6th series, 4 (1994), 50–2, 58–60.
[25] Serlo, 'De Capta Bajocensium Civitate', in *The Anglo-Latin Satirical Poets and Epigrammatists of the Twelfth Century*, ed. T. Wright, 2 vols., RS (London, 1892), ii, 241–51.
[26] For a clash at Maromme near Rouen, see OV, vi, 72.

This was taken up by a knight from Bayeux called Robert d'Arches, who killed Brun.[27] Henry thereupon stormed the town, and in the fire which broke out the cathedral and numerous other churches burned down. Gontier d'Aunay and the garrison were captured, and the men of Maine seized the spoils.[28] Henry clearly felt that the time had come for direct action, but the destruction of churches hardly accorded with the image of the church's protector which he was trying to project. The fighting then raged in the countryside between Bayeux and Caen.[29]

Unlike Bayeux, however, Caen was handed over without bloodshed, with the help of some leading townsmen, even though the duke himself was there. Wace, who evidently had access to local information, recounted the handover in detail. A group of leading townsmen was captured between Argences and Caen by Robert of Saint-Rémy. He took them to Robert FitzHaimon, who ransomed them and sent word to Henry, who was at Domfront. The two men met, and in return for the captives, Henry rewarded FitzHaimon with a grant of revenues and with hereditary custodianship of Caen. Henry was said by Wace to be very attached to FitzHaimon, who served him loyally. Henry promised to give the captives their freedom and land in addition; in return they promised to admit his forces into the city, giving hostages as proof of their good faith. The terms of the deal were kept secret from the people of Caen, because if they got wind of the treachery it was likely that they would resist, so ransom money was collected as if the captives were still in prison. The plan worked: a group of townsmen met in a garden near the church of Saint-Martin, and agreed to transfer their loyalty to the king. The duke was advised to retreat, and left through Porte Milet with his household knights. A gatekeeper robbed a chamberlain of one of the duke's bags, and other ruffians robbed the squires. The duke's castellan, Enguerran de Lacy, was expelled, and so the king gained control of the second capital of the duchy.[30]

Henry then tried to capture Falaise, but here he was not so lucky, because his ally Count Helias withdrew 'at the request of the Normans', presumably because Helias felt that on this occasion he could not be in action against the duke's forces.[31] Henry was compelled to lift the siege, but not before there had been casualties: a man named Roger of Gloucester, son of the Domesday sheriff of Gloucestershire, was killed during 'knightly jousting', and Robert FitzHaimon received a wound which deprived him of his senses, though

---

[27] Wace, *Roman de Rou* (ed. Holden), lines 10,957–11,060.
[28] Serlo, 'De Capta Baiocensium Civitate'; Wace, *Roman de Rou* (ed. Holden), lines 11,115–22.
[29] Ibid., lines 11,135–62.   [30] Ibid., lines 11,163–335.   [31] OV, iv, 154.

he did not die until March 1107.³² Henry met his brother near Falaise at Cintheaux in the week of Pentecost, but the meeting failed to resolve their differences, and fighting, the details of which are not recorded, continued until Michaelmas.

During this period Anselm was at Lyon, without the revenues from his see, and without the king's permission to return to England. He was growing tired of Henry's procrastination, and it was rumoured that he had begun excommunication proceedings against the king. He asked formally three times for the restitution of his property, making it clear that if it was not restored he would regard himself as having been disseised without judgement.³³ He also took the opportunity to alert the king's sister, Countess Adela, to the gravity of her brother's situation. Adela was a powerful and astute woman, guardian of Blois, Chartres, Châteaudun and Meaux on behalf of her young son.³⁴ She knew Anselm personally, having entertained him in 1103 when he had negotiated a truce in her dispute with the cathedral chapter at Chartres.³⁵ When he arrived at Blois, he found her recovering from illness, and took the opportunity to explain the situation, making no secret of the fact that he proposed to excommunicate Henry.³⁶ Adela had both personal and political reasons for getting involved. At a personal level she did not wish to see her brother excommunicated, and she may have preferred Henry to rule in Normandy.³⁷ At a political level, maintaining a strong alliance with the rulers of Normandy provided the counts of Blois with a powerful ally against their historic enemies, the counts of Anjou.

Adela warned her brother of the danger he faced, and Henry took her warning seriously.³⁸ On 21 July 1105 at l'Aigle close to the Norman frontier a personal reconciliation took place between the king and his archbishop, and Henry promised to restore the revenues of the archbishopric. When the king's companions tried to persuade Anselm to return to England, however, difficulties arose. Henry insisted that Anselm should not 'withhold his fellowship' from those who had already accepted investiture, but Anselm

---

[32] Ibid., vi, 80; WM, *GRA*, i, 722; 'Winchcombe Annals' (ed. Darlington), p. 122.
[33] Anselm, *Letters*, nos. 310, 316; Eadmer, *Historia Novorum*, pp. 163–4; Southern, *St Anselm*, p. 298.
[34] K. Lo Prete, 'The Anglo-Norman Card of Adela of Blois', *Albion*, 22 (1990), 569–89; even after Theobald assumed his majority Adela clearly remained very influential.
[35] Anselm, *Letters*, nos. 286–7, 299, 340; Eadmer, *Historia Novorum*, pp. 151–2.
[36] Anselm, *Letters*, no. 388.
[37] This is a point made by K. Lo Prete, 'Adela of Blois: Familial Alliances and Female Lordship', in *Aristocratic Women in Medieval France*, ed. T. Evergates (Philadelphia, 1999), pp. 7–43, at p. 32.
[38] The role of Adela as a peacemaker has been differently assessed. N. F. Cantor, *Church, Kingship, and Lay Investiture in England 1089–1135* (Princeton, NJ, 1958), pp. 221–6 played down her role; cf. Southern, *St Anselm*, p. 300; Vaughn, *Anselm of Bec and Robert of Meulan*, p. 289; and Lo Prete, 'The Anglo-Norman Card of Adela of Blois', 581.

refused. It was therefore decided that Anselm was to stay out of England for the time being until fresh envoys returned from Rome with the pope's adjudication of the issue, a postponement which would still give time for Anselm to attend the king's Christmas feast in England.[39] What is not made clear from the account of Eadmer, who was well placed to know what had happened, was whether the king had at last explicitly agreed to yield on the key issues of investiture and homage.[40] It is highly likely that he had agreed to the former, at least in principle; though if there had been a public announcement, it would surely have been reported by Anselm. Anselm himself may well have believed that any agreement between himself and the king would have to be ratified by the pope. When Anselm wrote to his friend Archbishop Hugh of Lyon in December 1105 he believed that the king had been convinced by the papal decrees on investiture, but he wished to retain homage, and had accordingly sent an appeal to Rome. Anselm thought that the king was likely to demand that both those who had accepted investiture from the king and those who had consecrated them should remain in office, and he asked for the archbishop's advice on this point.[41] Henry had had to come to terms with Anselm, but had succeeded in warding off the archbishop's excommunication of himself and of the count of Meulan, and there was always the chance that his emissaries to Rome would win further concessions.[42]

In August 1105 Henry returned to England, and in the autumn he travelled to the north, visiting Pontefract and York.[43] He may have been particularly concerned because those who had lost their lands, Robert de Bellême, his brothers Arnulf and Roger, and William count of Mortain, all had large estates in the north. Henry needed to secure the loyalty of their tenants, and to make sure he was not threatened in the north whilst preoccupied with Normandy.[44] Robert de Bellême visited England and attended the king's Christmas court 1105 at Westminster, for reasons that are not known. He may have been the duke's emissary, or he may have been trying to persuade Henry to restore his estates. Whatever his purpose was, it failed, and he left 'in a hostile fashion' and returned to Normandy.[45] The duke himself

[39] Eadmer, *Historia Novorum*, pp. 165–6.
[40] For the view that a deal was reached at this time see Vaughn, *Anselm of Bec and Robert of Meulan*, pp. 290–1; cf. Southern, *St Anselm*, p. 301; Cantor, *Church, Kingship, and Lay Investiture*, pp. 221–2.
[41] Anselm, *Letters*, no. 389.   [42] Ibid., nos. 364, 367, 368, 369, 370, 371.
[43] Ibid., no. 371; *RRAN*, ii, nos. 710–15.
[44] The fact that the king visited Pontefract, and that no reference is made to Robert de Lacy on that occasion, may indicate that Robert had lost his lands by this date, though all that is known for certain is that by 1114 he had been replaced by Hugh de Laval: W. E. Wightman, *The Lacy Family in England and Normandy 1066–1194* (Oxford, 1966), pp. 66–72.
[45] *ASC* E 1104, 1105.

arrived not long afterwards, in the early weeks of 1106, when the court was at Northampton. He asked Henry to return everything he had taken from him in Normandy, presumably the towns of Bayeux and Caen as well as Henry's lands as count of the Cotentin; but Henry, knowing he was in a strong position, simply refused. Robert departed, angry and empty-handed. The time for compromise was evidently past.[46]

At this juncture Bohemond, prince of Antioch, arrived in France to recruit men and supplies for the East, and asked Henry's permission to cross to England. This was not good news from Henry's point of view, because the last thing he needed was knights to leave England in any numbers, nor perhaps did he welcome any clarion call which would distract his followers from the struggle for Normandy. He advised against a winter voyage and said that he was proposing to cross to Normandy before Easter 1106 and would meet Bohemond there.[47] Bohemond instead made a triumphal progress through France during which, according to Orderic, many asked that he stand as godfather to their babies. He crowned his visit by his marriage to King Louis's daughter Constance at Chartres, where Countess Adela supplied a splendid wedding feast. From the pulpit of the cathedral Bohemond made a speech urging men to join him in an attack on the Emperor Alexius. His words hit home, and amongst those who took up arms were distinguished Normans, several of whom were named by Orderic.[48] This was hardly surprising given the Normans' response to the call to the First Crusade. It is not clear whether Henry did meet Bohemond, though Orderic implies that he did; but Bohemond certainly met Archbishop Anselm, at Rouen. There Anselm also met a master of knights called Ilgyrus, who regaled him with his war experiences and gave him two of the Virgin Mary's hairs.[49]

Henry told Anselm that he intended to cross to Normandy on Ascension Day, 3 May 1106,[50] though he may have crossed later than this. No specific reason for the delay is given in the sources, but he would have wished to be as well equipped as possible and the delay may simply have been a matter of logistics, given that this was the third successive year of campaigning. On 15 August Henry met Anselm at Bec. Anselm had experienced a frustrating wait; first the king's envoys to Rome had not finally left until December 1105,[51] and then came the disagreeable news that Henry had been exacting fines from clergy who had broken the decrees against clerical marriage laid down at the Council of Westminster. The pope's reply to the envoys who

---

[46] Anselm, *Letters*, no. 396. [47] OV, vi, 68–70. [48] Ibid., 70.
[49] Eadmer, *Historia Novorum*, pp. 180–1. [50] *ASC* E 1106. [51] Anselm, *Letters*, no. 397.

had been sent with news of the settlement at l'Aigle in 1105 finally arrived in late April 1106.[52] Anselm was told he could absolve those who had accepted investiture or done homage, and that those who did homage in future were not to be banned until the king could be persuaded to renounce this practice. In other words, although the pope was hoping that his concession on homage would be temporary, he was prepared to compromise, providing the king renounced investiture. However, just as the way was cleared for Anselm to return to England, he fell ill at Bec. Eadmer reported that when the king arrived in August he made further promises: that he would not exploit profits from vacant churches in the way his brother had done;[53] that married clergy who had not paid any part of their fine should be quit, and that those who had paid should have three years free of further liability. Finally, everything taken from the archbishopric during Anselm's absence was to be restored.[54] Anselm, having recovered from illness, was at last able to return to England, where the queen took special care to ensure that his lodgings were richly furnished.[55]

There is virtually no information about Henry's movements and strategy between May and August 1106. His position was strongest in the west of the duchy, and he had bridgeheads in lower Normandy, at Bayeux and Caen. His brother's support had dwindled and Robert was increasingly powerless to maintain order.[56] On the other hand, the duke's principal supporters, William of Mortain and Robert of Bellême, were holding firm, and there were other lords who still actively supported him or at the least were not prepared to come out openly for Henry. Robert's castellans still held Rouen and Falaise, and his support was holding up in the region on the right bank of the river Seine. The reality was that Henry would either have to persuade or compel more lords to transfer their loyalty to him, or provoke Robert to battle.

One incident reported by Orderic illustrates the cat-and-mouse game being played at this time. The abbot of Saint-Pierre-sur-Dives had died, and a monk of Saint-Denis near Paris had paid Duke Robert 140 marks to become the next abbot. He also built a castle there. He promised the duke, who was at Falaise, that he would bring Henry to him with only a few men so that he could be trapped. The abbot then went to Henry, who was at Caen, greeted him as a friend, and offered to hand over his castle at Saint-Pierre. He suggested that Henry did not need to come in force but with a

---

[52] Ibid., nos. 376, 391.
[53] This may have been a surrender of the kind of relief taken from the knights of Worcester in 1095, for which see *Select Charters*, ed. W. Stubbs, 9th edn (Oxford, 1913), p. 109.
[54] Eadmer, *Historia Novorum*, pp. 183–4.   [55] Ibid., p. 183.   [56] OV, vi, 86, 96.

few men only, to avoid raising suspicions. Robert had meanwhile installed two commanders at Saint-Pierre, Robert de Stuteville and Reginald de Warenne, with 140 knights, and prepared to send reinforcements. Henry thought the offer was promising, but he was also suspicious that he was being lured into a trap, so he set off at night with 700 knights, a very considerable force. He arrived unexpectedly at Saint-Pierre (some twenty kilometres away) at dawn, before the duke's reinforcements, and attacked the garrison. His knights proceeded to burn down both the abbey and the fortress. Reginald and Robert were captured, and many of their companions who had taken refuge in the church tower were burned to death. When the duke's reinforcements saw what had happened, they fled to Falaise. The abbot was captured, flung across a horse like a sack and taken to Henry, who banished him.[57] Henry had escaped the trap but was no nearer to a decisive outcome.

'That autumn was a stormy one in Normandy, with thunder and torrents of rain and wars.'[58] Henry was by this time in south-west Normandy, where Robert of Bellême and William of Mortain were still putting up strong resistance. He decided to besiege Tinchebray, a castle of William of Mortain. He built a siege castle and committed it to a man named Thomas de Saint-Jean, one of three brothers from Saint-Jean-le-Thomas near Mont-Saint-Michel who were active as military commanders for Henry.[59] Count William, however, brought up a force of knights and was able to provide the garrison with men and supplies whilst Henry's men could only look on. William's forces were so confident that they went out into the fields to cut green corn for fodder. They came and went with impunity, whilst the king's men, intimidated by William's leadership and the number of his knights, simply did not dare to leave their siege castle. Henry was not surprisingly very angry at the timorous attitude of his men, and he came to Tinchebray himself with his army to besiege the castle more closely.

Count William now appealed for help to the duke and to Robert de Bellême. The duke gathered his forces and demanded that his brother raise the siege or else he would declare war. Henry refused to agree, evidently in the belief that he could win a battle. The most detailed account of the events that followed is provided by Orderic.[60] Henry's army included Robert count of Meulan and Count William of Evreux, whose homage

---

[57] Ibid., 72, 80–2. The abbot became provost at Saint-Denis's priory at Argenteuil and was killed later in the same year.
[58] Ibid., 82.
[59] Ibid., 84, 194; Green, *GOE*, pp. 147–8. Thomas had perhaps entered Henry's service before 1100.
[60] OV, vi, 84.

had been transferred to Henry in 1104, plus Henry's allies, Counts Helias of Maine and Alan Fergant of Brittany; Earl William de Warenne, who had been restored to his English estates but had still not publicly sided with Henry before this; Rannulf *vicomte* of Bayeux; Ralph de Tosny (who, as we have seen, had been allowed to marry a daughter of Earl Waltheof: above, p. 70); Robert de Montfort, who had been one of those involved in the retreat from Vignats (above, p. 70); and Robert de Grandmesnil, an enemy of Robert de Bellême who had more to gain by supporting Henry than by siding with the duke.[61] Robert's army included Robert de Bellême, who arrived together with the recently released Robert de Stuteville, and William de Ferrers, lord of Ferrières-sur-Risle. The duke had fewer knights than Henry, it was said, but more footsoldiers.

As had been the case in 1101 efforts were made to avoid bloodshed. One notable figure in these efforts was Vitalis, a holy man who had been a chaplain of Count Robert of Mortain, then lived as a preacher and hermit, and eventually settled at Savigny.[62] Henry offered peace terms: he claimed to have come not out of greed or to deprive his brother of the rights of his duchy, but in response to the petitions of the poor. Robert was a duke in name only, mocked by his servants, and incapable of action. Henry asked his brother to hand over all the castles, all justice and management of the duchy and half of its land (perhaps lower Normandy where Henry was already strong). Robert could keep the remainder without labour or responsibility, and receive the value of the first half from Henry's treasury in England. Here then is the basis of Henry's claim to take over: that his brother did not really hold office at all, and Henry was intervening in response to the requests of the poor, and would undertake to restore peace and to protect God's people.

The idea of fitness for the responsibilities of earthly power was one which had been much discussed by polemicists during the contest between Pope Gregory VII and the Emperor Henry IV.[63] Hugh, a monk of Fleury-sur-Loire, who addressed to Henry I a treatise on royal power composed between about 1102 and 1105, picked up the same idea when he wrote that

---

[61] Ibid.; additional accounts of the battle are in H. W. C. Davis, 'A Contemporary Account of the Battle of Tinchebrai', *EHR*, 24 (1909), 728–32; Davis, 'The Battle of Tinchebrai: A Correction', *EHR*, 25 (1910), 295–6. The text was translated in *English Historical Documents*, ii, *1042–1189*, ed. D. C. Douglas and G. W. Greenaway, 2nd edn (London, 1981), pp. 329–30, and HH, p. 454. Henry of Huntingdon's account was followed by Robert of Torigny, *Chronicle*, 85.

[62] OV, vi, 86, and see also below, p. 124. For his possible appearance at the Council of Westminster in 1102, see E. Sauvage, 'Vitae BB. Vitalis et Gaufridi', *Analecta Bolliandiana*, i (1882), 373–4.

[63] A straightforward guide to the literature may be found in I. S. Robinson, *Authority and Resistance in the Investiture Contest. The Polemical Literature of the Late Eleventh Century* (Manchester, 1978), chapter 4.

rulers who were evil customarily lost their power.[64] Debate had ranged over issues of personal sin and the justification of rebellion against a tyrant rather than incompetence, which was the charge brought by Henry against his brother in 1104 and 1106, but the consequences were deemed to be the same: he who was unfit to wield power was to lose it.

The duke summoned his council and reported Henry's message. The council immediately rejected these terms, and opted for war. Henry's terms would have delivered the reins of power and half the duchy into Henry's hands. Perhaps Henry thought that the proposals were reasonable enough, given the territorial gains he had already made, but their effect would have been to reduce Robert's status to that of a mere dependant. Nor would the prospects of his supporters have been very rosy. It was hazardous for both brothers to risk all on the outcome of a battle, particularly for Robert whose army was evidently far outnumbered by his brother's force, estimated by an eye witness as some forty thousand men.[65] Why then did the duke offer battle? He too must have felt confident of victory over a younger brother, one who lacked his own experience of major battles gained on the crusade. Henry commended himself to God, asking for His help to bring victory to one who wished to protect His people.[66]

Henry then gave his instructions to his commanders, released Reginald de Warenne and others who had been captured at Saint-Pierre-sur-Dives, and pledged to restore the abbey. He drew up his army outside Tinchebray: the exact location of the battlefield is not known, but is thought to have been on the level ground in front of the count's castle.[67] Henry ordered his knights to fight on foot:[68] dismounted knights lost their speed and force, but fought more steadily.[69] There were three lines in Henry's army. The first, consisting of the men of Bayeux, Avranches, and Coutances, was commanded by Ranulf, *vicomte* of Bayeux; the second, with the king himself, by Robert of Meulan;[70] and the third, by William de Warenne.[71]

---

[64] Hugh of Fleury, 'Tractatus de Regia Potestate', *Monumenta Germaniae Historica, Libelli de Lite*, ii, 473.

[65] *English Historical Documents*, ii, 329.   [66] OV, vi, 88–9 and n.

[67] Anselm, *Letters*, no. 401. The count's castle, the traces of which have now disappeared, was built on the left bank overlooking the river Noireau: Louise, *La Seigneurie de Bellême*, ii, 291. For discussion of the battle's location, see J. Bradbury, 'Battles in England and Normandy, 1066–1154', *ANS*, 6 (1983), 6–7.

[68] HH, p. 454.

[69] On battle tactics, see S. Morillo, *Warfare under the Anglo-Norman Kings 1066–1135* (Woodbridge, 1994), pp. 144–74. It was said at the later battle of Bourgtheroulde (see below, p. 186), where Henry's knights also fought on foot, that they would be better prepared to fight to the bitter end.

[70] According to Orderic, Robert of Meulan commanded the second line: OV, vi, 88.

[71] Ibid., 88.

Finally, Count Helias, with about a thousand knights from Brittany and Maine, was stationed at a distance on the flanks.

The battle began at about nine in the morning. The trumpets sounded and the duke's smaller army attacked: 'experienced in the Jerusalem wars, he pushed back the royal line'.[72] The front line of his army was commanded by William count of Mortain, with Robert de Bellême in command of the rear. It clashed with that of Henry's army, and there was fierce fighting at close quarters. Then Count Helias with the Bretons and Manceaux attacked on the flanks, wreaking havoc amongst the duke's footsoldiers, and killing more than two hundred in the first assault. Seeing this, Robert de Bellême fled, and the battle was effectively over, having lasted little more than an hour.

The duke himself had the humiliation of being taken prisoner not by a knight but by Waldric, the king's chancellor, who despite his clerical status had accompanied the knights into battle.[73] The Bretons captured William of Mortain, and also captured were Robert de Stuteville, William de Ferrers and William III Crispin, lord of Neaufles. Amongst those fighting on the duke's side was his old friend, Edgar the Aetheling. After 1066, when briefly his claim to the English throne had been canvassed, Edgar's experiences had been chequered, as he moved between the courts of William the Conqueror and King Malcolm of Scots, and spent a period in Apulia.[74] At some stage he became a close friend of Robert Curthose and according to the Worcester chronicle, Robert had granted him land in Normandy. However, when Robert and William Rufus made peace in 1091, one of the conditions had been that Edgar was to lose his Norman estates and friends.[75] Edgar's exile was only temporary, however. A few months later, he was recalled by Duke Robert; the pair acted as mediators between William Rufus and King Malcolm of Scots, and they returned to Normandy together.[76] Edgar had subsequently been involved in the affairs of the children of Malcolm

---

[72] HH, pp. 454–5.
[73] OV, vi, 90. The presence at the battle of Nigel d'Aubigny was remembered at Byland abbey, founded by his son Roger de Mowbray: Dugdale, *Mon. Ang.* (1655 edn), i, 775.
[74] N. Hooper, 'Edgar the Aetheling: Anglo-Saxon Prince, Rebel and Crusader', *Anglo-Saxon England*, 14 (1985), 197–214.
[75] No reason is given for this decision. It may be surmised that Rufus was the driving force, and perhaps could have been concerned that Robert might use Edgar's claim to the English throne against that of his brothers, a suggestion made to me by N. Vincent.
[76] JW, iii, 58–60; *ASC* E 1091. In 1097 he was sent with a military force by William Rufus to help his cousin Edgar re-establish himself on the Scottish throne: JW, iii, 64. Edgar Aetheling also appeared in the Holy Land, probably in 1102: WM, *GRA*, ii, 466. For discussion of the date see David, *Robert Curthose*, pp. 236–7.

and Margaret, and he had gone to the Holy Land before returning to the West. After 1100 his niece was Henry's wife, and presumably he was in no danger at Henry's court. In 1106 he crossed the Channel to fight alongside the duke. When captured, he was soon set at liberty.[77]

From Henry's standpoint, the victory had been relatively bloodless. A report by an anonymous priest from Fécamp noted that the king had lost only two men dead and one wounded, Robert of Bonnebosc. Even if this represents the casualties amongst the knights only, not those from the rank and file, it is clear that losses were low. Many members of Robert's army were captured. Henry reported to Archbishop Anselm – doubtless with some exaggeration – that his forces had captured four hundred knights and ten thousand footsoldiers.[78]

The date of the battle is variously reported as 27, 28 or 29 September.[79] William of Malmesbury believed that it occurred on the eve of Michaelmas (viz. 28 September), and noted that the date was the fortieth anniversary of the Conqueror's landing at Pevensey. Was it the work of Providence, he wondered, that Normandy should submit to England on the very day the Normans had arrived to conquer that country?[80] As well as Providence, luck was also involved. Those who might have intervened on the duke's behalf did not do so. The king of France was old and inactive,[81] and the count of Anjou and his son were not prepared to get involved.[82] The count of Flanders, too, stood aloof, presumably persuaded not to intervene because of his treaty with Henry. Henry had been fortunate, too, in that his brother, though his forces were outnumbered, had been prepared to risk a pitched battle rather than leaving William of Mortain to his fate. It is possible to argue that the duke had made a fatal mistake because he had played directly into Henry's hands: if he had refused to fight, Henry would presumably have had to return to England for the winter, and all would have been to play for in the following year. Henry had also been lucky on the battlefield in that, after a short sharp encounter, the flanking attack of Count Helias had swung the battle his way at a crucial moment. Robert de Bellême, who might have been able to stiffen the resistance of the duke's army, had decided to leave whilst the going was good. The whole contest

---

[77] *ASC* E 1106.   [78] Anselm, *Letters*, no. 401.
[79] 27 September: *Chronique du Bec*, ed. A. A. Porée (Rouen, 1885), p. 5; *GND*, ii, 222; 28 September: *ASC* E 1106, JW, iii, 108–10 and WM, *GRA*, i, 722; 29 September: the priest of Fécamp. Davis, 'A Contemporary Account', 296; for discussion see OV, vi, 89n.
[80] WM, *GRA*, i, 722–4.
[81] Suger, *Vie de Louis VI* (ed. Waquet), pp. 80–2; OV, vi, 156.   [82] Ibid., 66–8.

was over quickly, with remarkably little loss of life, leaving the duke in Henry's custody. Henry's first experience of a pitched battle had thus been gloriously successful. The youngest of the three brothers, he had grown up in their shadow. Robert had achieved imperishable renown in the Holy Land and probably did not rate his youngest brother highly as a soldier; Rufus had been one of the greatest knights of the age; now the youngest of the Conqueror's sons, Henry, had been put to the test and was not found wanting.

Tinchebray proved to be a decisive military victory, in that Normandy and England were reunited in the hands of one man for almost three decades. How do we assess its significance? Some years ago Richardson and Sayles argued that its consequences for the history of England were far more important than those of the much more famous battle of Hastings.[83] By reuniting England with Normandy, the battle of Tinchebray, they argued, ensured 'the ascendancy of French speech' in England: its consequences, in other words, were linguistic and cultural rather than dynastic and political. This is to view the significance of the battle from too narrow a perspective. The priority which Henry gave to Normandy, reaffirmed by his victory, meant frequent and protracted absences from England, a determination to ensure order during those absences, and a relentless drive for English cash to meet the costs of war. Continuing close ties with the duchy ensured that, if some great cross-Channel complexes of land were broken up, others were created; and if some families divided into English and Norman branches, others based in England acquired a new stake across the Channel in Normandy. In the church, too, men were recruited on one side of the Channel to serve on the other side, and ties between Norman houses and their English dependencies remained strong.

For the Normans, too, Tinchebray represented a turning point. Had Robert remained duke, it is possible that noble power in Normandy would have been reconfigured, with the great families in some cases enjoying more autonomy from ducal authority, but in others finding that their power was increasingly challenged by local castellans. Norman society might have been more open to political, cultural and ecclesiastical influences from the duchy's neighbours. Instead, her frontiers were strongly defended by a ring of stone castles, and her fortunes were still closely bound with those of

---

[83] H. G. Richardson and G. O. Sayles, *The Governance of Mediaeval England from the Conquest to Magna Carta* (Edinburgh, 1963), p. 123.

the Normans in England.[84] Ducal rights were strongly defended, and the long period of Henrician rule played a part in sustaining the strong ducal authority that would later be revived under the Angevins. Henry was able to impose a measure of peace for the people and churches of Normandy, and as a result was duly praised by Orderic, though perhaps there was a price to be paid in terms of the vitality of intellectual life in Norman schools and the dynamism of Norman architecture. However, whilst Henry had breath in his body there was no question of giving Normandy up. He was determined to retain what he had won on the field of battle.

[84] For architectural trends see L. Grant, 'Architectural Relations between England and Normandy, 1100–1204', in *England and Normandy in the Middle Ages*, ed. D. Bates and A. Curry (London, 1994), pp. 117–29.

CHAPTER 5

Reform and reconstruction, 1107–1108

Henry's first priority after his great victory at Tinchebray was to take measures for the security of the duchy, and to reimpose order. These tasks were accomplished within a few months, and by Easter 1107 he had returned to England, where he was faced by matters which had been shelved whilst he had been preoccupied with war and at odds with Archbishop Anselm. The period between October 1106 and July 1108 was not marked by military victories or dramatic events, but was nevertheless of fundamental importance in establishing a mode of governing on each side of the Channel.

NORMANDY

Henry did not try to remove his brother formally from possession of the duchy, and it is hard to see how he could have done so.[1] Instead he imprisoned Robert and ruled in his place. Initially, at least, Henry may have avoided using the title 'duke of the Normans'. He was after all a king, and he could emphasise that he was the true heir of the Conqueror, and the guardian of Robert's son William Clito. Few however could have been in any doubt that he intended to keep what he had won. The immediate issue was securing custody of the ducal castles. The duke had given orders that the castle of Falaise, where his son William was staying, was only to be handed over to William de Ferrers. Accordingly he advised Henry to send William to take charge of the castle. Henry followed and received the castle and the fealty of the townspeople at the duke's command.[2] The king and the duke then went to Rouen together, and the castle was handed over by the castellan, Hugh de Nonant. Hugh may not have been reluctant to do so, for he had suffered loss of his lands through the activities of Robert de

---

[1] For what follows, see Green, 'Le gouvernement d'Henri Ier Beauclerc en Normandie'.
[2] OV, vi, 93.

Bellême. The duke released the other castellans from their allegiance, and they made their peace with Henry the 'conqueror'.[3]

There was no doubt about what had happened in Normandy. Orderic was able to write of events in 1107 'after King Henry had subjugated Normandy by war'.[4] In two other texts, his royal confirmation of the will of his friend, Robert count of Meulan, and a confirmation of a gift to the abbey of La Trinité at Caen, the message again was quite clear. In the former he confirmed to the younger of the count's twin sons 'whatever the count held in England in the second year after I subjugated Normandy to me by battle'. The elder twin was to receive the county of Meulan, the Beaumont estates in Normandy and the great manor of Sturminster in Dorset. However, if either twin died or was considered unsuitable to inherit, his share was to pass to the other. The emphasis here on suitability for inheritance clearly chimed with the case being made at Henry's court that his claim to the inheritance of William the Conqueror was superior because he, unlike Robert, was competent.[5] A similar phrase about the subjugation of Normandy occurs in a second text, the confirmation of a gift to La Trinité at Caen by Hawise, the widow of Robert Marmion, 'in the year in which Henry king of the English subjugated Normandy to himself'.[6]

How did the Normans react to the changed situation? It is not easy to weigh up the extent of the duke's support by 1106, or how far churchmen and lay lords came over to Henry after his victory, because the evidence is patchy. Orderic provides the principal narrative of events, and there is only a handful of documents issued by Robert or Henry relating to the duchy which have witness lists.[7] The only known defectors amongst the churchmen had been Serlo bishop of Sées and Ralph abbot of Sées, who had fled to Henry's court from the ravages inflicted by Robert de Bellême.[8] There was little alternative for churchmen but to accept the transfer of power from Robert to Henry, and churches had much to gain from the restoration of order. Some of the great lords had already made their choice. As early as 1104 Henry had been welcomed in Normandy by several, some of whom, like Robert of Meulan, had fought at his side in 1106. Others, however, especially those with few estates across the Channel, were more

---

[3] Ibid., 92. [4] Ibid., 136. [5] *RRAN*, ii, no. 843 and appendix, no. li.
[6] *Charters and Custumals of the Abbey of Holy Trinity, Caen* (ed. Walmsley), no. 8.
[7] Neither Archbishop William nor any of the Norman bishops appears in the witness lists of Henry's charters before Tinchebray, but too much should not be read into this as there was little occasion for them to do so. For an assessment of Robert's support base, see S. Mooers Christelow, '"Backers and Stabbers": Problems of Loyalty in Robert Curthose's Entourage', *Journal of British Studies*, 21 (1981), 1–17.
[8] OV, vi, 46.

cautious, and yet others remained loyal to the duke and his son and stayed away from Henry's court.

In this situation control of the ducal castles was to be crucial for Henry. Unlicensed castles were destroyed, and whenever Henry had the opportunity to recover possession of castles in the hands of powerful lords he did so. In this he was only reasserting one of the rights enjoyed by his father according to the inquest into ducal customs held by his brothers in 1091.[9] Nevertheless his insistence on having castles handed over undoubtedly upset the strategies of families which had held them, in some cases for several generations. Direct control of castles provided him with a network that was to be crucial when baronial loyalties faltered, as they did, especially in 1118.[10] Although their names are mentioned only occasionally in the sources, he placed his own men in charge of the garrisons, which were reinforced when necessary by knights from the royal household. The castles, strengthened and extended, were strongpoints along the frontiers and in the Norman towns where, even if the townsmen were equivocal about Henry's rule, the citadel could hold out.

In the months following Tinchebray, Henry summoned several large councils. The first was at Lisieux in October,[11] and the second at Falaise in January 1107. In March he was at Lisieux again, and he also held an assembly at Rouen attended by the queen.[12] The decrees passed at Lisieux in October were briefly reported by Orderic: the king ordered the establishment of a firm peace; robbery and plundering were to be suppressed; churches were to have such possessions as they had had on the day of his father's death; and all lawful heirs were to have their inheritances. Finally so far as the ducal estates were concerned, the clock was to be turned back to the day of his father's death, and grants made by Curthose were to be cancelled.[13] Henry's pledges of a firm peace and a condemnation of robbery and plunder recall the similar promise he had made at his coronation in 1100, though in Normandy the degree of disorder and the mechanisms for peacekeeping reflected the duchy's different traditions.

The promise that the possessions of churches were to be restored to the situation in 1087 was a recognition of losses experienced during the years of disorder, and it also implicitly set aside any actions of Henry's predecessor, who was thus being treated as if he had not been duke. Similarly any ill-judged grants Robert had made from the ducal demesne were cancelled. Restoring lost lands and rights to churches would necessarily take time; at

---

[9] Haskins, *Norman Institutions*, p. 282; J. Yver, 'Les châteaux forts en Normandie jusqu'au milieu du XIIe siècle', *Bulletin de la Société des Antiquaires de Normandie*, 53 (1955–6), 28–115.
[10] OV, vi, 222–4.   [11] Ibid., 92.
[12] Ibid., 136–8; *RRAN*, ii, no. 809, cf. nos. 807–8.   [13] OV, vi, 92–4.

least now 1087 was prescribed as the date by which lawful possession was to be judged.

The promise that lawful heirs were to have their inheritances was directed at those families which had suffered losses. Rufus' practice of making heirs 'buy back' their lands had been explicitly rejected by Henry in England, and it may be that both Robert and Rufus had had a hand in destabilising inheritance customs in Normandy, either by active intervention or by condoning violence. Noble sensitivity on this issue would hardly have been eased by Henry's violent overthrow of his elder brother, for by his actions he had overturned the natural order of succession amongst the Conqueror's sons. If he had not been freed from his homage to his elder brother – and not all believed he had[14] – then as a vassal he was also guilty of breaking his allegiance to his lord. It was crucial therefore for Henry to offer assurances about inheritances, though the very vagueness of the description 'lawful heirs' concealed the frequent difficulty, in disputed inheritances, of establishing who exactly the lawful heir was. Everyone knew this, and all Henry could do, as in England, was to offer assurances of a predisposition towards recognising inheritance.

Robert de Bellême was the most powerful of the duke's supporters who had escaped from the battlefield. He was still rich in men and castles, no fewer than thirty-four of them. He tried to get the support of Count Helias to help Duke Robert and his son, but Helias warned him against doing so.[15] Orderic offers the reader Helias's reasons for his own loyalty to Henry: the evils that had arisen in Normandy under the duke and men such as Robert de Bellême, and the judgement of God which had given Henry victory in battle. Helias believed that he should not offend God by rising up against Henry, though he did offer his services as a mediator for Robert de Bellême. Eventually a rapprochement between the king and Robert was achieved, but at a price. Robert had to surrender Argentan and other acquisitions from the ducal demesne. In return he was permitted to hold his father's *vicomté* of Falaise, though not the great ducal castle, and everything else that had belonged to his father. By November 1106 Robert was in attendance at Henry's court at Rouen, though he did not recover his lands across the Channel.[16] His brothers Arnulf and Roger were also reconciled and, although Arnulf did not regain his lands, Roger may have been restored to some small portion.[17] Henry was prepared to allow Robert

---

[14] Ibid., 94. [15] Ibid., 94–8. [16] *RRAN*, ii, no. 792.
[17] Anselm acted as a mediator for Arnulf: Anselm, *Letters*, no. 426. The *Life of St Anselm*, pp. 146–7, includes a story about Arnulf returning from Normandy to England when he was caught in a storm at sea; Arnulf called on St Anselm and was saved. Roger, who was lord of La Marche by right of his wife, was at a royal council at Nottingham in 1109: *RRAN*, ii, no. 919. For his possible recovery

his patrimonial lands in Normandy, and indeed would probably have been unable to do otherwise, but he was not prepared to allow Robert to become as belligerent in the southern marches of the duchy as he had been. In order to strengthen his own influence in the neighbourhood of Argentan, Henry placed there one of his key men, Nigel d'Aubigny, at Château-Gontier. He also permitted Nigel to hold Montbray, the castle of his wife's first husband.[18]

Robert de Montfort was less fortunate. He had inherited great estates in England, and had been a commander in William Rufus' army. He had appeared at Henry's court at the start of the reign, and at the siege of Vignats in 1102 had stirred up the duke's army to leave the scene.[19] He does not appear as a witness of Henry's documents after 1104, however, and it seems likely that around this time he went over to the duke's cause. If Orderic was right that Robert had a hereditary position as 'commander in the Norman army', it may be that he felt his overriding loyalty lay with the duke.[20] If so, then Orderic may have been mistaken about Robert's appearance in Henry's army at Tinchebray. At any rate, in 1107 he was charged by Henry with breach of fealty. Robert knew he was guilty, surrendered his lands, and joined Bohemond in Apulia, where he was warmly welcomed.

The great courts held by Henry in 1106 and 1107 gave opportunities for those Normans who had not yet sworn allegiance to do so. One welcome new arrival was William de Tancarville. His father, who held large estates on the right bank of the Seine,[21] had been chamberlain to William the Conqueror in Normandy, but neither he nor his son were major beneficiaries of the Conquest. William was one of the few Norman magnates to whom Henry was conspicuously generous in terms of grants of lands in England, which were used by William to enrich the college of secular canons at Saint-Georges-de-Boscherville, possibly in penance for a marriage he had contracted within the prohibited degrees of kinship.[22] This, with the consent of Henry I, was elevated to the status of a Benedictine abbey and colonised with monks from Saint-Evroult.[23] Henry was evidently involved in this project, which his generosity had helped to underwrite. Not all the

---

of lands, see C. P. Lewis, 'The King and Eye: a Study in Anglo-Norman Politics', *EHR*, 103 (1989), 583–4.

[18] *Charters of the Honour of Mowbray 1107–1191*, ed. D. E. Greenway, British Academy Records of Social and Economic History, New Series, 1 (1972), p. xix.
[19] OV, v, 246, 258; vi, 22; *RRAN*, ii, nos. 488, 544, 602, 621, 636, 663, 680.   [20] OV, vi, 100.
[21] *RRAN*, ii, no. 842 (and many other attestations).
[22] The marriage is referred to in a letter of Anselm, no. 419.
[23] *RRAN*, ii, no. 1012, pp. 324–6. In 1130 Rabel de Tancarville, William's son, was pardoned £4 11s. geld in Wiltshire, £2 6s. in Gloucs., and 15s. in Warwicks.: *PR 31 Henry I*, pp. 22, 80, 108.

Normans could be placated thus. William Crispin, for instance, who had been captured at Tinchebray, was released but did not remain quiet for long.

William Bonne-Ame, archbishop of Rouen, who might have stood out against the imprisonment of the duke, was an old man whom Henry had known all his life. He supported the cause of church reform, presiding over a council in 1096 when simony and the homage of priests to laymen were condemned, but he did not oppose Duke Robert directly over investiture. In 1105 he was suspended from office for an unknown reason, but restored after a hearing presided over by Archbishop Anselm acting as the pope's legate.[24] He was certainly in action in December 1107, when he consecrated a new abbot for Fécamp and ordained over a hundred priests, of whom Orderic himself was one, and over two hundred deacons.[25]

A matter of some urgency was to fill the bishoprics of Bayeux and Lisieux. Bishop Turold of Bayeux had been nominated by Rufus, but had failed to secure election by his chapter, or investiture.[26] Members of the chapter had appealed to Rome, and in 1104 he had been deposed by the pope. He managed to delay his deposition but a final hearing was ordered to take place before Archbishop Anselm in 1107, by which time Turold had decided to retire to the abbey of Bec. In his place Henry nominated Richard of Douvres, from a very distinguished clerical family. Richard's father Samson had been bishop of Worcester, and his brother was destined for York in the following year (see below, p. 110). Richard's connections with Henry's court could hardly have been stronger, and he had the added advantage of his local origins near Bayeux. Nevertheless his task there was a difficult one, for the see had suffered losses since the arrest of the redoubtable Odo in 1082, and Richard could do little to reverse this process. Moreover, the town of Bayeux, suffering from the effects of the fire of 1105, was threatened by the rising prominence of Caen, which was Henry's second capital in the duchy.

At Lisieux the situation was even more difficult. Ranulf Flambard had taken control of the temporalities and tried to secure the see first for one and then for another of his sons. After this the chapter had elected William, archdeacon of Evreux, but he had been unable to secure consecration from the archbishop of Rouen.[27] After Tinchebray, Henry's first thought was that he might bestow the see on Hervey the Breton, bishop of Bangor, who had been forced into exile, but Archbishop Anselm advised that this

---

[24] Anselm, *Letters*, no. 398.   [25] OV, vi, 140–2.
[26] S. E. Gleason, *An Ecclesiastical Barony of the Middle Ages. The Bishopric of Bayeux, 1066–1204* (Cambridge, Mass., 1936), pp. 17–23.
[27] OV, v, 322–3 and n.; Anselm, *Letters*, nos. 388, 397.

would be very difficult to achieve. Henry instead decided to nominate John, archdeacon of Sées, who had fallen foul of Robert de Bellême and crossed to England, where he became one of Henry's chaplains and a leading counsellor.[28] He was not only well known to the king, but was said to have excelled in legal cases, and the king may have envisaged at the time of his appointment that he would be able to deploy this talent in dealing with lawsuits referred to the duke's court.

Henry's determination to bring peace to the duchy depended on the fear and respect that he and his representatives could command and, if all else failed, on the use of coercive power. Those who desired justice in their lawsuits might seek him out personally when he was at Rouen or Caen, for instance, but there was also a panel of justices which met at Caen and which could dispense justice. Haskins long ago drew attention to reports of lawsuits in which the abbey of Saint-Etienne at Caen was involved, and which throw light on the operation of justice under Henry.[29] The first text can be no later than 1129 because of the reference to William de Tancarville, the chamberlain, who died in that year. The abbot made his case 'before the king and the whole court', viz. Bishop John of Lisieux, Robert de Courcy, William de Tancarville, William Peverel and Rainald of Arganchy.[30] In the second case, Roger son of Peter de Fontenay restored lands and tithes to the abbey in the castle at Caen 'in the presence of the whole justice', and gave security to the justice Geoffrey de 'Sublis'. The 'justice', viz. Bishop John, Robert de la Haye, Hugh de Montfort, Geoffrey de 'Sublis' and Roger Marmion, were witnesses. Hugh de Montfort was presumably the man of that name who rebelled in 1123 and was imprisoned thereafter, and Roger Marmion was dead by 1130.[31] Robert de la Haye was a royal steward in 1131.[32] A third case concerned the church of Secqueville. King Henry appointed a day for hearing the case, and on that day the abbot and monks obtained justice. The king and the 'justice' – that is, the body of justices, namely Bishop John, Robert de la Haye and Geoffrey de 'Sublis' – were witnesses, as were a number of barons. A word here is needed about the use of the noun *iusticia* in each of these three cases: it is being used not in the abstract sense of 'justice', but in that of people, in lieu of *iustitiarii*.[33] The king and justices seem to have constituted a panel which was collectively described as the 'justice', in the sense of a body of justices. Sessions were held in the king's presence, wherever he happened to be, at Caen, and, perhaps, elsewhere in the duchy.

[28] Anselm, *Letters*, no. 404; OV, vi, 142–4.   [29] Haskins, *Norman Institutions*, pp. 94–6.
[30] Ibid., p. 95 no. 5.   [31] *PR 31 Henry I*, p. 111.   [32] *RRAN*, ii, nos. 1688, 1693, 1698.
[33] For terminology see Haskins, *Norman Institutions*, pp. 93–4.

Later in the twelfth century Caen was the seat of the Norman exchequer, which met in the stone hall which Henry had built within the castle precincts, and it is tempting to associate the panel of justices mentioned above with that Norman exchequer. There is only one explicit reference to it, and this occurs in a copy of a charter inserted into a thirteenth-century cartulary of Merton priory, which refers to an exchequer apparently in Normandy.[34] It is a description of two court appearances by Bernard, a royal scribe, concerning land at Mathon. Bernard had obtained a judgement through the bishop of Lisieux, Robert de la Haye and many others 'at the exchequer' (location unspecified) against a man named Serlo the deaf. This judgement evidently had not done the trick: Serlo was placed 'in the king's mercy through the judgement of the barons of the exchequer because he had cultivated that land despite Bernard's title'. Those who were present when Bernard established his case included Robert de Courcy,[35] William FitzOdo[36] and Henry de Pomeroy,[37] William of Glastonbury,[38] Wigan the marshal, Robert, chaplain of the bishop of Lisieux, Robert of Evreux and Martin, scribe of the chapel.[39] Robert de Courcy is known to have been a steward; William FitzOdo and Henry de Pomeroy were constables, and William of Glastonbury a chamberlain. This account describes a court evidently very similar to those described in the account from Saint-Etienne, which could meet without the king being present, and deal with land disputes.

The description of the hearings does not make it absolutely clear that the exchequer in question was a separate exchequer meeting at Caen, but it seems most likely that it was, and that here we have a court presided over by a bishop on the lines of the English exchequer. While the role of this court, and that of Bishop John of Lisieux, may not have been precisely the same as its counterpart in England, it is likely that the basic functions of the two as courts of audit were the same, though there is no means of knowing which developed first.[40] If the accounts that Duke Robert was without cash are to be believed, ducal finances were in a woeful state in 1106, and it would have taken Henry time and persistence to recover lost

---

[34] London, British Library MS Cotton Cleopatra C vii ff. 99v–100r, printed J. H. Round, 'Bernard the King's Scribe', *EHR*, 14 (1899), 426 (no. 7).
[35] Green, *GOE*, pp. 242–3.   [36] Ibid., p. 253.   [37] Ibid., pp. 266–7.
[38] Ibid., p. 246.   [39] *RRAN*, ii, no. 1584.
[40] The view of most historians in recent years has been that the courts were established at roughly the same time on each side of the Channel. See, for instance, Hollister and Baldwin, 'The Rise of Administrative Kingship,' in *MMI*, pp. 232–6. This may well have been the case, but the evidence for an exchequer in early twelfth-century Normandy is one undated text: see Green, 'Unity and Disunity in the Anglo-Norman State', 118–21.

lands and rights for the ducal coffers. But as no rolls survive for this period from Normandy, there is no means of knowing even who accounted for revenue, and in what kind of coin.

Not only were ducal revenues doubtless smaller than those of the English crown, but such revenues may not have been paid in Norman coin. Normandy was a region where coins were widely used, but in the early twelfth century coins from neighbouring regions, Maine, Chartres and the Ile-de-France, circulated in addition to Norman coins, particularly near the frontiers of the duchy. Debased and false coins had been a problem in Normandy at the end of the eleventh century as they were in England, partly because silver itself was in short supply and partly because there was little that princes and kings could do in practice to punish those who were caught either debasing coins or in possession of such coins. According to the inquest held into the customs of William the Conqueror's day, the 'Customs and Rights of the Dukes of Normandy', coins in the duchy were supposed to be of good weight, that is, composed of fifty per cent silver; they were to be made only at Rouen and Bayeux; and heavy penalties could be imposed by the duke for those found with false coins.[41] The fundamental problem was the restricted supply of silver available in north-western Europe. In the 1120s, important deposits of silver at Alston near Carlisle began to be exploited (see below, pp. 175, 248), but before that all that could be done was to get hold of as much silver as possible from existing sources, and to punish those who were involved in debasement or forgery. As we have already seen (above, p. 79), in 1104, the year of Henry's first expedition to Normandy, heavy taxes had been levied in England, and on at least one famous occasion subsequently Henry is known to have paid off his knights in English coins (see below, p. 188).[42] Transporting large supplies of coined money across the Channel was risky and cumbersome, and such transhipments were presumably made only when necessary, and may imply that good quality silver coinage was not readily available in Normandy. If so, any profits that the duke might be able to make from the operations of Norman moneyers were likely to be limited.

Another obstacle in securing full payment of ducal revenues was the perennial problem of dishonest collectors, and here we have an illuminating story told by Abbot Suger, who in 1108 and 1109 was a young monk in

---

[41] *Consuetudines et Iusticie*, in Haskins, *Norman Institutions*, p. 283.
[42] F. Dumas, 'Les monnaies normandes des xe–xiie siècles avec un répertoire', *Revue Numismatique*, 21 (1979), 84–140; L. Musset, 'Réflexions sur les moyens de paiement en Normandie aux xie et xiie siècles', *Aspects de la société et de l'économie dans la Normandie médiévale (Xe–XIIIe siècles)*, *Cahier des Annales de Normandie*, 22 (1988), 81 (map).

charge of property belonging to the abbey at Berneval near Dieppe. The monks had the right to a valuable payment of fish from the local fishing boats, which had been appropriated by the duke's officer. The abbot of Saint-Denis and Suger as the local reeve pursued the matter through the courts, and finally secured a judgement in the abbey's favour. So profitable were the proceeds of the fish render that they financed a new feast (including roast meat, pastries and wine) to be celebrated at the abbey commemorating King Dagobert, which is why the story was recorded.[43] It was not surprising that Suger believed Henry's victory had inaugurated a new era of peace and justice: to those who plundered, wrote Suger, he promised that their eyes would be torn out and that they would swing from the gibbet, and what he promised, he performed. Neither nobles nor non-nobles dared to plunder or pillage.[44]

Ducal governance rested upon interlocking networks. In the first place there were the duke's own agents, those who collected his revenues and watched over his rights, and his castellans. Then there were those who held the titles of count and viscount, men of noble birth who possessed castles, lands and vassals. Such men owed allegiance to the duke, but at the same time might well resent Henry's insistence on garrisoning their castles or allowing his officials to intervene in their lands.[45] Moreover, on some honours, such as Breteuil, there were powerful local castellans who in 1103 were not prepared to accept a new lord from outside the honour.[46] Detailed studies of individual families, such as those of the Giroie (Géré) by Jean-Marie Maillefer and Pierre Bauduin,[47] and the lords of Bellême by the late Gerard Louise,[48] are helping to deepen our understanding of Norman society in the twelfth century, and, in the present context, the nature of the challenge faced by Henry I.

The archbishop, bishops and more important abbots were also key figures in Norman society. The archbishop was the person to whom in many cases Henry addressed writs and charters, presumably because he was held to

---

[43] R. Barroux, 'L'anniversaire de la mort de Dagobert à Saint-Denis au XIIe siècle: charte inédite de l'abbé Adam', *Bulletin Philologique et Historique du Comité des Travaux Historiques et Scientifiques*, 1942–3 (1945), 150; L. Grant, *Abbot Suger of Saint-Denis. Church and State in Early Twelfth Century France* (Harlow, 1998), pp. 90–1.

[44] *Vie de Louis* VI (ed. Waquet), p. 100.

[45] As count of Evreux, Amaury de Montfort fought (in vain) to secure the castle of Evreux, and resented the activities of Henry's officials (see below, pp. 180, 242).

[46] Crouch, *Beaumont Twins*, chapter 4; Bauduin, 'Le baron, le château et la motte'.

[47] J.-M. Maillefer, 'Une famille aristocratique aux confins de la Normandie: les Géré au XIe siècle', *Autour du pouvoir ducal normand Xe–XIIe siècles, Cahier des Annales de Normandie*, 17 (1985), 175–206; Bauduin, 'Une famille châtelaine'.

[48] Louise, *La Seigneurie de Bellême*.

be pre-eminent in ducal society. He and the bishops had the responsibility for punishing breaches of the Truce of God, a peacekeeping arrangement which had been introduced into Normandy in the eleventh century.[49] Some abbots, like those of Bec and Fécamp, had very considerable powers of justice either throughout the abbey's lands or in some portion of them.[50]

Some of the most important recent work on ducal Normandy has been concerned with the frontiers of the duchy. Pierre Bauduin's study of the formative era in the tenth and eleventh centuries offers a new view which highlights the nature of shifting power near the frontiers.[51] Daniel Power's study of the frontier in the Angevin era also stresses frontiers as zones rather than linear divisions between Normandy and her neighbours.[52] A detailed study, by Astrid Lemoine-Descourtieux, of a particular sector of the frontier that runs along the river Avre has demonstrated how Henry I had to buttress his authority in this sensitive region by strengthening Nonancourt and Verneuil.[53]

Thus ducal power was not consistent throughout Normandy, but varied from region to region. It was at its strongest in upper Normandy and those regions of lower Normandy spreading out from the great fortresses of Caen, Falaise, and Argentan. From Domfront ducal power extended south into the region of the Passais, and in the Cotentin there were important ducal estates. However, along the frontiers in the north, east and south ducal power had to contend with that of noble families. Here Henry's authority was most likely to be challenged by the frontier lords and, over time, steps were taken to strengthen ducal castles and to build new ones (see below, pp. 183, 233–4).

Henry had to return to England in 1107, and the security of his newly won duchy had to be ensured before he left. Very few of his documents can be securely dated to this period and this in itself is interesting, in that there was obviously no rush by churchmen to secure grants of confirmation of their lands and privileges. One document which Henry is known to have issued between 1107 and 1109 was granted at Caen. It was addressed to the

---

[49] M. de Boüard, 'Sur les origines de la trêve de Dieu en Normandie', *Annales de Normandie*, 9 (1959), 169–89; D. Barthélemy, *L'an mil et la paix de Dieu. La France chrétienne et féodale 980–1060* (Paris, 1999), pp. 521–36; *The Peace of God. Social Violence and Religious Response in France Around the Year 1000*, ed. T. Head and R. Landes (Ithaca, N.Y., 1992). For Henry's amendments to the Truce in Normandy, see below, p. 219.
[50] Ibid., p. 89 n. 21.   [51] Bauduin, *La première Normandie*, part III.
[52] D. Power, *The Norman Frontier in the Twelfth and Early Thirteenth Centuries*, Cambridge Studies in Medieval Life and Thought, 4th series, 62 (Cambridge, 2004).
[53] A. Lemoine-Descourtieux, 'La frontière normande de l'Avre de la fin du xe siècle au début du xiiie siècle: La défense et les structures du peuplement', thèse de doctorat, Université de Caen Basse-Normandie (2003).

archbishop of Rouen and to Robert de Candos (Chandos) and all his lieges of the district round Rouen, confirming a gift to the abbey of Jumièges of land in the forest of Roumare.[54] The primacy accorded to the archbishop in the address clause is not uncommon in such confirmations, as other documents show,[55] whilst Robert de Candos was either *vicomte* or castellan of Rouen.[56]

Henry presumably made some kind of arrangements for the government of the duchy during his absences, but this is not spelled out in the sources. The archbishop of Rouen, as already mentioned, was very old and probably not a suitable candidate. Bishop John of Lisieux was a newer appointment, though over time he achieved a pre-eminence comparable with that of Bishop Roger of Salisbury over royal administration in England. There was no obvious precedent for a deputy in Normandy. In 1066 the Conqueror had left his duchess, Matilda, in charge, assisted by senior magnates.[57] In 1096 Duke Robert had committed the duchy to his brother's guardianship, and Rufus is not known to have made arrangements for a regency council when he was in England. Henry therefore did not have a clear tradition to follow, and may not have made any formal arrangements, preferring to return in person as need arose.

ENGLAND

Henry returned to a situation very different from that at his departure in the previous year. Now he was returning 'victorious and strong for the first time'.[58] He spent the Easter feast of 1107 at Windsor, attended by the magnates of England and Normandy, who were said to be in great fear and trembling.[59] There was a backlog of business: decisions had to be made on the succession to lands and offices, and, if absolutely necessary, on a public declaration of his decision to renounce investitures. Henry was able to postpone this once again, however, because the pope had ordered royal representatives to attend a forthcoming council to be held at Troyes.[60]

Meanwhile this was the occasion to reward his friends, to distribute patronage and to fill vacant bishoprics and abbeys. The removal of Robert de Bellême and his brothers, and of Count William of Mortain, had opened up possibilities for changing the tenurial map in all areas of the country.

---

[54] *RRAN*, ii, no. 912. [55] Bates, 'The Earliest Norman Writs', 273.
[56] This Robert probably came from Candos, Seine-Maritime, not Candos, Eure. *RRAN*, ii, no. 1439, issued at Sainte-Vaubourg near Rouen, was witnessed by Robert de Candos and Roger his brother.
[57] OV, ii, 208, 210. [58] HH, p. 454. [59] ASC E 1107; Robert of Torigny, *Chronicle*, 88.
[60] Eadmer, *Historia Novorum*, pp. 184–5.

One region was Yorkshire, where Henry had already begun to insert his own men, such as Robert de Brus, into lands. A great new lordship was created for Nigel d'Aubigny, probably centred on York where he may have been the king's castellan, stretching across the Pennines as far as Kendal, and augmented by midland estates which had fallen to the crown since 1086.[61]

In the midland counties, the estates of Robert FitzHaimon, which were concentrated in Gloucestershire, were probably already earmarked for the king's illegitimate son Robert. Robert count of Meulan was allowed to adopt the title 'earl of Leicester' to consolidate his domination over this town and shire.[62] Gaps in the Norman lordships in Wales were plugged: Henry earl of Warwick was entrusted with Gower, and Roger of Salisbury with Kidwelly. Walter, sheriff of Gloucester, was put in charge of a new castle at Carmarthen, and a colony of Flemings was settled in Pembroke.[63]

In East Anglia too there were changes. Roger Bigod, a survivor of the Conquest who had done sterling service in the early years of Henry's reign, died, leaving a son who was a minor. This gave the king the opportunity to enrich William d'Aubigny, Nigel's brother. William married a daughter of Roger Bigod and thereby acquired a very generous endowment of Bigod lands in Norfolk.[64] The two most powerful lay lords in that county were now William d'Aubigny and William de Warenne. In Suffolk too there were changes: out went Robert de Montfort as lord of Haughley; these estates passed by marriage to Simon de Moulins, who married Robert's sister. (Moulins-la-Marche was a frontier castle abutting the river Sarthe, and it was important for Henry to strengthen his influence over the lords of this region.)[65] Out at some point, possibly in 1105, went Robert Malet lord of Eye; his estates for the time being were kept in the king's hands.[66] After the death of Roger Bigod, the shrievalty of Norfolk and Suffolk passed to Ralph de Belfou, a local baron.

In August 1107 a great council, postponed from Whitsuntide because Anselm had been ill, assembled at London.[67] First on the agenda was the issue of investitures, because the settlement between the king and Anselm

---

[61] *Charters of the Honour of Mowbray*, ed. Greenway, pp. xix–xxiv.
[62] OV, vi, 20.   [63] *Brut (RBH)*, p. 53; *(Peniarth)*, pp. 27–8.
[64] *Red Book of the Exchequer*, ed. H. Hall, 3 vols., RS (London, 1896), i, 397–8; Farrer, *Honors and Knights' Fees*, iii, 4; for discussion of the timing of this marriage see A. Wareham, 'The Motives and Politics of the Bigod Family, *c.* 1066–1177', *ANS*, 17 (1994), 231.
[65] For the family background of Simon of Moulins-la-Marche see E. Zack Tabuteau, 'The Family of Moulins-la-Marche', *Medieval Prosopography*, 13 (1992), 29–65.
[66] Hollister, 'Henry I and Robert Malet', in *MMI*, pp. 132–6.
[67] Eadmer, *Historia Novorum*, pp. 186–92; *Councils and Synods*, i, pt ii, 689–94.

needed ratification. Some of the bishops are said to have urged Henry not to surrender investiture. When Anselm appeared, however, the king declared publicly that no bishop or abbot would ever be invested at the hands of the king or any layman. In return Anselm conceded that no one should be deprived of ecclesiastical preferment because he had done homage to the king. Anselm thus made it clear that, although he did not approve of homage, he was not going to take sanctions against those who had performed it. However, the procedure for making appointments was not spelled out. Although there was an understanding that these should be made in accordance with canon law, that is, that they should be 'free', in practice what happened was that elections were held in the king's chapel.[68] In 1102 nine abbots had been deposed, indicating that Anselm was not prepared to accept those whose appointment was in some way tainted, so perhaps it was felt that his ability to veto dubious appointments was enough. At any rate, no dent was made in the king's decisive authority, and he now proceeded to fill bishoprics and abbacies. 'There were so many of them that there was nobody who remembered so many being given together.'[69]

At the Whitsuntide court in 1108 the king returned once again to church matters. The main issue once again was clerical marriage. There had been widespread evasion of the 1102 decrees on clerical marriage, though we are told also of the king's concern about the perfunctory way some priests performed services: Henry had clearly got the bit between his teeth.[70] Very strict regulations were now laid down about the clergy's association with women. They were not to allow women in their houses other than close relatives. Those who had kept their wives or been married since the council of 1102 were to put them away, and not to let them into their houses or let them live near the church. Those who were accused of breaking this decree could only clear themselves with competent witnesses: evidently too many had been promising to get rid of their wives and then not doing so; now they were to lose their benefices. Moreover, clergy in breach of the decrees were to suffer excommunication if they celebrated mass, and archdeacons and deans were to take oaths that they would not accept bribes to ignore breaches of the decree. Those who, having given up women and performed penance, lapsed from grace, were to lose all their goods and chattels, as were their womenfolk.[71] These regulations obviously went a good deal further than in the past, and showed that king and

---

[68] This at least was the procedure stated to have been the custom under Henry I, as described in clause 12 of the Constitutions of Clarendon: Stubbs, *Select Charters*, p. 166.
[69] *ASC* E 1107.　　[70] Eadmer, *Historia Novorum*, p. 193.
[71] *Councils and Synods*, i, pt ii, 694–703.

hierarchy meant business, though the situation on the ground was very slow to change. Moreover, there were some very prominent married clergy in the English church, most conspicuously the king's chief minister Roger of Salisbury. We can only assume that the king chose to turn a blind eye to such cases.

Archbishop Gerard of York had died shortly before the Council, and the king decided to nominate in his place Thomas, brother of Richard bishop of Bayeux. From one point of view Henry must have thought this was a safe choice, a man who would not cause trouble over a profession of obedience to Archbishop Anselm.[72] Yet this was not to be the case. Thomas was a popular choice at York: he had been provost of Beverley and, according to Hugh the Chanter, 'he had been brought up and well trained among us'.[73] In other words, he knew exactly the ins and outs of the defence of York against Canterbury's claim to primacy, and, in case he should have forgotten any detail, the chapter duly briefed him. Both the king and the new archbishop would have realised that, given Anselm's age, time was on their side. Thomas delayed making a profession and instead wrote to the pope with a request for his pallium, and thus managed to avoid making his profession before Anselm's death.[74]

Next on the agenda was a major reform of the way the court was provisioned, in order to bring to an end the uncontrolled spoliation which occurred as the court moved through the localities. In the early Middle Ages the court of the English king had, like other great households, moved from estate to estate eating the produce and renders of food collected there. It was a practice that suited a peripatetic court whose itinerary was relatively well known, so that large supplies could be gathered in anticipation, for instance, of the king's Christmas feast. It had become less practicable after the Conquest, however, as the size of the court grew, its itinerary became less regular, and (in Rufus' reign, at least) its activities were less disciplined. There is no way of knowing exactly how large the court was, but some idea perhaps may be gained from the fact that when the White Ship went down, it was only one of a flotilla of ships carrying the court back to England (below, p. 166). If the court arrived unexpectedly, provisions for men and horses had to be acquired and preferably paid for at a fair price, otherwise the effect on the locality could be like that of an army on the move. Under Rufus the indiscipline had become such a major problem that when news of the coming of the king's household spread, the locals

---

[72] For the context, see *Canterbury Professions* (ed. Richter).
[73] Hugh the Chanter, pp. 24, 26.   [74] Ibid., pp. 30–8.

fled to the woods. The members of his court had plundered and destroyed, wasting the supplies they could not consume or forcing hapless farmers to sell them, and they were reputed to have committed indecencies on wives and daughters. Such activities reflected on the king, because these were the members of his own household, for whom he, like any lord, was directly responsible.

At the start of his reign Henry had dismissed many of the hangers-on from his brother's day, and in the aftermath of Tinchebray he laid down strict new rules for the conduct and provisioning of the household. Those found guilty of misconduct were to be punished by blinding or mutilation,[75] and proclamations were issued about how much might be taken from country people as gifts, how much was to be paid for, and at what price.[76] Finally, fixed allowances of money, food, drink and candles were laid down for members of the court, as is known from a list entered into the thirteenth-century collections of material relating to the exchequer, 'the Constitution of the King's Household'.[77] This described the pay and allowances of principal officers of five departments of the household: the staff of the chapel, the hall, the buttery, the chamber and the constabulary.[78] Such regulations were probably not new,[79] but were rather an overhaul after the period of indiscipline under Rufus.[80]

There remained the problem of provisioning a large court. Wherever the king settled, supplies of food had to be brought in from neighbouring royal manors, or purchased, and wine might have to be transported over considerable distances. Farmers took supplies to the court, where they received cash payments in lieu, but there could be problems if the court did not follow a set itinerary. This indeed was the case by the early twelfth century, as the author of the *Dialogue of the Exchequer* explained.[81] All the officers of the household knew how much cash should be allowed for bread, meat or fodder, but clearly if the court did not arrive when expected, the farmers were not paid, and they complained either to the court or even to

---

[75] Eadmer, *Historia Novorum*, pp. 192–3.   [76] WM, *GRA* i, 742.
[77] *Dialogus de Scaccario*, p. 1 (discussed in more detail below, pp. 286–7); cf. Walter Map, *De Nugis Curialium*, p. 438.
[78] *Constitutio Domus Regis*, in *Dialogus de Scaccario*, pp. 129–35. Note that the headings for the different departments occur in the copy of the Black Book of the Exchequer, not the slightly earlier Red Book, but both are thought to have been copied from the same manuscript. A new edition and translation for Oxford Medieval Texts by Dr S. Church is in press.
[79] The treatise recalls Archbishop Hincmar's 'De Ordinatione Palatii', which is conveniently translated by D. Herlihy in *The History of Feudalism* (New York, 1970), pp. 208–27.
[80] William of Malmesbury's reference to the restoration of lights under Henry may be an elliptical reference to earlier allowances of candles which had been abandoned under Rufus: *GRA*, i, 714.
[81] *Dialogue of the Exchequer*, p. 40; for discussion see Green, *GOE*, pp. 63–4.

the king himself, presenting him with their ploughshares as a token.[82] The court's arrival was heralded by suitable publicity, which Henry was said to have provided, but ultimately his movements could not be tied.[83] He was sympathetic to the farmers' plight, and sent commissioners to survey the royal lands and to estimate the money value of food renders. These commissioners fixed sums for which the sheriffs were to be answerable at the exchequer. The commutation of food farms may have occurred later, but should be seen as a further step in the process of maximising cash revenues for the king as well as changing the way the household was provisioned. The problem was, as the author of the *Dialogue* recognised, that cash revenues were subject to the same depreciation due to inflation as all monies paid in cash rather than kind.[84]

Renewed efforts were made to get to grips with the problem of the English coinage, specifically of maintaining good quality and preventing forgery.[85] The efforts Henry had made at the start of his reign to restrict minting to certain locations, and to punish those who were found in possession of counterfeit money, had clearly not worked,[86] and, as we have seen, severe punishments could not get round the problem of a shortage of silver. Nevertheless those who made counterfeit money were now subjected to an even more severe punishment, that of losing their eyes and lower limbs.[87] To test their silver content, many coins were being broken or bent, and then rejected, so it was ordered that henceforth *all* coins were to be broken, so that they could not be rejected on that account. Eadmer's account of these measures refers to both pennies and halfpennies, an indication that the latter had come into being to serve a need for coins of a smaller denomination. The Worcester chronicler commented that Henry ordered that halfpennies should be round in his annals for 1108, and a similar statement occurs in the apocryphal 'Prophecies of Merlin' which were in circulation by the 1130s.[88] Examples of halfpennies have been found, and it has been suggested that they were in existence shortly before the decree of 1108.[89]

It is not long after the reforms of 1108 that the first explicit reference to the barons of the exchequer occurs, in a writ addressed to them notifying them

---

[82] This demonstration recalls the first of the king's nightmares, inserted by the Worcester chronicler in the year 1131, in which peasants appeared before the sleeping king and brandished their instruments at him: JW, iii, 200 (see frontispiece and below, pp. 310–11).
[83] Walter Map, *De Nugis Curialium*, pp. 470–2.   [84] *Dialogue of the Exchequer*, pp. 41–2.
[85] Blackburn, 'Coinage and Currency under Henry I', 62–4.   [86] *RRAN*, ii, no. 501.
[87] Eadmer, *Historia Novorum*, p. 193.
[88] JW, iii, 112–14; *The Historia Regum Britannie of Geoffrey of Monmouth*, i, ed. N. Wright (Cambridge, 1985), 76; OV, vi, 384; *Vie de Louis* VI (ed. Waquet), pp. 99–103.
[89] Blackburn, 'Coinage and Currency under Henry I', 63.

that the cathedral church of Lincoln was not to be liable to custom (tax) 'on account of the aid the king had thence on account of his daughter'. This is presumably a reference to an aid taken in 1110 to meet the costs of Matilda's betrothal and departure for Germany.[90] The wording of the address clause seems to presuppose that the barons of the exchequer were well known; they were clearly being addressed as a group, and in the context of liability to payment of revenue. The reference to the 'exchequer' shows that already the court was known by reference to the checked cloth covering the table around which the members of the court sat to hear the accounts presented by the sheriffs, though the court itself may have predated the checked cloth. The tradition reported by the author of the *Dialogue*, who was almost certainly the son of a former treasurer, was that the exchequer had been introduced from Normandy. Historians have long discussed whether this was true. There is no way of knowing for sure, but it is worth remembering that the reference in the *Dialogue* may be to the checked cloth only, not to regular meetings of a court of audit. The scale of royal finance, particularly when the great gelds were levied in the early eleventh century, has led some historians to the conclusion that the operation could not be run, in V. H. Galbraith's memorable phrase, 'from a box under the bed'.[91] There had been earlier efforts to keep an eye on receipts, because the *Dialogue* refers to the fact that the old name for the exchequer was 'the tallies'.[92] Tallies were the wooden sticks which were notched according to the amount paid over and then split, half being kept by each party as a receipt.[93] Bishop Roger of Salisbury presided over the meetings of the court, which were held twice each year, at Easter and Michaelmas, initially at Winchester but later, and possibly before 1135, at Westminster.[94] William of Malmesbury was to write of Roger that 'the king entrusted to his judgement the administration of justice throughout the realm, whether he were himself in England . . . or Normandy'.[95]

---

[90] *RRAN*, ii, no. 963.
[91] V. H. Galbraith, *Studies in the Public Records* (Edinburgh and London, 1948), p. 45.
[92] *RRAN*, ii, no. 1490, freeing the monks of Malvern from paying rent: four shillings 'are to be placed in my tallies' and they are to be quit, as ordered by William the Conqueror. This text is a fourteenth-century *inspeximus*. In another charter (or another version of the same) of Henry I for the same house, the four shillings are said to be quit 'at the exchequer'; for both, see Dugdale, *Mon. Ang.*, iii, 447–8.
[93] *Dialogus de Scaccario*, p. 7; for discussion see Campbell, 'The Anglo-Norman State in Administrative History', in *Essays in Anglo-Saxon History*, pp. 175–6.
[94] The possibility that the exchequer had moved to Westminster before 1135 rests on an allowance to the sheriffs of London for repairing the houses of the exchequer on the pipe roll of 1155–6: J. A. Green, 'Financing Stephen's War', *ANS*, 14 (1994), 110–111.
[95] WM, *GRA*, i, 738.

As in Normandy, so in England Henry's rule was to be celebrated for peace and justice, and it was from around this time that he seems to have thrown more weight behind the administration of justice. Contemporaries do not comment on the king's *personal* involvement, which surely they would have done if he devoted a good deal of time to hearing petitions: they were impressed by the awe and respect in which his authority was held.[96] The king had a duty to punish the most serious offences such as murder, rape and robbery; offences against him personally, his officials or his written orders also fell within the scope of his justice; and he had an appellate jurisdiction for those who felt that they had not obtained justice elsewhere.[97] To administer these rights there were men who were based locally, there were those who were sent by the king on judicial commissions, and there were a few who, like Bishop Roger, were called by contemporaries 'justices of all England'. Pleas could be heard before the king himself or at the exchequer; judicial commissions could hear pleas in the localities; and many pleas were heard in the shire court.

It was better, however, if men were deterred from wrongdoing in the first place by the deterrent value of severe punishments for those convicted, with death or mutilation for the most serious offences. Henry was said to have been particularly severe at the start of his reign, and switched later to taking fines in lieu.[98] Those who did offend, however, had to be brought to court and convicted. Indictment in many instances rested on personal accusation, either by the wronged party or a kinsman, or by a group of neighbours: by peer pressure, in other words. The incentives for bringing such accusations included a personal sense of injury, heightened by a sense of dishonour if injuries went unchallenged, or, in the case of peer pressure, fear of financial sanctions. Such incentives were not always sufficient, however, and by the early twelfth century official prosecutors were being used. In the church courts this was the responsibility of deans and archdeacons, and it may be that their role set a precedent for the use of comparable officers in the secular courts. At any rate, prosecutors were clearly being used by the reign of Henry I, and were evidently highly unpopular.[99] Convictions were secured either by using ordeals or, where appropriate, by the solemn swearing of oaths, in both cases invoking God's assistance. Those convicted were 'in the king's

---

[96] See however Walter Map, *De Nugis Curialium*, pp. 470–2 for the idealised picture of the king's day: open house to petitioners until the sixth hour.
[97] *Leges Henrici Primi*, cap. 10.   [98] WM, *GRA*, i, 742–4.
[99] R. C. Van Caenegem, 'Public Prosecution of Crime in Twelfth-Century England', in *Church and Government in the Middle Ages. Essays Presented to C. R. Cheney on His Seventieth Birthday* (Cambridge, 1976), pp. 41–76.

mercy', which meant that punishments could be assigned at the king's will and according to the severity of the offence. Those who falsified or debased the coinage were attacking royal authority and thus were subject to severe corporal punishment. Older ideas of compensation paid to the victims of crime or to the courtholder may not have disappeared entirely. They are certainly included in the contemporary *Laws of Henry I*, but as the rights of the injured kinsman were placed below those of the king, in practice there may have been little money left over to pay compensation. Forest law operated with particular severity. Justice as applied under Henry was selective, crude and punitive, but the very fear his authority engendered was better than lawlessness. 'No one dared injure another in his time. He made peace for man and beast' according to the famous epitaph in the Anglo-Saxon Chronicle.[100]

Given that the king's justice had to be administered on his behalf by others, much depended on their calibre. The giving of gifts was accepted and understood to be part of the way of doing business, but this could go too far. Amongst the charges brought by clergy at the Council of London in 1136 was that if anyone sought to defend his church and opposed the spoliation of vacant churches by the use of excommunication, he was persecuted by royal agents and would get no hearing for any request until he had oiled the king's palm.[101] Miles of Gloucester and Payn FitzJohn, leading officials in cases involving the court, were said to have been afraid to present themselves at King Stephen's court for fear of the poor and widows whom they had wronged.[102] It was not only the poor who were at risk for, as Henry of Huntingdon related, the great bishop of Lincoln, Robert Bloet, himself one of the 'justices of all England', found himself towards the end of his life being sued twice by the king before low-born officials.[103] Orderic Vitalis tells a story about Bricstan of Chatteris, who wanted to become a monk at Ely and was seeking to divest himself of his worldly goods, only to be accused of concealing the king's treasure by an official called Robert Malarteis before the royal justice Ralph Basset in the county court of Huntingdon.[104]

Sheriffs were in a particularly powerful position, and Henry had to take steps to ensure that they did not overstep the mark. There survives a writ issued at Reading which dates between May and July 1108. It was addressed to the bishop of Worcester and the sheriff, Urse d'Abetot, and ordered that the shire and hundred courts be held in those places and

---

[100] *ASC* E, 1135.
[101] *Gesta Stephani*, ed. and trans. K. R. Potter with an introduction and notes by R. H. C. Davis (Oxford, 1976), p. 26.
[102] Ibid., pp. 22–4.   [103] HH, p. 586.   [104] OV, iii, 346–58.

at those intervals that they had been in the reign of King Edward and not otherwise. In particular Henry instructed the sheriff not to summon such courts unless ordered to do so. The writ continued by stipulating in which courts different categories of lawsuits involving land were to be dealt with, and by what procedure.[105] The sheriff of Worcestershire had evidently been summoning shire and hundred courts on other than customary occasions, and presumably fining those who did not attend, and the bishop of Worcester is likely to have brought the matter to the king's attention. He was not the only bishop to do so. At an earlier date the sheriff of Hampshire had been warned to deal fairly with the bishop and monks of Winchester who had been summoned to attend shire and hundred courts they were not used to attend,[106] and in 1106, a panel of justices, including Ralph Basset, Geoffrey Ridel, Ranulf Meschin and Peter de Valognes, lord of Benington in Hertfordshire, was instructed to hear a complaint against the sheriff of Yorkshire about the liberty of Ripon, an ancient church held by the archbishops of York.[107]

Sheriffs were the most powerful of the royal officials who might transgress, but there were others. The archbishop of York complained about the failure of royal reeves at Driffield to pay the tithes they owed, and another royal writ ordered them to pay up or else.[108] Abbot Stephen of St Mary's Abbey at York was evidently having trouble with royal forest officials, and the king accordingly instructed the sheriff that the abbot had custody of the king's forests on his own lands.[109] Such writs were presumably issued in response to requests, and there may have been a growing need for them if royal officials were not prepared to accept customary rights without written title. Nevertheless, such complaints suggest that the king's rights were being administered with renewed vigour.

The king's commitment to maintain the laws of King Edward, combined with overlapping and potentially conflicting jurisdictions, helps to explain a contemporary interest in writing compendia of laws. A collection of laws was made by an anonymous author of the laws of English kings, supplemented by later additions such as Henry's Charter of Liberties and

---

[105] For the writ see *Die Gesetze der Angelsachsen*, i, 524. As for the dating, Richard of Beaumais was elected bishop of London in May 1108 and consecrated in July (Eadmer, *Historia Novorum*, p. 197); he witnessed this notification as bishop. It is addressed to Bishop Samson of Worcester and Urse d'Abetot, the sheriff, who died in 1108: 'The Winchcombe Annals', 122. The place of issue was Reading, and the king went abroad in about July: *RRAN*, ii, no. 892. I follow the translation of *divisio* and *occupatio* as allotment or seizure in Hudson, *Formation of the Common Law*, p. 24.
[106] *RRAN*, ii, no. 806.   [107] Ibid., no. 796.   [108] Ibid., no. 839.   [109] Ibid., nos. 836, 838.

the Ordinance on the Shire and Hundred Courts.[110] It was preceded by a dedication and a prefatory 'Argument'. This was apparently composed in about 1108,[111] because Henry was praised for defeating his enemies, evil officials were condemned, and mention was made of a recent royal council and the reform of the royal household. 'Not only has he given us back the law of King Edward . . . strengthened . . . by the improvements introduced by his blessed father . . . he has improved it with his own laws' (c. 27).[112] Henry was thus lauded not only for his stern justice, but also as a legislator. Yet even as Henry was perceived as a stern king on Old Testament lines, the reality was that law and justice were changing. More officials were bringing cases into royal courts, which were in turn taking cognisance of different kinds of cases. More reliance was being placed on the testimony of documents, creating a growing demand for royal writs and charters, and a market for those who could provide forgeries.

There were clear parallels between the measure of reform and reconstruction on both sides of the Channel in 1107 and 1108. Both in England and in Normandy the king's peace was proclaimed, and punishment for wrongdoers was promised. Roger bishop of Salisbury and John bishop of Lisieux had similar, though perhaps not identical, responsibilities, and presided over panels of justices. Ecclesiastical vacancies, numerous in England because of the king's quarrel with Anselm, were filled, and in England church councils were held in 1107 and 1108. Henry had to initiate reform measures in Normandy, and it was not surprising that he did much the same in England, where his hand had been strengthened by his victory over his enemies. Nevertheless, if there was one royal household, the two dominions otherwise remained separate, at least for the time being.

---

[110] Wormald, 'Quadripartitus', in *Law and Government in Medieval England and Normandy*, ed. Garnett and Hudson, pp. 111–47.
[111] R. Sharpe, 'The Prefaces of *Quadripartitus*', in ibid., pp. 148–72.
[112] Ibid., p. 167.

CHAPTER 6

Defence of his dominions, 1108–1115

The years between 1108 and 1116, when major trouble broke out in Normandy and the surrounding regions, were years when Henry, far from being able to relax, had to defend his dominions, especially Normandy, from those who wished to advance the claim to the duchy of his nephew William Clito. The state of affairs there led him to spend long periods of time away from England, and although there was no internal rebellion, there were evidently concerns about individuals' loyalty, and about the state of affairs in the north and in Wales. His hopes for the future were bound up in his son William, still the only legitimate son from his marriage, and it was with the goal of advancing his own son's claim that he sought to crush the hopes of his nephew.

Meanwhile a prestigious marriage was negotiated for his daughter: to the Emperor Henry V, who had succeeded his father in 1106, but was as yet unmarried. There was the prospect of a very large cash marriage portion of some ten thousand marks of silver, that is, £6,666 13s. 4d. This was very timely since Henry V was planning an expedition to Italy in the hope that he would be able to persuade the pope to crown him as emperor.[1] The emperor seems to have taken the initiative in opening negotiations, but the alliance had undoubted attractions for the king, too, in terms of both prestige and a powerful ally. Accordingly negotiations began, in which the queen – interestingly – took a leading role.[2]

The alliance was particularly opportune from the king's point of view. King Philip I of France died on 29 July 1108, which raised the question of Henry's relationship with the new French king, Louis VI, and specifically whether Henry was going to offer to perform homage. The customary practice, it was claimed, was for homage to be performed at the frontier, a form of homage called *hommage en marche* which, though formally recognising

---

[1] Leyser, 'England and the Empire in the Early Twelfth Century', pp. 204–6.
[2] Ibid., p. 194. *Bibliotheca Rerum Germanicarum*, v, ed. P. Jaffé (Berlin, 1869), *Monumenta Bambergensia*, no. 142, p. 259.

the suzerainty of the French king, did not involve any material diminution of the duke's effective power.³ In his youth, William the Conqueror had called on King Philip for help, but is not known to have performed homage to Philip.⁴ After William became king, he is known to have met Philip at least once, in 1079. Philip had sent Robert, King William's son, to the castle of Gerberoy in the Beauvaisis on the frontiers of Normandy, from which base the garrison plundered the surrounding district. The Conqueror, affronted by this challenge from his son, assembled an army and marched to Gerberoy, but King Philip arrived first, presumably – though the sources do not make this clear – repenting of his decision to help Robert. King Philip was amongst those who persuaded William to forgive his son.⁵ There is no indication, however, that William or Robert did homage on this occasion, though Robert may have done so.⁶ Henry's dilemma was that as a king himself he was not prepared to perform homage,⁷ but had to face the possibility that Louis might at some stage accept the homage of Robert's son, William Clito.

There was another more immediately aggravating cause of tension between Henry and Louis, namely the castles of the Vexin. At some stage, possibly when Prince Louis had visited Henry's court soon after the latter's accession,⁸ an agreement had been reached about Gisors and nearby Bray-et-Lu,⁹ whereby if either he or Henry came into possession of these castles, they were to be destroyed within forty days.¹⁰ Gisors was in the hands of the local lord, Theobald Payn, but at some point, probably after Tinchebray, Henry took the castle directly into his own hands, in accordance with his intention of resuming his father's lands and rights. This act angered Louis, who demanded that the castle should either be given up to him or destroyed, and he appointed a time and place for discussion.¹¹ Meanwhile he ravaged the lands of the count of Meulan, because the count was an ally of King Henry.¹²

---

³ J.-F. Lemarignier, *Recherches sur l'hommage en marche et les frontières féodales* (Lille, 1945), chapter 3.
⁴ D. Bates, *Normandy before 1066* (Harlow, 1982), pp. 59–62.   ⁵ OV, iii, 108–14.
⁶ *ASC* E, 1090, 1094; *GND*, ii, 206–7; JW, iii, 56, 70; WM, *GRA*, i, 548; HH, pp. 418–20. For the view that Robert probably did perform homage to Philip, see Hollister, 'Normandy, France and the Anglo-Norman Regnum', p. 213, and Lemarignier, *Hommage en marche*, p. 91 n. 60. The situation of the Norman kings within the British Isles is also worth noting in this context, though there is a similar difficulty in relying on later writers, who described such meetings using words which perhaps meant something different in their own day. King Malcolm III of Scots had recognised the overlordship of the Conqueror in 1072 at Abernethy: *ASC* E 1072; JW, iii, 20 (both use the phrase that Malcolm became William's man). For the quarrel between Malcolm and William Rufus at Gloucester in 1093, see above, p. 34.
⁷ WM, *GRA*, i, 758.   ⁸ See above, p. 40.
⁹ OV, vi, 50, and n. 2; Symeon of Durham, SD, *Opera Omnia*, ii, 232.
¹⁰ OV, v, 216; Suger, *Vie de Louis VI*, p. 102.   ¹¹ Ibid., p. 102.   ¹² Ibid., p. 104.

The two kings met at Planches-de-Neaufles, on the river Epte not far from Gisors, probably in March 1109.[13] Suger reported the confrontation in such detail that he must have been present: Louis's entourage included his uncle Robert, count of Flanders, Theobald count of Blois (King Henry's nephew), and the duke of Burgundy. A deputation was sent to Henry, reminding him that he had gained Normandy by the leave of the French king, and that the duchy had been granted 'as a fief'. A spokesman cited the terms of the agreement about the two castles, and continued that if any of Henry's men denied these terms, the French offered proof by battle. Some of the Normans returned with the French deputation, and appeared before King Louis. They denied the charges and demanded that the issue be tried by law. The French in their turn sent a second deputation of more powerful men, and nominated Robert count of Flanders as their champion. This achieved nothing, so Louis demanded that either the castle be destroyed or Henry fight for it in person. The two sides then began to quarrel over whose army was to cross the river. Some shouted out that the kings should fight on the bridge over the river, but Henry refused and said he would only fight when he was in a position where he could defend himself. Both forces then rushed to the river bank but were unable to cross, and retired for the night. On the following morning the French were quicker off the mark and forced the Normans to retreat into the castle. Suger thus presents the confrontation as a humiliation for Henry, because he refused to fight. On the other hand, he had not surrendered the castle, either, and it was obvious that Louis would not get it without a fight.[14] The standoff continued.

Henry was still in Normandy when the news reached him of the death of Archbishop Anselm. The relationship between the two since the council of London had been formal. In 1108 the ailing archbishop had travelled to the south coast to offer the king his blessing on his departure for Normandy. When Anselm was too unwell to appear at court, Henry had sent his son to receive the archbishop's blessing.[15] The York chronicler suggests that Henry never forgave Anselm for humiliating him over investiture, and he may have been right.[16] Nevertheless Henry was far too supple a politican to be betrayed into public exasperation with his archbishop such as his grandson was to utter, and which was to send Thomas Becket to his death, but he was in no rush to have the see of Canterbury filled, nor did he ever countenance the appointment of another archbishop like Anselm.

The negotiations for Princess Matilda's marriage had probably reached a successful outcome by the autumn of 1108, and at Whitsuntide 1109 the

[13] Ibid., p. 111n.   [14] Anselm, *Letters*, no. 461.
[15] Eadmer, *Historia Novorum*, p. 197.   [16] Hugh the Chanter, p. 130.

formalities took place at a splendid meeting of the court in London.[17] Henry of Huntingdon reported that the envoys who came from Germany were remarkable for their physical strength and splendid appearance.[18] In October 1109 Matilda was with her parents at a royal council at Nottingham, and early in the following year she was dispatched to her husband, arriving at Liège in February 1110.[19]

The marriage alliance with the emperor formed one strand in a web of diplomacy by which Henry sought to build up alliances with Normandy's neighbours. At Easter 1110, Counts Robert of Flanders and Eustace of Boulogne had both been at Utrecht for the betrothal of Matilda and the emperor, when negotiations for a renewal of the Anglo-Flemish treaty may have begun.[20] The terms of the treaty on this occasion were more generous to Count Robert than they had been in 1101. Robert was to produce only half the number of knights, 500 instead of 1,000 as stipulated in 1101, though he was to receive as much as £400 in return.[21] Count Eustace was to act as a mediator should Count Robert fail to meet his obligations.

By 1110 Henry needed his allies, because there were signs that storm clouds were gathering. Robert's son William Clito had survived infancy in the guardianship of Helias of Saint-Saëns, and his claim to be duke of Normandy could be advanced by Henry's enemies both inside the duchy and beyond. Henry evidently suspected the loyalty of some of the Normans, because in 1110 he is known to have exiled William Malet, William Baynard and Philip de Briouze.[22] Why these three? All had estates on both sides of the Channel. William Malet, son of Robert, whom Henry had made his chamberlain at the start of his reign, lost his English estates (but not those in Normandy) presumably for his support of the duke.[23] William Baynard

---

[17] Henry's letter to Archbishop Anselm reporting his disagreement with Louis VI had reported successful negotiations (on an unspecified subject) between himself and the emperor: *Letters*, no. 461: *Opera Omnia*, v, 410–11. For the betrothal, HH, p. 456.
[18] Ibid., p. 456. [19] *RRAN*, ii, no. 919; Chibnall, *Empress Matilda*, p. 22; OV, vi, 166–8.
[20] G. Meyer von Knonau, *Jahrbücher des deutschen Reiches unter Heinrich IV und Heinrich V*, 7 vols. (Leipzig, 1890–1909), vi, 119, as cited by Nip, 'The Political Relations between England and Flanders (1066–1128)', 162.
[21] Chaplais, *Diplomatic Documents*, pp. 5–8, no. 2; Van Houts, 'The Anglo-Flemish Treaty of 1101', 169–74.
[22] *ASC* E, 1110.
[23] For the disloyalty of Robert Malet, William's father, see OV, vi, 12; cf. Hollister, 'Henry I and Robert Malet', *MMI*, pp. 132–3; Lewis, 'The King and Eye', 569–87; C. Hart, 'William Malet and His Family', *ANS*, 19 (1996), 123–65; K. S. B. Keats-Rohan, 'Domesday Book and the Malets: Patrimony and the Private Histories of Public Lives', *Nottingham Medieval Studies*, 41 (1997), 20. Thompson pointed out that William Malet was a kinsman of William Crispin: 'Robert of Bellême Reconsidered', 279.

also lost his great estates and custody of Baynard's castle in London.[24] He too seems to have decided in favour of the duke, for he did not appear at Henry's court after 1101. Philip de Briouze was lord of Bramber in Sussex and Radnor in Wales. He may have fallen under suspicion for any reason, but if so, he was only to be out of favour for a time.[25]

Henry was evidently very concerned about the possibility of a rising to support the claim of William Clito, because he decided to remove the child from the custody of his guardian, Helias of Saint-Saëns. Henry sent Robert de Beauchamp, *vicomte* of Arques, to arrest the boy, but news of his intention preceded him. The boy's friends spirited him away, and he was subsequently joined by Helias.[26] Henry in retaliation confiscated the castle of Saint-Saëns, and this was entrusted to William de Warenne, whose own estates were in upper Normandy, and who was by this time fully restored to Henry's favour, having served in Henry's army at Tinchebray.[27] Helias did not abandon his young charge, but instead appealed for help to anyone who would listen: the king of France, and the dukes of Poitou, Burgundy and Brittany. Without powerful friends, the boy was doomed to the life of an exile.

A second important development was the death of Count Helias of Maine, on 3 July 1110. Maine, temptingly situated between Normandy and Anjou, had been subject to pressure from its powerful neighbours in both directions. Helias had been a staunch friend to Henry I, but he had no son, and his daughter, Eremburge, was married to Count Fulk of Anjou. On Helias's death Maine passed finally to the counts of Anjou. For the moment at least, from Henry's point of view that meant out of the hands of a friend and into those of an enemy.[28]

Moreover, relations with King Louis were still difficult. In 1111 Robert count of Meulan launched an attack on Paris, apparently in retaliation for King Louis's earlier attack on *his* lands. Details of the attack survive only in a much later account, but they paint a dramatic picture: the count's forces descended on the city, broke the bridges, captured the royal palace and

---

[24] For William Baynard see R. Mortimer, 'The Baynards of Baynard's Castle', *Studies in Medieval History Presented to R. Allen Brown*, ed. C. Harper-Bill, C. J. Holdsworth and J. L. Nelson (Woodbridge, 1989), pp. 241–53. For his attestations, *RRAN*, ii, nos. 532, 630, 749, 778, 863. The family is thought to have come from Saint-Leger-des-Rôtes, Eure: K. S. B. Keats-Rohan, *Domesday People. A Prosopography of Persons Occurring in English Documents, 1066–1166* (Woodbridge, 1999), p. 225. In 1106 the count and countess of Boulogne issued a charter 'in the house of William Baynard': *RRAN*, ii, no. 749.

[25] Ibid., no. 626 (concord of 1103 involving Philip de Briouze). Philip is mentioned in the 1130 pipe roll: *PR 31 Henry I*, pp. 72, 103, 126, 157.

[26] OV, vi, 162–6.   [27] Hollister, 'The Taming of a Turbulent Earl', *MMI*, p. 143.

[28] OV, vi, 172.

pillaged the houses. Louis returned in haste and only narrowly escaped capture whilst trying to cross the river Seine, but luckily the count retreated.[29] Count Robert, who had fought at Hastings, was elderly by now, but evidently the attack on his lands had to be avenged.

Henry himself seems to have remained in England, and at some time in the spring of 1111 he sent for Geoffrey the Breton, dean of Le Mans, to fill the vacant archbishopric of Rouen.[30] At first sight this looks a slightly surprising choice in that Geoffrey was an outsider. But he had a reputation for learning, and he was a reformer – both qualities that would recommend him to Henry, who wished to see the eradication of clerical marriage in Normandy as well as England.[31]

By the summer of 1111, Henry had decided that the situation in Normandy required his attention, and he crossed the Channel in August, probably to lend support to his nephew Theobald of Blois, who had come out against King Louis.[32] Having earlier in the year cooperated with Louis in besieging Hugh of Le Puiset, he now found himself at odds with him over the construction of a castle at Allaines. Theobald proceeded to build his own coalition of various lords who had their own reasons for fighting Louis. Lancelin de Bulles, described by Suger as lord of Dammartin, north-east of Paris, wanted right of passage through the Beauvaisis.[33] He was related to the Clare family, and his brother-in-law Odo de Dammartin was granted land in England by Henry I.[34] Payn of Montjay, east of Paris, wanted possession of the strategically significant castle of Livry.[35] With the support of his brother-in-law Miles of Montlhéry, Theobald won over Guy of Rochefort and Hugh of Crécy, whose lands lay to the south of Paris. The confederates waged war in the heart of France: on the right bank of the Seine, Theobald's allies controlled the region between Paris and Senlis,

---

[29] A. Luchaire, *Louis VI le Gros. Annales de sa vie et de son règne (1081–1137)* (Paris, 1890), no. 110, citing the chronicle of Philippe Mouskes, *Chronique Rimée de Philippe Mouskes*, ed. Frédéric-Auguste-Ferdinand-Thomas de Reiffenberg, 2 vols. (Brussels, 1836, 1838), ii, 232. For a discussion of the effect of this episode on Paris, see R. H. Bautier, 'Paris au temps d'Abélard', in *Abélard en son temps*, ed. J. Jolivet (Paris, 1981), p. 41.

[30] OV, vi, 172; for a review of his career see D. S. Spear, 'Geoffrey Brito, Archbishop of Rouen (1111–28)', *Haskins Society Journal*, 2 (1990), 125–6.

[31] OV, v, 236.   [32] *ASC* E 1111.

[33] J.-N. Mathieu, 'Recherches sur les premiers comtes de Dammartin', *Mémoires publiées par la Fédération des Sociétés Archéologiques*, 47 (1996), 25–31.

[34] Mathieu, 'Recherches sur les premiers comtes de Dammartin', 37–52; M. Bur, 'De quelques Champenois dans l'entourage français des rois d'Angleterre aux XIe et XIIe siècles', in *Family Trees and the Roots of Politics. The Prosopography of Britain and France from the Tenth to the Twelfth Century*, ed. K. S. B. Keats-Rohan (Woodbridge, 1997), pp. 342–6.

[35] Suger, *Vie de Louis VI* (ed. Waquet), p. 147.

whilst his vassal Ralph of Beaugency besieged the city of Orléans, and King Henry also raided French territory in support of his nephew.

One prominent casualty of the fighting was Count Robert of Flanders, who was fatally wounded, probably during an abortive attack on Dammartin with King Louis. As the king and his troops fled, the count fell and was trampled underfoot by the horses.[36] Robert had been a great crusader; since his return he had been an ally of Henry, but he also remained loyal to Louis. His successor Baldwin was by contrast a resolute opponent of Henry and a supporter of the cause of William Clito.

By 1112 Henry's enemies had united in a formidable coalition. Robert de Bellême had decided to throw in his lot with the opposition, together with William Crispin, lord of Neaufles, and William count of Evreux, both of whom Henry exiled, probably late in 1111. The situation in the south-east of the duchy was obviously difficult at this juncture. The lords of Châteauneuf-en-Thymerais had a history of fluctuating loyalty, and Henry decided to counteract the threat posed by their castle by building castles of his own at Nonancourt and Illiers-l'Evêque, and by taking over a third at Sorel.[37] Amaury de Montfort, lord of Montfort l'Amaury, also became involved. He was the nephew of William count of Evreux, and the brother-in-law of Count Fulk.[38] Against this coalition Henry had the support of the count of Blois-Chartres, and lords from the Ile-de-France. One of these was Hugh du Puiset, who, with the backing of five hundred knights, was besieged for a second time by King Louis. It was only after these knights' departure that Louis managed to take the castle.[39]

Henry's own movements during the first nine months of 1112 are known only in barest outline. However it was during this period that he issued charters in favour of a newly established monastic community at Savigny, the inspiration of Vitalis, the holy man who had tried to avert the battle at Tinchebray (see above, p. 90). For a time Vitalis had been based at Dompierre, in the Passais, and from 1105 he lived at Savigny, where the local lord Ralph de Fougères and his wife gave him land. The new community was situated in the diocese of Avranches but lay very close to the boundaries of the bishoprics of Rennes and Le Mans. It was right on the frontier, like Fontevraud which was coming into being around the same time in the diocese of Poitiers, but close to the boundaries of the dioceses of Angers and Tours.[40] Henry had everything to gain by getting involved with Savigny,

---

[36] OV, vi, 160–2.   [37] Ibid., 176. See map 3.   [38] Ibid., 176, 188.
[39] Suger, *Vie de Louis VI* (ed. Waquet), pp. 152–68.
[40] J.-M. Bienvenu, *L'étonnant fondateur de Fontevraud Robert d'Arbrissel* (Paris, 1981), pp. 81–2 (map).

as he could thus strengthen his authority in this remote corner of the duchy. Henry therefore exempted the food, property and chattels of Vitalis and his fellows from toll, custom and passage money,[41] and issued a solemn charter confirming the foundation, almost certainly on 2 March 1112.[42] This was a major initiative, because Henry had been cautious in his dealings with monastic communities in Normandy since 1106. Savigny was a new type of community, and the patronage of the king and other leading members of the aristocracy meant that it soon began to flourish, and Savignac communities were founded both in Normandy and in the British Isles.

By the autumn of 1112 Henry had decided to make a move against Robert de Bellême, and summoned his old enemy to his court at Bonneville-sur-Touques on 4 November 1112. Robert somewhat surprisingly turned up. He evidently believed he was under safe conduct as an envoy of Louis VI to demand the release of Duke Robert.[43] Instead Robert de Bellême was arraigned on a series of charges, of acting against his lord's interests, of failing to attend Henry's court, having been summoned three times, and of failing to render account for the revenues of three *vicomtés*, Argentan, Exmes and Falaise. He was probably technically guilty on all three charges, but in each case there was another point of view: he may not have felt it would have been safe to answer Henry's earlier summonses, and he may have regarded revenues from the three *vicomtés* as outright gifts. He had acted against Henry's interests, but it was debatable whether imprisonment and confiscation of land were appropriate penalties. By the sentence of the court he was condemned to imprisonment, however, first at Cherbourg[44] and then at Wareham in England.[45] He had been tricked, and the justification set out by Orderic, who was antipathetic and regarded Robert literally as public enemy number one ('incomparable in evil in the whole Christian era'), cannot conceal what had happened.

Robert's arrest sparked a backlash: his son William Talvas rebelled, and with him the nephews of William count of Mortain, who was still in prison, and the castellan families of Mortain who were still loyal to their lord.[46] Henry proceeded to besiege the town of Alençon, which was held against

---

[41] J. Van Moolenbroek, *Vital l'ermite, prédicateur itinérant, fondateur de l'abbaye normande de Savigny*, trans. Anne-Marie Nambet, *Revue de l'Avranchin*, 68 (1991), no. 1; B. Poulle, 'Savigny and England', in *Normandy and England in the Middle Ages*, ed. D. Bates and A. Curry (London, 1994), pp. 159–68.
[42] Van Moolenbroek, *Vital l'ermite*, no. 3: he prefers the date of 1113, but 1112 is more likely given the lack of any reference to a successor of William as count of Mortain.
[43] OV, vi, 256.   [44] JW, iii, 134.   [45] HH, p. 458; *ASC* E 1113; WM, *GRA*, i, 724.
[46] *Liber Monasterii de Hyda*, p. 308. For William Talvas, see Thompson, 'William Talvas, Count of Ponthieu', pp. 170–1; for the family of Avenel of Les Biards see Pouëssel, 'Les structures militaires du comté de Mortain', 49–56.

him by vassals loyal to Robert de Bellême,[47] and he spent Christmas 1112 in Normandy. As the new year began he made a breakthrough, though at some cost. He opened negotiations with Count Fulk of Anjou, and offered the tempting prospect of a marriage between his own son and the count's daughter. That Henry was prepared to offer such a prize is an indication of the importance of detaching Fulk from his alliance with Louis, and it would also head off the possibility that William Clito would marry a daughter of Fulk. From Henry's point of view it was a price worth paying, as it opened up the possibility of recovering Maine.

On 2 February 1113 Henry visited the abbey of Saint-Evroult, a visit described by Orderic who was evidently present.[48] The king held an inspection of the monks in the cloister and, liking what he saw, asked to receive the privilege of confraternity, which meant that he would share in the prayers of the monks. He granted the monks a charter confirming their lands and privileges and protecting them from being brought to court, except in the king's own court. He also gave them supplies of food which would go some way to pay for the costs of his visit, the logistics of which, especially in early February, would have presented a problem for the monks. This was an important visit for the monks, as well as a tremendous opportunity to catch the king's eye, but it was also important for the king to establish his authority in the region and his patronage over the abbey.

Shortly afterwards, in late February, Henry and Fulk met near Alençon, and an agreement was reached by which Fulk swore fealty and, if Orderic is to be believed, received Maine from Henry as his vassal.[49] This was a highly significant gain for Henry, who had thus asserted overlordship over Maine and stood between Fulk and King Louis. There was a price to be paid, as Prince William was betrothed to Matilda, Fulk's daughter, Count William of Evreux was restored to his lands, and Amaury de Montfort and William Crispin were pardoned, but not, however, William Talvas, who lost Bellême and his Norman lands, and was left with only his mother's small county of Ponthieu.[50]

With these manoeuvres Henry had cut the ground from under the feet of his enemies. King Louis had his own problems to deal with in the form of rebellions in the Ile-de-France, and was prepared to negotiate. The two kings accordingly met in the last week of March near Gisors.[51] The terms of the treaty were reported by Orderic. Louis recognised that the count of Anjou was to perform homage to the duke of Normandy for Maine,

---

[47] OV, vi, 178.   [48] Ibid., 174–6.   [49] Ibid., 180.
[50] Thompson, 'William Talvas, Count of Ponthieu', p. 171.
[51] Suger, *Vie de Louis VI* (ed. Waquet), p. 172.

and the count of Brittany for Brittany.[52] These were major concessions, because Louis was recognising the possibility that a new political entity, 'greater Normandy', was coming into being, in that he would take homage from the Norman duke for Maine and Brittany as well as Normandy. As Dominique Barthélemy has pointed out, this arrangement paralleled that taken by the dukes of Burgundy from lesser counts and lords.[53] Yet nothing – according to Orderic – was said about Normandy itself. It seems most likely that Louis agreed to these terms on the understanding that Prince William would perform homage for Normandy, as well as for Maine and Brittany. Suger associated William's homage with the cession to him of the castle of Gisors, by this treaty, though the ceremony did not take place until 1120, and only then after further vicissitudes.[54]

The treaty has been presented very much as a victory for Henry, but it was much more evenly balanced, if we accept that Henry had already signalled that his son would perform homage. It was crucial for the security of William's position that he should perform it, but homage by this time was not going to be simply a personal recognition of superiority: it had overtones of subordination for the territory concerned.[55] Although Henry might choose to regard Normandy as a largely independent duchy, the fact was that this act of homage would be a coup for Louis.

Although Robert de Bellême was safely in custody, some of his followers were fighting on, and it is a tribute to the loyalty this usually vilified leader could inspire that they did so. King Louis in effect washed his hands of the problem. Much of Robert's land was in Normandy but Bellême itself was held directly of the French king, and Louis now ceded this to Henry.[56] The castle at Bellême continued to hold out. Henry, with Counts Theobald of Blois, Rotrou of Perche and Fulk of Anjou, who had accepted peace terms, appeared before the castle on 1 May 1113. This was the feast of the Invention of the Holy Cross, and Henry had forbidden his men to fight. However, the knights of Theobald and Rotrou, who had not heard the king's edict, challenged the opposition to come out of the castle and fight in single combat. The knights of the garrison emerged, and as they did so the besiegers, against the spirit of their challenge, charged in force. As the defenders fled, they were cut down right in the entrance to the gateway of the castle, preventing the gates from closing and thus permitting the royal

---

[52] OV, vi, 180; Hollister, 'Normandy, France and the Anglo-Norman Regnum', *MMI*, p. 39.
[53] D. Barthélemy, *L'ordre seigneurial. XIe–XIIe siècle. Nouvelle histoire de la France médiévale*, iii (Paris, 1988), p. 235.
[54] Suger, *Vie de Louis VI* (ed. Waquet), pp. 110–12.
[55] As Lemarignier pointed out of the homage of 1120: *Hommage en marche*, p. 92.
[56] Ibid., p. 63 and n. 138.

army to enter and to capture most of the stronghold. The citadel held out, but the king's army burned the stronghold which his enemy had fortified long ago, and the war, for the time being at least, was over.[57]

Henry was able to return to England in the summer of 1113. He may then have travelled north,[58] but by Christmas he was at Windsor and turned his attention to the distribution of honours and the filling of vacancies in the church. One important beneficiary of his generosity was Stephen, the younger brother of Theobald of Blois, who had reached manhood and was to be provided for by his powerful uncle, who had ample reason to be grateful for Theobald's support. Stephen now received the honour of Eye and probably the bulk of estates of Roger the Poitevin, principally the whole of the later county of Lancashire, and estates in Yorkshire and Lincolnshire.[59]

At the same time the king allowed the queen's brother David to marry Matilda, widow of Simon de Senlis, one of the richest heiresses in the country. It was later claimed that this was at the queen's pleading, which may have been true,[60] but it is not necessary to assume that David owed his good fortune to his sister. Links between Henry and the children of Malcolm and Margaret went back before 1100. Their surviving sons are thought to have fled to Rufus' court in 1094 when Domnall Bán became king, and there Henry and David must have met.[61] After 1100 David appears at Henry's court and occasionally occurs as a witness to Henry's charters until 1107, after which time his movements are unknown.[62] He may have gone to

---

[57] OV, vi, 182.

[58] The suggestion that Henry may have travelled north arises from the tangled evidence relating to the establishment of Augustinian canons at Nostell, and the timing of Henry's assistance to his nephew David in securing lands bequeathed to him by his brother Edgar: A. A. M. Duncan, *The Kingship of the Scots 842–1292. Succession and Independence* (Edinburgh, 2002), p. 64.

[59] It is not clear precisely when Stephen arrived at his uncle's court, but he was with Henry when the latter visited Saint-Evroult in February 1113: OV, vi, 174. He had possibly joined Henry's court in 1111 or 1112. Christmas 1113 would therefore have been the first occasion on which Henry distributed honours in England since his spell in Normandy: a substantial number of magnates would have been present. For the timing of his receipt of the honour of Eye, see Lewis, 'The King and Eye', 580; E. King, 'Stephen of Blois, Count of Mortain and Boulogne', *EHR*, 115 (2000), 274–5.

[60] 'Vita et Passio Waldevi Comitis', in *Chroniques anglo-normandes*, ed. F. Michel, 3 vols. (Rouen, 1836–40), ii, 136–7; 'Life of Waltheof', in *Early Sources of Scottish History*, ed. A. O. Anderson, 2 vols., corrected edn (Stamford, 1990), ii, 147. For David's early life see the important new biography by R. Oram, *David I. The King Who Made Scotland* (Stroud, 2004), chapters 1–3; and G. W. S. Barrow in *Oxford DNB*. The starting point of any discussion of the Scottish kingdom in these years is now Duncan, *Kingship of the Scots*.

[61] Chronicle of Melrose, in *Early Sources of Scottish History*, ii, 89.

[62] Skeleton itinerary of David I, in *Charters of David I*, ed. G. W. S. Barrow (Woodbridge, 1999), p. 38; Kapelle, *Norman Conquest of the North*, p. 203. The views in Green, 'David I and Henry I', 3–4 need revision in the light of Duncan, *Kingship of the Scots*. *RRAN*, ii, no. 883 may date from 1108, but could have been earlier. King Edgar died in January 1107, whilst Henry was in Normandy.

Scotland after the accession of his brother Alexander, seeking perhaps the lands said to have been bequeathed him by Edgar, or possibly he may have spent part of the time in France.[63] If David had been involved in fighting for Henry, then the king may have been disposed to reward him by the time of his return to England in 1113.

By 1113, however, David was heir-presumptive to the Scottish throne, and it has been suggested that Henry may have decided to assist him to secure that territory in southern Scotland which, it was later claimed, had been bequeathed to him by Edgar but which he was only able to secure with the assistance of the Normans.[64] The implications of his marriage to Matilda were considerable. The bride was the king's kinswoman, and she transmitted a claim to Waltheof's earldom, both Northampton and Northumbria (Northumberland), which the Scots claimed. On the other hand, David was technically only a custodian of the lands and children of Simon and Matilda de Senlis, of whom the eldest would presumably inherit when he reached his majority, and Henry kept Northampton castle in his own hands. In the short term, David now had rich estates and vassals at his disposal, and there were soon signs of his presence in Cumbria and Teviotdale.[65] The warmth of David's relations with his brother, King Alexander, from this point may only be conjectured, but from Henry's perspective, such a complication was no bad thing, as both were bound to him. David's position in southern Scotland could almost be regarded as that of Henry's marcher lord, as Kapelle suggested.[66]

Also at the Christmas feast Theulf, a royal clerk and a canon of Bayeux, was nominated to the bishopric of Worcester. He would later confess on his deathbed to having purchased his appointment, and thus to having committed the sin of simony: an indication that Henry's behaviour may not always have been above reproach.[67] Abbots were nominated for Ramsey,

---

[63] For the suggestion that David's 'French period' ended in or not long before 1113, see Duncan, *Kingship of the Scots*, p. 63. Oram suggests that David may have acquired land at Querqueville in the Cotentin from Henry between about 1106 and 1113: *David I*, pp. 62–3. Querqueville was the identification suggested by G. W. S. Barrow for 'Karkarevil', the grant of whose church by Robert de Brus was confirmed by David between 1113 and 1124: see most recently *Charters of David I*, no. 1. Whilst it is possible that David was in France for some or most of the period between 1108 and 1113, it is odd that he does not occur as a witness to any of Henry's (admittedly few) Norman *acta* issued during these years. There are several unresolved questions here about the timing of David's 'French period' and the role of Robert de Brus. On the latter, see now R. M. Blakely, 'The Bruses of Skelton and William of Aumale', *Yorkshire Archaeological Journal*, 73 (2001), 21.
[64] The legacy was mentioned by Aelred of Rievaulx: *Relatio de Standardo*, in *Chronicles of the Reigns of Stephen, Henry II and Richard I*, ed. R. Howlett, 4 vols., RS (London, 1884–9), iii, 193. Henry himself could have travelled at least as far as York after his return to England in July 1113: Duncan, *Kingship of the Scots*, pp. 59–64.
[65] Ibid. [66] Kapelle, *Norman Conquest of the North*, p. 204.
[67] WM, *Gesta Pontificum Anglorum*, p. 290.

St Mary's York and Thorney; and soon afterwards the vacancy at Cerne was filled.[68] The most pressing vacancy, however, was Canterbury, and when the archbishop of York died in February 1114 it was possible to fill both Canterbury and York in succession. By filling Canterbury first, the precedence of Canterbury over York would be established, which *might* make it easier to secure a profession from York. Henry would have realised, however, that the chapter at York would try hard to ensure that their archbishop would not make a written profession to Canterbury. This was not a job which could be filled simply by choosing yet another member of the royal chapel, and Henry declared in public how difficult it would be to find someone of the calibre of preceding archbishops.[69]

A great council met at Windsor on 26 April where the matter was discussed. At the cathedral monastery of Christ Church Canterbury the preference was for another monk-archbishop. The king's first suggestion was his physician, Faritius, abbot of Abingdon.[70] However, the bishops of the southern province did not want a monk, though the last man not to have been a monk was Stigand, archbishop in 1066 – which was not exactly a happy precedent, since Stigand's appointment had never been regularised and his wealth affronted his contemporaries.[71] Roger of Salisbury and Robert of Lincoln, acting in concert, spoke out against Faritius, claiming that it would be improper to appoint as archbishop a physician who had examined the urine of women. They claimed that a worthy candidate could be found from the ranks of Norman clerks.[72] Perhaps Roger hoped for the highest office for himself, but if so, there is no evidence. A compromise candidate emerged in the person of Ralph d'Escures, bishop of Rochester. Ralph came from a noble family, and had entered the Benedictine monastery of Sées as a child. He rose to become abbot, and, having incurred the enmity of Robert de Bellême, went into exile at Henry's court in the company of the bishop of Sées. He had been promoted to Rochester in 1108, a see which in this period was usually filled at the archbishop's behest, so his elevation to Canterbury was in a sense an internal promotion.[73] The king said that he had no objection provided that the candidate was acceptable to the monks and people of Canterbury; he was, and was duly elected.[74] Ralph was said to be a man of great affability, but as soon as

---

[68] *ASC* H 1114. [69] WM, *Gesta Pontificum*, p. 125.
[70] Eadmer, *Historia Novorum*, p. 222. [71] WM, *Gesta Pontificum*, p. 126.
[72] *Chronicon Monasterii de Abingdon*, ed. J. Stevenson, 2 vols., RS (London, 1858), ii, 287.
[73] OV, vi, 46–8; Eadmer, *Historia Novorum*, p. 223; D. Bethell, 'English Black Monks and Episcopal Elections in the 1120s', *EHR*, 84 (1969) 675–6.
[74] Eadmer, *Historia Novorum*, p. 223.

he was consecrated, he took up the cause of the Canterbury primacy with great determination.[75]

When it came to filling the archbishopric of York, Henry did not feel the same need to take soundings. He chose Thurstan, a man who was very close to him, 'familiaris et acceptus et secretarius' (intimate, acceptable and the king's secretary) according to Hugh the Chanter.[76] Both Thurstan and his brother Audoin had been members of the royal household. Their father had been a prebendary of St Paul's cathedral in London,[77] and Audoin had been appointed to the bishopric of Evreux in 1113.[78]

Thurstan had little prior experience of northern England, though he is said to have been at Hexham in Northumberland when an Augustinian priory was set up there in 1113; perhaps this was a way of testing the waters in the north.[79] Henry knew that the York lobby would try to ensure that Thurstan would not make a profession to Canterbury, as his predecessor had done under pressure,[80] but he presumably hoped he had picked a man who would not cause trouble. This was a miscalculation. Initially, according to Hugh the Chanter, the king said he would not compel Thurstan to make the profession, and Thurstan was ordained deacon at Winchester, possibly in September 1114, shortly before the king's departure for Normandy in the same month. When Thurstan proceeded to York, he was briefed on the primacy, and decided his best plan was to appeal over the head of Canterbury to Rome. He crossed to Normandy to seek the king's permission, which was refused, and there the matter rested for a while.[81]

The number of vacant bishoprics and abbeys filled in the months after Henry's return had been exceptional, but of the appointees only one, Ealdwulf, abbot of Muchelney, seems from his name to have been English. The abbeys of Ramsey and Cerne were filled by monks of Caen, Thorney by a monk of Saint-Evroult, and of three other posts filled during 1114, St Edmunds was given to a monk of Bec, Peterborough to a monk of Sées, and Burton-on-Trent to a monk of the Old Minster at Winchester.[82] In his *History of Recent Events*, Eadmer, a monk at Christ Church, Canterbury, wrote despairingly of the employment prospects for the English at this time: if a candidate was found to be English, he was held to be of no virtue or

---

[75] At Rochester Ralph was replaced by Ernulf, who was skilled in canon law. At the time of his promotion Ernulf was abbot of Peterborough, and in the Peterborough version of the Anglo-Saxon Chronicle the king applied pressure on him to accept Rochester: *ASC* E 1114.
[76] Hugh the Chanter, p. 56.
[77] D. Nicholl, *Thurstan Archbishop of York (1114–40)* (York, 1964), p. 7.   [78] OV, vi, 174.
[79] John of Hexham; SD, *Opera Omnia*, ii, 404.   [80] Hugh the Chanter, pp. 40–50.
[81] Ibid., pp. 58, 60.   [82] *ASC* E 1114.

honour.[83] Even though Henry had an English wife and at least one English mistress, he evidently did not wish to see Englishmen in the upper echelons of the English church, and abbacies were still regularly awarded to monks from Normandy.

One of Henry's main concerns in 1114 was the security situation in Wales, where Norman lordships were coming under attack. The situation in mid-Wales was particularly unstable. Deaths had occurred amongst the Norman lords, and even more so amongst the Welsh of the midland principalities of Powys. The most recent atrocity there was the blinding of Madog, son of Rhirid ap Bleddyn, by his cousin Owain ap Cadwgan, to whose custody he had been handed over by Maredudd ap Bleddyn prince of Powys.[84] In north Wales the problem was the growing power of Gruffud ap Cynan, king of Gwynedd, which led the young earl Richard of Chester to complain about attacks on his lands. Gilbert FitzRichard, lord of Ceredigion, also complained, and the king was sufficiently disturbed to go to Wales in person with an army. The author of the *Brut* believed that Henry was intent on genocide; a more realistic aim was to impress his authority on the Welsh princes by a mixture of bribery and a show of force.

According to the *Brut*, three armies advanced into Wales. The first from the south was led by Gilbert FitzRichard, and included men from Cornwall and south Wales. The second was led by Alexander king of Scots, whose presence was a clear indication that he was prepared to acknowledge Henry's overkingship. Earl Richard advanced from the north to Pennant Bachwy, and the third army was led by the king into Powys as far as 'Murcastell', which has been identified as Tomen-y-Mur at Trawsfynydd in Merionethshire.[85] In the event, however, nothing happened. Owain ap Cadwgan treated for peace. Henry bought him off by offering to make him the greatest of all his family and to grant him his land free of tribute. When Gruffud ap Cynan heard that Owain had made peace he too sent messengers to treat for peace. In his case, however, he had to pay a large tribute, whereas Owain accompanied Henry to Normandy and, according to the Welsh chronicle, was knighted by Henry.[86]

Henry had done what he could short of embarking on a campaign of wholesale conquest: a show of military strength, and buying off those Welsh princes who were prepared to negotiate. Meanwhile he continued

---

[83] Eadmer, *Historia Novorum*, pp. 222–4.
[84] Maund, 'Owain ap Cadwgan: A Rebel Revisited'; see also appendix I, no. 8.
[85] *A Medieval Prince of Wales. The Life of Gruffudd ap Cynan*, ed. D. Simon Evans (Lampeter, 1990), p. 80 and note.
[86] *Brut (RBH)*, p. 81; *Brut (Peniarth)*, p. 38.

Defence of his dominions, 1108–1115

to insert his own men into the tenurial fabric along the Marches and in Wales. One was Alan FitzFlaad, a man of Breton extraction, who married the daughter of Warin the Domesday sheriff of Shropshire, and succeeded to Warin's lands and office.[87] Another was Payn FitzJohn, who seems to have arrived on the Marches at about this time, for he witnessed Henry's charter of confirmation to Geoffrey bishop of Hereford in 1115.[88] Payn's father John was a tenant-in-chief in England at the time of Domesday, and both Payn and his brother Eustace became very influential in the later years of Henry's reign, Payn in Herefordshire as the colleague of Miles of Gloucester, Eustace in the north as the colleague of Walter Espec.[89] Payn married Sibyl, daughter of Hugh de Lacy, and by this means acquired a good deal of the Lacy honour in Herefordshire.[90] William Peverel 'of Dover' (to distinguish him from William Peverel of Nottingham) was another man who rose under Henry I. He was established at Ellesmere in Shropshire in the early twelfth century.[91] Another Breton, Brian FitzCount, a son of Henry's friend Count Alan Fergant, who was brought up by Henry in the royal household as he himself later recounted, was possibly installed at Abergavenny around 1114. Brian's earliest attestation of a royal document was in 1114,[92] and he had acquired land in Wales by 1119.[93] Given that Henry's policy seems to have been to install men on the Marches or in Wales who had the resources to hold them, Brian's brilliant marriage to a great heiress, Matilda of Wallingford, had probably already taken place, as he was unlikely to have been given the Welsh command without resources of men and money.[94]

---

[87] Alan was described as sheriff in Henry II's charter for Shrewsbury abbey: *The Cartulary of Shrewsbury Abbey*, ed. U. Rees, 2 vols. (Aberystwyth, 1975), i, no. 36, pp. 42, 45. In Henry I's charter Alan, though not styled sheriff, confirmed his predecessor's gifts: ibid., no. 35, p. 34. For his ancestry see J. H. Round, 'The Origins of the Stewarts', in *Studies in Peerage and Family History* (London, 1901), pp. 115–31.
[88] *RRAN*, ii, no. 1101, cf. no. 1042.   [89] For synopses see Green, *GOE*, pp. 250–3.
[90] Wightman, *Lacy Family*, pp. 175–85.
[91] Hamo Peverel may have been established before 1100 since he appears in a charter of Earl Hugh of Shrewsbury (died 1098), but this text is not above suspicion. He married Sibyl de Tornai, whose father had been a tenant of Earl Roger in 1086, and first appears as a witness for Henry I in 1107: *RRAN*, ii, no. 828. William Peverel, who first witnessed for Henry in 1101 and was evidently more often at court, was established at Ellesmere: ibid., no. 516. Both occur as witnesses to ibid., no.1101, the charter confirming his lands to Geoffrey bishop of Hereford. There was a third brother, Payn, who received the lordship of Bourn in Cambridgeshire, c. 1122: I. J. Sanders, *English Baronies* (Oxford, 1960), p. 19. The family held land in west Normandy, for William gave the church of Le Buat and the vill of Lire to Bec: *RRAN*, ii, no. 1547.
[92] *RRAN*, ii, no. 1062. Walter de Beauchamp's origins have never been established.
[93] J. H. Round, 'The Family of Ballon and the Conquest of South Wales', in *Studies in Peerage and Family History* (London, 1931), p. 211.
[94] Keats-Rohan, 'Devolution of the Honour of Wallingford, 1066–1148', 315.

Finally, it was not long after the Welsh campaign that Henry decided to promote Bernard the queen's chancellor to the bishopric of St David's in south Wales, the first courtier in a Welsh bishopric (setting aside Urban, consecrated to Llandaff in 1107, who was Welsh), and a man who could aid the process of Normanisation of the Welsh church.[95] Bernard was ordained by Bishop William of Winchester at Southwark, but a dispute arose about the place of his consecration. Robert of Meulan, evidently still active as a defender of the king's rights over the church, said that it should be held, as was customary, in the royal chapel; Archbishop Ralph pitched in for Canterbury; the king pacifically (according to Eadmer) said that the archbishop should perform the consecration where he wished. Ralph thereupon proposed Lambeth, but the place finally settled on was Westminster abbey, so that the queen could attend.[96]

Next on Henry's agenda was to secure his heir's future. The best option here was to secure a formal recognition of his claim by the Norman magnates, of the kind received by his own father when *his* father, Duke Robert I, had left for the Holy Land, and which Robert Curthose had received in his turn.[97] Such a recognition for Prince William would presumably have been followed by William's homage to King Louis, which might have been agreed between the two kings at Gisors. Henry was probably spurred to action because the cause of his nephew William Clito had a new and powerful advocate in Count Baldwin of Flanders. Count Baldwin, as far as is known, had not been involved in the fighting in 1111 and 1112, nor had he been involved in the peace negotiations. At some stage he gave shelter to Helias and William Clito, and according to the Hyde chronicler, appeared at the court of King Louis to press the boy's claim.[98] This might have been in 1114, the same year in which Baldwin apparently contemplated an

---

[95] *St Davids Episcopal Acta 1085–1280*, ed. J. Barrow, Publications of the South Wales Record Society, no. 13 (Cardiff, 1998), pp. 2–4; W. S. Davies, 'Materials for the Life of Bishop Bernard of St David's', *Archaeologia Cambrensis*, 6th ser., 19 (1919), 306; *Episcopal Acts and Cognate Documents Relating to Welsh Dioceses 1066–1272*, ed. J. Conway Davies, 2 vols. (Cardiff, 1948–53), i, pp. 143–5. Gilla Espaic, bishop of Limerick, was also present, and a second anecdote also places him in the queen's circle: Matthew Paris reported that Abbot Richard of St Albans sent for Gilla Espaic to consecrate a chapel dedicated to Saints Cosmas and Damian in the abbey church, rather than going to his diocesan, with whom he was in dispute over the latter's rights to exercise episcopal jurisdiction in the abbey: *Gesta Abbatum*, i, 148. See M. Philpott, 'Some Interactions between the English and Irish Churches', *ANS*, 20 (1997), 202.

[96] Eadmer, *Historia Novorum*, pp. 235–6.

[97] Tabuteau, 'Role of Law', 148–52; G. Garnett, 'Ducal Succession in Early Normandy', in *Law and Government in Medieval England and Normandy* (ed. Garnett and Hudson), pp. 80–110; A. Lewis, *Royal Succession in Capetian France. Studies on Familial Order and the State* (Cambridge, Mass., 1981), pp. 20–32, 37–47, 50–4.

[98] *Liber Monasterii de Hyda*, p. 308.

expedition across the Norman frontier.[99] Baldwin formally knighted William Clito, though according to Hermann of Tournai this did not occur until 1116.[100] Baldwin's support for the young claimant thus brought an end to a period of quiescence in relations between the rulers of Flanders and England and Normandy. Baldwin either was not offered or did not accept a renewal of the treaty of 1110, and his wealth and the proximity of his lands to the Norman frontier meant that he was a formidable enemy.

For this reason, the quicker Henry's son was accepted as duke, the better. Henry accordingly crossed to Normandy from Portsmouth on 21 September 1114 and spent Christmas in Normandy. Early in 1115, whilst the court was still at Rouen,[101] he 'brought it about that all the chief men in Normandy did homage and swore oaths of allegiance to his son William'.[102] He then sent messengers to King Louis asking him to accept William's homage, and offering a large sum of money as a relief, which Louis accepted. It was at this point that things went wrong for Henry, because there were other voices at Louis's court. The count of Nevers in particular pointed out that Louis had made a prior commitment to William Clito.[103] Count Theobald in reprisal arrested the count of Nevers and, at his uncle's request, refused to release him.[104] Louis kept the money and a wrathful Henry returned to England in July 1115.

Meanwhile Count Theobald found himself in difficulty.[105] Not only was King Louis preparing to march against him, but he was excommunicated and his lands laid under interdict by the pope's legate, Cuno, at the request of King Louis. Those who helped Theobald were to be excommunicated, Louis himself was given permission to fight during Lent, and Ivo bishop of Chartres was given the responsibility of carrying out the sentence. Theobald protested that King Louis should have summoned him to *his* court, and not have allowed him to be condemned by ecclesiastical judges.

Henry felt he had to go to his nephew's aid. He began to gather his own forces, and returned to Normandy around Easter 1116. Before he did so, however, he had the magnates in England swear loyalty to his son at Salisbury in March 1116 in a ceremony which recalled that earlier oathtaking at Salisbury in 1086.[106] According to Eadmer, all made themselves the prince's men by fealty and oath. Archbishop Ralph and all the bishops and

---

[99] Warren Hollister drew attention to a charter of Baldwin issued at Ypres in 1114, 'where he had convened a meeting of many clerks and laity making arrangements for an expedition into Normandy': as cited in Hollister, 'Normandy, France and the Anglo-Norman Regnum', *MMI*, p. 40.
[100] Hermann of Tournai, p. 40.   [101] *RRAN*, ii, no. 1074.
[102] *ASC* E 1115; HH, p. 460.   [103] Luchaire, *Louis VI*, no. 203.
[104] Ibid.; Ivo of Chartres to Cuno, Migne, *Patrologia Latina*, cclxi, no. 275; OV, vi, 258.
[105] Luchaire, *Louis VI le Gros*, no. 203.   [106] Eadmer, *Historia Novorum*, p. 238; JW, iii, 138.

abbots swore fealty and by their oaths promised faithfully to transfer the kingdom and the crown to him. In the factors involved in royal succession, the wishes of a ruling king did count, whether expressed at the point of death or earlier. It is possible, for instance, that Edward the Confessor's presence in England in 1041 and 1042 in the lifetime of his half-brother, Harthacnut, was intended to promote the former's claim to the succession, but there is no reference to formal designation of the kind reported here,[107] and the origins of the ceremony seem to lie rather in Norman or French precedents.

Was Henry's intention to associate his heir with his rule on either side of the Channel, in the way Philip I of France had associated Prince Louis with his rule? Would Prince William in due course have been crowned? We can only speculate. William was much loved by his father (and, allegedly, overindulged), but so far had not been of an age to be much in the limelight.[108] He had appeared as a witness to a charter in December 1113; in September 1115 he was at a royal council at Westminster, and in December was with the king and queen when the abbey church at St Albans had been dedicated.[109] William was also with his father on 2 April 1116 when he witnessed a charter issued by the king at Odiham in Hampshire.[110] Matilda still acted as regent, though William was now an active participant in government, and stepped into her shoes after her death in 1118.[111]

Henry had believed he had a deal in 1113, whereby Normandy would pass safely into his son's hands, and, with it, the prospect of Maine. Now all had unravelled as Louis, having taking the money, had qualms

---

[107] *ASC* C, E, 1041.   [108] HH, p. 594.
[109] *RRAN*, ii, nos. 1091, 1092, 1103.   [110] Ibid., no. 1131.
[111] In the autumn of 1116 Matilda presided over a council of bishops at London, convened to discuss the implications of the imminent arrival in England of a papal legate and its implications for the autonomy of the English church: Eadmer, *Historia Novorum*, p. 239. She was also in London at the time Bricstan of Chatteris was miraculously freed from imprisonment: OV, iii, 356. The main source of evidence about viceregal arrangements comes from a group of documents entered into the cartulary of St Augustine's abbey, Canterbury. If we can take these at face value – and it would be reassuring if the evidence did not depend so heavily on a single source – Matilda may initially have resumed her role as regent, and William taken over from her either during the last months of her life or on her death, until he joined his father in Normandy in 1119: *RRAN*, ii, nos. 1189, 1190, 1191, 1202 (a fourteenth-century record of a charter by William for Odard of Bamburgh). It is not known when the queen's health began to deteriorate. It has been suggested that her brother David, who had been present at the Christmas court of 1115, visited his sister on a later occasion. The evidence is inferential: Matilda and William witnessed two confirmations by David for Durham, *Charters of David I*, nos. 9, 10. No. 10 was also witnessed by John bishop of Glasgow, the date of whose appointment is uncertain but, suggests Professor Barrow, unlikely to have been before 1116. It might also be argued that the fact that there are attestations by Matilda and William but not King Henry suggests the king was not in England at the time. If David did visit his sister again, possibly he had had news that her health was failing.

and refused to accept the homage of Henry's son William. It is easy to see why he had cold feet about doing so: there was not just the ethical question to consider, but also Louis doubtless felt a natural reluctance to recognise Henry's supremacy over Normandy. A grateful William Clito could make life very difficult for Henry, and for Louis that was no bad thing.

CHAPTER 7

Triumph and disaster, 1116–1120

Over the next few years Henry's fortunes veered sharply between triumph and disaster. He spent the whole period from Easter 1116 to November 1120 in France, and so was absent when his wife died on 1 May 1118. All other matters were subordinate to his main aims: to keep hold of the duchy, and to persuade Louis to accept the homage of his son William. He was eventually successful in both, but his enjoyment of his triumph was all too brief, because in November 1120 William and some three hundred members of the royal court were drowned in the wreck of the White Ship. Henry's happiness and his hopes for the future were destroyed in one night.

Henry's movements between Easter 1116 and 1118 are very difficult to reconstruct, as very few royal documents can be securely dated to that period. Orderic is less than informative: he began book XII of his *Ecclesiastical History* at Christmas 1118 with a retrospective but brief sketch of hostilities.[1] There was evidently fighting in several different areas. First, in 1117 'towards summer', Count Baldwin of Flanders invaded Norman territory, and met up with the forces of King Louis at Mortemer.[2] Secondly, King Louis attacked the forces of Stephen of Blois, who was acting as his brother's lieutenant, in the region of Brie. Louis also ravaged the region round Chartres.[3] Thirdly, fighting broke out in the Vexin. Otmund lord of Trie launched attacks across the river Epte into Norman territory. Henry's response was to seize the castle of Saint-Clair-sur-Epte on the French side of the river as a forward base, not far from his fortress at Château-sur-Epte.[4]

In response Louis planned a secret raid on Gasny, where the river Epte ran through the village before joining the Seine.[5] As Suger pointed out, its

---

[1] OV, vi, 184. [2] *ASC* E 1117; HH, p. 460; *Liber Monasterii de Hyda*, p. 311.
[3] Suger, *Vie de Louis VI* (ed. Waquet), p. 184.
[4] OV, vi, 184; *L'architecture normande au Moyen Age*, ed. M. Baylé, 2 vols. (Caen, 1997), ii, 283–4.
[5] Neither Suger nor Orderic gives precise dates for the attack. Orderic claims that the fighting lasted for about four years which, as Chibnall points out, might mean that it began in 1116: OV, vi, 186n.

capture would give the French easy access into Normandy. An advance party arrived disguised as monks, but when the villagers saw their swords they resisted fiercely, and it required Louis's arrival with reinforcements to rescue the situation; he captured the church and the churchyard. Orderic was scandalised when the French fortified the church, a priory of the monastery of Saint-Ouen at Rouen.[6] Louis called for support. Baldwin of Flanders soon arrived and so, according to Suger, did Count Fulk of Anjou.[7] The allies were able to raid, causing havoc – something, commented Suger, that did not usually happen when the king of the English was present. Louis left a garrison in the church at Gasny, and Henry had one siege castle, named Malassis (badly located), built on the next hill, together with another called Trulla Leporis (hare's form), with the aim of cutting the supply lines of the French and causing them to plunder their own land. Louis was forced to return, and attacked Malassis.

Henry's position deteriorated still further in 1118, the most difficult year of his rule in Normandy. As in the earlier phase of conflict between 1111 and 1113, the cause was a dangerous combination of external enemies and internal rebellion, but on this occasion the previous alliance of the king of France and the count of Anjou was joined by the count of Flanders. There was a progressive collapse of loyalty and order within Normandy, and a conspiracy within Henry's own household which led him to fear for his life. The trigger was the death in April of William count of Evreux without sons of legitimate birth. His closest male relative was his nephew, Amaury de Montfort, who claimed the succession to the county. This was not unexpected, but placed Henry in a difficult situation. Amaury was lord of Montfort l'Amaury, which was outside the borders of Normandy, though he held lands within the duchy, and he had been involved in the earlier phase of the fighting against Henry (above, p. 124). Strictly speaking, the title of count was the duke's to bestow or withhold, and on the advice of the bishop of Evreux, it was said, Henry refused to allow Amaury to succeed.[8] Amaury was well placed, however, to cause problems for Henry in south-east Normandy.

The death of Queen Matilda, on 1 May, followed quickly after that of Count William. It is not certain how long she was ill (see above, p. 136) and thus whether Henry had much warning of her death, but it is striking testimony of the pressing state of his affairs in Normandy that he did not hurry back to England. She had fulfilled her primary duty in bearing him a son, and she had conformed to contemporary models of a queen

---

[6] OV, vi, 184.   [7] Suger, *Vie de Louis VI* (ed. Waquet), p. 186.   [8] OV, vi, 188.

in her piety and works of charity. Her patronage had made a considerable impact on London, and she could safely be left to preside in England during Henry's absences. An elaborate funeral was conducted by Roger of Salisbury, who preached eloquently on her virtues. Thousands of masses, psalms and prayers were said for her soul, and alms were given in abundance.[9] On the king's orders she was buried in Westminster abbey, near Edward the Confessor and Queen Edith, though her own preference had been to be buried in Holy Trinity, Aldgate.[10] On her tomb was the inscription: 'Here lies the renowned queen Matilda the second, excelling both young and old of her day, she was for everyone the benchmark of morals, and the ornament of life.'[11] Matilda was to be remembered as 'Good Queen Maud',[12] and William of Malmesbury commented that 'her spirit showed by tokens more than ordinary that it inhabits heaven'.[13] After his return to England in 1120, Henry ordered that a halfpenny should be paid every day for a light before her tomb,[14] and in the 1130 pipe roll the sheriffs of London were allowed sums for oil for the light and a cloth for her tomb.[15]

Whilst some of the visitors to her tomb were interested in her as a potential saint, others may have reflected on her ancestry as a great-granddaughter of Edmund Ironside. Her brother David also made a grant, possibly at the time of her funeral, of thirty shillings a year from his manor of Tottenham to the monks, for candles, two by day and two by night, on the anniversaries of her death and those of his father and mother, together with special allowances of food and wine for the monks.[16] Her parentage was to be remembered by this gift, perpetuated in the coronation church of the Norman kings. Yet if there was popular interest in her cult, and backing from David for her commemoration, the monks were not enthusiastic in promoting her memory. Possibly they felt discouraged by the king. Henry may have been ambivalent about his wife's memory, in that her lineage could be traced back through her mother to a different, older, English royal line.

On 5 June a third death occurred, that of Robert count of Meulan.[17] Robert had been loyal to Henry from the start of his reign, and he was

---

[9] *Liber Monasterii de Hyda*, pp. 312–13.   [10] *Cartulary of Holy Trinity Aldgate*, no. 997.
[11] *Liber Monasterii de Hyda*, pp. 312–13.   [12] *Cartulary of Holy Trinity Aldgate*, pp. 224, 229–30.
[13] WM, *GRA*, i, 758; cf. Roger of Wendover, *Chronica sive Flores Historiarum*, ed. H. O. Coxe, 4 vols., English Historical Society (London, 1841–2), ii, 195; J. Bollandus and G. Henschius, *Acta Sanctorum Bollandiana* (Brussels etc., 1863–), 1 May, p. 4.
[14] *RRAN*, ii, no. 1377; *Westminster Abbey Charters*, no. 79.
[15] *PR 31 Henry I*, p. 144. The sum for oil was still being paid in Henry III's reign, as Robert Bartlett has pointed out: *England under the Norman and Angevin Kings* (Oxford, 2000), p. 601.
[16] *Charters of David I*, no. 13; *Regesta Regum Scottorum I. Acts of Malcolm IV*, ed. G. W. S. Barrow (Edinburgh, 1960), no. 6.
[17] OV, vi, 188.

initially the king's leading lay counsellor. His advice was particularly influential, whether on matters relating to the church, especially investiture, or on the number of formal daily meals to be eaten. Despite his advancing years he had fought at Tinchebray, and was again at the head of his troops in the attack on Paris. He was still active in old age, for he was one of a small delegation at the royal council at Salisbury in 1116 when Thurstan came under pressure to make a profession of obedience to Canterbury.[18] Although probably nearly twenty years older than Henry, he was one of the few men who could really be counted on, a staunch ally with great estates and castles in central Normandy and England, as well as the small but independent county of Meulan, and property in Paris. The bulk of his great estates was divided between his twin sons, Waleran and Robert, who were in their fourteenth year when their father died, and who were taken into the king's guardianship. The death of a great lord was a breach of continuity in any lordship; Henry had overall control, but he would have to hope that leading Beaumont vassals would remain loyal to the twins, and that their rivals would not take advantage of the interregnum to settle old scores.

Trouble was spreading quickly to other frontier regions as other lords seized their opportunity to rebel, sometimes in alliance with Normandy's neighbours. Henry spent the next months dealing with one revolt after another. In the north Henry count of Eu came out as a supporter of William Clito – not surprisingly perhaps, given his support for William's father in 1101 – and so too did Hugh de Gournay. Gournay was the centre of yet another frontier lordship, this time in the eastern sector of the Norman frontier. Hugh's father Gerard had been a companion of the duke on crusade; after Gerard's death his mother, Edith de Warenne, had married Drogo de Mouchy (-le-Châtel), who witnessed a number of Henry's charters,[19] a marriage which may well have been arranged by King Henry. Edith's son, Hugh, had been brought up and knighted by the king, so his disloyalty was a personal blow.[20] Count Henry and Hugh de Gournay were arrested at Rouen and made to surrender their castles. In June 1118, Hugh discussed with the king a marriage for his sister, Gundrada. The chosen bridegroom was Nigel d'Aubigny, one of Henry's inner circle, and this suggests that the king was already concerned about Hugh's loyalty. Indeed, Hugh left the wedding celebrations, went to the castle of Le Plessis, killed the castellan, who was loyal to the king (and to Hugh), and handed it over to his

---

[18] Hugh the Chanter, pp. 68–70. [19] *GND*, ii, 214–15; *RRAN*, ii, no. 956. [20] OV, vi, 190–2.

own kinsman, Hugh Talbot. Perhaps Henry had refused to allow Hugh to succeed to his father's castles as well as his lands.

Count Baldwin again advanced with an army into Normandy, burning villages as far as Arques and besieging Henry's garrison at Eu.[21] Count Stephen of Aumale now fortified his castles against the king, as did the vassals and friends of Hugh de Gournay.[22] Nearby Ponthieu was held by William Talvas, Robert de Bellême's son and no friend of Henry.[23] The allies were described by Orderic as bandits who preyed on the country people and took refuge in safe houses from which they emerged suddenly on their raids. Eighteen of the leading castellans of Normandy 'slumbered frozen in their perfidy, and rejoiced as the king's cause grew weaker'. Only William of Roumare, castellan of Neuf-Marché, resisted the rebels.[24]

There was trouble along the southern border, too. Robert Giroie had fought against Robert de Bellême after his return to Normandy in 1102, and this would have earned him some credit with Henry, but in 1118 he fortified the castle of Saint-Cénéri against Henry, and he persuaded Count Fulk of Anjou to besiege a former castle of Robert de Bellême in northern Maine, La-Motte-Gautier-de-Clinchamp. Fulk took the castle in only eight days. Henry's commanders, the brothers Roger and John de Saint-Jean, were in charge of the garrison; they surrendered, and retreated to the king's base at Alençon.

Henry was clearly very alarmed at the scale of the disorder, and sent out a military summons through the whole of Normandy. One specific concern was the possibility that the tenants of William Talvas would rise up in support of their lord, as they had done for his father Robert de Bellême in 1112 and 1113. It was possibly for this reason that Henry decided to transfer the lands to his nephew Theobald. Theobald handed them over to his younger brother Stephen, in return for the latter's share of the family lands in France.[25] On Stephen's shoulders now rested much of the Norman defence in the south, from Mortain to Sées, Alençon and La Roche-Mabille.

The next challenge came from Richer, lord of l'Aigle, who was seeking the succession to his father's estates in England. L'Aigle was situated on the southern border of Normandy; Gilbert, its lord, had been a faithful servant of Henry, and, probably after Tinchebray, had been rewarded with land in England, in Sussex.[26] Henry had refused to allow Richer to

---

[21] Ibid., 190.
[22] *Liber Monasterii de Hyda*, p. 313. The Hyde Chronicler is particularly well informed about affairs in this part of Normandy.
[23] Suger, *Vie de Louis VI* (ed. Waquet), p. 188.   [24] OV, vi, 194.
[25] Ibid., 194–6.   [26] Thompson, 'The Lords of Laigle', 182–6.

succeed, on the grounds that his brothers Geoffrey and Engenulf de l'Aigle had better claims because they served in the king's military household.[27] Richer left the court in anger and made an agreement with King Louis to transfer his allegiance to him if his inheritance was not restored quickly. Louis promised in return that if Richer were to support Louis's cause he would provide sixty knights for the garrison of l'Aigle, and Amaury de Montfort would supply another fifty. Under pressure Henry gave way, but too late to stop King Louis from securing the surrender of the castle of l'Aigle. Louis left a few days later, leaving Amaury de Montfort, his kinsman William Crispin and Hugh, lord of Châteauneuf-en-Thymerais, to face Henry. Henry himself hurried back to l'Aigle, but was diverted by William de Tancarville, who had come to warn him of the perilous state of affairs on the right bank of the Seine. There Hugh de Gournay and Stephen count of Aumale had established a castle outside Rouen and were waiting for the arrival of William Clito with a French army. Henry rushed off to Rouen, where he found that the gravity of the situation had been overestimated.

Rather than return to l'Aigle, however, Henry decided to try to deal with Hugh de Gournay's revolt. He marched to attack Hugh's castle of La Ferté-en-Bray, but was beaten off by torrential rain. He went instead to Neufbourg, a castle being held against him by its lord, a cousin of the Beaumont twins. Once again it appears that a family dispute lay behind the revolt, because Robert de Neufbourg had certain claims against his cousin Waleran of Meulan, and was unable to gain satisfaction because Waleran was the king's ward. Robert therefore rebelled; Henry stormed the castle and burned it to the ground.[28]

By this stage Henry's situation had become very difficult, and he found himself unable to trust his own men: 'those who ate with him favoured the cause of his nephew', and families were divided by the conflict.[29] There was a plot to kill him by members of his own household, reported only by Suger and William of Malmesbury. He was so alarmed that he often changed beds, increased the number of his guards, and slept with a shield and sword to hand each night. The unknown ringleader was caught, blinded and castrated. William of Malmesbury simply described him as 'a chamberlain born of a plebeian father who became prominent as a keeper of the royal treasures'.[30] According to Suger, one of the conspirators was a man he named only by his initial, 'H', further identified in a sixteenth-century manuscript of this work as Henry. A thirteenth-century French chronicle

---

[27] Ibid., 196–8.   [28] Ibid.   [29] Ibid.   [30] WM, *GRA*, i, 744.

named him as Hugh. Warren Hollister suggested that this may have been a chamberlain named Herbert, the only man, he believed, who was styled as treasurer at the time and the only chamberlain whose name is known to have begun with an H.[31] Suger wrote that the king never felt safe. Not only did he take the precaution of wearing his sword indoors, but he also fined his men heavily if they went out without theirs.[32]

On 7 October Henry held a great council at Rouen. It was attended by the archbishop, four of the Norman bishops and many abbots, plus the archbishop of Canterbury, who was still in Normandy after his visit to Rome.[33] It was also attended by the papal legate Cuno, cardinal bishop of Palestrina, who addressed the council on the subject of the emperor and the antipope. He asked for the prayers and donations of Norman churchmen. Cuno's presence was remarkable. He had summoned the clergy of Normandy to two legatine councils without success, and when they failed to attend a third, at Chalons-sur-Marne in 1115, had suspended and excommunicated them.[34] Nervousness at the curia about the possibility that Henry I would abandon Pope Paschal for the antipope may have prompted such severe action, though it did not actually happen. Whilst not relishing the appearance of a papal legate in Normandy, Henry may have allowed the legate's attendance in the hope that any peacemaking there would carry greater weight with his sanction.

On the very day of the council, however, a dramatic new development occurred at Evreux. Audoin bishop of Evreux had not attended the council because he was defending his see against attack from Amaury de Montfort. However, the constable of the castle of Evreux, believing that Amaury de Montfort had been unjustly deprived of his inheritance, had gone over to Amaury and was quickly joined by other local lords. The whole region was soon in turmoil. The castle garrison of Evreux sacked the town and the bishop's palace, and the bishop fled, spending about a year in exile.[35] Henry, however, decided to return to l'Aigle, in the second week of November. He proceeded to ravage the surrounding area, but when the knights of the garrison emerged they gained the upper hand. Count Theobald of Blois, who was unhorsed and captured, had to be rescued by the king and Theobald's brother Stephen, and in the ensuing engagement Henry was

---

[31] C. Warren Hollister, 'The Origins of the English Treasury', *EHR*, 93 (1978), 262–75; *MMI*, p. 214. However, Herbert FitzHerbert married Sibyl Corbet, Henry's mistress and the mother of two sons and at least one daughter, the queen of Scotland. If Herbert was the ringleader in 1118, it is unlikely that his son would have been allowed to marry Sibyl.
[32] Suger, *Vie de Louis VI* (ed. Waquet), p. 190. [33] Ibid., p. 202.
[34] On Cuno see Nicholl, *Thurstan*, pp. 60–1. [35] OV, vi, 202–4.

hit on the head with a stone, escaping serious injury only because of his helmet.[36]

Another setback occurred at Andely on the Seine, possibly in the last weeks of 1118.[37] The manor of (Le Grand) Andely on the right bank of the Seine belonged to the archbishop of Rouen. It was one of his most valuable estates, and of great strategic importance. It was here, or strictly speaking on the hillside above the village, that Richard the Lionheart would later locate his great stronghold of Château Gaillard. In 1118 the castle was under the command of Henry's (illegitimate) son Richard when a man named Ascelin son of Andrew offered to betray it to the French. Ascelin was for some reason at odds with Archbishop Geoffrey: he went to Louis and offered to let him into the town if Louis would come to take charge. Ascelin himself returned with some seasoned soldiers and let them into his grain store at night, whilst King Louis followed. In the morning the advance party burst out from their hiding place, crying out the English war cry. They rushed to the castle and as soon as they were inside the defences they changed to the French battle cry, 'Montjoie'. Thus the French were able to occupy the castle and the town. Richard and the garrison fled to the church, and were then permitted to make an honourable exit. Andely became a headquarters for several lords of the Vexin: Godfrey of Serans, Enguerrand of Trie, Aubrey of Boury and Baudry of Bray. Enguerrand of Trie was said to control all the region up from Andely to Pont-Saint-Pierre where the river Andelle joins the Seine. From this base he advanced to meet King Henry and mocked him.[38]

Whilst Henry was occupied at l'Aigle, trouble had also broken out in the south again, this time at Alençon, where the citizens rose in revolt against the rule of Stephen of Blois. He had not endeared himself by his exactions, but what had really outraged them was a demand for hostages, one of whom, the wife of a prominent citizen, had been committed to 'depraved men'. Her husband allied with other husbands in a similar plight who thought that Henry would not hear a complaint against Stephen – an interesting insight into the affection Henry was believed to have for his nephew. Accordingly they appealed for help to Count Fulk of Anjou through the mediation of Arnulf of Montgomery, Robert de Bellême's brother, who was evidently still in the area. Fulk entered the city and laid

---

[36] Ibid., 204.
[37] Orderic places the incident in 1119, but Suger, although he does not give a day, ascribes it to late 1118, for he says that Henry and Theobald went off to relieve the garrison at Alençon after being taunted by Enguerrand of Trie.
[38] Suger, *Vie de Louis VI* (ed. Waquet), pp. 190–2; OV, vi, 218.

siege to the castle. Henry summoned his forces, both Normans and English, and marched to Alençon to relieve the city.[39] Theobald and Stephen went ahead to try to fight their way in but were defeated by Fulk, who returned to the siege with his booty, and increased his pressure on the garrison by cutting the water supply. He also sent for help to the lords of Maine, and when they arrived they fought and roundly defeated King Henry's army. This was the first and, as it turned out, the only occasion on which Henry was defeated in pitched battle.[40] Stephen had not been able to establish his authority over the lands and castles of Robert de Bellême, and Henry's aim to set his nephew in the place of Robert de Bellême had failed. The whole year had been disastrous for Henry as rebellions had surfaced, now here, now there, with interventions from Flanders, from Anjou and Maine, and by the king of France. The count of Flanders had been wounded in September and lay seriously ill – dying as it proved – but otherwise the year ended much as it had begun.[41]

Henry's resources of men and money had been fully stretched. The Anglo-Saxon Chronicler wrote under that year of the 'numerous taxes from which there was no relief'. Part of the money may have been raised in the form of an aid, but how this was levied is not known.[42] Henry maintained a substantial military force in his own household, his *familia*.[43] Detachments might be stationed as castle garrisons: the garrison at Andely under the king's son Richard in 1118 was almost certainly a detachment of the royal household. Experts in castle construction, masons and labourers were all needed, often at short notice, when, for instance, siege castles had to be thrown up. Money was needed for scouts, weapons, provisions and bribes: the list is endless.

---

[39] *Chroniques des Comtes d'Anjou* (ed. Halphen and Poupardin), pp. 155–61.
[40] OV, vi, 206–8; *Chroniques des Comtes d'Anjou* (ed. Halpen and Poupardin), pp. 155–61.
[41] Accounts of Baldwin's final illness and its causes vary: see OV, vi, 190 (a wound received at Arques, compounded by a rich meal, drinking mead, and sexual intercourse); WM, *GRA*, i, 730 (brain damage from blows to his head, aggravated by a meal earlier that day and sex on the following night. Henry sent his best physician to his bedside); Suger, *Vie de Louis VI* (ed. Waquet), p. 194 (wounded at Arques); *Liber Monasterii de Hyda*, p. 315 (wounded at Arques by a sword thrust).
[42] *RRAN*, ii, no. 1192, issued by Prince William and therefore probably between May 1118 and May 1119, refers to 'this geld'. In the following year, between May and December, the monks of Abingdon sought to establish that they had 120 demesne hides quit of geld: *RRAN*, ii, no. 1211. The letter of Bishop Herbert of Norwich to Roger of Salisbury bewailing the £60 demanded for knights from his land may also belong to the period between 1116 and 1118, as he died in 1119: Richardson and Sayles, *Governance of Mediaeval England*, pp. 160–1.
[43] M. Chibnall, 'Mercenaries and the *Familia Regis* under Henry I', *History*, 62 (1977), 15–23; J. O. Prestwich, 'The Military Household of the Norman Kings', *EHR*, 96 (1981), 1–35; Morillo, *Warfare under the Anglo-Norman Kings*, pp. 60–6, 180–91.

As the war was not concentrated in any one area, and the situation was changing from day to day, Henry was constantly on the move, trying to deal with the most serious outbreaks of disorder, and watching his back the whole time as defections occurred. As Orderic pointed out, he could not mount a siege for any length of time because the tide of events was so changeable.[44] It is clear that sieges were usually short: the defenders were either taken by surprise, as at Andely where French soldiers penetrated in disguise, or they found themselves short of food or water, as at Alençon, and had to surrender. Henry had to rely on the intelligence with which he was provided, but when this proved to be faulty, as in the case of William de Tancarville, he lost time and momentum. His nephew Theobald did sterling service, but when he passed over the southern command to his younger brother Stephen, the latter was not up to the job. Henry still had the support of a nucleus of Norman magnates – who had interests across the Channel to consider – and his garrisons held the towns and cities of the duchy, but as the year closed, the outlook was bleak.

As the new year (1119) opened, the situation grew still more serious: 'everywhere evil was on the increase'.[45] There were fresh disturbances in the region of Ivry and Breteuil and continuing disorder in the southern marches. Since the clashes of 1103 and 1104, Breteuil had been held by Henry's daughter Juliana and her husband Eustace of Breteuil, who was now incited by Amaury de Montfort to claim custody of the ducal castle of Ivry, on the grounds that it had earlier been granted by Duke Robert to William of Breteuil.[46] Henry stalled, but he did not want to alienate Eustace. He tried to bind him closer by entrusting to his custody a hostage, the son of Ralph Harenc the castellan, and in return he held Eustace's two daughters, his own granddaughters, as hostages. Eustace put out the boy's eyes and sent him back to his father. Ralph Harenc went straight to the king. Henry, moved by the ill treatment of the boy, handed over his two granddaughters so that Ralph might take his revenge, which he did by blinding them and cutting off the tips of their noses. Whether Henry's decision should be regarded as cruel, even by the standards of this era, is discussed further below (pp. 314–16). Henry restored Ralph to the command of Ivry, and the news of their daughters' mutilation was sent to Eustace and Juliana. Eustace put his castles, Lire and Glos, Pont-Saint-Pierre and Pacy, in a state of defence, and sent Juliana with a force of knights to hold Breteuil. The citizens, fearful of their fate, sent word to Henry, who

---

[44] OV, vi, 200.   [45] Ibid., 208.   [46] Ibid., iv, 114.

arrived in haste. The citizens let him into the town and he then laid siege to the castle where Juliana was. Juliana asked for an interview with her father, and when he turned up unsuspecting she shot at him with a crossbow, but missed.

The incident is described by Orderic, but with little comment other than a biblical quotation that there is nothing so bad as a bad woman, so we can only speculate about the sense of desperation with which the daughter faced her father, and Henry's shock at a murderous assault by one of his children. He was obviously angry: he promptly had the drawbridge of the castle destroyed so that no one could enter or leave. Juliana had no option but to surrender. The only way of escape was by jumping off the castle wall into the moat, which she did, humiliating herself by showing her bare buttocks and getting soaked in the freezing waters of the moat, but she escaped to her husband at Pacy. Henry took his revenge on the treasonous pair by granting the whole of their inheritance, except Pacy, to Ralph de Gael, a nephew of William of Breteuil.[47]

Amaury de Montfort meanwhile refused Henry's offer of succession to the county of Evreux and the city, with the exception of the castle, and waged war ceaselessly, keeping his allies up to the mark, harassing villages, and carrying everything off.[48] The man who proved invaluable to Henry in this crisis was Ralph the Red of Pont-Erchenfray. He had already made his castle a bastion against rebel lords in 1118, and he also served with the king's household troops. On one occasion, when Ralph was serving in the Vexin with the king's son Richard, the latter was unhorsed. Ralph gave him his own horse and was himself captured by the French. Some fifteen days later Henry exchanged him for Walo of Trie, from the French Vexin.[49]

In the south there was more trouble as local garrisons at Exmes, Courcy and Montpinçon, hearing of desertions from Henry I, decided to desert too. The first magnate to do so was Reginald de Bailleul, a leading vassal of Roger of Montgomery, Robert de Bellême's father, who went to Henry at Falaise under the king's protection and formally renounced his fealty.[50] Henry thereupon demanded the surrender of his castle, but Reginald refused and returned there, hotly pursued by the king. Reginald had little option but

---

[47] Ibid., vi, 210–14. For the location of the places mentioned in this section, see map 3.
[48] OV, vi, 220.   [49] Ibid.
[50] Ibid., 214–16. Once again Orderic does not enlighten his readers about the context of Reginald's renunciation of fealty. He had held considerable estates in England under Roger of Montgomery; when he lost these is not clear.

to surrender, and Henry burned down his castle as an example to others who were tempted to defect.[51]

Orderic had first-hand experience of another local conflict. Richard of La Ferté-Fresnel, a vassal of Eustace of Breteuil,[52] fortified a castle at Anceins and from this base ravaged his neighbours' fields. On one occasion Richard joined forces with Eustace of Breteuil, Richer de l'Aigle, and William of La Ferté-Fresnel, and plundered the region, burning houses at Verneuces belonging to Orderic's own community at Saint-Evroult.[53] The castle of Le Ferté-Fresnel was not far from Pont-Erchanfray, and it was Ralph the Red who now dealt with Richard of La Ferté-Fresnel. When he saw the smoke of the burning houses at Verneuces, he collected the knights Henry had stationed at Le Sap and Orbec, and attacked a numerically superior force at the river Charentonne, seizing a good deal of booty and capturing a few knights. Ralph's advice to Henry was that the castle of La Ferté could now be taken, and so after Whitsuntide 1119 Henry approached and the men of La Ferté decided to surrender.[54]

Henry meanwhile was working to make peace with his enemies. A crucial move was to detach Count Fulk from his alliance with King Louis: if this could be achieved, it would allow Henry to concentrate on his other enemies, some of whom might be persuaded to lay down their arms. He succeeded by promoting a marriage between his heir, William, and a daughter of the count, Matilda. The count was tempted by the prospect of a grandson who might be king of England and duke of Normandy. The county of Maine was said to be Matilda's marriage portion,[55] though she also crossed to England in 1120 well supplied with money and equipment. There are no clues about when and how negotiations were conducted, but in May Prince William crossed to Normandy, and the wedding took place in the following month at Lisieux. Count Fulk, who set out for Jerusalem on pilgrimage, entrusted Maine to Henry I on the understanding that if he did not return, it should pass to his son-in-law.[56] The marriage paved the way for a general pacification in the south. At Count Fulk's request William Talvas was restored to all his father's lands in Normandy, but not the castles. Henry also pardoned Robert Giroie and restored his Norman fiefs of Montreuil and Echauffour.[57] Some held

---

[51] Ibid.
[52] Orderic refers to Eustace, surely in this context Eustace of Breteuil, as Richard's lord: ibid., 218.
[53] Ibid., 218–220. See map 3. [54] Ibid., 222. [55] WM, *GRA*, i, 758.
[56] Ibid. Fulk assisted at the consecration of Saint-Julien-du-Mans on 25 April 1119: *Actus Pontificum Cenomannensis in Urbe Degentium*, ed. G. Busson and A. Ledru, Société des Archives Historiques du Maine, ii (1902), pp. 415–17. He left for the Holy Land several days later: OV, vi, 310.
[57] Ibid., 224.

out a few weeks longer: Richer de l'Aigle, for instance, was evidently still in arms and had, it seems, attacked Cisai-Saint-Aubin near Gacé.[58] He came to terms in September, however, and received his father's lands in England.

On 17 June Count Baldwin of Flanders died of the wound he had received in the previous September. Henry announced the news of the death of one enemy, and his alliance with another, the count of Anjou, at a council summoned to Lisieux. It was news calculated to give the remaining rebels pause for thought. After this he went on the offensive and made a 'terrible progress' through Normandy, during which he burned the castle of Pont-Saint-Pierre, one of the castles of his son-in-law, Eustace of Breteuil.

He then went to Evreux, where the castle was still in the hands of Count Amaury's men. Despite arriving in force with his son Richard, Stephen of Blois and Ralph de Gael, he could not gain an entrance. The next step was to burn the town in order to put pressure on the castle garrison to surrender, but Henry obviously was concerned, perhaps recollecting the burning of Bayeux. Orderic reported that the king asked Bishop Audoin's advice: should he burn the city, destroying its churches and bringing suffering to the innocent, even though he promised to make amends by having the churches rebuilt even better than before?[59] The bishop, who had been driven out of his city, hesitated, but finally consented to the fire, on the grounds that the city would be freed from excommunicated traitors and restored to its lawful inhabitants. Ralph de Gael lit the first fire on the north side of the city, and it spread rapidly because everything was dry at the end of the summer.

Henry had hoped that news of the destruction of the city and the threat hanging over the castle garrison would spur Amaury to negotiate, but the garrison continued to hold out, and rejected the terms of surrender they were offered. Henry at first withdrew, but then returned at night with a great force of knights. He ordered a siege castle to be built by torchlight, which was then placed under the command of Ralph the Red, Simon de Moulins, and Gilbert of Exmes, his crack commanders. Amaury himself, with Eustace of Breteuil and knights from the French Vexin, based themselves at Pacy east of Evreux, and from here they led sorties against Henry's army.

---

[58] Ibid., 250.
[59] Henry appears to have kept his promise of restitution, because he granted to the bishop half the proceeds of the fair at Nonancourt, plus churches and tithes at Nonancourt, Verneuil and the port of Vernon, together with the grant of a manor in England: *RRAN*, ii, nos. 1356, 1554, 1673, 1700, 1830. The bishop's baggage was also freed from toll, and he was granted a house at Rouen which had belonged to William Brown the king's clerk: nos. 1555, 1910.

King Louis meanwhile was in the French Vexin. He besieged the castle of Dangu, and although the castellan resisted as best he could, he finally surrendered, after first burning the castle. Louis then tried to capture Château-sur-Epte, but here the defenders beat him off. At this point Amaury sent word to tell him of the burning of Evreux and to ask for help, and Louis accordingly withdrew.[60] Henry meanwhile had moved his army from Evreux to the Norman Vexin, and on 20 August he was at Noyon-sur-Andelle (Charleval). His men were cutting corn in the fields near Etrepagny for forage when his scouts, who were stationed at Mesnil-Verclives, spotted armed men with standards moving towards Noyon. This was the French army under the command of King Louis, who had based himself at Andely, hoping to meet Henry in battle. He was now to be given the opportunity.

Arguments were heard for and against engaging the enemy. On Henry's side William de Warenne and Roger FitzRichard of Bienfaite, a member of the Clare family, advised an attack, but William de Tancarville was more cautious. The Hyde Chronicler reported that William de Warenne offered to fight to the death to prove his fidelity against those who had suspected him, and asked the king to put him in the front line of the fighting.[61] On the French side, Burchard of Montmorency and others warned Louis not to engage in battle in Normandy, presumably because if he were defeated he stood the risk of being captured by men loyal to Henry (as indeed very nearly happened). On the other hand the knights of Chaumont in the French Vexin urged him to attack. Meanwhile, as scouts scurried to and fro, the armies grew closer. Henry sent out a force of knights and set fires which would throw the French into disarray.[62] He brought his army of five hundred knights, including two of his sons, Robert and Richard, and three earls, to a level field at Brémule near the hill of Mesnil-Verclives.

Accounts vary slightly about the disposition of the king's army.[63] According to Henry of Huntingdon there were three lines, nobles in the first, the king with his household (*familia*) in the second, and his sons with a great mass of footsoldiers in the third.[64] The Hyde Chronicler thought there were four lines, with William de Warenne, Walter Giffard and Roger FitzRichard in front, followed by a second line of nobles. A third line was composed of footsoldiers reinforced by knights including the king's sons, and the king was in the fourth line.[65]

---

[60] OV, vi, 228–34. [61] *Liber Monasterii de Hyda*, pp. 316–17.
[62] *Vie de Louis VI* (ed. Waquet), p. 196.
[63] Morillo, *Warfare under the Anglo-Norman Kings*, pp. 171–3.
[64] HH, p. 464; cf. OV, vi, 238; Suger, *Vie de Louis VI* (ed. Waquet), p. 196.
[65] *Liber Monasterii de Hyda*, pp. 316–17.

The French army of some four hundred knights seems to have attacked too hastily.[66] The first line, composed of the men of the Vexin, threw themselves against Henry's army. Reports about the next stage vary. According to Suger, the French were initially successful but then came up against the footsoldiers. Orderic's version was that William Crispin with eighty knights charged the Normans, but their horses were killed, so they were quickly cut off and many, including Otmund of Trie, were captured. The French then made a recovery, and the Norman line fell back, until it in turn recovered.[67] The French accordingly advised King Louis to retreat because of the superior numbers of the opposition and their own losses, which he did. The Normans then captured 140 knights and pursued the rest as far as the gates of Andely. William Crispin, however, caught sight of King Henry, and he rushed through the ranks to the man 'whom he specially hated'. He struck him on the head with his sword – twice according to Henry of Huntingdon.[68] The king was wearing a hauberk which the sword could not penetrate, but the blows forced the hauberk into the king's head and drew blood. The word Henry uses is *prorumperet*, gushed out: this may have been an exaggeration, because according to the Hyde Chronicler the king was only slightly hurt. There are discrepancies, too, about what happened next. Henry of Huntingdon thought that the king struck a mighty blow which, though it could not penetrate William Crispin's helmet, caused horse and rider to overturn, and that William was immediately captured at the king's feet. Orderic Vitalis claimed it was Roger FitzRichard who struck William Crispin down, and was then forced to protect him from the wrath of the king's friends who wanted to kill him.[69] Once again Henry had a lucky escape from death, and won a pitched battle with very few casualties. Orderic reported that of the nine hundred knights engaged on the field, only three were killed.

Meanwhile Louis, leaving while the going was good, lost his way and, meeting a peasant, he asked for directions and preferably a guide, whom he was willing to pay handsomely, to lead him back to Andely. Only when the French king's servants rushed out from Andely to greet the king did the peasant realise the identity of his companion, and that he could have obtained much more for his services elsewhere. Henry was said to have bought King Louis's standard for twenty marks of silver and kept it as a souvenir. On the day after the battle he returned the king's horse to him with its saddle and harness, and Prince William likewise returned William

---

[66] Suger, *Vie de Louis VI* (ed. Waquet), p. 196. Orderic's comment that the battle had taken place between Noyon and Andely without warning also points to a hasty attack: OV, vi, 240.
[67] Ibid., 238. [68] HH, p. 464. [69] OV, vi, 238.

Clito's horse. Henry pardoned some of the combatants who were the vassals of both kings, but others were imprisoned. Guy of Clermont died in prison at Rouen and Otmund of Chaumont was sent in chains to Arques. Some of the French escaped by tearing off their badges and pretending to be on the victorious side, shouting the Norman war cry, and praising King Henry. Of the Normans, only Robert (III) de Courcy, who was cut off from his companions whilst pursuing the French right into the town of Andely, was captured.

The outcome had been a humiliating defeat for the French, and it was costly because the captured knights had to be ransomed. Little had changed in strategic terms. Amaury de Montfort, who still held the castle of Evreux, conferred with King Louis at Paris and suggested that a joint expedition be launched against Breteuil.[70] If Breteuil fell, argued Amaury, it could be restored to their ally, Eustace of Breteuil. This in turn might encourage Ralph de Tosny to defect to their side, whereas at present he was too intimidated by the hostile garrison at Breteuil to offer any support. Louis was determined to show that he was not afraid to enter Normandy. He summoned contingents from all parts of his lands. Bishops, counts, magnates and parish priests were urged to answer the king's summons to wage war against a public enemy. Amaury himself offered to grant King Louis a safe escort.[71] The army set out, robbing churches and ill-treating monks and clergy, doing what it wished with impunity. Even though the bishops of Noyon and Laon were there, they apparently did not rein in their men because of their hatred of the Normans.[72]

Louis is said to have set fire to Ivry and approached Breteuil[73] with the twin aims of restoring Eustace's possessions and restoring the exiles who had lost their lands through loyalty to William Clito. The castle at Breteuil was under the command of Ralph de Gael, who marched boldly out and offered a fierce resistance. He ordered all the gates of the castle to be opened, but the fighting was so fierce that none of the French was able to gain entry. Henry sent a relief force of two hundred knights of the royal household, under the command of Ralph the Red and Rualon d'Avranches, which arrived at the height of the battle. Ralph the Red particularly distinguished himself, moving fast from one sector of the defences to another, and changing the badge he wore to confuse the enemy. He brought down many knights, capturing their horses, which he gave to his comrades rather than keeping them for himself, thus winning praise for his chivalry. Henry himself was

---

[70] Ibid., 242–6. [71] *Vie de Louis VI* (ed. Waquet), p. 198.
[72] OV, vi, 244–6. [73] *Vie de Louis VI* (ed. Waquet), p. 198.

advancing with his main army, so the French decided on this occasion that discretion was the better part of valour, and retreated. William of Chaumont and a force of some two hundred knights turned aside on their way back to France and tried to capture the castle of Tillières. This castle was held by Gilbert Crispin, a kinsman of that William Crispin who had fought at Brémule, but who, unlike William, had remained loyal to Henry. He lay in wait with his retainers, and ambushed and captured William of Chaumont along with several of his companions.[74]

Louis, still frustrated in his desire for revenge, turned his attention to Count Theobald and attacked Chartres, trying to burn the city. The clergy and townspeople pleaded to be spared, and brought with them a precious relic, the tunic worn by the Virgin when she gave birth to Christ. The king decided to give way, not wishing the cathedral to be burned, and he ordered the count of Flanders to pull back the army. It would appear, however, that trouble continued, and at least part of the city was burned.[75]

Two other disputes were brought to resolution through negotiated settlements. Richer de l'Aigle was reconciled with Henry through the intercession of his uncle, Count Rotrou of Perche, and received all his father's lands in England as well as Normandy.[76] Richer had been able to capitalise on the strategic importance of his border castle to bring pressure to bear upon Henry. His revolt, in other words, had been a successful means of attaining his desired end. The struggle within the honour of Breteuil, by contrast, continued. Ralph de Gael was still in possession of the castle of Breteuil itself, but was not sufficiently powerful to subdue either the castellans of Glos and Lire or Eustace of Breteuil, who was based at Pacy. It was only when Henry himself arrived in the district, with his army, that a settlement was negotiated. The castellans of Glos and Lire were persuaded to surrender their castles, and the rents of Glos were granted to Ralph the Red; Pont-Saint-Pierre was handed over to Ralph de Tosny; Eustace was allowed to keep Pacy, and the daughter of Ralph de Gael was betrothed to Henry's son, Richard.[77]

Meanwhile, however, on 18 October 1119, Pope Calixtus II arrived at Rheims to hold a council, to which clergy from all regions were summoned.[78] Attempts had been continuing to achieve a resolution of the Investiture Dispute with the emperor. Calixtus was a committed reformer who was nevertheless as keen to achieve a resolution as Henry V, and his plan was for a treaty to be ratified at Mouzon on the river Meuse. The

---

[74] OV, vi, 248.   [75] *La Chronique de Morigny*, ed. L. Mirot (Paris, 1909), p. 31.
[76] OV, vi, 250.   [77] Ibid., 294.
[78] M. Stroll, *Calixtus II (1119–1124). A Pope Born to Rule* (Leiden and Boston, 2004), chapter 23.

pope's council at Rheims put Henry in a difficult situation. He doubtless wished to remain uncommitted in public, either to the pope or to the emperor, in the search for a solution to the issue of investiture. He had to decide, however, whether to allow the bishops and abbots of England and Normandy to attend the council, despite having refused them permission to attend the recent legatine councils of Bishop Cuno. There was also the unresolved issue of Thurstan's consecration. The archbishop-elect was still obdurate in refusing to make any profession of obedience to Canterbury, appealing to the pope to effect his consecration. If Thurstan could reach the pope, however, it was possible that the pope would himself perform the consecration. Archbishop Ralph of Canterbury himself was now ill and unable to attend the council, and he urged the king to make sure that Thurstan could not reach the pope. Thurstan remained evasive until the pope's summons to the council arrived.[79]

In the end, Henry felt he had little alternative but to allow Thurstan to attend with the other archbishops and bishops. He may have believed that the pope would not consecrate Thurstan,[80] or that he had Thurstan's promise not to accept such a consecration.[81] The king gave the bishops permission to attend, but only if they did not take their disputes to the pope. He reminded them that each year he paid his dues to Rome (Peter's Pence) and upheld the privileges granted in ancient times.[82] In other words, Henry was making his own position about the king's rights over the church clear in advance of the council. However, Henry had other matters to worry about. The council would also be a perfect opportunity for a case to be made for William Clito, and Henry would need to have his counter-case prepared. He himself, however, decided not to attend.

Thurstan joined the pope at Tours on 22 September. His friends lobbied the pope to consecrate Thurstan, but, though evidently favourably disposed towards Thurstan, Calixtus at first demurred. He then decided to go ahead and on Sunday 19 October, the day before the council was due to begin, and before the English and Norman bishops had arrived, Thurstan was consecrated without a profession of obedience to Canterbury.[83] The pope had decided to bring this long-running saga to an end, even if he risked Henry's wrath by doing so. The English and Norman bishops had

---

[79] Hugh the Chanter, p. 108; Stroll, *Calixtus II*, chapters 5–6.
[80] This was the view put forward by Hugh the Chanter, who claimed that the bishop of Exeter had advised the king on this point: Hugh the Chanter, p. 114.
[81] Ibid., p. 120. The Canterbury version was that Thurstan had promised not to seek consecration without the king's consent: Eadmer, *Historia Novorum*, p. 255.
[82] OV, vi, 252. [83] Hugh the Chanter, pp. 118–20; Eadmer, *Historia Novorum*, p. 257.

an uncomfortable dilemma whether or not to acknowledge the new archbishop. It speaks volumes for their fear of Henry's anger that they decided unanimously not to speak to Thurstan during the council.

On Monday the formal proceedings began. King Louis entered, 'eloquent in speech, tall, pale, corpulent'.[84] He came, he said, to ask for guidance. He complained of wrongs done to him by King Henry, who had violently invaded Normandy, 'a part of my realm', and had treated his brother Duke Robert, Louis's vassal, without regard to justice or right; Henry had imprisoned Robert for many years; he had disinherited Robert's son and driven him into exile. He had arrested Robert de Bellême, Louis's envoy, in his own court and had kept him prisoner in a dungeon. Henry had also encouraged his nephew Count Theobald, another vassal of the French king, to rise in rebellion; and Theobald was responsible for the capture and imprisonment of Count William of Nevers. Archbishop Geoffrey of Rouen started to present Henry's case but was drowned out by cries of opposition, because his defence of the 'victorious prince' was displeasing to those who were present: eloquent testimony to Henry's unpopularity in the assembly.

The council then proceeded to other business. This included the complaint brought by Audoin bishop of Evreux against Amaury de Montfort for his expulsion from Evreux. One of Amaury's chaplains called the bishop a liar in front of the whole assembly, saying that Amaury had been disinherited by King Henry, and had recovered his honour as a brave knight should 'who is blessed with arms and friends'. It was King Henry who on the bishop's order had commanded all the churches and houses to be burned, though he had failed to capture either the citadel or the city. The French supported Amaury against Bishop Audoin, and a great uproar broke out, with everyone speaking at the same time.

The pope then spoke eloquently against violence and in favour of peace. He renewed the Truce of God preached by Pope Urban at Clermont. He announced his intention first to go to Mouzon to make peace with the emperor, while members of the council were to stay put. He would then visit Henry and Theobald and urge them to make peace with their enemies. In fact, negotiations with the emperor broke down, and the pope soon returned to Rheims, where the council resumed by debating the question of the abbey of Cluny's possession of monastic tithes, and ended with condemnations of the emperor, the antipope and their supporters, and of many ecclesiastical abuses, such as simony, lay investiture, hereditary succession

---

[84] OV, vi, 256–8.

to benefices, charging for chrism, clerical marriage and interference with pious donations.[85]

From Henry's point of view, the proceedings of the council had not gone well. His defence of the conquest of Normandy and his treatment of his nephew had been shouted down, as had the case brought by Bishop Audoin against Amaury, and Thurstan had been consecrated against Henry's wishes. However, Thurstan could not return to England without the king's permission, and Henry insisted that he would only grant permission if Thurstan made his profession.[86] Thurstan was no fool, however, and turned his negotiating skills towards arranging a meeting between Henry and the pope, which was fixed for November.

During the Council of Rheims, Henry had been camped with his army at the siege of Evreux, whilst his nephew Theobald worked to pacify the rebels.[87] Amaury de Montfort finally accepted the terms which Henry had offered earlier, namely, the county of Evreux minus custody of the castle. Eustace of Breteuil and Juliana meanwhile decided to seek a reconciliation with Henry. They were advised that the best approach was to present themselves before the king, unannounced and as barefoot penitents. The king expressed his astonishment at their effrontery, but Eustace replied that Henry was his 'natural lord' to whom he would offer faithful service and make amends as the king judged. Friends interceded, as did Juliana's brother, Richard. Henry's heart apparently softened, and he ordered Juliana to return to Pacy. Eustace went with him to Rouen, and was told that although he could not recover Breteuil, he could have lands in England worth two hundred pounds a year.[88]

Other rebels now came to terms, including Hugh de Gournay and Robert de Neufbourg, but Stephen count of Aumale continued to resist. Henry therefore brought his army to Eu in October 1119, and began to build a siege castle.[89] It was called 'Whore Humbler' as a deliberate slight against the Countess Hawise, who was believed to have persuaded her husband to rebel. Count Charles of Flanders decided to intervene on the count of Eu's behalf,[90] and the threat of renewed hostility there may have been one of the considerations prompting Henry to think of a marriage alliance with a family whose lands abutted the county of Flanders. Meanwhile he sent William de Warenne to the rebels, and it was perhaps a sign of the changed circumstances of 1119 that they came to terms. The count of Aumale was

---

[85] Ibid., 262–76. [86] Hugh the Chanter, pp. 122, 124. [87] OV, vi, 276–8.
[88] Ibid., 278–80. In 1130 Eustace was holding land in England, as may be seen from his remissions of geld in Wiltshire and Gloucestershire: *PR 31 Henry I*, pp. 22, 80.
[89] *Liber Monasterii de Hyda*, p. 320. [90] Ibid., pp. 320–1.

restored to his English estates, and Count Charles was granted an annual payment from England, which suggests that the treaties of 1101 and 1110 were renewed.[91]

William Clito was present during these negotiations with the rebels and, seeing his cause deserted by the great men, sent messengers to his uncle. He requested that his long-imprisoned father should be released into his care; conceded that Normandy would be surrendered absolutely and in perpetuity; and promised that he and his father would leave for Jerusalem, swearing never to return across the Alps or to stir up mischief. Henry however rejected these terms and instead offered his nephew money. William Clito, it was said, was moved by anger and grief, and declared that he would never take money or make peace with his uncle. He departed weeping, in the company of Helias of Saint-Saëns and his most loyal knights.[92] Henry might have been prepared to offer his nephew land or an income, but he was not going to free Duke Robert. Although his own fortunes had revived dramatically in 1119, the traumatic events of the previous year were evidently fresh in his mind.

Henry now only had to make peace with King Louis, and with this in mind met Pope Calixtus on 22 November in a church situated between Gisors and Chaumont.[93] William of Malmesbury believed that the pope had come with hostile intent to condemn the continuing captivity of Duke Robert, a pilgrim to the Holy Sepulchre,[94] and Henry might well have been concerned, given the hostile atmosphere at Rheims. He arrived therefore with his sons and with a great entourage; rich gifts were distributed; and Henry prostrated himself before the pope, greeting him with every reverence as the pastor of the universal church and his own kinsman.[95]

The pope then spoke.[96] He asked Henry to demonstrate the proverbial wisdom of Solomon and to make peace with his enemies. He continued that the synod of the faithful begged Henry to release his brother and to restore to him and his son the duchy of Normandy, on the grounds that God's law prescribed that each should be satisfied with what was lawfully his and should not covet the property of others, a direct comment on past events. According to Orderic, Henry argued in response that he had not deprived Robert of the duchy, but had laid a legal claim by battle to the inheritance of their father. Robert and William had never really possessed the duchy because it had been laid waste by bandits. The

---

[91] Ibid.
[92] Orderic says that William and Helias went into exile, but does not say where: OV, vi, 282.
[93] Stroll, *Calixtus II*, chapter 6.   [94] WM, *GRA*, i, 734.   [95] OV, vi, 282.
[96] For a version with slightly different emphases see WM, *GRA*, ii, 734–6.

church in particular had suffered for almost seven years, and churchmen had beseeched him to act. He had crossed to Normandy, where he had been received by distinguished counts; he had offered to help his brother to deal with men like Robert de Bellême but was spurned. He then took up arms and took Bayeux, Caen, and other fortified towns which his father had held in demesne but which Robert had handed over to lechers. He had fought his brother 'in the name of the Lord and for the protection of his native land', and with God's help had been victorious. He had striven to uphold his father's laws 'according to God's will and for the peace of his people'. He had treated his captive brother 'as a noble pilgrim, worn out with many hardships' and provided him with comforts, whilst his nephew had been entrusted to the guardianship of Helias. The latter had betrayed Henry, however: he had taken his nephew away and absconded, inciting the French and Burgundians to attack. Henry had frequently sent for his nephew under safe conduct to join his cousin, Henry's own son, at court and had even offered him three counties in England, but his offer had been rejected.[97]

Henry thus sidestepped the accusation of violent conquest by laying the blame for disorder in Normandy on his brother, and by emphasising the evils Curthose's rule had brought to the church and to Christian people. He himself had been spurred to action in response to the pleas of churchmen and then sought only to restore his father's laws. The imagery that he invoked for the honourable treatment accorded to his brother as a worn-out pilgrim countered the charge of imprisoning a valiant crusader, and he claimed to have offered his nephew wealth and position.

The pope then moved on to the conflict between Louis and Henry. Louis had complained that the treaty between them had been broken, that Henry's men had committed many acts of violence against him and his kingdom, and that the imprisonment of the count of Nevers had been ordered by Count Theobald. Henry's rejoinder was that Louis had been the first to break the treaty, and that he would follow the pope's recommendations for peace and advise his nephew to do the same.[98] Hugh the Chanter, who gave only an abbreviated account of the meeting, added the important detail that Henry offered to do willingly whatever the duke of Normandy owed to the king of France (homage, in other words).[99]

The other outstanding issue between the pope and Henry was the matter of Thurstan. The king once again discoursed on his customary royal rights over the English church. The pope confirmed these and, according to Hugh

---

[97] OV, vi, 282–6.   [98] Ibid., 288–90.   [99] Hugh the Chanter, p. 128.

the Chanter, promised that no legates would be sent to England, and that only those disputes which could not be settled by the archbishop of Canterbury were to be referred to the pope himself.[100] He then pleaded Thurstan's case, but the king replied that he had given his word that Thurstan would not enter the kingdom unless he made a personal profession to Archbishop Ralph.[101] The pope replied that he would free Henry from his promise, and Henry responded that he would have to take advice on this point. The upshot was that Thurstan was still not given permission to enter England, and the king sent orders that he should be deprived of the temporalities of his see.[102] Moreover, Anselm of St Saba, St Anselm's nephew, who had been appointed legate for England in 1116, was still not allowed to enter the country.[103]

The meeting was evidently carefully orchestrated, and included a debate between the youthful twin sons of Robert of Meulan and cardinals who were present. The twins, who still had to reach their majority, were said to have put on a dazzling display of dialectic, so that their opponents were forced to admit that skill in letters abounded in the western regions far more than they had believed.[104] Behind the king's self-justification and the pope's rhetoric for peace, the reality was that Henry was prepared to see that homage was performed for Normandy if Louis were prepared to accept it, but as yet he had not formally granted Thurstan permission to enter England.

The pope was not prepared to accept this rebuff, and in March 1120 he issued a privilege which awarded the palm of victory to Archbishop Thurstan.[105] The archbishop's suffragan bishops were confirmed, he was granted the right to use the pallium, and it was further decreed that the archbishop of Canterbury was not to make any demand for a profession from York, nor was York to make such a profession. Instead, according to the sixth-century plan of Pope Gregory the Great, precedence was to be accorded on the basis of seniority. Finally, the liberties and possessions of the church of York were to be protected from intervention from any person, lay or ecclesiastical. Those who flouted the papal decree were to be excommunicated after due warning.[106] In order that there could be no misunderstanding about his intention, the pope wrote at the same

---

[100] Eadmer, *Historia Novorum*, p. 258.   [101] Hugh the Chanter, pp. 130–2.
[102] Ibid., p. 132.   [103] Eadmer, *Historia Novorum*, pp. 239, 259.
[104] WM, *GRA*, i, 734–6. That such an entertainment was put on is intriguing. Twins of noble birth would have been a rare sight anyway, and even more so twins who had such skill in dialectic. The point was obviously being made that England and Normandy were not beyond the civilised world, but Henry may also have been trying to demonstrate his benevolent guardianship of the boys.
[105] Hugh the Chanter, pp. 146–9, 166–73.   [106] Ibid., pp. 166–72.

time to the archbishop of Canterbury explaining why he had consecrated Thurstan. He also wrote to the king to inform him of the sanctions to be taken against Ralph if Thurstan were not allowed to enter his see, and stating that there was to be an interdict upon both provinces, Canterbury and York, until Thurstan was restored.[107] The archbishops of Tours and Rouen were appointed as the pope's legates, the former to deliver the pope's letter to the king, the latter to join with him in exhorting the king to restore Thurstan. Cuno meanwhile was to deliver the pope's letter to Archbishop Ralph, and the pope also wrote to the York clergy informing them of his decision.[108]

Thurstan immediately left the papal court at Gap in Provence and headed north. He visited Countess Adela and Theobald of Blois, and briefed them on the situation and the documents he was carrying.[109] As in 1105, Adela was fully alive to the gravity of the sanctions facing her brother. The York chronicler makes it clear that there was still serious discord between Henry and Louis, and that Adela could see that her brother's excommunication would jeopardise peace negotiations. Thurstan obviously thought about going to King Louis's Easter court at Senlis to arrange for the delivery of the pope's letters to King Henry, but because of the hatred between the kings he sent a clerk instead. He remained with Adela, who was preparing to retire from the world to the abbey of Marcigny, and waited for the king's reply to letters which the pope and his legate had sent. The pope's letter was relatively conciliatory, merely asking the king to restore Thurstan. Henry still prevaricated, saying that he had first to consult his council. He continued to delay, and was reluctant to meet Cuno, with whom he was not on good terms. Cuno obviously felt the same, but a meeting of king and legate finally took place at Vernon, soon after Ascension Day 1120 (20 May).[110]

The meeting was evidently not easy: Henry restated his position that he could not obey the pope without breaking his word unless Thurstan made his profession to Archbishop Ralph, who had returned to England. Cuno reiterated that the king had been absolved from his oath; and that a great wrong had been done to the pope and the church in that an archbishop had been robbed of his see and exiled. Cuno told the king of the sentence

---

[107] Ibid., pp. 172–4. The news caused dismay at Canterbury, where a search was instituted to discover documentation for their privileges: Eadmer, *Historia Novorum*, pp. 260–1. The documents were the Canterbury forgeries. Historians are divided about the date they were produced: see Southern, *St Anselm*, pp. 259–64; M. Gibson, *Lanfranc of Bec* (Oxford, 1978), appendix C; and C. N. L. Brooke, 'The Canterbury Forgeries', *Downside Review*, 69 (1951), 210–31.
[108] Hugh the Chanter, p. 146. [109] Ibid., pp. 152–8. [110] Ibid., pp. 158–60.

he would soon receive. Even at this late stage Henry did not cave in. After much discussion, 'sometimes calm, sometimes angry', he did make one concession, that the temporalities of York should be restored to Thurstan. Even then he asked Thurstan to delay his return to England. Cuno found this unacceptable, seeing it as a further delaying tactic. Thurstan, who did not attend the meeting but was close by, somewhat surprisingly agreed.

Thurstan knew his former master, King Henry, and was able to read the political situation in Normandy with which his own prospects were now bound up. Henry almost certainly did intend that the issue of Thurstan's acceptance without a profession would be discussed at a council in England, much as the earlier deal with Anselm over investitures was discussed at the Council of London in 1107, and Archbishop Ralph would either be present or be represented. From Henry's point of view, the whole issue of whether the pope could order him to accept Thurstan was moot. However, Henry could not return to England without peace with Louis, and Louis still had to be persuaded to accept the homage of Henry's son for Normandy. If Thurstan could facilitate the peace, then Henry would be better disposed to accept him.[111] Thurstan evidently played an important part in the ensuing peace negotiations. The York chronicler believed that he was the man on the Norman side in whom King Louis had most confidence,[112] though William of Malmesbury emphasised the interventions of the counts of Anjou and Blois, and Countess Adela.[113]

During the following weeks peace negotiations between the various parties were successfully concluded. The counts of Flanders, Anjou, Ponthieu and Aumale, and Hugh de Gournay, all treated for peace, and the king of France 'restored' Normandy to Henry's son William.[114] Possibly around October,[115] and in an unrecorded location, Prince William performed homage.[116] This important act was not reported by Orderic, perhaps not surprisingly given Orderic's view that Robert was still the rightful duke, and because of the significance of such a recognition of the French king's authority. It may have taken place on the frontier, and have been viewed as a renewal of that 'hommage en marche' of earlier dukes, but its implications, in terms of the context – peacemaking after a conflict followed by homage

---

[111] SD, *Opera Omnia*, ii, 258. [112] Hugh the Chanter, p. 160.
[113] WM, *GRA*, i, 758. [114] *Liber Monasterii de Hyda*, pp. 319–20.
[115] Ibid., p. 319: 'in the month of October'. It is not precisely clear which of the following events took place in that month.
[116] WM, *GRA*, i, 734; SD, *Opera Omnia*, ii, 258; *Liber Monasterii de Hyda*, p. 319; for the ceremony at Senlis see Hugh the Chanter, p. 152. Philip was only three years old at the time. For discussion see Lewis, *Royal Succession in Capetian France*, pp. 55–6.

and cession of the duchy – broke new ground.[117] It is important therefore to ascertain exactly what occurred.

William of Malmesbury and Symeon of Durham believed that homage was paid to King Louis. The Hyde Chronicler, however, offers a different perspective: Henry granted a fixed annual rent each year from his English revenues to King Louis, in recognition of the fact that King Louis could not set aside the oath of William Clito which had been the cause of the war. Henry's son William paid homage to Philip, Louis's son, then a small child.[118] The Hyde Chronicler may well be accurate here. Some resolution of Louis's prior commitment to William Clito had to be found, and from Henry's perspective, it was homage performed by his heir (not himself) to King Louis's heir.

Henry was thus able to placate his other adversaries, leaving only Stephen count of Aumale, who was allied with the count of Flanders, to offer continued resistance, and they too were reconciled. Count Stephen had the prospect of the restoration of his lands, and the count of Flanders that of a renewal of the earlier treaties granting a cash payment in return for knights. Almost all William Clito's support had melted away.[119] Afterwards the Norman magnates performed homage and swore fealty to Henry's son William, an act which like no other could ensure that the succession to the duchy rested with him, and not with his cousin.[120]

Thus Henry had secured the succession to Normandy for his son, he had neutralised the enmity of Anjou, and he had beaten off a severe threat to his control in Normandy. A high price, homage for Normandy, had to be paid, and it had taken over four years of warfare, which had borne heavily on England as well as Normandy, to achieve this. Henry's robust defence of the Canterbury primacy had been trumped by papal intervention, and the issue of Thurstan's return was still unresolved. So too were the powers of papal legates in Normandy, an issue raised when Cuno, having summoned the bishops and abbots to a legatine council at Beauvais for the first anniversary of the Council of Rheims, threatened to excommunicate the Norman prelates and had to be dissuaded by Thurstan.[121] Cuno and Henry then met at Gisors, each reportedly in a happier frame of mind than at their earlier meeting, though Henry still refused to allow Thurstan to cross to

---

[117] Lemarignier, *Recherches sur l'hommage en marche*, p. 92. One commentator compared this homage with that of Rollo to Charles the Simple: *Ex Anonymi Blandinensis Appendicula ad Sigbertum, Recueil des Historiens de France*, xiv, 16.
[118] WM, *GRA*, i, 734; SD, *Opera Omnia*, ii, 258; *Liber Monasterii de Hyda*, p. 319.
[119] *Liber Monasterii de Hyda*, pp. 320–1, places William Clito's offer of terms to his uncle, and Henry's response with the offer of a subsidy, at this point in its account.
[120] SD, *Opera Omnia*, ii, 258.   [121] Hugh the Chanter, pp. 160–2.

England with him, saying that he proposed to confer with the archbishop of Canterbury at Christmas.[122] Henry then moved slowly westwards across Normandy, preparing to return to England by the western route, from the Cotentin peninsula. By late November he was at Barfleur, and as the preparations for his crossing were set in hand for his crossing he dispatched business, such as issuing a confirmation charter for the abbey of Cerisy.[123]

'NO SHIP EVER BROUGHT SUCH DISASTER TO ENGLAND'[124]

The wreck of the White Ship was the worst personal and political disaster of Henry's life. In one night he lost his son and heir, two other children, and many of his close friends and companions. For contemporaries it was a classic illustration of what William of Malmesbury called 'the mutability of human fortunes'.[125] Henry had triumphed over his enemies and was at last able to return to his kingdom, only to have the sweetness of victory snatched away, and the future of his own line placed once more in doubt. There is no suggestion of foul play in contemporary accounts,[126] amongst which that by Orderic is the most detailed.[127]

On 25 November, a man named Thomas son of Stephen went to the king; he offered a relief of one mark of gold (six pounds), and asked for his father's position.[128] Stephen had carried William to England in 1066 and had served him loyally for the rest of his life. Thomas had a fine vessel, the White Ship, excellently fitted out and ready for royal service. The boat

---

[122] Ibid., p. 164.   [123] *RRAN*, ii, no. 1233.   [124] WM, *GRA*, i, 760.   [125] Ibid., i, 758.

[126] See, however, the ingenious suggestion by Victoria Chandler that the evidence may be so ordered as to suggest that the wreck was engineered by William de Pirou, a royal steward, on behalf of Ranulf Meschin and William of Roumare: 'The Wreck of the *White Ship*: A Mass Murder Revealed?', in *The Final Argument: The Imprint of Violence on Society in Medieval and Early Modern Europe*, ed. D. J. Kagay and L. J. Andrew Villalon (Woodbridge, 1998), pp. 179–84. Her hypothesis cannot of course be totally disproved, but William de Pirou had no known link with Ranulf Meschin. The fact that Orderic included William de Pirou in the list of the drowned is most likely to have been a mistake, and the likeliest explanation for his disappearance from royal records after 1123 is death from natural causes.

[127] The most detailed account of the shipwreck is that by Orderic, OV, vi, 296–306, with which other early twelfth-century accounts are in broad agreement. Writing in the later twelfth century, Wace dwelt on the aftermath of the tragedy. He believed that the king had arrived safely at Southampton and had proceeded as far as Clarendon before the news was broken to him. William de Tancarville, 'a good vassal', urged him to rise and eat, saying that his grief gave succour to his enemies, and that it was for women to weep and wail. The young prince's bride, who had already gone to England, later returned to her father with the money, equipment and horses which formed part of her dowry: Wace, *Roman de Rou* (ed. Holden), lines 10, 205–72.

[128] OV, vi, 296: the word used by Orderic here is 'fief'. Thomas's father, Stephen son of Airard, had held land in England in 1086: DB, i, 636.

was probably like those on the Bayeux Tapestry and, according to Orderic, had some fifty rowers, with a side rudder, essentially the same, therefore, as Viking ships.[129] Stephen was probably the master-steersman who occurs in Domesday Book. It was his duty to produce a ship and to organise the availability of other ships to transport the royal entourage.[130] The king agreed to Thomas's request, but explained that he had already chosen a ship for himself. However, he said, he would entrust his sons William and Richard, and many nobles, to the White Ship. The sailors of the White Ship were delighted and asked William for drink, which he supplied in abundance.[131]

The harbour at Barfleur is about one and a half miles south of the Pointe de Barfleur (see map 6). It is tidal, and the tidal stream, or race (*raz*) of Barfleur, reaches as much as five knots off Barfleur at spring tides, making conditions difficult for ships entering and leaving the harbour. The passage to England, made without a compass, would have been easier by night than by day as ships could navigate by using the Pole Star, and would normally have taken between ten and twelve hours.[132] High water on 25 November was at 10.43 p.m, and conditions were calm, though dark, with a new moon.[133] If the ships had a draft of about two metres, it is unlikely that they would have been able to float much before 8 p.m., but at that time there would have been a strong current driving southwards towards the present Omaha beach. The pilots would therefore have waited until the race slackened.

About three hundred people had climbed aboard the ship, though a few disembarked because they realised that the young men had got out of hand. (One of those who stayed behind was Stephen of Mortain, who was suffering from diarrhoea.) There were about fifty experienced oarsmen and with them marine guards who were drunk and showing off. When priests

---

[129] OV, vi, 296; for discussion see Le Patourel, *Norman Empire*, p. 166. For the suggestion that the White Ship may have been about thirty to thirty-five metres long, and 3.5 to 4 metres in the beam, see T. Brett-Jones, 'The White Ship Disaster', *The Historian*, 64 (1999), 23–6. The Skuldelev longship had between forty and fifty-two rowers.

[130] For royal transfretations, see Le Patourel, *Norman Empire*, pp. 163–78.

[131] OV, vi, 296. The quantity here cited is three *muids*: a *muid* was a customary liquid measure, varying in volume but large nonetheless. Delisle suggested it was sixteen or thirty *sétiers* (a *sétier* was about eight pints): L. Delisle, *Etudes sur la condition de la classe agricole de Normandie au moyen âge* (Evreux, 1851), p. 566.

[132] Brett-Jones, 'The White Ship Disaster', 23.

[133] Ivan F. Nelson, 'Some Thoughts on the Loss of the White Ship, 25 November 1120', pers. comm. Orderic thought that there were about nine hours of moonlight, but he miscalculated: OV, vi, 298–9 and note.

arrived to bless them, they laughed and drove them away. The ship was carrying little cargo, and the passengers urged Thomas to try to overtake the king's fleet, which had already reached the open sea, possibly between about 11.30 p.m. and midnight.[134] Thomas agreed, and the rowers set off at full speed. They were presumably intending to follow the route to the north-east which avoids all dangers, but in working their way round to the north they hit a rock, stoving in two planks. The sailors tried to push the ship off, but she suddenly capsized. A boat was launched carrying Prince William and he might have escaped, but he turned back to try to save his sister, the countess of Perche, who was still aboard. As his boat returned, it was swamped by those who jumped down into it.[135] Two men who were in the sea caught hold of a spar and hung on for the best part of the night. Thomas surfaced and asked them what had become of the king's son. Hearing that the prince and all his companions had perished, Thomas preferred to drown rather than face the king's wrath. One of the two men, a son of Gilbert of l'Aigle, eventually slipped away and perished. His companion, a butcher of Rouen named Beroud, was wearing a pelisse, a sheepskin cloak, and in the morning he was rescued by three fishermen.

It is not easy even today to negotiate the route in and out of Barfleur harbour, as the approaches are dotted with rocks covered and uncovered by the tides. The rock on which the ship foundered is traditionally identified with the Quillebœuf Rock, which best seems to fit Orderic's description of a huge rock covered at high tide, though in fact there are other possibilities.[136] The Quillebœuf Rock is about one nautical mile from Barfleur and half a mile from the shore, about twenty minutes' rowing time at three knots. At midnight it would have been covered by about two metres of water, or less as the tide went out.[137] An alternative location is suggested by the comment of Robert of Torigny that the ship struck a rock at a place called *Catteraz*.[138] This seems to be the Raz de Barfleur, which is off the rocky point on which is situated the Gatteville lighthouse, slightly further away from Barfleur than the Quillebœuf Rock. The wreck occurred within earshot of the clergy who had blessed the voyage and were still waiting on the shore. The bishop of Coutances was there, having waved off his son, his brother and three nephews, all of whom were on the White Ship. King Henry and his companions, too, were said to have been able to hear the cries of those who were in fact drowning, though they did not know their cause.

---

[134] Nelson, pers. comm.   [135] WM, *GRA*, i, 760.
[136] Le Patourel, *Norman Empire*, pp. 177–8.
[137] This is Nelson's estimate (pers. comm.); cf. Brett-Jones, 'The White Ship Disaster', 25.
[138] *GND*, ii, 218.

The king's ship meanwhile had sailed safely on to England. Henry kept asking for news of his son, but no one dared to tell him.[139] On the following day and on Count Theobald's advice, a boy threw himself at the king's feet, weeping, and broke the news. The king fell to the ground overcome with grief, and had to be helped to a private room. He grieved for his sons, his companions in arms, and eminent nobles. Above all, we are told, he mourned for Ralph the Red and Gilbert of Exmes, his trusted captains, and he described their deeds of courage, weeping as he did so.

The casualties included, as well as the king's sons and daughter, his nieces, Matilda of Blois, her husband Richard earl of Chester, and Richard's half-brother, Othuer FitzCount, tutor of Prince William, who was reported to have flung his arms round the prince and drowned with him. The list of those drowned further included a young relative of the emperor, two sons of Ivo de Grandmesnil and William of Rhuddlan, who were travelling at the king's command to receive their fathers' lands in England, and members of the royal household: William Bigod, Geoffrey Ridel, Hugh de Moulins, Robert Mauduit and Gisulf the scribe.[140] Eighteen high-born women died: the daughters, sisters, nieces or wives of kings and counts. The local inhabitants dragged ashore the wreck. This still contained the king's treasure, almost everything, in fact, apart from the passengers and crew. Men hurried along the beach searching for bodies, and magnates tried to find divers to search for the bodies of their loved ones, but to little avail. The bodies of Earl Richard and a few others were found some days later a long way from the wreck, identified by their clothing, but that of Prince William was never recovered.

---

[139] Wace, *Roman de Rou* (ed. Holden), line 10,219.
[140] Here Orderic mistakenly included William de Pirou amongst the casualties: OV, vi, 304.

CHAPTER 8

Surviving the wreck, 1120–1124

The wreck of the White Ship was the turning point of Henry's reign. He had lost his beloved son and heir, two other children, and many friends and members of his court. We have no reason to be sceptical about accounts of Henry's grief. The love he had lavished on his only legitimate son had been genuine and the young man had died on the threshold of manhood, just married, and the recognised heir to his grandfather's lands. Henry is never known to have used Barfleur again as a port of transit.[1] There loomed a major problem over the succession, because he was a widower over fifty years of age. If he remarried and fathered a son, he would be old before that son reached manhood. His only legitimate daughter's marriage was still childless, though as there was no reason to think she could not bear children, his grandchildren, Henry's attention may have been turned in her direction again. His closest male heirs were now his nephews. It was inevitable that William Clito and his supporters should take fresh hope from the disaster, whilst Theobald of Blois might well have thought of himself at this time as his uncle's heir presumptive.

Whether a visit had been planned before the shipwreck or not, Theobald spent the Christmas feast with his uncle at the hunting lodge at Brampton in Huntingdonshire.[2] Henry proceeded to London and on the advice of Archbishop Ralph and the nobles, who assembled on 6 January 1121, the king announced his intention to marry Adeliza, daughter of Duke Godfrey of Lorraine.[3] Henry may have been grief-stricken at the loss of his heir, but he wasted no time in trying to father another. He had to be awake to every possibility, not retreat from the world.

The speed of this decision, and of the arrival of his bride in England, suggests that the marriage must have been in prospect before the wreck of the White Ship. Given that Queen Matilda had died in 1118, plans for a

---

[1] Le Patourel, *Norman Empire*, pp. 175–6.
[2] *ASC* E 1121; HH, p. 466 mentions the presence of Count Theobald.   [3] JW, iii, 148.

second marriage would not have been surprising; Henry may have been waiting until his return to England when his bride could be crowned. He could have opted for a bride from a royal or noble family in France, but once again his attention turned to the Empire. The planned match allied him with a neighbour of his enemy, Count Charles of Flanders, and strengthened ties of friendship with the imperial circle. His bride was very young: she was described as a girl at the time of her marriage and perhaps had been born in or around 1103. She was reportedly of great beauty and modesty.[4]

On 29 January the wedding took place at Windsor, possibly so that Bishop Roger of Salisbury, the diocesan bishop, could officiate.[5] The tactic backfired, because Archbishop Ralph, though too ill to officiate himself, insisted on his right to nominate a substitute, and deputed the bishop of Winchester in his place. Then the archbishop objected to King Henry placing the crown on his own head, so Henry removed it and the archbishop replaced it.[6] This incident, reported by Eadmer, may provide a clue about Henry's view: he could crown himself, and did not need to have the act performed by the archbishop.

Adeliza was endowed with lands and properties like her predecessors,[7] and she like Queen Matilda was a dedicatee of literary works, such as the *Bestiaire* of Philip de Thaon, the earliest known bestiary in Anglo-Norman.[8] Bestiaries were treatises, often illustrated, describing the appearance and qualities of animals and birds.[9] Adeliza (or her predecessor) also may have been the dedicatee of the poem *Brendan*, a translation into Anglo-Norman of the fabulous adventures of St Brendan and his companions.[10] She is said to have commissioned a biography of Henry I, which has been lost (see below, p. 297).

---

[4] Ibid. Cf. OV, vi, 308; HH, pp. 466–8; Eadmer, *Historia Novorum*, p. 290: 'of good morals and modest countenance'. For her life see L. L. Huneycutt, 'Adeliza (*c.* 1103–1151)', *Oxford DNB*; L. Wertheimer, 'Adeliza of Louvain and Anglo-Norman Queenship', *Haskins Society Journal*, 7 (1995), 101–15; Bartlett, *England under the Norman and Angevin Kings*, pp. 40–6; and K. Thompson, 'Queen Adeliza and the Lotharingian Connection', *Sussex Archaeological Collections*, 140 (2002), 57–64.
[5] JW, iii, 148. [6] Eadmer, *Historia Novorum*, pp. 292–3.
[7] Adeliza held the manor of Stanton Harcourt in Oxfordshire, which she gave to Reading Abbey, and Queenhithe in London: *Reading Abbey Cartularies*, ed. B. R. Kemp, 2 vols., Camden Society 4th series 31, 33 (1986, 1987), i, nos. 534–6, 459. She also held Waltham: see *The Early Charters of the Augustinian Canons of Waltham Abbey, Essex, 1062–1230*, ed. R. Ransford (Woodbridge, 1989), no. 16; for her geld exemptions see *PR 31 Henry I*, pp. 60 (Essex), 62 (Herts.), 102 (Bucks.), 104 (Beds.), 126 (Berks.), 152 (Middlesex).
[8] M. D. Legge, *Anglo-Norman Literature and its Background* (Oxford, 1963), pp. 18–26.
[9] For a recent survey see R. Baxter, *Bestiaries and their Users in the Middle Ages* (Stroud, 1998).
[10] Legge, 'L'influence littéraire', 683; for the text see Benedeit, *The Anglo-Norman Voyage of St Brendan*, ed. I. Short and B. Merrilees (Manchester, 1979).

She probably remained at Henry's side constantly between her marriage and the king's departure to Normandy in 1123, though she does not appear regularly as a witness to his charters. She was with him again in 1124 in Rouen when they viewed the relics of St Romanus, and again in England in 1126 and 1127, and she possibly travelled with him to Normandy on later trips, in 1128, 1129 and 1131.[11] Nevertheless there were no children of the marriage, though Adeliza was to bear at least seven children by her second husband, William d'Aubigny. Hildebert of Lavardin, bishop of Le Mans, wrote to commiserate with the queen on her childlessness,[12] but the problem may well have been on Henry's side. Whatever the cause, there would have been gossip and speculation in court circles. Henry showed himself very sensitive to ridicule from Luc de la Barre in 1124 (see below, pp. 186–7). Nothing was reported about the subject matter of the songs Luc composed, but they certainly hit a raw nerve, to judge from Henry's reaction.

One of Henry's major preoccupations in the early 1120s was the project to found, or, strictly speaking to refound, an abbey at Reading in Berkshire. Henry had already been generous to various religious communities, and he may have had the intention to establish an abbey for some time. If so the deaths of his wife and children may have acted as spurs to action.[13] The terms of the foundation charter, a text not without its problems,[14] show that the king's mind was directed towards his own mortality: by the counsel of his bishops and his other faithful men, for the salvation of his soul, those of his father, his brother William, his mother Matilda, and Matilda his wife and all his predecessors and successors, he had founded a monastery at Reading in honour of the Virgin and St John the Evangelist. Henry was interested in newer types of communities, like the Augustinians, and the eremetical groups at Savigny and Tiron, but his own project, in the traditions of his family, was for a great abbey which followed Cluniac observance.[15] Cluniacs had been his father's first choice for monks at Battle abbey in Sussex.[16] William Rufus had been a leading figure in the foundation of Bermondsey

---

[11] *RRAN*, ii, nos. 1280, 1292, 1301, 1303, 1391, 1427–8, 1467, 1489, 1559, 1569, 1587–8, 1701, 1874.
[12] Hildebert of Lavardin, *Letters*, Migne, *Patrologia Latina*, clxxi, cols. 135–312, no. 18.
[13] This suggestion was made by Southern, 'Place of Henry I', 162–3, and discussed by P. Stafford, 'Cherchez la Femme: Queens, Queens' Lands, and Nunneries: Missing Links in the Foundation of Reading Abbey', *History*, 85 (2000), 4–27.
[14] It has been suggested that the surviving text may be an 'improved' version of a charter originally given in 1125: *Reading Abbey Cartularies*, i, no. 1, pp. 35–6.
[15] B. Golding, 'The Coming of the Cluniacs', *ANS*, 3 (1980), 65–77, 208–12; F. Barlow, 'William I's Relations with Cluny', *Journal of Ecclesiastical History*, 32 (1981), 131–41.
[16] For the Conqueror's request to Abbot Hugh, see Anonymous II, *Vita S. Hugonis, Acta Sanctorum* III, 29 April 660–1; Migne, *Patrologia Latina*, clix, cols. 923–5.

priory,[17] and Countess Adela had retired to Marcigny, a nunnery of Cluniac observance, in 1120.[18] Henry had probably already been sending money to Cluny for some time,[19] and in 1121 eight monks were sent from Cluny who, with recruits from Lewes priory, which followed Cluniac observance, formed the nucleus of the new community at Reading.

At Reading there had been a monastery since the early Middle Ages, so from Henry's point of view the new endowment was an act of restoration. It was located in the south of England, not far from favoured royal residences at Windsor and Oxford, and situated with easy river access. The abbey was lavishly endowed: it received the lands of the former community at Reading, together with the church of Reading[20] and an estate there held by Tutbury priory,[21] as well as the lands of two other dissolved houses at Cholsey in Berkshire and Leominster in Herefordshire;[22] the churches of Wargrave and Cholsey, which had to be retrieved from the abbey of Mont-Saint-Michel; and, later, the church of Hanborough and probably the manor of Bucklebury and the manor and church of Pangbourne.[23] The abbey was also generously endowed with privileges: the intention seems to have been to give the abbey every privilege which the king could give, including that of a mint and a moneyer at Reading.[24]

The foundation was planned in such a way as to accord with reforming principles. Its lands were to be held 'freely', not burdened with the secular burdens of knight service; all goods were to be held in common, not divided between the abbot and convent; the prior and convent were to have custody during periods when there was no abbot; there were to be no hereditary offices; and the abbot was not to accept child oblates. It was to be fully independent, though in full communion with the mother house at Cluny. In 1123 Hugh of Amiens, prior of Lewes, was appointed the first abbot.[25]

---

[17] Bermondsey annals, *Annales Monastici*, iii, 427.   [18] Hugh the Chanter, p. 154.
[19] *The Letters of Peter the Venerable*, ed. G. Constable, 2 vols. (Cambridge, Mass. 1967), no. 89. We cannot be sure when Henry began to send money to Cluny, but it has been suggested that he may have taken over as the principal patron of the rebuilding of the church after the death of Alfonso VI in 1109; see Brooke, 'Princes and Kings as Patrons of Monasteries', pp. 136–7.
[20] Henry granted land at Appledram to the monks of Battle in return for the church they held at Reading: *The Chronicle of Battle Abbey*, ed. E. Searle (Oxford, 1980), p. 122.
[21] For the land held by Tutbury priory see *Reading Abbey Cartularies*, i, 49 n. 1.
[22] Ibid., 17. In 1086 Reading had been worth £48, Cholsey £47; Leominster was worth £60 after provision had been made for the nuns and was potentially valued at £120 in 1086: *DB*, i, 58, 56b–57, 180.
[23] Ibid., 16–17.   [24] Ibid., 18.
[25] Annals of Reading, 1121: Liebermann, *Anglo-Normannische Geschichtsquellen*, p. 10. For Hugh, see P. Hébert, 'Un (archévêque) de Rouen au xiie siècle. Hugues III d'Amiens', *Questions Historiques*, 64 (1898), 325–71; and Waldman, 'Hugh "of Amiens", Archbishop of Rouen (1130–64)'.

The church was built on a massive scale, some 450 feet long, including the later Lady Chapel.[26] Few of the buildings now survive, but its plan and size can be worked out, and there are some surviving sculpted capitals. The plan, like Cluny III, and Bermondsey and Lewes, also Cluniac, had double eastern transepts.[27] Some of the capitals, of Caen stone, have beakheads, and these are very early, possibly the earliest such examples in England.[28] We have no idea how much interest Henry took in the details of the building work, but it is apparent from the surviving remains that he wanted the biggest and the best, with no expense spared.

The scale and magnificence of the church give an indication of its role: it was intended to be a place for grand services, a place of resort for pilgrims, rather than a small intimate royal mausoleum. The foundation charter emphasises the use of the abbey's resources for caring for the poor and for pilgrims.[29] Pilgrims came to venerate relics, and the abbey soon acquired a fine collection, the jewel of which was the hand of St James the Apostle, brought back by the empress from Germany in 1125.[30] The king perhaps intended from the first that he would be buried in the abbey church, rather than alongside his first wife at Westminster Abbey.

Whilst building at Reading took shape over a period of years, a more immediate matter in 1121 was the backlog of business which had accumulated during the years of warfare in Normandy. Appointments to two bishoprics and two abbeys were made.[31] So far as great lordships were concerned, the most important decision was about the earldom of Chester, for Earl Richard had died in the White Ship. A strong earl was needed because the prince of north Wales, Gruffudd ap Cynan, was becoming ever more powerful and independent. As soon as the news of Earl Richard's death had spread, the Welsh raided Cheshire, burning two castles, killing and pillaging.[32]

---

[26] J. B. Hurry, *Reading Abbey* (London, 1901), p. 4.
[27] For an overview, see Grant, 'Architectural Relationships'.
[28] F. Henry and G. Zarnecki, 'Romanesque Arches Decorated with Human and Animal Heads', *Journal of the British Architectural Association*, 3rd series, 20–1 (1958), 25–7. For colour reproductions of some capitals see *English Romanesque Art 1066–1200*, ed G. Zarnecki, J. Holt and T. Holland, Arts Council (London, 1984), plates 129–31.
[29] *Reading Abbey Cartularies*, i, no. 1.
[30] K. Leyser, 'Frederick Barbarossa and the Hand of St James', originally published in *Transactions of the Royal Historical Society*, 5th series, 10 (1960), 61–83, reprinted in *Medieval Germany and Its Neighbours*, pp. 215–40; B. Kemp, 'The Miracles of the Hand of St James', *Berkshire Archaeological Journal*, 65 (1970), 3; Bethell, 'The Making of a Twelfth-Century Relic Collection'.
[31] Coventry and Lichfield (Robert Peche), and Richard (Hereford), plus Herbert (Westminster Abbey): Eadmer, *Historia Novorum*, pp. 290–1, and for Barking, *RRAN*, ii, no. 1242.
[32] SD, *Opera Omnia*, ii, 263–4.

Gruffudd had recently nominated a candidate for the north Welsh see of Bangor, vacant since Hervey the Breton had taken flight. Gruffudd was evidently not prepared to accept a candidate imposed by King Henry from England or Normandy, but he was willing to accept one David, whose name 'Scotus' suggests he may have been Irish rather than Scottish. Links between Gruffudd's court and Ireland in this period were strong.[33] Moreover, David was a man of some experience, in that he had been in the service of the emperor.[34] He was prepared to go to Canterbury for consecration, a concession which would have made him more acceptable to Henry. However, Gruffudd warned that if any obstacle was put in his way another candidate would be sought from Ireland.[35]

Henry thus had to handle the succession to the earldom of Chester with particular care. Earl Richard's closest male relative was his cousin, Ranulf, *vicomte* of Bayeux, lord of Carlisle and, by right of his wife, lord of Bolingbroke. Ranulf was not only the closest male relative of the dead earl: he was adult, experienced and loyal. Henry was willing to allow him to succeed to the title and lands of Chester, but not to keep Carlisle as well, which would have placed too great an assemblage of lands in the hands of one man.

Meanwhile Henry himself prepared an expedition to Wales. He spent Whitsuntide 1121 at Westminster, where he and his new queen wore their crowns.[36] Here he also received a papal legate, explaining that because of the forthcoming campaign it would not be possible for the legate to hold a council. He also pointed out that it had been agreed with the pope that no legates were to be sent to England during Henry's lifetime. The legate, Peter Pierleoni, thus had little option but to return, but not before he had spent three days at Christ Church Canterbury having his ear bent about the wrongs inflicted on Canterbury in its dispute with York.[37]

---

[33] M. T. Flanagan, '*Historia Gruffud vab Kenan* and the Origins of Balrothery, Co. Dublin', *Cambrian Medieval Celtic Studies*, 28 (1994), 85; see also Geoffrey of Burton, *Life and Miracles of St Modwenna*, ed. and trans. R. Bartlett (Oxford, 2002), pp. xxx–xxxvi.

[34] WM, *GRA*, i, 764; Leyser, 'England and the Empire in the Early Twelfth Century', *Medieval Germany and Its Neighbours*, p. 207. There is no proof that David was Irish rather than Scots, but his stay in Germany plus his recruitment by Gruffudd, who had spent a period of time in Ireland, makes this more likely than Scotland.

[35] *Life of Gruffudd ap Cynan*, p. 53; Eadmer, *Historia Novorum*, p. 260. David may have attended Henry's court in 1121: *RRAN*, ii, no. 1243, 1245 (*Cartulary of Shrewsbury Abbey*, i, no. 35). For the letter from Gruffudd and the people of Gwynedd, see *Episcopal Acts and Cognate Documents Relating to Welsh Dioceses*, i, 99–100.

[36] HH, p. 468.

[37] Eadmer, *Historia Novorum*, pp. 296–7; Brett, *The English Church under Henry I*, p. 41; *Westminster Abbey Charters*, nos. 187–8.

The king moved north-west to Shrewsbury, probably via Hereford and Bridgnorth.[38] At Shrewsbury he confirmed the endowments of the abbey, which had been founded by Roger of Montgomery and endowed by his tenants, and where a fresh assertion of royal authority and protection over the abbey was timely.[39] He then moved forward into mid-Wales, but retreated when he was wounded slightly by an arrow in an ambush by the men of Powys. According to William of Malmesbury he was startled into swearing his favourite oath, 'by the death of our Lord'.[40] The Welsh chronicler believed Henry was frightened off by this attack, but the reality was that he achieved a demonstration of armed might, which was all he could hope for. The men of Powys, having failed to secure the backing of Gruffudd ap Cynan, had little option but to offer to pay a tribute of ten thousand head of cattle.[41]

Since the fall of Robert de Bellême in 1102, Shropshire had been administered by Richard de Beaumais, bishop of London, who passed on the baton, possibly around this time, to the king's chamberlain, Payn FitzJohn. Payn had married Sibyl, daughter of Hugh de Lacy, and through his wife came to hold Ludlow and many of the Lacy lands in Herefordshire.[42] He worked closely with Miles, son and later successor of Walter, constable and sheriff of Gloucestershire, who also married advantageously. His bride was the daughter of Bernard of Neufmarché, lord of Brecknock, who in 1121 resigned his lands into the king's hands, whereupon Henry granted them to Miles, confirming the grant by charter.[43] The charter had been attested by Robert, the king's son, who by his marriage had received great estates in Gloucestershire and the lordship of Glamorgan in Wales. By September 1122 at the latest Robert had been created earl of Gloucester, one of the few new earldoms of the reign.[44] The title conferred superiority over Walter of Gloucester and other families in the shire; it established Robert as the key man in the region; and it may also have been granted in the hope of balancing the earldoms held by Stephen of Blois and Earl David.

---

[38] *RRAN*, ii, nos. 1295, 1294.
[39] *Cartulary of Shrewsbury Abbey*, i, no. 35. The words of Stephen's charter indicate that the charter of Henry I was confirmed at London in full council, and Rees, following Farrer, suggested a likely date of 29 May, when the king is known to have been at London and before his departure into Wales. He could, however, have confirmed the abbey's possessions when he was at Shrewsbury in the summer, and the formal charter could have been issued on his return.
[40] WM, *GRA*, i, 728.   [41] *Brut (RBH)*, pp. 104–8; *Brut (Peniarth)*, pp. 47–8.
[42] Wightman, *The Lacy Family in England and Normandy*, pp. 175–81.
[43] *Ancient Charters*, ed. J. H. Round, Pipe Roll Society, 10 (1888), pp. 8–10.
[44] Round argued for a date some time between 1121 and 1122: *Geoffrey de Mandeville* (London, 1892), pp. 420–36. This is probably correct, though the dating depends on references in charters which are in some cases not originals, and are not easy to date precisely.

By Michaelmas the king had returned from Wales. He presided over a great council, during which he put pressure on the recently returned Archbishop Thurstan to make a personal profession of obedience to Archbishop Ralph. He may have thought that once Thurstan was in England he would be more conciliatory, but if so he was mistaken.[45] Thurstan nevertheless was discreet in using the papal privilege dispensing him from the need to make a profession. He showed it to the king only in the presence of the bishop of Durham and Nigel d'Aubigny. Both the king and Nigel allegedly wept, the king because of Thurstan's expressions of affection and loyalty, and Nigel because he saw how upset the archbishop was, having hoped that on his return the quarrel would be left behind. The king's advice was that the archbishop should show the bishops the privilege; they refused to read it, and one of them falsely claimed that the bull was a forgery, a claim indignantly refuted by the York party.

In the early months of 1122 it appears that Henry was hoping to meet his daughter, the empress, for the first time since her marriage. Henry travelled into Kent to meet her during the month of May,[46] but she was prevented from attending by the refusal of Count Charles of Flanders to grant her safe passage across his lands.[47] It has been suggested that father and daughter had discussed the succession, and that this explains why Count Charles, a supporter of William Clito, would have refused her permission to cross his territory.[48]

Later in 1122 Henry went to the north of England. As in the case of Wales he needed to assert his authority along the borders of his realm after a lengthy absence from his kingdom. He had assumed direct lordship over Carlisle and its dependent region, and may have wished to make his presence felt personally. Moreover, at about this time valuable silver mines at Alston near Carlisle had been discovered, and Henry may have wished to ensure that the Scots did not take them over.[49] King Alexander had been exhibiting a sense of independence which was, from Henry's point of view, worrying. Like Gruffudd in north Wales, Alexander was seeking to bolster the independence of the church in his realm, in this case in the face of York's claim to primacy. The first sign of trouble had come with the consecration of John, David's chaplain, to the see of Glasgow,

---

[45] Hugh the Chanter, p. 178. The location of the council is not specified.
[46] HH, p. 468.   [47] Waverley Annals, *Annales Monastici*, ii, 218.
[48] K. Leyser, 'The Anglo-Norman Succession 1120–1125', *ANS*, 13 (1990), 234–5.
[49] For a discussion of the significance of these mines see I. Blanchard, '"Lothian and Beyond": the Economy of the "English Empire" of David I', in *Progress and Problems in Medieval England: Essays in Honour of Edward Miller*, ed. J. Hatcher and R. Britnell (Cambridge, 1996), pp. 23–45.

at some date between between 1114 and 1118. John steadfastly refused to make any profession to York. Then in 1120 Alexander invited Eadmer, the monk-historian of Canterbury, to become bishop of St Andrews, doubtless reckoning that Eadmer's background at Canterbury would ensure he would not entertain the idea of making a profession of obedience to Canterbury's rival, York. The scheme foundered, however, because Eadmer refused to perform homage to the Scots king or to receive investiture from him, and retired to Canterbury. Alexander was said to have declared that never in his lifetime would a Scottish bishop be subject to Canterbury.[50] In 1114 Alexander had accompanied his father-in-law to Wales, but he did not do so in 1121, and Henry might well have regarded this as an act of defiance which could not be ignored. Finally, in 1121 we hear of an assembly of northern magnates at Durham, when Durham's claim to Tynemouth priory was heard.[51]

Henry's immediate concern, however, may have been the consequence of the death of his daughter, the queen of Scots, in July.[52] Would King Alexander remarry? Even if he did, Henry must have wanted to ensure that the claim of David, his own ally, to the royal succession would be recognised. Yet Henry had his own position to consider, too, and there are signs of a concern with security along the river Tweed, where Bishop Ranulf built a castle at Norham, and Walter Espec at Wark.[53] Walter worked in partnership with Eustace FitzJohn, who was established at Alnwick in Northumberland.[54] The pair moved into the gap left by Nigel d'Aubigny, who had returned to active service in the king's household.[55] They were to dominate royal governance in the north-east in the way that Payn FitzJohn, Eustace's brother, and Miles of Gloucester did along the Welsh Marches.

Henry once again moved north, via Nottingham, York and Durham. 'Traversing Northumbria by long and muddy roads' he was at York on 6 December 1122, when monks from Saint-Evroult arrived, asking for confirmation of their choice of a new abbot.[56] Henry reached Carlisle, where he ordered the castle to be strengthened, perhaps beginning the building of

---

[50] Eadmer, *Historia Novorum*, pp. 279–88.
[51] SD, *Opera Omnia*, ii, 261–2.   [52] Oram, *David I*, pp. 70–2.
[53] Walter gave the church of Wark to the priory of Kirkham in Yorkshire, founded in about 1122: Dugdale, *Mon. Ang.*, vi, 208–9.
[54] Eustace's charter for Alnwick priory stated that his gift was being made 'for the soul of Ivo de Vesci and all his antecessors', and that of Eustace's son William referred to the souls of Eustace his father and Beatrice his mother: ibid., vi, 867–8. The founders' history states that Beatrice, the daughter of Ivo de Vesci, married Eustace FitzJohn. For Eustace's career, see Dalton, 'Eustace FitzJohn and the Politics of Anglo-Norman England'.
[55] Dalton, *Conquest, Anarchy and Lordship*, pp. 96–9, 101–2.   [56] OV, vi, 324.

the keep.[57] Steps were also taken to establish a community of Augustinian canons there.[58] This expedition thus gave Henry an opportunity to review his strategy in the north. Carlisle was to be kept in royal control. Norman lordship in the north-west was gradually consolidated, and a marriage alliance between Fergus, the native lord of Galloway, and a daughter of Henry was arranged.[59] Fergus had his own agenda, independent of the kings of Scots, and for this reason was a likely ally for Henry. Ranulf of Bayeux (Ranulf Meschin), who had been based at Carlisle since at least 1106, had extended his power north of Hadrian's Wall, and at some point lordships were established at Kirklinton and Burgh by Sands. Robert de Brus was established in Annandale, either on his own initiative or, more probably, on that of David of Scots, who confirmed his tenure in a charter.[60] Ranulf's departure to become earl of Chester would have left a gap in north-western society.[61]

Henry returned to the south of England during the month of December and spent Christmas at Dunstable, a royal manor situated at the crossing of Watling Street and the Icknield Way.[62] The court then moved on to Berkhamsted, where Ranulf the king's chancellor, who was escorting the king to the castle, fell from his horse, and died.[63] A few days later another death occurred, also in the king's presence. On 10 January 1123 the king had reached Woodstock, and was riding in the park with Roger of Salisbury on one side and Robert Bloet, bishop of Lincoln, on the other. Bishop Robert was reported to have sunk down and said to the king, 'Lord King, I am

---

[57] SD, *Opera Omnia*, ii, 267; M. R. McCarthy and H. R. T. Summerson, *Carlisle Castle, A Survey and Documentary History*, English Heritage (1990).
[58] Nicholl, *Thurstan*, p. 147 and n.; J. C. Dickinson, 'The Origins of Carlisle Cathedral', *Transactions of the Cumberland and Westmorland Antiquarian and Archaeological Society*, 45 (1946), 134–43; Dickinson, 'Walter the Priest and St Mary's, Carlisle', *Transactions of the Cumberland and Westmorland Antiquarian and Archaeological Society*, new series, 69 (1969), 102–14; *RRAN*, ii, no. 1431.
[59] The reference to a daughter of Fergus and an illegitimate daughter of Henry I, here named Elizabeth, occurs in a chronicle of the Isle of Man and the Isles: *Chronica Manniae et Insularum. The Chronicle of Man and the Sudreys from the Manuscript Codex in the British Museum, with Historical Notes by P. A. Munch*, revised by Dr. Goss, 2 vols., Manx Society (1874), p. 60; for discussion of the marriage see D. Brooke, 'Fergus of Galloway: Miscellaneous Notes for a Revised Portrait', *Transactions of the Dumfriesshire and Galloway Natural History and Antiquarian Society*, 3rd series, 65 (1990), 57–8; R. D. Oram, 'A Family Business? Colonisation and Settlement in Twelfth- and Thirteenth-Century Galloway', *Scottish Historical Review*, 82 (1993), 116.
[60] *Charters of King David I*, no. 16. The reference to the march of Ranulf Meschin's land seems to suggest, as Barrow points out, that Ranulf had been in possession in the recent past, and that David may have made the grant before 1124.
[61] Scott, 'Partition of a Kingdom', 21–30.
[62] R. A. Brown, H. M. Colvin and A. J. Taylor, *The History of the King's Works. The Middle Ages*, 2 vols. (London, 1963), ii, 924–5; *VCH Beds*., iii, 351; see also below, p. 302.
[63] HH, pp. 468–70.

dying'. The king dismounted, caught him in his arms, and had him carried back to his lodging.[64]

Bishop Robert had been one of Henry's stalwart supporters, second only to Roger of Salisbury, frequently at court and one of the select few described as a 'justice of all England' (see above, p. 114). Henry of Huntingdon wrote of the magnificent figure he presented: his knights and young nobles, his horses, the splendour of his clothes and of the meals set before him. Robert's influence had slipped toward the end of his life, when he twice suffered the indignity of being impleaded before a low-born judge. In the chronicler's presence he was seen to be shedding tears and when asked the reason, he claimed it was because of the fines levied against him. He despaired of the king's friendship, and when told that the king had in his absence praised him, said, 'The king only praises one of his men whom he has decided to destroy utterly.'[65] Henry now had to find a new chancellor, a new bishop, and, even more important, a new archbishop of Canterbury to replace Ralph d'Escures, who had died in October 1122. Accordingly writs were sent out to lay and ecclesiastical magnates ordering them to attend a council at Gloucester at Candlemas (2 February).[66]

The bishops told the king that they did not want a monk as archbishop, and although the monastic community at Canterbury resisted for two days, the monks were given a list of four names, from which they chose William of Corbeil, an Augustinian canon.[67] William had been a tutor to Ranulf the chancellor's sons, and had accompanied them to the fashionable cathedral school at Laon in northern France. He had also been a member of Anselm's inner circle, but even so this career history hardly made him a front runner.[68] It was said that the king had to ask Adelulf of Nostell who the candidate was, but the key point was his acceptability as a compromise candidate. Although he was a canon rather than a monk, he was at least acceptable to the Canterbury monks as a member of a religious order.[69] Even so, there were objections from a papal legate (who was in England at the time) to the promotion of a clerk over monks, and that the election had

---

[64] *ASC* E 1123; JW, iii, 152. [65] HH, pp. 586–8.
[66] *ASC* E 1123; see Bethell, 'English Black Monks'; *Councils and Synods*, i, pt ii, 725–7.
[67] D. Bethell, 'William of Corbeil and the Canterbury York–Dispute', *Journal of Ecclesiastical History*, 19 (1968), 145–59.
[68] Bethell discussed the suggestion that the Ranulf the chancellor in question was Ranulf Flambard: 'William of Corbeil and the Canterbury–York Dispute', 146. By the time of the account of the visit made by the canons of Laon to England, Flambard was bishop of Durham: *De Miraculis Sanctae Mariae Laudunensis Ecclesiae*, Migne, *Patrologia Latina*, clvi, col. 962. For the argument that the canons were in England in 1113, see J. S. P. Tatlock, 'The English Journey of the Laon Canons', *Speculum*, 8 (1933), 454–65.
[69] Hugh the Chanter, p. 184.

not taken place in the chapter house at Canterbury.[70] The Anglo-Saxon Chronicler, himself a monk, wrote of the Canterbury monks' unsuccessful struggle to have a monk-archbishop that 'it was of no avail, because the bishop of Salisbury was strong and controlled all England, and was against them with all his power and ability'. The bishop was riding high at this time: his nephew Alexander was nominated to the bishopric of Lincoln, and the new chancellor, Geoffrey Rufus, may have been a clerk in Roger's household.[71]

The new archbishop was finally consecrated at Woodstock by the bishop of London and his fellow bishops.[72] Both archbishops then set out for Rome to attend the Lateran council, Thurstan having been warned by Henry not to say anything which would injure the archbishop of Canterbury. According to the York version of events, various difficulties were raised at the curia about William's appointment, but he received his pallium. It looks as though the Canterbury party had decided that this was too good an opportunity to miss for pressing their claim to primacy over York, but the plan backfired, because when forged papal privileges were produced they were literally laughed out of court. Their next ploys were to try bribing the pope's chamberlain, and to threaten the York party. Eventually the archbishops were told that a day could be appointed for a judgement, but the archbishop of Canterbury claimed that he would have to consult the king, and so they left and returned to Normandy.[73]

By this time the situation in Normandy was giving rise to concern. The continuing childlessness of Henry's second marriage gave renewed hope to his enemies, and the prospects of his nephew William Clito were looking brighter.[74] A new coalition of Norman magnates began to form, headed by Waleran count of Meulan. He was a young man who had been in the king's protection after his father's death and whose betrayal must therefore have been a personal blow for Henry. The sources do not explain the explicit reason for Waleran's discontent. Orderic claimed he was carried away by dreams of glory and was unduly influenced by his steward, Morin du Pin.[75] Other possible reasons include a sense of injury because of a liaison between his sister and the king,[76] but there is no evidence that

---

[70] *ASC* E 1123; for Henry see C. Clark, '"This Ecclesiastical Adventurer": Henry of Saint-Jean d'Angély', *EHR*, 84 (1969), 548–60.
[71] *ASC* E 1123; for Alexander's career see A. Dyson, 'The Career, Family and Influence of Alexander le Poer, Bishop of Lincoln 1123–1148', B. Litt. thesis, Oxford (1971); for Geoffrey Rufus, Kealey, *Roger of Salisbury*, appendix 2 no. 4.
[72] Hugh the Chanter, pp. 184–6.   [73] Ibid., pp. 188–98.
[74] OV, vi, 328.   [75] Ibid., 356, 332, 350.
[76] *GND*, ii, 250. It is not known when the relationship occurred.

Waleran or his brothers saw this as a personal affront. Perhaps Waleran was aggrieved because his twin, not he, had been married to the heiress to the great honour of Breteuil.[77] To have allowed such a marriage would have put a great swathe of territory into the hands of one very young man. The king may reasonably have believed that Waleran would not object to such a marriage alliance for his twin, but if so he miscalculated, because Waleran promptly constructed a set of marriages which established alliances with lands and castles concentrated close to the valleys of the rivers Risle and Eure (see map 1).

First, one of his sisters married Hugh, lord of Montfort-sur-Risle. Hugh had been brought up in the royal household, but had an unrecognised claim to the great English estates confiscated from Robert de Montfort in 1107.[78] A second sister married William Louvel (Lovel), lord of Bréval just over the frontier in France, who had a claim to the honour of Ivry, which King Henry had committed to his half-brother, Robert Goel.[79] A third sister married Hugh FitzGervase of Châteauneuf-en-Thymerais, whose castle was strategically situated beside the river Avre south of Evreux and right on the frontier. He had been in arms against Henry I in 1118, when he held l'Aigle on behalf of Louis VI.[80] Hugh could provide an entrée for French forces, and his lands were close to the county of Evreux, now in the hands of Amaury de Montfort. Amaury was no friend of Henry I, but what angered him at this juncture, according to Orderic, was the activities of royal officials.[81] He had to watch men, described by Orderic as *prévôts* and tax collectors, imposing novel levies, perverting judgements to their will, and doing many wrongs to high and low by invoking fear of the king's authority. Henry was in England, unaware of what was going on.

There were lords elsewhere in Normandy with claims of their own to press. William of Roumare wanted his mother's land, the honour of Bolingbroke, which his stepfather had surrendered to the king on becoming earl of Chester in 1121.[82] Two of the lords of the Norman Vexin, Baudry de Bosco of Baudemont and Theobald Payn of Gisors, took the chance to pitch in.[83] The final dimension was the link between disaffected Norman lords and the hostile neighbours of the duchy. Count Fulk of Anjou sent emissaries to King Henry seeking the return of lands, cities and

---

[77] Crouch, *Beaumont Twins*, pp. 13–14.
[78] *GND*, ii, 175–7; OV, vi, 336; for the descent of Haughley, see Sanders, *English Baronies*, pp. 120–1.
[79] OV, iii, 208–10; vi, 228; *Complete Peerage*, viii, 208ff.
[80] OV, vi, 198.   [81] Ibid., 330–2.
[82] Ibid., 332. Orderic added that William also wanted Corby in Lincolnshire. The principal manor here had belonged to the bishop of Lincoln in 1086: *DB*, i, 344b.
[83] OV, vi, 332.

castles from the dowry of his widowed daughter, Matilda.[84] The emissaries left, 'thinking nothing of the gifts which had been offered'.[85] Hence a plan for William Clito to marry Sibyl, another of Count Fulk's daughters, met with a favourable reception. The count sent for William, and betrothed his daughter to him with Maine as her marriage portion until William recovered his inheritance.[86] Because of this marriage, King Louis was said to have renewed the charge that Henry was unjustly imprisoning his brother and had caused his nephew to flee Normandy.[87] At some stage, therefore, King Louis too lent his support to the coalition.

Finally, the situation of Eustace count of Boulogne had to be taken into account. He had made his peace with Henry in 1101, and thereafter occurs from time to time, chiefly in documents relating to the English lands of himself and his wife,[88] and as a witness to the renewal in 1110 of the treaty between Henry and the count of Flanders.[89] He was on sufficiently good terms with the king to receive additional English land formerly held by Eudo the steward, who died in 1120.[90] His county was strategically situated, and his control of Wissant, one of the few safe ports in the region, put him in a potentially powerful position. Not only that, but he had a claim to the crown of Jerusalem, which his brother Baldwin I had held until his death in 1118.[91] Eustace had no legitimate sons, but only a daughter, Matilda, whose marriage was therefore a matter of great moment, and had to be negotiated before the count, as he wished, retired from the world. Both arrangements had been made by 1125.[92] Negotiations presumably had taken time, and so it is possible that already in 1123 Henry, who was in a powerful position to influence the marriage, was planning a glittering match for his nephew Stephen of Blois.[93] This would at once safeguard the Boulogne inheritance and the port of Wissant, and offer Stephen the prospect of succeeding Baldwin II, himself childless, as king of Jerusalem. From the point of view

---

[84] SD, *Opera Omnia*, ii, 267.   [85] *ASC* E, 1121, 1123.   [86] OV, vi, 332.
[87] *ASC* E 1123.   [88] Viz. *RRAN*, ii, no. 665, 749, 775, 818.   [89] Ibid., no. 941.
[90] Round, 'The Counts of Boulogne as English Lords', pp. 163–4.
[91] For the background see A. V. Murray, *The Crusader Kingdom of Jerusalem. A Dynastic History 1099–1125*, Prosopographica et Genealogica (2000), chapter 5.
[92] In that year Count Eustace issued a charter to the abbey of Cluny in which he described himself as 'late count of Boulogne': Round, *C. D. F.*, p. 507. The marriage has been recently discussed by King, 'Stephen of Blois', 279–80.
[93] In this context it is worth noting that Stephen's whereabouts between 1122 and 1125 are not known. He was included in the address of a royal notification about the election of a new abbot of Saint-Evroult in December 1122 (OV, vi, 324), but is not mentioned in accounts of 1123 to 1125. King has suggested that he may have accompanied Henry to northern England in 1122. Symeon of Durham believed that Stephen had Savigniac monks brought to Tulketh in 1123, who later moved to Furness: King, 'Stephen of Blois', 279–80; SD, *Opera Omnia*, ii, 267.

of Theobald of Blois, Stephen's elder brother, it would mean that Stephen would be provided for without diminishing the family lands.

Henry was at Woodstock at the end of March 1123, and there he took counsel with his men. It was imperative that the marriage of William Clito be ended, and Henry is reported to have spent large sums to persuade the pope that it should be annulled. It was within the prohibited degrees, though no more so than that between his own son William and Fulk's daughter Matilda. Henry of Saint-Jean d'Angély, who was in England to collect Peter's Pence, may have acted as Henry's emissary in this respect.[94] After Easter, Henry sent his son Robert, earl of Gloucester, with Ranulf Meschin, *vicomte* of Bayeux and earl of Chester, to Normandy, with a large number of knights to reinforce his garrisons.[95] The king himself remained in England over Easter, crossing to Normandy on 11 June from Portsmouth, having 'committed all England to the care and government of Bishop Roger of Salisbury'.[96]

By this date Roger was one of the most experienced and certainly the most trusted of Henry's curial bishops. Ranulf Flambard of Durham and William Giffard of Winchester had seniority, but were not so close to the centre of affairs, and Queen Adeliza was evidently regarded as too young. As viceroy Roger had two main tasks: to ensure that there was no outbreak of revolt in England in support of William Clito or his father, and to respond to demands for money, men and materiel. Waleran of Meulan had inherited some land in England, notably the great Dorset estate of Sturminster Marshal, but most of his lands were in Normandy and France. His twin, Robert, had great estates in the midlands, and their cousin Roger was earl of Warwick. Robert had been at the royal court in the early months of 1123, but not, apparently, later in that year or in 1124.[97] It has been suggested that Earl Roger of Warwick too was suspected of disloyalty, and that the powerful treasury chamberlain, Geoffrey de Clinton, was established in Warwickshire as a watchdog, with a large tenancy provided for him by Earl Roger.[98] In fact, there is no indication of overt unrest in England.

Bishop Roger's other task was to keep the supply of money moving across the Channel. The year 1124 was reported by the Anglo-Saxon Chronicle

---

[94] S. B. Hicks, 'The Anglo-Papal Bargain of 1125: The Legatine Mission of John of Crema', *Albion*, 8 (1976), 304–5.
[95] SD, *Opera Omnia*, ii, 267.
[96] *ASC* 1123. John of Hexham, SD, *Opera Omnia*, ii, 272, 'proxima post Dominicam Pentecostes'.
[97] *RRAN*, ii, no. 1391; Crouch, *Beaumont Twins*, pp. 23–4.
[98] Crouch, 'Geoffrey de Clinton and Roger, Earl of Warwick', 116–18.

to have been 'troublous'. The weather was very bad so that the price of corn was high; the quality of coinage was very poor; and Ralph Basset and his colleagues held a famous or infamous court as a result of which forty-four men were hanged for theft and six blinded and castrated. The Chronicler reported that many thought the punishments were unjust, and that men who had any property were deprived of it 'by severe taxes and severe courts'.[99] How then was Roger to meet the king's demands for money? One tactic he employed was to appoint sheriffs, who paid for their offices, to hold them for shorter terms.[100] He also raised taxes of various kinds, and he made considerable use of travelling justices who went through the country in teams. Their concern was with the management of the king's rights. They both punished infringements and raised money for the king in the form of amercements (agreements for the king's favour) and levies called assizes. A key figure was Ralph Basset, and so active was he that the canons of Plympton priory secured a royal charter quitting their lands in Devon from the 'gelds and assizes of Ralph Basset'.[101]

The money raised in England was certainly needed in Normandy. Henry hired Breton mercenaries,[102] and he embarked on a major programme of strengthening the ducal castles. Robert of Torigny inserted a list of his building work at this point in his chronicle.[103] At Rouen Henry strengthened the wall, added battlements, and supplemented the buildings inside the wall. At Caen he was responsible for the keep and for strengthening the wall, and likewise at Arques, Gisors, Falaise, Argentan, Exmes, Domfront, Ambrières, Vire, Gavray and Vernon.[104] In fact there was a rolling programme of castle building (see below, pp. 303–4) and Robert fails to mention the castles most vulnerable if the conspirators decided to rise: Evreux, Breteuil, Pacy, Ivry and the frontier castles of Nonancourt, Tillières and Verneuil. As in 1118, the king needed to make sure his defences were in good order and his garrisons reinforced with knights from the royal household.

During September 1123, Waleran, Amaury and their co-conspirators met at La Croix-Saint-Leufroy. Henry got wind of the meeting: it was not easy, after all, for several nobles and their retinues to meet in this way without attracting comment. La Croix was the site of an abbey, and either then or later Count Waleran built a castle there.[105] The king gathered an army at Rouen and left the city without disclosing his intentions. What he did do was to summon one of the conspirators, Hugh de Montfort, to his

---

[99] *ASC* E 1124. [100] For the rest of this paragraph cf. Green, *GOE*, chapter 4.
[101] *RRAN*, ii, no. 1515. [102] SD, *Opera Omnia*, ii, 274.
[103] Robert of Torigny, *Chronicle*, 106–7.
[104] Roger of Wendover, *Flores Historiarum*, ii, 50. [105] OV, vi, 474.

presence, ordering him to hand over his stronghold of Montfort-sur-Risle. Henry presumably judged that Hugh would be most likely to crack under pressure and provide enough evidence for the king to round up the others. Hugh agreed to hand over the castle, and was dispatched with an escort to receive the keys. As soon as he was out of the king's sight, however, he spurred on ahead of his companions and, without dismounting, told his brother and his wife to guard the fortress well because the king was on his way with his forces. He galloped on to Waleran's castle of Brionne, and warned Waleran to arm himself for battle. The angry king decided to try to capture Montfort whilst it was unprepared; he succeeded in firing the town and secured all the fortifications except the citadel. Robert of Gloucester and Nigel d'Aubigny brought up a strong force from the Cotentin to besiege the castle. After a month, when they realised that no help would be forthcoming from their fellow conspirators, they decided to make peace, and handed over the tower.[106]

Henry now had to proceed against Waleran's castles one by one. He went to Pont-Audemer, where his forces attacked and burned the town, whilst the Bretons hunted for treasure concealed by the merchants in the wells and cellars. The castle was besieged, and the surrounding countryside for more than twenty miles was burned. The garrison of 140 knights included Frenchmen as well as Normans.[107] According to Orderic, Henry himself took personal charge of the siege. Like a *tiro*, a young knight, he rushed about providing help wherever it was needed. He gave instructions for the building of a siege tower or belfry, some twenty-four feet high, from which archers and slingers fought, and machines hurled rocks into the castle.[108] By December, when the siege had lasted seven weeks, the men of the garrison surrendered, and were allowed to leave with honour and with their full equipment. Many went to join Waleran at his castle of Beaumont, together with about two hundred from France, indicating that King Louis was actively supporting the rebels.[109] Although there is most information about the attacks on Montfort, Brionne and Pont-Audemer, the Durham chronicler mentions several attacks made by William Clito with the assistance of his father-in-law.[110]

Yet on the very day the garrison of Pont-Audemer surrendered, trouble broke out elsewhere, when an attempt was made to capture the castle of Gisors in the Vexin. The plan was to assassinate the castellan, Robert de Candos, on a day when it was known he would be unarmed, attending

---

[106] Ibid., 332–4.   [107] Ibid., 340–2.   [108] SD, *Opera Omnia*, ii, 274.
[109] OV, vi, 340–2.   [110] SD, *Opera Omnia*, ii, 274.

a lawsuit in the house of Theobald Payn of Gisors. At the same time the town was to be attacked by troops concealed in hiding. The plan went wrong: Robert was late and one of the conspirators, Baudry (possibly Baudry de Bray), threw off his hood and revealed his hauberk. Arriving at the market-place, Robert heard the commotion and when he saw fighting, he took refuge. Meanwhile the rebel commanders Amaury de Montfort and William Crispin climbed the hill facing the castle and tried to persuade the garrison to surrender. Robert de Candos had the town set on fire, and this drove the conspirators out of it.[111] A lull in the fighting ensued. According to Orderic, the king ordered a respite, because of the impact of the war on the ordinary people. He stationed detachments of his household troops in the captured castles of Montfort and Pont-Audemer. Ranulf (Meschin), *vicomte* of Bayeux, was stationed at Evreux. The constable Henry de Pomeroy was at Pont-Authou not far from the abbey of Bec, where there was a bridge across the river Risle, and a man named Odo Borleng was at Bernay, west of Beaumont-le-Roger. Odo, who was to play a prominent role in the battle which occurred in the following year, was evidently one of the captains of the knights of the royal household.

Hostilities resumed in March 1124. Waleran and his three brothers-in-law, under the overall command of Count Amaury, set out on 25 March to relieve the Beaumont castle of Vatteville, which was then being besieged by forces loyal to King Henry. They were blockading the citadel from a siege castle, which Waleran and his men captured in spectacular fashion, by snatching its commander from the rampart, by using an artificial hand with iron hooks. Waleran recovered his castle of Vatteville, which he handed over to trusted lieutenants. He ravaged the surrounding countryside for supplies for the garrison, and in one dramatic incident he punished peasants whom he found cutting wood in his forest of Brotonne by cutting off their feet, exacting a summary punishment for wrongdoing.[112]

Meanwhile Ranulf *vicomte* of Bayeux, still loyal to King Henry, was stationed in the castle at Evreux. He knew that Waleran was returning from the forest of Brotonne to his chief castle at Beaumont-le-Roger, and sent word to Henry's other commanders, Henry de Pomeroy, Odo Borleng and William of Pont-Authou, with about three hundred knights, to block Waleran's route.[113] Waleran's forces were numerically superior, and when

---

[111] OV, vi, 342–4.
[112] Ibid., 348. For discussion of Waleran's route, and the likelihood that Orderic was correct in siting the battle that ensued near Rougemontier, see Hollister, *Henry I*, pp. 299–300. Robert of Torigny located the battle at Bourgtheroulde: Robert of Torigny, *Chronicle*, 107.
[113] OV, vi, 348.

the king's men initially caught sight of them, their courage failed. Odo Borleng urged them to fight: he advised that the best plan would be for one section of the army to dismount and fight on foot, whilst the rest remained mounted. A force of archers stationed in the front line was to slow down the attack by wounding the horses, a tactic used with notable success at Brémule.[114] Odo had enough charisma to persuade the others to adopt this plan.

Meanwhile on the other side, the young Waleran was keen to fight, but Amaury de Montfort, who was with him, advised caution, saying that because the enemy had dismounted they would not surrender but fight to the death. However Waleran was dismissive of the risks and of the opposition, calling them 'country knights', not up to serious opposition.[115] He led a charge with a force of forty knights, but the archers once again proved to be the downfall, literally, of mounted knights, for they brought down the horses and the men were thrown off before they could strike a blow.[116] Waleran and two of his brothers-in-law, Hugh de Montfort and Hugh FitzGervase, were captured and imprisoned, with about eight other knights.[117] Amaury had a lucky escape because his captor took pity on him, and escorted him to Beaumont. William Louvel was captured by a peasant, but handed over his armour as a ransom and cutting his hair short (a chance piece of evidence that long hair was still not uncommon amongst knights) fled to the river Seine. There he gave his boots to a boatman for his passage money across the river and managed to reach home barefoot. Henry was at Caen when the battle took place, and was said to be so surprised at news of the victory that he had to go to the battlefield to see for himself.[118]

The king spent Easter 1124 at Rouen, where he sat in judgement on the rebels. The leaders, Waleran, Hugh FitzGervase and Hugh de Montfort, were sent to England in captivity, but a sterner fate awaited their lieutenants. Geoffrey de Tourville and Odard du Pin were blinded for the crime of treason, and Henry ordered the same punishment for Luc de la Barre. According to Orderic, the count of Flanders remonstrated that it was not customary to mutilate knights captured in war in the service of their lords,

---

[114] Morillo, *Warfare under the Anglo-Norman Kings*, pp. 156–7, 173–4.
[115] Waleran's description *pagenses et gregarii* is not easy to translate precisely, but the sense is clear: they were second-raters (OV, vi, 350–1); J. O. Prestwich, *The Place of War in English History 1066–1214*, ed. M. Prestwich (Woodbridge, 2004), p. 128n. and see note for a discussion of the translation of these terms.
[116] *GND*, ii, 234.
[117] HH, p. 472. According to this account, William de Tancarville may have had overall command.
[118] Robert of Torigny, *Chronicle*, 107.

only to be told that Geoffrey and Odard had been Henry's liege men and had broken their allegiance. Luc had never done homage. He had fought against Henry at Pont-Audemer, but, although he had been allowed to depart with his horses and baggage, he had then given his support to Henry's enemies (and in so doing had contravened the laws of war). In addition he had composed rude songs about the king and had sung them in public. The king's orders were carried out on the first two men, but Luc committed suicide by beating his brains out against the walls of his prison cell.

Henry's ruthlessness has to be understood not only in terms of personality, but also in context. This region of Normandy was difficult to rule, and holding the frontier was a military operation. Henry had been able to depend on the unswerving support of Robert of Beaumont, count of Meulan. He must have believed the count's twin sons would continue in the same tradition, and so had entrusted Breteuil to the younger twin. This was not an easy task, and it was by no means certain by 1123 that Robert (earl of Leicester) would succeed. There is no evidence that Robert was disloyal, but his elder twin had obviously decided to flex his muscles. Moreover, as in the case of Breteuil and Mortain in 1112, the problem was that even if Henry captured Waleran himself, there was no guarantee that his loyal castellans would not continue to fight, as was now the case. Morin du Pin had put his castles in a state of defence,[119] and Brionne and Vatteville were still holding out. Henry proceeded to besiege Brionne in April and built two siege castles there. The castle garrison finally surrendered, but not until the town had burned down. Vatteville surrendered next, and here the king ordered the castle to be razed to the ground. Henry then ordered Waleran to instruct Morin to surrender, which he did. Henry held the steward to have been responsible for inciting his young master to rebel, and so he was sent into exile.[120] Orderic relates that in the very week that the sentences were passed, the lords of seven castles in the region round Lisieux and the pays d'Ouche (see map 3) were planning to join the rebels.[121] Hugh du Plessis had seized Pont-Erchenfray for the rebels, and other castellans had come to terms because they were not strong enough to hold out.

Meanwhile Henry's efforts to annul his nephew's marriage were successful. The matter had been raised at Chartres in March, but without a conclusive outcome.[122] In June Cardinal John of Crema was appointed as the pope's legate to hear the matter, and the marriage was quickly recognised as falling within the prohibited decrees. It was annulled, and those districts

---

[119] OV, vi, 354.   [120] Ibid., 354–6.   [121] Ibid., 356.
[122] J. Chartrou, *L'Anjou de 1109 à 1151* (Paris, 1928), pp. 17–18.

where it continued to be recognised were threatened with interdict.[123] On 26 August, the pope ordered the bishops of Chartres, Orléans and Paris to proceed with interdicts against those who did not comply. Count Fulk was so angry he put the papal envoys in prison; as a consequence he was excommunicated and his lands were placed under interdict.[124] In fact the marriage plan might have been resurrected, because in December 1124 Pope Calixtus died, and with him his annulment of the marriage. However, without backers William Clito could get nowhere. In the words of Orderic, he was left to resume his wandering life with his faithful companions, Helias of Saint-Saëns and Tirel of Mainières.[125]

Henry had called for help in his present difficulties from his son-in-law, the emperor. In May at an imperial diet at Bamberg it had been decided to summon an army to be sent against Saxony.[126] The emperor decided instead, however, to march against Rheims, in order to help his father-in-law. The fact that he was prepared to do so in itself provides an interesting insight into the close relations between the two courts at this time: an attack on Rheims might divert Louis VI from launching an attack against Henry I.[127] Louis's response to the threat of invasion was to invoke the aid of Saint Denis, and then to take the standard of the Vexin, the county which, Suger claimed, Louis held in fief from the abbey of Saint-Denis, from the high altar of the abbey church. He rushed out against the enemy, calling upon the great lords of France, including Count Theobald, for assistance.

In fact the imperial army turned back at Metz without invading, but the episode allowed Suger to present his subject, King Louis, in a heroic light, whilst also emphasising the role of Saint Denis as the foremost protector of the realm. Meanwhile, Henry I and his son-in-law were still working in partnership, for whilst Louis was at Rheims to face the imperial army, Henry planned to seize, or at least to devastate, the Vexin with the help of Count Theobald. Amaury de Montfort, with support from the men of the Vexin, drove him off.

When the time came for Henry to pay his soldiers' wages, coin from England was used. It was found to be seriously debased, and the soldiers complained to the king. He was so infuriated that he sent an order to Bishop Roger that all the moneyers found guilty of debasement were to lose their

---

[123] Hicks, 'The Anglo-Papal Bargain of 1125', p. 307, citing the letter of Pope Calixtus, *Recueil des Historiens de France*, xv, 251; Stroll, *Calixtus II*, pp. 164–7.
[124] J. Chartrou, *L'Anjou de 1109 à 1151* (Paris, 1928), p. 18.
[125] OV, vi, 356–8.
[126] For the events mentioned in this paragraph see Suger, *Vie de Louis VI* (ed. Waquet), pp. 218–32.
[127] Leyser, 'The Anglo-Norman Succession', 237–9; Suger, *Vie de Louis VI* (ed. Waquet), pp. 218–30.

right hands and their genitals.[128] Accordingly, Bishop Roger summoned all the moneyers to Winchester, where each was duly mutilated.[129] Corporal punishment was the usual penalty for corrupt moneyers, though the scale of the reprisals on this occasion was exceptional. The author of the Anglo-Saxon Chronicle believed that it was nonetheless just, 'because they had ruined all the country with their great false-dealing'.[130]

The king's reaction to the intractable problem of maintaining the quality of the silver coinage had been once again to blame the moneyers. The evidence of the surviving coins on which the names of moneyers are recorded bears out the fact that an abnormally high number of the moneyers seem to have retired at this point.[131] The weight of coins seems also to have been brought under tighter control, and a number of smaller mints were closed, possibly because they were no longer profitable. A new issue of coins followed, probably in 1125, and it was not superseded before the end of the reign.[132] The switch to a fixed issue and the concentration of coining at fewer centres was a major departure from the pattern of frequent recoinages which went back to Edgar's reign. The king's direct profits from coining were probably reduced as a result, though this at the time may have seemed a price worth paying if the quality of the coins in which his revenues were paid improved as a result.

Henry had thus survived three years since the calamity of the White Ship, but he had achieved no lasting security. He had not fathered a son by his second marriage, and the rebellion of 1124 had shown that William Clito was an ever-present threat to his position in Normandy. He had managed to have William's marriage annulled, and he had defeated the rebels, but only if he could offer a realistic alternative to his nephew as his successor would he be able to breathe more easily.

---

[128] *GND*, ii, 236–8.
[129] *ASC* E 1125; JW, iii, 156–8; *Annales Monastici*, i, 11; ii, 47.   [130] *ASC* E 1125.
[131] There is a useful discussion of the pipe roll entries in Sir Ian Stewart, 'Moneyers in the 1130 Pipe Roll', *British Numismatic Journal*, 61 (1991), 1–8.
[132] Blackburn, 'Coinage and Currency under Henry I', 64–73.

CHAPTER 9

Matilda and the succession, 1125–1128

Henry seems to have stayed in Normandy for much if not all of the next two years. In the immediate aftermath of the revolt there was need to ensure that there was no further trouble, or, after the death of Pope Calixtus, that the new pope would not renege on the annulment of William Clito's marriage. In May 1125, however, the empress's husband died and, as a widow, she could have stayed in the empire or she could have remarried; instead she returned to her father.[1] She came back laden down with treasure, including a famous relic, the hand of St James, which she duly presented to Reading Abbey.[2] Matilda had a key role in her father's plans for the future.[3] Henry doubtless had not given up hope of having a son by his second wife, who was probably at his side in 1125, but if his own marriage proved childless, a remarried Matilda might yet produce an heir.[4]

Henry remained in Normandy during the first months of 1126. On 26 March he was at Sées for the consecration of the new cathedral in the company of the bishop, the archbishop of Rouen and the bishop of Lisieux. John archdeacon of Sées, the nephew of Bishop John of Lisieux, had been appointed as bishop of Sées, and in the next few years the bishopric and the chapter were reorganised, with the close personal involvement of the king. The bishopric was on the southern frontier of the duchy and part of it lay

---

[1] WM, *Historia Novella*, p. 4.
[2] For the treasures, see Leyser, 'Frederick Barbarossa, Henry II and the Hand of St James'. For a discussion of the Reading monks' claim that Henry had given them the relic, see *Reading Abbey Cartularies*, i, 19 and no. 5 and n. Matthew Paris, who may have been relying on a Reading source, claimed that the hand was sent by Henry at the time of his last crossing to Normandy: *Chronica Majora*, ed. H.R. Luard, 7 vols., RS (London, 1872–83), ii, 159; Kemp, 'Miracles of the Hand of St James', 1–2.
[3] WM, *Historia Novella*, p. 4.
[4] *RRAN*, ii, nos. 1427–8: the first of these is the foundation charter of Reading Abbey, a text which may have been improved; the second Henry's charter granting permission for the foundation of Kenilworth priory. Neither records a place of issue.

in Maine, so a loyal bishop would assist in strengthening ducal authority there.[5]

Meanwhile there was the empress's future to be sorted out, and what was to happen if Henry died without a son or before any as yet unborn child of Matilda's grew to maturity. Was she to rule in her own right or as guardian for a son? And how was her husband to fit into the scheme of things? At this time there was a preference for males over females in inheritance of land, but there were still tensions over the claims of collateral male heirs, such as brothers or nephews, as compared with those of daughters. Moreover, the succession to a crown raised issues of concern distinct from succession to land, which had been complicated by the successions of Rufus and Henry over the claims of their elder brother Robert.

It was not unheard of, though less usual, for women to exercise public authority, usually in their husbands' absences or, as widows, during the minority of their children.[6] Henry's own sister Adela was a case in point: as wife of Count Stephen of Blois-Chartres she had been able to rule in his absence on crusade; as a widow she had continued to do so, and when her son Theobald took over the reins of power, she had remained a formidable influence.[7] Adelasia of Sicily, widow of Count Roger the Great, ruled Sicily until her son Roger II came of age in 1112.[8] Much rarer were instances of queens regnant. Urraca, queen of Castile and wife of Alfonso king of Aragon, had ruled Castile in her own right, but not without opposition.[9] In contemporary eyes the claim of William Clito to Normandy had much to recommend it, and failing William, Henry's nephews, Theobald and Stephen, might well have been considered to take precedence over the empress. In promoting the claim of his daughter Henry was thus going against the expectations of the magnates, and it speaks volumes for his political dominance that he was able to secure their public commitment.

Although Henry put his daughter's claims forward when she was still a widow, everyone was aware that a second marriage could not be far away. Henry's decisions could not therefore be taken hastily or inadvisedly. He had to be sure that he could carry the leading men of England and Normandy with him, and evidently decided to announce his intentions

---

[5] Arnoux, 'Les Origines et le développement du mouvement canonical en Normandie', pp. 39–55. For the dedication of the chapter to the Augustinian rule, see below, p. 279.
[6] J. Martindale, 'Succession and Politics in the Romance-Speaking World, c. 1000–1400', in *England and her Neighbours 1066–1453*, ed. M. Jones and M. Vale (London, 1989), pp. 19–41.
[7] Lo Prete, 'Adela of Blois'.
[8] OV, vi, 428–432.
[9] B. F. Reilly, *The Kingdom of León-Castilla under Queen Urraca 1109–1126* (Princeton, 1982).

over the succession before making public any decision about Matilda's remarriage, though separating the two meant that there was the risk of a backlash if her husband proved unacceptable to the elite. One obvious possibility was that Henry might well wish to recreate that alliance with the Angevins which had been ended by the death of his son. However, such a marriage for a daughter was very different from that for a son: in contemporary eyes marriage would mean his daughter joined the kindred of the counts of Anjou, and such lands and rights as she inherited would be taken over by her husband. According to the Anglo-Saxon Chronicle, when the marriage took place it displeased the French as much if not more than the English; but Henry arranged it in order to secure the friendship of the count of Anjou, and to secure assistance against William Clito.[10] Moreover there was also the question of homage for Normandy: if such a marriage was arranged, could Henry be sure that King Louis would be prepared to take homage for Normandy – not, presumably, from the empress as a woman, but from her husband or from their son – and not to take homage meanwhile from William Clito?

How much of this could be foreseen in 1126 is not clear, and Henry may not have been irrevocably committed to the Angevin marriage, though the comment of Henry of Huntingdon that the king delayed his return to England until agreements with the princes of France had been arranged in a manner that was satisfactory suggests otherwise.[11] Also noteworthy is the reference made by Suger to the fact that between June and August 1126 Louis made an expedition to the Auvergne, and Henry is said to have been one of those who sent contingents.[12] This seems to have been the first occasion such a contingent was recorded. It was a symbolic recognition of the military obligation owed by the duke of Normandy to the king of France.

Meanwhile Henry still had to make sure that the magnates would consent to his plans. He returned to England in September 1126 in the company of Matilda, bringing with him the rebels captured in 1124: Waleran count of Meulan, Hugh FitzGervase, and Hugh de Montfort. Waleran was sent first to Bridgnorth and then to Wallingford, and Hugh FitzGervase was held at Windsor.[13] On the advice of the empress and King David, Duke Robert, the most distinguished prisoner of all, was moved from Devizes, where he had been in the custody of Roger bishop of Salisbury, to that of Robert of Gloucester, at Bristol.[14]

---

[10] *ASC* E 1127.   [11] HH, pp. 474–6.
[12] Suger, *Vie de Louis VI* (ed. Waquet), pp. 232–40.   [13] *ASC* E 1126.   [14] Ibid.

Matilda and the succession, 1125–1128

It is clear from the witness lists of documents datable to the autumn of 1126 that consultations were widely held with bishops and leading magnates.[15] Conan of Brittany's presence is mentioned by Hugh the Chanter.[16] King David of Scotland also appeared, the first time he had visited his brother-in-law's court since his accession to the throne.[17] He was naturally concerned about the succession to the English throne, and for his own part wanted to ensure that he would remain in possession of his wife's estates in England. There were other issues, too, such as the pressure which Archbishop Thurstan was continuing to apply for professions of obedience from the bishop of Glasgow and the bishop-elect of St Andrews.

The court spent Christmas at Windsor, and the celebrations were marred only by a quarrel between the archbishops of Canterbury and York over whose right it was to place the crown on the king's head, and whether the archbishop of York could have his cross carried before him into the king's chapel.[18] The king moved to London, and there on 1 January 1127, presumably in the great hall at Westminster, with his wife and his daughter present,[19] a ceremonial oathtaking occurred. Notwithstanding their earlier commitment to Matilda, many of those present were subsequently to pay homage and swear fealty to King Stephen. Not surprisingly, since it was reported after the event, memories of the exact terms of the oath differed, and sometimes on important points of detail. William of Malmesbury wrote from the perspective of the Angevin camp, as his *History of Recent Events* was dedicated to Robert earl of Gloucester.[20] He wrote:

[Henry] bound the nobles of all England, likewise the bishops and abbots, by oath, that if he died without a male heir they would immediately accept his daughter as their lady (*domina*). He said first what a disaster it been that William, to whom the realm belonged, had been taken away; now there remained only his daughter, to whom alone the succession rightfully belonged because her grandfather, uncle and father had been kings and on her mother's side she was descended from fourteen kings from the time of Egbert. Edward, the last of the race, had

---

[15] *RRAN*, ii, nos. 1448 (archbishop of Canterbury), 1449 (bishop of Lincoln and Ranulf earl of Chester), 1459, probably autumn 1126 (archbishop of York, bishops of Salisbury and Lincoln, Nigel, Roger's nephew, Robert of Gloucester, William de Tancarville, Brian FitzCount, Eustace FitzJohn), 1461 (Everard bishop of Norwich), 1466 (Geoffrey archbishop of Rouen, the bishop of Durham, Winchester, Lisieux and Evreux, the chancellor, Rotrou count of Perche, Roger earl of Warwick), 1467 (the queen).
[16] Rotrou, Archbishop Geoffrey and the two bishops witnessed *RRAN*, ii, no. 1466, and Conan's presence at court is mentioned by Hugh the Chanter, p. 216.
[17] 'After Michaelmas' according to *ASC* E, which presumably means that he set out for Henry's court as soon as he heard of the king's return to England.
[18] Compare the versions in Hugh the Chanter (p. 216) and JW, iii, 164–6.
[19] JW, iii, 178 refers to Matilda's presence.   [20] WM, *Historia Novella*, p. 2.

arranged the marriage of Malcolm and Margaret, and Matilda, mother of the empress, was their daughter.[21]

Matilda alone could succeed, therefore, because of her descent from kings on both her father's and mother's side, but it is also significant that the chronicler makes no reference to the crown. Matilda was to be *domina*. The version in John of Worcester is much more conditional: if the king died without an heir and the king's daughter *did* have an heir, she was to receive the English kingdom under Christ's protection with her lawful husband.[22] John of Hexham says that the magnates swore to secure the kingdom of England by hereditary right to Henry's daughter unless Henry left a son born in lawful marriage.[23] The shorter version of events in the Anglo-Saxon Chronicle has one significant difference, that the magnates swore to give Matilda England *and* Normandy after his death.[24] The speech reported to have been made by Henry of Blois, bishop of Winchester, to the Council of Winchester in 1141 similarly refers to Normandy as well as England.[25] One is forced to ask, therefore, whether those present believed that the oath was to apply to Normandy as well as to England, and whether indeed such a commitment could be made in respect of the duchy. Orderic and Henry of Huntingdon, by contrast, do not mention the oath at all, either because of misgivings about its terms, or, less probably, because they doubted its significance.

It was Roger of Salisbury who had the task of explaining the significance of the oath to those assembled.[26] The bishop must have had qualms about his own situation. He had always been loyal to King Henry, but was the empress as confident that he would support her? The fact that Duke Robert had been removed from his custody may be one indication that his loyalty was believed to be wavering.[27] According to William of Malmesbury, the bishop later said that he had only sworn the oath to Matilda on condition that the king would not give her in marriage to anyone outside the kingdom without consulting himself and the other chief men, and that no one had been involved in arranging that marriage, or had been aware that it would take place, except Robert earl of Gloucester, Brian FitzCount and Bishop John of Lisieux.[28] The bishop may have simply been excusing his action in doing homage to Stephen after Henry's death, but it may well be that he did

---

[21] Ibid., pp. 6–8.   [22] JW, iii, 176–8.   [23] SD, *Opera Omnia*, ii, 281–2.
[24] *ASC* E 1127, cf. Newburgh, i, 30.   [25] WM, *Historia Novella*, p. 92.   [26] Newburgh, i, 37.
[27] Hollister, 'The Anglo-Norman Succession Debate of 1126', *Journal of Medieval History*, 1 (1979), 19–39; *MMI*, pp. 155–9.
[28] WM, *Historia Novella*, p. 10.

disagree with the king's decision about the oath, even though he was not prepared to make any public statement. Another piece of circumstantial evidence points in the same direction. The monks of Malmesbury abbey appealed to the empress and King David for help in securing a restoration of the independent status of their community, which was then in the custody of Bishop Roger.[29] If the monks believed that the empress and the king would help them to secure permission to elect an abbot against the wishes of their powerful diocesan bishop, it may be that these two were perceived as having views different from the bishop's on other matters.

The first to take the oath was the archbishop of Canterbury. He was unlikely to refuse because his claim to primacy over York was still being supported consistently by the king. Henry also granted Archbishop William custody of Rochester castle in perpetuity, and allowed him to hold a legatine council at London in May 1127.[30] Next followed the archbishop of York and the bishops; then, instead of the abbots, King David, and Queen Adeliza.[31] The queen's own position at this juncture was clearly delicate: clearly the king wanted to ensure that if she did bear a son that son's rights would not be imperilled, so her public acceptance of the plan was important. It seems that her reward for compliance was the grant of royal rights over the county of Shropshire.[32] The magnates also swore that whatever the king gave to Queen Adeliza they would maintain.[33]

When it came to the lay magnates, Robert of Gloucester, seated by the left foot of the king, was called first. Bishop Roger is said to have admonished the earl thus: 'Get up, get up and swear the oath as the king wants'. Robert however replied that Stephen was the older and should go first, and a kind of competition broke out between the two.[34] The abbots were called last, a relegation which evoked a protest from Anselm, abbot of Bury St Edmunds.[35]

Meanwhile at his own court King Louis asked his nobles to aid William Clito. William was distinguished, handsome, daring and honourable, the king said, but he had suffered from misfortune since childhood. His mother had been poisoned whilst he was a baby; his father had been captured in battle at Tinchebray; and his uncle had taken possession of the duchy. He himself had been entrusted to Helias of Saint-Saëns, who had taken him off

---

[29] WM, *GRA*, i, 2–8.   [30] *RRAN*, ii, no. 1475; JW, iii, 166.   [31] JW, iii, 178.
[32] WM, *Historia Novella*, p. 6.   [33] SD, *Opera Omnia*, ii, 282.
[34] JW, iii, 178–80; cf WM, *Historia Novella*, p. 8. Later William claimed that Robert had taken the oath first of all the great men after King David (p. 112).
[35] JW, iii, 180.

to be brought up in France to be brought up by foreigners in great poverty. Many sought to kill him, others to restore him to his paternal inheritance, but the latter had achieved nothing. Queen Adelaide bestowed on him in marriage her half-sister Jeanne, daughter of Rainer count of Montferrat, and Louis announced that he had given him Pontoise, Chaumont, Mantes and 'all the Vexin'.[36] William's position was transformed from that of a landless exile to that of a man closely allied by marriage with the Capetian dynasty, and count of a strategically important frontier district whose lords would be only too ready to lend their support to his cause.

Henry and Louis probably each knew what was going to happen at each other's court, and it was perhaps inevitable that Louis should act on behalf of William Clito.[37] Louis for his part probably expected that Henry would die fairly soon without leaving a son, or hoped that if an heir was named, it would be William Clito. He may well have acted on the issue of principle, genuinely believing in William's claim, and feeling that Henry's action was outrageous. He probably believed that with a base in the Vexin William had a good chance of securing the whole of Normandy. The description of the ceded land was simply 'the Vexin', though the places mentioned were in the French Vexin. William marched quickly with a force of knights to Gisors, on the Norman side of the border, and there 'the Normans recognised him as their natural lord'.[38] The lords of the Norman Vexin would also have been predisposed to offer support given their restiveness under Henry's rule, and William would be well positioned to launch further attacks across the frontier.

Before Henry had time do much, however, on 2 March 1127 Count Charles of Flanders was murdered before the high altar of the church of St Donatian's in Bruges, where he had gone to hear mass at dawn. The count was lying prostrate on the floor with a service book in his hand. A man named Burchard, nephew of the provost of Bruges, crept up and put the blade of the sword across the count's neck; startled, he raised himself up and was then killed, together with as many of his other knights as the assassins could lay their hands on. The ringleader of the conspiracy was Bertulf, the provost of Bruges, who was the count's chancellor and receiver of his revenues; his brother, Desiderius Hacket, was castellan of Bruges. Their family, the Erembalds, were of humble origin, but they had acquired wealth and power, and it seems that when Count Charles began to make

[36] OV, vi, 370.
[37] S. B. Hicks, 'The Impact of William Clito upon the Continental Policies of Henry I of England', *Viator*, 10 (1979), 15.
[38] OV, vi, 370.

inquiries which were likely to result in Bertulf's loss of office, the family decided on the desperate pre-emptive action of assassination.[39]

Because the count was childless, a succession crisis ensued. There were a number of potential successors, including Baldwin IV count of Hainault; Arnold of Denmark, a nephew of Count Charles;[40] and Thierry count of Alsace (see appendix I, no. 6).[41] They also included Henry I, his daughter, and his nephews whose claims came from Henry's mother Matilda, a daughter of Count Baldwin V. Henry may never have intended very seriously to advance his own claim, but he was very concerned to ensure that the successful claimant should not be an enemy, and, most of all, should not be William Clito. After the murder, the assassins barricaded themselves in the church and adjoining residence. Bertulf made contact with one claimant, William of Ypres, an illegitimate son of Philip of Loos and a grandson of Count Robert I the Frisian (d. 1093),[42] who was alleged to have been lent by Henry I a large sum of money and three hundred knights to finance his candidature.[43] However, his illegitimate birth was an obstacle, and the situation was too volatile for him to establish himself permanently. There were too many interested parties for any easy resolution to the conflict.

Louis VI was overlord of Flanders, and as the county was technically without an heir, he summoned the Flemish barons to Arras on 20 March. In his letter of summons he wrote of the disorder that had occurred, saying that William d'Ypres intended to establish himself by force, but that the cities would not accept him because of his illegitimate birth: although his father was noble, his mother had been a wool carder. Louis had rejected the idea of granting the county to one of his sons, so he invited the barons to make their choice.[44] Baldwin of Hainault offered to defend his own claim by battle, through a judicial duel, but on the following day, thanks to the influence of Queen Adelaide his half-sister, the nobles elected William Clito, a great-grandson of Baldwin V, as their count.[45] This was a second blow for Henry: if his nephew succeeded in establishing himself as count of Flanders as well as count of the Vexin, he would have ample resources and bases on two fronts from which to launch attacks on Normandy.

Henry meanwhile had been offering subsidies to those who opposed William Clito, including Baldwin of Holland, Thomas de Coucy, lord of Marle, and William d'Ypres. Even Henry's father-in-law, Godfrey of

---

[39] Galbert of Bruges, *Murder of Charles the Good*, p. 131.
[40] Walter of Thérouanne, *Vita Karoli*, *Patrologia Latina*, clxvi, col. 937.
[41] Galbert of Bruges, *Murder of Charles the Good*, p. 161.
[42] Ibid., p. 144.　[43] Ibid., p. 190.　[44] Ibid., p. 187.
[45] Walter of Thérouanne, *Vita Karoli*, *Patrologia Latina*, clxvi, col. 936.

Louvain, had an interest, through his wife Clemence's dower lands in Flanders.[46] Henry supplied his nephew Stephen with cash to distribute, and placed an embargo on trade between England and Flanders.[47] The violence which the count's murder had sparked off could not be easily resolved because of the multiplicity of claimants and the complicated patchwork of lordships and towns in Flanders. Henry's tactic now was to keep the pot on the boil to prevent his nephew winning a decisive victory. For their part, William Clito and King Louis tried to win the support of the towns and cities. Messages were sent to Bruges promising that the citizens' rents and tolls would be reduced; then at Lille and at Ghent the king and the new count took homage.[48] They next advanced to Bruges, where they were met by a solemn procession of the canons of St Donatian's. King Louis read and confirmed the canons' privileges including that of a free election of the provost; and the count granted a charter promising remission of toll and rent; both swore to keep the terms of their charters.[49] Soon afterwards the new count offered similarly favourable terms to the townsmen of Saint-Omer. At the end of April, Louis and William Clito besieged Ypres, where they captured William of Ypres as well as the castle, and thus secured Aire and Cassel. In early May at Bruges sentence was passed on the murderers, and William Clito seemed to have the situation sufficiently in hand for the French king to leave.

Whilst these dramatic events unfolded in Flanders, Henry was seeking a renewal of the alliance between his dynasty and that of Fulk of Anjou, which had been shattered when Henry's son died in the White Ship, by arranging for his daughter to marry the count's son Geoffrey.[50] The marriage had gained added urgency from the sudden revival of William Clito's fortunes through the backing of King Louis, but the empress initially reacted badly to the prospect of marrying the son of a mere count (and one who was much younger than she was). Hildebert of Lavardin, archbishop of Tours, wrote to her and mentioned her disobedience to her father's wishes.[51] Yet

---

[46] Ibid., col. 937. Clemence was a sister of Pope Calixtus, and the widow of Count Robert II of Flanders. For a recent review of her career, see Stroll, *Calixtus II*, pp. 193–9.

[47] Walter of Therouanne, *Vita Karoli*, col. 937. Galbert of Bruges relates how the townsmen by March 1128 were complaining that Flemish merchants were hemmed in on account of William Clito: *Murder of Charles the Good*, pp. 270–1. There is a reference to losses incurred by William's supporters in the charter he granted to the citizens of Saint-Omer: G. Espinas, 'Le Privilège de Saint-Omer de 1127', *Revue du Nord*, 29 (1947), 47.

[48] Galbert of Bruges, *Murder of Charles the Good*, pp. 157, 198–9.

[49] Ibid., pp. 201–6.   [50] Hicks, 'The Impact of William Clito', 17.

[51] Hildebert, *Letters, Patrologia Latina*, clxxi, cols. 291–2; for the date, see Chibnall, *Empress Matilda*, p. 55n. An alternative possibility, 1129, is there discounted on the grounds that the letter indicates Matilda and Hildebert were on different sides of the Channel.

she herself had taken the decision to return to her father's court rather than having a marriage arranged for her in the empire, or retiring discreetly into religious life, and must have known that her father was unlikely to give her any say in the choice of a second husband. In May the king held a council in London,[52] followed immediately by a legatine council presided over by Archbishop William. Archbishop Thurstan, still angry over his treatment at Archbishop William's hands the year before, stayed away.[53] The canons were a repeat of those which had gone before, and once again simony and clerical marriage were condemned.[54] Matilda was dispatched to Normandy for the formal betrothal, which probably took place at Rouen on 22 May 1127,[55] whilst her father remained in England. The first priority was presumably to raise funds to send to his agents in Flanders, and for the cash dowry that would be expected with his daughter, but Henry nevertheless crossed the Channel in August.[56] Although no trouble in Normandy was reported, the situation in Flanders was still delicately poised. William Clito had gone on the offensive by condemning more than a hundred of the conspirators to death, and laying waste the county of Boulogne.[57] The possibility that William might succeed in Flanders must have given Henry cause for grave concern.

As the months passed, however, William found it difficult to maintain the momentum of his early successes in Flanders. In the first place, he needed money for his campaigns, but when he asked for it from the cities of Bruges and Lille, the citizens were not unsurprisingly resentful, in view of his earlier promises to lower rents and taxes.[58] In August 1127 the citizens of Lille had risen up against the count, who besieged the city and exacted a huge sum of money from the citizens.[59] By the early months of 1128 his castellans were facing opposition, and his rivals, Thierry of Alsace at Ghent, Baldwin of Hainault at Arras and Oudenarde, and Arnold of Denmark at Saint-Omer, were making headway.[60] On 30 March the citizens of Bruges elected Thierry as their count and expelled William, as did the citizens of Ghent.[61] In these expulsions the money of King Henry, 'my powerful and inveterate enemy' as his nephew described him, was alleged to have played a part. William wrote urgently to King Louis to ask him to come to help.[62] By 10 April Louis had arrived at Arras and wrote to the citizens of

---

[52] HH, p. 476.   [53] Hugh the Chanter, p. 218.   [54] *Councils and Synods*, i, pt ii, 743–9.
[55] HH, p. 476; OV, vi, 390n; Chartrou, *L'Anjou*, pp. 21–2.
[56] Symeon of Durham, *Opera Omnia*, ii, 282.
[57] Galbert of Bruges, *Murder of Charles the Good*, pp. 304–6; OV, vi, 372.
[58] Galbert of Bruges, *Murder of Charles the Good*, pp. 260–2.
[59] Ibid., pp. 264–6.   [60] Ibid., pp. 265–6, 271.   [61] Ibid., pp. 277–8.
[62] Luchaire, *Annales de la vie de Louis VI*, no. 404.

Ghent, urging them to send representatives to re-establish peace between themselves and William. The citizens were in no mood to comply, and were claiming that the king had nothing to do with choosing a count, which was the prerogative of the peers and the citizens.[63] The king held several meetings; he besieged Thierry at Lille, but then hurried away.[64]

The reason for Louis's hasty departure was a palace revolution – the dismissal of the king's chancellor and seneschal, Stephen de Garlande.[65] Stephen and his brothers, Gilbert the king's butler, Anselm and William, who had each held the office of seneschal before Stephen, were members of a family which had prospered greatly in the service of the French king and as a result attracted envy and hatred. Stephen had succeeded to the office of seneschal in 1120, but as a churchman could not transmit it to a son.[66] In 1127 he tried instead to steer the succession to his office towards his niece's husband, Amaury de Montfort, but this outraged the queen.[67] Stephen and his brother Gilbert lost their offices; Stephen took refuge in his castle of Livry, which was attacked by Louis and Count Ralph of Vermandois. On the basis that 'the enemy of my enemy is my friend', Henry I and Theobald helped Stephen and Amaury.[68] It may well have been at about this time that Henry made a dramatic raid into French territory, reaching Count Amaury's castle of Epernon, where he stayed for eight days.[69]

Meanwhile negotiations for the marriage of Matilda and Geoffrey were proceeding, albeit very slowly. This marriage was one of three being arranged by Count Fulk for his own future and that of his family. Fulk, a widower, planned to leave Anjou and marry the heiress to the Latin kingdom of Jerusalem. In late 1127 or 1128, an embassy had arrived in France from Baldwin king of Jerusalem, who, like Henry I, had no son to succeed him. Baldwin had four daughters and had chosen the eldest, Melisende, as his successor. He sent to France for a husband for her, and Fulk was the lucky man, having already been to the Holy Land in 1120 and being capable of bringing the necessary resources and leadership to the task of

---

[63] Galbert, *Murder of Charles the Good*, pp. 284–6.
[64] Ibid., p. 293.
[65] Few details survive. Suger was evidently reluctant to discuss the episode, for which the prinicpal source is the account in the *Chronique de Morigny* (ed. Mirot), pp. 42–3. For the Garlande family see E. Bournazel, *Le gouvernement capétien au XIIe siècle 1108–1180* (Paris, 1975), pp. 35–40; for the fall of Stephen, see Bautier, 'Paris au temps d'Abélard', pp. 68–71; Grant, *Abbot Suger of Saint-Denis*, pp. 124–9.
[66] St Bernard regarded Stephen's tenure of the seneschalcy as inappropriate: Bernard of Clairvaux, *Letters*, trans. B. S. James (Sutton, 1998), no. 80.
[67] *Chronique de Morigny*, p. 43.   [68] *Vie de Louis VI* (ed. Waquet), pp. 254–6.
[69] HH, p. 478. Luchaire suggested that this probably occurred in June or July, *after* Louis's expedition to Flanders: *Annales de la vie de Louis VI*, no. 414.

ruling the crusader kingdom. Fulk was given assurances about his future role: the delegation promised that within fifty days of his arrival in the Holy Land he would be given the hand of Melisende 'with the hope of the kingdom after the king's death'.[70] However, Fulk may have anticipated power even before his father-in-law's death, for Orderic believed that Baldwin had offered the crown to his son-in-law during his lifetime, and that Fulk had declined.[71] Fulk therefore planned to leave Anjou. Geoffrey was to be count there, whilst Helias, his younger son, was to marry Philippa, the heiress of Perche.[72] All three marriages thus depended on each other: Fulk had to be sure of his prospects in Jerusalem, and if either this marriage or that of Helias did not come off, the field would not be clear for Geoffrey to take over in Anjou. If Fulk did not leave the field clear for Geoffrey, the advantages of a marriage between Geoffrey and Matilda were, from Henry's point of view, diminished. Even though Henry needed to be sure, therefore, that the marriages took place, he must have been concerned about the delay, given that his own succession was still insecure until Matilda produced a son.

These discussions, and the arrival in the west of Hugh of Payens, the master of the crusading order of the Temple, aroused renewed interest in the crusade.[73] When Hugh reached Normandy Henry gave him many gifts and permitted him to cross the Channel. In both England and Scotland Hugh received many gifts of money which he could take back to Jerusalem, and many decided to follow him there.[74] It was a new departure for Henry to make such a public gesture of support for the crusade, but understandable in view of his concern that the crusading cause should not falter at this juncture (see also below, p. 278).

On 31 May (Ascension Day) 1128 Fulk took the cross at Le Mans, whilst on 10 June Henry was at Rouen to receive Geoffrey and thirty youths who were to be knighted with him. Great celebrations followed, described in some detail by the later chronicler, John of Marmoutier. A glittering world of wealth and chivalry is conjured up: the young men entered the hall where the king was sitting, surrounded by his knights. Contrary to his usual custom, Henry rose, kissed Geoffrey and, giving him his hand,

---

[70] William of Tyre, *Chronicon*, XIII 24; H. Eberhard Mayer, 'Studies in the History of Queen Melisende of Jerusalem', *Dumbarton Oaks Papers*, 26 (1972), 95–182.
[71] OV, vi, 390.
[72] K. Thompson, 'Dowry and Inheritance Patterns: Some Examples from the Descendants of King Henry I of England', *Medieval Prosopography*, 17 (1996), 55–6.
[73] For a good recent account of the order, see M. Barber, *The New Knighthood. A History of the Order of the Temple* (Cambridge, 1994).
[74] *ASC* E 1128.

asked him to be seated. He and his companions then took baths, a form of ritual cleansing, then they were anointed and richly dressed. Geoffrey wore robes of cloth of gold, a purple cloak, silken stockings, a helmet sparkling with precious stones, and a shield with a design of small lions. The young men were then equipped with horses, shields, lances and helmets. Finally from his own treasury Henry gave Geoffrey a sword of the finest workmanship believed to have been forged by Wayland the Smith. The celebrations which followed lasted for a week, and afterwards the count, his son and his daughter-in-law left for Le Mans, where the wedding ceremony was held, with further festivities.[75] The king conferred great honour on his son-in-law and his companions, five of whom are named: Jacqueline de Mailly, Robert de Semblençay, Arduin de St Medard, Robert de Bolio and Payn de Clairvaux.

It may safely be assumed that these celebrations were grand and protracted, but historians have obviously wondered whether this later chronicler embroidered some of the details. Some may be corroborated from other sources: the golden lions on Geoffrey's shield, for instance, are mirrored on those in his enamel portrait, which hung over his tomb and still survives. Moreover, it has been suggested that the golden lions had already been adapted as a badge by Henry, and thus been incorporated into the English royal coat of arms.[76] Secondly, the named companions of Count Geoffrey included Payn de Clairvaux, who is presumably to be identified with the man of that name who answered at the exchequer in 1130 for unpaid arrears from two years of the farm of Harting in Sussex.[77] This indicates that at least one Angevin had been granted a valuable estate in England: in 1086 Harting and Trotton had paid £120 and one mark of gold (six pounds).[78] The grant should probably not be viewed simply as largesse: it may have been part of the security arrangements for the married couple's future. Geoffrey and Matilda would need safe bases in southern England after Henry's death.

Exactly what security arrangements *were* made is not mentioned in the Norman and English sources, but the Angevins would have been very concerned about Geoffrey's position both before and after his

---

[75] John of Marmoutier, *Historia Gaufredi Ducis Normannorum et Comitis Andegavorum, Chroniques des Comtes d'Anjou*, ed. L. Halphen and R. Poupardin (Paris, 1913), pp. 177–81.
[76] For comment, see A. Ailes, 'Heraldry in Twelfth-Century England: The Evidence', in *England in the Twelfth Century*, ed. D. Williams (Woodbridge, 1990), p. 14; Ailes, *The Origins of the Royal Arms of England*, Reading Medieval Studies, monograph no. 2 (1982), p. 47; for a sceptical view that the lions had originated with Henry I rather than the counts of Anjou, see D. Crouch, *The Image of Aristocracy in Britain 1000–1300* (London, 1992), pp. 223–4.
[77] *PR 31 Henry I*, p. 42.   [78] *DB*, i, 23.

father-in-law's death. Matilda was granted castles as her dowry, of which her husband would have expected to take possession.[79] When her father died, Geoffrey would have expected to rule Normandy and England in his wife's name, but this may well not have been what Henry had in mind at all. Henry's interest was in grandsons, and he may have envisaged his daughter ruling (as his sister Adela as a widow had done in Blois) until her eldest son came of age. How much was spelled out before the wedding is not clear; the fact that the marriage broke down so quickly is perhaps an indication that Geoffrey's view of his situation did not accord with that of his father-in-law.

The marriage of Geoffrey and Matilda took place at Le Mans on 17 June, and was celebrated by the bishop of Le Mans, assisted by the bishop of Sées.[80] The Angevin marriage was achieved, but not without great financial cost, both for the wedding festivities and in providing the dowry which Matilda would surely have taken to her new husband. There are some indications of pressure on Henry's English resources at about this time, because the solitary surviving pipe roll records an audit of the treasure at Winchester taken by the two magnates who had most to do with the marriage, Robert earl of Gloucester and Brian FitzCount, who were sent to Winchester between Michaelmas 1128 and Michaelmas 1129 to review the situation.[81] In the following financial year there were sweeping changes in the ranks of the sheriffs and a marked improvement in the payment of the sheriffs' farms.[82] Count Fulk, accompanied by his sons Geoffrey and Helias, had a last interview with his daughter Matilda, now a nun at Fontevraud, before he left for Jerusalem.[83] If, as we might assume, Geoffrey was accompanied by his wife, it may have been on this occasion that the empress's interest in Fontevraud was aroused, leading her father to make a munificent grant to the abbey (see below, p. 209).

Within weeks came yet another swift turn of events: William Clito, whose cause had been prospering, was wounded and died, and with his death the focus of opposition to Henry's rule in Normandy was removed, for Duke Robert was now an old man, and still in prison. On 21 June William had inflicted a defeat on his rival Thierry of Alsace at Axspoele even though his forces were outnumbered.[84] Shortly after this, he escaped assassination, having been warned by his mistress while she was washing his hair.[85] He then joined forces with Godfrey of Louvain, and they besieged Aalst, where Godfrey's vassal was supporting Thierry. Many flocked to join

[79] OV, vi, 444.　[80] Chartrou, *L'Anjou*, pp. 21–2.　[81] *PR 31 Henry I*, p. 130.
[82] Green, *GOE*, pp. 65, 203–4.　[83] Chartrou, *L'Anjou*, p. 24.
[84] HH, pp. 480–2.　[85] OV, vi, 374.

William, prepared to leave their native land, such was their faith in him.[86] He was a brave and courageous leader who all too often fought alongside his men. Whilst riding to head off a relief force and urging his men to the attack, he seized a lance, which pierced the fleshy part of his hand. He showed the wounds to his friends and complained of pain striking his heart. Within days the wound had turned gangrenous, and he died. William's father, Duke Robert, still in prison, dreamed that he was wounded and lost his right arm. When he awoke he realised that his son, whom he had not seen for more than twenty years, was dead.[87]

Helias of Saint-Saëns and the other members of his household concealed William's death until the castle garrison had been forced to surrender. The lord of Aalst was taken to William's tent by the Normans and was shown the young count's body. He burst into tears, and returned with an escort which took the corpse for burial to the abbey church of Saint-Bertin at Saint-Omer. Over the tomb was an epitaph which began 'William, most nobly born and famous knight'. The news was carried to King Henry by a son of Odo of Bayeux, who brought with him sealed letters from William. The dying man asked his uncle's pardon for all the wrongs he had done him, and for the restoration of all of his supporters who were prepared to renew their loyalty to Henry. The king agreed, and was reconciled with many;[88] others, however, took the cross and set out for Jerusalem. Thierry of Alsace emerged as the successful claimant to the county of Flanders. According to Galbert of Bruges, Thierry was invested with all that Count Charles had held by both King Louis and King Henry, a statement which suggests that Henry renewed the treaties of 1101 and 1110.[89] Some years later and with the advice of King Henry, Thierry married Sibyl of Anjou, the promised bride of William Clito, and in this way Thierry stepped into William's shoes both as count and as Sibyl's husband.[90] Henry himself saw to the task of pacifying Stephen of Boulogne.[91]

William was clearly highly regarded by his contemporaries: 'Mars had died on earth, the gods lament an equal god', reported Henry of Huntingdon, who saw the young count as a hero.[92] William could inspire loyalty, especially from Helias of Saint-Saëns, who stayed with him throughout his life, and also from Normans who were not prepared to see the claims of William and his father set aside. As William grew to manhood,

---

[86] Ibid., 374.   [87] Ibid., 380.
[88] Amongst those who took the opportunity to be reconciled with the king was William of Roumare: ibid., 380.
[89] Galbert of Bruges, *Murder of Charles the Good*, p. 312.
[90] OV, vi, 378.   [91] Ibid.   [92] HH, p. 48.

his charisma and courage made him a focus of support. With his death, however, 'all the power and daring of those who had supported him against his uncle crumbled away'.[93] William's death had thus removed the danger to Henry's rule in Normandy, and also the prospect of a hostile count in Flanders.

By November 1128 the king was at Rouen, where he permitted the papal legate, Matthew of Albano, to hold a council. The bishops and abbots of Normandy in the king's presence heard the legate condemn clerical marriage; a priest who refused to separate from his wife was not to hold a church; and none of the faithful were to hear any such priest say mass. Pluralism, and lay possession of churches and tithes, were also condemned. The king also issued a confirmation charter for Saint-Evroult at the request of Robert de Grandmesnil and Robert Giroie, representatives of the abbey's two founding families.[94] There are problems about the authenticity of this charter, but the attestation of William Talvas, son of Henry's old enemy Robert de Bellême, is suggestive of a recall to court at this time, possibly on the insistence of Geoffrey of Anjou.[95] Once again there are few hard facts about Henry's whereabouts during the winter months that followed, though he may have been at Argentan at Christmas.[96] What Henry needed to hear, however, was that his daughter was expecting a child, but as the weeks wore on, there was still no prospect of a happy event.

---

[93] OV, vi, 380.   [94] *RRAN*, ii, no. 1553.
[95] Geoffrey was William's overlord for Peray and Mamers: OV, vi, 446.
[96] *RRAN*, ii, nos. 1556–7. Note however that these documents cannot be dated precisely.

CHAPTER 10

Rescuing the marriage, 1129–1135

Henry spent the first months of 1129 in Normandy. Despite the lack of a legitimate son or grandson to succeed him, his affairs were prospering. He was at peace with King Louis and the new count of Flanders,[1] and thus felt able to show magnanimity towards some of his opponents. He sent for Count Waleran of Meulan and Hugh FitzGervase, who were still in prison in England and, after providing hostages, they were freed from captivity. When the king returned to England in July, Waleran went with him, and was restored to all his lands but not the castles.[2] Count Theobald was also a member of the royal party,[3] and not long afterwards his brother Henry of Blois, abbot of Glastonbury, was nominated to the wealthy bishopric of Winchester. The king was thus distributing patronage to his favourites, perhaps in part with an eye on the succession. However, no sooner had he returned to England than he was told that his daughter had been repudiated by her husband and had returned to Rouen.[4] This was terrible news for the old king, who had little option but to try to repair the damage as quickly as possible.

There is no contemporary explanation of the reasons for the quarrel. The Durham chronicler believed that Matilda had been thrown out by her husband,[5] but did not specify the reason. Dr Chibnall has drawn attention to letters by Hildebert of Lavardin, archbishop of Tours, one of which referred to a reconciliation between the count and his father-in-law, stating that the count had now agreed to his father-in-law's wishes.[6] This certainly strengthens the impression of a conflict between the count's expectations and those of King Henry. The breach is unlikely to have been trivial, because Matilda knew how much hung on its consequences, and that she would have to face her father's disappointment.

---

[1] SD, *Opera Omnia*, ii, 283.   [2] *ASC* E 1129.   [3] *RRAN*, ii, no. 1607.
[4] SD, *Opera Omnia*, ii, 283.   [5] Ibid.   [6] Chibnall, *Empress Matilda*, pp. 57–8.

Financial matters had been on the king's mind, and concerns about revenue may have played a part in arousing his suspicions about his chamberlain, Geoffrey de Clinton, who was accused of treason at the Easter court of 1130. The matter is only briefly reported in the narrative sources without any comment about the background. Geoffrey had risen from a relatively modest family to become exceedingly wealthy as one of the two 'treasury chamberlains' who provided the essential links between the itinerant royal household and the sources of treasure stored in royal castles. He had served in the household for many years in this capacity and in addition was sheriff of Warwickshire. Geoffrey and William de Pont-de-l'Arche (his colleague as treasury chamberlain), Bishop Roger of Salisbury and his nephew Nigel, formed a key group which managed the king's finances. The treasury audit may have raised initial disquiet about fiscal management, especially if there had been problems in raising the money promised for Matilda's dowry. Then, in 1129, Geoffrey's nephew Roger, archdeacon of Buckingham, was nominated to the bishopric of Coventry and Lichfield. Uncle and nephew thus possessed a very powerful base in the midlands. Moreover, the Durham chronicler believed that Roger had 'bought' the bishopric for 3,000 marks, a huge figure for what was a relatively impoverished see.[7] Perhaps it was intimated to the king that Geoffrey had overreached himself, like Provost Bertulf in Bruges and Stephen de Garlande at the court of Louis VI (see above, pp. 196, 200). The assassination of Count Charles could certainly be viewed as a warning to princes about overmighty subjects.

Geoffrey was indicted on the basis of suspicion or *infamia*, and the question naturally arises about the grounds of the charge: he may have threatened the king's life, or he may have been accused of being in league with Henry's enemies. The king may have instigated the charge, or he may have been spurred on by someone else. The suggestion has been made that Geoffrey's downfall was engineered by Roger earl of Warwick, who had particular reason to resent an upstart who had been foisted on him as a tenant, and who had the effrontery to build a castle only a few miles from the earl's own castle at Warwick.[8] Geoffrey doubtless had many enemies, and the earl may have been glad to see the back of him, but there is no evidence that his trial was engineered by the earl or by his powerful cousins, the Beaumont twins. According to Henry of Huntingdon, the charge was false.[9] The evidence of the pipe roll shows that Geoffrey was still in possession of his offices and most of his lands at Michaelmas 1130,

---

[7] SD, *Opera Omnia*, ii, 283.
[8] Crouch, 'Geoffrey de Clinton and Roger Earl of Warwick', 119–20.
[9] HH, p. 486.

and he was at court in 1131,[10] though he dropped out of sight not long afterwards, and by 1133 had been succeeded by his son.[11]

There must have been much anxious discussion at court during the winter of 1129–30 about the royal succession. King David had travelled south to his brother-in-law's court, where at Easter 1130 he presided over the trial of Geoffrey de Clinton. David himself, as a great-grandson of Edmund Ironside, had a direct personal interest in the succession. After Easter Peter the Venerable, abbot of Cluny, arrived in England. He is known to have travelled to Peterborough abbey, and to the alarm of the monks it was rumoured that the king had promised to subject the abbey to Cluniac observance.[12] He may also have been laying the groundwork for the first general chapter of all Cluniac priors, which was to be held in 1132.[13]

An issue of great importance to both the king and the abbot was the disputed papal election which had occurred in February 1130. One party of cardinals, including a number from northern Europe, had elected Gregorio Papareschi (Innocent II), whilst a rival group, chiefly from Rome and southern Italy, had elected Pietro Pierleoni, cardinal priest of Santa Maria Trastevere (Anacletus II).[14] Through the wealth and connections of his family, Anacletus was able to establish himself in Rome and he gained the support of Roger II of Sicily, to whom he granted a crown. Innocent accordingly had left Rome and travelled north of the Alps. He was welcomed in France by the monks of Cluny, for he was himself a Cluniac monk; he was then recognised as pope by a council of the French church in May 1130. By September he was at Cluny, where he consecrated the abbey church.[15]

It was by no means inevitable that Henry would follow King Louis in throwing his weight behind Innocent II. The English bishops are thought to have favoured Anacletus, as did King David, and there was support for him in France from, for example, Hildebert of Lavardin, now archbishop of Tours.[16] There were evidently misgivings and even cynicism in England about the goings-on in Rome. William of Malmesbury included in his *History of Recent Events* a letter from Peter, cardinal bishop of Porto, to the four bishops who were behind the election of Innocent, denouncing

---

[10] *RRAN*, ii, no. 1687, 1688, 1715–16: issued at Northampton in September 1131; no. 1798 may be later than this.
[11] Ibid., nos. 1933, 1744.   [12] *ASC* E 1130.   [13] Knowles, *Monastic Order in England*, p. 157.
[14] *Councils and Synods*, i, pt ii, 754–7; I. S. Robinson, *The Papacy 1073–1198* (Cambridge, 1990), pp. 69–78.
[15] OV, vi, 418–20.
[16] St Bernard wrote to Hildebert to try to persuade him to back Innocent: *Letters*, no. 127, in *Opera*, ed. J. Leclercq and C. H. Talbot, 8 vols. in 9 (Rome, 1975–7), vii, 305–7.

the illegality of the election.[17] For the Worcester chronicler the schism was the outcome of the rival ambitions of the Emperor Lothar III and Roger II for the control of southern Italy.[18] However, there was some support for Innocent II. Agents of Urban bishop of Llandaff seem to have been at Rome in February, and they accepted Innocent immediately.[19] In September Urban's men were once again in attendance on Innocent at Genoa.[20] Such unilateral action should not, however, obscure the fact that the final decision rested with the king.

Other voices raised in support of Innocent were loud and persuasive, including those of Peter the Venerable and St Bernard.[21] Both were influential figures, but what may have weighed most strongly with Henry was Innocent's relatively moderate views on investitures as compared with those of Anacletus. In other words Innocent was unlikely to overturn the settlement of the investiture dispute in England, whereas Anacletus might have done so. By the close of the year at any rate Henry had made up his mind to recognise Innocent, and he travelled to Chartres, where on 13 January 1131 he prostrated himself before the pope.[22]

Amongst the matters discussed by the pope and the king must have been the breakdown of the empress's marriage. The pope may well have wished to assist its repair, with the prospects for peace in France and recruiting support for the crusade in mind. We know that it was at Henry's request that the pope confirmed a charter in favour of the abbey of Fontevraud in Anjou.[23] Only a year earlier Henry had made a generous cash gift to the abbey, which may never have been put into effect possibly because the empress's marriage had broken down.[24] The terms of the new charter, said to have been issued in 1130, reveal clearly the king's preoccupation with dynastic matters, because the gift was made for the souls of his parents, his relatives, for the redemption of his soul, and for the prosperity of his whole realm. It may have been around this time that his daughter Juliana entered the community there, an added reason for generosity.[25] When the gift was renewed in 1130, the sums promised were slightly different and the second charter was witnessed by the archbishop of Rouen and all the Norman bishops bar one, as well as by Robert de Sigillo, Count Theobald, Robert of Gloucester, William de Warenne, Rabel de Tancarville, Hugh Bigod, Brian

---

[17] WM, *Historia Novella*, pp. 14–18.   [18] JW, iii, 232.
[19] *Councils and Synods*, i, pt ii, 754–7.   [20] Jaffé, *Regesta Pontificum Romanorum*, i, nos. 7421–2.
[21] *Vita Petri Venerabilis*, Migne, *Patrologiae Latina*, clxxxix, 20; for comment see OV, vi, 418–21.
[22] Ibid., 420.   [23] *RRAN*, ii, no. 1687.   [24] Ibid., nos. 1580–1.
[25] OV, vi, 278. For Juliana's presence at Fontevraud, see *Grand cartulaire de Fontevraud*, ed. J.-M. Bienvenu *et al.*, i (Poitiers, 2000), nos. 99, 223.

FitzCount, Geoffrey de Clinton and Count Theobald's steward, Andrew de Baudemont.[26] It is tempting to suppose that the renewal of the gift and its confirmation by the pope were signs of hope that the marriage could be restored (see also below, p. 281).

By May 1131 Henry was at Rouen where, in an illustrious company that included cardinals, the archbishops of Tarragona and Rouen, the bishops of Chartres, Lisieux and Sées, and the abbots Suger, Bernard and Peter the Venerable, he met the pope once again.[27] The king, his nobles and, according to William of Malmesbury, the Jewish community of the city also presented the pope with gifts.[28] A major church council was then held in the city. On this occasion the king assigned to the abbey of Cluny one hundred marks of revenue in England, sixty marks from the farm of London and forty from the farm of Lincoln. Both Henry and the empress, who was with her father, appended their crosses to the document.[29] Like the gift to Fontevraud, this was a gift of revenue, not of land, and was perhaps made in response to a request from Peter the Venerable towards the costs of the great building work at Cluny.

It was probably not long afterwards that the king issued a charter for the abbey of La Trinité Caen, confirming its possession of the manor of Horsted given by William II, and of his own very valuable gift of Tilshead in Wiltshire.[30] Henry was obviously very conscious of family ties. Not only had Holy Trinity been founded by his mother, but his sister Cecilia was now abbess. Henry issued other charters of confirmation around this time, but it is the outright gifts, money to Fontevraud and Cluny and to La Trinité Caen, which are so striking, and which have led to the suggestion that Henry was experiencing a second 'spiritual crisis' around this time.[31]

There is no doubt about the munificence of his gifts, but this was what might be described as focussed generosity. Those to Fontevraud were obviously related to one daughter's marriage, and possibly another's entry into

---

[26] If this was, as is most likely, Geoffrey de Clinton the elder, then he was still at court. He was also present in the following month, at Rouen, when the king confirmed his own gift to the church of Saints Gervase and Protase of Sées, this second charter being also witnessed by the Beaumont twins and by Robert de la Haye the steward: *RRAN*, ii, no. 1688.

[27] *RRAN*, ii, no. 1691 n.

[28] WM, *Historia Novella*, p. 18. There was a large and important Jewish community in Rouen by this date: N. Golb, *The Jews in Medieval Normandy* (Cambridge, 1998), p. 201.

[29] *RRAN*, ii, no. 1691 and n.; later in the same year, probably at the council of Northampton, the king issued another charter confirming this gift, ibid., no. 1713.

[30] Ibid., no. 1692; *Charters and Custumals of the Abbey of Holy Trinity Caen, Part 1, The English Estates*, ed. M. Chibnall, British Academy Records of Social and Economic History, New Series, v (1982), p. 33. Tilshead had been worth £100 in 1086: *DB*, i, 65.

[31] Made by Southern in the earlier version of his Raleigh Lecture, 'Place of Henry I in English History', 163n. For further discussion of this issue, see below, p. 312.

the community there. His gift to Cluny was the latest instalment of a stream of generosity which over the last few years had been marked by the promotion of Cluniacs: Henry of Saint-Jean-d'Angély to the abbey of Peterborough, Abbot Hugh of Reading to the archbishopric of Rouen, and Henry of Blois to the bishopric of Winchester. Henry's munificence to La Trinité Caen can again be interpreted in terms of family piety. This was the house founded by his mother and where his sister had been abbess until her death in 1127. It may indeed have been her death that acted as a spur to Henry's generosity.

Other beneficiaries of Henry's generosity in 1131 were the monks of Cîteaux. The Cistercians were yet another new form of the religious life; while they had been going from strength to strength in France, as yet they had scarcely penetrated England or Normandy. The bishop of Winchester had been responsible for the first Cistercian house in England, at Waverley in 1128, but Henry's meeting with St Bernard at Rouen in May 1131 opened the door to their future expansion in England. Possibly around this time he granted exemption from toll on food, clothing and other necessities for the Cistercian monks of Pontigny.[32] St Bernard wrote announcing his intention to send monks to England, and in 1131 the king issued instructions to his officials, and especially to his reeves of Southampton, Hastings, Dover, Barfleur, Caen, Ouistreham and Dieppe, that the horses, goods and men of the abbey of Cîteaux were to be quit of toll, passage and pontage.[33] In the following year the king also issued charters to the fledging Cistercian house at Rievaulx in Yorkshire.[34] In 1134, probably as one of the last major benefactions he made, he gave a site at Mortemer in Normandy to a community which was struggling to get on its feet, and later was to adopt the Cistercian rule.[35]

Henry had returned to England in the summer of 1131, and it was possibly on this occasion that he had a near escape from shipwreck, and, according to the Worcester chronicler, promised to remit geld for seven years and to visit the shrine of St Edmund at Bury.[36] His daughter was still in his company, and at some point Geoffrey of Anjou decided to make his peace with his wife. Not only was she a great heiress, but the wealth and prestige of her

---

[32] *Le premier cartulaire de l'abbaye cistercienne de Pontigny (XIIe–XIIIe siècles)*, ed. M. Garrigues (Paris, 1981), no. 3.
[33] St Bernard, *Letters*, no. 92: *Opera*, vii, 241; *RRAN*, ii, no. 1720.
[34] Ibid., no. 1720, 1961, nos. 1740–1.
[35] P. F. Gallagher, 'The Monastery of Mortemer-en-Lyons in the Twelfth Century – Its History and Its Cartulary', PhD thesis, University of Notre Dame (1970), pp. 8–14.
[36] HH, p. 486; *ASC* E 1131; 'before autumn, after the earlier Feast of St Peter'; for the story of the perilous sea crossing see JW, iii, 202. This passage is discussed further below, p. 311.

father would assist Geoffrey's efforts to hold his rebellious Angevin lords in check. Henry, however, did not send her straight back to Anjou. Instead he decided to air the question of her marriage before a meeting of his council, which was duly summoned to Northampton on 8 September. There it was formally decided that Matilda should be restored to her husband 'who was asking for her'.[37] Then she received an oath of fealty from those present, both those who had taken it on the earlier occasion and those who had not.[38] The oath was clearly deemed to be crucial, because now the magnates could not claim, as Bishop Roger was later to do,[39] that on the first occasion they had given their allegiance only on the understanding that Matilda was not to be married outside the kingdom without their consent. The council was particularly well attended: both archbishops were there as well as the cardinal-priest of San Silvestro, ten bishops of English sees, seven abbots, the chancellor and his deputy Robert de Sigillo, Nigel, Bishop Roger's nephew, five earls, and a strong contingent from the aristocracy and the royal household, including, it would appear, Geoffrey de Clinton.[40]

On this occasion Bishop Roger received yet another mark of the king's favour. He received a charter confirming the possession of Malmesbury abbey 'as his demesne and own seat'.[41] The pleas of the monks for the election of an abbot so that they might regain their independent status had evidently fallen on deaf ears. The archbishop of Canterbury too received a mark of favour – a grant of the possessions of the collegiate church of St Martin's Dover – with the aim that an Augustinian priory should be founded there.[42] Both bishop and archbishop would of course be key figures in the transmission of power after Henry's death, the bishop because he controlled royal administration, and the archbishop as the person who would crown the empress.

Henry spent the next eighteen months in England. As always he was on the move: we find him at Dunstable,[43] at Woodstock, then at London.[44] At some stage in 1132 he gave the monks of Peterborough a fright by reviving the idea of turning their community into a Cluniac house. Henry of Saint-Jean-d'Angély had by now been ejected from Saint-Jean in Poitou; he had returned to Cluny and, so the monks of Peterborough alleged, promised that if he were to visit England he would be able to make this abbey Cluniac. He must have been very persuasive, because the king did indeed send for

---

[37] HH, pp. 486–8.   [38] WM, *Historia Novella*, pp. 18–20.   [39] Ibid., p. 10.
[40] *RRAN*, ii, no. 1715.   [41] Ibid.   [42] Ibid., ii, no. 1736.
[43] Ibid., nos. 1826–7. In the latter he granted the manor, borough, market and schools of the vill to the canons, reserving for himself the houses and garden.
[44] HH, p. 488; *Councils and Synods*, i, pt ii, 757–61.

the monks, and it was only when the bishops of Salisbury and Lincoln explained what had been going on, and that the abbot had been behaving treacherously, that the king bade him surrender Peterborough and leave the country.[45]

Henry may have visited eastern England in 1132,[46] and it is not impossible that he took the opportunity to visit the shrine of St Edmund at Bury, perhaps in fulfilment of the vow attributed to him by the Worcester chronicler.[47] By Christmas he was at Windsor and there, according to Henry of Huntingdon, he fell ill.[48] This was the first and only occasion on which he is reported as having been in ill health before the last week of his life, which is a tribute to what was basically a robust constitution, as he was now over sixty years of age. His illness must have heightened concerns about the succession: his daughter was pregnant, but there was no guarantee she would give birth to a son. Stephen of Blois was with the king, and it looks as though it was at about this time that he began to associate himself more closely with the royal court.[49] Stephen acted so quickly and decisively when the king did die in 1135, crossing to England and persuading the archbishop of Canterbury to crown him, as to suggest that his actions were premeditated. His plans may not have been widely known, because a meeting of Norman barons, having heard of the old king's death, would proceed to elect Theobald as their duke.[50] Theobald himself may have planned to make a bid for the throne, but we shall never know.[51]

Intimations of mortality must have sharpened Henry's anxieties about his daughter's pregnancy, but on 25 March, at Le Mans, Matilda gave birth safely to a son, named Henry after her father.[52] The king was spending the Easter festival 'at the new hall' in Oxford, that is, at Beaumont Palace.[53] His relief must have been profound, though he had bitter experience of how nothing was certain in dynastic planning. The baby was baptised on Easter eve at the cathedral church of Saint-Julian-du-Mans. Matilda gave a pallium to the cathedral, and her father gave a rent in England.[54]

---

[45] *ASC* E 1132.
[46] *RRAN*, ii, no. 1906; and see for comments Greenway's introduction, HH, p. clxviii. There was a vacancy at Ramsey between 1131 and 1133.
[47] See *RRAN*, ii, no. 1733. Hugh de Waterville may have been the custodian of the abbey during the vacancy. W. Farrer assigned this writ to spring 1132: 'An Outline Itinerary of Henry I', originally published in *EHR*, 34 (1919), 303–82, 505–79, no. 668. (Later published as a pamphlet.)
[48] HH, p. 488. [49] King, 'Stephen of Blois', 291. [50] OV, vi, 454.
[51] Theobald was said to have been angry that the Norman barons, having heard that Stephen had been crowned king, then decided to acknowledge the younger brother as their duke: ibid., 454.
[52] Robert of Torigny, *Chronicle*, 123. [53] HH, p. 488.
[54] *Actus Pontificum Cenomannensis*, ii (ed. Busson and Ledru), 432; *Chronica Sancti Albini Andegavensis*, in *Chroniques des Eglises d'Anjou*, ed. P. Marchegay and E. Mabille (Paris, 1869), p. 33.

Henry may have decided to cross the Channel once again as soon as he heard the news, but first there was business to attend to. His decisions indicate that he was placing a good deal of trust in Roger of Salisbury and his nephews. Alexander had been bishop of Lincoln since 1123. He was an important figure at Henry's court and a royal justice, and the king now strengthened the bishop's authority within his diocese. Alexander had built a castle at Newark in Nottinghamshire, and the service of his knights who formerly owed garrison duty at the royal castle of Lincoln was transferred to Newark.[55] He also possessed a castle at Sleaford in Lincolnshire,[56] and the king assigned to him custody of the east gate of the city of Lincoln.[57] The king may have been building up Alexander's power to balance that of two locally powerful magnates, Ranulf II earl of Chester and his half-brother William of Roumare.[58] Nigel the treasurer was promoted to the bishopric of Ely,[59] and Durham went to the king's chancellor Geoffrey Rufus, who may earlier have been a member of Roger's household.[60] Finally, the first bishop of Carlisle was consecrated by Archbishop Thurstan: this was the last English see to be created before the Reformation (see below, p. 272).

The news that Henry was once again intending to cross the Channel in 1133 reached Wulfric of Haselbury, a recluse in Somerset. Wulfric was said to have commented, 'He will go, but he will not come back; or if he does, it will not be safe and sound.' The prophecy was repeated to the king, who took it badly and checked to make sure that Wulfric had indeed said this. Wulfric bravely replied that he had no regrets, because he was not talking about himself.[61] Wulfric was an Englishman who had been a local priest and then decided to become a recluse. He was able to perform cures, one of which had brought him to the attention of the king and queen,[62] and he was able to foresee the future, though it was a fair bet (given the king's age) that he might not return from his visit to Normandy.

---

[55] *RRAN*, ii, no. 1791. The bishop was also granted a fair and permission to build a bridge at Newark: ibid., nos. 1773, 1770.
[56] WM, *Historia Novella*, p. 80.   [57] *RRAN*, ii, no. 1784, cf. nos. 1792, 1771–2.
[58] Ranulf succeeded to his father's estates in 1129; William de Roumare had inherited the honour of Bolingbroke from his mother. Both tried to asssert their power in Lincolnshire in Stephen's reign: P. Dalton, 'Aiming at the Impossible: Ranulf II Earl of Chester and Lincolnshire in the Reign of King Stephen', in *The Earldom of Chester and its Charters*, Chester Archaeological Society, lxxi (1991), 109–34.
[59] HH, p. 488.
[60] A man of this name witnessed Roger's charter for Kidwelly priory: Kealey, *Roger of Salisbury*, pp. 232–3.
[61] *The Life of Wulfric of Haselbury by John, Abbot of Ford*, ed. M. Bell, Somerset Record Society, xlvii (1933), pp. 116–17.
[62] Ibid., pp. 63–5; for background see H. Mayr-Harting, 'Functions of a Twelfth-Century Recluse', *History*, 60 (1975), 337–52.

The Anglo-Saxon Chronicler and John of Worcester date the king's crossing to 2 August, the anniversary of Henry's accession.[63] William of Malmesbury also gives the day of the week as Wednesday, but believes that it was 5 August, the anniversary of his coronation: 'God's providence jested strangely then with human affairs, that he [Henry] should go on board, never to return alive, on the day when he had been crowned in the distant past to reign so long and so happily.'[64] Worse was to come. On that very day there was an eclipse of the sun, described by William of Malmesbury and in graphic detail by John of Worcester.[65] The king had travelled to the south coast and had deferred his crossing even though the weather was fine. He was on the seashore waiting for a favourable wind when a sudden cloud appeared, the size of which had never been seen before. The day grew dark, so that men had to use candles to go about their business. The king and his companions watched the skies and saw the sun shining like the new moon, and then change its shape, growing both wider and narrower. The Anglo-Saxon Chronicler believed that the eclipse took place when the king was actually sleeping on board ship.[66] Though the sea had been calm and the wind slight, the king's ships at anchor were violently disturbed. It was said churches in Yorkshire were exuding moisture as though perspiring.[67] On the following Friday there was an earthquake, and on 8 August the moon seemed to change in shape within a short space of time during the evening. William knew what to make of this: the 'elements accompanied with their sorrow the last crossing of so great a prince'.

These descriptions have to be taken with a pinch of salt by the modern reader. Medieval chroniclers had a genius for being wise after the event, and the belief that natural phenomena were channels through which God's will could be revealed to man was part and parcel of their world picture. Eclipses, earthquakes, floods and storms not only proved how vulnerable mortal men were; they were prognostications of the future. A modern reader might well consider that if the weather conditions had been so dramatic, a king who had lost three children in a shipwreck was unlikely to embark on that day!

Despite the unfavourable omens, Henry crossed the Channel safely. In February 1134 the news came that his brother Robert had died at Cardiff,

---

[63] *ASC* E 1133; JW, iii, 208. [64] WM, *Historia Novella*, p. 22.
[65] Ibid.; JW, iii, 208–109. [66] *ASC* E 1135.
[67] This recalled a Sibylline prophecy, noted by John of Salisbury: *Policraticus*, I-IV, ed. K. S. B. Keats-Rohan, Corpus Christianorum Continuatio Mediaevalis, ccxviii (Turnhout, 1993), II, 15, p. 95; translated selections by Joseph B. Pike, *Frivolities of Courtiers and Footprints of Philosophers*, reprint (New York, 1972), p. 77.

whither he had been moved from Bristol, and he was buried with due ceremony at St Peter's abbey, Gloucester.[68] Henry made a donation of the manor of Rodley to the abbey to provide funds for a light before the high altar in memory of his brother.[69] Robert was an old man by the time he died, but while William Clito was alive, the king evidently felt it was too dangerous to release him, and after William's death it was simpler to leave things as they were. The contrast between the fate of Robert, imprisoned for over twenty-seven years, and that of Edgar the Aetheling, who had after 1070 made his peace with the Normans and lived on into the 1120s, is striking.[70] Edgar evidently ceased to be regarded as a political threat: he had an honourable career as a soldier, and a modest estate on which to live. By contrast, Henry had had no compunction about keeping his own brother securely imprisoned, though Robert was said to have been provided with every kind of delicacy to eat.[71] It was only later that the story that Henry had had his brother blinded began to circulate, and perhaps arose because Duke Robert was confused with William of Mortain.[72] Later too came stories that Robert had been given or taken liberty and had tried to raise a force against Henry. The French chronicler Geoffrey de Vigeois, writing before 1184, claimed that Henry had paroled his brother on certain conditions, but that Robert had raised a force and been recaptured. The chronicler adds that he did not need to be recaptured a third time, that is, that there was no point in further escapes.[73] A similar story was repeated by the St Albans chroniclers, Roger of Wendover and Matthew Paris, no friends of strong kings.[74] It is not impossible that Robert did try to escape: after all, Ranulf Flambard had successfully escaped from the Tower of London in 1101. Blinding was a way of ensuring that rivals were no longer a threat, though it seems unlikely Robert was deliberately blinded on the king's orders. Little would be achieved by it, since his son was still free.

---

[68] JW, iii, 212.
[69] *Historia et Cartularium Sancti Petri Gloucestriae*, ed. W. H. Hart, 3 vols., RS (London, 1863–7), i, 110–11.
[70] WM, GRA, i, 416; Hooper, 'Edgar the Aetheling', 211.
[71] WM, GRA, i, 706. Two entries in the 1130 pipe roll under London and Middlesex were payments for an allowance for bread and for ornaments for an unnamed count of the Normans: *PR 31 Henry I*, pp. 144, 148. These may have been for Robert, but it seems unlikely that the sheriffs of London would have been responsible for purchasing bread for Robert, who was then, so far as is known, in prison in the west.
[72] Roger of Howden, *Gesta Henrici Secundi Benedicti Abbatis*, ed. W. Stubbs, 2 vols., RS (London, 1867), i, 330: 'excaecavit eum'; HH, pp. 698–9.
[73] *Recueil des historiens des Gaules et de la France*, xii, 432, and see above.
[74] Roger of Wendover, *Flores Historiarum*, ii, 39; Matthew Paris, *Historia Anglorum, sive, ut vulgo dicitur, historia minor. Item, ejusdem abbreviatio chronicorum Angliae*, ed. F. Madden, 3 vols., RS (London, 1866–9), i, 212–13; *Chronica Majora*, ii, 133.

What may well have happened, of course, is that his eyesight failed as he grew old. It is interesting nevertheless that within fifty years it was believed that Henry was capable of such an act.

Matilda had joined her father in Rouen in 1134 during her second pregnancy, when her eldest son, Henry, may have been with her. On 3 June her second son was born at Rouen, and was named Geoffrey after his father. Matilda fell desperately ill, and her life was despaired of. She distributed her wealth to orphans, widows, the poor, and particularly churches and to monasteries. To Bec she gave gold, silver and precious stones, and expressed her wish to be buried there. Her father, however, initially refused to grant her wish and said that Rouen, the resting place of Rollo and William Longsword, was more appropriate as her final resting place. He finally agreed to her wishes, and in the event she recovered her health.[75]

Henry remained in Normandy, delighting, it was said, in his grandsons, but as the empress recovered, relations with her father deteriorated. Roger of Howden, writing much later, claimed that the earls and barons of all Henry's dominions were commanded to swear fealty to the empress and her son Henry. If such a ceremony occurred, it presumably took place in Normandy.[76] There were various problems over the custody of castles, which would be crucial in any contested succession. One was over the castles of Robert de Bellême, who probably died about this time, for Henry allowed Robert's son William Talvas to inherit the lands, but not the castles.[77] Secondly, Matilda's marriage portion was said to have included the custody of certain castles, and it appears her father had refused to hand these over.[78] Thirdly, however, it was reported by Robert of Torigny that Geoffrey and Matilda wanted Henry to take an oath of allegiance about the custody of *all* the castles of England and Normandy.[79] If this version is correct, then what Geoffrey and Matilda wanted was a public ratification of the succession, in which Geoffrey's role was acknowledged, and this the king was simply not prepared to do. Henry evidently wished attention to be focussed on the prospects of his grandson, perhaps hoping that he himself would live long enough for young Henry to be able to govern himself immediately, or after only a short regency. Yet contemporaries would have assumed that after the old king's death Geoffrey ought to rule by right of his wife. Matilda herself seems to have come round to this point of view, for Henry of Huntingdon certainly believed that she stirred up the disagreement which soured the

---

[75] Robert of Torigny, *Chronicle*, 123–4.
[76] Roger of Howden, *Chronica*, i, 187; Chibnall, *Empress Matilda*, p. 61.
[77] Roger of Howden, *Chronica*, i, 128. Robert was still living in 1130: *PR 31 Henry I*, p. 112.
[78] OV, vi, 444.   [79] Robert of Torigny, *Chronicle*, 128.

last months of the king's life.[80] Henry's refusal to give assurances, and the resulting estrangement from his daughter, made it much harder to ensure a peaceful transition of authority after his death.[81]

On this issue contemporaries may well have believed Henry was wrong not to give pledges for the future. If Matilda was to succeed without opposition, she would need to command the loyalty of those who held royal and ducal castles. As part of the supposed agreement between Duke William and Harold Godwinson in Normandy in 1064 when Harold swore to recognise William as Edward the Confessor's heir, Harold is said to have agreed to fortify Dover at his expense for William's knights, and to supply the garrisons of other castles to be fortified in places chosen by the duke.[82] This agreement could have served as a model for that negotiated at the time of Matilda's wedding: she would have expected at the least that the castles in the towns that were part of her dowry, Argentan, Exmes, and Domfront, would be handed over, and some kind of security given about the transfer of other important strongholds.[83] Henry, however, was not prepared to surrender any power to his daughter and her husband, though there are signs that he may have been trying to ease the way for her, by ensuring Dover was in the custody of her brother, for example, and possibly by making concessions to the citizens of London.

Henry's stubborn retention of his daughter's dowry angered his son-in-law, who proceeded to flout Henry's wishes, and annoyed him further by besieging another son-in-law, Roscelin of Beaumont-sur-Sarthe, and burning his castle to the ground. At this juncture, according to Orderic, the king was so enraged that he was tempted to return to England taking his daughter-in-law with him.[84] Henry perhaps envisaged a regency council in England which would include Matilda's brother Robert of Gloucester, the archbishop of Canterbury, and the bishop of Salisbury, until her son Henry was old enough to be crowned.

The future fate of Normandy in Henry's plans is not clear: presumably the duchy was to pass with the kingdom to his grandson Henry, but trouble was brewing in Normandy. Roger de Tosny in particular fell under suspicion, and the king sent his own knights to garrison Roger's castle of Conches.[85] The situation along the southern frontier was uneasy. William Talvas was aggrieved because of the king's failure to concede custody of his family's

---

[80] HH, p. 490; Robert of Torigny, *Chronicle*, 125.   [81] WM, *Historia Novella*, pp. xli–xlii.
[82] *The Gesta Guillelmi of William of Poitiers* (ed. Davis and Chibnall), p. 70.
[83] These castles were handed over to Matilda immediately after her father's death by Wigan 'Algason', King Henry's *vicomte*: OV, vi, 454.
[84] Ibid., 444.   [85] Ibid.

castles, and he repeatedly refused to answer Henry's summons to court. Eventually Henry disseised him, and in September he went over formally to the count of Anjou.[86]

One indication of trouble was Henry's renewal and strengthening in 1135 of the Truce of God legislation.[87] Promulgated at Rouen before 1 August, this confirmed the basic principles of the Truce: that peace was to be maintained at certain times of the week and of the year, and that violence against particular groups of people was proscribed.[88] From the time of the Conqueror, the dukes had thrown their weight behind the Truce. Although the bishops were charged with dealing with breaches of the peace, they were reinforced when necessary by the duke's *vicomte*. In 1135, when men suspected of breaking the Truce were challenged to trial by battle, that procedure was to take place in the king's court. If anyone was convicted, the diocesan bishop was to have the first £9 of the fine, any extra going to the king.[89]

The situation was beginning to look serious in Normandy, and although the king was warned that there was also trouble in Wales, he postponed leaving the duchy.[90] From the start of August until All Saints (1 November) Henry prowled through the region round Sées, took into his own hands Alençon and Almenêches and others of William Talvas's castles, and strengthened the defences of Argentan.

By 25 November, however, he was in the north-east of the duchy, hunting in the forest of Lyons and at the castle of Lyons (-la-Forêt).[91] He came back from hunting at Saint-Denis in the forest of Lyons and had dinner, eating a dish of lampreys, though this was against his doctors' advice.[92] The king had intended to go hunting on the following day – he had ordered his huntsmen to be ready – but he fell ill during the night. Henry of Huntingdon described the king's symptoms: a chill, a convulsion, followed by fever.[93] Archbishop Hugh of Rouen was summoned to the king's bedside. Henry had earlier made his confession to his chaplains, but now he turned to the archbishop. The archbishop later wrote to the pope with an account of the king's last three days, and his account was conveyed to Abbot Peter of Cluny, who in

---

[86] OV, vi, 446.
[87] *Coutumiers de Normandie*, ed. E.-J. Tardif, 2 vols. (Rouen and Paris, 1903, 1896), i (i), 65.
[88] See above, pp. 105–6.　[89] *Coutumiers de Normandie* (ed. Tardif), i (i), 65.
[90] OV, vi, 446.　[91] Ibid., 448.
[92] HH, p. 490. Saint-Denis was identified by T. Arnold as Saint-Denis-le-Ferment near Gisors in Henry of Huntingdon, *Historia Anglorum*, ed. Arnold, RS (London, 1979), p. 254; for comment see *RRAN*, ii, xxxi. For discussion of the story about lampreys, see above, p. 6.
[93] HH, p. 490.

turn wrote to the king's sister, Adela.[94] According to this account, Henry confessed his sins once again, beating his breast, renouncing all evil desires and promising to mend his ways. The archbishop gave him absolution three times during those three days. Henry adored the crucifix, received the sacrament, and made arrangements for the payment of his debts and the distribution of alms to the poor. The archbishop asked him for permission to perform the anointing of the sick, to which Henry agreed. 'So he died in peace. God grant him peace, for peace he loved.'[95]

This is clearly an account of a 'good death', with no references to any unpleasant physical symptoms. The payment of debts and the distribution of charity was conventional, and mirrored what the Conqueror had done in 1087.[96] Orderic's account of Henry's last days supplies a few additional details: on the archbishop's advice, Henry revoked all sentences of forfeiture, and allowed exiles to return and the disinherited to recover their inheritances (his father too had freed prisoners). Robert of Gloucester was instructed to take sixty thousand pounds from the king's treasure at Falaise to pay the wages and gifts for his father's servants and knights. The king had ordered that his body should be taken for burial to Reading, and that all should devote themselves to the preservation of peace and the protection of the poor.[97] He died on Sunday 1 December, either as night fell (according to Orderic) or during the hours that followed.[98]

News of Henry's illness soon brought the nobles to his bedside. Amongst these were Robert of Gloucester, William de Warenne, Rotrou of Perche, the Beaumont twins and the bishop of Evreux.[99] When the king was asked about his successor 'he assigned all his lands on both sides of the sea to his daughter in lawful and lasting succession, being somewhat angry with her husband because he had vexed the king by not a few threats and insults'.[100] In this account Henry wanted his daughter – no reference to his son-in-law – to succeed. The author was at pains to show that there had not been any last-minute change of mind in favour of Stephen, as the latter's party later claimed, though the dying man could have made a gesture which was so interpreted.[101]

---

[94] WM, *Historia Novella*, pp. 24–6; *Letters of Peter the Venerable* (ed. Constable), i, no. 15, translated in R. H. C. Davis, *King Stephen*, 3rd edn (London, 1990), pp. 12–13.
[95] On contemporary descriptions of death, attitudes and rituals, see D. Crouch, 'The Culture of Death in the Anglo-Norman World', in *Anglo-Norman Political Culture and the Twelfth-Century Renaissance*, ed. C. Warren Hollister (Woodbridge, 1997), pp. 157–80.
[96] OV, iv, 80.   [97] Ibid., 448.   [98] Ibid.; WM, *Historia Novella*, p. 24.
[99] OV, vi, 448.   [100] WM, *Historia Novella*, pp. 24–5.
[101] *Liber Eliensis*, p. 285; John of Salisbury, *Historia Pontificalis* (ed. Chibnall), p. 85.

When Henry's old rival, Louis VI, died in 1137, he was buried at Saint-Denis, as he had wished; and as Abbot Suger pointed out (quoting from Lucan), 'Happy is the man who knows in advance the exact place where he will lie when the whole world totters into ruins.'[102] Yet Henry's wish to be buried at Reading meant a major effort to transport the body, at a time when leading lords had to look to the security of their lands and castles. Archbishop Hugh and Bishop Audoin had made the five earls and counts present swear an oath that they would not leave the king's body, except by common consent, but would provide an honourable escort as far as the coast,[103] perhaps to ensure that there would not be any disorder of the kind that had followed the Conqueror's death.[104]

On Monday 2 December the body was moved from the castle at Lyons-la-Forêt to Rouen accompanied by a huge cortège. At Rouen there were services in the cathedral, and then at night in the archbishop's chamber the body was embalmed, and filled with balsam.[105] Henry's intestines, brains, and eyes[106] were taken to Emendreville in an urn and buried there in one of his favourite churches, Notre-Dame-du-Pré.[107] This was the first recorded occasion on which body parts had been removed from the corpse of an English king, though it had been the practice for those of German emperors in the eleventh century. All the Salian emperors were buried at Speyer, and their entrails were buried in important churches near their places of death.[108] The rest of Henry's body was cut all over with knives, sprinkled with a great deal of salt, and wrapped in ox hides to keep down the smell which, according to Henry of Huntingdon, was already causing the deaths of those who watched over it.[109] It even, he wrote, killed the man who had been paid a great fee to cut off the head and take out the brain, although he had wrapped linen cloths round his head: 'He was the last of many whom King Henry had put to death.'[110]

The shortness of Henry's last illness meant that the leading contenders in the succession were dispersed, and uncertainty about the future only served to heighten the tension of an interregnum. The empress went quickly into southern Normandy and the castles of Argentan, Exmes and Domfront

---

[102] Suger, *Vie de Louis VI* (ed. Waquet), p. 286.   [103] OV, vi, 448–50.   [104] Ibid., 449n.
[105] On the subject of royal burials, see E. M. Hallam, 'Royal Burial and the Cult of Kingship in France and England, 1060–1330', *Journal of Medieval History*, 8 (1982), 359–380.
[106] HH, p. 702.   [107] WM, *Historia Novella*, p. 26.
[108] D. Schäfer, *Mittelalterlicher Brauch bei der Überführung von Leichen. Sitzungsberichte der Preussichen Akademie der Wissenschaften* (1920), 478–98, as cited by Hallam, 'Royal Burial and the Cult of Kingship', 364.
[109] HH, p. 702; for a modern account of embalming, see J. Litten, *The English Way of Death. The Common Funeral since 1450* (London, 1991), p. 37.
[110] HH, p. 702.

were handed over to her. Her husband followed with William Talvas, and was received at Sées and other castles loyal to William, but they made little further headway.[111] Stephen of Blois, who had been in his county of Boulogne at the time of his uncle's death, crossed to England and with some neat footwork secured the contents of the treasury at Winchester. On 22 December he was crowned by the archbishop of Canterbury.[112] Robert of Gloucester meanwhile had proceeded to Falaise to carry out his father's wishes for the payment of his household and mercenaries.[113]

The great men of Normandy were also meeting to discuss the future. One assembly, variously reported as taking place at Neufbourg (by Orderic) or Lisieux (by Robert of Torigny), concluded that Theobald of Blois, not Stephen, should be the next duke. In Orderic's version it was at this meeting that a monk sent from England arrived with the news that Stephen had been crowned, and because the assembled Normans held lands on both sides of the Channel, they decided to accept the *fait accompli*.[114] Robert of Torigny believed that Theobald had proceeded to Rouen and was in negotiation with the earl of Gloucester when news of Stephen's coronation arrived. Earl Robert duly handed over the old king's treasure to Stephen's men, and with his great estates in England and Wales to consider, he had little alternative.[115]

Henry's cortège, now composed of his household and knights from England, had proceeded from Rouen via Pont-Audemer and Bonneville to Caen. There was a long wait of about four weeks for a wind to facilitate the Channel crossing, and during this Christmas period, the king's body was placed in the choir of Saint-Etienne. Elaborate prayers were said: matins for the dead, lauds and vespers.[116] By this time it was becoming evident that the embalming process had not been entirely successful, for Henry of Huntingdon reported that despite the salt and wrappings of hide, a black fluid leaked through the hides and had to be collected by attendants, 'faint with dread'.[117] Finally the body was shipped across the Channel, with an escort of monks from Saint-Etienne. King Stephen, we are told, went to meet the funeral party, and by reason of the love he bore his uncle he carried the bier on his shoulders, and with his barons accompanied it to Reading, where the body was laid out.[118] After the celebration of masses and the distribution of alms to multitudes of poor people, the body was finally laid to rest before the high altar, in the presence of King Stephen, Archbishop

---

[111] OV, vi, 454. [112] WM, *Historia Novella*, pp. 26–8; *Gesta Stephani*, pp. 10–12.
[113] OV, vi, 448. [114] Ibid., 454. [115] Robert of Torigny, *Chronicle*, 128–9.
[116] P. Binski, *Medieval Death. Ritual and Representation* (Avon, 1996), pp. 53–4.
[117] HH, p. 702. [118] JW, iii, 216.

William of Canterbury, and many bishops and nobles.[119] No descriptions of the tomb survive: it may initially have had a slab, but at some point an effigy was placed on it, and there is a reference to its having been repaired in Richard II's day.[120] Henry's obsequies were thus much more protracted and elaborate than those of his father or William Rufus, or indeed those of Louis VI as reported by Suger,[121] in part because of the protracted journey to Reading, but also, perhaps, to mark the passing of a great king.

---

[119] WM, *Historia Novella*, p. 30; for a recreation of the funeral (with a reproduction of a picture of the funeral presented to the Mayor and Corporation of Reading) see J. B. Hurry, *King Henry Beauclerc and Reading Abbey* (London, 1917).
[120] *Reading Abbey Cartularies*, i, 107. [121] Suger, *Vie de Louis VI* (ed. Waquet), pp. 282–6.

CHAPTER II

The ruler

The best-documented aspects of Henry's life relate to his exercise of power. This chapter is concerned with his approach to rule, the limits of his dominions, domestic changes, political management, governance and wealth. His rights over the church are separately discussed in chapter 12. The aim has been not to provide a detailed account of governance in the kingdom and the duchy, but to explore how Henry tackled the challenge of power, and the significance of that rule for the development of the kingdom and the duchy, as well as for the link between them, strengthened by almost three decades of condominium. The approach adopted is thematic: the first section is concerned with frontiers and consolidation, the second with what might be called man-management, the third with governance, and the fourth with wealth and the economic context of rule. The picture of Henry which emerges here differs substantially on some points from that of other historians.

FRONTIERS AND CONSOLIDATION

As king of the English Henry had inherited territory and also claims to superiority over other peoples within the island of Britain.[1] He wore an imperial crown of a type inherited from King Edward the Confessor, and with it he inherited the idea of rule over different peoples. How effectively that authority could be exercised at any moment depended on circumstance, but it meant that the boundaries of his kingdom were not fixed immutably. When he took over Normandy from his brother, he had perforce to take into account his relations with the king of France. The boundaries of the duchy could be precisely drawn, and relations with Normandy's neighbours were on a very different footing from those with the Welsh princes or the Scottish kings. Naked territorial aggression was hardly going to work,

[1] For a succinct account see Davies, *First English Empire*, chapter 1.

and the techniques for extending power were alliances, especially through marriage, and the recognition of overlordship; yet Henry's situation in Normandy was not so fundamentally different from that in England as might be supposed, and on both sides of the Channel he was awake to every opportunity for expansion.

It has been argued that in the eleventh century the Normans had been aggressive land-takers, whereas Henry, either through inclination or necessity, sought only to protect what he had inherited.[2] Whereas his father had been able to invade England because the king of France and the counts of Anjou and Flanders were not prepared to make life difficult for him, Henry had to struggle against the hostility of all three. The term 'imperial overstretch' has been applied to the situation in which he found himself, and it has been claimed that even with all his skill and financial reserves Henry could do little more than maintain the status quo.[3]

However, when circumstances permitted, Henry could be every bit as aggressive as his brother and father had been. There was much more opportunity for Henry to extend the boundaries of his realm in Britain than as ruler of Normandy, and the claims of English kings to overkingship, already in existence in 1066, could be deployed against the Welsh and Scots. The ecclesiastical primacies claimed by the archbishops of Canterbury and York, and the perceived need to reform the churches of Wales and Scotland, gave added justification for intervention.[4] Churchmen, particularly those at Canterbury who nursed their own dreams of an ecclesiastical primacy over all the churches of the British Isles, were alert to these claims.[5] It is clear from their actions that the Conqueror and Rufus did not regard the frontiers of their realms as excluding expeditions against the Welsh and Scots, nor, in the case of the former, as preventing land-taking by Normans. The case of Scotland was more contentious. English kings' claims to superiority over kings of Scots were recognised from time to time, and the backing which Rufus gave to Malcolm III's son Edgar had strengthened the latter's material dependence on him, but the implications of acts of submission shifted over time and according to circumstance. Moreover, personal acts by kings of

---

[2] Hollister and Keefe, 'Making of the Angevin Empire', *MMI*, p. 250.
[3] Stringer, *Reign of Stephen*, p. 10.
[4] For the Normans in Wales see R. R. Davies, *The Age of Conquest. Wales 1063–1415* (Oxford, 1987), chapter 2; for relations with the Scots, J. A. Green, 'Anglo-Scottish Relations, 1066–1174', in *England and Her Neighbours 1066–1453*, ed. M. Jones and M. Vale (London, 1989), pp. 53–73; for Ireland Davies, *First English Empire*, pp. 7–9; B. T. Hudson, 'William the Conqueror and Ireland', *Irish Historical Studies*, 29 (1994–5), 145–58.
[5] M. T. Flanagan, *Irish Society, Anglo-Norman Settlers, Angevin Kingship: Interactions in Ireland in the Late Twelfth Century* (Oxford, 1989), pp. 44–9.

Scots, whether or not they could be construed to subordinate not only the person of the king but also the kingdom, were complicated by territorial issues. The boundary between the two kingdoms was not immutably fixed as in the west, local and conflicting centres of power followed in the wake of the old kingdom of Strathclyde, and in the east English and Scots vied for influence over the southern regions of Lothian.[6]

Henry was far from indifferent to claims of overkingship, and pressed them as and when circumstances allowed. He made two expeditions in person against the Welsh, in 1114 and 1121, taking submission from Welsh princes, and his relations with successive kings of Scots, though strengthened by his marriage to Matilda, did not prevent a continuance of claims to superiority.[7] His treatment of the Welsh, as we have seen (pp. 69, 132, 173), was adapted to meet the situation applying in different regions. In the south, Norman lordship was consolidated and extended where possible, into Ceredigion (Cardigan), which Henry granted to Gilbert FitzRichard,[8] and into Rhos, in south-west Wales, where he established a colony of Flemings (see map 9).[9] In mid-Wales his policy was one of divide and rule between the various competing families, offering inducements, and taking submissions, as circumstances dictated. Only in the north was Gruffudd ap Cynan able to maintain the independence of his kingdom of Gwynedd, aided by the mountainous topography of the area and by the fact that for the first twenty years of Henry's reign there was no vigorous earl based at Chester.[10]

In the north of England, Normans were moving beyond Hadrian's Wall by the early twelfth century: Richer de Boivill was established at Kirklinton to the north of Carlisle, Robert de Trivers at Burgh by Sands to the north-west, and Turgis Brundos at Liddel to the north-east.[11] It is

---

[6] G. W. S. Barrow, 'The Anglo-Scottish Border', *Northern History*, 50 (1966), 21–42; reprinted in *The Kingdom of the Scots*, pp. 139–61.
[7] On the death of King Edgar in 1107 Alexander succeeded 'with the consent of King Henry': HH, p. 457. There is no direct reference to David as king swearing allegiance to Henry, but he was present and swore the oath to the empress in January 1127: WM, *Historia Novella*, p. 8. For discussion see Green, 'Anglo-Scottish Relations', pp. 61–2.
[8] *Brut (RBH)*, pp. 71–3, *Brut (Peniarth)*, p. 34.   [9] *Brut (RBH)*, p. 53, *Brut (Peniarth)*, p. 27.
[10] R. R. Davies, 'Henry I and Wales', *Studies in Medieval History Presented to R. H. C. Davis*, ed. H. Mayr-Harting and R. I. Moore (London, 1985), pp. 132–47; for Gruffudd, see *Gruffudd ap Cynan: A Collective Biography*, ed. K. L. Maund (Woodbridge, 1996), especially the essays by D. Moore, 'Gruffudd ap Cynan and the Medieval Welsh Polity', pp. 1–59, at 39–46, and C. P. Lewis, 'Gruffudd ap Cynan and the Normans', pp. 61–77, at pp. 73–7.
[11] For the suggestion that Richer de Boiville came from the Norman estates of Ranulf Meschin, then lord of Carlisle, see G. W. S. Barrow, *The Anglo-Norman Era in Scottish History* (Oxford, 1980), p. 176; for Robert de Trivers, Sanders, *English Baronies*, p. 23; and for Turgis Brundos, T. H. B. Graham, 'Turgis Brundos', *Cumberland and Westmorland Antiquarian and Archaeological Society*, new series, 29 (1929), 49–56.

not clear whether or not they were acting on their own initiative, perhaps with the backing of Ranulf Meschin, lord of Carlisle, or, indeed, of David, prince of Cumbria.[12] At some stage, possibly around 1120, Robert de Brus was established by David in Annandale.[13] David was a close ally of his brother-in-law King Henry, and their friendship was strengthened when in 1113 David was granted permission to marry a great heiress, the daughter of Earl Waltheof (see above, pp. 128–9). Henry was related both to King Alexander, his son-in-law, and David, his brother-in-law. David's situation with regard to Alexander was not straightforward, and from one perspective he was an ally of Henry whose lands constituted a great march between the northern and southern kingdoms. Moreover, Henry, by arranging a marriage between one of his daughters and Fergus of Galloway, formed an alliance with Fergus, who, as recent research has indicated, acted with a degree of independence from the king of Scots.[14] From Henry's perspective, David and Fergus were allies who could perhaps in the future be brought more securely under southern influence.

To the west, in the Irish Sea region, there were further possibilities and dangers which Henry could not afford to ignore. The Norse king, Magnus Barelegs, had ambitions towards the Isles, Man, and the Norse settlements of Ireland, and had inflicted a defeat on the Normans of north Wales in 1098. Moreover Norse fleets were still a reality, trading with the east coast ports of England: Magnus' treasure was after all stored in Lincoln.[15] His death in 1103 marked the end of an era (see above, p. 69),[16] but Henry was not to know this, and he maintained links with the ruler of Man and the earl of Orkney. He was also alive to the possibility that Irish forces might be recruited by his enemies. This threat was most immediate in 1102, when Arnulf of Montgomery sought to raise troops in Ireland to help his brother, Robert de Bellême. There remained the further possibility that Welsh princes would look to Ireland for support against the Normans.[17]

---

[12] The date at which David secured Cumbria is thought to have been between 1108, when he last occurs as a witness to a charter of Henry I, and Christmas 1113. For the suggestion that David obtained Cumbria and Teviotdale in 1113 with the assistance of Henry see Duncan, *Kingship of the Scots*, pp. 59–64 and Oram, *David I*, pp. 60–7. See also above, p. 129.
[13] *Charters of David I*, no. 16.
[14] R. D. Oram, 'Fergus, Galloway and the Scots', in *Galloway: Land and Lordship* (Edinburgh, 1991), ed. R. D. Oram and G. P. Stell, pp. 117–30; R. D. Oram, *The Lordship of Galloway* (Edinburgh, 2000), chapter 2; J. G. Scott, 'The Partition of a Kingdom: Strathclyde 1092–1153', *Transactions of the Dumfries and Galloway Natural History and Antiquarian Society*, 72 (1997), 11–40.
[15] OV, vi 48–50.
[16] R. Power, 'The Death of Magnus Barelegs', *Scottish Historical Review*, 73 (1994), 216–22.
[17] A. Candon, 'Muirchertach ua Briain, Politics and Naval Activity in the Irish Sea, 1075–1119', in *Keimelia: Studies in Medieval Archaeology and History in Memory of Tom Delaney*, ed. G. Mac Niocaill and P. F. Wallace (Galway, 1988), pp. 397–415.

Henry's policy in Normandy was the product of a very different situation. Louis VI was determined to secure homage from the great princes of France. When Henry refused, this opened up the possibility that Louis would turn instead to William Clito; hence if he himself refused to pay homage, Henry knew that his own son would have to do so. This was a major turning point after many years of *de facto* independence for the dukes of Normandy. That Henry should have been prepared to make such a surrender, which he finally did in 1120, only a few months before William's death, demonstrates the price he was prepared to pay to safeguard his son's prospects.

Ultimately Normandy could only be protected by judicious alliances to ring the frontiers with allies, and by looking further afield to amicable relations with neighbouring counts and with the king of France. Here Henry used every means at his disposal: marriages were arranged between his illegitimate daughters and key lords, especially along the southern frontiers, and his English resources could also be used to promote and reward loyalty. Relations with Brittany were good. Henry was able to secure the allegiance of the Breton count, Alan Fergant. Conan, son of the count, married yet another of Henry's daughters;[18] and Brian, an illegitimate son, was reared by Henry and provided with lands in England and Wales, as we have seen. He recruited knights from Brittany,[19] and the most prominent were given land in England.[20]

Henry was on good terms also with Helias count of Maine, but Helias's daughter and heiress was married to Fulk count of Anjou, so that when Helias died the county passed to Fulk, a redoubtable enemy of Henry. According to Orderic, in 1113 King Louis nevertheless conceded that the count of Anjou was to perform homage to Henry for Maine, and in 1128 the marriage of Matilda and Geoffrey effectively resolved the contest between Normandy and Anjou over Maine.[21] Henry also continued to cultivate close relations with the castellan families of northern Maine. He arranged a marriage for one of his illegitimate daughters to Guy de Laval, lord of Beaumont-sur-Sarthe.[22] Hugh de Laval, probably the uncle of Guy, was

---

[18] *GND*, ii, 250–1; P. Jeulin, 'L'Hommage de Bretagne en droit et dans les faits', *Annales de Bretagne*, 41 (1934), 411–13.
[19] WM, *GRA*, i, 728.
[20] For Henry's promotion of Bretons see Round, *Studies in Peerage and Family History*, pp. 124–5. The work of K. S. B. Keats-Rohan on this subject is of great importance, especially 'The Bretons and Normans of England 1066–1154: the Family, the Fief and the Feudal Monarchy', *Nottingham Medieval Studies*, 36 (1992), 42–78 and 'Le rôle des Bretons dans la politique de colonisation normande de l'Angleterre', and see also *Domesday Descendants*, pp. 14–18.
[21] OV, vi, 180 (1113).
[22] For the marriage of Guy de Laval to Emma, see Hollister, 'Anglo-Norman War and Diplomacy', *MMI*, p. 282; for that of Constance, ibid., pp. 282–3; *GND*, ii, 250–1.

granted the lands of Robert de Lacy, lord of Pontefract.[23] The lords of Mayenne had to surrender custody of the castles of Ambrières and Gorron, but in return received land in England.[24] Geoffrey of Gorron, a kinsman of the lords of Gorron and of Richard de Lucy, the future justiciar of Henry II, became abbot of St Albans.[25] Such alliances – and there may have been others[26] – helped to strengthen Norman influence in northern Maine, but ultimately it was to be Henry's diplomatic manoeuvring which finally brought the county into the family firm.

To the north-east, Normandy was bordered by the small, notionally independent counties of Boulogne, Ponthieu, Eu and Aumale (see map 1). In practice these were too small to be serious threats, and their counts held land in England and Normandy, which meant that they were tied into the interests of the Anglo-Norman state. Henry had a castle at Lyons-la-Forêt, and the surrounding forest was one of his favoured hunting grounds. Another important ducal castle was that of Neuf-Marché, and this was committed to the custody of William of Roumare who, although in revolt for a time, had been reconciled with Henry and married Matilda de Redvers.[27] The lords of Gournay commanded an important sector of the frontier. Hugh II de Gournay succeeded as a minor, and his lands were in the custody of his stepfather, Drogo de Mouchy-le-Châtel, an ally of Henry. When Hugh reached manhood he rebelled for a time, but was reconciled in 1119.[28] In the Oise region, Henry continued his predecessor's policy of building links with local families like the lords of Dammartin and Clermont.[29] He was also a benefactor of the abbey of Saint-Germer de Fly, which was situated in the diocese of Beauvais.[30]

The Vexin (see map 5) was more problematic, however, because it was politically divided between the Norman duke and the French king, and

---

[23] Wightman, *Lacy Family in England and Normandy*, pp. 66–7. [24] *Book of Fees*, i, 86, 97.
[25] Geoffrey was descended from Geoffrey FitzRivallon of Dol: Keats-Rohan, 'Le rôle des Bretons dans la politique de colonisation normande de l'Angleterre', 202. The brother of Richard de Lucy the justiciar, later abbot of Battle, was described in the *Chronicle of Battle Abbey* (p. 142) as a kinsman of Abbot Geoffrey: E. Amt, 'Richard de Lucy, Henry II's Justiciar', *Medieval Prosopography*, 9 (1988), 61–87.
[26] The origins of Geoffrey 'de Sublis', the prominent Norman justice, have never been established: *RRAN*, ii, nos. 1352, 1593, 1897. He could have been related to the lords of Sablé. Robert II de Sablé had a younger son called Geoffrey: A. Angot and E. Laurain, *Généalogies féodales mayennaises* (Laval, 1942), p. 759. For Guy de Sablé in Normandy under Duke Geoffrey, and his possible links with this family, see Power, *Norman Frontier in the Twelfth and Early Thirteenth Centuries*, pp. 500–1.
[27] OV, vi, 380. [28] OV, vi, 190–4 and see above, p. 141.
[29] Mathieu, 'Recherches sur les premiers comtes de Dammartin'; M. Bur, 'Quelques champenois dans l'entourage français des rois d'Angleterre'.
[30] For Henry's benefactions to the abbey of Saint-Germer de Fly, see D. Lohrmann, 'Saint-Germer-de-Fly und das Anglo-Normannische Reich', *Francia*, 1 (1973), 193–256.

it was too close to Rouen and Paris to be neglected. The locally powerful families had estates and kinsfolk on both sides of the river Epte, and the lords of the Norman Vexin for the most part had little reason to be grateful to Henry. Henry therefore had to hold the region militarily despite determined opposition, and the number of castles and frequency of conflict meant in turn that the local lords, like William Crispin and Theobald Payn of Gisors, became more alienated.[31]

In the south-east (see map 4), the Norman frontier ran from the great castle of Vernon on the Seine to Pacy on the Eure, thence following the course of the rivers Avre and Iton. For Henry, this sector proved to be particularly problematic. Henry had staunch allies in Count Rotrou of Perche and William Gouet, both of whom were his sons-in-law, Gilbert Crispin, lord of Tillières, and his nephew Theobald count of Blois-Chartres. Local lords had interests across the border, and their loyalty could not always be counted on. The deaths without male heirs of key Norman lords such as William of Breteuil in 1103 and William count of Evreux in 1118 caused major headaches. In the latter year particularly Henry was in acute difficulties, which were exploited by the disaffected.

Then there were the hostile neighbours of Normandy to be considered. For King Louis, the wealth and independence of Henry in Normandy, and his rule over the Norman Vexin, were to be resisted. To that end Louis allied with the count of Anjou and disaffected Normans. Henry thus had every incentive to counterbalance the Franco-Angevin alliance by keeping on excellent terms with his sister, Countess Adela of Blois, and advancing the careers of her sons. The eldest, Count Theobald, had to steer a very careful course in the conflicts between his uncle and King Louis. Henry's generosity to the younger brother, Stephen, in granting him vast estates confiscated from others in England and Normandy meant that Theobald did not have to diminish his own resources to provide for his brother, and from Henry's point of view a loyal nephew was substituted for the disloyal Norman lords William of Mortain, Roger the Poitevin, and William Malet. Yet Theobald cannot have relished the prospect of an alliance between Henry and the count of Anjou, a historic rival of his own family.

Within existing boundaries, too, Henry also sought to consolidate and strengthen his authority. In England there were striking successes in the growing signs of Norman colonisation and settlement in the northern counties. Here Henry used the great tranches of land confiscated from his enemies to insert his own men into the tenurial fabric. Ranulf Flambard

---

[31] Green, 'Lords of the Norman Vexin', pp. 53–61.

made the bishopric of Durham into a bastion of Norman influence; some Normans settled in Northumberland; and Carlisle stood as a potent symbol of Norman claims to the southern parts of the old kingdom of Strathclyde. Castles were built and religious houses founded in this area, and although links with Lothian and the Scottish court remained strong, the northern English counties (viewed from a southern perspective) were more securely tied into the southern kingdom than before. Norman lordships in Wales, especially in the south, were also put on a stronger footing. Henry's practice was to grant lordships to men with ample resources to throw into the defence of their Welsh territories. The Welsh were fighting back, especially in the last year of Henry's life. Nevertheless, fortification and settlement, the foundation of religious houses and the establishment of territorial dioceses were all making progress.

In Normandy, Henry's rule had greatest effect in the reshaping of political society in the southern marches. Henry assisted the reorganisation of the diocese of Sées, and showed generosity to the abbeys of Savigny and Saint-Evroult. He built up good relations with local lords, especially those who had suffered at the hands of Robert de Bellême, and in general sought to stabilise what had previously been, from the duke's point of view, a remote and turbulent region.[32]

HENRY AND THE MAGNATES

At the very heart of a ruler's success lay his ability to command respect and loyalty, as the chronicler William of Malmesbury understood. When William drew his pen portrait of Henry I, he praised the king for his consistency in friendships and hatreds, for rewarding his friends and punishing his enemies. At the start of his reign he had used corporal punishment, but later he tended to use fines and by this means, in William's eyes, he won the respect of the nobles. He sought by every means to win over those who faltered in their loyalty, and punished all who challenged his dignity. The chronicler pointed out that even during Henry's lengthy absences in Normandy no one dared raise his head in revolt in England. When Henry faced rebellion from his nobles, only once was he betrayed by one of his servants. Otherwise he remained secure all his life, for all men feared him in their hearts while having words of love on their lips.[33] Consistency rather than caprice, and the fear of condign punishment for those who were

---

[32] I hope to explore these themes in more detail in a forthcoming paper.
[33] WM, *GRA*, i, 742–4.

disloyal, were thus seen to be crucial. So too was information. Orderic Vitalis commented on Henry's desire to know everything that was going on, and in particular all the affairs of his officials.[34] Henry certainly used private agents, for Orderic mentioned those who collected evidence against Robert de Bellême.[35] Respect had to be at the heart of the nobles' view of their king, and respect had to be won by an ability to assess the hopes and fears of individuals, and to reward and punish accordingly. Henry undoubtedly showed remarkable acumen in weighing up political odds, yet that in turn depended on information: only if he knew what was going on would his decisions be soundly based.

Dealing with the magnates was a complicated game of chess, played in a context that was ever-changing: the dynastic politics of Welsh princes, Scottish kings, the counts of Anjou and Flanders and the king of France all affected Henry's decisions, as well as the shifting fortunes of his own family. Less dramatic and obvious were the changes in law and custom that affected how men viewed inheritance and lordship, and thus the range of Henry's patronage, and the circumstances in which it could be exercised. The church's law on marriage, especially on the binding nature of the union and the restrictions on the choice of partners, had repercussions for views of legitimate succession. The idea that daughters should share an inheritance – which, it is thought, applied in Normandy – was at some stage introduced into Anglo-Norman practice. The principles of inheritance grew stronger, not least because of increasing resort to law and the courts, in which development Henry played a part.

Historians use the term 'the magnates', but it is not a term which can be precisely defined, as historians use different, sometimes overlapping, criteria for identifying those at the summit of Anglo-Norman society. One is the amount of land they held, and its geographical location. Some held large, cross-Channel, complexes of land, whilst the interests of many others lay basically on one side of the Channel or the other. Secondly, there was possession of a title. A small minority of magnates were distinguished by the title 'earl' in England or 'count' in Normandy; the same Latin word (*comes*) was used for both, but their powers, although similar, were not identical. Thirdly, in England there was status as a tenant-in-chief of the king. Fourthly, there was perception of noble status based on illustrious descent.

When Henry became king, many of the Anglo-Norman magnates, as we have seen, came to pay homage, and after he had faced down his brother

---

[34] OV, vi, 100. [35] Ibid., 20.

in 1101 and routed his principal enemies, he grew stronger. As the years went by, he refashioned the aristocracy, bringing to England men from west Normandy and Brittany, promoting individuals who remained loyal, and providing for his many children. Many of the faces at the top came and went, and undoubtedly the composition of the aristocracy had changed by the end of the long reign. Both before and after 1100, theirs remained a competitive and envious society. The old idea that there was a gulf between a court circle and the great Anglo-Norman magnates under Rufus, which Henry I then 'healed', was based on an analysis of charter attestations. It did not take account of the pattern of surviving documents, and has been shown to be misleading.[36] There were naturally some individuals who prospered under Rufus and Henry, but it was the younger brother who was the consummate master of political management. What ultimately Henry could not do was to order men's behaviour after his death, and, despite his best efforts, very few of the 'English' Norman magnates initially came out in support of his daughter.

The situation in Normandy presented a different kind of challenge for Henry as ruler, partly because of the intrinsic character of political society there, but also owing to the nature of ducal authority and the fact that some continued loyal to the cause of Duke Robert and his son, a loyalty which could be combined with the pursuit of personal and family claims to encourage opposition to Henry. On the first point, the character of political society, in general ducal power was strongest in upper Normandy (see map 1) and most fragile in frontier regions. Duke Robert retained a hard core of support, which was reinforced by the return to Normandy of Robert de Bellême and William count of Mortain, who lost their lands in England. Henry had his own bases in the Cotentin and a nucleus of support from most of the magnates with lands in England, and he was also able to use his own resources – either land or marriages to one of his many daughters – to build alliances, notably with Eustace of Breteuil, Rotrou count of Perche, Ralph de Tosny and William count of Evreux. After 1106, he continued to ally with Norman families, especially those with lands in the sensitive frontier regions. His success was inevitably less complete than in England. The lords of the Norman Vexin in particular remained aloof, as did William Talvas, son of Robert de Bellême.

Custody of castles was a very contentious matter. In theory castles, whether built directly by the king or duke or by magnates, were at the

---

[36] Hollister, *Henry I*, chapter 9; D. Bates, 'The Prosopographical Study of Anglo-Norman Royal Charters', and for a rejoinder, Hollister, *Henry I*, Appendix.

ruler's disposal.[37] In England after 1102, the king's right to custody was not challenged directly. In Normandy, however, the issue was not quite so clear-cut: Henry's insistence on custody conflicted with family desires to retain hereditary possession of castles, arousing resentment and opposition. One such case was his resumption of the key castle of Gisors. Another was his conflict with Amaury de Montfort over the citadel at Evreux, though the king did allow Amaury to succeed to his lands. Where a castle had been built by a lord's ancestor, as in the case of William Talvas's castles in Normandy, Henry's retention seemed to contravene custom, as a comment of Robert of Torigny makes clear.[38]

In addition to keeping such fortresses under his own control, Henry also added to the strength and number of ducal castles in a major programme of fortification. Most striking were the keeps or *donjons* which he had built in Normandy (and also in England). They were of different shapes and sizes and fulfilled different functions, but in total they represented Henry's major legacy as ruler of Normandy. The duchy was now studded with seriously fortified castles which could be garrisoned by royal knights and provide bridgeheads from which to ride out trouble. In 1119, as Orderic noted, it was the castles and fortified towns which remained loyal.[39] Frontier defences in particular had been strengthened: the Passais was brought more firmly under control; the frontier sector that ran along the river Avre was strengthened by the building of Nonancourt (*c.* 1112) and Verneuil (*c.* 1124);[40] and in the Vexin Henry was responsible for Noyon-sur-Andelle (modern Charleval).[41] In the far west, adjacent to the river Couesnon which formed the boundary between Normandy and Brittany, he was responsible for the castle-town of Pontorson.[42]

In coming to an overall view of Henry's 'management of the magnates' we have to remember that decisions had to be taken on a case-by-case basis, and in consultation. Patronage decisions involved balancing the aims of one family against another, and were contingent on dynastic accident,

---

[37] Yver, 'Les châteaux forts en Normandie jusqu'au milieu du xiie siècle'. The whole issue of the rights of a ruler or overlord over castles has been subjected to a re-evaluation by C. Coulson, *Castles in Medieval Society. Fortresses in England, Ireland and France in the Central Middle Ages* (Oxford, 2003); see especially pp. 66–70, and part II section 3.
[38] *GND*, ii, 252. [39] OV, vi, 222.
[40] *GND*, ii, 250. Lemoine-Descourtieux, 'La frontière normande de l'Avre', part II.
[41] OV, vi, 218. Robert of Torigny refers to Henry having restored the castle at Châteauneuf-sur-Epte (*GND*, ii, 250).
[42] Ibid. The earliest reference to the *bourg* at Pontorson seems to have been the confirmation by Henry II of a grant to the burgesses there of the customs granted by his grandfather to the burgesses of Verneuil: *Ordonnances des Rois de France de la troisième race*, ed. E.-J. Laurière, 21 vols. (Paris, 1723–1849), iv, 638.

unexpected deaths and the lack of male heirs. In that sense, the decisions made in the aftermath of the White Ship were important and were reached in peculiarly tragic circumstances. One important question is how far, from the perspective of noble society and patronage, England and Normandy were regarded as a unit, 'one homogeneous, aristocratic community'.[43] There were already some very important 'cross-Channel complexes'. Henry added a few more: Nigel d'Aubigny, for instance, was given a great northern lordship in England and then, in the aftermath of Tinchebray, the lordship of Montbray in Normandy.[44] Robert of Gloucester stepped into the shoes of Robert FitzHaimon, and thus gained a lordship that stretched from Glamorgan in Wales via Gloucester and Kent to the Bessin in Normandy. Stephen of Blois had vast estates in England, the county of Mortain and then, by marriage, the county of Boulogne. Henry's illegitimate son Richard was to be lord of Breteuil and perhaps, if he had not died in the White Ship, he too would have been given land in England.

Moreover, there are other instances where Henry gave estates in England to men, whether Normans or their neighbours, whose loyalty he wished to promote. It has been pointed out, for example, that his daughters were provided with estates as marriage portions when their marriages were arranged.[45] Other instances could be cited where a great Norman lord was given a modest estate in England, and probably vice versa, doubtless for convenience as the court moved between the two realms. There is one example of a great Norman lord who was given a good deal of land in England after 1106: William de Tancarville. The extent of his lands, a good many of which were soon transferred to Saint-Georges-de Boscherville, was exceptional.[46] On the whole, what Henry did *not* do was to lavish his English wealth on Norman magnates as a group.[47] Thus by the end of his life there remained some 'cross-Channel magnates', but many more whose estates were chiefly situated on one side of the Channel or the other.

GOVERNANCE

Whilst historians have generally been agreed that the reign of Henry I made an important contribution to the development of royal administration and

---

[43] Le Patourel, *Norman Empire*, p. 195; for discussion see Green, 'Unity and Disunity in the Anglo-Norman State', 129–34; D. Crouch, 'Normans and Anglo-Normans: A Divided Aristocracy', in *England and Normandy in the Middle Ages*, ed. D. Bates and A. Curry (London, 1984), pp. 51–67.
[44] *Charters of the Honours of Mowbray*, p. xviii.
[45] Thompson, 'Dowry and Inheritance Patterns'. [46] Round, *C. D. F.*, p. 66.
[47] J. A. Green, 'Henry I and the Aristocracy of Normandy', in *La France anglaise au Moyen Age, Actes du IIIe Congrès des Sociétés Savantes* (Paris, 1988), pp. 161–73.

justice, there has been less unanimity about the nature of that contribution, and justifiable scepticism about the king's personal involvement.[48] There has been a good deal of research on royal finance, law and justice, and on royal agents (see above, p. 14). Some have drawn attention to specialisation, in terms of the emergence of the court of the exchequer, of routine, and even of government predicated on a rational approach.[49] Royal justice, it has been suggested, had developed to such a degree by 1135 as to lay foundations for its take-off in the later twelfth century.[50] There has been much less written about Henry's regime in the duchy. The starting point still remains the chapter in Haskins' *Norman Institutions* in which the evidence relating to a Norman exchequer and the work of ducal justices is discussed, from which it would appear that ducal administration was developing along parallel lines to royal administration.[51] The increasing use of writs in the later years of Henry's life might lead at first sight to an impression that the duchy was being treated in much the same way as the kingdom, though in fact the number and subject matter of such writs differed from those issued for England.[52] Here, as in England, there were new men whose rise to power so scandalised Orderic Vitalis.

Questions remain, however, about the extent of deliberate innovation, of routine, and of the quality of royal justice, especially in England, and these questions impact on any assessment of Henry I. Should we see his reign as crucial in the emergence of the medieval state, marked by the emergence of specialised agencies, greater use of documents, and full-time officials, or rather as a much more traditional king, using whatever means came to hand to ensure that his revenues were collected and his rights administered?

The person on whom Henry most depended in England was Roger d'Avranches, who had managed his household for him before 1100 and within months of Henry's accession was appointed first royal chancellor and then bishop of Salisbury.[53] As royal chancellor he was at the king's side, and saw to the drawing up of documents ordered by the king. As bishop, his diocesan responsibilities did not prevent him from spending long periods at court in the king's service. In the charter he issued for

---

[48] For recent reappraisals see recent discussions by D. Crouch, *The Reign of Stephen 1135–54* (Harlow, 2000), pp. 15–16, 320–1, and Matthew, *King Stephen*, chapter 3, and pp. 133–7.
[49] Hollister, 'Anglo-Norman Political Culture and the Twelfth-Century Renaissance', pp. 9–16.
[50] Hudson, *Formation of the English Common Law*, p. 117.
[51] Haskins, *Norman Institutions*, chapter 3; see, for example, the statement on p. 85 that 'Parallels and connections with England will inevitably suggest themselves.'
[52] Bates, 'Earliest Norman Writs', 270–82.
[53] For details of his career see Kealey, *Roger of Salisbury*. Roger is thought to have been nominated to the bishopric in September 1101 (ibid., pp. 13–14).

Reading abbey, Roger styled himself the king's *procurator*, the man who made sure the king secured his revenues, a term which had earlier been used of Ranulf Flambard, Rufus' chief financial minister.[54] Roger came to preside over the exchequer, and during the king's absences was one of those who assisted the queen.[55] When Henry left England for Normandy in 1123, he appointed Roger as viceroy during his absence. Roger also supervised the oathtaking ceremony in 1127.[56] Any concerns the king may have had about a shortfall in his English revenues were not, or only briefly, laid at the bishop's door, and he and his family continued to prosper in the last years of the reign.[57]

Under Bishop Roger, the court of the exchequer met each year to audit the accounts presented by the sheriffs and other financial officials. The members of this court included the leading officers of the royal household and their clerks, and here the accounts were heard and, if necessary, penalties imposed. Written records were kept, so that year on year the scribes knew what was paid and how much remained outstanding. English kings had a relatively developed administrative infrastructure: their sheriffs sat in the shire courts, supervised the collection of royal revenues, ensured that the local policing groups or tithings (the system known as frankpledge) were being kept up,[58] and were the first point of contact for royal orders, transmitted through an ever-growing number of royal writs.[59] The king's rights of justice and jurisdiction were vigorously upheld, not only by sheriffs but also by justices: individuals who were deputed to act in specific cases or, by the 1120s, to visit groups of counties in localised eyres. In Normandy the person whose authority seems most nearly to have approximated to that of Bishop Roger was Bishop John of Lisieux. He was archdeacon of Sées, and a man who, according to Orderic, was expert both as a judge and in ecclesiastical business. He had taken refuge at Henry's court, and the king had come to know and trust him.[60] Appointed to the bishopric of Lisieux

---

[54] *Reading Abbey Cartularies*, i, 144–5; for discussion see D. M. Stenton, 'Roger of Salisbury, *Regni Angliae Procurator*', *EHR*, 39 (1924), 79–80; OV, iv, 107 (Flambard).

[55] Kealey, *Roger of Salisbury*, chapter 2; Green, *GOE*, chapter 3.

[56] *Newburgh*, i, 23, 26–9; WM, *Historia Novella*, p. 10.

[57] Green, *GOE*, p. 47. For Henry's charter confirming Roger's possession of the abbey of Malmesbury, see *RRAN*, ii, no. 1715; Roger's nephew Nigel was appointed bishop of Ely in 1133. Another nephew, Alexander, had already been appointed bishop of Lincoln in 1123, and Adelelm, either Roger's nephew or his son, was archdeacon of Dorset. For these and other members of Roger's family, see Kealey, *Roger of Salisbury*, appendix 3.

[58] Frankpledge, whose origins lay in pre-Conquest England, was a system whereby groups of ten (sometimes twelve) men were responsible for each other's lawful behaviour and for producing any one of their number in court, if need be.

[59] Green, *GOE*, chapter 8.   [60] OV, vi, 142–4.

in 1107, he, like Bishop Roger in England, was at the heart of a court which took care of ducal finances and justice. This court, meeting at Caen, was probably already known as the exchequer, and like its English counterpart probably conducted an annual audit of ducal revenues.

Thus on both sides of the Channel there were moves to ensure that revenues were collected and rights upheld. More detail is available for revenues from England than Normandy because of the survival of the 1130 pipe roll, and the overriding impression gained from this is of fixed and customary annual revenues, paid in coins which were being checked with increasing rigour for quality, together with a very important category best summarised as 'justice and jurisdiction'. This comprised judicial fines, but the largest sums came from agreement negotiated with individual tenants-in-chief. These were highly lucrative but also politically sensitive. The size of the agreements made reflected various factors: the precise nature of the privilege being sought, its acceptability to other members of the elite, and the individual's ability to pay. In Normandy ducal revenues differed in detail from those of English kings, most strikingly in the smaller proportion derived from demesne lands.[61] The units of administration were different: the Norman *vicomtes* do not seem to have played such an important role as English sheriffs, and it seems likely that some important ducal castles were already centres of governance from which revenues were collected and ducal rights administered, as they were later in the twelfth century.

In the 'Prophecies of Merlin', an apocryphal text circulating in the early twelfth century, Henry was identified as the 'lion of justice' at whose roar the dragons trembled.[62] His justice was admired for the peace he brought, and the severity with which he punished lawbreakers.[63] In both England in 1100 and Normandy in 1106 he committed himself to the maintenance of good laws and the punishment of evildoers in a way that was traditional, but also essential if he were to win support. Chroniclers expressed admiration for his effectiveness, and their communities benefited. It is less easy, however, to be sure of the *quality* of that peace and justice: questions about its even-handedness, and Henry's ability to temper justice with mercy, are hard to answer. Perhaps this was a reign of terror, in which men obeyed because they feared retribution, capital or corporal punishment, imprisonment or loss of their lands.

---

[61] L. Delisle, 'Des revenus publics en Normandie au xiie siècle', *Bibliothèque de l'Ecole des Chartes*, 10 (1848–9), 173–210, 257–89; 11 (1849), 400–51; 13 (1852), 97–135. For a comparison of English and Norman pipe rolls, see V. Moss, 'Normandy and England in 1180: the Pipe Roll Evidence', in *England and Normandy in the Middle Ages*, ed. D. Bates and A. Curry (London, 1994), pp. 185–95.

[62] Geoffrey of Monmouth, *History of the Kings of Britain*, p. 174.   [63] OV, vi, 98.

What is best documented are Henry's dealings with the great, and the care with which his court was used as a forum in which proceedings were taken against his enemies, and where differences could be submitted to arbitration. From one point of view, such an impression is hardly surprising, given the character of the surviving records. These were in any case usually compiled by the winning side and may give a slanted view of the king's role as arbitrator and conciliator. Nevertheless, behind the language of such reports lies the fact that the possibility of an intervention by Henry was evidently very real. The cartulary of Abingdon abbey provides a vivid insight into the way one community under its abbot, Faritius, a man high in the favour of Henry I, was able to use his privileged position to secure a whole battery of writs and charters confirming lands and property, buttressing jurisdictional claims and defending the abbey's interests against others.[64] Abbot Faritius of Abingdon was obviously very adept at using his high standing with the king to secure dozens of writs to protect the abbey's lands and rights.

One well-documented lawsuit recorded the resolution of a dispute between the great abbey of Mont-Saint-Michel and one of its barons, Thomas de Saint-Jean, a man who was particularly close to Henry I.[65] Thomas was accused of laying waste the abbey's woods and lands; the monks' response was, according to the report, to pray to God for vengeance, a prospect which induced Thomas to negotiate, and a detailed settlement was worked out. Thomas arrived at the abbey in the presence of the bishop of Avranches, promising that neither he nor his heirs would try to recover the disputed land, offering gifts and requesting the privilege of fraternity for himself, his parents and his brothers. He later reaffirmed his oath before King Henry himself. This dispute, we may assume, had gone on for some time. The monks had resorted to the power of prayer, and only then was their opponent brought to terms. Even when both Thomas and his sons promised not to try to recover the land in question, the monks remained suspicious, and it was at this point that recourse was had to King Henry, a powerful figure who might be able to ensure that Thomas would keep his word.

A second Norman lawsuit which is well documented is that between the bishop of Sées and the abbot of Marmoutier over the bishop's rights over

---

[64] *Historia Ecclesie Abbendonensis*, ii, 65–225.
[65] London, British Library, Additional Charters no. 66, 980; Avranches, Bibliothèque Municipale, ms. 210, f. 36 (Cartulary of Mont-Saint-Michel); J. Boussard, 'Thomas de Saint-Jean-le-Thomas et l'abbaye du Mont-Saint-Michel (début du xiie siècle)', in *Droit privé et institutions régionales. Etudes historiques offertes à Jean Yver* (Paris, 1976), pp. 87–96; Round, *C. D. F.*, no. 724, pp. 261–2.

churches held by the abbey in his diocese. The background here was the effort by Bishop John to reorganise his see (below, p. 270), which brought him into conflict with the influential abbey of Marmoutier in the diocese of Tours, a house with which William the Conqueror and Henry had special relations. Marmoutier had supplied the monks for the Conqueror's abbey at Battle, and Henry seems to have been treated by the monks as one of their number. In 1126 one dispute was settled by the mediation of 'the glorious and worshipful king of the English, Henry', as 'father and brother of the church of Marmoutier'.[66] The conflict between the bishop and the abbey was over the abbey's churches within his diocese of Sées, and particularly the status of Marmoutier's priory of Saint-Léonard at Bellême.[67] One text, which survives in the original, relates how the dispute was resolved at Sées in 1127; the testatory sign of King Henry was recorded, and it was noted that this had occurred when 'he gave his daughter to Geoffrey the younger, count of the Angevins'.[68] In the last analysis, Henry was appealed to because of a belief that he could make judicial decisions effective. It was this that had particularly impressed the young Suger, when he was *prévôt* of Saint-Denis's property at Berneval near Dieppe in 1108 or 1109 (see above, p. 104). In these lawsuits Henry had put his authority behind the settlement, but he was also concerned to see that his rights of jurisdiction were upheld. Royal documents were increasingly addressed to unnamed 'justices' in Normandy who, like their colleagues in England, had a duty to ensure that the duke's rights were observed and any fines were collected.

In the case of disputes over lands, property and rights, Henry as king and duke reacted in response to requests for his intervention, whether through the issue of orders or documents, or, on rare occasions, by a personal appearance: on both sides of the Channel his intervention at the behest of one side in a legal dispute was by 1135 a far from remote possibility.[69]

Disputes between the rich and powerful surface in the written records in a way that crime and violence do not, yet clearly contemporaries believed that both kingdom and duchy were more peaceful under Henry I, certainly than they were to be after his death. The Anglo-Saxon Chronicle, which was to provide the classic picture of violence after Henry's death, wrote of the king: 'He was a good man, and was held in great awe. In his days no man dared to wrong another. He made peace for man and beast.'[70] In Normandy both Orderic and Suger commented on Henry's love of peace

---

[66] *RRAN*, ii, no. 1439; Round, *C. D. F.*, no. 1191, p. 430.   [67] *RRAN*, ii, 360–1.
[68] Henry crossed to Normandy on 26 August 1127, so if he did indeed visit Sées in that year, it must have been in the autumn. Alternatively his consent may have been recorded later.
[69] For England, see Hudson, *Formation of the Common Law*, p. 22.   [70] *ASC* E 1135.

and his severity.[71] That peace depended in no small measure on ensuring that others carried out their responsibilities: that those with armed retinues kept them in order; in Normandy, that bishops upheld the Truce of God; and that local communities as far as possible policed themselves. Only a narrow range of the most serious offences, and those which constituted an attack on the ruler's authority, were the immediate concern of the king and duke. Those found guilty were placed 'in his mercy' and subjected to corporal or pecuniary punishments.

Local mechanisms for peacekeeping may have differed between England and Normandy. In the kingdom, the pre-Conquest system of suretyship which had covered much of the country had evolved into a compulsory system of pledging groups of males of free status, supervised by the sheriffs. Tithing groups were subdivisions of the hundreds or wapentakes, which had their own courts, and these in turn were subdivisions of the shires. In Normandy peacekeeping probably rested to a greater extent on local lords, whilst the bishops were given the responsibility of punishing those who broke the Truce or Peace of God, which had been introduced in the eleventh century. By 1135 it appears that there were problems in making the Truce work effectively, and in the last year of Henry's life it was decreed that where an individual was charged with homicide during the Truce and was challenged to trial by battle, the trial should take place in the king's court (see above, pp. 106, 219).[72] In other words, Henry himself was taking direct responsibility for making the Truce work. Another striking difference between the kingdom and the duchy was in the way forest law worked. In England the royal monopoly of forests and forest law was much more exclusive than the duke's in Normandy, where many of the great lords had private forests. Exactly how this had come about, and how far Henry himself extended the bounds of royal forests, is a story still to be told.

In the last analysis the maintenance of peace and order was less systematic and even-handed than has sometimes been suggested. In the report of the king's nightmares inserted into the Worcester chronicle, Henry is assailed on different occasions by each of the three orders of medieval society: the peasants with their ploughshares, knights with their swords, and churchmen who prod him with their staffs.[73] The dreams suggest that to many, Henry's regime was oppressive and his officials rapacious. In 1124 the Anglo-Saxon Chronicle reported that 'the man who had any property was deprived of it by severe taxes and severe courts'. Sometimes it was the vulnerable who

---

[71] OV, vi, 98; Suger, *Vie de Louis VI* (ed. Waquet), p. 100.
[72] *Coutumiers de Normandie* (ed. Tardif), i (i), 65.
[73] JW, iii, 198–200; for further discussion of the nightmares, see below, pp. 310–11.

suffered, like Jews of London, who were fined an immense sum 'for a sick man whom they killed'.[74] The hapless Bricstan of Chatteris, trying to dispose of his worldly goods before becoming a monk, fell under suspicion from the royal official 'Malarteis'.[75] After Henry's death churchmen at the Council of London were vociferous about the persecution of those who had objected to the oppression of the church.[76] In some cases even the great found themselves impleaded: men like Robert Bloet bishop of Lincoln or Baldwin de Redvers, whose fine for killing a stag was recorded in the 1130 pipe roll.[77] In Normandy Amaury de Montfort was angered by the activities of Henry's officials. Orderic commented that the officials did many wrongs to both high and low by invoking the power of the king and the fear he inspired: 'unscrupulous officials are worse than robbers', he concluded.[78] Henry of Huntingdon was still more blunt: 'royal business is wickedness'.[79]

What struck contemporaries particularly about these officials was Henry's use of 'new men', whose careers have since been much discussed.[80] Orderic conveniently provides a short list of those whom he believed fell into this category: Geoffrey de Clinton, Ralph Basset, Hugh of Buckland, Guillegrip, Rainer of Bath, William Trussebut, Haimo of Falaise, Wigan Algason (the marshal), and Robert of 'Bostare'.[81] Hugh of Buckland may have been a clerk, and possibly married. He had London connections, and there was a prebendary of St Paul's of this name with whom he may be identified.[82] In fact, several men who made careers as sheriffs were clerks, who possessed skills of literacy and numeracy: Osbert the priest, sheriff of Yorkshire and Lincolnshire,[83] and Richard of Winchester.[84] Richard of Beaumais was originally a clerk in the household of Roger of Montgomery before passing into the king's service, holding the shrievalty of Shropshire and then becoming bishop of London.[85]

---

[74] *PR 31 Henry I*, p. 149. [75] Ibid., p. 149; for Bricstan, see above, p. 115.
[76] *Gesta Stephani*, pp. 24–8. [77] HH, pp. 586–8; *PR 31 Henry I*, p. 153.
[78] OV, vi, 330–2. [79] HH, p. 604.
[80] See above, p. 14, references cited in the footnote. [81] OV, vi, 16.
[82] J. Le Neve, *Fasti Ecclesiae Anglicanae 1066–1300, I, St Paul's Cathedral*, compiled by D. E. Greenway (London, 1968), p. 51; C. N. L. Brooke with G. Keir, *London 800–1216. The Shaping of a City* (London, 1975), p. 204.
[83] J. A. Green, *Medieval English Sheriffs to 1154* (London, 1990), pp. 14–15.
[84] There was a man named Richard of Winchester who was a prebendary of Willesden: Le Neve, *Fasti, St Paul's*, p. 86. He may have been the man of that name who was sheriff of Bedfordshire in the 1120s: *PR 31 Henry I*, p. 100.
[85] J. F. A. Mason, 'The Officers and Clerks of the Norman Earls of Shropshire', *Transactions of the Shropshire Archaeological Society*, 56 (1957–60), 253–4. There may have been others who were also (married) clerks. Ralph Basset was the presiding justice at the meeting of the shire court of Huntingdon when

Others were what had been called in an earlier age *fiscalini*, men who had some connection with the management of royal and ducal demesnes.[86] Again there are possible examples in Orderic's list: Geoffrey de Clinton's name derived from Glympton near Woodstock, one of Henry's favourite hunting lodges, and it is possible that this connection brought him to the king's attention.[87] Ralph Basset held land as an under-tenant of the honour of Robert d'Oilly, and may have come to Henry's attention during the period the future king spent at Abingdon abbey (see above, p. 23), or when Henry took over Domfront in about 1091 or 1092, for the Basset estate at Montreuil-au-Houlme was not far away.[88] Haimo of Falaise, whose career is not well documented but was clearly important, may have been recruited from Falaise.[89] The most famous example not on Orderic's list was William de Pont-de-l'Arche, whose name indicates that he came from the place where there was an important fortified bridge across the Seine. Some of these new men were referred to simply by their nicknames, such as William Trussebut and Guillegrip. William became constable of Bonneville, and came into possession of the Yorkshire honour of Warter,[90] but Guillegrip remains obscure.[91]

The kind of services that men such as these performed for the king was the adminstration of his rights of justice and jurisdiction and the collection of his revenues by officials such as Geoffrey de Clinton and Ralph Basset. Men of this kind presiding over courts must have affronted noble sensibilities, as is indicated by Bishop Robert Bloet's complaints about being impleaded by a low-born official of the king.[92] The author of the *Gesta Stephani* wrote disparagingly of Miles of Gloucester and Payn FitzJohn as

---

Bricstan was brought before it, according to Orderic (OV, iii, 350). In the *Liber Eliensis* version, however, the presiding officer is said (p. 268) to have been Ralph the chaplain. Geoffrey FitzPayn, who granted the church of Tockwith to Nostell priory in Yorkshire, is described as a royal chaplain: Nicholl, *Thurstan*, p. 130n. Although Geoffrey acquired substantial lands in his lifetime they passed after his death to the Trussebut family, and if he had been a clerk this might explain why he did not establish a landed family.

[86] S. Airlie, 'Bonds of Power and Bonds of Association in the Court Circle of Louis the Pious', in *New Perspectives on the Reign of Louis the Pious*, ed. P. Godman and R. Collins (Oxford, 1999), pp. 197–8.
[87] Green, *GOE*, p. 142n.
[88] For Ralph's lands, see W. T. Reedy, 'The First Two Bassets of Weldon', *Northamptonshire Past and Present*, 4 (1966–72), 241–5, 295–8; for the estates held of the honour of Wallingford, see *The Boarstall Cartulary*, ed. H. E. Salter, Oxford Historical Society, 88 (1930), p. 319; for the castle at Montreuil, see OV, vi, 466–8; for the family, see *Basset Charters c. 1120–1250*, ed. W. T. Reedy, Pipe Roll Society, new series, l (1995), pp. xxvii–xxx.
[89] This Haimo, or a man of the same name, was pardoned 13s. danegeld in Warwickshire in 1130 (*PR 31 Henry I*, p. 108). Robert de Brus, who came from Brix, a large ducal demesne in the Cotentin, may have been owed his entrée to Henry's service to this fact.
[90] OV, vi, 526; *Early Yorkshire Charters*, x, 5–22.
[91] The name occurs in Domesday Shropshire: *DB*, i, 254, 258b.
[92] HH, pp. 586–8.

low-born members of the court who had been advanced as *archiministri palatinorum* (chiefs of the palace officials), responsible for cases impleaded at the king's court, and afraid of presenting themselves at Stephen's court because of the cries of the widows and orphans whose lands they had misappropriated.[93] To be brought before men of a lower social origin was insulting to men of high birth, yet Henry's new men were too powerful to be flouted.

Miles and Payn, however, were rather different from men like Ralph Basset and Geoffrey de Clinton, in that Miles's father had been a court constable and constable of Gloucester, and had held Carmarthen for the king.[94] Miles was not exactly a new man, therefore, and nor was Payn, whose father John, nephew of Waleran, is mentioned as a tenant-in-chief in Domesday Book.[95] Miles himself held the office of constable as well as a sheriff, and he was lord of Brecknock by right of his wife.[96] He was a military man as well as a sheriff, and this pattern was not uncommon. There were different, overlapping career patterns, and the 'newness' in some cases was relative. Men like Miles and Payn, his brother Eustace FitzJohn, and Walter Espec were what Southern described as men 'from a middle station in society'.[97] Moreover, if more were known about individuals' career paths, it is not impossible that that those who appear to have been 'new' would in fact turn out to be kin or associates of 'old' men, to whom they may have owed their introduction to royal circles.[98]

Some evidently spent most of their time as military men. Nigel d'Aubigny is perhaps the most spectacular example here. He was the brother of William d'Aubigny, who had risen under Rufus. Nigel himself may have been sent by Rufus to the north before 1100.[99] When Henry came to the throne his rise continued, and after 1100 he received a great lordship in the north, probably with the custody of York, and a lordship in south-west Normandy.[100] Nevertheless he continued as one of Henry's chief captains, and seems to have been at his side for long periods, to judge from the frequency of his

---

[93] *Gesta Stephani*, pp. 22–4.
[94] For the careers of Walter and Miles see D. Walker, 'Miles of Gloucester, Earl of Hereford', *Transactions of the Bristol and Gloucestershire Archaeological Society*, 77 (1958), 66–96.
[95] John nephew of Waleran was a tenant-in-chief in Essex and Norfolk; for the careers of Payn and Eustace see Green, *GOE*, pp. 251–2.
[96] For Miles's marriage settlement see *Ancient Charters*, p. 9.
[97] Southern, 'Place of Henry I', p. 218.
[98] R. V. Turner, *Men Raised from the Dust. Administrative Service and Upward Mobility in Angevin England* (Philadelphia, 1988), pp. 145–6.
[99] Barlow, *William Rufus*, p. 291; Green, *Aristocracy of Norman England*, p. 114.
[100] *Charters of the Honour of Mowbray*, pp. xvii–xxvi.

charter attestations. A man whose career in Normandy was not dissimilar was Ralph the Red, lord of Pont-Erchenfray.[101]

If origins and career patterns varied, so too did the scale of rewards. Orderic was generalizing when he referred to the men on his list as 'raised from the dust above earls and illustrious castellans', because on the whole the men raised from the dust were not allowed to acquire great estates either through direct royal grant or by marriage. Thus Geoffrey de Clinton and William de Pont-de-l'Arche acquired great wealth, but the vast majority of their estates were held either as life tenancies or as under-tenancies and did not pass to their heirs, though Geoffrey's son held a substantial estate by virtue of his marriage to a daughter of the earl of Warwick.[102] Ralph Basset secured for his son Richard custody of the lands of Geoffrey Ridel, and marriage to a Ridel daughter. These estates passed into the hands of his grandsons, but the two lordships in question, Drayton in Staffordshire and Great Weldon in Leicestershire, were not of the first rank.[103]

The rise of men who were in effect administrators was a social phenomenon of some importance, and it was not confined to England. As we have seen (above, pp. 196–7, 200), in Flanders the Erembald clan rose to commanding heights under Count Charles, as did the Garlande family at the court of King Louis VI.[104] Their prominence was a reflection of a growing need by rulers for men to collect their revenues and keep a watchful eye on their rights. The times were changing, and providing growing opportunities for the enterprising.

Such men were envied and hated, and it could hardly be otherwise. The most telling testimony comes from the pen of William of Malmesbury, who, when Roger bishop of Salisbury died in 1139, allowed himself a measure of candour when he came to write Roger's obituary. The bishop, he wrote, had begun by managing Count Henry's affairs before he became king; afterwards the king denied him nothing. Roger pleaded the legal cases, controlled the expenditure, and kept the treasure, whether the king was in England or not. Anything bordering his property that he wanted he exacted 'by prayer or price', or by force. Even the greatest, however, could be broken. Roger had no forewarning of his fall, only a few years after Henry I's death. He was actually arrested in Stephen's chamber; one of his

---

[101] OV, vi, 40–1, 70, 100, 104, 198, 220–2, 230–2, 246, 250, 302.
[102] Southern, 'Place of Henry I', pp. 214–18; J. H. Round, 'A Great Marriage Settlement', *Ancestor*, 11 (1904), 153–7.
[103] *Basset Charters*, no. 47.
[104] For the Erembalds, see Galbert of Bruges, *Murder of Charles the Good*, pp. 97–8; for the Garlande family, see Luchaire, *Annales de la vie de Louis VI*, chapter 3; Bournazel, *Le Gouvernement capétien au XIIe siècle*, pp. 35ff.

nephews fled, another was arrested, a third was put in chains, and only when Roger's castles were surrendered was he freed.[105] Similarly Geoffrey de Clinton was accused of treason in 1130; he was cleared, but his son never enjoyed the same prominence.[106] In Flanders, the fall of the Erembalds was even more complete. The clan, aware that the count had decided to challenge their status, had decided to make a pre-emptive strike by killing the count, and they themselves perished in the civil war that followed.[107] In France, Stephen de Garlande did survive, though not unscathed. After the king had besieged his castle, and he and Louis were reconciled, Stephen recovered the chancellorship but lost the seneschalcy.[108]

Henry's new men have to be understood in context. Like any king, he wanted his own people. Some were established magnates, whilst others were men of lesser status. Only the most successful from already established families were promoted into great lordships. The men of modest origins, like Geoffrey de Clinton, were allowed to acquire great wealth, but they did not rise to the heights of the great nobles. At the end of the long reign there were many new families which had risen, whilst others had been casualties of war or politics.

In his Raleigh Lecture, Sir Richard Southern suggested that Henry's use of royal patronage was important not just in his own day, but in shaping the longer-term development of English society by ensuring that its middle orders were relatively thickly populated.[109] Whilst it was certainly the case that the middling orders were relatively numerous in the early twelfth century, it is not clear that Henry's patronage was decisive in ensuring that they remained so. Relatively little is known about this social group as compared with the great men, but it is tempting to see their presence from before the Norman Conquest and through the twelfth century as a continuum, rather than attributing to any single ruler a decisive impact on their numbers.

A rather different point has been made by Dr Keats-Rohan, who has argued that ideas of nobility were altered by Henry's patronage. She has argued that perceptions of nobility shifted because of the way he endowed his servants with great wealth and power, so that greater emphasis than hitherto was placed on officeholding and service.[110] Again, we may wonder how much actually changed in Henry's reign. If there was anything new

---

[105] WM, *Historia Novella*, pp. 64–70.
[106] Crouch, 'Geoffrey de Clinton and Roger earl of Warwick', 120–2.
[107] Galbert of Bruges, *Murder of Charles the Good* (ed. Ross), pp. 316–17.
[108] Luchaire, *Annales de la vie de Louis VI*, pp. xlv–liv.
[109] Southern, 'Place of Henry I', pp. 208–9.   [110] Keats-Rohan, *Domesday Descendants*, pp. 8–38.

about Henry's new men, it surely lay in the kinds of careers a few, but by no means all, pursued. Even by this criterion, it was not that justices and sheriffs had not prospered before 1100 in royal service, it was rather that the numbers who did so had achieved a critical mass under Henry which made them noticeable to contemporaries.

There was thus a great deal of administrative activity by growing numbers of officials, yet in all of this, it is hard to find concrete evidence of Henry's personal involvement. He clearly did like to know all the affairs of his officials, as Orderic commented, but to assume that he supervised their activities closely may be assuming too much. Often they must have been left unchecked to administer his rights and collect his revenues.[111]

Henry's own approach to ruling was based on the maintenance of tradition. He claimed to be his father's legitimate heir, promised to restore good laws, and proclaimed his peace. In carrying out these pledges he naturally used the apparatus and the men to hand: auditing procedures, writs and justices; bishops as ministers; and new men. In that sense he did not seek self-conscious innovation, nor was there any drive towards rule based on a rational rather than a reactive, essentially pragmatic, response.[112] The suggestion that royal administration took its cue from the intellectuals who can be found at times at Henry's court overlooks the immediacy with which responses to problems were devised. This was after all the king who, when his mercenaries complained about the poor quality of the coins in which they had been paid, ordered Bishop Roger in England to mutilate all the moneyers.[113]

Nevertheless, the cumulative impact of administrative activity was to have important consequences in England and in Normandy. In England a long period of peaceful rule brought greater intensification of royal authority, along broad lines of development that had already been set. In 1100 royal administration was already relatively centralised, with channels of communication going outwards to the sheriffs through writs. But by 1135 the Norman settlement of England was much more secure than it had been in 1100, especially in the northern counties, and royal justice was vigorous, and its role in settling disputes over land and property had greatly expanded. In Normandy too it may be argued that Henry's regime renewed ducal administration and helped to make Normandy one of the most closely administered regions of France in the twelfth century.

---

[111] OV, vi, 100.
[112] Cf. Hollister, 'Anglo-Norman Political Culture and the Twelfth-Century Renaissance', pp. 9–16.
[113] ASC E 1125 (*recte* 1124).

WEALTH

Henry's wealth, and his love of riches, impressed contemporaries deeply. Wealth was displayed at his court, showered on his favourites, and poured out in the construction of castles and churches, payment of subsidies, and the wages of knights.[114] As noted above, a good deal of information about his English revenues derives from the invaluable 1130 pipe roll, though there are relatively few details for Norman revenues. Moreover revenues do not provide the whole picture: was Henry so rich because, as his critics claimed, he was greedy?[115] To what extent was his wealth based on developing new sources of wealth, and to what extent on exploiting those which already existed? How far was he the beneficiary of an English economy that was expanding rapidly in the early twelfth century? How disruptive to the regional economy in Normandy were the conflicts of the early twelfth century? There are no clear answers to any of these questions, but the economic context of his rule is a topic that deserves more attention than it has received.

In the early twelfth century there are signs of growing economic activity in England, as demonstrated by 'managerial confidence' amongst landlords and their interest in towns, tolls and trade.[116] On the other hand, there is no doubt that shortages of silver were placing constraints on the availability of high-quality coins both in England and in Normandy, and this is why the opening up of important new mines at Alston in Cumbria was so important.[117] Normandy, especially outside the Cotentin, was a prosperous region, and Rouen an important trading centre both regionally and over longer distances.[118] On the other hand, the Flemish wool towns were booming, and the trade fairs of Champagne were beginning their meteoric rise: it could be argued that Normandy was sandwiched between two regions which in their different ways were beginning to prosper even more than the duchy.

Moreover, the key question here is not about economic growth, but the extent to which Henry was able to tap the wealth of his realms. The revenue

---

[114] The classic study of this topic remains J. O. Prestwich, 'War and Finance in the Anglo-Norman State', *Transactions of the Royal Historical Society*, 5th series, 4 (1954), 19–43.
[115] HH, p. 700.
[116] E. King, 'Economic Development in the Early Twelfth Century', in *Progress and Problems in Medieval England. Essays in Honour of Edward Miller*, ed. R. Britnell and J. Hatcher (Cambridge, 1966), pp. 1–22.
[117] For a speculative discussion of the economic impact of the silver mines at Alston on Cumbria and Lothian see Blanchard, '"Lothian and Beyond"'.
[118] L. Musset, 'Rouen au temps des francs et sous les Ducs (Ve siècle–1204)', in *Histoire de Rouen*, ed. M. Mollat (Toulouse, 1979), pp. 59–72.

from the royal manors was largely finite.[119] It was let out at rents fixed by custom, and was used in a variety of ways to provision the household, to support the royal family and to reward the king's men, as well as to supply income. The king had the ability to levy geld, essentially a land tax, but again there were limits to what could be asked and who was prepared to pay, hence the importance of tapping the wealth of those who had it: the churchmen, the magnates and the towns. Towns were particularly important to the king and duke for rents and tolls, and because of the merchant communities who could be persuaded to contribute to Henry's coffers on one pretext or another. It also led Henry to work closely with the richer members of the towns.[120]

London occupied a crucial place in Norman England. Not only was it the largest city, but it was already politically important. Control of London was indispensable for William the Conqueror in 1066, and in 1141 for his granddaughter. The Conqueror had been prepared to confirm the Londoners' privileges, and his original writ still survives.[121] In the period immediately after the battle of Hastings the city was a dangerous place for the Normans, and it may have taken time before the Conqueror and Rufus felt more secure there, but by the early twelfth century the royal court was more in evidence. The city too made a substantial contribution to royal revenue through the farm (a consolidated payment) paid by its sheriffs, and by an additional large sum each year by way of an aid, which in 1130 was £120.

Henry showed remarkable favour to the city in 1130 when he allowed the citizens to purchase the right of choosing those who would act as sheriffs.[122] He may also have reduced the farm they paid from the very large figure of over £500 to the £300 which had apparently been customary in his father's day, though the evidence for such a reduction is contained only in his charter to the Londoners, the authenticity of which is problematic.[123] The sheriffs who had been in office in London in 1130, and who had evidently been unable to collect much by way of cash revenue, seem to have been

---

[119] For royal revenue see Green, *GOE*, chapter 4.   [120] For Winchester see below, pp. 299–300.
[121] London, Corporation of London Records Office, Charter no. 1A.   [122] *PR 31 Henry I*, p. 148.
[123] The lower figure is mentioned in the second charters of the empress and Stephen to Geoffrey II de Mandeville (*RRAN*, iii, nos. 275, 276). It is the figure mentioned in the charter allegedly granted by Henry to the Londoners, the authenticity of which has been much discussed: see C. N. L. Brooke, G. Keir and S. Reynolds, 'Henry I's Charter for the City of London', *Journal of the Society of Archivists*, 4 (1972), 558–78. Warren Hollister followed J. C. Russell in arguing for a date of 1133: 'London's First Charter of Liberties: Is It Genuine?', *Journal of Medieval History*, 6 (1980), 290–2; cf. J. C. Russell, 'The Date of Henry I's Charter for London', in *Dargan Historical Essays (Historical Studies presented to Marion Dargan)*, ed. W. M. Dabney and J. C. Russell, University of New Mexico Publications in History, no. 4 (Albuquerque, 1952), 9–16; Green, 'Financing Stephen's War'.

citizen-sheriffs who were willing to pay a fine to lay down their office. Their fellow citizens, however, paid a sum to keep the privilege of free election, a privilege which may have seemed worthwhile if it enabled Henry to keep on good terms with the Londoners, both for his sake and, looking ahead, for his daughter's.

Secondly, there were links between the royal court and the money men – the goldsmiths and moneyers. Several of the latter held royal offices, or *ministeria*. William FitzOtto, who was responsible for cutting the dies used to stamp the silver coins, was a man of substance, with rural estates as well as city property.[124] Payments due to the king in most counties had to be paid in coins of the current issue, and it seems that the king may have benefited from the process of ensuring that only such coins reached the king. It has been pointed out that in 1130, for example, Adelulf the Fleming and Geoffrey Bucherell each made payments in connection with some kind of exchange.[125] In Stephen's reign it is clear that Flemish merchants were a very important source of credit, and there is no reason to suppose that their role did not date back before 1135.[126]

There was an important Jewish community in London, which had settled in the wake of the Normans, and it is clear from the pipe roll that the king had already assumed the role of 'protector' of the Jews.[127] Already the Jews were lending to members of the nobility; they made payments at the exchequer for the king's help in recovering their debts, and they had undertaken to pay an enormous fine of £2,000.[128] The fine suggests that Jewish physicians were already active, and its size indicates that they were extremely wealthy and that their wealth could be tapped for the royal coffers.

The vast majority of major towns and cities belonged to the king, and Henry took care not to add more than a handful (Colchester, Leicester and Reading) to the few in private hands.[129] Each year these towns paid an annual fixed contribution to the king, and by 1130 they were also paying an additional sum called an 'aid', which supposedly voluntary but clearly had become an annual impost.[130] Those which received royal charters confirming their customs presumably paid for the privilege, and at least one,

---

[124] Nightingale, 'Some London Moneyers'; for William FitzOtto see Green, *GOE*, p. 280.
[125] *PR 31 Henry I*, p. 145; Nightingale, 'Some London Moneyers', 46.
[126] Green, 'Financing Stephen's War', 105–6.
[127] For the rising Jewish communities see J. Hillaby, 'Jewish Colonisation in the Twelfth Century', in *The Jews in Medieval Britain. Historical, Literary and Archaeological Perspectives*, ed. P. Skinner (Woodbridge, 2003), pp. 19–20.
[128] *PR 31 Henry I*, p. 149.   [129] *RRAN*, ii, no. 552; Kemp, *Reading Abbey*, p. 15; OV, vi, 18–20.
[130] Green, *GOE*, p. 76.

Lincoln, had made an agreement to pay their annual farms independent of the royal sheriff.[131]

Rouen had prospered under the dukes as a great entrepôt, trading in slaves, wine, fish and salt. Its merchants had enjoyed a monopoly of trade between Normandy and Ireland, whence came slaves and hides, and they also had a privileged position at London.[132] The city was a centre of ducal power: the dukes had a castle there, where treasure was stored. As trade prospered, so did the dukes, by imposing tolls, especially on wine, and their right to 'fat fish', or whales.[133] It was important for Henry to establish good relations with the leading men. Soon after the battle of Tinchebray he confirmed the liberties of the citizens, and some impression of these privileges may be gained from the confirmation issued by his grandson in 1151.[134] Amongst the wealthy men of the city was an important Jewish community, as we have seen (above, p. 210).[135]

What probably mattered most to the merchants was that once again the duchy and the kingdom were in one pair of hands, which meant that trade could flow freely. Thomas Becket's father Gilbert, for instance, came from Rouen but moved to London, becoming sheriff possibly at the end of the reign.[136] There are tantalising glimpses of the links between the merchant patriciate and the Norman kings. Two prominent citizens of Rouen, Baldwin son of Clarus and Anselm *vicomte* of Rouen, were successively sheriffs of Berkshire.[137] Anselm, whose widow Emma may still be traced in business in the later twelfth century, was at once a key figure in Rouen and the holder of one of the largest sheriff's farms. A third individual, William FitzAnsger, was adressed in a royal document and may have been a ducal justice.[138]

Caen, too, continued to prosper.[139] Henry was a frequent visitor, building continued at the castle and the abbeys, and Caen stone was exported across the Channel to southern England.[140] Other centres where there were

---

[131] *PR 31 Henry I*, pp. 114–15.
[132] *RRAN*, iii, no. 729: Henry FitzEmpress confirmed the liberties of the citizens of Rouen.
[133] L. Musset, 'Quelques notes sur les baleiniers normands du Xe au XIIe siècle', *Revue d'Histoire Economique et Sociale*, 42 (1964), 147–61.
[134] *RRAN*, iii, no. 729. [135] Golb, *The Jews of Medieval Normandy*, chapter 3.
[136] *Materials for the History of Thomas Becket*, iii, 14.
[137] *PR 31 Henry I*, p. 122; Green, *Government of England*, p. 213.
[138] William was mentioned as one of the leading citizens at the time of the 1090 revolt (OV, iv, 226); he was included in the address of a document of Henry I (Haskins, *Norman Institutions*, p. 98).
[139] For a detailed study see L. Jean-Marie, *Caen aux XI et XIIe siècles. Espace urbain, pouvoirs et société* (Condé-sur-Noireau, 2000).
[140] T. Tatton Brown, 'La pierre de Caen en Angleterre', in *L'Architecture normande au moyen âge*, ed. M. Baylé, 2 vols. (Caen, 1997), i, pp. 305–14.

both ducal castles and adjacent towns, like Falaise and Argentan, may also have expanded. On the vulnerable frontier along the river Avre, places like Verneuil and Nonancourt played a key role in border defences. Sometimes the townsmen remained loyal to Henry even if the castellan did not. Townsmen were also able to offer very considerable financial backing, but if they were pushed too hard, trouble could ensue, as Stephen of Blois found to his cost at Alençon in 1118.[141] However, not all Norman towns prospered, and some suffered badly from warfare: Bayeux was burned in 1105,[142] as was Evreux in 1119 and Gisors in 1123.[143] A good deal of attention has necessarily been paid to Henry's dealings with the great nobles of England and Normandy, and rightly so, yet in his dealings with towns and traders surely lay the secret of those vast supplies of money which so impressed contemporaries.

The picture that has emerged here of Henry as a ruler has diverged at several points from much of the prevailing orthodoxy of the last few years. The suggestion that Henry broke with his father's and brother's expansionist wars, and was content with what he had inherited, ignores the evidence for further expansion in the British Isles and the tenacity with which alliances with neighbours were pursued. Today's ally presented opportunities for stronger intervention tomorrow, and no one understood the game of dynastic politics better than Henry. His daughters were the commodity by means of which those alliances were forged: few could resist a bride of royal, albeit illegitimate, birth. England and Normandy came to be ringed with allies, who defended the frontiers and offered opportunities for Normans to expand into Wales and Scotland. Maine, long a target for takeover by the Normans, was subsumed into Anjou, and then brought into the Anglo-Norman world through the marriage of Geoffrey and Matilda.

In territorial terms, internal consolidation was perhaps even more important in the long run than expansion. If Henry had not maintained Rufus' alliance with the kings of Scots, Normans would have met more resistance in Cumbria and Northumberland than they did, and even upland Yorkshire might have been at risk. Instead castles were built and religious houses were founded. In the southern marches of Normandy, too, the removal of Robert de Bellême was followed by a reshaping of political society, a reorganisation of the diocese of Sées, alliances with those who were prepared to be allies rather than enemies, and the strengthening of the border fortresses.

Henry's view of his inheritance was thus more traditional and arguably less pacific than has been supposed. In other ways, too, his mode of ruling

---

[141] Ibid., pp. 204–8.   [142] OV, vi, 78.   [143] Ibid., 228, 344.

has been portrayed here as traditional and reactive, rather than innovatory and constructive. The description 'administrative kingship', if by that is meant a new form of kingship based on specialisation of function and administrative routine, and the rise of those who might, for want of a better word, be described as bureaucrats, is premature, though such a long and powerful regime did generate important innovations.[144]

'Normandy', wrote William of Malmesbury, 'was the principal cause of Henry's wars.'[145] It was a great thing to be a king, but the sheer determination Henry showed in gaining the duchy, and then holding it against every attack, is instructive about his priorities. Yet whilst he was resolute in his aim to hold on to Normandy, he did not consciously seek to incorporate the duchy into an 'Anglo-Norman state'. Each remained distinct, though inevitably influenced by almost three decades of rule by one man.

---

[144] For the phrase see Hollister and Baldwin, 'Rise of Administrative Kingship'.
[145] WM, *GRA*, i, 744.

CHAPTER 12

'Guardian of the church'

At his coronation in 1100, Henry had sworn to protect the church and the whole Christian people. In his Charter of Liberties he had further promised 'freedom' to the church, spelling out that he would not take anything from the demesne of a church until a new archbishop, bishop, or abbot was appointed (see above, p. 45). Though the position of the duke in Normandy was theoretically different from that of a king, in practice William the Conqueror had been the effective lay power over the church within the duchy, and it was that power which Henry assumed in 1106. In Normandy too, Henry affirmed similar ideas of protecting churches and restoring to them lands taken away from their demesnes since his father's death (above, p. 98). The ideal of protection, to which Orderic's epithet 'guardian of the church' cited in the title of this chapter refers,[1] was central to contemporary ideas of rule; what it meant in practice was very differently interpreted by lay rulers and churchmen, and it changed over time. Henry's long life encompassed more than a common share of personal felicities and misfortunes which were construed in a context of Christian belief and changing religious practice. During his lifetime the western church became much better organised under an increasingly influential and self-confident papacy: vibrant cathedral schools were breaching new frontiers in theology and law, scholars were bringing knowledge of Greek and Arabic texts into northern Europe, and preachers were calling the faithful to follow Christ in new ways. By exploring the evidence – relatively abundant in comparison with other areas of his life – for Henry's response to these changes, we can assess their impact on him both as ruler and as private individual.

The subject is dealt with here thematically, but it is important to recognise differences in religious practice and ecclesiastical organisation between England, Wales and Normandy. In England two new dioceses, Ely and Carlisle, were created in Henry's reign. In Wales the process of creating

[1] OV, vi, 452.

territorial dioceses and introducing non-native religious communities was only just beginning. In Normandy the revival of diocesan activity and religious life after the Viking era had begun earlier and had peaked under Duke William. Yet if there were some differences between Henry's territories, there were also features in common. Common goals of reform and renewal, and the interchange of personnel, chiefly from Normandy to England but also some movement in the reverse direction, and both into and out of the Anglo-Norman world, must all be taken into account.

RULE BY THE GRACE OF GOD

A suitable starting point is to consider perceptions of royal or ducal authority, and the implications of changing ideas about the exercise of power in the church, as well as changing realities in the practice of kingship. The strong desire of reformers in the eleventh century to separate the clerical order from the laity had prompted a fundamental reappraisal of the location of authority and power, and the quarrel between Pope Gregory VII and the Emperor Henry IV had led to a propaganda war of claim and counter-claim even on the most fundamental of questions: could popes depose emperors or vice versa?[2]

William the Conqueror, who had transferred from Normandy to England his view that reform of the church, and particularly the eradication of clerical marriage, should be effected under the guidance of the lay ruler, had established a good working relationship with his new archbishop of Canterbury, Lanfranc, and had pressed ahead with reform of the English church with due recognition to the authority of Pope Alexander II (1061–73).[3] Gregory VII (1073–85) had tried to bring the English and Norman churches within the scope of his programme for a reorganised and revitalised church under papal leadership. One key aspect of the process by which bishops and abbots were appointed came to centre on the denunciation of the practice by laymen of investiture of bishops and abbots with their staffs.[4] When Gregory came up against the Conqueror's robust defence of his prerogatives, he had little option but to back away from a confrontation whose consequences could only add to his troubles.[5] In the

---

[2] For a good guide in English see Robinson, *Authority and Resistance in the Investiture Contest*.
[3] The best review of the subject remains Barlow, *English Church 1066–1154*.
[4] See C. Morris, *The Papal Monarchy. The Western Church from 1050 to 1250* (Oxford, 1989), pp. 105–8, 115, 125, 155–73.
[5] H. E. J. Cowdrey, 'Pope Gregory VII and the Anglo-Norman Church and Kingdom', *Studia Gratiana*, 9 (1972), 79–114 (reprinted in *Popes, Monks and Crusaders*, London, 1984, x); Cowdrey, *Pope Gregory VII 1073–1085* (Oxford, 1998), pp. 459–67.

last years of his life, the Conqueror had not formally recognised either the pope or the antipope, and Rufus in England was able to avoid a commitment for some years, until pushed out of an isolationist stance by his new archbishop's request in 1095 to receive his pallium from Urban II, whom he had recognised when he was abbot of Bec.[6] In Normandy there had been some contact with Urban II, because a quarrel had erupted between the archbishop of Rouen and the abbey of Fécamp which had resulted in an intervention by Urban II. Then in 1095 Robert had responded personally to Urban's call to the crusade.[7] Yet neither in Normandy or England had reformed ideas about the prince's authority over the church made much impact in a practical way: the decisive voice in appointments remained with king and duke, who both continued to practise investiture.[8]

Coronation and crown-wearings were a crucial aspect of the Norman regime in England, not least because of the circumstances in which the Conqueror had come to the throne. They embodied ideas of sanctification and responsibility: the king was changed by his anointing with chrism into a new person, with God-given power, and he swore to protect church and people. The re-enactment of the coronation ceremony by crown-wearings, which were held three times a year when the king was in England,[9] reinforced the specialness of his role, elevated and distinct from those around him. The singing of royal acclamations to the king and the queen, in the great churches of Normandy as well as England, underlined their position in the celestial hierarchy of saints and angels.[10] So far as the ritual of coronation was concerned, the old ideology of sacral kingship had barely been dented by reforming ideas by the time that Henry I was crowned king.

One of the most famous compilations of ecclesiastical polemics was drawn up within the Anglo-Norman world, probably around 1100: 'the Anglo-Norman Anonymous'.[11] Attempts to identify the author or authors of the treatises in this collection have so far failed, but the most reasonable guess is that some of them emanated from the cathedral chapter at Rouen.[12] That referred to by historians as J 24 is concerned directly with

---

[6] Eadmer, *Historia Novorum*, pp. 53ff.   [7] David, *Robert Curthose*, pp. 82, 88–91.
[8] The evidence for England comes from Eadmer, *Historia Novorum*, pp. 111–12; for Normandy there is the case of Roger of Le Sap, who was invested as abbot of Saint-Evroult by Duke Robert (OV, iv, 254). Pope Paschal II reproached the duke for having performed an investiture: W. Levison, 'Aus englischen Bibliotheken. II, Ein Schreiben Paschalis II an Robert von Normandie', *Neues Archiv der Gesellschaft für ältere deutsche Geschichtskunde*, 35 (1909), 427; David, *Robert Curthose*, pp. 154–5.
[9] *ASC* E 1087.
[10] H. E. J. Cowdrey, 'The Anglo-Norman Laudes Regiae', *Viator*, 12 (1981), 37–78, and see below, p. 289.
[11] *Die Texte des Normannischen Anonymous*, ed. K. Pellens (Wiesbaden, 1966).
[12] H. Böhmer, *Kirche und Staat in England und in der Normandie im XI. und XII. Jahrhundert* (Leipzig, 1899); G. H. Williams, *The Norman Anonymous of A. D. 1100*, Harvard Theological Studies, no. 18

the relationship between royal and episcopal authority. This is a defence of the old position: kings and priests are sanctified with the same oil; royal authority comes from God, whereas that of priests comes from Christ and thence from God; kings can institute priests and grant them the ring and the staff, though when they do so it has to be recognised that they conveyed only temporal things; and kings can summon councils. Had Henry heard these views, he would certainly have approved.

Hugh, a monk at Saint-Benoît at Fleury-sur-Loire, addressed his treatise on 'royal power and priestly dignity' to Henry, 'the most glorious king of the English'.[13] In this, Hugh declares that he has been moved to write in response to those who seek to separate royal and priestly dignity. However, he restates the view that royal power is ordained by God, and a king's duty is to correct the people from error and summon them back to the way of equity and justice.[14] This traditional formulation was again surely one to which Henry would have subscribed.

Henry recognised the importance of coronation and of ritual crown-wearings even if he abandoned his father's regular tri-annual ceremonies (see below, pp. 289–90). He also recognised the special importance of Westminster abbey as the coronation church, and as a burial place of royalty. He did not seek to have Rufus buried there, presumably because it would have delayed his own coronation at a time when speed was essential to the success of his plans, but it was on his order that his first wife Matilda was buried there (see above, p. 14), close to the tombs of Edward the Confessor and Queen Edith.[15] When Matilda was buried, the abbacy was vacant, and when a new abbot was appointed in 1121, a clutch of confirmations and grants was issued, two of which were made for the souls of King Henry and of Edward the Confessor,[16] and a third for the wellbeing of Henry's family.[17] Henry ordered a light to burn at his wife's tomb in perpetuity, and King David made a grant of land to fund the keeping of anniversaries of his sister and his parents.[18] Both grants may have prompted

---

(Cambridge, Mass., 1951); Cantor, *Church, Kingship and and Lay Investiture in England*; R. Nineham, 'The So-Called Anonymous of York', *Journal of Ecclesiastical History*, 14 (1963), 31–45; K. Pellens, *Das Kirchendenken des Normannischen Anonymus* (Wiesbaden, 1973). For helpful comparison with Ivo of Chartres see Lynn K. Barker, 'Ivo of Chartres and the Anglo-Norman Cultural Tradition', *ANS*, 13 (1990), 32.

[13] See *Monumenta Germaniae Historica, Libelli de Lite*, ii, 465–94.   [14] Ibid., ii, 468.
[15] Edith had been buried there on the order of King William: WM, *GRA*, i, 702.
[16] *Westminster Abbey Charters*, nos. 76, 78; E. Mason, 'Westminster Abbey and the Monarchy between the Reigns of William I and John (1066–1216)', *Journal of Ecclesiastical History*, 41 (1990), 209–10; Mason, 'The Site of King Making and Consecration: Westminster Abbey and the Crown in the Eleventh and Twelfth Centuries', in *The Church and Sovereignty c. 590–1918. Essays in Honour of Michael Wilks*, ed. D. Wood, Studies in Church History, 9 (1991), 57–76.
[17] *Westminster Abbey Charters*, no. 77.   [18] Ibid., nos. 79, 99; *Charters of David I*, no. 13.

the veneration at Matilda's tomb remarked on by William of Malmesbury.[19] How far Henry himself was interested in the cultic potential of his late wife, or of King Edward, is hard to know. It appears that Edward's tomb was opened in 1102, but neither the king nor the queen was said to have been present.[20]

That Henry chose to attend the great ceremonies for the translation of relics and the consecration of churches (below, p. 291) suggests that he was aware of the value of associating with the saints of pre-Conquest England.[21] Amongst those saints whose relics were honoured were sainted kings, such as Oswald of Northumbria: one possible reason for Henry's involvement in the establishment of Nostell priory in Yorkshire was its association with St Oswald.[22] Bury in Suffolk, home to the cult of the martyred royal saint St Edmund, was an important abbey which Henry visited on at least two occasions:[23] the second visit in 1132 is said to have been made as a thank-offering for his escape from shipwreck (see above, p. 213).

Marc Bloch suggested that Henry may have been the first English king to touch for the king's evil,[24] but this is unlikely.[25] There is no indication that Henry ever did engage in such practices, or even came into contact with those suffering from skin diseases, unlike the Capetian kings. In France the belief that kings could cure those who suffered from scrofula, the practice of 'touching for the king's evil', may be traced back to the reign of Robert the Pious (996–1031).[26] In England the miracles attributed to Edward the Confessor included one in which the king is said to have cured a sufferer from a skin disorder, though it is not clear whether this was indeed scrofula.[27] This miracle was known to William of Malmesbury, who pointed out that Edward had performed similar miracles on many occasions whilst

---

[19] WM, *GRA*, i, 458.

[20] F. Barlow, *Edward the Confessor* (London, 1970), p. 267, discusses this episode.

[21] For Louis VI, see T. G. Waldman, 'Saint-Denis et les premiers Capétiens', in *Religion et culture autour de l'an mil: royaume capétien et Lotharingie. Actes du Colloque Hugues Capet (987–1987)*, ed. D. Iogna-Prat and J.-C. Picard (Paris, 1990), pp. 191–7.

[22] Nicholl, *Thurstan*, pp. 130–7.

[23] *RRAN*, ii, nos. 759–62 (1100/1107, possibly 1106); 1733 (c. 1129/1133, possibly 1132).

[24] M. Bloch, *Les rois thaumaturges* (Paris, 1961 edn), p. 61; trans. J. E. Anderson, *The Royal Touch* (London and Montreal, 1973), p. 25.

[25] As Barlow pointed out (*Edward the Confessor*, p. 272).

[26] The classic account is that by Bloch, *Les rois thaumaturges*; see more recently F. Barlow, 'The King's Evil', *EHR* 95 (1980), 3–27; J. Le Goff, 'Aspects religieux et sacrés de la monarchie française du xe au xiiie siècle', in *La royauté sacrée dans le monde chrétien. Colloque de Royaumont, mars (1989)*, ed. A. Boureau and C. S. Ingerflom (Paris, 1982), pp. 19–28; P. Buc, 'David's Adultery with Bathsheba and the Healing Power of the Capetian Kings', *Viator*, 24 (1993), 101–20.

[27] *The Life of King Edward Who Rests at Westminster*, p. 93. It has been suggested that his may have been a false insertion: J.-P. Poly, 'Le capétien thaumaturge: genèse populaire d'un miracle royal', in *La France de l'an mil*, ed. R. Delort (Paris, 1990), p. 305.

living in Normandy before he became king, and that his curative power was a reflection of his *personal* sanctity, not royal blood.[28] Guibert, abbot of Nogent in northern France, writing in the early twelfth century, mentioned that he had once seen Louis VI of France touch the scrofulous, and that his father Philip I had done so until he lost his power because of his sins; but Guibert believed that the English kings had never attempted such a cure.[29]

It is possible, however, that *Matilda's* touch could have been thought to have curative powers. She, like her mother, was said to have washed the feet of the sick in her chamber.[30] This was a *topos* derived from the 'Life of St Radegund' but this text, like the 'Life of St Margaret', gives no indication of the precise nature of the illnesses from which those cured had suffered. By the mid-twelfth century, however, it was believed that Matilda had washed the feet of lepers, and that she had been found doing so by her brother David.[31]

The idea that the king's person was special was reflected in the comment by Orderic about the crime committed by William Crispin at the battle of Brémule in raising a sword against the king's head, which had been anointed with holy chrism and crowned by bishops.[32] If the king's person was special in life, it had been less so in death. One of the early defining experiences for Henry must have been his father's funeral, and the less than dignified incidents which had taken place then: the fact that the body could not be fitted into the coffin, and the protest made at the ceremony itself about ownership of a plot of land. Rufus' body had been carried to Winchester in a cart, and the funeral was apparently conducted quickly. After Henry's own death, however, his body was honoured by a series of ceremonies as it was moved from Lyons to Rouen, Caen and thence to Reading abbey for its final interment.[33] Ongoing debates in the church about the location of authority and the exercise of power were bound to affect older ideas about sacral kingship in the long term, but Henry was still concerned to associate

---

[28] *GRA*, i, 406–8. [29] 'De Pignoribus Sanctorum', Migne, *Patrologia Latina*, clvi, col. 616.
[30] WM, *GRA*, i, 758; 'The Life of St Margaret', translated Huneycutt in *Matilda of Scotland*, p. 173.
[31] Ailred of Rievaulx, 'Genealogia Regum Anglorum', Migne, *Patrologia Latina*, cxcv, col. 736.
[32] OV, vi, 238. Orderic, interestingly, did not make such a comment when he mentioned the killing of Malcolm III Canmore, a king, but not anointed and crowned in the same way: OV, iv, 270. For rituals associated with the king see S. Bertelli, *The King's Body*, translated R. Burr Litchfield (Philadelphia, 2001).
[33] For the rise of rituals associated with the deaths of kings see A. Erlande-Brandenburg, *Le Roi est Mort. Etude sur les funérailles les sépultures et les tombeaux des rois de France jusqu'à la fin du XIIIe siècle*, Bibliothèque de la Société Française d'Archéologie, 7 (Geneva and Paris, 1975), chapters 1 and 2.

himself with ritual and with shrines, especially those of the most important English saints.[34]

Long before Henry's reign, historians of the Normans and their dukes had discussed the nature of ducal authority and power. Dudo of Saint-Quentin wrote around the turn of the millennium, when ideas of sacral rulership were potent in northern France. His portrayal of Rollo, the Viking leader, placed his conversion to Christianity centre stage: Rollo and his followers, the founders of Normandy, were to be Christian rulers. Rollo's son William Longsword (c. 929–43) was a Christian martyr;[35] Richard I (943–96) had saintly attributes, and under his rule the refoundation of monasteries had got under way.[36] The story of Christian rule was thus interwoven by Dudo into the history of a Christian people. When his story of the Normans was taken up by William, a monk of Jumièges in Normandy, these ideas were incorporated, though William's attention shifted to the story of the interlocking histories of Normandy and England, culminating in Duke William's epic conquest.[37] These historians did have views about the responsibilities of Christian rulership, and their focus was on the story of the Norman dukes, but there was no Norman monastery which ever assumed the role Saint-Denis was to assume in relation to Capetian kingship. The abbey of Fécamp, which had been re-established by Duke Richard II and was also his burial place, was a possible candidate, but its history took a different course in the later eleventh century, as it began to promote its custody of the relic of the Holy Blood.[38]

The rise of crusading fervour provided a fresh dimension to the portrayal of princely responsibilities. Duke Robert had covered himself with glory

---

[34] For similar points made in connection with the Angevin kings, see N. Vincent, 'The Pilgrimages of the Angevin Kings', in *Pilgrimage: The English Experience from Becket to Bunyan*, ed. C. Morris and P. Roberts (Cambridge, 2002), pp. 12–45. The work of J. L. Nelson is of fundamental importance: some of her more important articles are collected in *Politics and Ritual in Early Medieval Europe* (London, 1986). For a critique of historians' study of ritual, see P. Buc, *The Dangers of Ritual: Between Early Medieval Texts and Social Theory* (Princeton, 2002), and a rejoinder by G. Koziol, 'The Dangers of Polemic: Is Ritual Still an Interesting Topic of Historical Study?', *Early Medieval Europe* 11 (2002), 367–88.

[35] Dudo of St Quentin, *History of the Normans* (trans. Christiansen), pp. 60–3, 109, 115.

[36] Ibid., p. 109: 'holy, religious, good, and pious'; p. 167: 'we . . . declare him for his merit to be blessed and holy'; p. 173: and, of his body, 'most holy'.

[37] Duke William I was described as 'the most sacred', and 'the most pious and blessed': *GND*, i, 94, 98. The author did not, however, view Duke Richard I in the same light, though he was praised for his mode of life.

[38] For a discussion of the community's changing evaluation of its relics see C. Beaune, 'Les ducs, le roi et le Saint-Sang', in *Saint-Denis et la royauté. Etudes offertes à Bernard Guenée*, ed. F. Autrand, C. Gaward and J.-M. Moeglin (Paris, 1999), pp. 711–32; J. A. Green, 'Fécamp under the Norman Kings', *Tabularia*, www.unicaen.fr/mrsh/crahm/revue/tabularia, May, 2002; for a discussion of the Holy Blood, see N. Vincent, *The Holy Blood. King Henry III and the Westminster Blood Relic* (Cambridge, 2001), chapter 4.

at Antioch and Jerusalem, and he was not oblivious of the potential for added prestige that his exploits commanded. On his return to Normandy in 1100 he made a solemn pilgrimage to Mont-Saint-Michel,[39] the shrine of St Michael, the greatest of the warrior saints, and he presented to the abbey of La Trinité at Caen a banner he had captured from the Saracens.[40] When Henry's party had to justify his invasion of the duchy, it is therefore significant that Robert's achievements in the Holy Land were not denigrated, but passed over. Instead the focus was put on the duke's indolence after his return: by his sloth Robert had failed to protect the church and the Christian faithful, whereas Henry would ensure that churches had their lands and rights as they had enjoyed them at the death of his father. Protection of the church remained a theme of Orderic's discussion of Henry's rule over Normandy and, as noted above, it figured prominently in the chronicler's obituary of the king. Although the duke of Normandy was not a crowned king with all the symbolic power emanating from coronation, the historians of the Normans did see their leaders as having responsibilities to exercise power according to Christian precept, and a duty of care to the Christian souls over whom they ruled.

In the longer term the debate about the right relationship between secular and ecclesiastical power obviously affected ideas of imperial and royal rule, but it is hard to see that they had much effect on the way Henry viewed his own position. Coronation, acclamations, religious rituals were symbolic of older ideas, but they did not necessarily conflict with the new.[41] If some ecclesiastics in England or Normandy thought Henry old-fashioned in his views about his rights and responsibilities, they were hardly likely to say so. Henry was often on the defensive to protect his rights, but his continuing power over appointments, combined with his record in trying to root out married clergy, and as a benefactor, served to silence criticism and to win him the respect of men like Abbots Suger and Peter the Venerable, and Archbishop Hugh of Rouen.

HENRY AND THE CHURCHMEN

Central to the roles of the king and duke was the process of appointing archbishops, bishops and abbots. As soon as the news arrived of the death

---

[39] OV, v, 300. [40] Wace, *Roman de Rou* (ed. Holden), lines 9,691–9,698.
[41] A point also made by Vincent, 'Pilgrimages of the Angevin Kings', pp. 39–45. For a different view, see G. Koziol, 'England, France, and the Problem of Sacrality in Twelfth-Century Ritual', in *Cultures of Power. Lordship, Status and Process in Twelfth-Century Europe*, ed. T. N. Bisson (Philadelphia, 1995), pp. 124–48.

of a bishop or abbot, an officer was sent to take charge of the revenues.[42] The ruler could fill or prolong vacancies more or less as he wished, and it was in his financial interests to do the latter. It was over the length of and profts made from ecclesiastical vacancies that Rufus attracted such criticism from contemporary chroniclers.[43] In 1100 Henry promised that he would not take anything from the demesne of vacant churches, but he made no commitment on the length of vacancies, nor did he promise to relinquish his rights over the revenues. Nevertheless, on the whole Henry had a better record than Rufus. His officials were said to have been reasonable about apportioning revenues for monks, for instance, and vacancies were not usually protracted.[44] The major exception here was the long vacancy at Canterbury following Anselm's death. The delay was probably caused by several reasons: the king had been engaged in war between 1111 and 1113, the selection of an archbishop needed special care, and the king was profiting financially from the long vacancy. As indicated above, however (p. 13), by delaying until after the death of the archbishop of York, it was possible to fill Canterbury before York, so that the new archbishop in the south could legitimately claim seniority and on that basis consecrate his new colleague in the north.

Selection

On both sides of the Channel Henry had a decisive voice in nominations to archbishoprics, bishoprics and abbeys. In the case of the archbishopric of Canterbury, we know that it was power exercised with circumspection, and that on both occasions the see was filled, the choice of a new archbishop was debated at meetings of a great council. The wishes of the monks of Christ Church and of the bishops of the southern province also had to be taken into account. On the first occasion, in 1114, Henry's initial choice was Faritius, abbot of Abingdon, who might have been acceptable at Canterbury, but was rejected by the bishops of Salisbury and Lincoln. The man eventually chosen was a monk, Ralph d'Escures, bishop of Rochester (see above, p. 13). On the second occasion, once again the southern bishops and the monks of Christ Church Canterbury had different views. Four names were presented

---

[42] For example, William de Pont-de-l'Arche was sent to Durham after the death of Bishop Ranulf in 1128: *PR 31 Henry I*, p. 131. In 1125 Richard Basset and Walter the archdeacon of Oxford were sent to Peterborough to make a survey of the abbey's revenues after the abbot's death: *The Peterborough Chronicle of Hugh Candidus*, ed. W. T. Mellows (Oxford, 1949), p. 99.

[43] M. Howell, *Regalian Right in Medieval England* (London, 1962), pp. 5–29.

[44] *Chronicle of Battle Abbey*, p. 116; L. H. Jared, 'English Ecclesiastical Vacancies', 362–93.

to the king, from which he chose that of an Augustinian canon, William of Corbeil. William was the first archbishop since Stigand who was not a monk, but from the point of view of the Canterbury monks he was at least a member of a religious order, and from the king's point of view, he was an educated man.

At York all three appointments were of seculars, men who were or had been members of the royal household, all of them members of those clerical families who in this period achieved what has been described as 'a near stranglehold on royal patronage'.[45] The first, Gerard, was a former royal chancellor and already bishop of Hereford, and he was translated, according to later gossip, as a reward for having officiated at Henry's coronation.[46] Relatively little is said about him by the York chronicler, doubtless because he was at odds with his chapter, but he was a learned man.[47] His successor, Thomas, provost of Beverley and nephew of an earlier archbishop, was the candidate the canons themselves wanted, according to Hugh the Chanter. The king had intended to appoint him to London, but was persuaded instead to give him York.[48] Finally there was Thurstan, who had been a royal chaplain and who, like his father and brother, was a prebendary of St Paul's, with relatively little prior experience of northern affairs.[49] The three appointments, of past or present royal servants who were recruited from a small pool of clerical families, thus bear more comparison with the majority of Henry's appointments to bishoprics in England and Normandy than to Canterbury, but in one case at least – that of Thomas – Henry had been sensitive to local wishes.

Henry's two appointments to the archbishopric of Rouen were of reformers and outsiders. The first, Geoffrey Rufus, was Breton by origin, and a brother of the bishop of Saint-Malo; he was an educated man who had been dean of Le Mans, and tried to impose celibacy on the Norman clergy.[50] His successor, Hugh of Amiens, was a Cluniac monk, prior of Saint-Martial at Limoges, then of Lewes, and finally abbot of Reading. He too was a distinguished intellectual and reformer, and he was so well regarded at Rome that the pope was intending to keep him there, until Henry made his wish for Hugh's return very clear.[51] In neither case do we hear of any process of prior consultation, and the appointment of non-Normans was a departure from the recent past.

---

[45] Brett, *The English Church under Henry I*, p. 110. [46] Walter Map, *De Nugis Curialium*, p. 470.
[47] Hugh the Chanter, p. 12; V. H. Galbraith, 'Girard the Chancellor', *EHR*, 46 (1931), 77–9.
[48] Hugh the Chanter, p. 15.   [49] For Thurstan see Nicholl, *Thurstan*, chapter 1.
[50] Spear, 'Geoffrey Brito, Archbishop of Rouen'.
[51] Hébert, 'Un archevêque de Rouen au XII siècle'; Waldman, 'Hugh "of Amiens"'.

Appointments to bishoprics again reflected the king's wishes, though on occasion he was reported as having taken soundings. Only rarely was the accusation of simony voiced: Theulf, bishop of Worcester, for instance, confessed to the sin on his deathbed, and complaints about simony were voiced at the council of London in 1136.[52] The most prominent group of appointees was made up of former royal clerks and chaplains. Only two were monks, and at least one if not both were appointed for special reasons. Henry of Blois, appointed to Winchester in 1129, was the king's nephew; and his predecessor as abbot of Glastonbury, Seffrid (Siegfried) d'Escures, who had been appointed to Chichester four years earlier, was a half-brother of the archbishop of Canterbury, and had accompanied the archbishop to Rome in 1123 (though his appointment may have been motivated partly by the desire to free Glastonbury for Henry of Blois).[53] Another kinsman of the king was Richard, son of Robert of Gloucester and Isabelle of Douvres, and nephew of Richard II bishop of Bayeux. The younger Richard was nominated to Bayeux, but the archbishop delayed his consecration for two years, because of his illegitimate birth.[54]

As well as the Augustinian archbishop of Canterbury there were three nominations of Augustinians to bishoprics: Robert of Béthune, prior of Llanthony, to Hereford; Adelulf, prior of Nostell, to Carlisle; and Algar, prior of Bodmin, to Coutances. Robert was chosen after consultation with Miles of Gloucester, and the king said of him that he wanted to leave at least one good bishop behind him.[55] Adelulf was said to have been the king's confessor; he was prior of Nostell when appointed first bishop of Carlisle in 1133.[56] Algar, a pupil of Anselm of Laon, was in charge of Bodmin priory (*procurator*), then a canon there, before moving to Coutances.[57] Robert of Béthune was a man of some learning; another was Gilbert 'the Universal', a canon of Auxerre, who had supported the Canterbury primacy at Rome

---

[52] WM, *Gesta Pontificum*, p. 290n.; *Gesta Stephani*, p. 26. According to Symeon of Durham, Geoffrey de Clinton gave his nephew the enormous sum of three thousand marks 'to make him more worthy of the bishopric (of Lichfield)': SD, *Opera Omnia*, ii, 283.

[53] ASC E 1123. The other reason was obviously the favour in which Henry regarded Ralph and his family. The archbishop's nephew John became successively archdeacon of Canterbury, and bishop of Rochester in 1125. He had protested in 1119 at the Council of Rheims against the papal consecration of Thurstan without a profession.

[54] OV, vi, 428–9, 442.

[55] *Anglia Sacra*, ed. H. Wharton, 2 vols. (London, 1691), ii, 304–5; *English Episcopal Acta. VII. Hereford 1079–1234*, ed. J. Barrow (Oxford, 1993), pp. xxxvii–xl.

[56] Nicholl, *Thurstan Archbishop of York*, pp. 134, 147, 150.

[57] Algar was at Bodmin when the canons of Laon visited: Hermann, 'De Miraculis S. Mariae Laudunensis', Migne, *Patrologia Latina*, clvi, col. 983; see also M. L. Colker, 'The Life of Guy of Merton by Rainald of Merton', *Medieval Studies*, 31 (1969), 259–61.

in 1126 and was nominated to London in 1128.[58] The king also offered a bishopric to the distinguished intellectual, Robert Pullen.[59] So although former royal servants remained predominant in the episcopate, by the end of his life Henry was choosing men from a wider pool, possibly motivated by a desire for men of intellectual distinction, and possibly recognising, as in the case of Gilbert Foliot, the value of bishops skilled in canon law.

As in the nomination of bishops, so too in the selection of abbots the king's voice was decisive.[60] Orderic related the way a new abbot was chosen for Saint-Evroult in 1122. The monks chose one of their own number and then went to find the king, who was at York. The king then 'gave' the abbey to the monks' nominee, and issued a charter granting him all the abbey's lands and rights.[61] In the case of Malmesbury after the death of the abbot in 1118, for instance, he allowed Bishop Roger of Salisbury to keep the revenues from the abbey, ignoring the monks' pleas for a new abbot, and in 1131 he granted the possessions of the abbey to Bishop Roger (see above, p. 212). By contrast, in 1109 the abbey of Ely was finally detached from the see of Lincoln and elevated to the seat of a new bishopric, with the approval of the pope.[62] And it was with the king's active involvement (at a price) that in 1110 the monks of the New Minster at Winchester moved to a different, more commodious, site outside the city.[63]

The king's choices did not always prove to be satisfactory. On the day of his coronation in 1100 two nominations were self-evidently pledges to win the backing of their families. Robert, an illegitimate son of Earl Hugh of Chester,[64] was appointed to Bury in 1100, but was deposed at the council of London in 1102. Richard, son of Richard FitzGilbert of Clare, was nominated to Ely; he also was deposed in 1102, perhaps because of the way he had been chosen, but was subsequently reinstated by the pope.[65]

In Normandy Henry had difficult dealings with the monks of Mont-Saint-Michel, who were unhappy when outsiders were nominated as abbots. In 1085, according to the annals of the abbey, a monk of Caen had been nominated 'by earthly power'.[66] After the battle of Tinchebray, the abbot

---

[58] JW, iii, 176–7; B. Smalley, 'Gilbertus Universalis, Bishop of London (1128–34), and the Problem of the "Glossa Ordinaria"', *Recherches de Théologie Ancienne et Médiévale*, 7 (1935), 24–60.
[59] SD, *Opera Omnia*, ii, 319.
[60] For Henry I and the abbots of Benedictine houses in Normandy, see Gazeau, 'Recherches sur l'histoire de la principauté normande (911–1204). I, Les abbés bénédictins de la principauté normande', chapter 6.
[61] OV, vi, 320–4.   [62] *Liber Eliensis*, pp. 224–8.
[63] *Annales Monastici*, ii, 44. It has been pointed out that the initiative may well have been the bishop's: *English Episcopal Acta. VII. Winchester 1070–1204*, ed. M. J. Franklin (Oxford, 1993), p. xxxiii.
[64] OV, iii, 236–8.   [65] *Liber Eliensis*, pp. 225–7.
[66] Robert of Torigny, *Annales du Mont-Saint-Michel*, in *Chronique* (ed. Delisle), ii, 222–4.

had Henry distribute some of the monks to other Norman abbeys, whereupon the remainder complained to Henry, who ordered the return of the monks. The abbot then handed back his pastoral staff, and Henry nominated Roger, prior of Jumièges, as abbot 'by the force of royal majesty'. Again the monks did not consent, and in 1123 Roger too was replaced.[67]

Sometimes the king granted free elections, and then monks might choose one of their own number. Other abbots came from a small group of Norman houses: Bec,[68] Saint-Etienne in Caen[69] and Saint-Evroult.[70] The choice of Cluniacs at Mont-Saint-Michel, and of Henry of Saint-Jean-d'Angély at Peterborough in 1127, were other manifestations of the king's love of Cluniacs.[71] The appointment of Henry of Saint-Jean illustrates a third feature, that Henry liked to recruit talented outsiders into his realm. Another example was Anselm abbot of Saint Saba, nephew of Archbishop Anselm, who had come to the king's notice as a papal emissary sent to collect arrears of Peter's Pence, and was appointed abbot of Bury St Edmunds.[72]

Investiture and homage

The story of Henry's battle with Archbishop Anselm over homage and investiture, and its outcome in Henry's formal surrender of investiture at the council of London in 1102, has already been told (above, pp. 52–3, 66, 81, 86, 88, 108). No comparable formal condemnation of investiture was made in Normandy, probably because by 1106 it must have been apparent that Henry

---

[67] Ibid., 224.
[68] Viz. Battle (Ralph, 1107); Bury (Alebold, monk of Bec and prior of Sainte-Nicaise, Meulan 1114); Canterbury, St Augustine's (Hugh, before 1126); Colchester (Gilbert 1117) and Ely (Richard 1100–2, c. 1103–7): all from D. Knowles, C. N. L. Brooke and V. Landon (eds.), *The Heads of Religious Houses, England and Wales. I, 940–1216*, 2nd edn (Cambridge, 2001), pp. 29, 32, 36, 40, 45. Cormeilles (Benedict, early twelfth century): Robert of Torigny, 'De Immutatione Ordinis Monachorum', Migne, *Patrologia Latina*, ccii, col. 1317. Mont-Saint-Michel, 1131: J. Laporte, 'Les listes abbatiale et priorale du Mont-Saint-Michel', in *Millénaire Monastique du Mont-Saint-Michel*, 5 vols. (Paris, 1967–93) i, 268–84. Conches (Gilbert, 1130): Robert of Torigny, 'De Immutatione', col. 1316. Lyre (Ralph, 1130): ibid., col. 1316. Lessay (Warin, early twelfth century): Robert of Torigny, *Chronique* (ed. Delisle), ii, 202. Bec: 'Lives of Abbots William and Boso': S. Vaughn, *The Abbey of Bec and the Anglo-Norman State* (Woodbridge, 1981), pp. 139–43.
[69] Cerne (William, 1114), Glastonbury (Herluin, 1100), Ramsey (Reginald, 1113 or 1114): Knowles, Brooke and Landon, *Heads*, pp. 37, 51, 62; Caen (Eudo 1107): OV, vi, 138.
[70] Crowland (Geoffrey 1109), S. Benet of Holme (William, 1127), Thorney (Robert, 1113 or 1114): OV, iv, 256; Knowles, Brooke and Landon, *Heads*, pp. 42, 68, 75. Orderic mentions these three monks as abbots in England, and adds three in Normandy: Warin, who became abbot of Saint-Evroult, Louis, abbot of Saint-Georges de Boscherville, and Gilbert of Glos, abbot of Lire (OV, iv, 256–7).
[71] *ASC* E 1127.
[72] Ibid., E 1115. Anselm returned as legate in the following year: Eadmer, *Historia Novorum*, p. 239; for Henry as legate, see *ASC* E 1123.

would not be able to invest prelates in the duchy, given the condemnation his eldest brother had already attracted. In England Henry continued to take homage from bishops and abbots. Bishops of the southern province made written professions of obedience to the archbishop of Canterbury.[73]

In Normandy, however, it seems that the king could take homage from bishops, but experienced resistance to homage from the abbots-elect of privileged houses.[74] We learn this from the accounts kept by the monks of Bec, who guarded their privileges jealously. The monks relate how in 1124 they chose their prior, Boso, as their new abbot, but that Boso refused steadfastly to do homage to Henry, and he also refused to make a written profession of obedience to the archbishop of Rouen. The bishops of Lisieux and Evreux were angry at the refusal to perform homage which they themselves had performed, but Henry was eventually forced to accept the situation, preferring to avoid trouble. Archbishop Geoffrey however was not so pliable, and continued to demand a written profession from Boso. It took the intervention of John of Crema, the papal legate, to secure a form of words which was sufficiently acceptable to both Boso and the archbishop.[75]

Archbishop Geoffrey's successor, Hugh, continued the struggle to extract written professions of obedience. When he became archbishop, the abbots of three great houses had not yet been blessed. Two, the abbots of Saint-Ouen and Jumièges, were persuaded to make their professions, having appeared before the pope at Rheims in 1131. This resulted in an indignant protest from the king to Pope Innocent II, on the grounds that the issue had been decided outside the duchy, and that Hugh had infringed the traditional rights of the duke.[76] The pope in response wrote to the archbishop recommending moderation: an insight into the benefits (from Henry's point of view) of good relations with Innocent II.[77] The issue of homage by abbots-elect in Normandy to the duke was thus complicated by

---

[73] *Canterbury Professions* (ed. Richter).
[74] M. Chibnall, 'From Bec to Canterbury: Anselm and Monastic Privilege', *Anselm Studies. An Occasional Journal*, 1 (1983), 23–44.
[75] Miles Crispin, 'Vita Bosonis Abbatis Beccensis Quarti', Migne, *Patrologia Latina*, cl, cols. 723–34, trans. Vaughn in *Abbey of Bec*, pp. 126–33. Cf. 'De Libertate Beccensis Monasterii', *Annales Ordinis Sancti Benedicti* (Paris, 1745), v. 601–5; 'On the Liberty of Bec', in Vaughn, *Abbey of Bec*, pp. 134–43. For discussion see J. Potter, 'Monastic Freedom vs. Episcopal and Aristocratic Power in the Twelfth Century: Context and Analysis of the *De libertate Beccensis*', in *Negotiating Secular and Ecclesiastical Power*, ed. H. Teunis and A. Wareham (Turnhout, 1999), pp. 73–85. In 'On the Liberty of Bec', the archbishop wanted Boso to say 'profiteor' (I profess), but Boso wished only to acknowledge his obedience, and it was on the intervention of the papal legate that the latter formulation was accepted.
[76] Migne, *Patrologia Latina*, clxxix, cols. 669–70.   [77] Ibid., cols. 150–1.

a parallel campaign by the archbishops, and in this situation Henry backed the abbots against the archbishops.

Ecclesiastics and governance in England and Normandy

Archbishops, bishops and abbots remained central figures in contemporary governance, and often controlled large complexes of land over which they had considerable powers of jurisdiction. In Durham their power went still further, for they controlled the appointment of the sheriffs.[78] Abbots of the major Benedictine houses figure less frequently in the witness lists to Henry's documents than do many of the bishops, but they remained important figures in local society.[79] In England particularly some of the older abbeys possessed extensive estates which owed knight service to the king, the patronage of many livings, and powers of jurisdiction. The abbey of Bury St Edmunds, for instance, was lord of eight and a half hundreds in west Suffolk.[80] In Normandy Henry sought to build up good relations with the important Benedictine abbeys by confirming and sometimes augmenting their lands and privileges. He issued charters of confirmation and gave lands and privileges to many of the leading Norman houses. Bec (see map 1) was particularly important, and Henry issued a charter of confirmation of donations even before his victory at Tinchebray.[81] The value of good relations with the community was demonstrated in 1124 when he stayed at the abbey whilst suppressing the revolt headed by Waleran count of Meulan.[82] In the following year he granted extensive rights of justice and the right to take custom in the town, and confirmed these rights in subsequent charters.[83]

The abbey of Saint-Pierre-sur-Dives (see map 1), whose buildings were destroyed by Henry shortly before the battle of Tinchebray, also received a grant of very important powers.[84] The abbey of Saint-Evroult (see map 3), situated close to the sphere of operations of Robert de Bellême, was another house with which good relations helped Henry to consolidate his authority, this time in the southern marches of the duchy (see above, p. 231). In the

---

[78] Green, *English Sheriffs*, p. 38.
[79] K. L. Shirley, *The Secular Jurisdiction of Monasteries in Anglo-Norman and Angevin England* (Woodbridge, 2004).
[80] An impression of the regalian rights in the abbey's 8½ hundreds may be gained from *The Kalendar of Abbot Samson of Bury St Edmunds and Related Documents*, ed. R. H. C. Davis, Camden Society, 3rd series, lxxxiv (1954).
[81] *RRAN*, ii, no. 860.   [82] OV, vi, 354.   [83] *RRAN*, ii, nos. 1434, 1900–1.   [84] Ibid., ii, no. 905.

west Montebourg (see map 2), begun by his father, was favoured,[85] and so were the two abbeys at Caen.

Bishops in particular were key figures at the king's court, where their counsel counted, and not simply on ecclesiastical matters. The archbishops crossed the Channel on occasion, and if the presence of the English archbishops in Normandy might sometimes be explained as a staging post en route to Rome, the presence of Archbishop Geoffrey of Rouen in England cannot. The timing of his visits – 1115–16, 1121–2, 1126–7 – strongly suggests that with the succession in mind, the king was particularly concerned to have the archbishop present at court.[86] Individual bishops such as Roger of Salisbury, Robert of Lincoln, John of Lisieux and Audoin of Evreux moved easily between the king's court and their dioceses.[87]

Individual bishops enjoyed peculiarly important regional roles, or had particular areas of expertise. Ranulf Flambard, for instance, may never have enjoyed Henry's favour after his endeavours on behalf of Duke Robert, but when he returned to his diocese he proved to be a bastion of Norman influence in Durham, which prior to his arrival had strong ties with the Scots.[88] William Warelwast was highly regarded as an emissary to the pope, and even after he became bishop of Exeter and, in later life, was suffering from blindness, he was nevertheless dispatched to Rome.[89] Some bishops gained reputations for their study of law, both the law of the church and secular law. One of these was Ernulf of Rochester, who was possibly responsible for the great legal collection, the *Textus Roffensis*.[90] Bishop Robert Bloet had years of experience in legal matters, and was the king's justiciar in Lincolnshire, a position inherited by his successor, Bishop Alexander.[91] In England some bishops controlled castles: Ranulf Flambard, for instance,

---

[85] *RRAN*, ii, no. 1953.
[86] Ibid., nos. 1091, 1104, 1124, 1127 (1115–16), 1244, 1247, 1248, 1256, 1265, 1289, 1290, 1294 (all 1121–22), 1356 (1113/1122), 1466, 1474 (1126–7).
[87] For the attendance of the English bishops see E. U. Crosby, 'The Organization of the English Episcopate under Henry I', in *Studies in Medieval and Renaissance History*, 4, ed. W. M. Bowsky (University of California, Davis, 1967), p. 7; for Audoin, *RRAN*, ii, 1204, 1256, 1356, 1427–9, 1432–3, 1439, 1441–2, 1447, 1450, 1466, 1546–5, 1554–5, 1578, 1580–1, 1591, 1656, 1673, 1680, 1687, 1688–90, 1693, 1697–8, 1700–1, 1830, 1892, 1900–2, 1908, 1910, 1932, 1948.
[88] Offler, 'Rannulf Flambard as Bishop of Durham'.
[89] 1115–16: Eadmer, *Historia Novorum*, p. 234; Hugh the Chanter, p. 76; 1119: Hugh the Chanter, pp. 119, 124; 1120: ibid., pp. 142–4.
[90] *Peterborough Chronicle*, pp. 96–7. For Ernulf's possible responsibility for the *Textus Roffensis*, see P. Wormald, 'Laga Eadwardi: The *Textus Roffensis* and its Context', *ANS*, 17 (1994), 264.
[91] *RRAN*, iii, no. 490. Alexander has been suggested as the possible author of a legal glossary of old English terms preserved in the Red Book of the Exchequer: *Red Book of the Exchequer* (ed. Hall), iii, ccclvi–ccclxiii.

held Durham and built another castle at Norham,[92] and Bishop Roger held the royal castle at Salisbury and built others at Sherborne and Devizes.[93] Similarly, the grant of custody of Rochester castle to the archbishop of Canterbury in 1127 may have been with an eye partly on security, and partly as an inducement for the archbishop's loyalty.[94]

In Normandy relatively little is heard about the bishops of the western dioceses of Avranches and Coutances, though after the appointment of bishop Algar to the latter see, Henry did issue a charter restoring the church of St Mary on the island of Alderney to the canons of Coutances, in 1134.[95] At Bayeux, Lisieux, Sées and Evreux, the king's preference for choosing bishops from a small handful of clerical families is particularly striking. Two sons of Samson, bishop of Worcester, became bishops in turn: Richard of Douvres became bishop of Bayeux in 1107, and Thomas became archbishop of York in 1108. John of Lisieux was, as noted above (p. 102), a key figure in presiding over the Norman justices and the exchequer. His nephew John was appointed to Sées in 1124, where he promptly starting reorganising his bishopric with the king's active support.[96] Audoin of Evreux was the brother of Archbishop Thurstan, and a staunchly loyal figure in a region where Henry had considerable political and military difficulties. Audoin accepted with resignation the destruction of the city and his cathedral by fire in 1119, but his continuing loyalty to the king brought rewards for his see in the form of half the proceeds of the fair at Nonancourt, plus the churches and tithes of Nonancourt, Verneuil and Vernon, freedom for his baggage from toll, the manor of Bramford in Suffolk, and land and a house in Rouen.[97] The continuing importance in governance of bishops and abbots of the larger Benedictine houses is not in itself unusual, but in Normandy particularly it helped Henry to assert his authority over the duchy.

One of the issues in which Henry could not avoid becoming embroiled was that of the primatial claims of the archbishops of Canterbury and

---

[92] M. Leyland, 'The Origins and Development of Durham Castle', in *Anglo-Norman Durham 1093–1193*, ed. D. Rollason, M. Harvey and M. Prestwich (Woodbridge, 1994), pp. 415–16; P. Dixon and P. Marshall, 'The Great Tower in the Twelfth Century: The Case of Norham Castle', *Archaeological Journal*, 140 (1993), 410–32; Offler, 'Rannulf Flambard', 20.
[93] R. Stalley, 'A Twelfth-Century Patron of Architecture: A Study of the Buildings Erected by Roger, Bishop of Salisbury 1102–39', *Journal of the British Archaeological Association*, 3rd series, 34 (1971), 62–83.
[94] *RRAN*, ii, no. 1475.   [95] Ibid., ii, no. 1902.
[96] For John, bishop of Sées, see OV, vi, 340, 366.
[97] *RRAN*, ii, nos. 1356, 1554–5, 1673, 1700, 1830, 1910.

York.[98] The primatial claims of Canterbury encompassed all the churches of the British Isles, and as such provided useful ammunition for ideological or, indeed, territorial claims to an imperial concept of rule over different peoples, the rhetoric of which bolstered the claims of kings to overlordship or imperial rule (see above, p. 224). For the archbishops of Canterbury the pressing issue was that of securing written professions of obedience from their colleagues at York. The quarrel had essentially begun in 1070 when the newly appointed Lanfranc had demanded a written profession of obedience from the newly elect archbishop of York, Thomas. When the latter refused, the case was referred to Rome and was circumspectly referred back by Pope Alexander for settlement at a royal council in England. Lanfranc was not satisfied with the decision in his favour at Winchester in 1072, and sought a papal privilege to put his claim beyond question, but did not succeed. The issue remained a recurring problem as each archbishop of Canterbury tried to secure a written profession from newly appointed archbishops of York. At the start of his reign, Henry was lucky in that Archbishop Gerard of York was able to avoid making a profession, on the grounds that he had already made one as bishop of Hereford.[99] His successor Thomas procrastinated and avoided making a profession during Anselm's lifetime, only to be compelled to do so by the king after Anselm's death.[100] The issue of a written profession became serious in 1114 when Archbishop Ralph of Canterbury demanded a profession from Thurstan, who stood out against all the king's threats and preferred to go into exile rather than to comply. The ensuing conflict was graphically chronicled by Hugh the Chanter.[101] Thurstan was finally consecrated by the pope without making a profession, but he then had to face the king's anger as well as that of Archbishop Ralph, and it was only because of his usefulness as an envoy between Henry and Louis VI in 1120 that Henry was prepared to allow him to cross to England and finally to enter his see. Even then the Canterbury lobby was not prepared to let the matter rest, sending another legation to Rome in 1123, though their collection of alleged papal privileges in support of the primacy was laughed out of court by the cardinals.[102] From Henry's point of view, the problem by this time was not only that Archbishop Ralph was a sick man, unable to present the best case he could, but also that by the early

---

[98] Primacy over the archdiocese of Rouen was claimed by the archbishops of Lyon. For the bulls of Gregory and Urban II see *Gallia Christiana*, iv, Instrumenta, xi, xiii; for Paschal II, see Migne, *Patrologia Latina*, clxiii, col. lxi; for Calixtus, *Regesta Pontificum Romanorum*, i, no. 6888.
[99] Hugh the Chanter, pp. 56–7 and n.
[100] Ibid., pp. 40–50.   [101] Ibid., pp. 56–105.   [102] Ibid., pp. 192–4.

twelfth century popes were not prepared to accept that some archbishops had primacy over others. This was therefore a battle which Canterbury was unlikely to win, even when William of Corbeil took the case to Rome in person.[103]

Whilst the archbishops of Canterbury had no success in securing their demands for written professions from the archbishops of York, they had some in exercising superiority over the Welsh and Irish churches. In Wales particularly, the process whereby territorial dioceses were being established in the place of earlier structures gave archbishops of Canterbury the opportunity for intervention: they consecrated Urban for Llandaff (1107), Bernard for St David's (1115), and David the Scot for Bangor (1120) (see above, pp. 134, 173). Such appointments may be seen as part of growing Norman influence over Wales, in which castles were built and religious houses were founded by the new lords, part of a continuing push westwards from England under Henry which was emphasised in the previous chapter (above, p. 226). Canterbury's primatial claims over the Irish church, too, had political connotations which, from Henry's point of view, might one day be useful. Although the currents of reform were flowing strongly within Ireland, it was by no means clear that Canterbury's influence had had its day.

In northern England and Scotland, too, older patterns of ecclesiastical organisation were being superseded, and here too reform and reorganisation had potential for territorial expansion. The archbishops of York had claims to primacy over the whole of north Britain. Thus when David, lord of Cumbria, the future king of Scots, requested Archbishop Thomas II to consecrate a man named Michael as bishop of Glasgow, he did so.[104] However, although Michael's successor, John, was similarly consecrated at York, he steadfastly refused to make a profession of obedience to Thurstan.[105] As kings, Alexander and David were concerned to support claims for a Scottish church independent of both York and Canterbury. As we have seen (above, p. 193), Henry put pressure on Archbishop Thurstan to consecrate a bishop for St Andrews in 1126 without securing a profession of obedience.[106] In the case of Carlisle, however, Henry was not prepared to be conciliatory and backed the creation of a new diocese. Thurstan accordingly consecrated the first bishop in 1133.[107] The northern archbishops, like their colleagues

---

[103] Bethell, 'William of Corbeil and the Canterbury-York Dispute'.
[104] This is at least is the version reported at York by Hugh the Chanter, pp. l, 52–3.
[105] Ibid., pp. xlv–liv; 124–5, 202–3, 206–7, 212–17.   [106] JW, iii, 174–5.
[107] For the bull see *Historians of the Church of York and its Archbishops* (ed. J. Raine), iii, 40; for the see, Nicholl, *Thurstan*, pp. 140–50.

at Canterbury, could see the possibilities for establishing new dioceses or reviving old ones, and sometimes these were, from Henry's point of view, potentially promising: we have seen how he allied with Fergus of Galloway (above, pp. 177, 227), and it is not surprising to learn that Archbishop Thurstan consecrated a bishop for Whithorn in south-west Scotland.[108] Archbishop Thomas II had consecrated a bishop of Orkney,[109] and he consecrated a bishop for the independent kingdom of Man.[110] Such bishops may have had only nominal authority, but they cannot be left out of account in any assessment of Henry's claims to an imperial authority over the British Isles.

HENRY AND REFORM

Henry, like his father, believed in reform and renewal based on close cooperation between ruler and ecclesiastics. When William became duke there was still much to do to restore the diocesan church, especially in western Normandy, and by the appointment of able and vigorous bishops the episcopal church was revitalised: cathedrals were rebuilt, prebends were created and archdeacons were appointed. The archbishops of Rouen in conjunction with the duke held councils at which canons on simony and clerical marriage, the twin goals of reformers, were condemned. Hand in hand with reform of the secular clergy went the revival of monastic life. Dukes Richard I and Richard II had led the way in monastic benefactions, followed by William, Matilda and leading members of the aristocracy.[111]

The situation in England in 1066 was rather different. The diocesan church was relatively conservative in temper, and as yet untouched by contemporary reforming ideas. Archbishop Stigand, an intruder and pluralist, was deemed, in restrospect, a disgrace. In southern and parts of central and eastern England there were wealthy monasteries, which in some respects (though not all historians agree on this point) had lost the reforming zeal of the days of Dunstan and Aethelwold; in the north there were still clerical communities, but monastic life had been deeply affected in the Viking era. With Lanfranc as archbishop of Canterbury and new Norman bishops the diocesan church was overhauled. Some chapters were already monastic; others became so. Some cathedrals were relocated to larger towns; all were

---

[108] Gillaldan was consecrated between 1128 and 1140: *Fasti Ecclesiae Scoticanae Medii Aevi ad annum 1638*, 2nd draft by D. E. R. Watt, Scottish Record Society, new series, i (1969), 128; R. D. Oram, 'In Obedience and Reverence: Whithorn and York *c.* 1128–*c.* 1250', *Innes Review*, 42 no. 2 (1991), 83–100.
[109] Hugh the Chanter, pp. xlviii–xlix, 52–3, 118–19, 122–3, 132–3.
[110] Ibid., p. xlvi n.   [111] OV, ii, 10.

rebuilt. Archdeacons were appointed, and the lengthy process of disentangling ecclesiastical and secular jurisdiction began with the prohibition of ecclesiastical pleas in the hundred courts. Reforming councils were held, and here too clerical marriage was condemned. Nor did the English monasteries escape the winds of change; here resistance was on occasion violent, and as yet little progress had been made towards reviving monasticism in the north.

In the last decade of the eleventh century the situation was changing still further as different approaches to the Christian life were explored. One approach to the religious life which met with a ready response was that of communities of canons, who were celibate and lived according to a rule which they believed was inspired by St Augustine. This proved highly attractive to recruits and benefactors, first in England and then in Normandy. The ideal of celibacy was central, and the communities were flexible: they could incorporate earlier communities of hermits or clerks; they could be attached to schools or hospitals; and they could also form cathedral chapters. Some developed reputations for scholarship, others for practical works of charity; some were richly endowed, others more modestly.

The progress of reform suffered a check after the deaths of the Conqueror and Lanfranc. If Rufus' reputation for irreligion was perhaps overdone by contemporary chroniclers, he was nevertheless not particularly interested in reform. He refused to allow ecclesiastical councils to be summoned, and his quarrel with Anselm left the English church leaderless. In this climate it is unlikely that further progress on eradicating clerical marriage could be made. In contrast Henry was much more committed to reform in England and Normandy, first by appointing men of stature, some of whom were notable reformers, to bishoprics, secondly by permitting and participating in councils, and thirdly by the active encouragement of canons, Cluniacs and the new orders, as well as Bec.

It would appear, however, that the conciliar decrees against clerical marriage enacted at the council of Westminster in 1102 were as widely disregarded as earlier prohibitions, and so in 1105 the king went further, and fined married clergy. Eadmer described the plight of the clergy: 'extortion, frightful and cruel, beat down like a raging storm upon all'. Those who had nothing to give were driven from their cottages, or their sticks of furniture were removed. The king was determined to punish those who had kept wives during Anselm's exile: when not enough clergy were found guilty, a levy was nevertheless placed on each parish to be paid by the priest. Those who could not or would not contribute were imprisoned and allegedly tortured. A deputation met the king and asked for pity, and he drove them away. They asked the queen to intercede on their behalf; she was sympathetic, but too frightened to intervene.[112] Further action was urged by the king in 1108, and procedures were set up for enforcing the rules.[113] There the matter rested for a few years, but the attack was resumed in 1125,[114] 1127[115] and 1129.[116] Henry of Huntingdon reported that the council of 1129 had been summoned to deal with the issue of priests' wives. The archbishop of Canterbury had naively handed the issue over to royal jurisdiction, with the result that the king took fines and allowed the clergy to keep their wives. In the chronicler's view the prelates had been deceived and the lower clergy humiliated.[117] In Normandy, too, clerical marriage was condemned at councils in 1119[118] and 1128.[119]

The difficulty of making headway on this issue, especially at the grassroots level, is thus apparent, but it is surely significant that Henry, either out of principle or because he was unwilling to countenance the rebuff to his authority, continued to throw his weight behind the drive for clerical celibacy. There was a certain irony here, for not only was the king's own sexual conduct far from spotless, but neither was that of some leading bishops. Ranulf Flambard, bishop of Durham, had a mistress and several children,[120] and Richard of Beaumais, bishop of London, had a son and several nephews.[121] Even the great Bishop Roger of Salisbury had a mistress and a son.[122]

King Henry's view of reform was thus moulded by that of his father, subscribing to the ideal of clerical celibacy and ensuring the creation of dioceses where they were needed; but it was very much a vision in which the lay ruler was at the forefront and the pope a distant but venerated figure. The Conqueror had presided over councils in Normandy, and continued to do so in England. He had been able to rebuff or evade efforts by Pope Gregory VII to intervene more directly in ecclesiastical affairs in England and in Normandy. Henry continued to defend as best he could those customary rights over the churches which he had inherited, but the papacy by the early twelfth century had become much more of a force to be reckoned with, even in the affairs of his own family. Henry personally met Pope Calixtus II in 1119 to defend himself against the charges which had been brought by King Louis VI at the papal council at Rheims. It was Pope Honorius'

---

[112] Eadmer, *Historia Novorum*, pp. 171–3. [113] *Councils and Synods*, i, part ii, 694–704.
[114] Ibid., i, part ii, 730–41; HH, pp. 472–4. Henry, himself the child of a clerical marriage, retailed a scandalous story that the legate was discovered with a whore.
[115] *Councils and Synods*, i, part ii, 743–9. [116] ASC E 1129. [117] HH, pp. 482–4.
[118] OV, vi, 290–4. [119] Ibid., 388–90. [120] Offler, 'Rannulf Flambard', 22–3.
[121] Brooke and Keir, *London 800–1216*, pp. 345–7. [122] OV, vi, 532–3.

intervention in 1125 that resulted in the dissolution of the marriage between Henry's nephew, William Clito, and Sibyl of Anjou on the grounds of consanguinuity. The possibility of a similar intervention by the pope when the empress married Sibyl's brother Geoffrey could not be discounted, since bride and groom were related in the same degree as William and Sibyl. When in 1130 there was another contested election to the papacy, Henry could not afford to remain detached, and he presumably sought reassurances from Innocent II that he would not intervene to dissolve the marriage between Geoffrey and the empress.

By the early twelfth century the flow of embassies and legations between Normandy, England and Rome was much greater than in Henry's father's day, and in one sense it is hardly surprising that Henry helped to fund the costs of building a road through the Alps.[123] Henry was awake to the need for envoys like William Warelwast[124] and Bernard, bishop of St David's, who could best represent his interests at Rome.[125] There were far more contacts between English and Norman churchmen and Rome in this period than before, over investiture, the Canterbury primacy, and the claims of some monasteries to exempt status.[126]

However, some aspects of these growing contacts between the papacy and churches in England and Normandy challenged Henry's inherited rights. Attendance at papal councils could be problematic: thus in 1119 Henry was concerned that if Thurstan attended the papal council at Rheims, the pope might intervene on Thurstan's behalf.[127] When in 1123 Calixtus summoned a general council, according to Hugh the Chanter the archbishops of York and Canterbury were summoned, but the king delayed, sending instead a clerk and two of the Norman bishops.[128]

The arrival of papal legates might also be a matter for concern to both the king and the archbishop of Canterbury, who believed that the primacy of his see rendered legates superfluous.[129] Some of the legates sent to England

---

[123] *GND*, ii, 254–6.   [124] Eadmer, *Historia Novorum*, p. 234.   [125] Hugh the Chanter, p. 188.
[126] For exemptions in Normandy, see J.-F. Lemarignier, *Etude sur les privilèges d'exemption et de juridiction ecclésiastique des abbayes normandes jusqu'en 1140* (Paris, 1937). For the dispute at Bec in 1124 see above, p. 267. For the situation in England see D. Knowles, 'Essays in Monastic History IV. The Growth of Exemption', *Downside Review*, 31 (1932), 201–31, 396–436; Knowles, *Monastic Order*, pp. 575–87.
[127] Hugh the Chanter, pp. 110–14.
[128] Ibid., p. 187. Innocent II also summoned a general council to Rheims in 1131, but there are no details about the attendance of prelates from England or Normandy: OV, vi, 422; cf. Suger, *Vie de Louis VI* (ed. Waquet), p. 268.
[129] Eadmer, *Historia Novorum*, p. 126. For legates see S. Weiss, *Die Urkunden der päpstlichen Legaten von Leo IX. bis Coelestin III. (1049–1198)* (Cologne, Weimar, Vienna, 1995); Brett, *English Church*, pp. 35–50.

seem to have been concerned partly or wholly with the collection of arrears of Peter's Pence, but others, who had broader remits, were thwarted by Henry. In 1121, for instance, Henry sent Bernard, bishop of St David's, and a royal clerk, John son of Odo bishop of Bayeux, to the legate Peter Pierleoni, to transmit the king's order that the legate was not to enter any monastery or church or take procurations. Peter was then taken to the king, who explained that, having led an army in Wales, he had nothing left to give him. He also explained the customs of England, and sent him away with gifts.[130] Only in 1125 was the legate John of Crema allowed to hold a legatine council in England, possibly in thanks for his efforts in scotching the marriage of William Clito.[131]

In Normandy too Henry objected to the efforts of the papal legate, Cuno of Palestrina, to force the Norman bishops to attend a legatine council at Châlons-sur-Marne. When Cuno suspended the bishops for not attending, Henry was irate at what he saw as an infringement of his rights.[132] Yet Matthew, cardinal-bishop of Albano, the pope's legate in France and England, was allowed to hold a legatine council at Rouen in 1128. According to Orderic, the context was the lengthy illness of Archbishop Geoffrey, and the legate, by the king's command, summoned the bishops and abbots of Normandy to hear reforming decrees condemning clerical marriage, pluralism and the gifting of churches and tithes by laymen directly to monks.[133] Matthew was a Cluniac monk, formerly prior of the abbey of Saint-Martin des Champs at Paris, and a kinsman of Abbot Hugh of Reading, who may have recommended him to the king.[134]

RELIGIOUS PATRONAGE

Those who wrote about Henry after his death paid tribute to his generosity as a patron and benefactor, both to existing and to new churches.[135] The scale, direction and timing of his gifts reveal mixed motives: dynastic and political concerns, and personal tastes. Charters confirming lands, rights or privileges, or grants of exemption from toll or of the right to hold fairs, were occasions for strengthening bonds with the greater churches of England and Normandy, and cost Henry relatively little. It was important to support churches particularly associated either with past kings, like Bury

---

[130] Eadmer, *Historia Novorum*, pp. 294–6. [131] *Councils and Synods*, i, part ii, 730–2.
[132] Ibid., p. 234.   [133] OV, vi, 388–90.
[134] A. Clark Frost in Hollister, *Henry I*, pp. 431–2; D. Ursmer Berlière, 'Le Cardinal Matthieu d'Albano (c. 1085–1135)', *Revue Bénédictine*, 18 (1901), 113–40, 280–303.
[135] For details, see Green, 'The Piety and Patronage of Henry I'.

St Edmunds, or Westminster abbey, or with important saints, like St Albans, or Durham (St Cuthbert), or, in Normandy, Mont-Saint-Michel. He was scrupulous, too, towards the houses founded by his parents, Saint-Etienne and La Trinité at Caen, Montebourg and Battle abbey. He shared his parents' affection for the abbey of Bec, and was generous to the priory of Notre-Dame-du-Pré. Like his father, he was generous to churches outside Normandy and England, such as the abbey of Marmoutier, and, most of all, to the abbey of Cluny in Burgundy. There could be no clearer indication of the Norman kings' wealth and prestige than the fact that they could fund grand gestures outside their own territory. Henry gained glowing opinions for his subventions to the building work at the abbey of Cluny, and he also provided funds for Saint-Martin-des-Champs at Paris, which was Cluniac in observance.[136] In 1128 Henry made gifts to the Templars, whose master, Hugh of Payens, was in the west trying to raise men and money for the crusade,[137] possibly because of his concern to ensure the success of Count Fulk of Anjou's expedition to Jerusalem.

Of all the monastic houses Henry patronised, Cluny took pride of place. His father had tried to secure monks from Cluny for the abbey he founded at Battle. Rufus' foundation at Bermondsey was an offshoot of La Charité-sur-Loire. Adela his sister became a nun at Marcigny in 1122, and her son Henry became a monk at Cluny.[138] As just noted, King Henry sent funds to Cluny for the building of the abbey church (exactly when is not known), and it is possible that he intended to endow Cluniac Montacute, after the downfall of his kinsman William of Mortain, until he decided instead on a major initiative of his own at Reading. After 1120 the favour Henry showed to the Cluniacs increased. Not only was wealth showered on Reading abbey, but, as we have seen, the king took his nephew Henry under his wing and nominated him first to the richest abbey, and then to the richest bishopric, in England. One Cluniac, Henry of Saint-Jean-d'Angély, was nominated to the abbacy of Peterborough, and another, Hugh of Amiens, to the archbishopric of Rouen. To judge from the direction of his patronage, Henry was genuinely attracted by Cluniac ideals, and he liked their elaborate ritual and commemoration of the dead.

As well as monks, Henry was also a notable patron of canons. There were various reasons why such communities were favoured by benefactors. Converting communities of clerks into Augustinian canons was one way of bringing them into line with reforming ideals. Such houses could be set up

---

[136] *GND*, ii, 254–5; for discussion, see Frost in Hollister, *Henry I*, pp. 413–18, 453–4.
[137] *ASC* E 1128.
[138] Barlow, 'William I's Relations with Cluny'; Golding, 'The Coming of the Cluniacs'.

in towns and cities, where they might become famous as centres of learning, or in the countryside, where they might act as centres for evangelism, as, for instance, at Nostell in Yorkshire. Cathedral chapters could adopt the Augustinian rule, as at Sées in Normandy and Carlisle in northern England. Augustinian houses were being founded in England from the late eleventh century, and, as we have seen (above, p. 58), Queen Matilda's foundation at Holy Trinity Aldgate, London, seems to have inspired her husband to found other houses. He was credited with the foundation of at least five in England: Cirencester,[139] Dunstable,[140] Carlisle cathedral priory,[141] Wellow by Grimsby[142] and St Denys at Portswood near Southampton,[143] and also played a role in the foundation of others, such as Nostell[144] and Merton.[145] In Normandy Henry was actively involved in the regularisation of the chapter at Sées.[146] The lead of the king and queen was followed by other members of their court, and in Normandy as well as England houses of canons were set up.[147] As yet little is known about contacts between the early English and Norman houses, and their links in turn to the 'independent' houses of Saint-Victor in Paris or Prémontré near Laon, founded by St Norbert.[148]

Henry is also credited with a part in the foundation of the hospital of Mont-aux-Malades outside Rouen,[149] and he also made a gift to the Grand Beaulieu at Chartres, patronised by his sister – possibly when he visited the city in 1131.[150] Such foundations were proliferating. They were both a way

---

[139] *The Cartulary of Cirencester Abbey, Gloucestershire*, ed. C. D. Ross, 3 vols. (London, 1964–77), i, xix–xxii.
[140] *RRAN*, ii, nos. 1826–7.
[141] Dickinson, 'The Origins of Carlisle Cathedral'; *RRAN*, ii, no. 1491, where a date of 1127 is suggested; Nicholl, *Thurstan*, pp. 140–1.
[142] *RRAN*, ii, no. 1737.
[143] *Ibid.*, ii, nos. 1507–8; *The Cartulary of St Denys near Southampton*, ed. E. O. Blake, 2 vols., Southampton Record Series, xxiv, xxv, (1981), ii, appendix 1, nos. 1–2.
[144] Nicholl, *Thurstan*, pp. 127–37.
[145] For Henry's grant of the royal manor see *RRAN*, ii, no. 1301, and for the foundation see M. L. Colker, 'Latin Texts Concerning Gilbert, Founder of Merton Priory', *Studia Monastica*, 12 (1970), 241–71.
[146] Arnoux, 'Les origines', pp. 120, 142–4, 215–20.
[147] For England see J. C. Dickinson, *The Origins of the Austin Canons and Their Introduction into England* (London, 1950), chapter 3; for Normandy see Arnoux, 'Les origines'.
[148] Dickinson, *Origins of the Austin Canons*, chapter 4; Arnoux, *Des clercs au service de la réforme*, chapter 3. Henry is said to have given a chalice, vestments and money to the abbey of Mariënweerd in Frisia, whose first abbot was his kinsman: H. M. Colvin, *The White Canons in England* (Oxford, 1951), p. 27.
[149] A grant of forty shillings (Rouennais) by Henry to Mont-aux-Malades was referred to in a confirmation by Duke Geoffrey: *RRAN*, iii, no. 730.
[150] *Cartulaire de la léproserie du Grand Beaulieu*, ed. R. Merlet and M. Jusselin (Chartres, 1909), no. 1; *RRAN*, ii, no. 1917. This grant was confirmed by Innocent II in 1131, and was made 'for the soul of his father, all his kindred, remission of his sins, and the welfare and security of his kingdom of England and duchy of Normandy'.

of removing lepers from the streets, and away from the sight of the well to do, and a form of practical charity.[151] Leper hospitals were a particular development of the late eleventh and early twelfth centuries, and possibly the earliest leper house in England, at St Giles, Holborn, near London, was founded by Queen Matilda.[152]

In the early twelfth century there was increasing interest in providing for women's vocations, and here Henry's interest may have been prompted by his wife and sisters. In England Henry showed most favour towards the abbey of Romsey, perhaps persuaded by his first wife, who had spent some time there before her marriage.[153] Queen Matilda also seems to have taken an interest in Malling, in Kent, and the nuns received the grant of a market from the king at her request.[154] In Normandy he was generous to La Trinité Caen, where his sister had spent most of her life and was later abbess. The nuns were granted the great royal manor of Tilshead in Wiltshire, possibly partly in exchange for other land.[155] He also granted certain rights and exemptions on their land in England to the nuns of Marcigny, the house where his sister Adela was to end her days. The grant was witnessed by her son, Henry of Blois, and Andrew de Baudemont, steward of Count Theobald.[156] Of the Norman nunneries, that of Saint-Amand at Rouen received wine from Henry's cellar and alms from Vaudreuil.[157]

In the early twelfth century in northern France charismatic religious leaders who preached revival attracted bands of followers who set up communities, often in the great forests. Two of these, the Savigniacs and the Tironensians, settled not far from the frontiers of Normandy, and both were favoured by Henry.[158] In the case of the Savigniacs, he issued charters exempting the monks' goods from toll and custom, confirmed the foundation of the abbey and granted them vines at Avranches, land at

---

[151] R. I. Moore, *The Formation of a Persecuting Society. Power and Deviance in Western Europe 950–1250* (Oxford, 1987), pp. 45–65.
[152] Dugdale, *Mon. Ang.*, vi, ii, 635–6: charter of Henry II confirming a grant of sixty shillings a year given by his grandmother for the hospital of St Giles.
[153] *RRAN*, ii, nos. 630, 802, 811, 874, 883, 1160, 1634.
[154] Ibid., ii, nos. 634–5, 791, 943, 1081, 1271, 1398.
[155] Ibid., ii, nos. 1692, 1928; see *Charters and Custumals of the Abbey of Holy Trinity, Caen. Part 1, The English Estates*, pp. xxvi–xxviii.
[156] *RRAN*, ii, no. 1599a.
[157] Ibid., ii, nos. 829, 1271, and see also no. 1962. For Saint-Paul at Rouen, see no. 1965; for the nuns of Villers-Canivet, no. 1919. In England for the nuns of Barking, see nos. 798, 1242, 1453; and for Shaftesbury, nos. 1165, 1347.
[158] On this subject see H. Leyser, *Hermits and the New Monasticism* (London, 1984).

Dompierre, Saint-Alveus, and a house at Frenouse. He confirmed a settlement between the monks of Caen and Savigny, and grants made by other benefactors.[159] Piety and self-interest went hand in hand, for Henry's patronage helped to strengthen his authority in one of the more remote corners of the duchy.

Bernard of Tiron was another charismatic leader who finally settled at Thiron in the diocese of Chartres and was taken under the wing of Rotrou count of Perche, Henry's son-in-law. Rotrou, Henry's sister Adela and her son Theobald were all benefactors. Henry himself joined this family circle of benefactors, issuing a charter confirming a gift by Adam de Grémonville to the abbey as early as 1115.[160] In addition he gave fifteen marks of silver a year for shoes for the community, as well as exempting their demesnes from toll and helping with the costs of building the dorter.[161] A third religious leader was Robert of Arbrissel. His followers had originally included men and women, but soon evolved into a community of nuns of aristocratic birth at Fontevraud in Anjou.[162] As we have noted above (pp. 209–10), Henry was spectacularly generous to this community following the marriage of his daughter Matilda, and possibly around the time his daughter Juliana became a nun there.

Of the new orders, the notable absentees until the end of Henry's reign were the Cistercians, and this might at first sight seem odd considering the role of the Englishman Stephen Harding in the foundation of Cîteaux. However, we have seen in the case of the other new 'orders' that Henry did not take the initiative in founding houses, but rather responded to fashion. Moreover, to outside observers the Savigniacs must have seemed very like the Cistercians in their austere way of life and preference for remote locations, and the Savigniacs were favoured by Henry and leading members of his court. The Cistercians' breakthrough into royal favour seems to have come when Henry met Saint Bernard in 1130 and then received him at Rouen in the following year. Henry probably made a grant for Pontigny, possibly at the time of their meeting,[163] and later one for the monks of

---

[159] Van Moolenbroek, *Vitale l'ermite*, no. 346, nos. 1, 3, 6, 8, *RRAN*, ii, nos. 1003, 1015, 1183, 1212. See also nos. 1016, 1588, 1433, 1973.

[160] *RRAN*, ii, no. 1074, dated on the day that William, the king's son, was presented to the Norman barons.

[161] For Henry's own gift, see *Cartulaire de l'abbaye de la Saint-Trinité de Tiron*, ed. L. Merlet, 2 vols. (Chartres, 1883), i, 27 (*c.* 1117); *RRAN*, ii, nos. 1236, 1169; see also nos. 1187, 1223, 1294, 1874–5.

[162] J.-M. Bienvenu, *L'étonnant fondateur de Fontevraud Robert d'Arbrissel* (Paris, 1981).

[163] *Le premier cartulaire de l'abbaye Cistercienne de Pontigny (XIIe–XIIIe siècles)*, p. 86 no. 3.

Cîteaux,[164] and then one for the monks of Rievaulx.[165] At the very end of his life Henry rescued a struggling community of monks and gave them a new site at Mortemer in Normandy; after his death they adopted the Cistercian rule.[166]

In his lifetime and after his death Henry achieved a great reputation as a benefactor of the church. The amounts he gave, his choice of beneficiaries, and even, in some cases, the terminology of his charters, convey a sense of his motives, personal, dynastic and political. What remains elusive is any insight into his concern for his immortal soul: was he plagued by fears of damnation, over and beyond those of his fellow men?[167] Perhaps he was, but the rise of the practice of more frequent confession and penance, emphasised by contemporary writers, may have misled historians into thinking that Henry was unusually sensitive on the issue.[168]

At the council of London in 1136 a remarkable attack was launched on the state of the English church in Henry's reign: the church had been downtrodden, churchmen subjected to litigation, taxes exacted, appointments made under the influence of money, a blind eye turned to adultery, lands taken from the church during vacancies, offerings to the church diverted, and all dissent and criticism repressed.[169] Many of these criticisms were true: churchmen suffered as well as benefited from the rigorous assertion of royal justice. The financial burdens on the church are visible in the 1130 pipe roll, and direct accusations of simony, though rare, do occur (above, pp. 45, 129, 207). The 'marriage' of Roger of Salisbury was evidently ignored. Roger's wealth, and his treatment of (for instance) the abbey of Malmesbury, whose transfer to the bishopric was confirmed with a royal charter, shows that the king was prepared to allow a good deal of latitude to favoured ecclesiastics. Henry's outlook was traditional, and that involved him in defending rights which many in the church outside England and Normandy were coming to regard as outmoded.

Yet Henry's views were not antipathetic to reform, and he devoted considerable efforts to the eradication of clerical marriage in both England and Normandy. New dioceses were founded, and others, such as Sées,

---

[164] *RRAN*, ii, no. 1720.   [165] Ibid., ii, nos. 1740–1, 1961.
[166] Gallagher, 'Monastery of Mortemer-en-Lyons in the Twelfth Century – Its History and Cartulary' (dissertation), chapter 1; for the foundation history of the abbey see A. de Monstier, *Neustria Pia* (Rouen, 1663), pp. 768–78; J. Bouvet, 'Le récit de la fondation de Mortemer', *Collectanea Ordinis Cisterciensium Reformatorum*, 22 (1960), 149–68.
[167] Southern, 'Place of Henry I', pp. 232–3.
[168] Crouch, 'The Troubled Deathbeds of Henry I's Servants'.
[169] *Gesta Stephani*, p. 26.

were reorganised. The calibre of the bishops was usually respectable, and sometimes better than respectable, and he was a generous patron to individual bishops and to cathedral communities and religious houses. With this record, it is easy to see why chroniclers looking back on his reign from the troubled years after 1135 were more inclined to accord him glowing tributes.

CHAPTER 13

Court and court culture

In recent years historians, including medievalists, have come to appreciate how much may be learned about power, culture and personal taste by studying courts and court culture.[1] Relatively little has been written about the court of Henry I,[2] though its way of life, style and patronage provide invaluable insights into his personality and preferences. The evidence is much fuller for some aspects of court life than others. It is very hard, for instance, to capture tone and atmosphere. Historians have been sceptical, for instance, of Gaimar's claim that he could tell much about the jokes and feasts at Henry's court, given that king's capacity for sternness and, some would argue, cruelty.[3] The sources also say little about the dividing line between the king's 'public' and 'private' life, or about the participation of women in court life. Nevertheless there is sufficient evidence, not only to illustrate the composition and working of the court, but also to suggest ways in which Henry's court not only reveals much about the king himself, but also helped to shape cultural development in twelfth-century England and Normandy.

INSIDERS AND OUTSIDERS

The court was at once the setting for the king's daily life and the principal instrument of his rule over England and Normandy. It was a large body of people: as already noted, when the White Ship went down in 1120, it

---

[1] The work which more than any other acted as a stimulus here was N. Elias, *The Court Society*, trans. E. Jephcott (Oxford, 1983). For a good review of recent work on early medieval court culture, see C. Cubitt, 'Introduction', in *Court Culture in the Early Middle Ages. The Proceedings of the First Alcuin Conference. Studies in the Early Middle Ages*, ed. C. Cubitt, iii (Turnhout, 2003), 1–16.
[2] As pointed out by Hollister, 'Anglo-Norman Political Culture and the Twelfth-Century Renaissance'.
[3] Gaimar, *Lestoire des Engleis* (ed. Bell), lines 64995–6501; for comment: Southern, 'Place of Henry I', p. 230; J. Gillingham, 'Kingship, Chivalry and Love. Political and Cultural Values in the Earliest History Written in French: Geoffrey Gaimar's *Estoire des Engleis*', in *Anglo-Norman Political Culture* (ed. Hollister), pp. 33–58.

was only one of a fleet of ships taking the king and the court back to England (above, p. 166). Its numbers waxed and waned according to the time of the year and what the king was doing. At the great festivals of the Christian year the numbers of magnates would be swollen by those who came to wait upon the king. Absence, unless authorised, was foolish and sometimes dangerous. If the king was on campaign, the numbers of knights included in the *familia* would be augmented. There were probably always numbers of youths being reared in the royal household, not only receiving an education in arms but also building alliances which would serve them well in adult life.

Already we can see how those who lived at court were conscious of being insiders. Henry of Huntingdon recounted the salutary tale of Simon, son of Robert Bloet bishop of Lincoln, a youth who had been lucky enough to have been brought up or *nutritus* by the king. He possessed all the virtues likely to be appreciated at court: he was quick-witted, a good speaker, handsome, charming and discreet. Not surprisingly he advanced in the king's friendship and was appointed dean of Lincoln whilst he was still young. Then things began to go wrong. Simon made accusations against others, and they turned on him and destroyed his influence with the king; he was imprisoned and, after escaping through a sewer (which the author evidently thought highly appropriate), went into exile. The moral of the story was that those who were brought up in beds of roses were surrounded by manure.[4] A sense of living according to a common code of values was fostered by status, 'nearness to the king', outward signs such as dress and hairstyles, and a shared sense of humour. By the late eleventh century a more ostentatious way of dressing and the custom of men wearing their hair long were spreading.[5] Clerical commentators were scandalised about goings-on at court, but in fact this was a milieu where laymen and clergy mixed, and the effects may be seen in the kind of literary works being composed.[6]

The terms used to describe the court reveal its different aspects: the *domus* was the king's domestic household; the term *familia* was used for the bigger entity and, especially in the chronicle of Orderic Vitalis, for the knights of the royal household; and the term *curia* was used of the

---

[4] HH, pp. 596–7.
[5] Gillingham, 'Kingship, Chivalry and Love'; Barlow, *William Rufus*, pp. 103–9, 105–8; Bartlett, 'Symbolic Meanings of Hair in the Middle Ages'.
[6] This is a wide field of research. For a particularly influential view, see S. C. Jaeger, *The Origins of Courtliness: Civilising Trends and the Formation of Courtly Ideals, 939–1210* (Philadelphia, 1985); cf. A. Scaglione, *Knights at Court. Courtliness, Chivalry, and Courtesy from Ottonian Germany to the Italian Renaissance* (Berkeley, Los Angeles and Oxford, 1991).

formal court. The staff of the domestic household basically fell into two categories, indoor and outdoor. We are well informed about the staff of the domestic household because of the survival of a treatise that deals with the pay and allowances of its principal members, *The Constitution of the King's Household*.[7] The indoor staff was divided into the three main departments common to royal and noble households: the hall, under the stewards and butler; the chamber, under the chamberlains; and the chapel, headed by the chancellor and the chaplains. The outdoor staff in the charge of the marshals included the officers of the stables, kennels and mews. The lay heads of department were themselves magnates, but it was still important for them to maintain their duty of personal service, and thus their access to the king and their status in the hierarchical world of the court.

There is little here that distinguished the royal household from any other great household, save its size, but this in itself posed major logistical problems in terms of discipline, provisioning and accommodation. We have seen how Henry set major reforms in hand after his return from Normandy in 1107: he tried to give due notice of the arrival of the court in a particular locality, prescribed the sums to be paid for provisions, set scales of pay and allowances, and punished offenders severely.[8] Supplying such a large number of people could also offer opportunities. According to Walter Map, Henry's itinerary was so well publicised that merchants followed the king about.[9] We know, incidentally, that the sole survivor of the White Ship was a butcher from Rouen who was travelling with the court to England.[10] The presence of the court at Westminster or Winchester may have been a stimulus to local suppliers of provisions and to merchants. Luxury goods were often imported through the wharves at London, one of which, Queenhithe, was part of the queen's dower. Another, Dowgate, was reserved for merchants from Rouen.[11] In London a royal chamberlain was in charge of collecting the levy or prise on wine and of providing wine for the king's use.[12] There was a whole network of local officials: reeves of royal estates, those who looked after the meadows used for fodder, the foresters and those responsible for the royal stud farms.

Two departments of the domestic household were already evolving into departments of central government. First, the chapel was headed by a

---

[7] *Constitutio Domus Regis*, in *Dialogus de Scaccario*, pp. 129–35.
[8] *Dialogus de Scaccario*, pp. 38–42; see above, p. 111.
[9] *De Nugis Curialium*, p. 438.   [10] OV, vi, 298–300.
[11] For the wharves see Brooke and Keir, *London 800–1216*, pp. 265, 318.
[12] *PR 31 Henry I*, p. 145; for his office see W. Kellaway, 'The Coroner in Medieval London', in *Studies in London History Presented to Philip Edmund Jones*, ed. A. E. J. Hollaender and W. Kellaway (London, 1969), pp. 76–7.

chancellor who was ultimately responsible for custody of the king's seal and supervised those who drew up documents on the king's behalf, the royal scribes. It is thought that there may have been two scribes working together in the first half of the reign, and at least four by the end.[13] These scribes must have travelled with the royal court, whilst others must have been based at Winchester to deal with the drawing up of documents relating to the collection of royal revenues. The chamber, secondly, was the financial department of the household, as well as looking after the king's clothes and personal belongings.[14] Finally, the travels and accommodation of members of the household, stabling, and fodder for the horses were the responsibility of the master-marshal and his four deputies. This must have been a gargantuan task, and the possibilities for self-enrichment manifold.[15]

Henry's passion for hunting meant that his court included very large numbers of huntsmen and their staff. Some were stationed at favourite royal forests, whilst others were in more or less regular attendance. Henry spent weeks at a time on an occupation which combined display, excitement and exercise as well as providing food.[16] In late November 1135, aged about sixty-eight, he was in the forest of Lyons, ready to go off hunting, when he fell ill. Deer were hunted either by chasing them towards the hunting party, or by driving them into enclosures where they could be killed, perhaps with the bow, a method which left less to chance.[17] It was evidently this method that was being used on the day William Rufus met with his fatal accident. The best hawks came from Norway, and in 1130 a man named Outi of Lincoln accounted at the exchequer for a hundred Norway hawks and a hundred gerfalcons, indicative of a large-scale trade.[18]

The royal court also included the king's own retinue of knights. The king's personal military retinue was as old as kingship.[19] Its size presumably

---

[13] Bishop, *Scriptores Regis*, p. 30.   [14] Green, *GOE*, p. 33.
[15] OV, vi, 16, 450, and see above, p. 111.
[16] For comments on the importance of such rituals for Carolingian rulers see Janet L. Nelson, 'The Lord's Anointed and the People's Choice: Carolingian Royal Ritual', in *Rituals of Royalty. Power and Ceremonial in Traditional Societies*, ed. D. Cannadine and S. Price (Cambridge, 1987), pp. 166–72.
[17] For a general survey see J. Cummin, *The Hound and the Hawk. The Art of Medieval Hunting* (London, 2001 edn); J. Steane, *The Archaeology of the Medieval English Monarchy* (London, 1993), pp. 146–52, considers the archaeological evidence. For the Norman period see Barlow, *William Rufus*, pp. 121–32. Earl Hugh of Chester was very fond of hunting: OV, ii, 262. Adelard of Bath wrote a treatise on falconry; see D. Evans, 'Adelard on Falconry', in *Adelard of Bath. An English Scientist and Arabist of the Early Twelfth Century*, ed. C. Burnett, Warburg Institute Surveys and Texts, xiv (London, 1987), pp. 25–7.
[18] *PR 31 Henry I*, p. 111.
[19] For what follows see Chibnall, 'Mercenaries and the *Familia Regis*'; Prestwich, 'The Military Household of the Norman Kings'; and Prestwich, *Place of War in English History*, pp. 127–8. Much may also be learned from S. D. Church, *The Household Knights of King John* (Cambridge, 1999).

fluctuated according to the needs of the moment, but contemporaries certainly thought that Henry's military entourage was substantial: Suger for instance remarked how the English king in France was usually accompanied by many knights.[20] Orderic describes the activities of detachments of Henry's household knights as stationed in castles over the winter of 1123, and describes them as crucial to the victory of his forces over the rebels at Bourgtheroulde, in a way that again suggests they were not inconsiderable in number.[21] Some were of relatively modest origins, like Odo Borleng, one of the commanders at Bourgtheroulde, whereas others were from noble families, for example, William of Grandcourt, son of the count of Eu, who was also at this battle.[22] Two sons of Roger earl of Hereford were mentioned by Orderic as fighting in the royal household in the hope that one day they might recover their father's confiscated lands.[23] Exactly what proportion of household knights fought for pay in the Norman period is not clear, but what is indisputable is Henry's ability to recruit knights for wages. As we have seen (above, pp. 188–9), at the end of the campaign in 1124 he paid off many knights with English coin.

Young boys began their military training probably at about seven years of age. The ties formed in those years were important social connections, and those reared by the king, the greatest of lords, were bound by special ties to him and to their companions. They were *nutriti*, men raised by the king, who might rise to positions of wealth and power. Brian FitzCount, an illegitimate son of Count Alan Fergant of the Bretons, was later to refer to himself as having been brought up in Henry's household; he had remained loyal to Henry's daughter, and impoverished himself on her account.[24] Amongst others sent to Henry's court were Raymond, son of the count of Poitou,[25] and Olaf, son of the king of Man.[26] A kinsman of the Emperor Henry V was amongst those who took passage on the White Ship, together with two sons of Ivo de Grandmesnil and their cousin William of Rhuddlan.[27] There was again nothing new about the practice of accepting boys into a great household for military training, but the fact that other rulers sent children to Henry's court was a reflection of his prestige. It is a reminder too of the different generations there. It was not always easy to keep these young

---

[20] Suger, *Vie de Louis VI* (ed. Waquet), p. 186. [21] OV, vi, 348–50.
[22] Ibid., xxiv–xxv, 348–52. [23] Ibid., ii, 318–19.
[24] H. W. C. Davis, 'Henry of Blois and Brian FitzCount', *EHR*, 24 (1910), 302–3; for a recent discussion, E. King, 'The Memory of Brian fitz Count', *Haskins Society Journal*, 13 (1999), 75–98.
[25] William of Tyre, *Chronique* (ed. Huygens), 14, 9. Raymond was pardoned seven shillings in 1130 from the payment made by the Londoners to have a sheriff of their own election (*PR 31 Henry I*, p. 148); see also J. P. Phillips, 'A Note on the Origins of Raymond of Poitiers', *EHR*, 106 (1991), 66–7.
[26] *Chronica Manniae et Insularum*, i, 61. [27] OV, vi, 304.

men in check, as Henry found in 1113 at Bellême. The king had ordered the army not to fight because it was the feast of the Invention of the Holy Cross, but the knights of Counts Theobald and Rotrou took on some of the knights of the garrison in single combat, and matters got out of hand somewhat.[28] Feats of arms and military exercises were part of the way of life of such young men. Elsewhere in Europe tournaments were becoming popular, but not in Normandy or England, presumably because they were already discouraged.[29]

RITUAL, PRECEDENCE AND GIFTS

Courts were theatres in which rituals demonstrating legitimacy, power and generosity could all be acted out. The year was punctuated by the great Christian festivals, each with solemn church services, feasting and entertainment, and by the holding of councils. Here were the great continuities of court life, when the king's wealth and power were very publicly on view, but each king could also adapt or alter the rituals and ceremonies at his court. Thus William the Conqueror may have been (historians do not agree) the first to have held solemn crown-wearing ceremonies three times each year when he was in England: Easter at Winchester, Whitsuntide at Westminster, and Christmas at Gloucester. Mass would be sung, including acclamations to all the powerful of heaven and earth, including the king and queen.[30] Many ecclesiastics and magnates attended, and great feasts were held. These ceremonies were held in places which emphasised the Conqueror's position as heir of the old royal line and, in the case of Westminster, the fact that he had been crowned in the abbey re-established by the Confessor himself. The regalia, the king's clothing, the lavishness of the feast and the richness of the vessels displayed the king's wealth. There was a story told of a jester who, seeing the Conqueror wearing cloth of gold, cried out 'Behold, I see God', only to be sternly rebuked for his temerity by Archbishop Lanfranc.[31]

According to William of Malmesbury, Henry initially followed his father's practice, but then the ordered sequence was interrupted.[32] Henry is known to have worn his crown on occasion, for instance in 1121 soon

---

[28] Ibid., 182. [29] For what sounds like a tournament in 1119, however, see OV, vi, 230.
[30] Cowdrey, 'The Anglo-Norman Laudes Regiae'.
[31] 'Vita Lanfranci', Migne, *Patrologia Latina*, cl, col. 53, trans. by Vaughn, in *The Abbey of Bec and the Anglo-Norman State*, p. 107.
[32] WM, *GRA*, i, 508; *Vita Wulfstani*, ii, 12; M. Biddle, 'Seasonal Festivals and Residence: Winchester, Westminster and Gloucester in the Tenth to Twelfth centuries', *ANS*, 8 (1985), 51–72.

after his second marriage.³³ It was important that the young queen, whom it was hoped would be the mother of his children, should appear publicly wearing her crown. Similarly he wore his crown at the Christmas feast in 1126, prior to the taking of oaths to his daughter.³⁴ Thus it was the regularity of the tri-annual ceremonies that changed, not the practice of solemn crown-wearing.

Solemn oathtakings were important, too. Henry may himself have been present at the great oathtaking at Salisbury in 1086 when 'all the landholding men of any account' bowed down before his father.³⁵ This oath is thought to have followed the precedent of those sworn to Carolingian rulers. It was clearly related to the particular circumstances of 1086: a follow up to the Domesday Inquest, and preparatory to the king's expedition to France in August. The oathtakings of Henry's reign, however, were directed more specifically towards the succession. In the early weeks of 1115 Henry had presented his son William to the Norman magnates as his heir, and about a year later he did the same before an assembly of magnates at Salisbury (see above, pp. 135–6). Then early in 1127 and in the autumn of 1131 there were assemblies at London and Northampton when the assembled magnates swore oaths to accept the empress as her father's successor (see above, pp. 193–5, 212). Spectacular festivities might also occur on the occasion of dubbing to knighthood. Henry himself had been dubbed by his father in 1086, and Rufus was said to have performed a group knighting at the great feast he held at Westminster in 1099;³⁶ we have also heard how in 1128 Henry dubbed his new son-in-law, Geoffrey of Anjou, and his companions at Rouen, accompanied by much celebration.

Rituals associated with royal deaths were also becoming more elaborate.³⁷ As we have seen (above, pp. 25, 26), the Conqueror's death and funeral had been marred by unseemly incidents, and Rufus' body was transported from the New Forest to Winchester on a cart, it was said. By contrast, when Queen Matilda died in 1118 her obsequies, conducted by Roger of Salisbury, were elaborate, as were the king's own in December 1135 and January 1136. The large and solemn cortège which accompanied the king's body from Lyons-la-Forêt to Caen was itself a highly visible tribute to Henry, and on the other side of the Channel, the mark of respect shown by King Stephen in helping to carry his uncle's bier before the solemn ceremonies at Reading abbey was again a sign of changing times, compared with the disruption of the Conqueror's funeral at Caen. We hear too of other ecclesiastical rituals.

[33] HH, p. 468. [34] JW, iii, 164–7; Hugh the Chanter, p. 216.
[35] ASC E 1086. [36] Gaimar, *Lestoire des Engleis* (ed. Bell), line 5972ff.
[37] Crouch, 'Culture of Death in the Anglo-Norman World', pp. 20–6.

Channel crossings, with all their potential for danger, were preceded by ceremonies of blessing. In 1108 Archbishop Anselm travelled to the south coast to administer a blessing to Henry on the eve of the king's departure to France, and in 1120 the bishop of Coutances blessed the White Ship on the eve of its fateful voyage for England.[38]

The king for his part participated in great occasions such as the consecration of new abbey or cathedral churches. With the queen and their son William, Henry attended the consecration of the abbey church at St Albans abbey in 1115.[39] He was present at Sées for the consecration of the cathedral in 1126.[40] In 1130 he was at Christ Church Canterbury, where the ceremonies were reportedly the greatest since the dedication of the temple of Solomon, and on the following day he moved on to Rochester, for the consecration of the cathedral there.[41] In fact, as Vincent has noted, the monks of Canterbury were so well versed at laying on ceremonies when royal visitors arrived that Henry II had to order them to desist when in 1174 he visited Becket's shrine as a penitent.[42]

The ceremonies attendant on the display of relics, or their movement to new shrines, presented further opportunities for participation by the king. Henry presumably took the opportunity to visit shrines: the possibility that he went to St Edmunds to venerate the martyred king in 1132 has been noted above (p. 213). In 1124 he was at Rouen when in the presence of the papal legate the relics of St Romanus were solemnly displayed.[43]

Above all the great courts were occasions of political moment and for the demonstration of power. Here men came to offer their counsel and service, and to receive reward or punishment. It was here at the start of his reign that Henry received homage and allegiance from the great men, and here decisions were made about the grant of lands or the marriage of widows and heiresses. In 1131 at Northampton it was decided that the empress should be returned to her husband, the public discussion perhaps a tacit admission that the issue should have been discussed at a great council before she went to her betrothal in Normandy. Here too Henry took action against his enemies, for instance, arresting Robert de Bellême in 1112, dealing with the rebels of 1124 and hearing the case against his chamberlain, Geoffrey de Clinton. Such great courts were attended by both laymen and clergy, and it is clear that ecclesiastical councils either tended to follow on from, or were

---

[38] OV, vi, 300.   [39] *RRAN*, ii, no. 1102.   [40] OV, vi, 366.
[41] Gervase of Canterbury, *Actus Pontificum, Opera*, ii, 383.
[42] Edward Grim, *Materials for the History of Thomas Becket*, ii, 445, as cited in Vincent, 'Pilgrimages of the Angevin Kings of England', p. 16.
[43] Rouen, Archives Départementales, Seine-Inférieure G. 3666.

merged seamlessly with, the royal council, and that the king presided over both.

Performance and precedence were intrinsic to court ritual. The archbishop of Canterbury was careful to insist on his right to place the crown on the king's head at crown-wearings. In 1121 he insisted on his right to officiate at the king's wedding, and made King Henry, who had put on his own crown, take it off, so that he could be solemnly crowned by the archbishop.[44] The oath to Matilda in 1127 was administered by Roger of Salisbury, and the order of priority in which people took it reflected status. First came the archbishop of Canterbury, then the bishops and abbots. King David was the first layman to swear. Next Stephen of Blois and Robert of Gloucester vied to take the oath. Acording to one account Stephen sat on the king's right, and Robert, who sat on his left, accorded Stephen precedence as the elder.[45] As mentioned above (p. 195), the fact that the abbots took the oath after the laymen provoked a protest from one of their number.

Another important change was a reduction in the number of formal meals each day from two to one. Here it would appear that the king did not set the trend, but followed it. According to William of Malmesbury, Robert count of Meulan was so influential that when he decided to dine only once each day, the king and other nobles followed suit. Robert himself was allegedly copying the practice of the Byzantine emperor, and in doing so his motive was not parsimony but ease of digestion, though two lengthy meals each day must have been time-consuming as well.[46] Nevertheless the idea that the imperial court at Constantinople set a standard for civilised eating followed in the West is intriguing. According to William of Malmesbury, Henry in fact was not interested in culinary delicacies, eating essentially for sustenance and drinking only to quench his thirst.[47] This may or may not have been true: clearly the author wished to portray the king as moderate and able to exercise self-discipline, but if he had been a notorious gourmand, this surely would have been reported.

The way men and women conducted themselves in public was of course crucial as an indication of deference and respect. The king's behaviour gave a lead, and where he led others followed, most dramatically at Carentan in 1105 when he presented himself to the bishop of Sées for a haircut. Deference was crucial: monks who received the king, for instance, were to genuflect as if to a bishop or an abbot.[48] Acts of homage were public acts of submission,

---

[44] Eadmer, *Historia Novorum*, pp. 292–3.   [45] JW, iii, 178; cf. WM, *Historia Novella*, p. 9.
[46] WM, *GRA*, i, 736.   [47] Ibid., 746.
[48] *The Monastic Constitutions of Lanfranc*, trans. D. Knowles, revised edn by C. N. L. Brooke (Oxford, 2002), p. 106.

hence Henry's reluctance to perform homage for Normandy to Louis VI; on the other hand Henry did prostrate himself before the pope in 1119 and 1131. Public displays of anger conveyed a message to those who witnessed them: cross me, and you will regret it.[49] Thus when Henry's daughter Juliana and her husband wished to be reconciled, they were advised to present themselves as penitents, and approached the king barefoot, supplicating his pardon.[50]

Access to the king was regulated partly by his officials, and partly by the physical arrangement of accommodation within castles and palaces.[51] The hall was the space where the household ate together, whereas access to the king's private accommodation was more carefully controlled. When the news of the wreck of the White Ship was broken to Henry, he fell to the ground, and had to be helped to a private chamber.[52] Yet a king had to be open to members of his court, and Walter Map praised Henry's practice of being available to the senior members of his court before dinner and the younger folk in the afternoons. This arrangement was implicitly contrasted with the empress's advice to Henry II, that he should be much in his chamber and little in public.[53]

Arrivals and departures from court involved seeking permission. A surviving letter of Geoffrey, abbot of Vendôme, to Henry, 'his dearest lord and most cordial friend', acknowledges that, since the king did not wish him to make a journey for which he had obviously asked permission (presumably to cross to Normandy), he was going to change his plans.[54] When the empress had wished to travel across Flanders to see her father, Count Charles's refusal similarly made her change her arrangements.[55] Henry was particularly angry when his brother Robert appeared in England in 1103 without prior agreement, and sent Robert of Meulan to make contact with the duke. Robert de Bellême believed he was acting as Louis VI's envoy when he appeared at Henry's court in 1112, only to be disabused when Henry arrested him (above, p. 125). Departures from court in particular required consent, and without it could be construed as acts of defiance.[56]

---

[49] On this subject see *Anger's Past. The Social Uses of an Emotion in the Middle Ages*, ed. B. H. Rosenwein (Ithaca, New York, 1998).
[50] OV, vi, 278; for the subject see G. Koziol, *Begging Pardon and Favour: Ritual and Political Order in Early Medieval France* (Ithaca, NY, 1992).
[51] For a general survey see J. Steane, *The Archaeology of Power. England and Northern Europe AD 800–1600* (Stroud, 2001), chapter 2.
[52] OV, vi, 300.   [53] *De Nugis Curialium*, pp. 438, 478.
[54] Geoffrey of Vendôme, *Letters*, no. 17, Migne, *Patrologia Latina*, clvii, col. 200.
[55] Waverley annals, *Annales Monastici*, ii, 218.
[56] S. D. B. Brown, 'Leavetaking: Lordship and Mobility in England and Normandy in the Twelfth Century', *History*, 79 (1994), 199–215.

Anselm repeatedly asked Rufus for permission to go to Rome, and when he finally left England, after protracted discussions with the king, he suffered the ignominy of having his bags searched; after his departure his property was seized by royal officials.[57]

The giving and receiving of gifts was an important aspect of court ritual.[58] Henry loved precious objects: those who wished to gain his favour sent him presents, especially exotic animals of all kinds.[59] These included lions, lynxes, camels and even a porcupine, which William of Malmesbury describes as if he had actually seen it.[60] Such gifts were viewed as a sign of a king's prestige:[61] King Edgar of Scots, for instance, sent the king of Leinster a camel.[62] However, Henry obviously liked his menagerie, which he housed at his hunting lodge at Woodstock in Oxfordshire.[63]

Henry's interest may be viewed partly as a reflection of his personal taste, and also of a growing preoccupation with the natural world, which was manifest in various lines of scholarly inquiry. One sign of this is a renewed interest in Pliny's *Natural History*. It has recently been suggested that the Augustinian scholar Robert of Cricklade, who was responsible for making an abbreviation of Pliny's *Natural History*, may have dedicated his manuscript in the first instance to Henry I.[64] Another indication was the writing of bestiaries, manuscripts in which the qualities of real and mythical beasts were described.[65] De luxe illuminated bestiaries were destined for elite circles. Some were written in Latin, but as we have noted (above, p. 169), a text in the (Anglo-Norman) vernacular survives which was written by a man named Philip de Thaon and dedicated to Queen Adeliza: persuasive testimony that there was an interest in such matters at court.

Henry in his turn made generous gifts. Sometimes these took the form of money, such as the presents he made to the master of the Templars in

---

[57] Eadmer, *Historia Novorum*, pp. 86–9.
[58] The *locus classicus* for this subject is M. Mauss, *The Gift: Forms and Functions of Exchange in Archaic Societies* (London, 1970 edn).
[59] WM, *GRA*, i, 740.   [60] Ibid., ii, 372–3.
[61] For gifts to Charlemagne, see *Einhard and Notker the Stammerer, Two Lives of Charlemagne* (trans. Thorpe), p. 70; see also Widukind, *Rerum Gestarum Saxonicarum Libri Tres*, ed. G. Waitz *et al.*, Monumenta Germaniae Historica, Scriptores Rerum Germanicarum in Usum Scholarum (Hanover, 1935), p. 135.
[62] *Annals of Inisfallen*, ed. with a translation by Seán Mac Airt (Dublin, 1951), p. 262; Ritchie, *Normans in Scotland*, p. 160.
[63] WM, *GRA*, i, 740.
[64] E. Van Houts, 'The Prologues of Robert of Cricklade's *Defloratio Plinii Naturalis Historiae*', forthcoming. I should like to thank Dr Van Houts for kindly sending me a copy of her paper in advance of publication. This manuscript appears to be the only one explicitly dedicated to Henry I.
[65] For bestiaries see Baxter, *Bestiaries and Their Users*.

1128, or to the pope in 1119 and 1131, or to the abbot of Bec.[66] Sometimes they took the form of precious objects, like the gems he gave to his nephew Theobald, which ended up being incorporated into the great cross made for the abbey of Saint-Denis,[67] or the gold cup he was later said to have given to Juhel de Mayenne.[68] The silver basins used for water for washing the king's hands were given to the chamberlain William de Tancarville, who passed them on to the priory of Sainte-Barbe en Auge.[69] According to Walter Map, Henry gave clothes three times each year to Louis VI and several of his princes.[70] Sometimes weapons were given, such as the sword bestowed on Geoffrey of Anjou in 1128.[71] Sometimes gift-giving took the form of relics, such as those from the emperor which Henry passed on to Matilda and she in turn gave to Holy Trinity Aldgate.[72]

This then was a court for the ostentatious display of wealth. Clearly there was an element of personal preference here as Henry liked to acquire high-status objects of many kinds, but ostentation served to make an important point about power. King Louis could certainly not compete in this respect: if the Capetian court had been as grand as Henry's we surely would have heard so from Suger, who was not averse to describing the splendours of Saint-Denis. Henry's court would have borne comparison with that of the counts of Anjou, and the wedding celebrations in 1128 may well have been making a deliberate point. The Normans were a new royal dynasty, and royal ritual served to remind their subjects of their kingship. Of the western rulers, only perhaps the court of Roger II of Sicily, himself an *arriviste*, was more exotic or more conspicuous in its luxury.

COURT AND CULTURE

Wealth could be used for cultural patronage, a dimension of court culture in which historians have also shown much interest. The term 'patronage' raises further questions (which cannot, alas, be answered for Henry I)

---

[66] *ASC* E 1128; *GND*, ii, 250; WM, *Historia Novella*, p. 18; *GND*, ii, 254.
[67] Suger, 'De Rebus in Administratione Sua Gestis', ii, 32, in *Œuvres complètes*, ed. Lecoy de la Marche, p. 195. According to the Life of St Bernard, the gems had been part of great vessels which were placed on the table before the king on feast days when he wore his crown: *Vita Prima*, Migne, *Patrologia Latina*, cclxxxv, cols. 301–2. Two enamelled candlesticks which had belonged to Henry I were found in the cathedral treasury at Rouen after the death of Archbishop Rotrou in 1183: 'Inventaire du trésor de la cathédrale après la mort de l'archevêque Rotrou', in *La Cathédrale de Rouen. Seize siècles d'histoire*, ed. J.-P. Chaline, Société de l'Histoire de Normandie, 70 (1996), pp. 114–17.
[68] *Book of Fees*, i, 97. [69] Walter Map, *De Nugis Curialium*, pp. 490–1. [70] Ibid., p. 470.
[71] John of Marmoutier, 'Historia Gaufredi Ducis', in *Chroniques des Comtes d'Anjou* (ed. Halphen and Poupardin), p. 179.
[72] *The Cartulary of Holy Trinity Aldgate*, pp. 224–5.

about whether kings were simply purchasers of objects or expertise, or whether they exercised taste. Did they set trends, or did they merely follow them? Such questions are particularly tantalising in relation to the scholars who are known to have had some kind of connection with the court of Henry I.

Several men are identified as having been Henry's physicians, and these included Petrus (Peter) Alfonsi, a famous scholar who played a crucial role in bringing knowledge of Greek and Arabic texts into northern Europe.[73] The reference is incidental, and there is no means of knowing how important the connection was. Adelard of Bath was another scholar who helped to transmit knowledge of Arabic science. His name indicates his place of origin, and his family held land from the bishops of Bath.[74] He grew up into a man of diverse intellectual interests who spent some time at Henry's court, and to whom the king showed some favour.[75] Amongst his written works was a treatise on falconry which referred to 'King Harold's books', possibly a reference to King Harold Godwinson. He also wrote a treatise on the abacus, a tool for calculation using the numbers one to nine, with a blank for zero. The exchequer employed the same method of calculation, to get round the problem that the Roman system of numeration which was then in use did not have a symbol assigned to zero.[76] Although the role of scholars such as Adelard in bringing skill in computation to bear on accounting procedures was less innovatory than used to be thought, in that it has become clear that knowledge of the abacus was well established in England by the late eleventh century, awareness of the practical utility of arithmetic in royal administration clearly is significant.[77]

Why did Henry have men like Petrus Alfonsi and Adelard of Bath at his court? He may simply have wanted to appear civilised, a king at whose court the erudite received hospitality and favour; he may have valued them as scholars or, in the case of the former, as a physician. However, in both cases it may have been above all their ability to predict the future that was most valued.[78] Belief in astrology and other methods of foretelling

---

[73] C. H. Haskins, *Studies in the History of Medieval Science* (Cambridge, Mass., and London, 1927), pp. 113–20.

[74] L. Cochrane, *Adelard of Bath. The First English Scientist* (London, 1994); *Adelard of Bath*, ed. Burnett. For Adelard's background, see M. Gibson, 'Adelard of Bath', in *Adelard of Bath* (ed. Burnett), pp. 7–16.

[75] *PR 31 Henry I*, p. 22.   [76] Cochrane, *Adelard of Bath*, pp. 24–8.

[77] G. R. Evans, 'Schools and Scholars: the Study of the Abacus in English Schools *c.* 980–*c.* 1150', *EHR*, 94 (1979), 71–81; Haskins, *Studies in the History of Medieval Science*, pp. 327–55.

[78] For Adelard's possible authorship of horoscopes which seem to have been connected with Henry FitzEmpress, see J. D. North, 'Some Norman Horoscopes', in *Adelard of Bath* (ed. Burnett), pp. 147–61.

the future was widespread.[79] John of Salisbury, who wrote about different ways of foretelling the future in his *Policraticus*, discussed astrology, and also several other ways of predicting events.[80] From Henry's point of view, it must have been difficult to know whether the predictions of a holy man like Wulfric of Haselbury were to be believed, or rather those of an astrologer or a soothsayer, but as a great and wealthy king he could afford to take advice from different sources, and he did. Again this fits in with the idea that he always tried to be forewarned of events. Many churchmen disapproved of prophecy that was not divinely inspired, but it was obviously difficult for a layman to be sure which prophecies fitted into that category.

There must have been crowds, too, of entertainers and musicians looking for work, who came and went.[81] Queen Matilda's known love of music meant that many 'scholars who were famous for their songs or verses' are said to have crowded her court.[82] In this case it seems that the queen had a personal love of music, but in the case of literary dedications it is hard to be sure whether Henry's wives were personally particularly interested, or were being addressed as potential patrons. In the case of William of Malmesbury's *Deeds of the Kings of the English*, however, the author tells us that his work owed its origin to Queen Matilda's desire to know more about her descent from St Aldhelm.[83] *The Voyage of St Brendan* by Benedeit was possibly dedicated first to Queen Matilda, then to Queen Adeliza.[84] Henry's second wife has already been referred to as a patron of Philip de Thaon (above, p. 169), and of David the Scot.[85]

It has been pointed out that this court was a milieu where Latin, French and English culture intermingled, and where stories from Wales or Ireland were picked up and retold; the resulting form of French, or Anglo-Norman, was in literary terms relatively well developed.[86] While it is not always easy

---

[79] R. W. Southern, 'History as Prophecy', *Transactions of the Royal Historical Society*, 5th series, 22 (1972), 159–80. For episcopal prognostics, see G. Henderson, '*Sortes Biblicae* in Twelfth-Century England: the List of Episcopal Prognostics in Cambridge, Trinity College MS R. 7. 5', in *England in the Twelfth Century*, ed. D. Williams (Woodbridge, 1990), pp. 113–29.

[80] John of Salisbury, *Policraticus*, II, chapters 10–29 (ed. Keats-Rohan), pp. 89–171.

[81] J. Southworth, *The English Medieval Minstrel* (Woodbridge, 1998), chapter 4.

[82] WM, *GRA*, i, 756.   [83] Ibid., 4–8.

[84] Benedeit, *The Anglo-Norman Voyage of St Brendan*, ed. I. Short and B. Merrilees (Manchester, 1979). Nothing is known about the author, nor is it certain whether the original dedicatee was Matilda, who occurs in one manuscript, or Adeliza (pp. 4–6). C. Sneddon has argued that it was Adeliza, and that the use of Irish material was a means of conveying independent status: 'Brendan the Navigator: A Twelfth-Century View', in *The North-Sea World in the Middle Ages. Studies in the Cultural History of North-West Europe*, ed. T. R. Liska and L. E. M. Walker (Dublin, 2001), pp. 211–28.

[85] Gaimar, *Lestoire des Engleis* (ed. Bell), lines 6480–4.

[86] On the subject of languages in England see the work of I. Short, especially 'On Bilingualism in Anglo-Norman England', *Romance Philology*, 33 (1980), 467–99; 'Patrons and Polyglots: French Literature in Twelfth-Century England', *ANS*, 14 (1992), 229–49.

to assess the contribution made by Henry himself, or by his wives, the sheer wealth and longevity of his court provided opportunities for the ambitious. Not only that, but the way of life at court was emulated by leading members of his court. Bishops like Alexander of Lincoln, and laymen like Robert earl of Gloucester and Waleran count of Meulan, were patrons of scholars and men of letters. Although the political troubles of the following reign may have disrupted the development of a court culture for a time, when Henry II and Queen Eleanor came to the throne that culture flourished once again.

SETTING

The restless travels of medieval kings and their courts are notorious, yet each king's itinerary naturally reflected his own concerns and preferences. The court's movements may be reconstructed from chronicles and charters.[87] Between 1100 and 1104 Henry stayed in England; thereafter he crossed the Channel back and forth, spending more time in Normandy than in England. He also made two expeditions to Wales, in 1114 and 1131, and visited Chartres in 1131. Transporting the court across the Channel was a major undertaking, as John Le Patourel has pointed out.[88] Whereas the Conqueror and Rufus tended to use the shorter sea crossings, Henry preferred to cross from the vicinity of Portsmouth or Southampton. Le Patourel links Henry's preference for this route to the convenience of access to Winchester and the royal treasury. Although the western routes were longer, Henry might have felt more secure sailing directly to Ouistreham, or a port in his 'own' territory of the Cotentin, than from Dover to Wissant or Dieppe. By Henry's reign there is known to have been a royal galley and at least one or possibly more officers 'of the galley', who was probably responsible for impressing other ships to carry the rest of the king's household. These officers seem to have held land by virtue of their offices.[89] Thus when the owner of the White Ship requested the right to transport the king from Barfleur in 1120 he was asking to succeed to his father's land, and said that he had a suitable ship already fitted out.[90]

The king was on the move every week or two, unless he was actually on the south coast waiting for winds and tides for a Channel crossing, and it

---

[87] S. Mooers Christelow, 'A Moveable Feast: Itineration and the Centralization of Government under Henry I', *Albion*, 27 (1995), 187–228. The forthcoming edition of the writs and charters of Henry I will throw fresh light on the details of the royal itinerary.

[88] Le Patourel, *Norman Empire*, pp. 165–78.

[89] Haskins, *Norman Institutions*, pp. 121–2.   [90] OV, vi, 296.

is clear that although from time to time he visited outlying regions of his realms, in practice his travels tended to follow a certain pattern. It is also possible to see what were evidently personal preferences. In England Westminster became more important, Winchester perhaps less so, by the end of the reign; Windsor and Woodstock were evidently personal favourites. Henry's passion for hunting took him often to the forests, especially those in Hampshire, Wiltshire, Oxfordshire and Northamptonshire. He tended not to visit Canterbury or Dover, perhaps because he used the harbours in Hampshire instead,[91] and he visited Gloucester less than his father or William Rufus. In Normandy his presence was most often recorded at Rouen and Caen; his itinerary elsewhere in the duchy is not known in as much detail as it is in England because there are fewer surviving documents which mention the places he visited. In any case his movements were more directly affected by the periods of disorder there, so statistics are not very helpful. As he grew older, the number of places he visited became fewer, though he was still on the move during the last months of his life.[92]

Henry inherited a wide variety of accommodation, from palaces to castles, hunting lodges, houses and even tents, though how often the king himself as opposed to his courtiers slept under canvas is not clear.[93] It is possible to classify his residences into three broad and overlapping categories: first, the relatively large and commodious complexes, best described as palace complexes, with halls and chambers;[94] secondly, castles built since the mid-eleventh century; and thirdly, rural accommodation, such as lodges and houses. In the first category Winchester remained a very important centre, and in Henry's reign it had the added convenience of proximity to the king's usual route for crossing to Normandy, from harbours in Hampshire.[95] A castle had been built after the Conquest, and there was also a palace complex which had been enlarged by the Conqueror.[96] The vast Norman cathedral and palace could be used for the rituals of crown-wearings and the great feasts which followed. The fact that Winchester was a substantial city meant that goods and services, and accommodation for members of the court, were all available. Because of the survival of two early twelfth-century surveys of Winchester, it has been possible for historians to trace in very great detail who lived where, and it is clear that royal officials

---

[91] Le Patourel, *Norman Empire*, pp. 175–6.   [92] OV, vi, 446–8.
[93] *Constitutio Domus Regis, Dialogus de Scaccario*, p. 135.
[94] W. J. Blair, 'Hall and Chamber: English Domestic Planning 1000–1250', in *Manorial Domestic Building in England and Northern France*, Society of Antiquaries, Occasional Paper no. 15 (London, 1994), 1–5.
[95] Le Patourel, *Norman Empire*, p. 167.   [96] *Winchester Studies*, I, 292–7.

made up a fair proportion of the landlords in the city.[97] Royal treasure was stored there, conveniently for transport down to the coast and thence to Normandy. In 1111 Queen Matilda presided over 'her court and that of her husband' in the treasury at Winchester, and from the names of those present with her, it is probable that this was a meeting of the exchequer.[98]

Westminster was a royal centre of growing importance during the reign. Between 1100 and 1104 Henry spent Christmas there and Easter at Winchester. He visited Westminster relatively frequently, and it was here in January 1127 that oaths were sworn to his daughter Matilda. The palace buildings were dominated by Rufus' great hall, which was conveniently close to the abbey. Merchants came to London bringing luxury goods which would find a ready market at court: the 1130 pipe roll mentions purchases of herrings, nuts, oil, wine, spices, pepper, towels and basins.[99] By the end of the reign it is possible that the court of the exchequer met at Westminster, because there is a reference to expenditure for repairing the 'houses of the exchequer' in the pipe roll account of 1156, which could suggest that the houses had not been used in the recent past (say, if the exchequer sessions had been disrupted), and needed repair.[100] Moreover, Brand has pointed out that the only two documents issued by Henry which refer to judicial action by the barons of the exchequer were both in favour of Westminster abbey, and it is at least a possibility that the abbot obtained them because of his proximity to the exchequer.[101]

Queen Matilda's patronage made a very considerable impact on London. Two or three stone bridges were said to have been built at her wish;[102] she seems to have been responsible for the building of a public bathhouse and latrine complex;[103] and she was evidently interested in helping sufferers from leprosy, a disease of particular concern in this era, and one for which benefactors were beginning to endow specialist hospitals.[104] Her

---

[97] Ibid., 387–92.   [98] *RRAN*, ii, no. 1000.   [99] *PR 31 Henry I*, p. 144.
[100] *PRs 2–4 Henry* II, p. 4; Green, 'Financing Stephen's War', pp. 110–11.
[101] P. Brand, '"Multis Vigiliis Excogitatam et Inventam": Henry II and the Creation of the English Common Law', *Haskins Society Journal*, 2 (1990), 206–7; E. Mason, *Westminster Abbey and Its People c. 1050–c. 1216* (Woodbridge, 1996), p. 163.
[102] *VCH Essex*, vi, 44–5; 59–60; *VCH Surrey*, ii, 72.
[103] *Munimenta Gildhallae Londoniensis*, ed. H. T. Riley, 3 vols., RS (London, 1859–62), iii, 445–9.
[104] Ailred, 'Genealogia Regum Anglorum', Migne, *Patrologia Latina*, cxcv, col. 736. For the hospital of St Giles, Holborn, see Dugdale, *Mon. Ang.*, vi.ii, 635–6: charter of Henry II confirming a grant of sixty shillings a year given by his grandmother to the hospital. For a medieval illustration see *The Illustrated Chronicles of Matthew Paris. Observations of Thirteenth-Century Life*, trans. and ed. with an introduction by R. Vaughn (Stroud, 1993), p. 103. D. Knowles and R. N. Hadcock, *Medieval Religious Houses: England and Wales* (Cambridge, 1953), p. 253, suggest 1101 as the year of foundation, but in a note point out that Stow suggested *c.* 1117. Matilda may also have been responsible for the foundation of the hospital of St Mary and St James at Chichester: ibid., p. 263.

most important project, however, was the foundation of an Augustinian priory, on the advice of Archbishop Anselm. The new foundation was situated, like the leper hospital, outside the city walls, on a site where Waltham abbey had a church.[105] The queen bought out the abbey's rights and gave the new foundation Aldgate and the land belonging to it, plus two-thirds of her rents from the city of Exeter.[106] The contribution made by Matilda's patronage to easing the transition of London to Norman rule is not to be underestimated. The Londoners had continued to offer resistance to the Conqueror after the battle of Hastings, and three castles had to be built in the city, two in the west (Baynard's and Mountfitchet's) and one in the east (the Tower).[107] Westminster was soon the site of a great palace complex close to the abbey, and a great new cathedral (St Paul's) went up, as well as Holy Trinity and other new churches. By the time Henry died, the landscape of London had been transformed.

The scale and character of building work was conditioned by the site and what was there already, by the frequency of the king's visits, and by the security situation. Years of peace in southern England meant that the kind of fortification needed at Carlisle, for instance, was not required, and this may well have affected the king's decisions about when and where to stay, and thence his movements. Why live in a confined (and noisy) tower-keep when luxurious accommodation with private apartments was available in a rural setting, as at Woodstock? This was one of Henry's favourite residences, the 'favourite seat of his retirement and privacy', where his menagerie of wild animals was kept.[108] He may have been responsible for ordering a stone wall to be built round the park.[109] Woodstock is only some seven miles from Oxford, where there was a royal castle in the custody of the d'Oilly family. By the end of the reign Henry had built a stone hall at Beaumont, not far geographically from the keep and probably part of the same defended complex.[110] Although derelict houses in Oxford were reported in 1086 in Domesday Book, by the early twelfth century the town seems to have been reviving,[111] and there were several religious establishments. A collegiate church had been founded in the castle chapel dedicated to St George, and,

---

[105] *Cartulary of Holy Trinity Aldgate*, pp. 223–4.   [106] Ibid., pp. 224–5.   [107] *Carmen*, pp. 40–8.
[108] *Gesta Stephani*, p. 138. The fact that the empress was said to have constructed a castle here suggests that the site had been only modestly defended up to that point.
[109] HH, p. 488; *History of the King's Works*, ii, 986.
[110] HH, p. 488 refers to the king's new hall at Oxford. For the castle see *Oxford Before the University*, ed. A. Dodd, Oxford Archaeology, Thames Valley Landscapes Monograph no. 17 (2003), pp. 46–50 (the castle); p. 59 (Beaumont).
[111] *DB*, i, 154; H. E. Salter, *Medieval Oxford*, Oxford Historical Society, c (1936), 20–39; R. H. C. Davis, 'The Ford, the River and the City', in *From Alfred the Great to King Stephen* (London, 1991), pp. 281–91.

with the assistance of Bishop Roger of Salisbury, the ancient church of St Frideswide was converted into an Augustinian priory.[112] In about 1129 a second Augustinian house was established at Osney by Robert d'Oilly, constable of the castle, and his wife, a royal mistress.[113] Just outside the town a nunnery was founded at Godstow, with the assistance of Henry I.[114] The schools associated with the religious houses were already thriving, and the numbers of clerks there doubtless looked to the royal court for possible employment.[115]

Dunstable was another favoured residence. It was situated at the crossing of two great roads, Watling Street and the Icknield Way, and was a useful staging post on the route to Northampton.[116] Henry cleared the site and founded a borough, reserving nine acres for himself. Here he spent Christmas 1122, and some ten years later founded an Augustinian priory. The combination of residence and priory or abbey is paralleled elsewhere, in both England and Normandy. When Henry attended the consecration of the abbey church at St Albans in 1115, he may have stayed either in the abbey or at the nearby royal residence of Kingsbury.

Henry obviously liked the midland forests in Northamptonshire. He visited Rockingham,[117] where there was an important royal castle, with lodges at Geddington,[118] Brampton,[119] King's Cliffe[120] and Brigstock,[121] as well as the castle at Northampton[122] and accommodation at nearby Kingsthorpe.[123] It cannot be without significance, however, that he did not issue documents from the New Forest, and it is hard to doubt that he saw this forest, where two of his brothers had died, as unlucky. The buildings at these lodges have disappeared, indicating that they were probably of timber

---

[112] The early history of the priory has been reviewed by W. J. Blair, 'St Frideswide's Monastery: Problems and Possibilities', *Oxoniensia*, 53 (1988), 221–58. Bishop Roger exchanged lands with Abingdon abbey in order to provide the canons with a suitable site: *RRAN*, ii, no. 1128; J. C. Dickinson, *Origins of the Austin Canons*, pp. 113–14.

[113] D. Postles, 'The Foundation of Oseney Abbey', *Bulletin of the Institute of Historical Research*, 53 (1980), 242–4; for the foundation charter, see *The Cartulary of Oseney Abbey*, ed. H. E. Salter, 6 vols., Oxford Historical Society (1929–36), i, no. 1.

[114] *The English Register of Godstow Nunnery*, ed. A. Clark, 3 vols., Early English Text Society, cxxix, cxxx, cxl (1905–11), i, 26; L. Smith, 'Benedictine Women at Oxford: The Nuns at Godstow', in *Benedictines in Oxford*, ed. H. Wansbrough and A. Marett-Crosby (London, 1997), pp. 95–100, 293–4.

[115] Theobald of Etampes was one of the masters there probably before 1100: R. W. Southern, 'From Schools to University', in *The History of the University of Oxford*, ed. T. H. Aston, i, *The Early Oxford Schools*, ed. J. Catto (Oxford, 1984), pp. 5–6.

[116] *History of the King's Works*, ii, 924–5; *VCH Beds.*, iii, 351.

[117] *RRAN*, ii, nos. 741–5, 1031, 1120, 1320, 1458–1463; *History of the King's Works*, ii, 815. In 1095 Rockingham was the location of an important royal council when Rufus confronted Anselm.

[118] *History of the King's Works*, ii, 943.   [119] Ibid., 901.   [120] Ibid., 969.

[121] Ibid., 902.   [122] Ibid., 750.   [123] Ibid., 977.

construction, as were the many houses mentioned as places where the king evidently attended to business whilst waiting for favourable winds to take him across the Channel, such as Westbourne, Rowner, Wartling, Eastling, Portsmouth and Fareham.

Some royal residences were more appropriate to certain functions than others. Large assemblies needed large halls, of the kind built by William Rufus at Westminster. Crown-wearings necessitated clergy and a church or chapel where the ceremony could be performed. This might be Winchester or Westminster, but could be held elsewhere: we know that Henry wore his crown three times at the hunting lodge at Brampton in Northamptonshire, where a chapel was built,[124] and there may have been a great wooden hall, as at Cheddar, a royal residence since Anglo-Saxon times.[125]

Henry's programme of castle-building in Normandy was essentially rooted in security considerations, but these could not be separated from either residential needs or the public exercise of authority, so as well as building and strengthening tower keeps, there was work on residential accommodation and on halls. Thus at Rouen, Henry is reported to have strengthened the wall, adding battlements and extra buildings inside the enclosure.[126] At Caen, he is thought to have been responsible for raising the walls and for building a stone keep and a stone hall, all of which survive.[127] At Argentan, at the very end of his life, he ordered the strengthening of the walls.[128] Even if Henry perforce had to be resident at Rouen, he evidently liked to hunt in the ducal forests nearby. At Notre-Dame-du-Pré, for instance, there was a priory of the abbey of Bec founded by his parents, where parts of his body were later interred (see above, pp. 221, 278). Here he had a residence which was said to have gilded roofs.[129]

The most obvious feature about all this building activity is its cost. The sheer number of castles, on both sides of the Channel, where building work occurred through the construction of either tower-keeps, halls or curtain walls, is striking, and in itself makes a point about power and wealth. Secondly, there is the question of type. Henry followed in his father's and brother's footsteps in building halls, whether these were grand, stand-alone halls or part of a hall-chamber block, with residential accommodation attached. The origins of hall-chamber blocks are thought to go

---

[124] *Placitorum in Domo Capitulari Westmonasteriensi Asservatorum Abbreviatio*, ed. W. Illingworth for the Record Commission (London, 1811), p. 95, cited in *History of the King's Works*, ii, 901.
[125] P. A. Rahtz, *The Saxon and Medieval Palaces at Cheddar* (1979).
[126] Robert of Torigny, *Chronique*, p. 106.
[127] M. de Boüard, *Le Château de Caen* (Caen, 1979).   [128] OV, vi, 446.
[129] Stephen of Rouen, 'Draco Normannicus', *Chronicles of the Reigns of Stephen, Henry II, and Richard I*, ii, 713.

back to Anglo-Saxon England, and to have passed into Normandy after 1066, though naturally it is hard to be certain whether English customs affected Normandy or vice versa. One of the earliest of such blocks in Normandy was that at Domfront, possibly constructed on Henry's orders before 1100.[130] The question of the origins of new trends in building is hard to answer precisely. Henry shared also his father's and brother's preference for building on a large scale. He particularly liked large keeps, as at Falaise, which must have been very expensive, and Falaise in turn seems to have been an influence on the keep at Norwich.[131] At Norwich the keep's external ornamentation still survives, though heavily restored.[132] If, as has been suggested, Henry I rather than his grandson was responsible for beginning the polygonal keep within a curtain wall at Gisors, then this was a new departure.[133] Moreover, if many of these buildings were utilitarian, some were comfortable and even perhaps luxurious: it would be odd if the buildings at Notre-Dame-du-Pré had gilded roofs but were otherwise spartan.

Moreover, the building of castles and palaces was only one dimension of the architectural patronage of Henry and Queen Matilda, for the ecclesiastical buildings they sponsored were even more obviously statements of wealth and ostentation.[134] Research on Holy Trinity Aldgate, for instance, has demonstrated its size and the fine quality of the masonry.[135] The size of Reading abbey, and the quality of the surviving sculpture, again speak volumes about the king's view of what 'his' abbey church should look like: money was no object (see above, p. 172).

The final point to be made about the physical setting of the royal court is that numerous, large and high-quality buildings set a standard to which others could aspire. To deal in detail with trends in architecture, sculpture and decorative detail in buildings sponsored by nobles and churchmen in England and Normandy is beyond the scope of this chapter, but, looking at the buildings which can be associated with leading members of the court,

---

[130] M. Wood, *Norman Domestic Architecture* (London, 1974); E. Impey, 'La demeure seigneuriale en Normandie entre 1125 et 1225 et la tradition anglo-normande', in *L'architecture normande au moyen âge*, ed. M. Baylé, 2 vols. (Caen, 1997), i, 217–41.

[131] Ibid., 239.

[132] T. A. Heslop, *Norwich Castle Keep: Romanesque Architecture and Social Context*, The Centre of East Anglian Studies, University of East Anglia (Norwich, 1994).

[133] J. Mesqui and P. Toussaint, 'Le château de Gisors aux XIIe et XIIIe siècles', *Archéologie Médiévale*, 29 (1999), 253–317.

[134] For context see E. Fernie, *The Architecture of Norman England* (Oxford, 2000); R. Plant, 'Ecclesiastical Architecture c. 1050–1200', in *A Companion to the Anglo-Norman World*, ed. C. Harper-Bill and E. Van Houts (Woodbridge, 2003), pp. 215–53; Grant, 'Architectural Relationships between England and Normandy'.

[135] For an isometric view, see J. Schofield, *The Building of London from the Conquest to the Great Fire*, 3rd edn (Stroud, 1994), p. 48.

it is hard to avoid the conclusion that what might best be described as a courtly style was beginning to emerge. The court was a competitive world where the wealthy enjoyed huge riches, some of which were poured out on buildings. Those of Bishop Roger of Salisbury, for instance, have been studied in some detail. At Sherborne, Bishop Roger constructed a castle of the hall-chamber type. It consisted of buildings round a courtyard; surviving sculptural fragments suggest that no expense was spared.[136] Of the same bishop's castle at Devizes, Henry of Huntingdon said there was no castle more splendid in Europe.[137] Roger also had custody of the royal castle at Salisbury, and here work on the keep was recorded on the 1130 pipe roll. Close by was the cathedral which the bishop had rebuilt and extended.[138] His nephew, Bishop Alexander of Lincoln, was another notable patron of architecture and so, though his buildings date from a slightly later period, was Bishop Henry of Winchester.[139] The great lay lords, too, were engaged in building in stone, and over the course of decades castle complexes, often incorporating hall-chamber blocks, took shape. Here buildings in Normandy were of the same type as in England, and it has been suggested that after about 1120 we may talk of an Anglo-Norman style of seigneurial architecture.[140]

Furthermore, it has been argued that under Henry I the construction of stone castles was seen as a hallmark of the upwardly mobile. Geoffrey de Clinton, the king's chamberlain and sheriff of Warwickshire, was probably responsible for starting the stone keep at Kenilworth, one of the first stone castles in the county.[141] Richard Basset, the king's sheriff and justice, 'bursting with the wealth of England' to quote from Orderic, returned to

---

[136] R. A. Stalley, 'The Patronage of Roger of Salisbury', MA dissertation, Courtauld Institute, University of London (1969); Stalley, 'A Twelfth-Century Patron of Architecture'.
[137] HH, p. 720.   [138] *PR 31 Henry I*, p. 13; for the cathedral WM, *GRA*, ii, 738.
[139] For Alexander see HH, p. 748; Dyson, 'Career, Family and Influence of Alexander le Poer', chapter 4; for his work at Lincoln, HH, p. 748; R. Gem, 'Lincoln Minster: Ecclesia Pulchra, Ecclesia Fortis', in *Medieval Art and Architecture at Lincoln Cathedral*, British Archaeological Association (1986), pp. 9–28; G. Zarnecki, *Romanesque Sculpture at Lincoln Cathedral*, Lincoln Minster Pamphlets (1970), reprinted in *Studies in Romanesque Sculpture* (London, 1979); for Newark, HH, p. 720; for Bishop Henry of Blois as a patron see Y. Kusaba, 'Henry of Blois, Winchester, and the Twelfth-Century Renaissance', in *Winchester Cathedral: Nine Hundred Years, 1093–1993* (Chichester, 1993), pp. 69–80; G. Zarnecki, 'Henry of Blois as a Patron of Sculpture', in *Art and Patronage in the English Romanesque*, Society of Antiquaries, Occasional Paper, new series, no. 8 (London, 1986), pp. 159–72; for buildings in Winchester, see *Winchester Studies*, i, 325–86 (Wolvesey), *VCH, Hampshire*, ii, 193–4 (St Cross); and for Bishop Henry's castles M. W. Thompson, 'Recent Excavations in the Keep of Farnham Castle, Surrey', *Medieval Archaeology*, iv (1960), 81–94 (Farnham). For his work at Glastonbury see Adam of Domerham, *Historia de Rebus Gestis Glastoniensibus*, ed. T. Hearne, 2 vols. (London, 1727), ii, 316–18.
[140] Impey, 'La demeure seigneuriale – Normandie', p. 241.
[141] Crouch, *Image of Aristocracy in Britain*, p. 260.

Normandy and built a stone keep on his ancestral fief at Montreuil-au-Houlme, an event which the chronicler clearly thought was remarkable.[142]

Any great king might be presumed to have held great courts marked by feasting, hunting and the exchange of gifts, yet at the same time he could exercise choice in the manner of his life, and where he chose to spend most time. Henry evidently was passionate about the hunt and liked to live in his rural hunting lodges. The scale of his building programme, and the money poured out, not only on castles (which were needed for defensive purposes) but also on great churches, suggests too the exercise of choice: like his father and elder brother, he liked big buildings. Yet the court of Henry I has a historical significance beyond the insights it supplies into personal taste. It is clear that the combination of wealth and duration served to generate a common code, where those who belonged shared similar values and saw themselves as insiders. This is not new, but it stood out in northern Europe in the early twelfth century, and it played a part in the rise and dissemination of courtly values in twelfth-century Europe.[143]

---

[142] OV, vi, 468.

[143] These ideas are more fully developed in 'Henry I and the Origins of the Court Culture of the Plantagenets', forthcoming in the proceedings of the 2004 Conference 'Plantagenêts et Capétiens, confrontations et héritage', Poitiers and Fontevraud 2004.

CONCLUSION

'Once the peace and glory of the world'

William of Malmesbury tells us that in extreme moments Henry I was wont to swear 'By our Lord's death', an incidental detail which beguiles the reader: why should the author have made this up?[1] This biography began with a discussion of the difficulty of knowing when biographical details are to be taken literally, and when narrative authors are doling out commonplaces, or indulging in irony. Issues of fact are reasonably straightforward, and some personality traits are not difficult to establish, but others are much harder to estimate and ultimately depend on personal judgement. At this point, having reviewed as much of the evidence as possible, we must try to answer the question: what kind of man was Henry?

Three great loves of Henry's life were wealth, hunting and sex (not necessarily in that order). From all sides, that love of wealth mentioned by the chroniclers is borne out. He liked money, and acquiring all kinds of precious things, including exotic animals. Wealth was power, and although he was accused by Henry of Huntingdon of cupidity, in fact he lavished wealth on his favourites and on those he wished to impress. Wealth was showered on religious communities for a mixture of motives, religious, personal and dynastic, political and propagandist. Wealth could be used for display, for embellishing his many residences, and for securing for his court the services of the best physicians and scholars. He evidently wanted to show that his court was no uncivilised backwoods affair when in 1119 he had the Beaumont twins, neither destined for the church, offer a display of rhetoric to the pope and cardinals.

He loved the hunt, as did his father and his brother William Rufus. If we are to believe the mid-twelfth-century chronicler Wace, he was so skilled at tracking that his kinsman, Count William of Mortain, called him 'Stag's foot' and claimed that he could tell from a stag's tracks how many

---

[1] WM, *GRA*, i, 728. The description constituting the chapter title is by Robert of Torigny is *GND*, ii, 258.

antlers it had.[2] The king's itinerary demonstrates his many visits to forests, as repeatedly writs and charters are said to have been drawn up at locations in or near forests such as Brampton in Huntingdonshire or Woodstock in Oxfordshire. The English forests seem to have been enlarged during Henry's reign, and may indeed have been well on their way to their maximum size. Not only were the forests in England and Normandy extensive, but the law applied there was strict, and, according to Orderic Vitalis, Henry was disinclined to relax his rights sufficiently to allow the nobility the right to hunt on their own lands. He also made those who had land near the bounds of the forest mutilate their dogs so that they could not hunt the deer.[3] Orderic does not make clear whether in this context he was writing of the situation in Normandy as well as England, but if he was, then this was a marked tightening of the previous situation, as great lords do more commonly seem to have enjoyed the right to have private forests in Normandy than they did in England.

'He gave way too easily to the sin of lust; from boyhood to old age he was sinfully enslaved by this vice, and had many sons and daughters by his mistresses.'[4] Henry acknowledged an exceptional number of children, by comparison with his father and brothers: the Conqueror may not have had any children outside wedlock, Rufus may have been homosexual, and Robert is known to have had only two children.[5] Henry, however, acknowledged an exceptional number (see appendix I, no. 2), and these may have been only the children born to women of sufficiently high status that their claims could not be ignored. Henry's earliest known liaison was with Ansfrida, and it possibly went back to the time he spent at Abingdon in 1084, when he was about sixteen (see above, p. 26). Thereafter his mistresses included at least one of high rank, Isabel, daughter of his close friend Robert of Meulan.[6] Although she bore the king a child, she was subsequently married to a man of noble status.[7] Henry is also said to have had a liaison with Nest, a Welsh princess, on whom it was claimed he fathered a child.[8] Other mistresses included two with English names, Edith, mother of the countess of Perche, who occurs in the 1130 pipe roll, and Ede, daughter of the Northumbrian thegn Forne, who was to marry Robert d'Oilly, constable of Oxford castle.[9] There are glimpses of the way such liaisons were formed.

[2] Wace, *Roman de Rou* (ed. Holden), lines 10,517–40.   [3] OV, vi, 100.
[4] OV, vi, 99; Thompson, 'Affairs of State: The Illegitimate Children of Henry I'.
[5] OV, v, 282.   [6] *GND*, ii, 250–1.
[7] *Complete Peerage*, xi, appendix D, p. 117; Thompson, 'Affairs of State', 133.
[8] *Complete Peerage*, xi, appendix D, p. 110. Thompson, 'Affairs of State', 131, suggests that this may have been a short liaison and that the king may not have been the father of a son by Nest.
[9] *Complete Peerage*, xi, appendix D, pp. 108–13; Thompson, 'Affairs of State', 132.

Ansfrida sought out the young prince for his help in securing her property after her husband's death. Isabel must have come to his attention when in the company of her father, Count Robert. If Orderic is correct, Henry remained promiscuous in old age. At least two of his illegitimate sons were young at the time of his death, and so their births may have occurred in 1120 or later.[10] Nevertheless the possibility was raised above (p. 170) that he may well have had problems in fathering children by the time of his second marriage. His illegitimate children were clearly important politically. His eldest sons, Robert and Richard, seem to have been intended to assist his son William: Robert as earl of Gloucester and Richard as lord of Breteuil. His daughters were the means by which alliances could be made, especially with those whose lands adjoined the kingdom or the duchy.

The sources on the whole are silent about his feelings for his children, with the exception of his son William, on whom he clearly doted, and who had acquired the reputation of being a spoilt young man. He probably saw much less of his daughters than his sons, for the girls would probably have been betrothed at an early age. Matilda was sent off to Germany in 1110 at only eight years of age, and may not have seen her father again until her return to Normandy in 1125. She was evidently a woman of spirit: as the widow of an emperor she was said not to have liked the prospect of marrying the son of a mere count, but she finally obeyed her father. When her marriage ran into difficulty, she retired to Normandy, but then returned to her husband when it had been so decreed and approved in a royal council.

The sources are also silent about Henry's feelings for the women in his life. His two wives were richly endowed with lands and property, and, after she had produced a son, Matilda was trusted to represent Henry's authority in England during his absence. He did not, however, bring forward his return from Normandy in 1118 when she died. His second wife was much younger than he was, and the pair did not succeed in conceiving a child. The desperate importance of doing so may have been part of the problem of conception, but the fact that Adeliza was able to bear several children to her second husband does raise questions about her relationship with King Henry.

Orderic's description of Henry as 'a man of tremendous energy' is borne out by his itinerary. He travelled as far north as Carlisle, twice into Wales, and crossed the Channel on a number of occasions, and was hunting in the forest of Lyons at the time of his death. He evidently enjoyed robust good health until quite late in life, and it is interesting that his brother Robert

---

[10] OV, vi, 100.

did not die until 1134, and Adela not until 1137. His itinerary does show a slowdown in his travels towards the end of his life, but only one period of illness is reported, by Henry of Huntingdon, in 1132.[11] The names of some of the king's physicians have been noted, and there are contemporary drawings of one of them, Grimbald, holding aloft bottles and writing tablets.[12] What is not clear is whether the king employed physicians because of physical need, or anxiety about his health.[13] Whatever the reason, he could afford the best.

Henry showed courage when it was needed, a crucial factor for kings in this era. He was with his army at the major battles in 1106 and in 1119. He evidently did not have the passion for war of his father and brothers, and probably was not their equal as a warrior. It cannot have been easy for Henry growing up as the son of the renowned William the Conqueror, and the brother of Robert, the crusader, and Rufus, the great captain of knights. Henry's expulsion from Mont-Saint-Michel as a young man in 1091 must have been very humiliating. There is even a hint that Duke Robert may not have taken his youngest brother seriously: when he arrived in England in 1103 unannounced and without permission, he does not seem to have anticipated Henry's anger, or the price that would have to be paid. William of Malmesbury commented that Henry preferred to attain his ends by peaceful means wherever possible.[14]

Sudden death was always a possibility for rulers, and in 1118 Henry's situation was particularly precarious. He feared assassination, and took to sleeping with his weapons at hand, changing the position of his bed each night.[15] This was the year when, it was alleged, a conspiracy against his life by some of his household officials was uncovered, and the ringleader put to death.[16] In 1119 his daughter Juliana tried to murder him by shooting him with a crossbow after he had mutilated her daughters.[17] In Wales, too, in 1121 he came under attack but escaped, thanks to the protection of his mail coat.[18]

It is not easy to weigh up whether Henry was especially concerned about his health, or sudden death, or the prospect of hell-fire that awaited him thereafter. The drawings of Grimbald the king's physician were included in the Worcester chronicle because the author inserted in his account of the events of 1130 an illustrated account of the nightmares of Henry I. These were said to have been observed by Grimbald, and related to Abbot Godfrey at Winchcombe in the writer's presence. In the first vision peasants

[11] HH, p. 488. [12] JW, iii, plates 1–3. [13] Southern, 'Place of Henry I', p. 232.
[14] WM, *GRA*, i, 742. [15] *Vie de Louis VI le Gros* (ed. Waquet), p. 190. [16] Ibid.
[17] OV, vi, 210–14. [18] WM, *GRA*, i, 726.

appeared brandishing their implements before the king, who lay sleeping in bed. In the second he saw knights fully armed, who wanted to kill him. Prelates stood by searching for the property belonging to their churches. In the third prelates appeared again, holding their pastoral staffs, with which they wanted to attack him.[19]

These anecdotes were followed in the chronicle by a description of the king's escape from shipwreck on his return voyage to England, and his promise to remit 'the Danish tribute' (i.e. geld) for seven years, and to visit the shrine of St Edmund. However, the annals dealing with the years 1128 to 1131 were revised and continued down to 1140, which means that the author knew at the time of writing about the troubles which broke out after Henry's death. The whole section of the chronicle between 1128 and 1135 included meteorological phenomena, especially in 1133 on the eve of what was to be the king's last crossing to Normandy: the sun shone like a new moon, then changed its shape – some claimed this as a solar eclipse – followed by tremors affecting the sea, perspiration from the walls of churches in the north, and an earthquake.[20] Such phenomena were a particular interest of the monks of Worcester, but by placing these details after stories – first that of the king's experiences, secondly of Saint Odilia and her father's penance, and thirdly that of the pious end of the precentor of Worcester – the author has heightened the emotional tension of the writing and the reader's sense of the need for repentance. Henry may well have had nightmares. These three visions may have been loosely based on reality, but that he should dream so precisely of the three orders into which, it was believed at the time, society was divided suggests that this was a deliberate literary device. In other words, the author was using his account of Henry's reign as a vehicle to urge upon his readers the need for repentance. Churchmen in the early twelfth century were urging the need for confession and penance, and the Worcester chronicler's story should be understood in this context.

That having been said, it would have been only natural if the wreck of the White Ship did not heighten Henry's sense of the fragility of human life and happiness and, perhaps, a sense that he was being punished for past sins. His lavish endowment of Reading abbey may in part have reflected these feelings, though it seems likely that he would have made a grand gesture anyway, like his father at Saint-Etienne Caen and Battle abbey. Henry's bereavement and remarriage, with the urgent need for the blessing of a son, may simply have spurred on his efforts.[21]

---

[19] JW, iii, 198–202.   [20] Ibid., 210.
[21] Stafford, 'Cherchez la Femme'; Green, 'Piety and Patronage of Henry I', 4–7.

More remarkable perhaps than the foundation of Reading was the scale of Henry's patronage between about 1128 and 1131, particularly his generosity to Cluny, to Fontevraud and to the Templars. The continuing childlessness of his second marriage, and the complicated negotiations for his daughter's marriage with the great men of England and Normandy and with Count Fulk of Anjou, who was negotiating his own role in the kingdom of Jerusalem, were difficult enough. The death of Henry's nephew, William Clito, removed one serious danger, but when the empress's marriage ran into turbulence, the prospect of a grandson for Henry must have seemed less and less likely. The possibility that Geoffrey of Anjou wished to escape from the marriage was another complication, as was the papal schism, for Henry had to ensure that neither pope nor antipope would prevent the repair of his daughter's marriage.

Henry's dramatic escape from shipwreck is said to have occurred after his meetings with Pope Innocent II, and before the council in 1131 at which the decision that Matilda should return to her husband was taken. The timing of Henry's lucky escape was a reminder of his advancing years and the precariousness of the succession. In this context, a promise to remit danegeld for seven years and a visit to the shrine of St Edmund, otherwise unrecorded, are entirely possible. Only when his daughter gave birth to two healthy sons, Henry and Geoffrey, did the future look brighter to their grandfather. It may be therefore that the timing and generosity of Henry's religious patronage reflect the ups and downs of his life, yet the image of a king subject to night terrors, 'consumed by fear and haunted by his troubles' in Henry of Huntingdon's words, may say more about the concerns of twelfth-century chroniclers than about the king's temperament.

In other respects Henry seems to have had strong nerves. In 1101 he had to wait for his brother's arrival in England, fearing that many of the greatest magnates would desert his court for that of Robert. His best hope was to remain confident and to ignore intrigues.[22] An ability to conceal his feelings was also mentioned in an anecdote told by Henry of Huntingdon of Bishop Robert Bloet. The author, seated next to the bishop at dinner, saw him in tears because his servants, who had formerly been richly clothed, were now dressed in woollens. When he was told that the king had praised him in his absence, the bishop remarked that the king only praised those whom he had decided to destroy utterly, for the king was a man of the greatest animosity and inscrutability of mind.[23]

---

[22] Ibid., 7–16.   [23] HH, pp. 566–8.

He was also extremely tenacious in his defence of his rights, as the earlier chapter on the church makes clear. He tried hard to avoid giving way on investiture in England. He was only persuaded of the need to do so by the gravity of his position in Normandy, and even then hoped to resume the practice. He did his utmost to prevent Thurstan from being consecrated archbishop until he had made a profession of obedience, and even after the consecration refused for many months to grant Thurstan permission to enter his see. The ability to procrastinate, and to use anger as a weapon, is vividly illustrated in the detailed accounts of his tussles with his archbishops, Anselm of Canterbury and Thurstan of York.

Orderic's description of Henry as a 'curious inquirer' (*curiosus perscrutator*), who wanted to know about everything that was going on, also has the ring of truth about it.[24] Orderic had had first-hand experience of the king's inquiring nature when Henry visited the abbey of Saint-Evroult in 1113. The king, seated in the cloister, had interrogated the monks about their conduct before granting the abbey a charter confirming its lands and privileges, and requesting the privilege of confraternity with the monks. However, Orderic made his comment about the king's inquisitiveness in the context of his desire to know what his officials were doing, and so to be forewarned of conspiracies. Henry had Robert de Bellême watched for more than a year by private spies, who wrote down his misdeeds in detail, before he summoned him to answer forty-five charges in 1102.[25] In 1123 he was forewarned of the conspiracy of Waleran of Meulan and his confederates, and, without giving his knowledge away, summoned one of them, Hugh de Montfort, to his court.[26]

According to William of Malmesbury, the king's hatreds and friendships were maintained to extremes, the one serving as outlets for his great fits of rage, the other for his generosity to his friends, to whom he gave great wealth.[27] This too sounds credible. William count of Mortain was never forgiven, and is thought to have endured a long captivity. Robert de Bellême managed to patch up his relations with Henry after Tinchebray, but it is hard to believe that he was secure, or that his ultimate downfall was not merely a matter of time. Once arrested he was never released; nor would Henry release his own brother, despite representations from William Clito.

Those who were members of Henry's inner circle remained correspondingly loyal, like Robert count of Meulan, his brother Henry earl of Warwick, Richard de Redvers, Robert FitzHaimon and Nigel d'Aubigny. A man like Nigel was able to refer to the king as his 'dearest lord', and referred to his

---

[24] OV, vi, 100. [25] Ibid., 20. [26] Ibid., 334. [27] WM, *GRA*, i, 742.

love for Henry.[28] Wealth was lavished on those closest to the king, most obviously the great wealth given to his nephews Stephen and Henry of Blois.

Henry was fortunate in becoming king as a mature adult, in that he was experienced in the ways of his world; but he also chose his friends and advisers carefully. Robert count of Meulan was the chief of these, particularly at the start of the reign.[29] The count came from an older generation, having fought at Hastings as a youth. William of Malmesbury described how, because he had risen to pre-eminence under Henry, his advice was particularly persuasive: he was the architect of victory in war, one who ensured that the laws were strictly obeyed, and absolutely loyal.[30] The count evidently stiffened Henry's resolve to stand out on the issue of investitures, but when the king had to give way, the settlement was backed both by Robert and by Richard de Redvers, another man who was close to the king.[31] Roger bishop of Salisbury fulfilled a different role, as the archetypal servant who had served Henry before 1100 and was still in his service in 1135. He may not have counselled on peace and war, but he was influential over the choice of archbishops for Canterbury in 1114 and 1123.[32]

Henry was certainly a harsh ruler, and there has been some discussion as to whether his severity was exceptional for his times.[33] A. L. Poole believed that this was a reign of 'calculated terror',[34] and Sir Richard Southern argued that Henry punished with 'a Byzantine ferocity already outmoded'.[35] The problem lies partly in comprehending contemporary expectations of kings and the sanctions they imposed. Kings had to be severe to be effective, but were all offences, and all transgressors, to be treated with equal severity? The Anglo-Saxon Chronicler, for instance, thought that the moneyers who were mutilated on the king's orders in 1125 deserved their fate, but the hanging of forty-four thieves and castration of six more in the previous year by the king's justice Ralph Basset provoked the comment that many thought a great injustice had been done.[36]

Most of the material relating to Henry's cruelty arises in the context of revolt. The earliest was the summary death dealt out by Henry to Conan of Rouen in 1090. Both Orderic and William of Malmesbury saw this as just retribution,[37] and neither blamed Henry. The tower at Rouen was a seat of

---

[28] *Charters of the Honour of Mowbray*, no. 2.   [29] OV, vi, 328.   [30] WM, *GRA*, i, 736.
[31] Anselm, *Letters*, no. 230.   [32] *Chronicon Monasterii de Abingdon*, ii, 287; *ASC* E 1123.
[33] Hollister, 'Royal Acts of Mutilation'.   [34] Poole, *From Domesday Book to Magna Carta*, p. 155.
[35] Southern, 'Place of Henry I', p. 231.   [36] *ASC* E, 1124, 1125.
[37] OV, iv, 224–6; WM, *GRA*, i, 712–14.

ducal power and justice; summary punishment for manifest treachery was permissible, and perhaps the place of death was regarded as appropriate in the circumstances. It was also perhaps a reflection of the fact that Conan was not a noble but a townsman, who had used money to build up an armed retinue. Nevertheless, Henry's action was a revealing indication of his character.

Periods of long imprisonment for royal or noble rebels was not unheard of, but sentences of death or mutilation were exceptional by the early twelfth century in Henry's world. The rumour that Count William of Mortain, the king's kinsman, had been blinded on Henry's orders reached the chronicler Henry of Huntingdon, who cited it in his criticism of the king.[38] King Henry did not even flinch from allowing corporal punishment to be meted out to his granddaughters, who were blinded and lost the tips of their nostrils to punish their parents, who had killed a hostage entrusted to them. He certainly was not acting on a whim, and it has been suggested above (p. 147) that the situation facing him at the time was extremely serious. If he had failed to respond to the appeal from the aggrieved father, then the situation in south-eastern Normandy might have spiralled further out of control. Orderic made no comment about the mutilation, and one possible inference is that, although he remained silent, he felt the punishment was too severe.

Orderic is also the source of the most detailed account of the punishment of the vanquished rebels of 1124 (see above, pp. 186–7). Henry ordered three of the captured rebel castellans – Odard du Pin, Geoffrey de Tourville and Luc de la Barre – to be blinded though the leaders of the revolt were only imprisoned. According to Orderic, this severity provoked a protest from the count of Flanders, who protested that it was not usual in his country for knights who followed their lord into battle to be punished in this way.[39] The king's reply was that the first two had become Henry's liege men (presumably whilst the Beaumont lands were in his hands), and thus were fatally compromised when they committed treason. Luc by contrast had not performed homage. He had fought against Henry at Pont-Audemer, and had been pardoned by Henry when peace was declared. He had been allowed to leave with his horses and baggage, but had violated the terms of his safe conduct by continuing to aid the enemy. To compound this offence he had composed scurrilous songs about the king. When Count Charles had heard the charges against Luc he remained silent, because, according to Orderic, he had no reasonable counter-argument. Luc, knowing he was

---

[38] HH, p. 604.　　[39] OV, vi, 352.

to suffer the punishment of blinding, chose to commit suicide. On this occasion there was a case for Henry's actions, but the fact that Orderic invents a speech from the count of Flanders may indicate that there was disquiet, because it was more usual to ransom knights (as occurred after the battle of Brémule in 1119) than to inflict capital or corporal punishment on them.[40] It is clear that Henry was concerned because, even with the leaders in prison, their castellans would fight on: indeed Morin of Le Pin, tutor of Waleran of Meulan, continued to hold Beaumont until Waleran ordered him to surrender.[41] The independence of castellans had already been demonstrated in the lordship of Breteuil after the death of William of Breteuil, and in the county of Mortain after the imprisonment of Count William (see above, pp. 73, 125). The context in which each of these incidents occurred was different, but by exploring them in detail we can see that Henry's decisions were not capricious. Nevertheless, some contemporaries evidently did regard his decisions as cruel: there is a sharp contrast here with, for example, the behaviour of King Louis VI.

Key aspects of Henry's personality thus stand out clearly in the written record, whilst others are ambiguous or remain hidden, especially those which relate to his temperament and disposition. Something of the effect he had on others is also clear: respected and feared, he was also capable of inspiring loyalty and perhaps affection. Above all it is a sense of his political acumen which shines through the record. He was well able to calculate political odds, and was tenacious in negotiation and resilient in recovering from setbacks. Constantly on the move, he understood the need to be present in person for the successful exercise of power.

Those who wrote about Henry after his death were unanimous in recognising that amongst his greatest achievements was the peace he brought to his realms.[42] Despite his methods, and the irregularities of his personal life, the years of peace experienced in both England and Normandy stood out by comparison with the rule of Rufus in England and Robert in Normandy, and the disorder on both sides of the Channel which followed Henry's death. Rufus stood condemned for his exploitation of the church, and Robert for weakness and irresolution. In contrast the Henrician era appeared much less troubled.

---

[40] Strickland, *War and Chivalry*, provides a searching discussion of the subject. Chapters 1, 7 and 9 are particularly relevant here.
[41] OV, vi, 354–6.
[42] For the obituaries, see D. Lohrmann, 'Der Tod König Heinrichs I. von England in der mittellateinischen Literatur Englands und der Normandie', *Mittellateinisches Jahrbuch*, 8 (1973), 90–107.

Moreover the marriage of Henry to a princess descended from the pre-Conquest English kings, and the birth of their son William, perhaps augured a brighter future for the English. For William of Malmesbury at least, William's birth seemed to fulfil Edward the Confessor's prophecy about a green tree which would unite the Normans and English.[43] The notion that by the early twelfth century Normans and English were growing closer together, and that this process was symbolised by Henry's marriage and his liaisons with English women, was taken up in the nineteenth century by Edward Augustus Freeman. Under Henry, he wrote, 'England became England once again.'[44] Henry, it has been suggested here, was alive to the importance of his own birth to crowned parents, aware of the monarchy's associations with certain places and shrines, and personally associated with individual women of English birth, but it is not demonstrably clear that he was an Anglophile.[45] Henry may indeed have resented any jibes that came from his brother's Norman friends to the effect that he had 'gone native'. As has been pointed out, the process of assimilation of Normans and English took place over a long time scale, and was a complex process.[46] Individuals had a sense of different identities and, in Henry's case, we cannot be sure of his personal feelings.

By 1135 certainly Norman rule was more securely rooted, especially in northern England, than it had been at the start of Henry's reign. The relations between Henry and the sons of Malcolm III helped to prevent Scots incursions, so that Normans began to settle in the northern counties, to build castles and to found religious houses. The tenurial landscape of the north was radically restructured in the wake of large-scale confiscations of land, so that the new elite, men like Nigel d'Aubigny, Walter Espec and Eustace FitzJohn, were Henry's creations. At Durham the reorganisation of the bishopric continued, and at Carlisle a new bishopric was established. In the southern marches of Normandy a similar process followed the downfall of William count of Mortain and Robert de Bellême. Stephen of Blois replaced William, and Robert's patrimonial lands passed to his son William Talvas, but Henry was able to strengthen his castles, reward those families who were loyal to him, and offer patronage to Savigny, to the bishop of Sées and to the abbey of Saint-Evroult. In reordering political society in these regions of England and Normandy, the rule of Henry I was of lasting significance.

[43] WM, *GRA*, i, 758.
[44] Freeman, *Norman Conquest of England*, v, 148–50; Freeman, *William Rufus*, ii, 457.
[45] Crouch, *Normans*, pp. 159–160.
[46] Thomas, *The English and the Normans*, chapter 5; Marritt, 'Coincidences of Names', pp. 159–65.

Henry's regime in Normandy was also significant for the strengthening of ducal castles, especially those near the frontiers of the duchy. As we have seen, the political frontiers of the duchy were in one sense precisely defined, yet in terms of political loyalties they were zones rather than linear boundaries, where families mingled with their neighbours, bound by ties of family and lordship.[47] In a British context, the frontiers of Henry's kingdom can also be regarded as zones, and here too he sought to establish allies whose role was both to be defensive and, if circumstances permitted, to serve as bases for further expansion. Although Henry may have been less overtly aggressive than his brother Rufus, he too accepted that their father's legacy was not simply Normandy and England, but a bundle of rights and claims to be pursued when possible.

The late John Le Patourel pointed out that under Henry's rule Normandy and England came closest to constituting a Norman 'empire'.[48] There were imperial overtones to Henry's rule over different peoples, as noted above (p. 224), epitomised in the imperial crown of the kings of the English. Henry's entourage was and remained the focal point of administration for the kingdom and the duchy, and undoubtedly an extended period of condominium affected both England and Normandy. His early experiences in western Normandy created bonds with the men of that region who were established in England after 1100, and, although some of the great cross-Channel complexes of land broke up, others were created. Anglo-Normans were selected for preferment in the churches of Normandy as well as England. The movement of ecclesiastics was not simply one way, from Normandy to England, though native Englishmen continued to feel a sense of exclusion from the higher echelons of the church. Study of manuscripts and buildings again shows continuing interactions, doubtless facilitated because the two realms were under one ruler.[49] It could be

---

[47] On this subject see especially D. J. Power, 'Introduction. Frontiers: Terms, Concepts, and the Historians of Medieval and Early Modern Europe' and 'French and Norman Frontiers in the Central Middle Ages', in *Frontiers in Question: Eurasian Borderlands 700–1700*, ed. D. J. Power and N. Standen (London, 1999), pp. 1–12, 28–31, 105–31; Power, *Norman Frontier in the Twelfth and Thirteenth Centuries*, part 1; Bauduin, *La première Normandie*; Demoine-Descourtieux, 'La frontière normande de l'Avre'.

[48] Le Patourel, *Norman Empire*, p. 354.

[49] For manuscripts see especially R. Gameson, *The Manuscripts of Early Norman England* (Oxford, 1999); J. J. G. Alexander, *Norman Illumination at Mont St Michel 966–1100* (Oxford, 1970); *Manuscrits et enluminures dans le monde normand (Xe–XVe siècle)*, ed. P. Bouet and M. Dosdat, Colloque de Cerisy-la-Salle (Caen, 1999); for architecture, the essays in *England and Normandy in the Middle Ages* (ed. Bates and Curry) by Fernie and Grant are particularly helpful; see also Plant, 'Ecclesiastical Architecture c. 1050–to c. 1200'.

suggested here, however, that England and Normandy remained distinct in terms of administration, custom and justice.

Henry's governance was a mixture of old and new. If in many respects his outlook was traditional, and more so than has usually been allowed in recent years, it evolved in ways that were to have profound consequences for England and Normandy. Henry came to the throne using the traditional rhetoric of English kings: he promised to maintain good laws and to protect the church. In Normandy too he portrayed himself as the true heir of the Conqueror, the defender of the Norman church. At his court the traditional rituals of feasts and hunts and gift-giving continued. As king and duke he presided over ecclesiastical councils, exercised close control over appointments, and sought to evade the legations of papal envoys.

In all of this there was little that was very new, yet the context in which these rights were maintained was changing. In England, there was a great renaissance in the collection and recording of law, and an upsurge in the demand for documentation and especially for royal writs. In Normandy, the duke's claim to control castles conflicted with local families' views that custody belonged to them. The increasing power of local castellans made it difficult for Henry to impose outsiders as lords of Norman honours. Above all, the maintenance of royal and ducal customs over the church came up against growing papal influence. The surrender of lay investiture was only the most obvious sign of a changing world. By the time Henry died, there was much more contact between the ecclesiastics of England and Normandy and those of Rome.

A new style of ruling has been attributed to Henry, described as 'administrative kingship',[50] based on settled routine, documentation, a growing army of administrators and increasing specialisation of function. It has been suggested, however, that change was incremental, involving further developments along pre-existing lines rather than a radical change of direction. Historians should not be too ready to anticipate the rise of bureaucracy and routine, or to assume that the work of royal agents was orderly or even closely supervised. Nevertheless, some three decades of vigorous rule meant an intensification of administrative activity. In England recent work has demonstrated the importance of the reign for the growth of the common law; and in Normandy the continuing strength of ducal customs in the twelfth century, still marked at the time the duchy was taken over by

---

[50] Hollister and Baldwin, 'Rise of Administrative Kingship', reprinted in *MMI*.

King Philip Augustus in 1203–4, surely owed something to the efforts of Henry I to impose order on the duchy.

William of Malmesbury pointed out that Normandy was the chief cause of Henry's wars,[51] and it certainly gave him the most trouble. After 1106 he spent lengthy periods there, and his English wealth was poured out for the defence of the duchy. Above all he wanted to ensure that neither his brother Robert nor Robert's son William would hold Normandy, and at every step his decisions were made with this end in sight. Henry's goals were those of all dynasts: put crudely, he wanted to secure and to keep the lands, rights and claims he had inherited, perhaps to add to them, and certainly to bequeath them to his heirs. Henry failed to secure a peaceful transition of power to an adult son. In this of course he was far from unique. The emperor Henry V had died without a legitimate son, and Louis VI's heir had died suddenly in 1131 when his horse stumbled over a pig in the streets of Paris.[52] Having no son at all, or too few, was a mischance. After the deaths of William Clito in 1128 and Duke Robert himself in 1134, the magnates of England and Normandy had no real alternative but to accept either Matilda and her young sons, or one of Henry's adult nephews, Theobald or Stephen.

Henry had done his best to assure Matilda's succession in England, but in Normandy the situation was made more difficult because of his refusal either to hand over the castles that were her marriage portion, or to swear an oath concerning custody of all the castles, with the result that at the time of his death father and daughter were estranged. This was particularly unfortunate because Stephen was thereby alerted to the possibility that swift action on his part might be successful, as indeed it was. If this reconstruction is correct, not only were Matilda and Geoffrey wrong-footed, but so also was Theobald, who found that the Norman magnates would no longer back his claim to the duchy of Normandy when the news of Stephen's coronation arrived. Nevertheless, Henry FitzEmpress was to be the ultimate victor in the wars over the legacy of Henry I, and if this is what his wily grandfather had hoped for, ultimately he was successful.

Henry I was not an administrator or a social engineer. He was an extremely able ruler who understood the art of propaganda, of playing a waiting game, and of manipulating the hopes and fears of men. His nature was calculating, determined, even ruthless; he loved material possessions, and was self-evidently a man of strong sexual appetites. Yet there was more to Henry than political cunning: this was a man who, if feared by some,

---

[51] WM, *GRA*, i, 744.　[52] Suger, *Vie de Louis VI* (ed. Waquet), p. 266.

could win and keep the loyalty of others. He possessed a clear sense of what it was to rule England and Normandy, and took his role as protector of the church in his realms very seriously. The churchmen who knew him, such as Peter the Venerable and Archbishop Hugh, and those who wrote about him, like Orderic Vitalis, recognised that in an imperfect world, peace and security in England and Normandy had come to rest on his shoulders.[53]

[53] OV, vi, 452.

Appendix I
Inheritances and family trees

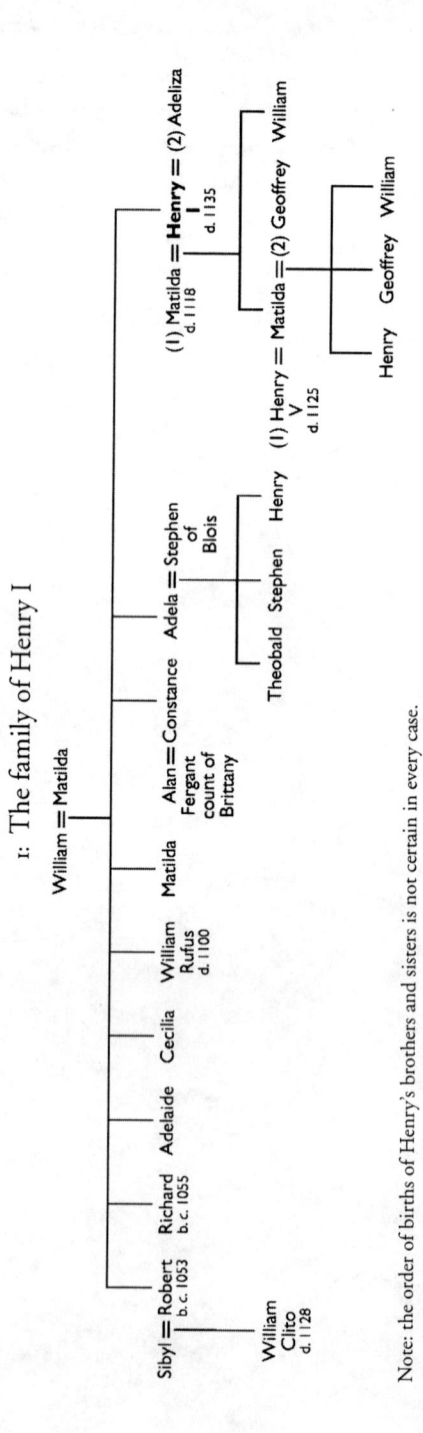

1: The family of Henry I

William = Matilda

- Robert b. c. 1053 = Sibyl
  - William Clito d. 1128
- Richard b. c. 1055
- Adelaide
- Cecilia
- William Rufus d. 1100
- Matilda
- Alan Fergant count of Brittany = Constance
- Adela = Stephen of Blois
  - Theobald
  - Stephen
  - Henry
- Henry d. 1135 = (1) Matilda d. 1118 / (2) Adeliza
  - (1) Henry V d. 1125 = Matilda = (2) Geoffrey
    - Henry
    - Geoffrey
    - William
  - William

Note: the order of births of Henry's brothers and sisters is not certain in every case.

2: The illegitimate children of Henry I

Henry I

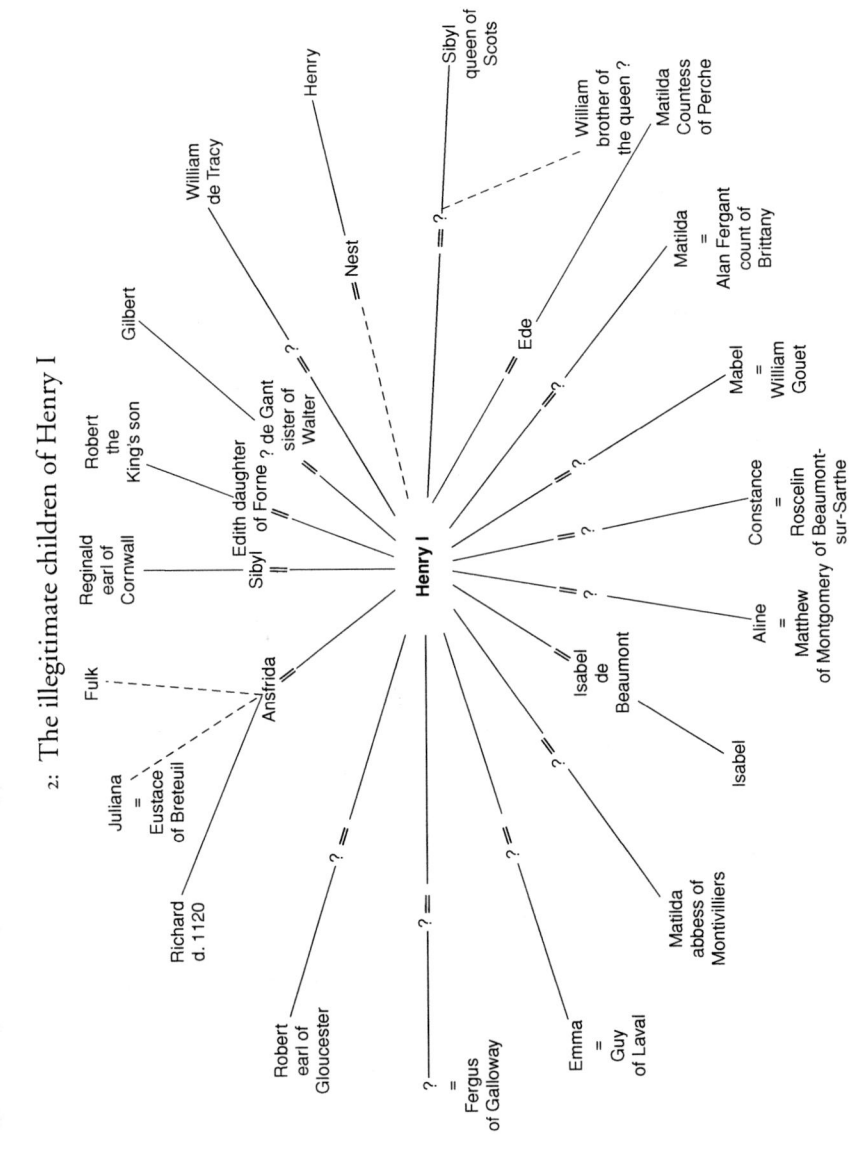

- Ansfrida
  - Fulk
  - Juliana = Eustace of Breteuil
  - Richard d. 1120
- ? = Robert earl of Gloucester
- ? = Fergus of Galloway
- ? = Emma = Guy of Laval
- Matilda abbess of Montivilliers
- Isabel de Beaumont
  - Isabel
- ? = Matthew of Montgomery of Beaumont-sur-Sarthe
  - Aline
- Constance = Roscelin
- ?
  - Mabel = William Gouet
- ?
  - Matilda = Alan Fergant count of Brittany
- Ede
- ? = William brother of the queen
  - Matilda Countess of Perche
- ? = Sibyl queen of Scots
- Nest
  - Henry
  - William de Tracy
- Sibyl = Reginald earl of Cornwall
- Edith daughter of Forne
- ? de Gant sister of Walter
  - Robert the King's son
  - Gilbert

This diagram is designed to illustrate some of Henry's illegitimate children and their mothers, where known. It includes those listed in Appendix D (by G. H. White) to *Complete Peerage*, xi, as revised by Thompson, Affairs of State: The Illegitimate Children of Henry I'. The identities of some of the mothers and children are not certain. Juliana of Breteuil and Fulk may not have been the children of Ansfrida, and the king may not have fathered Nest's son Henry.

3: The family of Queen Matilda

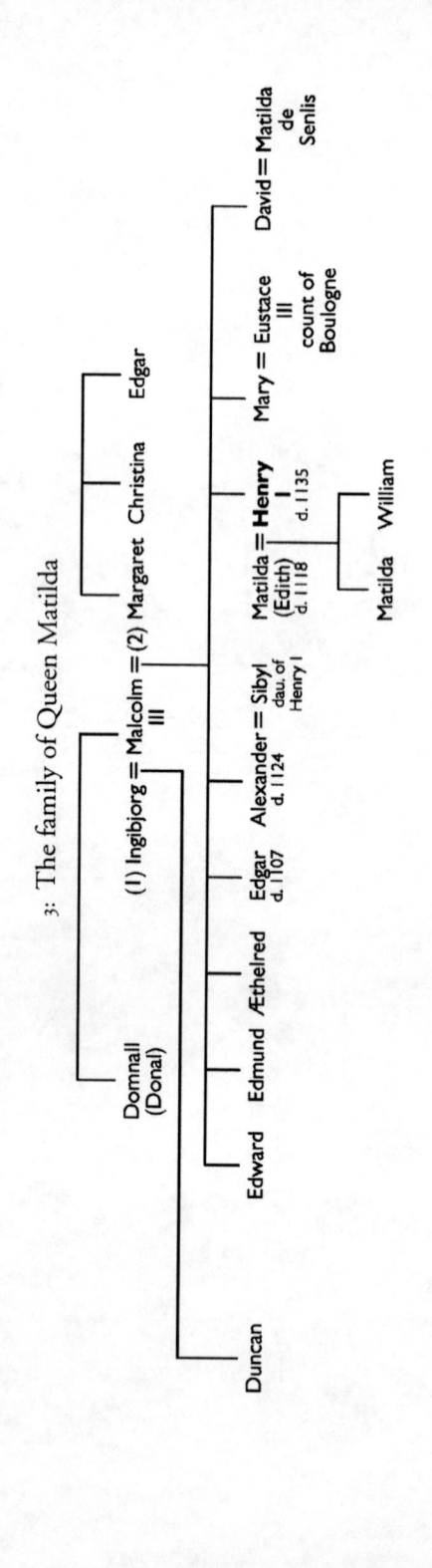

```
                    (1) Ingibjorg = Malcolm III = (2) Margaret    Christina    Edgar
                    ┌──────┘              └──────────────────────────┐
                    │                                                │
        ┌───────┬───────┬────────┬─────────┬──────────┐    ┌─────────┼─────────┬──────────┐
     Duncan  Edward  Edmund  Æthelred  Edgar    Alexander = Sibyl  Matilda = Henry I   Mary = Eustace III   David = Matilda
       Domnall                          d. 1107    d. 1124  dau. of  (Edith)   d. 1135         count of              de Senlis
       (Donal)                                              Henry I  d. 1118                   Boulogne
                                                                      │
                                                                ┌─────┴─────┐
                                                             Matilda    William
```

4: Claimants to the honour of Breteuil

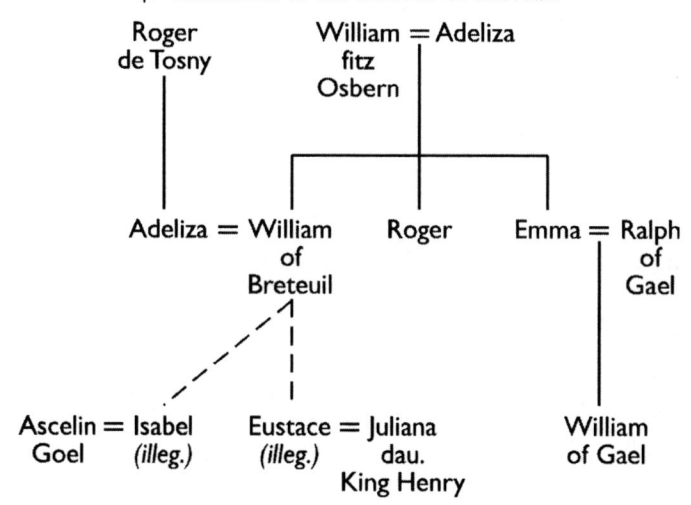

```
      Roger              William  =  Adeliza
    de Tosny              fitz
                         Osbern
        |          ┌────────┼────────┐
    Adeliza  =  William      Roger      Emma  =  Ralph
                  of                              of
               Breteuil                          Gael
                  ╱ |
                ╱   |
              ╱     |
  Ascelin = Isabel   Eustace = Juliana        William
   Goel    (illeg.)  (illeg.)   dau.          of Gael
                              King Henry
```

5: The counts of Evreux

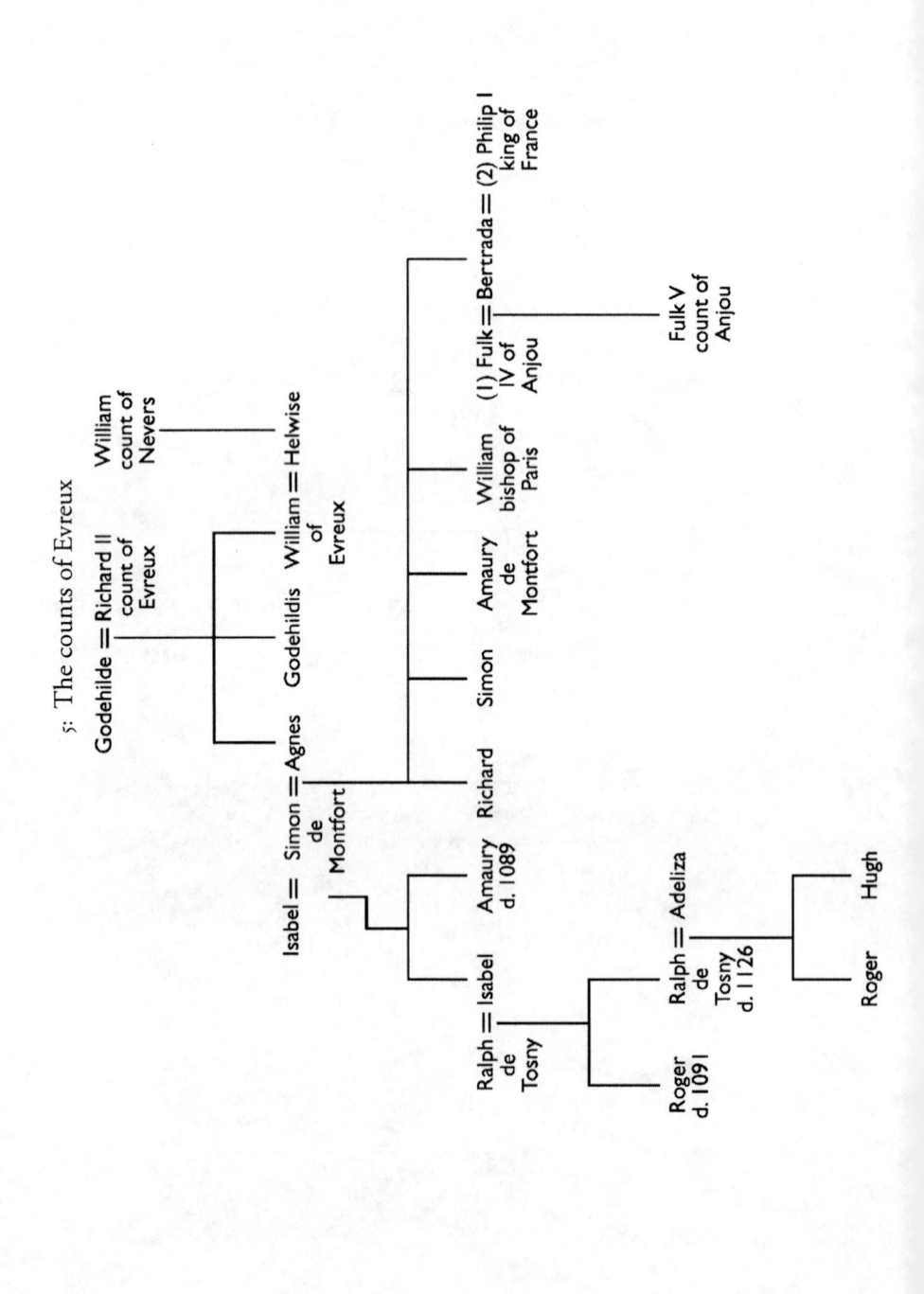

```
Godehilde = Richard II       William
            count of         count of
            Evreux            Nevers
            |                    |
    ┌───────┼────────────┐       |
Godehildis   William = Helwise
             of
             Evreux
```

```
Isabel = Simon = Agnes
         de Montfort
         |
   ┌─────┴──┬────────┬──────────┬──────────────┬────────────────────────┐
Richard   Simon   Amaury     William         (1) Fulk = Bertrada = (2) Philip I
                  de         bishop of            IV of                king of
                  Montfort   Paris                Anjou                France
                                                  |
                                              Fulk V
                                              count of
                                              Anjou
```

```
      ┌────────────┐
Ralph = Isabel   Amaury
de Tosny         d. 1089
|
┌──────┬──────────┐
Roger          Ralph de Tosny = Adeliza
d. 1091        d. 1126
               |
          ┌────┴────┐
         Roger    Hugh
```

6: Claims to the county of Flanders in 1128

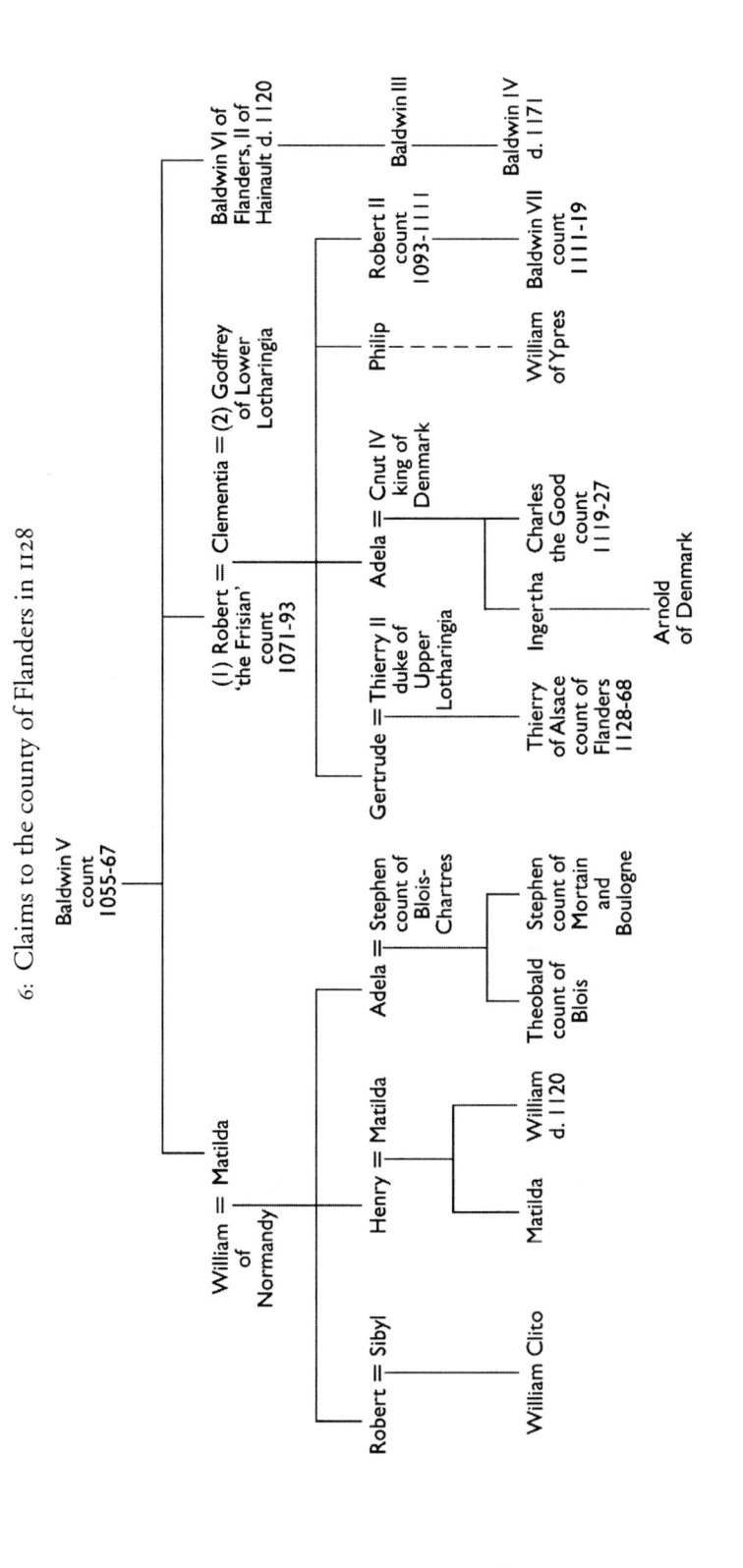

7: The Capetian kings

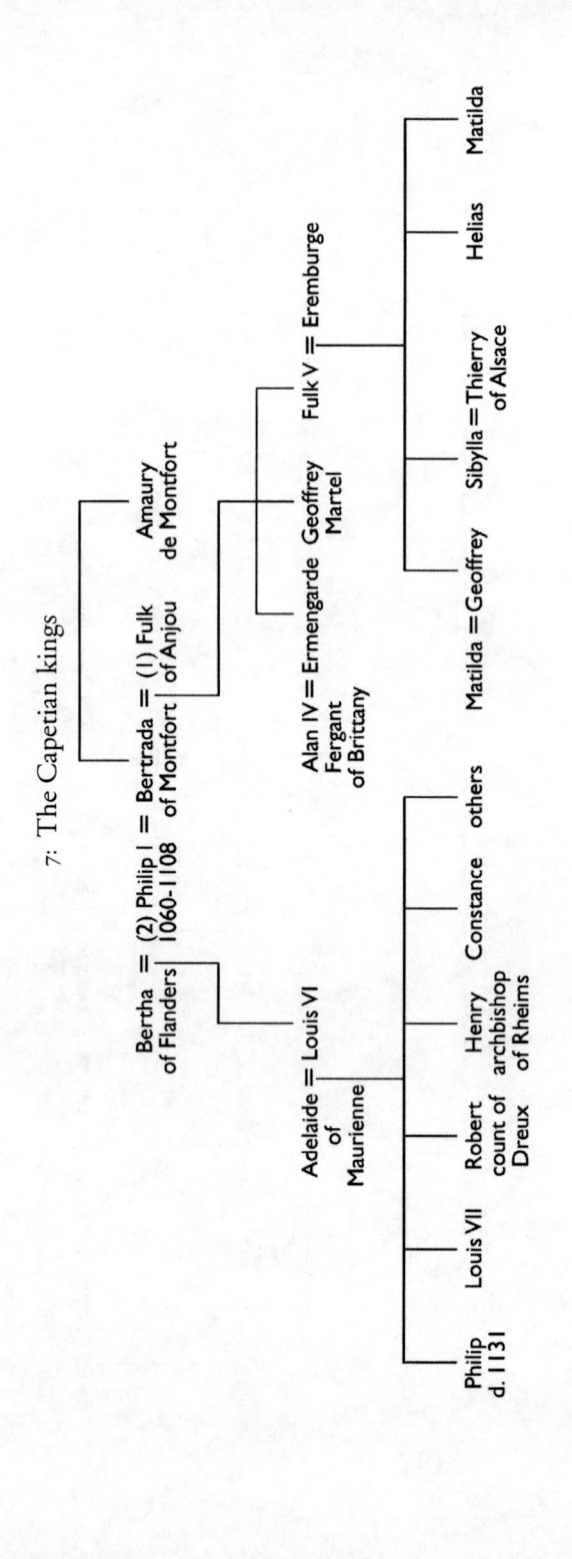

```
                    Bertha  = (2) Philip I = (1) Fulk     Amaury
                    of Flanders  1060-1108   of Anjou    de Montfort
                                             Bertrada
                                             of Montfort
          ┌──────────┘                       │
  Adelaide = Louis VI      Alan IV = Ermengarde  Geoffrey   Fulk V = Eremburge
  of                       Fergant                Martel
  Maurienne                of Brittany
                                    │                        │
                           Matilda = Geoffrey    Sibylla = Thierry  Helias  Matilda
                                                          of Alsace

  ┌──────┬──────────┬──────┬──────────┬──────────┐
Philip  Louis VII  Robert  Henry     Constance  others
d.1131           count of  archbishop
                 Dreux    of Rheims
```

8: The dynasty of Powys

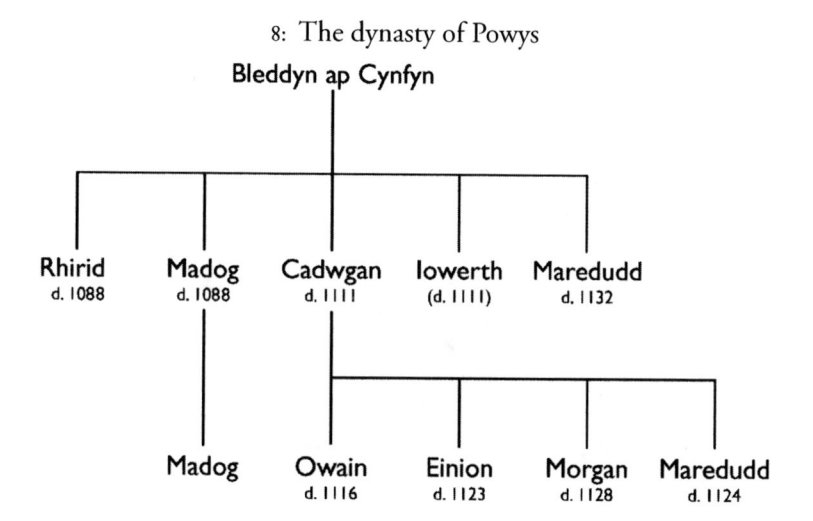

Bleddyn ap Cynfyn

- **Rhirid** d. 1088
- **Madog** d. 1088
- **Cadwgan** d. 1111
  - Madog
  - Owain d. 1116
  - Einion d. 1123
  - Morgan d. 1128
  - Maredudd d. 1124
- **Iowerth** (d. 1111)
- **Maredudd** d. 1132

9: Robert de Bellême and his family

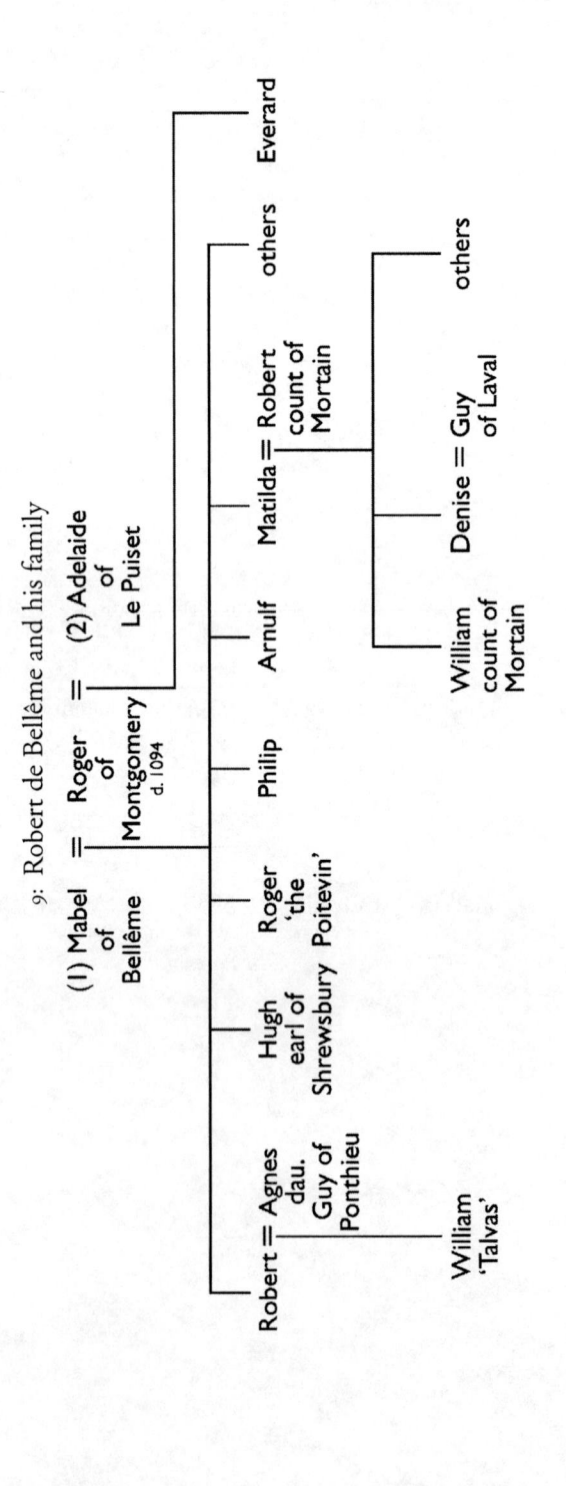

```
                    (1) Mabel  =  Roger       =  (2) Adelaide
                        of        of                of
                        Bellême   Montgomery        Le Puiset
                                  d.1094
    ┌───────┬──────────┬──────────┬──────┬────────┬─────────┬─────────┐
  Robert=Agnes  Hugh    Roger     Philip  Arnulf  Matilda=Robert    others
         dau.   earl of 'the                              count of
         Guy of Shrewsbury Poitevin'                      Mortain
         Ponthieu                                  ┌──────┴──────┐
    │                                           William        Denise=Guy     others
  William                                       count of              of Laval
  'Talvas'                                      Mortain
```

Appendix II
Maps

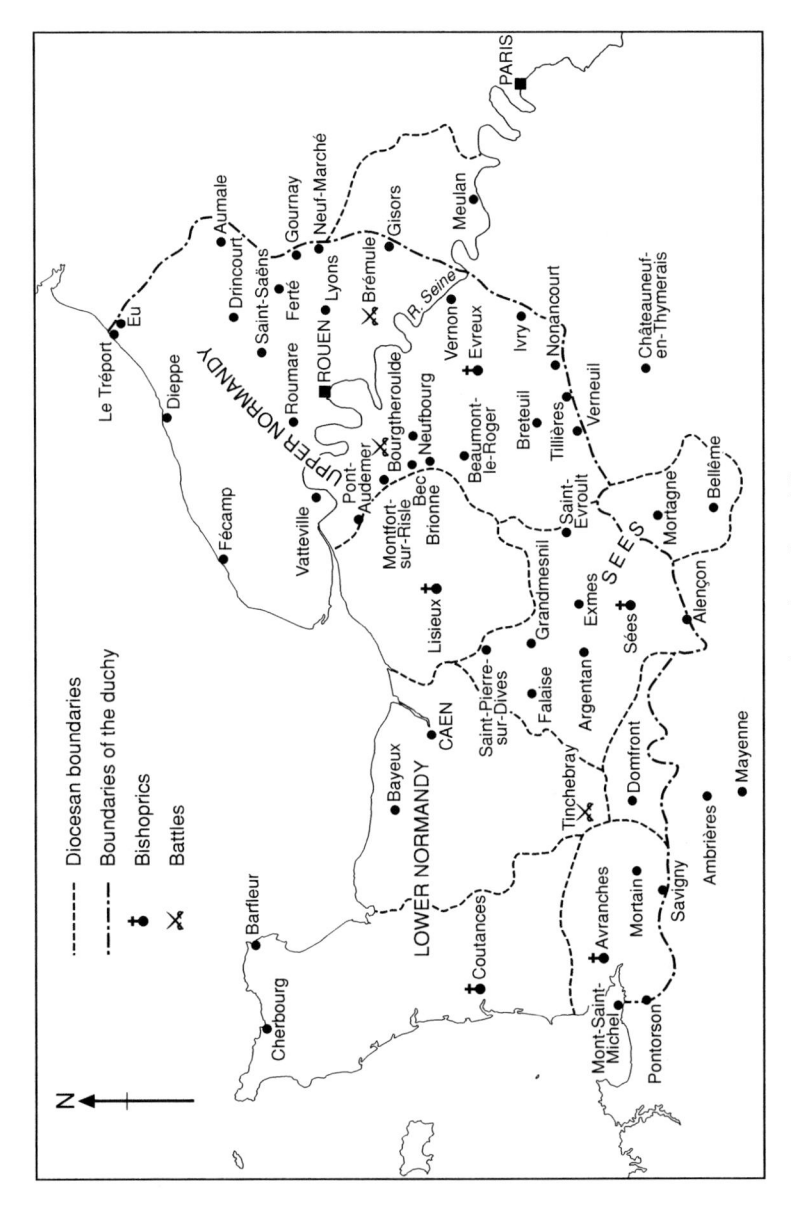

Map 1: Normandy in the early twelfth century

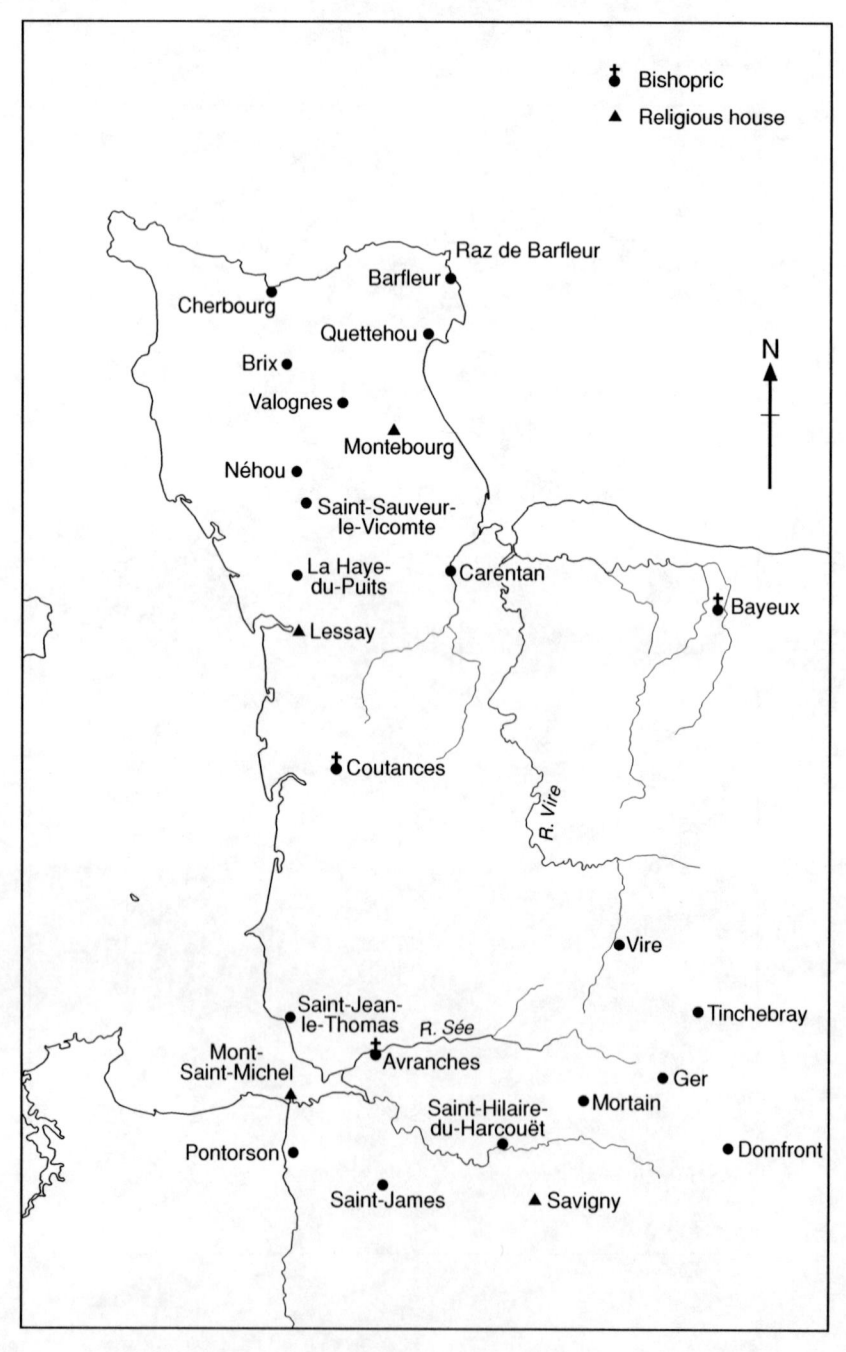

Map 2: Western Normandy

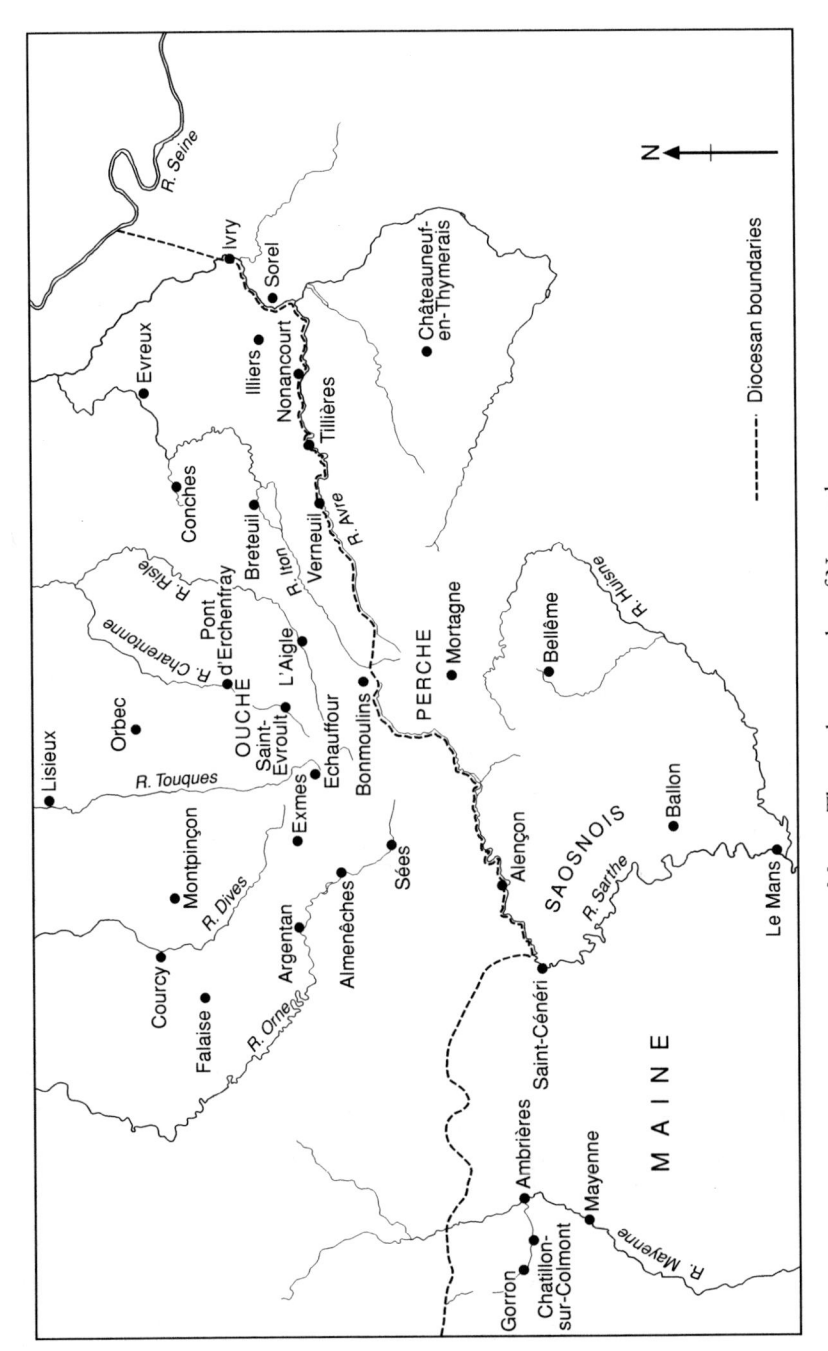

Map 3: The southern marches of Normandy

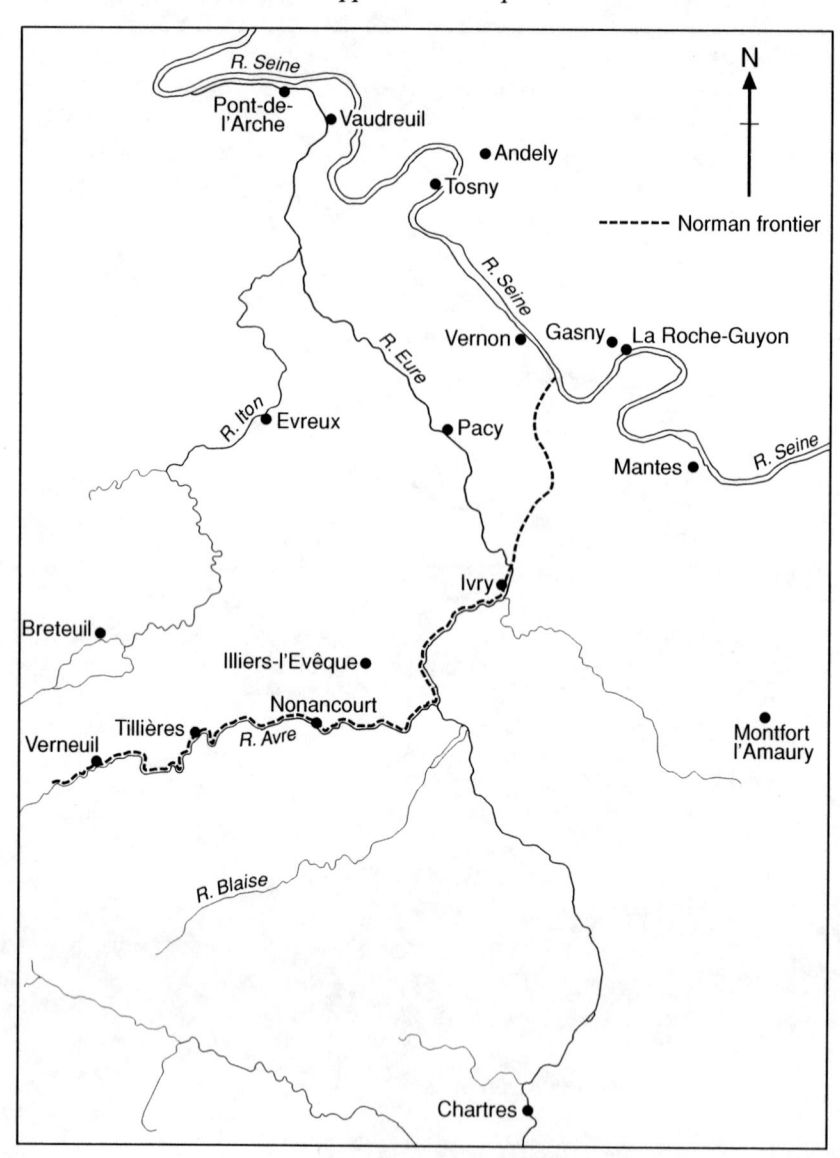

Map 4: Evreux and the valley of the river Eure

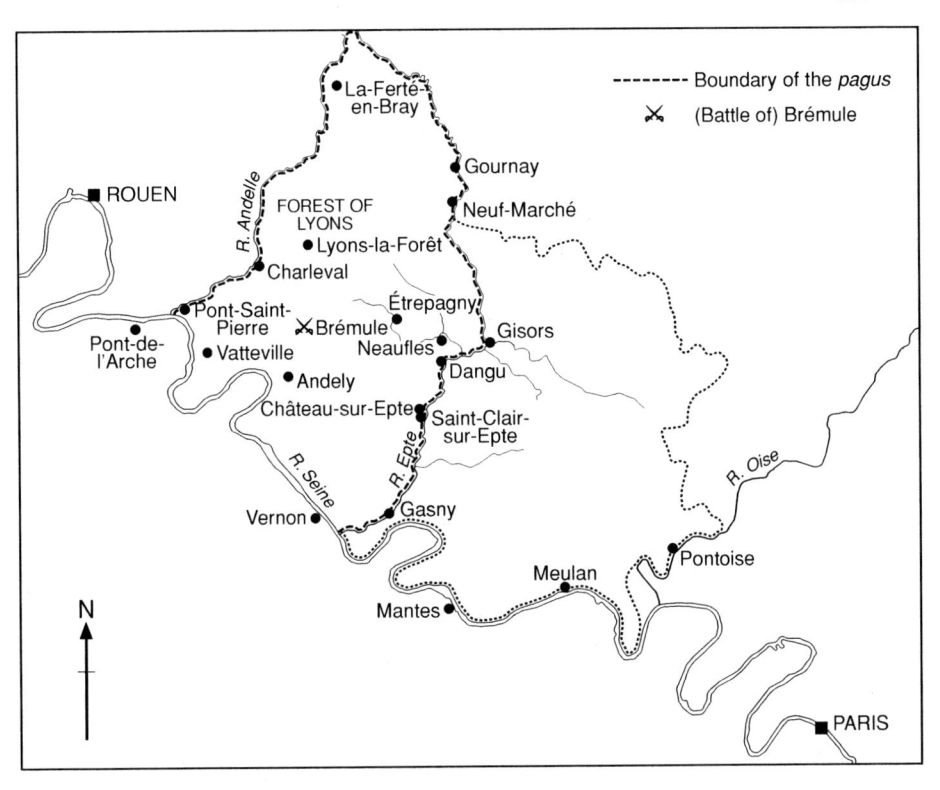

Map 5: The Vexin

Appendix II: Maps

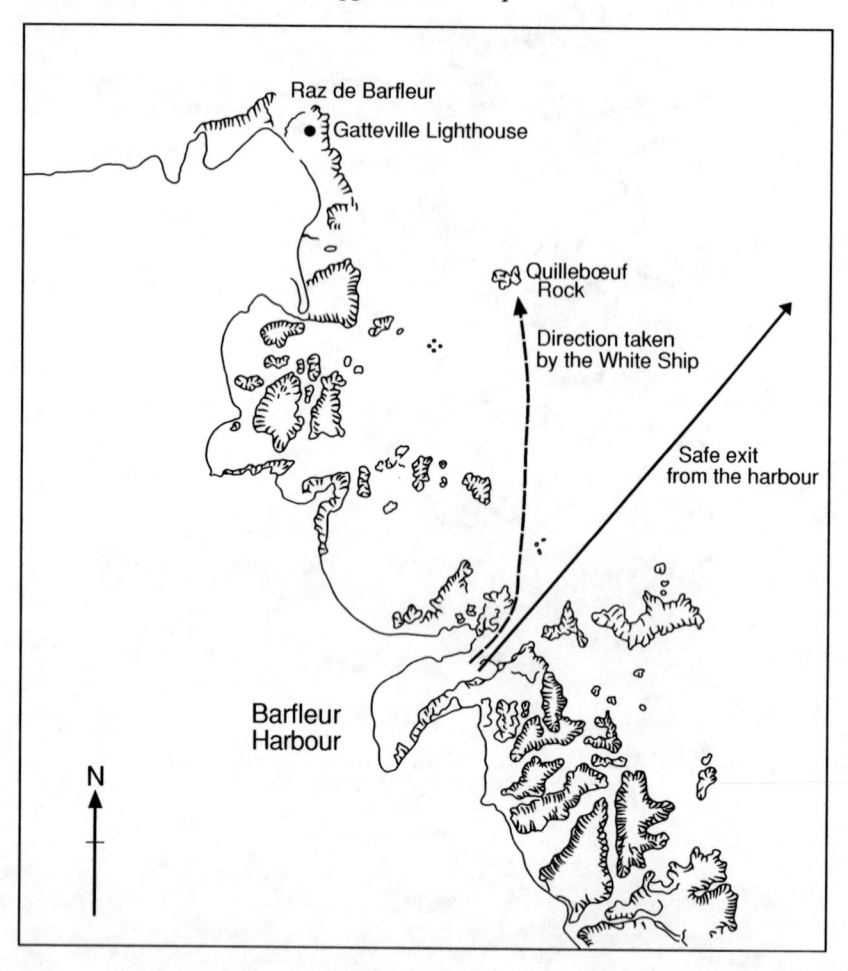

Map 6: Barfleur

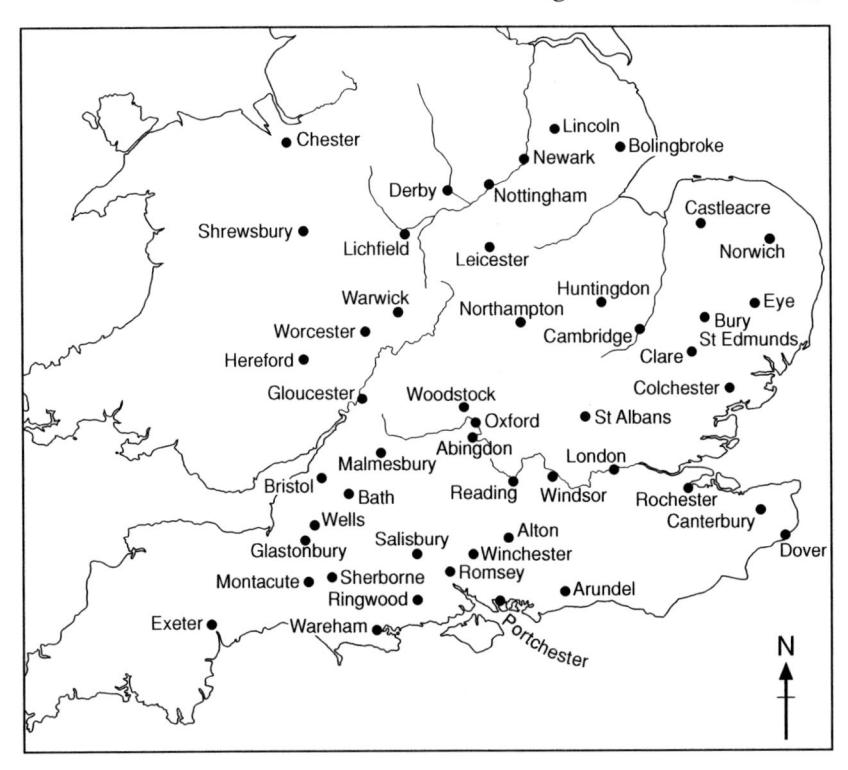

Map 7: The midlands and southern England

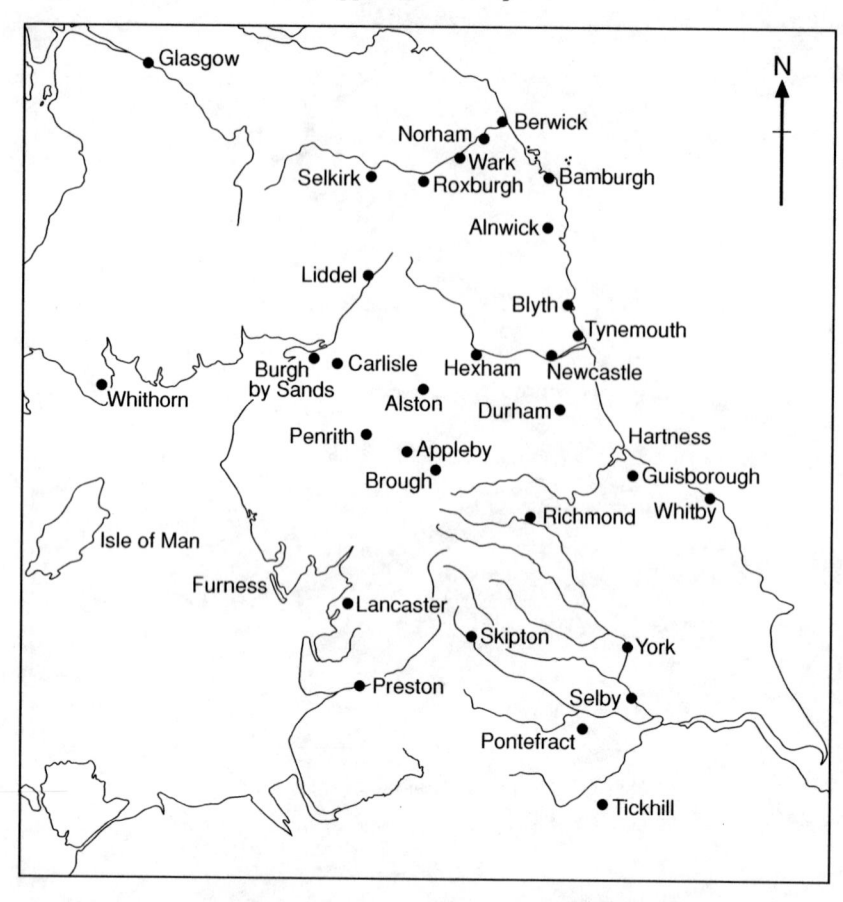

Map 8: Northern England and southern Scotland

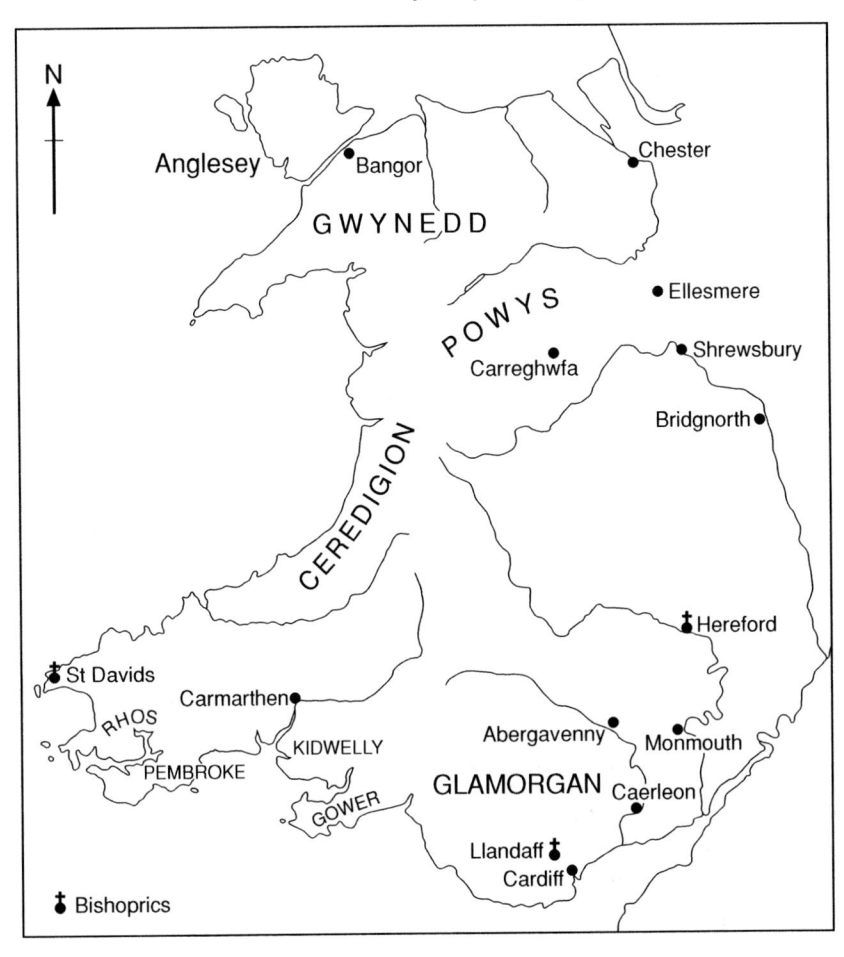

Map 9: Wales in the early twelfth century

Bibliography

MANUSCRIPT SOURCES

London, British Library, Additional Charter no. 66,980.
London, British Library, MS Cotton Cleopatra C vii.
London, Corporation of London Records Office, Charter no. IA.

UNPUBLISHED DISSERTATIONS

Bauduin, P., 'La frontière normande au Xe–XIe siècles: Origine et maîtrise politique de la frontière sur les confins de la haute Normandie (911–1087)', thèse de doctorat de l'Université de Caen Basse-Normandie (1998).

Chanteux, H., 'Recueil des actes d'Henri Beauclerc, duc de Normandie', thèse inédite de l'Ecole des Chartes (1932).

Dyson, A., 'The Career, Family and Influence of Alexander le Poer, Bishop of Lincoln 1123–1148', B. Litt. thesis, Oxford (1971).

Gallagher, P. F., 'The Monastery of Mortemer-en-Lyons in the Twelfth Century – Its History and Its Cartulary', PhD thesis, University of Notre Dame (1970).

Gazeau, V., 'Recherches sur l'histoire de la principauté normande (911–1204). I. Les abbés bénédictins de la principauté normande. II. Prosopographie des abbés bénédictins (911–1204)', dossier d'habilitation, Université de Paris, I – Panthéon-Sorbonne (2002).

Lemoine-Descourtieux, A., 'La frontière normande de l'Avre de la fin du xe siècle au début du xiiie siècle: La défense et les structures du peuplement', thèse de doctorat, Université de Caen Basse-Normandie (2003).

Spear, D. S., 'The Norman Episcopate under Henry I, King of England and Duke of Normandy (1106–1135)', PhD thesis, University of California, Santa Barbara (1982).

Stalley, R. A., 'The Patronage of Roger of Salisbury', Courtauld Institute, Univ. of London, MA dissertation (1969).

Waldman, T. G., 'Hugh "of Amiens", Archbishop of Rouen (1130–64)', DPhil thesis, University of Oxford (1970).

PRINTED PRIMARY SOURCES

Actus Pontificum Cenomannensis in Urbe Degentium, ed. G. Busson and A. Ledru, Société des Archives Historiques du Maine, ii (1902).
Adam of Domerham, *Historia de Rebus Gestis Glastoniensibus*, ed. T. Hearne, 2 vols. (London, 1727).
Ailred of Rievaulx, 'Genealogia Regum Anglorum', Migne, *Patrologia Latina*, cxcv, cols. 711–738.
 The Priory of Hexham, Its Chroniclers, Endowments, and Annals, ed. J. Raine, 2 vols., Surtees Society, xliv, xlvi (1864, 1865).
 Relatio de Standardo, in *Chronicles of the Reigns of Stephen, Henry II and Richard I*, ed. R. Howlett, 4 vols., RS (London, 1884–9), iii, 181–99.
Ancient Charters, ed. J. H. Round, Pipe Roll Society, 10 (1888).
Anglia Sacra, ed. H. Wharton, 2 vols. (London, 1691).
The Anglo-Latin Satirical Poets and Epigrammatists of the Twelfth Century, ed. T. Wright, 2 vols., RS (1892).
The Anglo-Saxon Chronicle, a Revised Translation, ed. D. Whitelock, D. C. Douglas and S. I. Tucker (London, 1961).
Annales Monastici, ed. H. R. Luard, 5 vols., RS (London, 1864–9).
Annals of Inisfallen, ed. with a translation by Seán Mac Airt (Dublin, 1951).
Anselm, *Anselmi Opera Omnia*, ed. F. S. Schmitt, 6 vols. (Seckau, Edinburgh, 1938–61).
Basset Charters c. 1120 to 1250, ed. with an introduction by W. T. Reedy, Pipe Roll Society, new series, l (1995).
Benedeit, *The Anglo-Norman Voyage of St Brendan*, ed. I. Short and B. Merrilees (Manchester, 1979).
Bernard of Clairvaux, *Letters*, trans. by B. S. James (Sutton, 1998).
 Opera, ed. J. Leclercq and C. H. Talbot, 8 vols. in 9 (Rome, 1975–7).
Bibliotheca Rerum Germanicarum, ed. P. Jaffé (Berlin, 1869), *Monumenta Bambergensia*, v.
The Boarstall Cartulary, ed. H. E. Salter, Oxford Historical Society, 88 (1930).
Bollandus J. and Henschius, G., *Acta Sanctorum Bollandiana* (Brussels etc., 1863–).
The Book of Fees, Commonly Called Testa de Nevill, Reformed from the Earliest MSS by the Deputy Keeper of the Records, 3 vols. (London, 1920–31).
The Brevis Relatio de Guillelmo Nobilissimo Comite Normannorum Written by a Monk of Battle Abbey, edited with an historical commentary by E. M. C. Van Houts, *Chronology, Conquest and Conflict in Medieval England*, CAMDEN MISCELLANY XXXIV, Camden Miscellany, 5th series, x (1997), 1–48.
Brut y Tywysogyon or the Chronicle of the Princes. Peniarth MS 20 version, ed. and trans. T. Jones, 2 vols. (Cardiff, 1941–52).
Brut y Tywysogyon or the Chronicle of the Princes. Red Book of Hergest Version, ed. and trans. T. Jones (Cardiff, 1955).
Burton, J., *Monasticon Eboracense* (York, 1758).
Calendar of Documents preserved in France, Illustrative of the History of Great Britain and Ireland, i, A. D. 918–1216, ed. J. H. Round (London, 1899).

Canterbury Professions, ed. M. Richter, Canterbury and York Society, lxvii (1973).
Carmen de Hastingae Proelio of Guy bishop of Amiens, ed. F. Barlow (Oxford, 1999).
Cartulaire de l'abbaye de la Saint-Trinité de Tiron, ed. L. Merlet, 2 vols. (Chartres, 1883).
Cartulaire de la léproserie du Grand Beaulieu, ed. R. Merlet and M. Jusselin (Chartres, 1909).
Cartulaire de Saint-Martin de Pontoise, ed. J. Depoin, Publications de la Société Historique du Vexin (1909).
The Cartulary of Cirencester Abbey, Gloucestershire, ed. C. D. Ross, 3 vols. (London, 1964–77).
Cartulary of Holy Trinity Aldgate, ed. G. A. J. Hodgett, London Record Society, 10 (1970).
The Cartulary of Oseney Abbey, ed. E. H. Salter, 6 vols., Oxford Historical Society (1929–36).
The Cartulary of St Denys Near Southampton, ed. E. O. Blake, 2 vols., Southampton Record Series, xxiv, xxv (1981).
The Cartulary of Shrewsbury Abbey, ed. U. Rees, 2 vols. (Aberystwyth, 1975).
Charters and Custumals of the Abbey of Holy Trinity Caen, Part 1, The English Estates, ed. M. Chibnall, British Academy Records of Social and Economic History, New Series, v (London, 1982).
Charters and Custumals of the Abbey of Holy Trinity Caen. Part 2, The French Estates, ed. J. Walmsley, British Academy Records of Social and Economic History, New Series, xxii (London, 1994).
The Charters of the Anglo-Norman Earls of Chester c. 1071–1237, ed. G. Barraclough, Record Society of Lancashire and Cheshire, cxxvi (1988).
The Charters of David I. The Written Acts of David I King of Scots, 1124–1153, and of His Son Henry, Earl of Northumberland, 1139–52, ed. G. W. S. Barrow (Woodbridge, 1999).
Charters of the Honour of Mowbray 1107–1191, ed. D. E. Greenway, British Academy Records of Social and Economic History, New Series, 1 (1972).
Charters of the Redvers Family and the Earldom of Devon 1090–1217, ed. R. Bearman, Devon and Cornwall Record Society, new series, xxxvii (1994).
Chronica Manniae et Insularum. The Chronicle of Man and the Sudreys from the Manuscript Codex in the British Museum, With Historical Notes by P. A. Munch, revised by Dr Goss, 2 vols., *Manx Society*, xxii, xxiii (1874).
Chronica Sancti Albini Andegavensis, in *Chroniques des Eglises d'Anjou*, ed. P. Marchegay and E. Mabille (Paris, 1869).
The Chronicle of Battle Abbey, ed. E. Searle (Oxford, 1980).
Chronicles of the Reigns of Stephen, Henry II and Richard I, ed. R. Howlett, 4 vols., RS (London, 1884–9).
The Chronicles of Scotland compiled by Hector Boece, 2 vols., Scottish Text Society, 3rd series, x, i.e. vol. i (1938 for 1936), ed. R. W. Chambers and E. C. Batho; xv, i. e. vol. ii (1941), ed. E. C. Batho and H. W. Husbands.
Chronicon Monasterii de Abingdon, ed. J. Stevenson, 2 vols., RS (London, 1858).
La Chronique de Morigny, ed. L. Mirot (Paris, 1909).

Chronique du Bec, ed. A. A. Porée (Rouen, 1885).
Chroniques des Comtes d'Anjou et des Seigneurs d'Amboise, ed. L. Halphen and R. Poupardin (Paris, 1913).
Complete Peerage, by G. E. C., revised edn V. Gibbs, H. A. Doubleday, G. H. White, 13 vols. in 12 (London, 1910–59).
The Coucher Book of Selby, 2 vols., i, ed. J. T. Fowler, ii, ed. C. C. Hodges, Yorkshire Archaeological Society, Record Series, x, xiii (1892, 1893).
Councils and Synods with Other Documents Relating to the English Church, i, part ii, *1066–1154*, ed. D. Whitelock, M. Brett and C. N. L. Brooke (Oxford, 1981).
Coutumiers de Normandie, ed. E.-J. Tardif, 2 vols. (Rouen and Paris, 1903, 1896).
Darlington, R. R., 'Winchcombe Annals 1049–1181', in *A Medieval Miscellany for Doris Mary Stenton*, ed. P. M. Barnes and C. F. Slade, Pipe Roll Society, new series, xxxvi (1960), 111–37.
'De Libertate Beccensis Monasterii', *Annales Ordinis Sancti Benedicti* (Paris, 1745), v, 601–5.
Dialogus de Scaccario. The Course of the Exchequer by Richard FitzNigel and Constitutio Domus Regis. The Establishment of the Royal Household, ed. and trans. C. Johnson with corrections by F. E. L. Carter and D. E. Greenway (Oxford, 1983).
Diplomatic Documents preserved in the Public Record Office, i, *1101–1272*, ed. P. Chaplais (London, 1972).
Domesday Book, ed. A. Farley for the Record Commission, 4 vols. (London, 1783–1816).
Dudo of St Quentin, *De Moribus et Actis Primorum Normanniae Ducum*, ed. J. Lair (Caen, 1865); translated as *The History of the Normans*, ed. E. Christiansen (Woodbridge, 1998).
Dugdale, W., *Monasticon Anglicanum*, new edn., 6 vols. in 8 (London, 1817–30).
Eadmer, *Historia Novorum*, ed. M. Rule, RS (London, 1884).
Eadmer, *The Life of St Anselm Archbishop of Canterbury*, ed. and trans. R. W. Southern (Oxford, 1979).
The Early Charters of the Augustinian Canons of Waltham Abbey, Essex, 1062–1230, ed. R. Ransford (Woodbridge, 1989).
Early Yorkshire Charters, i–iii, ed. W. Farrer (Edinburgh, 1914–16); iv–xii, ed. C. T. Clay, Yorkshire Archaeological Society, Record Series, Extra Series, i–iii, v–x, 1935–65. Extra Series vol. iv is index to first three vols., ed. C. T. Clay and E. M. Clay, 1942.
Einhard and Notker the Stammerer, *Two Lives of Charlemagne*, translated L. Thorpe (Harmondsworth, 1969).
Encomium Emmae, ed. A. Campbell, Camden Society, 3rd series, lxxii (reprinted 1998).
English Episcopal Acta. VII. Hereford 1079–1234, ed. J. Barrow (Oxford, 1993).
English Episcopal Acta. VIII. Winchester 1077–1204, ed. M. J. Franklin (Oxford, 1993).
English Historical Documents, ii, ed. D. C. Douglas and G. W. Greenaway, 2nd edn. (London, 1981).

English Lawsuits from William I to Richard I. I. William I to Stephen, ed. R. C. Van Caenegem, Selden Society, cvi (1990).
The English Register of Godstow Nunnery, ed. A. Clark, 3 vols., Early English Text Society, cxxix, cxxx, cxl (1905–11).
Episcopal Acts and Cognate Documents Relating to Welsh Dioceses 1066–1272, ed. J. Conway Davies, 2 vols. (Cardiff, 1948–53).
Gaimar, *Lestoire des Engleis*, ed. A. Bell (Oxford, 1960).
Galbert of Bruges, *The Murder of Charles the Good*, trans. and ed. J. B. Ross, Harper Torchbook edition (New York, 1967).
Gallia Christiana in Provincias Ecclesiasticas Distributa, ed. P. Piolin, 16 vols. (Paris, 1715–1865).
Geoffrey of Barton, *Life and Miracles of St Modwenna*, ed. and trans. R. Bartlett (Oxford, 2002).
Geoffrey of Monmouth, *The Historia Regum Britannie of Geoffrey of Monmouth*, i, ed. N. Wright (Cambridge, 1985).
  The History of the Kings of Britain, trans. L. Thorpe (Harmondsworth, 1966).
Geoffrey of Vendôme, *Letters*, Migne, *Patrologia Latina*, clvii, cols. 33–212.
Gerald of Wales, *Opera*, 8 vols., i–iv, ed. J. S. Brewer, v–vii, ed. J. F. Dimock, and viii, ed. G. F. Warner, RS (London, 1861–91).
Gervase of Canterbury, *The Historical Works of Gervase of Canterbury*, ed. W. Stubbs, 2 vols., RS (London, 1879–80).
The Gesta Normannorum Ducum of William of Jumièges, Orderic Vitalis and Robert of Torigni, ed. E. M. C. Van Houts, 2 vols. (Oxford, 1992, 1995).
Gesta Stephani, ed. and trans. K. R. Potter with an introduction and notes by R. H. C. Davis (Oxford, 1976).
Grand cartulaire de Fontevraud, ed. J.-M. Bienvenu with Robert Favreau and Georges Pon, i (Poitiers, 2000).
Guibert of Nogent, 'De Pignoribus Sanctorum', Migne, *Patrologia Latina*, clvi, col. 607–680.
  Self and Society in Medieval France. The Memoirs of Abbot Guibert of Nogent (1064?–c. 1125), ed. J. F. Benton, trans. C. C. Swinton Bland (rev. J. F. Benton) (New York, 1970).
Die Gesetze der Angelsachsen, ed. F. Liebermann, 3 vols. (Halle, 1903–16).
Gesta Stephani, ed. and trans. K. R. Potter, R. H. C. Davis, with a new introduction and notes by R. H. C. Davis (Oxford, 1976).
Henry of Huntingdon, *Historia Anglorum*, ed. T. Arnold, RS (London, 1879).
  Historia Anglorum, ed. and trans. D. Greenway (Oxford, 1996).
Hermann, 'De Miraculis S. Mariae Laudunensis', Migne, *Patrologia Latina*, clvi, cols. 973–988.
Hermann of Tournai, *The Restoration of the Monastery of Saint Martin of Tournai*, translated with an introduction and notes by L. H. Nelson (Washington, 1996).
Hildebert of Lavardin, *Carmina Minora*, ed. A. B. Scott (Leipzig, 1969).
  Letters, Migne, *Patrologia Latina*, clxxi, cols. 135–42.

Historia Ecclesie Abbendonensis. The History of the Church of Abingdon, ii, ed. and trans. J. Hudson (Oxford, 2002).
Historia et Cartularium Sancti Petri Gloucestriae, ed. W. H. Hart, 3 vols., RS (London, 1863–7).
The Historians of the Church of York and its Archbishops, ed. J. Raine, 3 vols., RS (London, 1879–94).
Hugh of Flavigny, *Chronicon*, Migne, *Patrologia Latina*, cliv, cols. 21–404.
Hugh of Fleury, 'Tractatus de Regia Potestate', *Monumenta Germaniae Historica, Libelli de Lite*, ii, 465–494.
Hugh the Chanter, *The History of the Church of York 1066–1127*, ed. C. Johnson, revised edn by M. Brett, C. N. L. Brooke and M. Winterbottom (Oxford, 1990).
Ivo of Chartres, *Letters*, Migne, *Patrologia Latina*, clxii, cols. 11–288.
Jaffé, P., *Regesta Pontificum Romanorum*, 2nd edn by S. Loewenfeld, F. Kalterbrunner and P. Ewald, 2 vols. (Leipzig, 1885–8).
John of Hexham, Continuation of Symeon of Durham, *Historia Regum, Opera Omnia*, ed. T. Arnold, 2 vols., RS (London, 1882–5), ii, 284–332.
John of Marmoutier, 'Historia Gaufredi Ducis Normannorum et Comitis Andegavorum', in *Chroniques des Comtes d'Anjou et des Seigneurs d'Amboise*, ed. L. Halphen and R. Poupardin (Paris, 1913), pp. 172–238.
John of Salisbury, *The Historia Pontificalis of John of Salisbury*, ed. and trans. M. Chibnall (reprinted Oxford, 1986).
  Policraticus, i–iv, ed. K. S. B. Keats-Rohan, Corpus Christianorum Continuatio Mediaevalis, ccxviii (Turnhout, 1993). English translation (selection) in *Frivolities of Courtiers and Footprints of Philosophers*, ed. J. B. Pike (New York, 1972).
  Vita Anselmi, Migne, *Patrologia Latina*, cxcix, cols. 1009–1040.
John of Worcester, *The Chronicle of John of Worcester*, vol. ii, ed. R. R. Darlington, and P. McGurk, vol. iii, ed. P. McGurk (Oxford, 1995, 1998).
The Kalendar of Abbot Samson of Bury St Edmunds and Related Documents, ed. R. H. C. Davis, Camden Society, 3rd series, lxxxiv (1954).
Leges Henrici Primi, ed. L. J. Downer (Oxford, 1972).
Le premier cartulaire de l'abbaye Cistercienne de Pontigny (XIIe–XIIIe siècles), ed. M. Garrigues (Paris, 1981).
The Letters and Charters of Gilbert Foliot, ed. A. Morey and C. N. L. Brooke (Cambridge, 1967).
Letters of Lanfranc, ed. H. Clover and M. Gibson (Oxford, 1979).
The Letters of Peter the Venerable, ed. G. Constable, 2 vols. (Cambridge, Mass., 1967).
Liber Eliensis, ed. E. O. Blake, Camden Society, 3rd ser., xcii (1962).
Liber Monasterii de Hyda, ed. E. Edwards, RS (London, 1866).
The Life of Gundulf, Bishop of Rochester, ed. R. Thomson (Toronto, 1977).
The Life of King Edward Who Rests at Westminster, ed. F. Barlow, 2nd edn (Oxford, 1992).

'The Life of St Margaret', trans. L. L. Huneycutt, *Matilda of Scotland. A Study in Medieval Queenship* (Woodbridge, 2003), pp. 161–78.

'Life of Waltheof', in *Early Sources of Scottish History*, ed. A. O. Anderson, 2 vols., corrected edn (Stamford, 1990).

The Life of Wulfric of Haselbury by John, Abbot of Ford, ed. M. Bell, Somerset Record Society, xlvii (1933).

Llandaff Episcopal Acta 1140–1287, ed. D. Crouch, Publications of the South Wales Record Society, no. 5 (Cardiff, 1988).

Marbod of Rennes, *Letters*, Migne, *Patrologia Latina*, clxxi, cols. 1465–92.

Materials for the History of Thomas Becket, 7 vols., i–vi ed. J. C. Robertson, vii ed. J. C. Robertson and J. B. Sheppard, RS (London, 1875–85).

Matthew Paris, *Chronica Majora*, ed. H. R. Luard, 7 vols., RS (London, 1872–83).
  Historia Anglorum, sive, ut vulgo dicitur, historia minor. Item, ejusdem abbreviatio chronicorum Angliae, ed. F. Madden, 3 vols., RS (London, 1866–9).
  Flores Historiarum, ed. H. O. Coxe, 4 vols. (London, 1841–4).
  The Illustrated Chronicles of Matthew Paris. Observations of Thirteenth-Century Life, trans. and ed. with an introduction by R. Vaughn (Stroud, 1993).

A Medieval Prince of Wales. The Life of Gruffudd ap Cynan, ed. D. Simon Evans (Lampeter, 1990).

Memorials of St Edmund's Abbey, ed. T. Arnold, 3 vols., RS (London, 1890–6).

Miles Crispin, 'Vita Bosonis Abbatis Beccensis Quarti', Migne, *Patrologia Latina*, cl, cols. 723–34.

The Monastic Constitutions of Lanfranc, trans. D. Knowles, revised edn by C. N. L. Brooke (Oxford, 2002).

Munimenta Gildhallae Londoniensis, ed. H. T. Riley, 3 vols., RS (London, 1859–62).

Orderic Vitalis, *The Ecclesiastical History of Orderic Vitalis*, ed. M. Chibnall, 6 vols. (Oxford, 1969–80).

Ordonnances des Rois de France de la troisième race, ed. E.-J. Laurière, 21 vols. (Paris, 1723–1849).

Patrologia Latina, ed. J.-P. Migne, 221 vols. (Paris, 1844–64).

The Peterborough Chronicle of Hugh Candidus, ed. W. T. Mellows (Oxford, 1949).

Philippe Mouskes, *Chronique Rimée de Philippe Mouskes*, ed. Frédéric-Auguste-Ferdinand-Thomas de Reiffenberg, 2 vols. (Brussels, 1836, 1838).

Pipe Roll 31 Henry I, ed. J. Hunter for the Record Commission (London, 1833).

Placitorum in Domo Capitulari Westmonasteriensi Asservatorum Abbreviatio, ed. W. Illingworth for the Record Commission (London, 1811).

Reading Abbey Cartularies, ed. B. R. Kemp, 2 vols., Camden Society, 4th series, xxxi, xxxiii (1986, 1987).

Recueil des actes des ducs de Normandie de 911 à 1066, ed. M. Fauroux (Caen, 1961).

Recueil des Historiens des Gaules et de la France, ed. M. Bouquet and others, 24 vols. (Paris, 1869–1904).

Red Book of the Exchequer, ed. H. Hall, 3 vols., RS (London, 1896).

Regesta Regum Anglo-Normannorum. The Acta of William I (1066–1087), ed. D. Bates (Oxford, 1998).

Regesta Regum Anglo-Normannorum 1066–1154, 4 vols., i ed. H. W. C. Davis, ii ed. C. Johnson and H. A. Cronne, iii and iv ed. H. A. Cronne and R. H. C. Davis (Oxford, 1913–69).
Regesta Regum Scottorum I. Acts of Malcolm IV, ed. G. W. S. Barrow (Edinburgh, 1960).
Richard of Hexham, 'De Gestis Regis Stephani et de Bello Standardii', *Chronicles of the Reigns of Stephen, Henry II and Richard I*, ed. R. Howlett, 4 vols., RS (London, 1894–9), iii, 137–78.
Robert of Torigny, *Chronicle*, in *Chronicles of the Reigns of Stephen, Henry II and Richard I*, ed. R. Howlett, 4 vols., RS (London, 1894–9), iv, 81–315.
   Chronique suivi de divers opuscules historiques de cet auteur, ed. L. Delisle, 2 vols., Société de l'Histoire de Normandie, Rouen (1872–3).
   'De Immutatione Ordinis Monachorum', Migne, *Patrologia Latina*, ccii, cols. 1309–20.
Roger of Howden, *Chronica*, ed. W. Stubbs, 4 vols., RS (London, 1868–71).
   Gesta Henrici Secundi Benedicti Abbatis, ed. W. Stubbs, 2 vols., RS (London, 1867).
Roger of Wendover, *Chronica sive Flores Historiarum*, ed. H. O. Coxe, 4 vols., English Historical Society (London, 1841–2).
Rouleaux des Morts du IXe au XVe siècle, ed. L. Delisle, Société de l'Histoire de France (1866).
St Davids Episcopal Acta 1085–1280, ed. J. Barrow, Publications of the South Wales Record Society, no. 13 (Cardiff, 1998).
Select Charters, ed. W. Stubbs, 9th edn (Oxford, 1913).
Serlo, 'De Capta Bajocensium Civitate', in *The Anglo-Latin Satirical Poets and Epigrammatists of the Twelfth Century*, ed. T. Wright, 2 vols., RS (London, 1892), ii, 241–51.
The Song of Roland, trans. D. L. Sayers (Harmonsdworth, 1957).
Stephen of Rouen, 'Draco Normannicus', *Chronicles of the Reigns of Stephen, Henry II and Richard I*, ed. R. Howlett, 4 vols., RS (London, 1994–9), ii, 585–71.
Suger, *Œuvres complètes de Suger, recueillies, annotées et publiées d'après les manuscrits*, ed. A. Lecoy de la Marche (Paris, 1865).
   Vie de Louis le VI le Gros, ed. H. Waquet (Paris, 1929), trans. R. C. Cusimano and J. Moorhead, *The Deeds of Louis the Fat* (Washington, 1992).
Symeon of Durham, *Historia Regum, Opera Omnia*, ed. T. Arnold, 2 vols., RS (London, 1882–5).
Die Texte des normannischen Anonymus, ed. K. Pellens (Wiesbaden, 1966).
Ungedrückte Anglo-Normannische Geschichtsquellen, ed. F. Liebermann (Strassburg, 1879).
Vitae BB. Vitalis et Gaufridi, ed. E.-P. Sauvage, *Analecta Bollandiana*, i (1882), 355–90.
'Vita et Passio Comitis Waldevi', in *Chroniques anglo-normandes*, ed. F. Michel, 3 vols. (Rouen, 1836–40), ii, 99–142.
'Vita Lanfranci', Migne, *Patrologia Latina*, cl, cols. 19–58.

Vita Petri Venerabilis, Migne, *Patrologia Latina*, clxxxix, cols. 15–28.
Vita Prima (of St Bernard), Migne, *Patrologia Latina*, clxxxv, cols. 226–466.
(Anonymous) *Vita S. Hugonis, Acta Sanctorum*, III, 29 April 660–1.
Wace, *Le Roman de Rou de Wace*, ed. A. J. Holden, Société des Anciens Textes Français (Paris, 1970–3); for an English translation see Wace, *The Roman de Rou*, trans. G. S. Burgess, Société Jersiaise (2002), revised and reprinted Woodbridge, 2004.
Walter of Thérouanne, *Vita Karoli*, Migne, *Patrologia Latina*, clxvi, col. 873–1046.
Walter Map, *De Nugis Curialium. Courtiers' Trifles*, ed. and trans. M. R. James, rev. edn by C. N. L. Brooke and R. A. B. Mynors (Oxford, 1983).
Westminster Abbey Charters 1066–c. 1214, ed. E. Mason with J. Bray, London Record Society, xxv (1988).
Widukind, *Rerum Gestarum Saxonicarum Libri Tres*, ed. G. Waitz *et al.*, Monumenta Germaniae Historica, Scriptores Rerum Germanicarum in Usum Scholarum (Hanover, 1935).
William of Malmesbury, *Gesta Pontificum*, ed. N. E. S. A. Hamilton, RS (London, 1870), translated by D. Preest, *The Deeds of the Bishops of England* (Woodbridge, 2002).
  Gesta Regum Anglorum, vol. i, ed. R. A. B. Mynors, R. M. Thomson and M. Winterbottom; vol, ii, general introduction and commentary by R. M. Thomson (Oxford, 1998, 1999).
  Historia Novella, ed. E. King and trans. K. R. Potter (Oxford, 1998).
  Saints' Lives: Lives of SS. Wulfstan, Dunstan, Patrick, Benignus and Indract, ed. and trans. M. Winterbottom and R. M. Thomson (Oxford, 2002).
William of Newburgh, *Historia Rerum Anglicarum, Chronicles of the Reigns of Stephen, Henry II and Richard I*, ed. R. Howlett, 4 vols., RS (London, 1994–9), i, 1–408; ii, 1–385.
William of Poitiers, *The Gesta Guillelmi of William of Poitiers*, ed. and trans. R. H. C. Davis and M. Chibnall (Oxford, 1998).
William of Tyre, *Chronicon*, ed. R. B. C. Huygens, Corpus Christianorum, Continuatio Mediaevalis, 2 vols. (Turnhout, 1986), trans. by E. A. Babcock and A. C. Krey, *A History of Deeds Done Beyond the Sea by William Archbishop of Tyre*, 2 vols. (New York, 1943, 1976).

SECONDARY SOURCES

Adelard of Bath. An English Scientist and Arabist of the Early Twelfth Century, ed. C. Burnett, Warburg Institute Surveys and Texts, xiv (London, 1987).
Ailes, A., *The Origins of the Royal Arms of England*, Reading Medieval Studies, monograph no. 2 (1982).
  'Heraldry in Twelfth-Century England: the Evidence', *England in the Twelfth Century*, ed. D. Williams (Woodbridge, 1990), pp. 1–16.
Aird, W., *St. Cuthbert and the Normans. The Church of Durham, 1071–1153* (Woodbridge, 1998).

Airlie, S., 'Bonds of Power and Bonds of Association in the Court Circle of Louis the Pious', in *New Perspectives on the Reign of Louis the Pious*, ed. P. Godman and R. Collins (Oxford, 1999), pp. 191–204.
Alexander, J. J. G., *Norman Illumination at Mont St Michel 966–1100* (Oxford, 1970).
Alexander, J. W., 'Herbert of Norwich, 1091–1119: Studies in the History of Norman England', *Studies in Medieval and Renaissance History*, 6 (1969), 119–227.
Amt, E., 'Richard de Lucy, Henry II's Justiciar', *Medieval Prosopography*, 9 (1988), 61–87.
Anger's Past. The Social Uses of an Emotion in the Middle Ages, ed. B. H. Rosenwein (Ithaca, NY, 1998).
Angot, A., and Laurain, E., *Généalogies féodales Mayennaises* (Laval, 1942).
L'architecture normande au Moyen Age, ed. M. Baylé, 2 vols. (Caen, 1997).
Arnoux, M., 'Les origines et le développement du mouvement canonical en Normandie', in *Des clercs au service de la réforme. Etudes et documents sur les chanoins réguliers de la province de Rouen*, ed. M. Arnoux, Bibliotheca Victorina, xi (Turnhout, 2000), pp. 11–189.
Barber, M., *The New Knighthood. A History of the Order of the Temple* (Cambridge, 1994).
Baring, F. H., 'The Making of the New Forest', *EHR*, 16 (1901), 427–38.
Barker, L. K., 'Ivo of Chartres and the Anglo-Norman Cultural Tradition', *ANS*, 13 (1990), 15–33.
Barlow, F., *Edward the Confessor* (London, 1970).
  The English Church 1066–1154 (London, 1979).
  'The King's Evil', *EHR*, 95 (1980), 3–27.
  'William I's Relations with Cluny', *Journal of Ecclesiastical History*, 32 (1981), 131–41.
  William Rufus (London, 1983).
  'William II (c. 1060–1100)', *Oxford DNB*.
Barlow, F., Biddle, M., Feilitzen, O. von and Keene, D. J., *Winchester in the Early Middle Ages*. Winchester Studies I, ed. M. Biddle (Oxford, 1976).
Barroux, R., 'L'anniversaire de la mort de Dagobert à Saint-Denis au XIIe siècle: charte inédite de l'abbé Adam', *Bulletin Philologique et Historique du Comité des Travaux Historiques et Scientifiques* 1942–3 (1945), 131–51.
Barrow, G. W. S., 'The Anglo-Scottish Border', *Northern History*, 50 (1966), 21–42.
  'Scotland's "Norman" Families', in *The Kingdom of the Scots* (London, 1973), pp. 315–36.
  'The Pattern of Lordship and Feudal Settlement in Cumbria', *Journal of Medieval History*, 1 (1975), 117–38.
  The Anglo-Norman Era in Scottish History (Oxford, 1980).
  'David I (c. 1085–1153)', *Oxford DNB*.
Barthélemy, D., *L'ordre seigneurial. XIe–XIIe siècle. Nouvelle histoire de la France médiévale*, 3 (Paris, 1988).
  L'an mil et la paix de Dieu. La France chrétienne et féodale 980–1260 (Paris, 1999).
Bartlett, R., *England under the Norman and Angevin Kings* (Oxford, 2000).

'Symbolic Meanings of Hair in the Middle Ages', *Transactions of the Royal Historical Society*, 6th series, 4 (1994), 43–60.

Barton, R. E. *Lordship in the County of Maine c. 890–1160* (Woodbridge, 2004).

Bates, D., *Normandy before 1066* (Harlow, 1982).

'The Earliest Norman Writs', *EHR*, 100 (1985), 266–84.

'A Neglected English Charter of Robert Curthose, Duke of Normandy', *Historical Research*, 59 (1986), 121–4.

'The Prosopographical Study of Anglo-Norman Royal Charters', in *Family Trees and the Roots of Politics. The Prosopography of Britain and France from the Tenth to the Twelfth Century*, ed. K. S. B. Keats-Rohan (Woodbridge, 1997), pp. 89–102.

Re-ordering the Past and Negotiating the Present in Stenton's First Century, Stenton Lecture 1999 (Reading, 2000).

Bauduin, P., 'Une famille châtelaine sur les confins normanno-manceaux: les Géré (xe–xiiie siècles)', *Archéologie Médiévale*, 22 (1992), 309–56.

'Le baron, le château et la motte: baronnage et maîtrise du territoire châtelain dans la seigneurie de Breteuil (xie–xiie siècles)', 'Autour du château médiéval' (Rencontres historiques et archéologiques de l'Orne), *Société Historique et Archéologique de l'Orne. Mémoires et documents*, 1 (1998), 37–53.

La première Normandie (Xe–XIe siècles). Sur les frontières de la Haute Normandie: identité et construction d'une principauté (Caen, 2004).

Bautier, R. H., 'Paris au temps d'Abélard', in *Abélard en son temps*, ed. J. Jolivet (Paris, 1981), pp. 21–77.

Baxter, R., *Bestiaries and Their Users in the Middle Ages* (Stroud, 1998).

Beaune, C., 'Les ducs, le roi et le Saint-Sang', in *Saint-Denis et la royauté. Etudes offertes à Bernard Guenée* (Paris, 1999), pp. 711–32.

Berg. D., *England und der Kontinent. Studien zur auswärtigen Politik der anglonormannischen Könige im 11. und 12. Jahrhundert* (Bochum, 1987).

Berlière, D. Ursmer, 'Le Cardinal Matthieu d'Albano (c. 1085–1135)', *Revue Bénédictine*, 18 (1901), 113–40, 280–303.

Bertelli, S., *The King's Body*, translated R. Burr Litchfield (Philadelphia, 2001).

Bethell, D., 'William of Corbeil and the Canterbury-York Dispute', *Journal of Ecclesiastical History*, 19 (1968), 145–69.

'English Black Monks and Episcopal Elections in the 1120s', *EHR*, 84 (1969), 673–98.

'The Making of a Twelfth-Century Relic Collection', *Popular Belief and Practice, Studies in Church History*, 8 (1971), 61–72.

Biddle, M., 'Seasonal Festivals and Residence: Winchester, Westminster and Gloucester in the Tenth to Twelfth Centuries', *ANS*, 8 (1985), 51–72.

Bienvenu, J.-M., *L'étonnant fondateur de Fontevraud Robert d'Arbrissel* (Paris, 1981).

Binski, P., *Medieval Death, Ritual and Representation* (Avon, 1996).

Bishop, T. A. M., *Scriptores Regis* (Oxford, 1961).

Bisson, T. N., *Conservation of Coinage. Monetary Exploitation and Its Restraint in France, Catalonia, and Aragon c. 1000–1225 A.D.* (Oxford, 1979).

'The "Feudal Revolution"', *Past and Present*, 142 (1994), 6–42.

Blackburn, M., 'Coinage and Currency under Henry I: A Review', *ANS*, 13 (1990), 49–81.
Blacker, J., *The Faces of Time. Portrayal of the Past in Old French and Latin Historical Narrative of the Anglo-Norman Regnum* (Austin, Texas, 1994).
Blair, W. J., 'St Frideswide's Monastery: Problems and Possibilities', *Oxoniensia*, 53 (1988), 221–258.
   'Hall and Chamber: English Domestic Planning 1000–1250', *Manorial Domestic Building in England and Northern France*, Society of Antiquaries, Occasional Paper no. 15 (London, 1994), 1–21.
Blakeley, R., 'The Bruses of Skelton and William of Aumale', *Yorkshire Archaeological Journal*, 73 (2001), 19–28.
Blanchard, I., '"Lothian and Beyond": the Economy of the "English Empire" of David I', in *Progress and Problems in Medieval England: Essays in Honour of Edward Miller*, ed. J. Hatcher and R. Britnell (Cambridge, 1996), pp. 23–45.
Bloch, M., *Les rois thaumaturges* (Paris, 1961 edn), trans. J. E. Anderson, *The Royal Touch* (London and Montreal, 1973).
Böhmer, H., *Kirche und Staat in England und in der Normandie im XI. und XII. Jahrhundert* (Leipzig, 1899).
Boureau, A., *La Loi du royaume. Les moines, le droit et la construction de la nation Anglaise (XIe–XIIIe siècles)* (Paris, 2001).
Bournazel, E., *Le gouvernement capétien au XIIe siècle 1108–1180* (Paris, 1975).
Boussard, J., 'Thomas de Saint-Jean-le-Thomas et l'abbaye du Mont-Saint-Michel (début du XIIe siècle)', in *Droit privé et institutions régionales. Etudes historiques offertes à Jean Yver* (Paris, 1976), pp. 87–96.
Bouvet, J., 'Le récit de la fondation de Mortemer', *Collectanea Ordinis Cisterciensium Reformatorum*, 22 (1960), 149–68.
Bradbury, J., 'Battles in England and Normandy, 1066–1154', *ANS*, 6 (1983), 1–12.
Brand, P., '"Multis Vigiliis Excogitatam et Inventam": Henry II and the Creation of the English Common Law', *Haskins Society Journal*, 2 (1990), 197–222.
Brett, M., *The English Church under Henry I* (Oxford, 1975).
Brett-Jones, T., 'The White Ship Disaster', *The Historian*, 64 (1999), 23–6.
Brooke, C. N. L., 'The Canterbury Forgeries', *Downside Review*, 69 (1951), 210–31.
   The Saxon and Norman Kings (London, 1967).
   'Princes and Kings as Patrons of Monasteries', in *Il monachesimo e la riforma ecclesiastica (1049–1122). Settimana internazionale di studio. Quarta Passa della Mendola, 1968. Miscellanea del Centro di studi medioevali*, 6 (Milan, 1971), 125–44.
Brooke, C. N. L., with Keir, G., *London 800–1216: The Shaping of a City* (London, 1975).
Brooke, C. N. L., Keir, G. and Reynolds, S., 'Henry I's Charter for the City of London', *Journal of the Society of Archivists*, 4 (1972), 558–78.
Brooke, D., 'Fergus of Galloway: Miscellaneous Notes for a Revised Portrait', *Transactions of the Dumfriesshire and Galloway Natural History and Antiquarian Society*, 3rd series, 65 (1990), 47–58.
Brown, R. A., *Castles from the Air* (Cambridge, 1989).

Brown R. A., Colvin, H. M. and Taylor, A. J., *The History of the King's Works, The Middle Ages*, 2 vols. (London, 1963).

Brown, S. D. B., 'Leavetaking: Lordship and Mobility in England and Normandy in the Twelfth Century', *History*, 79 (1994), 199–215.

Brown, T. Tatton, 'La pierre de Caen en Angleterre', in *L'Architecture normande au moyen age*, ed. M. Baylé, 2 vols. (Caen, 1997), i, pp. 305–314.

Brückmann, J., 'The *Ordines* of the Third Recension of the Medieval English Coronation Order', in *Essays in Medieval History Presented to Bertie Wilkinson*, ed. T. A. Sandquist and M. R. Powicke (Toronto, 1969), pp. 99–115.

Buc, P., 'David's Adultery with Bathsheba and the Healing Power of the Capetian Kings', *Viator*, 24 (1993), 101–20.

The Dangers of Ritual: Between Early Medieval Texts and Social Scientific Theory (Princeton, 2001).

Bur, M., 'De quelques Champenois dans l'entourage français des rois d'Angleterre aux xie et xiie siècles', in *Family Trees and the Roots of Politics. The Prosopography of Britain and France from the Tenth to the Twelfth Century*, ed. K. S. B. Keats-Rohan (Woodbridge, 1997), pp. 333–59.

Campbell, J., 'Observations on English Government from the Tenth to the Twelfth Century', *Transactions of the Royal Historical Society*, 5th ser. 25 (1975), 39–54 (reprinted in *Essays in Anglo-Saxon History*, pp. 155–70).

'The Anglo-Saxon State in the Administrative History of Western Europe,' in *Histoire Comparée de l'Administration (IVe–XVIIIe siècles). Actes du XIV Colloque Historique Franco-Allemand, Tours 1977*, Beihefte der *Francia* (Munich, 1980), pp. 117–34, reprinted in *Essays in Anglo-Saxon History*, pp. 171–89.

Essays in Anglo-Saxon History (London, 1986).

'The Late Anglo-Saxon State: a Maximum View', *Proceedings of the British Academy*, 87 (1994), 39–65.

Candon, A., 'Muirchertach ua Briain, Politics and Naval Activity in the Irish Sea, 1075–1119', in *Keimelia: Studies in Medieval Archaeology and History in Memory of Tom Delaney*, ed. G. Mac Niocaill and P. F. Wallace (Galway, 1988), pp. 397–415.

Cantor, N. F., *Church, Kingship and Lay Investiture in England 1089–1135* (Princeton, N.J., 1958).

La Cathédrale de Rouen. Seize siècles d'histoire, ed. J.-P. Chaline, Société de l'Histoire de Normandie, 70 (1996).

Chandler, V., 'The Last of the Montgomerys: Roger the Poitevin and Arnulf', *Historical Research*, 62 (1989), 1–14.

'The Wreck of the *White Ship*: A Mass Murder Revealed?', in *The Final Argument: The Imprint of Violence on Society in Medieval and Early Modern Europe*, ed. D. J. Kagay and L. J. Andrew Villalon (Woodbridge, 1998), pp. 179–84.

Chaplais, P., 'The Seals and Original Charters of Henry I', *EHR*, 75 (1960), 260–75.

Chartrou, J., *L'Anjou de 1109 à 1151* (Paris, 1928).

Chibnall, M., 'Mercenaries and the *Familia Regis* under Henry I', *History*, 62 (1977), 15–23.

The Empress Matilda. Queen Consort, Queen Mother, and Lady of the English (Oxford, 1991).
'From Bec to Canterbury: Anselm and Monastic Privilege', *Anselm Studies. An Occasional Journal*, 1 (1983), 23–44.
Christelow, S. Mooers, '"Backers and Stabbers": Problems of Loyalty in Robert Curthose's Entourage', *Journal of British Studies*, 21 (1981), 1–17.
'Familial Clout and Financial Gain in Henry I's Later Reign', *Albion*, 14 (1982), 267–92.
'Patronage in the Pipe Roll of 1130', *Speculum*, 59 (1984), 284–307.
'A Moveable Feast? Itineration and the Centralization of Government under Henry I', *Albion*, 28 (1996), 187–228.
Church, S. D., *The Household Knights of King John* (Cambridge, 1999).
Clanchy, M. T., *From Memory to Written Record* (London, 1979).
Abelard (Oxford, 1997).
Clark, C., 'This Ecclesiastical Adventurer": Henry of Saint-Jean d'Angély', *EHR*, 84 (1969), 548–60.
Cochrane, L., *Adelard of Bath. The First English Scientist* (London, 1994).
Colker, M. L., 'The Life of Guy of Merton by Rainald of Merton', *Medieval Studies*, 31 (1969), 250–61.
'Latin Texts Concerning Gilbert, Founder of Merton Priory', *Studia Monastica*, 12 (1970), 241–71.
Colvin, H. M., *The White Canons in England* (Oxford, 1951).
Constable, G., *Letters and Letter Collections*, Typologie des Sources du Moyen Age Occidental, fasc. 17 (Turnhout, 1976).
Cooper, A., '"The Feet of Those that Bark Shall Be Cut Off": Timorous Historians and the Personality of Henry I', *ANS*, 23 (2000), 47–67.
'The Rise and Fall of the Anglo-Saxon Law of the Highway', *Haskins Society Journal*, 12 (2002), 39–69.
Coulson, C., *Castles in Medieval Society. Fortresses in England, Ireland and France in the Central Middle Ages* (Oxford, 2003).
Court Culture in the Early Middle Ages. The Proceedings of the First Alcuin Conference. Studies in the Early Middle Ages, ed. C. Cubitt, iii (Turnhout, 2003).
Cowdrey, H. E. J., 'Pope Gregory VII and the Anglo-Norman Church and Kingdom', *Studia Gratiana*, 9 (1972), 79–114, reprinted in *Popes, Monks and Crusaders* (London, 1984).
'The Anglo-Norman Laudes Regiae', *Viator*, 12 (1981), 37–78.
Pope Gregory VII 1073–1085 (Oxford, 1998).
Crosby, E. U., 'The Organization of the English Episcopate under Henry I', *Studies in Medieval and Renaissance History*, 4, ed. W. M. Bowsky (University of California, Davis, 1967), 3–88.
Crouch, D., 'Geoffrey de Clinton and Roger Earl of Warwick: New Men and Magnates in the Reign of Henry I', *[Bulletin of the Institute of] Historical Research*, 55 (1982), 113–24.
The Image of Aristocracy in Britain 1000–1300 (London, 1992).

'Normans and Anglo-Normans: A Divided Aristocracy', in *England and Normandy in the Middle Ages*, ed. D. Bates and A. Curry in (London, 1984), pp. 51–67.

The Beaumont Twins, Cambridge Studies in Medieval Life and Thought, 4th ser. i (Cambridge, 1986).

'The Culture of Death in the Anglo-Norman World', in *Anglo-Norman Political Culture and the Twelfth-Century Renaissance*, ed. C. Warren Hollister (Woodbridge, 1997), pp. 157–80.

'Robert of Gloucester's Mother and Sexual Politics in Norman Oxfordshire', *Historical Research*, 72 (1999), 323–33.

The Reign of Stephen 1135–54 (Harlow, 2000).

The Normans. The History of a Dynasty (London, 2002).

'The Troubled Deathbeds of Henry I's Servants: Death, Confession, and Secular Conduct in the Twelfth Century', *Albion*, 34 (2002), 24–36.

The Culture of Christendom: Essays in Medieval History in Memory of Denis L. T. Bethell, ed. M. A. Meyer (London, 1993).

Cultures of Power. Lordship, Status and Process in Twelfth-Century Europe, ed. T. N. Bisson (Philadelphia, 1995).

Cummin, J., *The Hound and the Hawk. The Art of Medieval Hunting* (London, 2001 edn).

Cunliffe, B., and Munby, J., *Excavations at Portchester Castle*, IV, *Medieval. The Inner Bailey*, Reports of the Research Committee of the Society of Antiquaries of London (London, 1985).

Dalton, P., 'Aiming at the Impossible: Ranulf II Earl of Chester and Lincolnshire in the Reign of King Stephen', in *The Earldom of Chester and its Charters*, Chester Archaeological Society, lxxi (1991), 109–34.

Conquest, Anarchy and Lordship. Yorkshire 1066–1154, Cambridge Studies in Medieval Life and Thought, 4th ser. 27 (Cambridge, 1994).

'Eustace FitzJohn and the Politics of Anglo-Norman England: the Rise and Survival of a Twelfth-Century Royal Servant', *Speculum*, 71 (1996), 358–83.

Damian-Grint, P., *The New Historians of the Twelfth Century* (Woodbridge, 1999).

David, C. W., *Robert Curthose Duke of Normandy* (Cambridge, Mass., 1920).

'The Claim of King Henry I to Be Called Learned', in *Anniversary Essays in Medieval History by Students of Charles Homer Haskins*, ed. C. H. Taylor and J. L. LaMonte (Boston and New York, 1929), pp. 45–56.

Davies, H. W. C, 'A Contemporary Account of the Battle of Tinchebrai', *EHR*, 24 (1909), 728–32.

'The Battle of Tinchebrai: A Correction', *EHR*, 25 (1910), 295–6.

'Henry of Blois and Brian FitzCount', *EHR*, 24 (1910), 297–303.

Davies, R. R., 'Henry I and Wales', in *Studies in Medieval History Presented to R. H. C. Davis*, ed. H. Mayr-Harting and R. I. Moore (London, 1985), pp. 132–47.

The Age of Conquest. Wales 1063–1415, paperback edn (Oxford, 1987).

The First English Empire. Power and Identities in the British Isles 1093–1343 (Oxford, 2000).

Davies, W. S., 'Materials for the life of Bishop Bernard of St David's', *Archaeologia Cambrensis*, 6th ser., 19 (1919), 299–322.
Davis, R. H. C., *King Stephen*, 3rd edn (London, 1990).
'The Ford, the River and the City', in Davis, *From Alfred the Great to King Stephen* (London, 1991), pp. 281–91.
De Boüard, M., 'Sur les origines de la trêve de Dieu en Normandie,' *Annales de Normandie*, 9 (1959), 169–89.
Le château de Caen (Caen, 1979).
Delisle, L., *Etude sur la condition de la classe agricole en Normandie au moyen âge* (Evreux, 1851).
Histoire du château et des sires de Saint-Sauveur-le-Vicomte (Paris, Caen, 1867).
'Des revenus publics en Normandie au xiie siècle', *Bibliothèque de l'Ecole des Chartes*, 10 (1848–9), 173–210, 257–89; 11 (1849), 400–51; 13 (1852), 97–135.
De Monstier, A., *Neustria Pia: seu de omnibus et singulis Abbatiis et prioratibus totius Normannie* (Rouen, 1663).
Des Clercs au service de la réforme. Etudes et documents sur les chanoins réguliers de la province de Rouen, sous la direction de M. Arnoux, Bibliotheca Victorina, xi (Turnhout, 2000).
Dickinson, J. C., 'The Origins of Carlisle Cathedral', *Transactions of the Cumberland and Westmorland Antiquarian and Archaeological Society*, 45 (1946), 134–43.
The Origins of the Austin Canons and their Introduction into England (London, 1950).
'Walter the Priest and St Mary's, Carlisle', *Transactions of the Cumberland and Westmorland Antiquarian and Archaeological Society*, new series, 69 (1969), 102–14.
Dixon, P. and Marshall, P., 'The Great Tower in the Twelfth Century: The Case of Norham Castle', *Archaeological Journal*, 140 (1993), 410–32.
Donnelly, J., 'The Earliest Scottish Charters?', *Scottish Historical Review*, 68 (1989), 1–22.
Douglas, D.C., *William the Conqueror. The Norman Impact upon England* (London, 1964).
Downham, C., 'England and the Irish-Sea Zone in the Eleventh Century', *ANS*, 26 (2003), 55–73.
Dumas, F., 'Les monnaies normandes des xe–xiie siècles avec un répertoire', *Revue Numismatique*, 21 (1979), 84–140.
Duncan, A. A. M., 'The Earliest Scottish Charters', *Scottish Historical Review*, 37 (1958), 103–35.
'Yes, the Earliest Scottish Charters', *Scottish Historical Review*, 78 (1999), 1–38.
The Kingship of the Scots 842–1292. Succession and Independence (Edinburgh, 2002).
'Alexander I (d. 1124)', *Oxford DNB*.
Elias, N., *The Court Society*, trans. E. Jephcott (Oxford, 1983).
English, B., 'William the Conqueror and the Anglo-Norman Succession', *Historical Research*, 64 (1991), 221–36.

English Romanesque Art 1066–1200: Hayward Gallery, London, 5 April–8 July 1984, ed. G. Zarnecki, J. Holt and T. Holland, Arts Council (London, 1984).

Erlande-Brandenburg, A., *Le Roi est Mort. Etude sur les funérailles, les sépultures et les tombeaux des rois de France jusqu'à la fin du XIIIe siècle*, Bibliothèque de la Société Française d'Archéologie, 7 (Geneva and Paris, 1975).

Espinas, G., 'Le Privilège de Saint-Omer de 1127', *Revue du Nord*, 29 (1947), 43–9.

Evans, G. R., 'Schools and Scholars: the Study of the Abacus in English Schools c. 980–c. 1150', *EHR*, 94 (1979), 71–81.

Farrer, W., 'An Outline Itinerary of Henry I', *EHR*, 34 (1919), 303–82, 505–79, later reprinted as a pamphlet.

Honors and Knights' Fees, 3 vols. (London and Manchester, 1923–5).

Fernie, E., 'Architecture and the Effects of the Norman Conquest', in *England and Normandy in the Middle Ages*, ed. D. Bates and A. Curry (London, 1994), pp. 105–16.

The Architecture of Norman England (Oxford, 2000).

Feuchère, P., 'Une tentative manquée de concentration territoriale entre Somme et Seine: la principauté d'Amiens-Valois au xie siècle', *Le Moyen Age*, 60 (1954), 1–37.

Flanagan, M. T., *Irish Society, Anglo-Norman Settlers, Angevin Kingship: Interactions in Ireland in the Late Twelfth Century* (Oxford, 1989).

'*Historia Gruffud vab Kenan* and the Origins of Balrothery, Co. Dublin', *Cambrian Medieval Celtic Studies*, 28 (1994), 71–94.

Foreville, R., 'Le sacre des rois anglo-normands et angevins et le serment du sacre (xie–xiie siècles)', *ANS*, 1 (1978), 49–62.

La France de l'an mil, ed. R. Delort (Paris, 1990).

Freeman, E. A., *The History of the Norman Conquest of England* (5 vols. and index) (Oxford, 1867–79).

The Reign of William Rufus, 2 vols. (Oxford, 1882).

Galbraith, V. H., 'Girard the Chancellor', *EHR*, 46 (1931), 77–9.

Studies in the Public Records (Edinburgh and London, 1948).

Gameson, R., *The Manuscripts of Early Norman England* (Oxford, 1999).

Garnett, G., '*Franci et Angli*: the Legal Distinction between Peoples after the Conquest', *ANS*, 8 (1985), 109–37.

'Ducal Succession in Early Normandy', in *Law and Government in Medieval England*, ed. G. Garnett and J. Hudson (Cambridge, 1994), pp. 80–110.

'The Third Recension of the English Coronation *Ordo*: the Manuscripts', *Haskins Society Journal*, 11 (1998), 43–71.

Gauthiez, B., 'Paris, un Rouen capétien? (Développements comparés de Rouen et Paris sous les règnes de Henri II et Philippe Auguste)', *ANS*, 16 (1993), 117–36.

Gazeau, V., 'Les abbés bénédictins de la Normandie ducale', *ANS*, 26 (2003), 75–86.

Gem, R., 'Lincoln Minster: Ecclesia Pulchra, Ecclesia Fortis', in *Medieval Art and Architecture at Lincoln Cathedral*, British Archaeological Association (1986), pp. 9–28.

Gibson, M., *Lanfranc of Bec* (Oxford, 1978).
Gillingham, J., 'Kingship, Chivalry and Love. Political and Cultural Values in the Earliest History Written in French: Geoffrey Gaimar's *Estoire des Engleis*', in *Anglo-Norman Political Culture and the Twelfth-Century Renaissance*, ed. C. Warren Hollister (Woodbridge, 1984), pp. 47–61.
Gleason, S. E., *An Ecclesiastical Barony of the Middle Ages. The Bishopric of Bayeux, 1066–1204* (Cambridge, Mass., 1936).
Golb, N., *The Jews in Medieval Normandy* (Cambridge, 1998).
Golding, B., 'The Coming of the Cluniacs', *ANS*, 3 (1980), 65–77, 208–12.
'"Tribulationes Ecclesiae Christi": The Disruption Caused at Canterbury by Royal Confiscations in the Time of St. Anselm', *Spicilegium Beccense*, 2 (1984), 125–45.
Government, Religion and Society in Northern England 1000–1700, ed. J. C. Appleby and P. Dalton (Stroud, 1997).
Graham, T. H. B., 'Turgis Brundos', *Cumberland and Westmorland Antiquarian and Archaeological Society*, new series, 29 (1929), 49–56.
Gransden, A., *Historical Writing in England c. 550–c. 1307* (London, 1974).
Grant, L., 'Architectural Relations between England and Normandy, 1100–1204', in *England and Normandy in the Middle Ages*, ed. D. Bates and A. Curry (London, 1994), pp. 117–29.
Abbot Suger of Saint-Denis. Church and State in Early Twelfth Century France (Harlow, 1998).
Green, J. A., 'Lords of the Norman Vexin', in *War and Government in the Middle Ages. Studies in Honour of J. O. Prestwich*, ed. J. Gillingham and J. C. Holt (Woodbridge, 1984), pp. 47–61.
The Government of England under Henry I, Cambridge Studies in Medieval Life and Thought, 4th series, ii (Cambridge, 1986).
'Henry I and the Aristocracy of Normandy', in *La France anglaise au Moyen Age, Actes du IIIe Congrès des Sociétés Savantes* (Paris, 1988), pp. 161–73.
'Anglo-Scottish Relations, 1066–1174', in *England and Her Neighbours 1066–1453*, ed. M. Jones and M. Vale (London, 1989), pp. 53–73.
'Unity and Disunity in the Anglo-Norman State', *Historical Research*, 62 (1989), 114–34.
'Aristocratic Loyalties on the Northern Frontier of England, c. 1100–1174', in *England in the Twelfth Century* (Woodbridge, 1990), pp. 83–100.
Medieval English Sheriffs to 1154 (London, 1990).
'Financing Stephen's War', *ANS*, 14 (1994), 91–114.
'David I and Henry I', *Scottish Historical Review*, 75 (1996), 1–19.
The Aristocracy of Norman England (Cambridge, 1997).
'Robert Curthose Reassessed', *ANS*, 22 (1999), 95–116.
'The Piety and Patronage of Henry I', *Haskins Society Journal*, 10 (2001), 1–16.
'Le gouvernement d'Henri Ier Beauclerc en Normandie', in *La Normandie et l'Angleterre au moyen âge*, ed. P. Bouet et V. Gazeau, Colloque de Cerisy-la-Salle (Caen, 2003), pp. 61–73.

'"A Lasting Memorial": The Charter of Liberties of Henry I', in *Charters and Charter Scholarship in Britain and Ireland*, ed. M. T. Flanagan and J. A. Green (Houndmills, 2005), pp. 53–69.

'Networks and Solidarities at the Court of Henry I Beauclerc', in *Liens personnels, réseaux, solidarités en France et dans les îles Britanniques (XIe–XXe siècle), Actes de la Table Ronde organisée par le GDR 2136 et l'Université de Glasgow (10–11 mai, 2002)*, forthcoming, Publications de la Sorbonne, 2005.

'Henry I and the origins of the Court Culture of the Plantagenets', forthcoming in the proceedings of the 2004 Conference 'Plantagenêts et Capétiens, confrontations et héritage', Poitiers and Fontevraud, 2004.

Gruffudd ap Cynan: A Collective Biography, ed. K. L. Maund (Woodbridge, 1996).

Haahr, J. G., 'The Concept of Kingship in William of Malmesbury's *Gesta Regum* and *Historia Novella*', *Medieval Studies*, 38 (1976), 351–71.

Hallam, E. M., 'Royal Burial and the Cult of Kingship in France and England, 1060–1330', *Journal of Medieval History*, 8 (1982), 359–80.

Hart, C., 'William Malet and His Family', *ANS*, 19 (1996), 123–65.

Haskins, C. H., *Norman Institutions* (Cambridge, Mass., 1918).

Studies in the History of Medieval Science (Cambridge, Mass., and London, 1927).

Hébert, P., 'Un archévêque de Rouen au XIIe siècle. Hugues III d'Amiens', *Questions Historiques*, 64 (1898), 325–71.

Henderson, G., '*Sortes Biblicae* in Twelfth-Century England: the List of Episcopal Prognostics in Cambridge, Trinity College MS R.7.5', in *England in the Twelfth Century*, ed. D. Williams (Woodbridge, 1990), pp. 113–35.

Henry, F. and Zarnecki, G., 'Romanesque Arches Decorated with Human and Animal Heads', *Journal of the British Architectural Association*, 3rd series, 20–1 (1958), 1–3.

Herlihy, D., *The History of Feudalism* (New York, 1970).

Heslop, T. A., *Norwich Castle Keep: Romanesque Architecture and Social Context*, The Centre of East Anglian Studies, University of East Anglia (Norwich, 1994).

Hicks, S. B., 'The Anglo-Papal Bargain of 1125: the Legatine Mission of John of Crema', *Albion*, 8 (1976), 301–10.

'The Impact of William Clito upon the Continental Policies of Henry I of England', *Viator*, 10 (1979), 1–21.

Hillaby, J., 'Jewish Colonisation in the Twelfth Century', in *The Jews in Medieval Britain. Historical, Literary and Archaeological Perspectives*, ed. P. Skinner (Woodbridge, 2003), pp. 15–40.

Hollister, C. Warren, *The Military Organization of Norman England* (Oxford, 1965).

'The Anglo-Norman Civil War: 1101', *EHR*, 88 (1973), 315–34, reprinted *MMI*, pp. 77–96.

'Magnates and "Curiales" in Early Norman England', *Viator*, 4 (1973), 115–22, reprinted *MMI*, pp. 97–115.

'The Misfortunes of the Mandevilles', *History*, 58 (1973), 315–33, reprinted *MMI*, pp. 117–27.

'The Strange Death of William Rufus', *History*, 9 (1973), 22–9, reprinted *MMI*, pp. 59–75.

'The Anglo-Norman Succession Debate of 1126', *Journal of Medieval History*, 1 (1975), 19–39, reprinted *MMI*, pp. 145–69.

'Normandy, France and the Anglo-Norman Regnum', *Speculum*, 51 (1976), 202–42, reprinted *MMI*, pp. 17–57.

'The Taming of a Turbulent Earl: Henry I and William de Warenne', *Réflexions Historiques*, 3 (1976), 83–91, reprinted in *MMI*, pp. 137–44.

'Henry I and Robert Malet', *Viator*, 8 (1977), 63–81, reprinted in *MMI*, pp. 129–36.

'The Origins of the English Treasury', *EHR*, 93 (1978), 262–75, reprinted *MMI*, pp. 209–22.

'Royal Acts of Mutilation: The Case against Henry I', *Albion*, 10 (1978), 330–40, reprinted *MMI*, pp. 291–301.

'London's First Charter of Liberties: Is It Genuine?', *Journal of Medieval History*, 6 (1980), 289–306, reprinted *MMI*, pp. 191–208.

'War and Diplomacy in the Anglo-Norman World: the Reign of Henry I', *ANS*, 6 (1984), 72–88, reprinted *MMI*, pp. 273–289.

'Henry I and the Invisible Transformation of Medieval England', *Studies in Medieval History Presented to R. H. C. Davis*, ed. H. Mayr-Harting and R. I. Moore (London, 1985), pp. 303–16.

Monarchy, Magnates and Institutions in the Anglo-Norman World (*MMI*) (London, 1986).

'William II, Henry I and the Church: Difference in Style or Change in Substance?', *Peritia*, 6–7 (1987–8), 119–40.

'The Vice-Regal Court of Henry I', in *Law, Custom, and the Social Fabric. Essays in Honour of Bryce Lyon*, ed. B. S. Bachrach and D. Nicholas (Kalamazoo, 1990), pp. 131–44.

'The Rouen Riot and Conan's Leap', *Peritia*, 10 (1996), 341–50.

'Anglo-Norman Political Culture and the Twelfth-Century Renaissance', in *Anglo-Norman Political Culture and the Twelfth-Century Renaissance. Proceedings of the Borchard Conference on Anglo-Norman History, 1995*, ed. C. Warren Hollister (Woodbridge, 1997), pp. 1–16.

Henry I, edited and completed by A. Clark Frost (New Haven and London, 2001).

'Henry I (1068/9–1135)', *Oxford DNB*.

Hollister, C. Warren and Baldwin, J. W., 'The Rise of Administrative Kingship: Henry I and Philip Augustus', *American Historical Review*, 83 (1978), 867–905, reprinted in *MMI*, pp. 223–45.

Hollister, C. Warren and Keefe, T. K., 'The Making of the Angevin Empire', *Journal of British Studies*, 12 (1973), 1–25, reprinted in *MMI*, pp. 247–71.

Holt, J. C., 'Feudal Society and the Family in Early Medieval England: II. Notions of Patrimony', *Transactions of the Royal Historical Society*, 5th series, 33 (1982), 193–220.

Colonial England, 1066–1215 (London, 1997).

Hooper, N., 'Edgar the Aetheling: Anglo-Saxon Prince, Rebel and Crusader', *Anglo-Saxon England*, 14 (1985), 197–214.

Howell, M., *Regalian Right in Medieval England* (London, 1962).

Hudson, B. T., 'William the Conqueror and Ireland', *Irish Historical Studies*, 29 (1994–5), 145–58.

Hudson, J., *Land, Law and Lordship in Anglo-Norman England* (Oxford, 1994).

The Formation of the English Common Law. Law and Society in England from the Norman Conquest to Magna Carta (London, 1996).

'Henry I and Counsel', in *The Medieval State. Essays Presented to James Campbell*, ed. J. R. Maddicott and D. M. Palliser (London, 2000), pp. 109–26.

Huneycutt, L. L., *Matilda of Scotland. A Study in Medieval Queenship* (Woodbridge, 2003).

'Adeliza (*c.* 1103–51)', *Oxford DNB*.

'Matilda (1080–1118)', *Oxford DNB*.

Hurry, J. B., *Reading Abbey* (London, 1901).

King Henry Beauclerc and Reading Abbey (London, 1917).

Impey, E., 'La demeure seigneuriale en Normandie entre 1125 et 1225 et la tradition anglo-normande', *L'architecture normande au moyen age*, ed. M. Baylé, 2 vols. (Caen, 1997), i, 217–41.

Jaeger, S. C., *The Origins of Courtliness: Civilising Trends and the Formation of Courtly Ideals, 939–1210* (Philadelphia, 1985).

Janssen, W., *Die Päpstlichen Legaten in Frankreich vom Schisma Anaklets II bis zum Tode Coelestins III (1130–1198)*, Kölner Historische Abhandlungen Band, 5/2 (1961).

Jared, L. H., 'English Ecclesiastical Vacancies during the Reigns of William II and Henry I', *Journal of Ecclesiastical History*, 42 (1991), 362–93.

Jean-Marie, L., *Caen aux XIe et XIIe siècles. Espace urbain, pouvoirs et société* (Condé-sur-Noireau, 2000).

Jessee, W. Scott, 'Urban Violence and the *Coup d'Etat* of Fulk le Réchin in Angers, 1067', *Haskins Society Journal*, 7 (1995), 75–82.

Jeulin, P., 'L'Hommage de Bretagne en droit et dans les faits', *Annales de Bretagne*, 41 (1934), 380–473.

Jewell, H. M., *The North–South Divide. The Origins of Northern Consciousness in England* (Manchester, 1984).

Kantorowicz, E. H., *The King's Two Bodies: A Study in Medieval Political Theology* (Princeton, 1957).

Kapelle, W. E., *The Norman Conquest of the North* (London, 1979).

Kealey, E. J., *Roger of Salisbury. Viceroy of England* (Berkeley, Los Angeles and London, 1972).

Keats-Rohan, K. S. B., 'The Devolution of the Honour of Wallingford, 1066–1148', *Oxoniensia*, 54 (1989), 311–18.

'The Bretons and Normans of England 1066–1154: the Family, the Fief and the Feudal Monarchy', *Nottingham Medieval Studies*, 36 (1992), 42–78.

'Two Studies in North French Prosopography', *Journal of Medieval History*, 20 (1994), 25–57.

'Le rôle des Bretons dans la politique de colonisation normande de l'Angleterre (vers 1042–1135)', *Mémoires de la Société d'Histoire et d'Archéologie de Bretagne*, 74 (1996), 183–216.

'Domesday Book and the Malets: Patrimony and the Private Histories of Public Lives', *Nottingham Medieval Studies*, 41 (1997), 13–56.

Domesday People. A Prosopography of Persons Occurring in English Documents, 1066–1166, I (Woodbridge, 1999).

Domesday Descendants. A Prosopography of Persons Occurring in English Documents 1066–1166, II (Woodbridge, 2002).

Kellaway, W., 'The Coroner in Medieval London', in *Studies in London History Presented to Philip Edmund Jones*, ed. A. E. J. Hollaender and W. Kellaway (London, 1969), pp. 75–91.

Kemp, B. R., 'The Miracles of the Hand of St James', *Berkshire Archaeological Journal*, 65 (1970), 1–19.

Kern, F., *Kingship and Law in the Middle Ages* (Oxford, 1939).

King, E., 'Economic Development in the Early Twelfth Century', in *Progress and Problems in Medieval England. Essays in Honour of Edward Miller*, ed. R. Britnell and J. Hatcher (Cambridge, 1966), pp. 1–22.

'The Memory of Brian fitz Count', *Haskins Society Journal*, 13 (1999), 75–98.

'Stephen of Blois, Count of Mortain and Boulogne', *EHR*, 115 (2000), 271–96.

Knowles, D., 'Essays in Monastic History IV. The Growth of Exemption', *Downside Review*, 31 (1932), 201–231, 396–436.

The Monastic Order in England, 2nd edn (London, 1966).

Knowles, D., Brooke, C. N. L. and London, V. (eds.), *The Heads of Religious Houses in England and Wales 940–1216*, 2nd edn (Cambridge, 2001).

Knowles, D., and Hadcock, R. N., *Medieval Religious Houses: England and Wales*, 2nd edn (Cambridge, 1971).

Koziol, G., *Begging Pardon and Favour: Ritual and Political Order in Early Medieval France* (Ithaca, NY, 1992).

'England, France, and the Problem of Sacrality in Twelfth-Century Ritual', in *Cultures of Power. Lordship, Status and Process in Twelfth-Century Europe*, ed. T. N. Bisson (Philadelphia, 1995), pp. 124–48.

'The Dangers of Polemic: Is Ritual Still an Interesting Topic of Historical Study?', *Early Medieval Europe*, 11 (2002), 367–88.

Kusaba, Y., 'Henry of Blois, Winchester, and the Twelfth-Century Renaissance,' in *Winchester Cathedral. Nine Hundred Years, 1093–1993* (Chichester, 1993), pp. 69–80.

Laporte, J., 'Les listes abbatiale et priorale du Mont-Saint-Michel', in *Millénaire monastique du Mont-Saint-Michel*, 5 vols. (Paris, 1967–93), i, 268–84.

Legg, L. G. Wickham, *English Coronation Records* (London, 1901).

Legge, M. D. *Anglo-Norman Literature and its Background* (Oxford, 1963).

'L'influence littéraire de la cour d'Henri Beauclerc', in *Mélanges offerts à Rita Lejeune*, ed. F. Dethier, 2 vols. (Gembloux, 1969), i, 679–87.

Le Goff, J., 'Aspects religieux et sacrés de la monarchie française du xe au xiiie siècle', in *La royauté sacrée dans le monde capétien. Colloque de Royaumont, mars 1989*, ed. A. Boureau and C. S. Ingerflom (Paris, 1982), pp. 19–28.

Lemarignier, J.-F., *Etude sur les privilèges d'exemption et de juridiction ecclésiastique des abbayes normandes jusqu'en 1140* (Paris, 1937).

— *Recherches sur l'hommage en marche et les frontières féodales* (Lille, 1945).

Le Neve, J., *Fasti Ecclesiae Anglicanae 1066–1300, I, St Paul's Cathedral*, compiled by D. E. Greenway (London, 1968).

Le Patourel, J., 'Henri Beauclerc, Comte du Cotentin, 1088', *Revue Historique de Droit Français et Etranger*, 4th series 53 (1975), 167–8.

— *The Norman Empire* (Oxford, 1976).

Levison, W., 'Aus englischen Bibliotheken. ii, Ein Schreiben Paschalis II an Robert von der Normandie', *Neues Archiv der Gesellschaft für ältere deutsche Geschichtskunde*, 35 (1909), 427–31.

Lewis, A. W., *Royal Succession in Capetian France. Studies on Familial Order and the State* (Cambridge, Mass., 1981).

Lewis, C. P., 'The King and Eye: a Study in Anglo-Norman Politics', *EHR*, 103 (1989), 569–87.

— 'Gruffudd ap Cynan and the Normans', *Gruffudd ap Cynan: A Collective Biography*, ed. K. L. Maund (Woodbridge, 1996), pp. 61–77.

Leyland, M., 'The Origins and Development of Durham Castle', in *Anglo-Norman Durham 1093–1193*, ed. D. Rollason, M. Harvey and M. Prestwich (Woodbridge, 1994), pp. 407–24.

Leyser, H., *Hermits and the New Monasticism* (London, 1984).

Leyser, K., 'England and the Empire in the Early Twelfth Century', *Transactions of the Royal Historical Society*, 5th series, 10 (1960), 61–83, reprinted in Leyser, *Medieval Germany and Its Neighbours 900–1250* (London, 1982), pp. 191–214.

— 'Frederick Barbarossa and the Hand of St James', *Transactions of the Royal Historical Society*, 5th series, 10 (1960), 61–83, reprinted in *Medieval Germany*, pp. 215–40.

— 'Some Reflections on Twelfth-Century Kings and Kingship', Leyser, *Medieval Germany*, pp. 241–67.

— 'The Anglo-Norman Succession 1120–1125', *ANS*, 13 (1990), 225–41.

Litten, J., *The English Way of Death. The Common Funeral since 1450* (London, 1991).

Lohrmann, D., 'Der Tod König Heinrichs I. von England in der mittellateinischen Literatur Englands und der Normandie', *Mittellateinisches Jahrbuch*, 8 (1973), 90–107.

— 'Saint-Germer-de-Fly und das Anglo-Normannische Reich', *Francia*, 1 (1973), 193–256.

— 'Pierre le Vénérable et Henri Ier', in *Pierre Abélard, Pierre le Vénérable: les courants philosophiques, littéraires et artistiques en occident au milieu du XIIe siècle* (Paris, 1975), pp. 191–203.

Lo Prete, K., 'The Anglo-Norman Card of Adela of Blois', *Albion*, 22 (1990), 569–89.
— 'Adela of Blois: Familial Alliances and Female Lordship', in *Aristocratic Women in Medieval France*, ed. T. Evergates (Philadelphia, 1999), pp. 7–43.
Louise, G., *La Seigneurie de Bellême Xe–XIIe siècles*, 2 vols., *Le Pays Bas Normand*, 101, 102 (1990, 1991).
Luchaire, A., *Louis VI le Gros. Annales de sa vie et de son règne (1081–1137)* (Paris, 1890).
Maillefer, J.-M., 'Une famille aristocratique aux confins de la Normandie: les Géré au XIe siècle', in *Autour du pouvoir ducal normand Xe–XIIe siècles, Cahier des Annales de Normandie*, 17 (1985), pp. 175–206.
Manuscrits et enluminures dans le monde normand (Xe–XVe siècle), ed. P. Bouet and M. Dosdat, Colloque de Cerisy-la-Salle (Caen, 1999).
Marritt, S., 'Coincidences of Names, Anglo-Scottish Connections and Anglo-Saxon Society in the Late Eleventh Century', *Scottish Historical Review*, 83 (2004), 150–70.
Martindale, J., 'Succession and Politics in the Romance-Speaking World, c. 1000–1400', in *England and her Neighbours 1066–1453*, ed. M. Jones and M. Vale (London, 1989), pp. 19–41.
Mason, E., 'The King, the Chamberlain, and Southwick Priory', *Historical Research*, 53 (1980), 1–10.
— 'Westminster Abbey and the Monarchy between the Reigns of William I and John (1066–1216)', *Journal of Ecclesiastical History*, 41 (1990), 199–216.
— 'The Site of King Making and Consecration: Westminster Abbey and the Crown in the Eleventh and Twelfth Centuries', in *The Church and Sovereignty c. 590–1918. Essays in Honour of Michael Wilks*, ed. D. Wood, Studies in Church History, 9 (1991), 57–76.
— 'William Rufus and the Historians', *Medieval History*, 1 (1991), 6–22.
— *Westminster Abbey and Its People c. 1050–c. 1216* (Woodbridge, 1996).
Mason, J. F. A., 'The Officers and Clerks of the Norman Earls of Shropshire', *Transactions of the Shropshire Archaeological Society*, 56 (1957–60), 244–57.
Mathieu, J.-N., 'Recherches sur les premiers comtes de Dammartin', *Mémoires publiées par la Fédération des Sociétés Archéologiques*, 47 (1996), 7–59.
Matthew, D., *King Stephen* (London, 2002).
Maund, K. L., 'Owain ap Cadwgan: A Rebel Revisited', *Haskins Society Journal*, 13 (1999), 65–74.
Mauss, M., *The Gift: Forms and Functions of Exchange in Archaic Societies* (London, 1970 edn).
Mayer, H. Eberhard, 'Studies in the History of Queen Melisende of Jerusalem', *Dumbarton Oaks Papers*, 26 (1972), 95–182.
Mayr-Harting, H., 'Functions of a Twelfth-Century Recluse', *History*, 60 (1975), 337–52.
McCarthy, M. R., and Summerson, H. R. T., *Carlisle Castle, A Survey and Documentary History*, English Heritage (1990).

McDonald, R. A., 'Matrimonial Politics and Core–Periphery Interactions in Twelfth- and Early Thirteenth-Century Scotland', *Journal of Medieval History*, 21 (1995), 227–47.

Mesqui, J. and Toussaint, P., 'Le château de Gisors aux XIIe et XIIIe siècles', *Archéologie Médiévale*, 29 (1999), 253–317.

Metcalf, D. M., 'The Taxation of Moneyers under Edward the Confessor and in 1086', in *Domesday Studies*, ed. J. C. Holt (Woodbridge, 1986), pp. 279–93.

Miguet, M., *Templiers et Hospitaliers en Normandie*, Comité des travaux historiques et scientifiques (Paris, 1995).

Moore, R. I., *The Formation of a Persecuting Society. Power and Deviance in Western Europe 950–1250* (Oxford, 1987).

Morillo, S., *Warfare under the Anglo-Norman Kings* (Woodbridge, 1994).

Morris, C., *The Papal Monarchy. The Western Church from 1050 to 1250* (Oxford, 1989).

Morse, R., *Truth and Invention in the Middle Ages* (Cambridge, 1991).

Mortimer, R., 'The Baynards of Baynard's Castle', *Studies in Medieval History Presented to R. Allen Brown*, ed. C. Harper-Bill, C. J. Holdsworth and J. L. Nelson (Woodbridge, 1989), pp. 241–53.

Moss, V., 'Normandy and England in 1180: the Pipe Roll Evidence', in *England and Normandy in the Middle Ages*, ed. D. Bates and A. Curry (London, 1994), pp. 185–95.

Murray, A. V., *The Crusader Kingdom of Jerusalem. A Dynastic History 1099–1125*, Prosopographica et Genealogica (2000).

Murray, M., *God of the Witches* (London, 1933).

Musset, L., 'Quelques notes sur les baleiniers normands du xe au XIIe siècle', *Revue d'Histoire Economique et Sociale*, 42 (1964), 147–61.

'Rouen au temps des Francs et sous les Ducs (Ve siècle–1204)', in *Histoire de Rouen*, ed. M. Mollat (Toulouse, 1979), pp. 59–72.

'Une aristocratie d'affaires anglo-normandes après la conquête', *Etudes Normandes*, 35 (1986), 7–19.

'Réflexions sur les moyens de paiement en Normandie aux xie et xiie siècles', *Aspects de la société et de l'économie dans la Normandie médiévale (Xe–XIIIe siècles), Cahier des Annales de Normandie*, 22 (1988), 65–89.

Nelson, J. L., *Politics and Ritual in Early Medieval Europe* (London, 1986).

'The Lord's Anointed and the People's Choice: Carolingian Royal Ritual', in *Rituals of Royalty. Power and Ceremonial in Traditional Societies*, ed. D. Cannadine and S. Price (Cambridge, 1987), pp. 166–72.

Neveux, F., *La Normandie des ducs aux rois Xe–XIIe siècle* (Rennes, 1998).

Nicholl, D., *Thurstan Archbishop of York (1114–40)* (York, 1964).

Nightingale, P., 'Some London Moneyers and Reflections on the Organization of English Mints in the Eleventh and Twelfth Centuries', *Numismatic Chronicle*, 142 (1982), 34–50.

'The London Pepperers' Guild and Some Twelfth-Century English Trading Links with Spain', *[Bulletin of the Institute of] Historical Research*, 58 (1985), 123–32.

Nineham, R., 'The So-Called Anonymous of York', *Journal of Ecclesiastical History*, 14 (1963), 31–45.
Nip, R., 'The Political Relations between England and Flanders (1066–1128)', *ANS*, 21 (1998), 145–67.
North, J. D., 'Some Norman Horoscopes', in *Adelard of Bath. An English Scientist and Arabist of the Early Twelfth Century*, ed. C. Burnett, Warburg Institute Surveys and Texts, xiv (London, 1987), pp. 147–61.
O'Brien, B., 'Forgery and the Literacy of the Early Common Law', *Albion*, 27 (1995), 1–18.
— 'From *Morðor* to *Murdrum*: The Pre-Conquest Origin and Norman Revival of the Murder Fine', *Speculum*, 71 (1996), 74–110.
— *God's Peace and King's Peace. The Laws of Edward the Confessor* (Philadelphia, 1999).
Offler, H. S., 'Rannulf Flambard as Bishop of Durham (1099–1128)', *Durham University Journal*, 64; new series, 33 (1971–2), 14–25.
Oram, R. D., 'Fergus, Galloway and the Scots', in *Galloway: Land and Lordship*, ed. R. D. Oram and G. P. Stell (Edinburgh, 1991), pp. 117–30.
— 'In Obedience and Reverence: Whithorn and York c. 1128–c. 1250', *Innes Review*, 42 no. 2 (1991), 83–100.
— 'A Family Business? Colonisation and Settlement in Twelfth- and Thirteenth-Century Galloway', *Scottish Historical Review*, 82 (1993), 111–45.
— *The Lordship of Galloway* (Edinburgh, 2000).
— *David I. The King Who Made Scotland* (Stroud, 2004).
Oxford before the University, ed. A. Dodd, Oxford Archaeology, Thames Valley Landscapes Monograph no. 17 (2003).
Oxford Dictionary of National Biography: From the Earliest Times to the Year 2000, ed. H. C. G. Matthew and B. Harrison, 60 vols. (Oxford, 2004).
Palais Médiévaux (France–Belgique), ed. A. Renoux, Publications de l'Université du Maine (1994).
The Peace of God: Social Violence and Religious Response in France Around the Year 1000, ed. T. Head and R. Landes (Ithaca, N.Y., 1992).
Pellens, K., *Das Kirchendenken des normannischen Anonymus* (Wiesbaden, 1973).
Phillips, J. P., 'A Note on the Origins of Raymond of Poitiers', *EHR*, 106 (1991), 66–7.
Philpott, M., 'Some Interactions between the English and Irish Churches', *ANS*, 20 (1997), 187–204.
Plant, R., 'Ecclesiastical Architecture c. 1050– c. 1200', in *A Companion to the Anglo-Norman World*, ed. C. Harper-Bill and E. Van Houts (Woodbridge, 2003), pp. 215–53.
Pollock, F., and Maitland, F. W., *The History of English Law*, 2 vols., 2nd edn (Cambridge, 1968).
Poly, J.-P., 'Le capétien thaumaturge: genèse populaire d'un miracle royal', in *La France de l'an mil*, ed. R. Delort (Paris, 1990), pp. 282–308.
Poole, A. L., *From Domesday Book to Magna Carta*, 2nd edn (Oxford, 1955).

Postles, D., 'The Foundation of Oseney Abbey', *Bulletin of the Institute of Historical Research*, 53 (1980), 242–4.
"'Patronus et Advocatus Noster": Oseney Abbey and the Oilly Family', *Historical Research*, 60 (1987), 100–2.
Potter, J., 'Monastic Freedom vs. Episcopal and Aristocratic Power in the Twelfth Century: Context and Analysis of the *De Libertate Beccensis*', in *Negotiating Secular and Ecclesiastical Power*, ed. H. Teunis and A. Wareham (Turnhout, 1999), pp. 73–85.
Pouëssel, J. 'Les structures militaires du comté de Mortain (xie et xiie siècles)', *Revue de l'Avranchin*, 58 (1981), 11–74, 81–156.
Poulle, B., 'Savigny and England', in *Normandy and England in the Middle Ages*, ed. D. Bates and A. Curry (London, 1994), pp. 159–68.
Power, D. J. 'Introduction. Frontiers: Terms, Concepts, and the Historians of Medieval and Early Modern Europe', in *Frontiers in Question: Eurasian Borderlands 700–1700*, ed. D. J. Power and N. Standen (London, 1999), pp. 1–12, 28–31.
'French and Norman Frontiers in the Central Middle Ages', ibid., pp. 105–31.
The Norman Frontier in the Twelfth and Early Thirteenth Centuries, Cambridge Studies in Medieval Life and Thought, 4th series, 62 (Cambridge, 2004).
Power, R., 'The Death of Magnus Barelegs', *Scottish Historical Review*, 73 (1994), 216–22.
Prestwich, J. O., 'War and Finance in the Anglo-Norman State', *Transactions of the Royal Historical Society*, 5th series, 4 (1954), 19–43.
Review of Hollister, *Military Organization of Norman England*, EHR, 81 (1966), 103–10.
'The Military Household of the Norman Kings', *EHR*, 96 (1981), 1–35.
The Place of War in English History 1066–1214, ed. M. Prestwich (Woodbridge, 2004).
Rahtz, P. A., *The Saxon and Medieval Palaces at Cheddar* (1979).
Reedy, W. T., 'The First Two Bassets of Weldon', *Northamptonshire Past and Present*, 4 (1966–72), 241–5, 295–8.
Reilly, B. F., *The Kingdom of León-Castilla under Queen Urraca 1109–1126* (Princeton, 1982).
Religion et culture autour de l'an mil: royaume capétien et Lotharingie: actes du colloque Hugues Capet (987–1987), ed. D. Iogna-Prat and J.-C. Picard (Paris, 1990).
Renoux, A., 'Résidences et châteaux ducaux normands au xiie siècle', in *L'Architecture normande au moyen âge*, ed. M. Baylé, 2 vols. (Caen, 1997), i, 197–217.
Richardson, H. G. and Sayles, G. O., *The Governance of Mediaeval England from the Conquest to Magna Carta* (Edinburgh, 1963).
Ritchie, R. L. G., *The Normans in Scotland* (Edinburgh, 1953).
Robinson, I. S., *Authority and Resistance in the Investiture Contest. The Polemical Literature of the Late Eleventh Century* (Manchester, 1978).
The Papacy 1073–1198 (Cambridge, 1990).
Round, J. H., *Geoffrey de Mandeville* (London, 1892).

'Bernard the King's Scribe', *EHR*, 14 (1899), 417–30.
Studies in Peerage and Family History (London, 1901).
'The Origins of the Stewarts', in *Studies in Peerage and Family History* (London, 1901), pp. 115–31.
'A Great Marriage Settlement', *Ancestor*, 11 (1904), 153–7.
The King's Serjeants and Officers of State (London, 1911).
'The Family of Ballon and the Conquest of South Wales', *Studies in Peerage and Family History* (London, 1931), pp. 181–215.
'Walter Tirel and His Wife', *Feudal England* (London, 1964 edn).
Le Royauté sacrée dans le monde chrétien. Colloque de Royaumont (mars 1989), ed. A. Boureau and C. I. Ingerflom (Paris, 1982).
Russell, J. C., 'The Date of Henry I's Charter for London', in *Dargan Historical Essays (Historical Studies Presented to Marion Dargan)*, ed. W. M. Dabney and J. C. Russell, University of New Mexico Publications in History, 4 (Albuquerque, 1952), pp. 9–16.
Salter, H. E., *Medieval Oxford*, Oxford Historical Society, c (1936).
Sanders, I. J, *English Baronies* (Oxford, 1960).
Sassier, Y., *Royauté et idéologie au Moyen Age. Bas-Empire, monde franc, France (IVe–XIIe siècle)* (Paris, 2002).
Scaglione, A., *Knights at Court. Courtliness, Chivalry, and Courtesy from Ottonian Germany to the Italian Renaissance* (Berkeley, Los Angeles, and Oxford, 1991).
Schieffer, T., *Die päpstlichen Legaten in Frankreich vom Vertrag von Meersen (870) bis zum Schisma von 1130*, Eberings Hist. Stud. 263 (Berlin, 1935).
Schofield, J., *The Building of London from the Conquest to the Great Fire*, 3rd edn (Stroud, 1994).
Schramm, P. E., *A History of the English Coronation*, trans. G. Wickham Legg (Oxford, 1937).
Scott, J. G., 'The Partition of a Kingdom: Strathclyde 1092–1153', *Transactions of the Dumfries and Galloway Natural History and Antiquarian Society*, 72 (1997), 11–40.
Sharpe, R., 'The Prefaces of *Quadripartitus*', *Law and Government in Medieval England and Normandy*, ed. G. Garnett and J. Hudson (Cambridge, 1994), pp. 148–72.
'The Use of Writs in the Eleventh Century', *Anglo-Saxon England*, 32 (2003), 247–61.
'Address and Delivery in Anglo-Norman Royal Charters', *Charters and Charter Scholarship in Britain and Ireland*, ed. M. T. Flanagan and J. A. Green (Houndmills, 2005), pp. 32–52.
Shirley, K. L., *The Secular Jurisdiction of Monasteries in Anglo-Norman and Angevin England* (Woodbridge, 2004).
Short, I., 'On Bilingualism in Anglo-Norman England', *Romance Philology*, 33 (1980), 467–99.
'Patrons and Polyglots: French Literature in Twelfth-Century England', *ANS*, 14 (1992), 229–49.

Smalley, B., 'Gilbertus Universalis, Bishop of London (1128–34), and the Problem of the "Glossa Ordinaria"', *Recherches de Théologie Ancienne et Médiévale*, 7 (1935), 24–60.

Smith, L., 'Benedictine Women at Oxford: The Nuns at Godstow', in *Benedictines in Oxford*, ed. H. Wansborough and A. Marett-Crosby (London, 1997), pp. 95–100, 293–4.

Sneddon, C., 'Brendan the Navigator: A Twelfth-Century View', in *The North-Sea World in the Middle Ages. Studies in the Cultural History of North-West Europe*, ed. T. R. Liska and L. E. M. Walker (Dublin, 2001), pp. 211–28.

Southern, R. W., 'Ranulf Flambard and Early Anglo–Norman Financial Administration', *Transactions of the Royal Historical Society*, 4th series, 16 (1933), 98–128, reprinted in *Medieval Humanism and Other Studies* (Oxford, 1970), pp. 183–205.

'The Place of Henry I in English History', *Proceedings of the British Academy*, 47 (1962), 127–69, reprinted in *Medieval Humanism and Other Studies*, pp. 206–33.

'History as Prophecy', *Transactions of the Royal Historical Society*, 5th series, 22 (1972), 159–80.

'From Schools to University', in *The History of the University of Oxford*, ed. T. H. Aston, i, *The Early Oxford Schools*, ed. J. Catto (Oxford, 1984), pp. 1–36.

Saint Anselm. A Portrait in a Landscape (Cambridge, 1990).

Southworth, J., *The English Medieval Minstrel* (Woodbridge, 1998).

Spear, D. S., 'Les doyens de Rouen au cours de la période ducale', *Annales de Normandie*, 33 (1983), 91–119.

'Les archidiacres de Rouen au cours de la période ducale', *Annales de Normandie*, 34 (1984), 15–50.

'Les dignitaires de la cathédrale de Rouen pendant la période ducale', *Annales de Normandie*, 37 (1987), 121–47.

'Geoffrey Brito, Archbishop of Rouen (1111–28)', *Haskins Society Journal*, 2 (1990), 123–37.

'Les chanoines de la cathédrale de Rouen pendant la période ducale', *Annales de Normandie*, 41 (1991), 135–76.

Stafford, P., 'The Laws of Cnut and the History of Anglo-Saxon Royal Promises', *Anglo-Saxon England*, 10 (1981), 173–90.

'Cherchez la Femme: Queens, Queens' Lands, and Nunneries: Missing Links in the Foundation of Reading Abbey', *History*, 85 (2000), 4–27.

Stalley, R. A., 'A Twelfth-Century Patron of Architecture: A Study of the Buildings Erected by Roger, Bishop of Salisbury 1102–39', *Journal of the British Archaeological Association*, 3rd series, 34 (1971), 62–83.

Steane, J. M., *The Archaeology of the Medieval English Monarchy* (London, 1993).

The Archaeology of Power. England and Northern Europe AD 800–1600 (Stroud, 2001).

Stenton, D. M., 'Roger of Salisbury, *Regni Angliae Procurator*', *EHR*, 39 (1924), 79–80.

Stephenson, W., 'An Inedited Charter of Henry I', *EHR*, 21 (1906), 505–9.

Stewart, I., 'Moneyers in the 1130 Pipe Roll,' *British Numismatic Journal*, 61 (1991), 1–8.
Strevett, N., 'The Anglo-Norman Civil War of 1101', *ANS*, 26 (2003), 159–71.
Strickland, M., *War and Chivalry. The Conduct and Perception of War in England and Normandy, 1066–1217* (Cambridge, 1996).
Stringer, K. J., 'Some Documents Concerning a Berkshire Family and Monk Sherborne Priory, Hampshire', *Berkshire Archaeological Journal*, 63 (1967), 23–67.
The Reign of Stephen. Kingship, Warfare and Government in Twelfth-Century England (London, 1993).
Stroll, M., *Calixtus II (1119–24). A Pope Born to Rule* (London and Boston, 2004).
Stubbs, W., *Constitutional History of Medieval England*, 3 vols., i, 6th edn (Oxford, 1897).
Tabuteau, E. Zack, *Transfers of Property in Eleventh-Century Norman Law* (Chapel Hill and London, 1988).
'The Role of Law in the Succession to Normandy', *Haskins Society Journal*, 3 (1991), 141–69.
'The Family of Moulins-la-Marche', *Medieval Prosopography*, 13 (1992), 29–65.
Tatlock, J. S. P., 'The English Journey of the Laon Canons', *Speculum*, 8 (1933), 454–65.
Thomas, H. M., *The English and the Normans. Ethnic Hostility, Assimilation, and Identity 1066–c. 1220* (Oxford, 2003).
Thompson, J. W., *The Literacy of the Laity in Norman and Angevin England* (New York, 1960).
Thompson, K., 'Une confirmation supposée de Guillaume le Bâtard', *Annales de Normandie*, 34 (1984), 411–12.
'Robert de Bellême', *ANS*, 13 (1990), 263–86.
'William Talvas, Count of Ponthieu, and the Politics of the Anglo-Norman Realm', in *England and Normandy in the Middle Ages*, ed. D. Bates and A. Curry (London, 1994), pp. 169–84.
'The Lords of Laigle: Ambition and Insecurity on the Borders of Normandy', *ANS*, 18 (1995), 177–99.
'Note de recherche. Arnoul de Montgomery', *Annales de Normandie*, 45 (1995), 49–53.
'Dowry and Inheritance Patterns: Some Examples from the Descendants of King Henry I of England', *Medieval Prosopography*, 17 (1996), 45–61.
Power and Border Lordship in Medieval France. The County of the Perche, 1000–1226 (Woodbridge, 2002).
'Queen Adeliza and the Lotharingian Connection', *Sussex Archaeological Collections*, 140 (2002), 57–64.
'Affairs of State: The Illegitimate Children of Henry I', *Journal of Medieval History*, 29 (2003), 129–51.
'Robert Duke of Normandy (b. in or after 1050, d. 1134)', *Oxford DNB*.
Thompson, M. W., 'Recent Excavations in the Keep of Farnham Castle, Surrey', *Medieval Archaeology*, 4 (1960), 81–94.

Tillmann, H., *Die päpstlichen Legaten in England bis zur Beendignung der Legation Gualas (1218)* (Bonn, 1926).
Turner, R. V., *Men Raised from the Dust. Administrative Service and Upward Mobility in Angevin England* (Philadelphia, 1988).
Turvey, R., *The Welsh Princes 1063–1283* (London, 2002).
Van Caenegem, R. C., 'Public Prosecution of Crime in Twelfth-Century England', in *Church and Government in the Middle Ages. Essays presented to C. R. Cheney on His Seventieth Birthday* (Cambridge, 1976), pp. 41–76.
Van Houts, E. M. C., 'Latin Poetry and the Anglo-Norman Court 1066–1135: The *Carmen de Hastingae Proelio*', *Journal of Medieval History*, 15 (1989), 39–62.
'Wace as Historian', in *Family Trees and the Roots of Politics*, ed. K. S. B. Keats-Rohan (Woodbridge, 1997), pp. 103–32, reprinted in *The History of the Norman People. Wace's Roman de Rou* (trans. Burgess), pp. xxxv–lxii.
'The Anglo-Flemish Treaty of 1101', *ANS*, 21 (1998), 169–74.
'The Warenne View of the Past', *ANS*, 26 (2003), 103–21.
Van Moolenbroek, J., *Vital l'ermite, prédicateur itinérant, fondateur de l'abbaye normande de Savigny*, trans. Anne-Marie Nambet, *Revue de l'Avranchin*, 68 (1991).
Vaughn, S., *Anselm of Bec and Robert of Meulan. The Innocence of the Dove and the Wisdom of the Serpent* (Berkeley, Los Angeles and London, 1987).
The Abbey of Bec and the Anglo-Norman State, 1034–1136 (Woodbridge, 1981).
Victoria History of the Counties of England (London, 1901–).
Vincent, N., *The Holy Blood. King Henry III and the Westminster Blood Relic* (Cambridge, 2001).
'The Pilgrimages of the Angevin Kings of England, 1154–1272', in *Pilgrimage. The English Experience from Becket to Bunyan*, ed. C. Morris and P. Roberts (Cambridge, 2002), pp. 12–45.
Von Knonau, G. Meyer, *Jahrbücher des deutschen Reiches unter Heinrich IV und Heinrich V*, 7 vols. (Leipzig, 1890–1909).
Waldman, T. G., 'Saint-Denis et les premiers Capétiens', in *Religion et culture autour de l'an mil: royaume capétien et Lotharingie. Actes du Colloque Hugues Capet (987–1987)*, ed. D. Iogna-Prat and J.-C. Picard (Paris, 1990), pp. 191–7.
Walker, D., 'Miles of Gloucester, Earl of Hereford', *Transactions of the Bristol and Gloucestershire Archaeological Society*, 77 (1958), 66–96.
Ward, J., 'Royal Service and Reward: the Clare Family and the Crown, 1066–1154', *ANS*, 11 (1988), 261–78.
Ward, P. L., 'The Coronation Ceremony in Medieval England', *Speculum*, 14 (1939), 160–78.
Wareham, A., 'The Motives and Politics of the Bigod Family, c. 1066–1177', *ANS*, 17 (1994), 223–42.
Warren, W. L., 'The Death of William Rufus', *History Today*, 9 (1959), 22–9.
'The Myth of Norman Administrative Efficiency', *Transactions of the Royal Historical Society*, 5th series, 34 (1984), 113–32.
Watt, D. E. R., *Fasti Ecclesiae Scoticanae Medii Aevi ad annum 1638*, 2nd draft, Scottish Record Society, new series, 1 (1969).

Weiss, S., *Die Urkunden der päpstlichen Legaten von Leo IX. bis Coelestin III. (1049–1198)* (Cologne, Weimar and Vienna, 1995).
Wertheimer, L., 'Adeliza of Louvain and Anglo-Norman Queenship', *Haskins Society Journal*, 7 (1995), 101–15.
West, F. J., *The Justiciarship in England 1066–1232* (Cambridge, 1966).
'The Colonial History of the Norman Conquest', *History*, 84 (1999), 219–36.
Wightman, W. E., *The Lacy Family in England and Normandy 1066–1194* (Oxford, 1966).
Williams, A., 'Some Notes and Considerations on Problems Connected with the English Royal Succession, 860–1066', *ANS*, 1 (1978), 144–67, 225–33.
Williams, G. H., *The Norman Anonymous of A.D. 1100*, Harvard Theological Studies, no. 18 (Cambridge, Mass., 1951).
Williamson, H. Ross, *The Arrow and the Sword: An Essay in Detection*, 2nd edn (London, 1955).
Wood, M., *Norman Domestic Architecture* (London, 1974).
Wormald, P., 'Laga Eadwardi: The *Textus Roffensis* and its Context', *ANS*, 17 (1994), 243–66.
'Quadripartitus', in *Law and Government in Medieval England and Normandy. Essays in Honour of Sir James Holt*, ed. G. Garnett and J. Hudson (Cambridge, 1994), pp. 113–32.
The Making of English Law. King Alfred to the Twelfth Century. Legislation and Its Limits (Oxford, 1999).
J. Yver, 'Les châteaux forts en Normandie jusqu'au milieu du xiie siècle, contribution à l'étude du pouvoir ducal', *Bulletin de la Société des Antiquaires de Normandie*, 53 (1955–6), 28–115.
Zarnecki, G., *Romanesque Sculpture at Lincoln Cathedral*, Lincoln Minster Pamphlets (1970), reprinted in Zarnecki, *Studies in Romanesque Sculpture* (London, 1979), xv, 1–24.
'Henry of Blois as a Patron of Sculpture', in *Art and Patronage in the English Romanesque*, Society of Antiquaries, Occasional Paper, new series, no. 8 (London, 1986), pp. 159–72.
'Romanesque Sculpture of Lincoln Cathedral and the Continent', *England and the Continent*, ed. J. Mitchell assisted by M. Moran, *Harlaxton Medieval Studies*, 8 (Stamford, 2000), pp. 28–34.

WEBSITES

Green, J. A., 'Fécamp under the Norman Kings', *Tabularia*, www.unicaen.fr/mrsh/crahm/revue/tabularia, May, 2002.

Index

Aalst 203
abbots, precedence of 195
Abergavenny 133
Abetot, *see* Urse d'Abetot
Abingdon:
   abbey 28, 67
   cartulary-chronicle of 7, 23, 26, 239
   Henry's favour to 7
   Henry's visit (1084) 22, 23, 308
Achard 32
Adam de Grémonville 281
Adela, countess of Blois 21, 85, 87, 161, 162, 180,
    191, 203, 220, 230, 279, 281
   death 310
   retires to Marcigny 171, 278, 280
Adelaide of Maurienne, queen of France 196
Adelasia, countess of Sicily 191, 196
Adelard of Bath 296
Adeliza, queen of England 168, 170, 182, 195
   appearance 169
   childlessness 170, 309
   dower 169
   literary patronage 169, 294, 297; commissions
     biography of Henry 169
   takes the oath (1127) 195
Adelulf, bishop of Carlisle 178, 214, 264
Adelulf the Fleming 250
Aethelred, king of England 46
Aethelred, son of Malcolm III, king of Scots 53
Aethelwold, bishop of Winchester 273
Aigle, l' 21, 85, 88, 142, 143, 144, 145, 180
   see also Engenulf, Geoffrey, Gilbert, Richer
Aire 198
Alan I, lord of Richmond 54
Alan Fergant, count of Brittany 90, 127, 133,
    228, 288
Alan FitzFlaad 133
Alderney, church of St Mary 270
Aldhelm, St 297
Alençon 119, 126, 142, 145, 147, 252, 269
   castle 219

Alexander bishop of Lincoln 179, 213, 214, 268,
    298, 305
Alexander I king of Scots 129, 132, 175, 176, 227,
    272
   on Welsh expedition (1114) 176
Alexander II, pope 68, 255, 271
Alexius, emperor 87
Alfonso I king of Aragon 191, 264
Algar bishop of Coutances 270
Allaines 123
Almenêches:
   castle 219
   nunnery 75
Alnwick 176
Alston 104, 175, 248
Alton 64
   treaty of 64, 68
Amaury de Montfort 74, 124, 126, 143, 144, 153,
    156, 157, 180, 183, 185, 186, 234, 242
   advises King Louis 153
   based at Pacy 150
   claims county of Evreux 139
   drives Henry's forces from Vexin 188
   and Eustace of Breteuil 147
   his men at Evreux 150
   joins conspiracy (1123) 180, 185
   and l'Aigle 143
   refuses terms 148
   and Stephen de Garlande 200
Ambrières 183, 229
Anacletus II, antipope 208, 209
Anceins 149
Andelle, river 24, 145
Andely 145, 146, 151, 152, 153
Andrew de Baudemont 210, 280
Angers, diocese of 124
Angevins 83
Anglesey 69
Anglo-Saxon Chronicle 38, 52, 65, 78, 79, 115,
    146, 179, 183, 189, 192, 194, 215, 240, 241,
    314

372

Index

Anjou 82, 146, 163, 200, 209, 230, 252, 281
  count of 29, 85, 93, 192, 225, 295
  see also Fulk, Geoffrey Martel, Geoffrey 'the Bearded'
Annandale 177, 227
Anselm, St, archbishop of Canterbury 21, 38, 43, 44, 51, 58, 60, 61, 62, 64, 66, 67, 73, 74, 81, 85, 93, 101, 108–9, 110, 116, 178, 291, 313
  abbot 256
  adviser to queen 58, 64, 65, 66
  and Bohemond 87
  and council of London (1102) 72; (1107) 109, 162
  death 120, 262, 271
  and Henry's marriage 55, 56
  illness 88
  invested as archbishop 52
  as legate 101
  quarrel with Rufus 274, 294
  recognises Urban II 256
  reconciled with Henry 85
  refuses homage 52, 67
  returns to England (1100) 52, 58; (1106) 88
  and Rome 74
Anselm *vicomte* of Rouen 251
Anselm de Garlande 200
Anselm of Laon 264
Anselm of St Saba, abbot of Bury St Edmunds 160, 195, 266
Ansfrida, Henry's mistress 26, 27, 308
Antioch 87, 261
antipope, see Gregory VIII
Apulia 92, 100
Arduin de St Médard 202
Arganchy, see Rainald of Arganchy
Argences 84
Argentan 70, 75, 99, 106, 125, 183, 205, 218, 252, 303
  castle 35, 219, 221
  vicomte of 125
Arnold III count of Flanders and Hainault 197
Arnold of Denmark 197, 199
Arnoux, M. 18
Arnulf of Montgomery 62, 68, 69, 71, 72, 86, 99, 107, 145, 227
Arques 142, 153, 183
  vicomte of 122
Arras 197, 199
Arsic, see Manasser Arsic
Arthur, King 7
Arundel 70
Ascelin Goel 73
Ascelin son of Andrew 145
Ascelin son of Arthur 26

Aubigny, see Nigel d'Aubigny, William d'Aubigny
Audoin bishop of Evreux 131, 139, 144, 150, 156, 157, 220, 267, 269, 270
  at Henry's deathbed 220, 221
Augustinian canons 18, 170, 177, 178, 264, 278–9
  see also under names of individual communities: Carlisle, Cirencester, Dover, Dunstable, Hexham, London Holy Trinity Aldgate, Merton, Nostell, Oxford, St Frideswide's, Sainte-Barbe-en-Auge, St Denys Portswood, Sées, Wellow by Grimsby
Aumale:
  count of, see Stephen court of Aumale
  county 229
Aunay, see Gontier d'Aunay
Auvergne 264
Avon, river 69
Avranches 91, 281
  bishops of, see Roger d'Avranches, Rualon d'Avranches
  castle 31
  diocese 124, 270
Avranchin 28
Avre, river 106, 180, 230, 234, 252
Axspoele 203

Baldwin V count of Flanders 61, 197
Baldwin VII count of Flanders 124, 134–5, 154
  death 150
  incursions into Normandy 138, 139, 140, 142
  wounded 146
Baldwin count of Hainault 197, 199
Baldwin I king of Jerusalem 181
Baldwin II king of Jerusalem 181, 200
Baldwin de Redvers 242
Baldwin FitzGilbert 50
Baldwin of Holland 197, 251
Baldwin son of Clarus 251
Bamberg 188
Bangor 173
  bishops of, see David 'Scotus', Hervey of Bangor
Barfleur 82, 164, 165, 166, 168, 211, 298
Barking 57
Barthélemy, Dominique 127
Basset family, see Ralph Basset, Richard Basset
Bath 66
Battle abbey 11, 170, 240, 278, 311
Baudry de Bosco, of Baudemont 180
Baudry of Bray 145, 180, 185
Bauduin, P. 17, 105, 106

374 Index

Bayeux 36, 82, 83, 84, 87, 88, 91, 101, 159
  burning of (1105) 101, 264, 270
  bishopric 101, 264, 270
  bishops of, *see* Richard of Douvres, Turold
  cathedral 8; canon of, *see* Wace
  mint 104
  Tapestry 165
  vicomte, *see* Ranulf Meschin
Baynard, *see* William Baynard, Baynard's castle
Baynard's castle 122
Beauchamp, *see* Hugh de Beauchamp, Robert de Beauchamp
Beaumont-le-Roger 185, 186
  castle 184, 185, 316
  estates 74, 97, 315
  lords of, *see* Henry de Beaumont, Robert de Beaumont, Waleran de Beaumont
Beaumont-sur-Sarthe 228
Beaumont twins 17, 97, 141, 143, 160, 195, 207, 220, 307
  vassals of 141
  see also Robert earl of Leicester, Waleran count of Meulan
Beauvais:
  council (legatine) at 163
  diocese of 229
  region 119, 123
Bec, abbey of 6, 87, 88, 101, 106, 131, 185, 217, 266, 278, 303
  abbots of, *see* Anselm, Boso
  monk of 135
Bellême 33, 105, 126, 127, 289
  castle 127
  lords of, *see* Robert de Bellême, Roger of Montgomery, William Talvas
Bellencombre 76
Benedeit 297
Benington 116
Berkhamsted 177
Berkshire 23, 67, 171, 251
  forests 299
Bermondsey priory 170–1, 172, 278
Bernard, St, abbot of Cîteaux 209, 210, 281
  meeting with Henry 211
Bernard, bishop of St David's 134, 272, 275–6, 277
Bernard of Neufmarché 174
Bernard of Tiron 281
Bernard the king's scribe 103
Bernay 185
Berneval 105, 240
Bertulf (Erchembald family) 196, 207
Bessin 36, 235
bestiaries 169
Beverley 110, 263

Bienfaite 151
  lord of, *see* Roger FitzRichard
Bigod, *see* Hugh Bigod, Roger Bigod
Bisson, T. N. 15
Bleddyn ap Cynfyn, ruler of Powys 71
  Iowerth, his son 71
Bloch, Marc 258
Blois 85, 124
  count of, *see* Stephen
  countess, *see* Adela
  see also Stephen king of England
Bodmin
  prior, *see* Algar bishop of Coutances
Bohemond 87, 100
Bolingbroke 173, 180
Bonneville-sur-Touques 125, 222, 243
Boso abbot of Bec 267
Boulogne
  count of, *see* Eustace III
  county of 199, 229, 235
Bourgtheroulde 288
Bramber 122
Bramford 270
Brampton 168, 302, 303, 308
Brand, P. 300
Bray-et-Lû 119
Brecknock 174, 244
Brémule, battle of 151, 154, 186, 259, 316
Brendan, Voyage of 169, 296, 297
Breteuil 73, 74, 105, 147, 153, 154, 157, 180, 183, 187, 235, 309, 316
  lords of, *see* Eustace of Breteuil, William FitzOsbern, William of Breteuil
Bretons 83, 92, 133, 183, 184
Bréval 180
Brian FitzCount 133, 194, 203, 210, 228, 288
Bricstan of Chatteris 115, 242
Bridgnorth 68, 70, 71, 174, 192
Brie 138
Brigstock 302
Brionne 184, 187
Briouze 122
  see also Philip de Briouze
Bristol 192, 216
Brittany 32, 73, 82, 122, 127, 228
  counts or dukes of, *see* Alan Fergant, Stephen count of Brittany
Brix 33
  see also Robert de Brus
Brotonne, forest of 185
Bruges 198, 199, 207
  church of St Donatian 196, 198
Brun, a knight 83
Brut y Tywysogyon 7, 132, 174
Bucklebury 171

Burchard (Erembald family) 196
Burchard of Montmorency 151
Bures-en-Bray 35
Burgh by Sands 177, 226
Burgundy 73, 122, 278
  duke of 120
Burton on Trent, abbey 131
Bury St Edmunds:
  abbey 67, 68, 134, 258, 268, 278, 291
  abbots, *see* Anselm of St Saba, Robert abbot of Bury St Edmunds
  shrine of St Edmund 211, 213, 311, 312

Caen 25, 27, 36, 70, 82, 84, 87, 88, 101, 102, 103, 106, 131, 159, 172, 186, 211, 222, 251, 299
  abbey of La Trinité 21, 97, 210, 211, 261, 269, 278, 280
  abbess of, *see* Cecilia, Henry's sister
  abbey of Saint-Etienne 25, 102, 222, 259, 265, 266, 269, 278, 281, 290, 311
  castle 91, 102, 106, 303
  exchequer at 238
Calixtus II, pope 154, 155, 158, 160, 188, 190, 275, 276
Campbell, J. 15
Canterbury 74, 299
  archbishops of 173, 262; appointment of 130, 262, 314; primatial claims of 110, 130, 141, 155, 163, 173, 179, 225, 265, 270, 271–2, 276
  cathedral 134, 291
  cathedral priory 6, 11, 51, 130, 131, 173, 176
  monks of 178, 262
Cardiff 215
Carentan 82, 292
Carlisle 104, 175, 176, 177, 214, 226, 227, 231, 309
  bishop of, *see* Adelulf
  castle 34, 301
  diocese 254, 272, 317
  priory 177, 279
Carmarthen 108, 244
Carreghwfa 69
Cassel 198
Castile 191
castles:
  custody of 233
  ducal 98, 238, 303
Cecilia, Henry's sister, abbess of La Trinité 21, 210, 280
Ceredigion 71, 132, 226
Cerisy 164
Cerne, abbey 130, 131
Chaise-Dieu, La 51
Châlons-sur-Marne 144, 277
Champagne 246

chancellors:
  of king, *see* Geoffrey Rufus, Gerard archbishop of York, Robert Bloet, Roger d'Avranches, Waldric, William Giffard
  of queen, *see* Bernard bishop of St David's
Channel crossings 298, 299
Charentonne, river 149
Charité-sur-Loire, La 278
Charlemagne, emperor 5, 6
Charles count of Flanders 39, 154, 157, 158, 162, 163, 169, 175, 186, 197, 204, 245, 293, 315–16
  murder of 196, 207
Charleval, *see* Noyon-sur-Andelle
  coronation charter *see* under Henry I
Chartres 85, 87, 104, 138, 139, 154, 187, 209, 298
  bishop of 188, 210
  diocese of 281
  hospital of Le Grand-Beaulieu 279
Château-Dun 85
Château Gaillard 145
Château-Gontier 35, 70, 75, 100
Châteauneuf-en-Thymerais 124, 180
  lord of, *see* Hugh FitzGervase
Château-sur-Epte 138, 151
Chaumont-en-Vexin 37, 151, 158, 196
  lord of, *see* Otmund
Cheddar 303
Cherbourg 31, 125
Cheshire 35, 172
Chester:
  bishops of, *see* Robert bishop of Chester, Roger bishop of Chester
  earldom of 172, 173, 226
  earls of, *see* Hugh earl of Chester, Ranulf Meschin, Richard earl of Chester
Chibnall, Marjorie 206
Cholsey 171
Christina, aunt of Queen Matilda 53
Cintheaux 85
Cirencester 279
Cisai-Saint-Aubin 150
Cistercians 281
Cîteaux, abbey of 211, 213, 281, 282
Clare 50
  family 40, 50, 123, 151
  see also Gilbert FitzRichard, Roger FitzRichard
Clemence countess of Flanders 198
Clermont, council of 35, 156
Clermont, lords of 229
Cluniacs 263, 266
  observance 170
Cluny, abbey of 39, 156, 171, 172, 208, 210, 278, 312
  abbots of, *see* Hugh abbot of Cluny, Peter the Venerable

Cnut, king 46
  lawcode of 1, 46, 48
coinage:
  Chartrain 104
  English 14, 47, 79, 104, 112, 188
  Ile-de-France 104
  Manceau 103–4
  Norman 103–4
  see also moneyers
Colchester 250
Conan son of Alan Fergant 193, 228
Conan son of Pilatus 29–31, 314–15
Conches 37, 218
constables, royal, *see* Henry de Pomeroy, Miles of Gloucester, Walter of Gloucester
Constance, daughter of Louis VI 87
Constantinople 292
Constitution of the King's Household 12, 111, 286
Conversano, count of, *see* Geoffrey count of Conversano
coronation 256
  king's 44
  queen's 56
Cornwall 132
Cotentin 28, 33, 36, 52, 82, 87, 106, 164, 184, 233, 248, 298
  count of, *see under* Henry I
Couësnon, river 234
councils:
  ducal: Falaise (1107) 98; Lisieux (1106, 1107) 98, 150; Rouen (1107) 98; (1118) 144
  ecclesiastical: English: London (1102) 72, 87, 117, 265; London (1107) 108, 162; (1108) 109; (1136) 115, 282; Norman: of Lisieux (1118) 98, 150; Rouen (1128) 205
  legatine: Châlons-sur-Marne (1115) 144, 277; London (1127) 199; Rouen (1128) 205; Winchester (1141) 194
  papal: Clermont (1095) 35, 156; Rheims (1119) 154, 156, 158, 163, 267, 275, 278
  royal: Northampton (1131) 212, 312; Nottingham (1109) 121; Windsor (1123) 130
Courcy:
  castle garrison 148
  family 62
  see also William de Courcy
court, royal 19
  culture of 1, 19, 298
  reform of 110
Coutances 91, 270
Coventry 67
Creully 82
Crispin, *see* Gilbert Crispin, Miles Crispin, William Crispin

Croix-Saint-Leufroy, La 183
Crouch, D. 16, 17
crown 224
crown-wearings 169, 257, 289, 299
Cumbria 129, 227, 248, 252
Cuno, cardinal archbishop of Palestrina, papal legate 135, 144, 155, 161–2, 163, 277
'Customs and Rights of the Dukes of Normandy' 103, 104
Cuthbert, St 278

Dagobert, king of the Franks 105
Dammartin 123, 124, 229
Dangu, castle 151
David I, king of Scots, earl of Huntingdon 174, 177, 193, 195, 208, 227, 257, 292
  favours Anacletus 208
  marriage 128
  piety 14
  prince of Cumbria 227, 272, 297
  and Queen Matilda 140, 259
  and Scottish church 272
David 'Scotus', bishop of Bangor 173, 272, 297
David, Charles Wendell 76
Desiderius Hacket (Erembald family) 196
Devizes, castle 192, 270, 305
Devon 183
Dialogue of the Exchequer 111, 113
Dieppe 105, 211, 240, 298
Dijon, abbot of Saint-Bénigne at 36
documents issued in Henry I's name 9
Dolfin of Carlisle 34
Domesday Book 12, 165, 244, 301
  Inquest 23, 290
Domfront 27, 32, 33, 63, 64, 80, 82, 84, 106, 183, 218, 222, 243, 304
  strategic location of 32
Domnall Bán, king of Scots 35, 36, 128
Dompierre 124, 281
Dorset 97, 182
Douvres family, *see* Richard bishop of Bayeux, Samson bishop of Worcester, Thomas archbishop of York
Dover 51, 52, 211, 213, 218, 298, 299
  St Martin's church at 212
Drayton 245
Driffield 116
Drogo de Mouchy-le-Châtel 141, 229
Dudo of St Quentin 260
Duncan king of Scots 34, 35
Dunois 80
Dunstable 177, 212, 302
  priory 279, 302
Dunstan archbishop of Canterbury 273

Durham 34, 176
  bishopric of 231, 267, 268
  bishops of, *see* Geoffrey Rufus, Ranulf Flambard
  castle 270
  cathedral priory 11, 278
  claim to Tynemouth priory 176
  diocese of 317; temporalities of 317
  historical writing: *History of the Kings* 7
  see also Symeon of Durham
Dyfed 71

Eadmer 6, 51, 52, 55, 57, 58, 64, 66, 86, 88, 131, 134, 135, 169, 176, 274
  Life of Anselm 39
  refuses homage to Alexander 176
Ealdwulf, abbot of Muchelney 131
Eastling 303
Echauffour 149
Ede, daughter of Forne 27, 308
Edgar king of England 189
Edgar king of Scots 36, 53, 54, 129, 225, 294
Edgar Aetheling 36, 55, 92–3, 216
  captured at Tinchebray 93
  on crusade 93
Edith queen of England, tomb 140, 257
Edith de Warenne 141
Edith, mother of the countess of Perche 27, 308
Edith, wife of Henry I, *see* Matilda II queen of England
Edmund Ironside, king of England 140, 208
Edmund, St 258, 311, 312
Edmund, son of Malcolm III, king of Scots 53
Edward I king of England 7
Edward the Confessor, king of England 47, 69, 116, 136, 193, 194, 218, 224
  miracles attributed to 258
  prophecy of the green tree 75, 317
  tomb 140, 257
  see also law, law of King Edward
Edward, son of Malcolm III, king of Scots 53, 54
Egbert king of Wessex 193
Eleanor (of Aquitaine), queen of England 298
Ellesmere 133
Ely:
  abbey of 115
  abbot of, *see* Richard abbot of Ely
  bishops of, *see* Hervey, Nigel
  diocese of 254, 265
Emendreville 221
emperor:
  Byzantine 292, 295
  German, *see* Henry IV, Henry V
Engenulf de L'Aigle 143

English 83, 131, 146
Enguerran de Lacy 84
Enguerrand of Trie 145
Epernon 200
Epte, river 24, 120, 138, 230
Erembald family 196, 245, 246
  see also Bertulf, Burchard, Desiderius Hacket
Eremburge countess of Anjou 122, 228
Ernulf bishop of Rochester 269
Escures *see* Ralph d'Escures, Seffrid d'Escures
Etrepagny 151
Eu 35, 142, 157, 229
  count of, *see* Henry count of Eu
  county of 31
Eudo the Steward 49, 62
Eure, river 180, 230
Eustace III count of Boulogne 52, 61, 65, 121, 181
Eustace FitzJohn 133, 176, 244, 317
Eustace of Breteuil 73, 74, 147, 149, 150, 152, 153, 154, 157, 233, 293
Evrécin 24
Evreux 144, 150, 157, 252
  archdeacon of, *see* William archdeacon of Evreux
  bishops of 270; *see also* Audoin, Gilbert
  castle 144, 150, 153, 183, 185, 234
  count of, *see* Amaury de Montfort
  county of 148, 157, 180
  diocese of 156
exchequer:
  English 15, 237; barons of 112
  Norman 102–3, 236, 238
Exeter 301
Exmes 75, 125, 148, 183, 218, 221
  vicomté 125
  see also Gilbert of Exmes
Eye, honour of 108

Falaise 84, 88, 89, 98, 106, 125, 148, 183, 220, 222, 243, 252
  castle 96, 304
  vicomté 99, 125
Fareham 303
Faritius abbot of Abingdon 7, 67, 130, 239, 262
Fécamp, abbey of 31, 256, 260
  abbot of 101, 106
  priest from 93
  see also relics, relic of the Holy Blood
Fergus lord of Galloway 177, 227, 273
Ferrières-sur-Risle 90
  see also William de Ferrers
Ferté-en-Bray, La 143
Ferté-Fresnel, La 147, 149
Finchampstead 38

378 Index

Flanders 135, 146, 196–200, 204, 226, 245, 246, 293
  counts, see Baldwin V, Baldwin VII, Charles count of Flanders, Robert count of Flanders, Thierry of Alsace
Flemings 108, 226
Fontenay, see Roger son of Peter de Fontenay
Fontevraud abbey 124, 203, 209, 210, 281, 312
forests 48, 299, 308
  law of 241
  officials 199
Forne son of Sigulf 27, 308
Fourches 70
France 87, 195, 200, 225, 246, 258
Freeman, E. A. 16, 317
Frenouse 281
Frost, Amanda Clark 15
Fulk IV 'le Rechin', count of Anjou 37, 43
Fulk V count of Anjou 122, 124, 126, 127, 139, 142, 145, 149, 162, 163, 180, 188, 192, 198, 200, 201, 203, 228, 278

Gacé 150
Gael 73
Gaimar, see Geoffrey Gaimar
Galbert of Bruges 204
  Murder of Charles the Good 8
Galbraith, V. H. 113
Galloway 227
  see also Fergus of Galloway
Gap 161
Garlande family 245
  see also Anselm de Garlande, Gilbert de Garlande, Stephen de Garlande, William de Garlande
Gasny 138, 139
Gavray 183
Gazeau, V. 17
Geddington 302
geld 311
Genoa 209
Geoffrey abbot of Vendôme 293
Geoffrey bishop of Hereford 133
Geoffrey Bucherell 250
Geoffrey count of Anjou 198, 205, 219, 320
  besieges Roscelin 218
  knighting 201–2, 290, 295
  marriage 200, 201, 203, 228, 240, 252, 276; marriage breakdown 211, 312
  quarrels with Henry 217
Geoffrey count of Conversano 38
Geoffrey son of Geoffrey count of Anjou 217, 312
Geoffrey de Clinton 182, 207–8, 210, 212, 242, 243, 244, 245, 246, 291, 305

Geoffrey de l'Aigle 143
Geoffrey 'de Sublis' 102, 229
Geoffrey de Tourville 186–7, 315
Geoffrey Gaimar 7, 284
Geoffrey of Gorron, abbot of St Albans 229
Geoffrey of Monmouth 7
  History of the Kings of Britain 7
Geoffrey of Vigeois 8, 216
Geoffrey Ridel 116, 167, 245
Geoffrey Rufus, bishop of Durham, chancellor 179, 212, 214
Geoffrey 'the Bearded', count of Anjou 43
Geoffrey Martel, count of Anjou 83
Geoffrey the Breton, archbishop of Rouen 123, 145, 156, 190, 263, 269
Ger 78
Gerard, archbishop of York, chancellor, bishop of Hereford 43, 58, 62, 67, 68, 73, 110, 262, 263, 271
Gerard de Gournay 141
Gerard de Saint-Hilaire 70
Gerberoy 119
Germany 121, 172, 309
Gervase of Canterbury 75
Gesta Stephani 243
Ghent 198, 199, 200
Giffard family see Walter Giffard, William Giffard
Gilbert Becket 251
Gilbert bishop of Evreux 35
Gilbert Crispin 154, 230
Gilbert de l'Aigle 30, 142
  son of 166
Gilbert de Garlande 200
Gilbert FitzRichard 40, 50, 62, 132, 226
Gilbert Maminot, bishop of Lisieux 26, 132
Gilbert of Exmes 150, 167
Gilbert the Universal, bishop of London 264–5
Giroie 105
  see also Robert Giroie
Gisors 126, 134, 158, 163, 183, 196, 252
  castle 37, 40, 119, 120, 127, 184, 234, 304
Gisulf the Scribe 167
Glamorgan 174, 235
Glasgow, bishop of, see John bishop of Glasgow, Michael bishop of Glasgow
Glastonbury 263
  abbot of see Henry of Blois, Seffrid
Glos 147, 154
Gloucester 299
  abbey 11, 38, 216
  abbot see Serlo
  castle 244
  constables, see Miles of Gloucester, Roger of Gloucester, Walter of Gloucester

council at 178
court at 34
crown-wearings at 289
earldom of 174, 235
Gloucestershire, sheriff of 84, 175
Glympton 243
Godfrey abbot of Winchcombe 310
Godfrey of Louvain, duke of Lorraine 168, 197–8, 203
Godfrey of Serans 145
Godstow 302
Goel, *see* Ascelin Goel
Gontier d'Aunay 82, 83, 84
Gorron 229
  lords of 229
Gouffern, forest of 75
Gournay 29, 141, 229
Gower 108
Grandmesnil
  family, *see* Ivo de Grandmesnil, Robert de Grandmesnil
  lands 68
Great Weldon 245
Gregorio Papareschi, *see* Innocent II, pope
Gregory I, pope 160
Gregory VII, pope 90, 255, 275, 276
Gregory VIII, antipope 144
Grimbald, Henry's physician 310
Gruffud ap Cynan 132, 172, 174, 226
Guibert of Nogent 259
Guillegrip 242
Gundrada de Gournay 141
Gundulf bishop of Rochester 75
Guy de Laval 228
Guy of Clermont 153
Guy of La Roche Guyon 37
Guy of Rochefort 37, 123
Gwynedd 132, 226

'H', conspirator 143
Hadrian's Wall 177, 226
Haimo of Falaise 242
Haimo the Steward 50, 62
Hampshire 48, 53, 136
  forests of 299
  sheriff of 116
Hanborough 171
Harold Godwinson, king of England 69, 218, 296
Harthacnut king of England 136
Harting 202
Haschier 32
Hasculf of Saint-James 33
Haskins, C. H. 102, 236
Hastings 63, 211
  battle of 94, 123, 301, 314
Haughley 108
Hawise countess of Aumale 157
Hawise Marmion 97
Haye-du-Puits, La *see* Robert de la Haye
Helias, lord of La Flèche, count of Maine 37, 83, 84, 90, 92, 99, 122, 228
Helias of Saint-Saëns 121, 122, 134, 158, 159, 188, 195–6, 204
Helias son of Fulk V of Anjou 201, 203
Henry count of Eu 63, 80, 141, 157
Henry IV, emperor 90, 255
Henry V, emperor 118, 154, 188, 190, 288, 320
Henry I, king of England, duke of Normandy:
character and personal traits:
  acquisitiveness 4, 307–16; Anglophilia (supposed) 16, 317; consistency to friends and enemies 3, 313; courage 310; curiosity 313; eating habits 292; employs spies 68, 232, 313; energy 309; favourite oath 174, 307; fear of assassination 310; general comments about 1, 2, 307; generosity to friends 3, 313; grief at wreck of White Ship 6, 167; health 1, 309; love of hunting 1, 287, 299, 307; piety 14, *see also* religious patronage; preferred residences 299; severity and alleged cruelty 3, 13, 15, 114, 284, 314; sexual appetites 3, 4, 308; snores 5
life:
  birth 20; childhood and education 21, 22; knighted 23; his father's bequest 25; as count of the Cotentin 28, 245; dealings with his brothers 29, 30; killing of Conan 30; besieged at Mont-Saint-Michel 31, 310; in exile 32; crosses to England (1094) 35; remains with Rufus 35, 36–7; at time of Rufus' death 39–41; accession 42; coronation 44; issues coronation charter (Charter of Liberties) 42, 45–9, 116, 254; and Anselm's return 51; marriage 53, 317; brother's challenge for the throne (1101) 60; moves against his opponents (1102) 68–72; meets his brother (1103) 76; in Normandy (1104) 80; (1105) 82–6; (1106) 87–9; victory at Tinchebray 89–95; and governance of Normandy; and governance of England 107; and Louis VI (1108–9) 118; and security of Normandy (1110–13) 121; visits Saint-Evroult (1113) 3, 126, 313; and English affairs 128; Welsh expedition (1114) 132; and his heir 134; campaigns in Normandy (1116–18) 138–47; defeat at Alençon 146;

Henry I, king of England (*cont.*)
    and Juliana 147; victory at Brémule 151; meets Calixtus II 158; peacemaking 162; wreck of the White Ship 164–7, 168; remarries 168; expedition to Wales (1121) 173–4; revolt of 1123–4 179; orders punishment of moneyers 188; plans for succession 190; Flemish succession 196; knights Geoffrey 198–201; meets Innocent II 209; escapes shipwreck 213, 311; illness 213; and his grandsons 217; quarrels with Geoffrey and Matilda 217; final illness and death 1, 219
    personal relationships:
    Adeliza 309; Anselm 120; children 27, 309; mistresses 27; Matilda 54, 58, 309; parents 23, 25; siblings 27, 28, 41, 216; Thurstan 131
    other topics:
    achievements 316; Channel crossings 298; and the church, *see* chapter 12 *passim*; claim to throne 43; governance 235; itinerary 10, 286; justice 1, 238; and London 249; and magnates 11, 14, 231, 313; new men of 14, 242; nicknames: 'Beauclerc' 23; 'Godric' 61; 'Stag's foot' 307; patronage: architectural 2, 304, 306; political 14, 16, 49–50, 107, 128, 173; religious 13, 170, 201, 209, 311; reform of court 110, 286; style of ruling 247, 319
Henry II, king of England 4, 5, 15, 120, 213, 217, 218, 286, 291, 293, 298, 312, 320
Henry I, king of France 21, 312
Henry de Beaumont, earl of Warwick 43, 61, 108, 313
Henry de Pomeroy 103, 185
Henry de Port 42
Henry of Blois, bishop of Winchester, abbot of Glastonbury 206, 211, 264, 278, 280, 314
    architectural patronage 305
    as a monk at Cluny 194
Henry of Huntingdon:
    History of the English 4–5, 6, 121, 151, 152, 178, 192, 194, 204, 207, 217, 242, 285, 305
    on Henry I 4, 18, 213, 275, 307, 310, 312, 315; his death 6, 219, 221, 222
    on Robert Bloet, bishop of Lincoln (q.v.) 115, 312
Henry abbot of Saint-Jean d'Angély 182, 211, 212, 266, 278
Herbert bishop of Thetford 67, 68
Hereford 174
Herefordshire 35, 133, 171
Herluin 25
Hermann of Tournai 55, 56, 135

Hertfordshire 116
Hervey the Breton, bishop of Bangor, Norwich 101, 173
Hexham priory 131
Hildebert of Lavardin, bishop of Le Mans, archbishop of Tours 170, 198, 206, 208
Holderness 62, 72
Hollister, C. Warren 11, 15, 18, 144
Holy Trinity, Aldgate *see under* London
Honorius II, pope 275
Horsted 210
hospitals, *see* Chartres, Le Grand-Beaulieu, London, St Giles Holborn, Rouen, Mont-aux-Malades
Houlme 35
Hugh abbot of Cluny 38
Hugh archbishop of Lyon 74, 86
Hugh Bigod 210
Hugh de Beauchamp 62
Hugh de Gournay 141, 142, 143, 157, 162, 229
Hugh de Lacy 133, 174
Hugh de Laval 228
Hugh de Montfort 102, 180, 183–4, 186, 192, 313
Hugh de Montpinçon 70
Hugh de Moulins 167
Hugh de Nonant 96
Hugh du Plessis 187
Hugh du Puiset 123, 124
Hugh earl of Chester, *vicomte* of Avranches 28, 31, 33, 49, 61
Hugh earl of Shrewsbury 69
Hugh FitzGervase of Châteauneuf-en-Thymerais 143, 180, 186, 192, 206
Hugh Maminot 62
Hugh of Amiens, archbishop of Rouen, previously prior of Saint-Martial, Limoges, Lewes, and abbot of Reading 171, 209, 210, 211, 219, 221, 261, 263, 267, 277, 278, 321
Hugh of Buckland 242
Hugh of Crécy 123
Hugh of Fleury 90, 123, 257
Hugh of Payens, master of the Temple 201, 278
Hugh Talbot 142
Hugh the Chanter, precentor of York 6, 110, 120, 131, 159, 161, 162, 179, 193, 263, 271, 276
Hunter, Joseph 12
Huntingdon 115
Huntingdonshire 168, 308
Hyde abbey, chronicle attributed to 7, 63, 134, 151, 152, 163

Icknield Way 177, 302
Ile-de-France 80, 104, 124, 126
Ilgyrus 87
Illiers-l'Evêque 124

Innocent II, pope 208, 209, 267, 276, 312
Investiture Dispute (Contest) 154
investitures 52–3, 66, 67, 81, 85, 86, 88, 108, 266, 313
Iowerth 71
Ireland 69, 227, 272
Irish 173
Irish Sea 69, 227
Isabel daughter of Robert of Meulan 27, 179, 308, 309
Isabelle of Douvres 264
Italy 118, 208, 209
Iton, river 230
Ivo bishop of Chartres 135
Ivo de Grandmesnil 68
  his sons 167, 288
Ivry 73, 147, 153, 180, 183

Jacqueline de Mailly 202
Jeanne, daughter of Rainer count of Montferrat 196
Jerusalem 38, 149, 158, 181, 200, 201, 203, 204, 261, 312
Jews:
  London 242, 250
  Rouen 210
John king of England 45
John, bishop of Lisieux, archdeacon of Sées 102, 103, 107, 117, 190, 194, 237, 267, 269, 270
John bishop of Glasgow 175–6, 193, 272
John bishop of Sées 190, 203, 210, 239, 270, 317
John de Saint-Jean 142
John of Crema, papal legate 187, 267, 268, 277
John nephew of Waleran 133, 244
John of Hexham 194
John of Marmoutier 8
  Deeds of the Counts of Anjou 8, 201
  History of Duke Geoffrey 8
John of Salisbury 39, 296, 297
John of Worcester 194, 215, 241
  see also Worcester, chronicle composed at
John son of Odo, bishop of Bayeux 277
Juhel de Mayenne 295
Juliana daughter of Henry I 74, 147–8, 157, 209, 281, 293, 310
Jumièges:
  abbey of 107, 267
  chronicler, *see* William of Jumièges
  prior, *see* Roger abbot of Mont-Saint-Michel
justice:
  ducal 12, 19
  royal 12, 14, 15, 19, 114
justices:
  ducal 102, 236, 237
  royal 15, 115, 237, 243

Kapelle, W. E. 129
Keats-Rohan, K. S. B. 16, 246
Kendal 108
Kenilworth, castle 305
Kent 50, 62, 175, 235, 280
Kidwelly 108
Kingsbury 302
King's Cliffe 302
Kingsthorpe 302
Kirklinton 177, 226

Lacy family, *see* Enguerran de Lacy, Hugh de Lacy, Robert de Lacy, Sibyl de Lacy
  estates in Herefordshire 133, 174
Lambeth 56, 134
Lancashire 128
Lancellin de Bulles 123
Lanfranc archbishop of Canterbury 22, 23, 25, 56, 68, 255, 269, 273, 289
Laon 279
  bishop of 153
  cathedral school 178
Laval, *see* Guy de Laval, Hugh de Laval
law 1
  English 12, 14, 19
  Norman 12, 19
legal literature 9, 13; *Laws of Henry I* 13, 115; laws of King Edward 13, 16, 48, 116; Ordinance on Shire and Hundred Courts 116; *Quadripartitus* 13, 116
legates, papal, *see* St Anselm, Anselm of St Saba, Cuno, John of Crema, Matthew of Albano, Peter of Pierleoni, William of Corbeil
Leicester 250
  earls *see* Robert count of Meulan, Robert earl of Leicester
Leicestershire 245
Leinster, king of 69
  see also Muirchertach Uí Briain
Lemoine-Descourtieux, Astrid 106
Leominster 171
Le Patourel, John 18, 298, 318
Lewes priory 171, 263
Leyser, Karl 6
Liddel 227
Liège 121
Lille 198, 199, 200
Limoges, priory of Saint-Martial 263
Lincoln 214, 227
  bishops of, *see* Alexander bishop of Lincoln, Robert Bloet
  castle 214
  diocese 265
  farm of 210, 251
Lincolnshire 128, 214, 269

Lire 147, 154
Lisieux 98, 222
  bishop of 101, 210, 270
  council of (1118) 150
  region (Lieuvin) 187
Livry 123, 200
Llandaff, bishop of, *see* Urban bishop of Llandaff
Llanthony, prior of 264
London 35, 43, 44, 61, 67, 120, 193, 212, 249, 251, 290, 300–1
  bishops of, *see* Gilbert the Universal, Maurice bishop of London, Richard of Beaumais
  castles: Baynard's 122, 301; Mountfichet's 301; the Tower 51, 60, 216, 301
  cathedral, St Paul's 301; cathedral chapter 131, 242, 263
  chamberlain, king's 286
  citizens of 218
  councils at (1102) 265; (1107) 162; (1127), (1136) 195, 199, 242, 264, 282
  farm of 210
  hospital of St Giles, Holborn 280
  priory of Holy Trinity Aldgate 58, 140, 279, 280, 295, 301, 304; chronicle of 7
  sheriffs of 140, 249, 251
  wharves (Dowgate and Queenhithe) 286
Longueville 35, 49
Lothar III, emperor 209
Lothian 34, 226, 231
Louis VI, king of France 39, 40, 59, 87, 118, 119, 120, 122, 125, 126, 127, 129, 134, 135, 136, 138–9, 143, 145, 149, 151, 153, 156, 158, 161–3, 192, 195, 206, 208, 228, 245, 258, 271, 275, 293, 295, 316
  life:
  defeat at Brémule 4, 151–2; attacks Chartres 275; makes peace 162; takes homage from Henry's son William 138, 163; supports rebels (1123–4) 181, 184; and imperial army 188; grants Vexin to William Clito 196; and Flemish succession 8, 197, 198, 204; and the Garlande family 200, 207; death of his son 320; death and burial 221, 223; compared with Henry I 230
Louise, Gerard 105
Luc de la Barre 170, 186, 315
Ludlow 174
Lyon 44, 74, 85
  archbishop of, *see* Hugh archbishop of Lyon
Lyons, forest of 219, 287, 309
Lyons-la-Forêt 1, 219, 221, 229, 259, 290

Madog, son of Rhirid ap Bleddyn 132
Magnus Barelegs 69, 227

Maine 29, 31, 32, 34, 37, 61, 65, 80, 82, 83, 84, 92, 104, 122, 126, 142, 146, 154, 181, 191, 228, 252
  count of, *see* Helias, lord of La Flèche
Maillefer, Jean-Marie 105
Malarteis 242
  see also Robert Malarteis
Malcolm III, king of Scots 16, 34, 53–4, 55, 92, 93, 128, 225, 317
Malet, *see* Robert, William
Malling, nunnery 280
Malmesbury abbey 57, 195, 212, 265, 282
Maminot, *see* Hugh Maminot
Man, Isle of 227, 273
Manasser Arsic 62
Mandeville, *see* Roger de Mandeville, William de Mandeville
Mans, Le 29, 37, 201, 202, 203, 213
  bishop of 203; *see also* Hildebert of Lavardin
  bishopric of 124
  cathedral of Saint-Julian 213
  dean 263; *see also* Geoffrey the Breton, archbishop of Rouen
Mantes 24, 196
Marbod bishop of Rennes 57
Marche, La 72
Marcigny 161, 171, 278, 280
Maredudd ap Bleddyn 132
Margaret, St, queen of Scots 53, 54, 55, 93, 128, 194, 259
Margaret of Maine 29
Marle 197
Marmion, *see* Hawise Marmion, Robert Marmion, Roger Marmion
Marmoutier 239–40, 278
Martin, scribe of the chapel 103
Mary countess of Boulogne 54, 65
Mathon 103, 104
Matilda, empress 55, 172, 175, 192, 195, 197, 207, 211, 217, 249, 288, 293, 309
  life:
  birth 67; betrothal and marriage 113, 120, 121, 190, 309; as Henry's successor 191, 193–5, 320; betrothal and second marriage 198, 199, 200, 203, 228, 240, 252, 276, 281; marriage breakdown 206, 209; reconciliation 212, 312; children 211, 213; quarrels with her father 217; actions after his death 221
Matilda I, queen of England 20, 22, 23, 107, 197, 273
Matilda II (Edith), queen of England 14, 53, 54, 55, 64, 75, 88, 170, 194, 259, 291, 300, 309
  character and personality 57–8
  appearance 57; impact of, on London 300; love of music 297; piety 14, 259;

patronage: architectural 304; literary: 2, 169, 297; religious 7, 57, 279, 280, 295
life:
lineage 53; birth and upbringing 53–4; meeting with her father 54; marriage 226; coronation 56; as regent 79, 136; intercedes for clergy 275; visits Normandy 58, 98; death 138, 139, 168; funeral 140, 290; burial 257; tomb 140, 257–8; assessment of 139–40
other topics:
nicknamed 'Godiva'; veneration of 140
Matilda III, queen of England 181
Matilda daughter of Fulk of Anjou 126, 149, 181, 182, 203, 281
Matilda of Blois, countess of Chester 167, 181
Matilda countess of Perche 80, 166
Matilda de Redvers 229
Matilda de Senlis, queen of Scots 128, 129
Matilda of Wallingford 133
Matthew, D. 15
Matthew of Albano, papal legate 205, 277
Matthew Paris 9, 216
Maurice bishop of London 43
Mayenne 229
Meaux 85
Melisende queen of Jerusalem 200
Merionethshire 132
Merlin, 'Prophecies of' 112
Merton priory 103, 279
Mesnil-Verclives 151
Metz 188
Meulan 74
counts of, *see* Robert count of Meulan, Waleran count of Meulan
county of 43, 97, 141
Meuse, river 154
Michael, St 261, 272
Michael bishop of Glasgow 272
Miles Crispin 23, 62
Miles of Gloucester 115, 133, 174, 176, 243, 244, 264
Miles of Montlhéry 123
monetagium 47
moneyers 188, 247, 250
Montacute priory 278
Montbray 100, 235
Montebourg abbey 269, 278
Montfort l'Amaury 124, 139
lord of, *see* Amaury de Montfort
Montfort-sur-Risle
castle 184, 185
lords of, *see* Hugh de Montfort, Robert de Montfort

Montgomery:
brothers, *see* Arnulf, Hugh earl of Shrewsbury, Robert de Bellême, Roger the Poitevin
estates 69
Montpinçon 148
see also Hugh de Monpinçon
Montreuil-au-Houlme 243, 306
Montreuil-l'Argillé 149
Mont-Saint-Michel 28, 31, 52, 89, 171, 239, 261, 265, 266, 278, 310
Morin du Pin 179, 187, 316
Mortain 142, 187
castellan families of 125
castle 78, 142
counts of, *see* Robert of Mortain, William of Mortain
county of 187, 235, 316
Mortemer 138, 211, 282
Motte-Gautier-de-Clinchamp, La 142
Moulins-la-Marche 108
Mouzon 154, 156
Mowbray, *see* Robert de Mowbray
Muchelney abbey 131
Muirchertach Uí Briain, king of Leinster 69, 294
Murcastell 132

Neaufles 92
Planches de 120
lord of, *see* William Crispin
Nest wife of Gerald of Windsor 27, 308
Neufbourg 143, 222
lord of, *see* Robert de Neufbourg
Neuf-Marché 142, 229
Newark castle 214
New Forest 21, 40, 48–53, 290, 302
new men 242
Newnham on Severn 58
Nigel d'Aubigny 100, 108, 141, 175, 176, 184, 235, 244, 313, 317
Nigel bishop of Ely 207, 212, 214
Nigel of Saint-Sauveur 28
Nonancourt 106, 124, 183, 234, 252, 270
Norbert, St 279
Norfolk 108
shrievalty of (with Suffolk) 108
Norham castle 176, 270
Northampton 87, 290, 291
castle 302
council (1131) 212, 312
earls of, *see* Simon earl of Northampton, Waltheof
Northamptonshire, forests of 299, 303
Northumberland 131, 176, 252

Northumbria 129, 176
  earl of, see Robert de Mowbray, Waltheof
Norwich 68, 304
Nostell priory 258
Notre-Dame-du-Pré priory 6, 30, 221, 278, 303, 304
Nottingham 179
  council (1109) 121
Nottinghamshire 214
Noyon, bishop of 153
Noyon-sur-Andelle (Charleval) 151, 153, 234

oathtakings 135, 193, 212, 290
Odard du Pin 186–7, 315
Odiham 136
Odilia, St 311
Odo bishop of Bayeux 24, 28, 29, 101
  his son 204, 277; see also John son of Odo
Odo Borleng 185–6, 288
Odo de Dammartin 123
d'Oilly family 301
  see also Robert d'Oilly
Oise region 229; river 24
Olaf son of the king of Man 288
Orbec 149
Orderic Vitalis 3–4, 6, 21, 22, 25, 30, 32, 35, 38, 42, 43, 49, 60, 64, 65, 71, 80, 81, 82, 87, 88, 95, 97, 98, 100, 101, 115, 126, 127, 138, 139, 142, 147, 149, 152, 158, 162, 179, 180, 184, 185, 187, 188, 194, 201, 222, 228, 232, 234, 237, 254, 259, 265, 277, 285, 288, 314, 321
  comments on Henry I:
  burning of Evreux 150; death 220; love of peace 240; new men 236, 242, 243, 305; personality 4, 6, 247, 309, 313; 148, 309; protection of hunting 308; punishment of his granddaughters 148, 315; and revolt of 1124 179, 180, 184, 185, 186, 187, 315; rule in Normandy 261; self-defence 158
  comments on other key events and people:
  death of Conan 30, 314; Duke Robert 4, 29, 79, 162; Robert de Bellême 4, 70, 125; Treaty of Alton 65; White Ship 164
  life and work 3, 40
  contribution to *The Deeds of the Dukes of the Normans* 3 (see also under William of Jumièges); *The Ecclesiastical History* 3; ordained 101; view of Norman history 3–4
Orkney 227, 273
Orléans 124
  bishop of 188
Osbert the priest, sheriff 242
Osmund bishop of Salisbury 22
Osney abbey 302
Oswald, St 258

Othuer FitzCount 167
Otmund of Chaumont 152, 153
Otmund of Trie 138, 152
Ouche, *pays* 187
Ouistreham 211, 298
Outi of Lincoln 287
Owain ap Cadwgan 132
Oxford 171, 213
  Beaumont Palace 213, 301
  castellan of, see Robert d'Oilly
  castle 301
  collegiate church of St George's 7, 302
  St Frideswide's priory 301
Oxfordshire 27
  forests 299, 308

Pacy 147, 148, 150, 154, 157, 183, 230
Pangbourne 171
Paris 32, 122, 123, 141, 153, 230, 320
  abbey of Saint-Martin des Champs 277, 278
  abbey of Saint-Victor 279
  bishop of 188
Paschal II, pope 51, 81, 87, 101, 144
Passais 32, 33, 106, 124
Payn de Clairvaux 202
Payn FitzJohn 115, 133, 174, 176, 243, 244
Payn of Montjay 123
Peace of God, see Truce of God
Pembroke 62, 69, 108
penance 14
Pennant Bachwy 132
Pennines 108
Perche
  count of, see Rotrou count of Perche
  countess of, see Matilda countess of Perche
  county of 80, 201
Peter Alfonsi 296
Peterborough abbey 131, 208, 212, 278
  chronicle of 7
Peter, cardinal bishop of Porto 208
Peter de Valognes 116
Peter Pierleoni, cardinal priest of Santa Maria Trastavere 173, 208, 277
  see also Anacletus II, antipope
Peter's Pence 67, 155, 182, 266, 277
Peter the Venerable, abbot of Cluny 208, 209, 210, 219–20, 261, 321
Pevensey 63, 93
Peverel, see William Peverel (of Dover); William Peverel (of Nottingham)
Philip I king of France 24, 35, 37, 40, 62, 83, 93, 119, 136
  alleged curative powers of 259
  at Gerberoy 119
  death 118

Philip II Augustus king of France 320
Philip de Briouze 121, 122
Philip de Thaon 169, 294, 297
Philip of Loos 197
Philippa of Perche 201
Philip son of King Louis 163
physicians, royal, *see* Faritius, Grimbald, Peter Alfonsi
pipe roll (1130) 1, 9, 12, 13, 238, 248
Plessis, Le 141
Plympton priory 183
Poitiers, diocese of 124
Poitou 72, 212
  duke of 122
Poix, priory of Saint-Denis 39
Pont-Audemer 184, 185, 187, 222, 315
Pont-Authou 185
Pontefract 86, 229
Pont-Erchenfray 147, 148, 149, 187
  see also Ralph the Red
Ponthieu 76, 126, 142, 229
Pontigny 211, 281
Pontoise 37, 39, 196
Pontorson 234
Pont-Saint-Pierre 145, 147, 150, 154
Poole, A. L. 314
Port family, *see* Henry de Port
Portsmouth 63, 135, 182, 298, 303
Power, Daniel 17, 106
Powys 71, 132, 174
Prémontré 279
primacies 225
  see also Canterbury, York
Provence 161

Rabel de Tancarville 210
Radegund, St
  Life 259
Radnor 122
Rainald of Arganchy 102
Rainer of Bath 242
Ralph Basset 115, 116, 183, 242, 243, 244, 245, 314
Ralph count of Vermandois 200
Ralph de Belfou 108
Ralph d'Escures, archbishop of Canterbury, abbot of Sées, bishop of Rochester 76, 97, 130, 134, 135, 144, 155, 160, 161, 162, 164, 168, 169, 175, 178, 262, 271, 292
Ralph de Fougères 124
Ralph de Gael 148, 150, 153, 154
Ralph de Tosny 31, 73, 74, 90, 153, 154, 233
Ralph Harenc 147
Ralph of Beaugency 124
Ralph the Red of Pont-Erchenfray 148, 149, 150, 153, 154, 167, 245

Ramsey abbey 129, 131
Ranulf I Meschin, earl of Chester, *vicomte* of Bayeux, lord of Carlisle 90, 91, 116, 173, 177, 180, 182, 185, 214, 227
Ranulf II earl of Chester 214
Ranulf Flambard, bishop of Durham 45, 50, 60, 63, 68, 101, 175, 176, 182, 216, 230, 237, 269–70, 275
Ranulf the chancellor 177, 178
Raymond son of the count of Poitou 288
Reading 115, 250
  abbey 3, 170–2, 220, 222, 223, 237, 259, 263, 278, 290, 304, 311
  relics 14
Redvers, *see* Baldwin de Redvers, Matilda de Redvers, Richard de Redvers
Reginald de Bailleul 148
Reginald de Warenne 30, 76, 89, 91
Reginald of Grancey 73
relics 172
  hand of St James 172, 190
  Holy Blood 260
  of St Romanus 170
Rennes:
  bishop of, *see* Marbod
  bishopric 124
revenue:
  ducal 103–4, 105, 112, 238
  royal 12, 112, 238
Rheims 188
  papal council at 154–7, 158, 163, 267, 275, 276, 278
Rhirid ap Bleddyn 132
Rhos 226
Richard abbot of Ely 50, 265
Richard I duke of Normandy 260, 273
Richard II duke of Normandy 260, 273
Richard I king of England 145
Richard II king of England 223
Richard Basset 305–6
Richard son of Henry I (illegitimate) 25, 145, 146, 148, 150, 151, 157, 309
  betrothal 154
  death in White Ship 165, 235
Richard, son of Henry I (legitimate) 75
Richard, son of William the Conqueror 20, 21, 28
Richard de Lucy 229
Richard de Redvers 28, 33, 61, 313, 314
Richard earl of Chester 80, 132, 167, 172, 275
Richard FitzBaldwin 50
Richard of Beaumais, bishop of London 174, 179, 242, 275
Richard of Douvres, bishop of Bayeux 101, 110, 264, 270

Richard of La Ferté-Fresnel 149
Richard of Winchester 242
Richard son of Robert of Gloucester 264
Richardson, H. G. 94
Richer de L'Aigle 142, 149, 150, 154
Richer de Boivill 226
Richmond, lord of, *see* Alan I
Ridel see Geoffrey Ridel
Rievaulx 211, 282
Ripon 116
Risle, river 180, 185
Robert I duke of Normandy 134
Robert II (Curthose) duke of Normandy 21, 22, 27, 34, 40, 42, 53, 60, 70, 81, 82, 88, 96, 98, 99, 100, 101, 119, 125, 158, 159, 162, 316, 320
   as duke (to 1095) 28, 30, 31, 34, 37, 50
   cause 96, 156, 158, 182, 233
   claim to Normandy 24
   claim to throne 42–3, 191
   death and burial 215–16, 310, 320
   expedition to England (1101) 63–6; return visit (1103) 75, 76, 293
   godfather of Edith (Matilda) 53
   imprisonment 8, 192, 194, 203, 216, 313; meets Henry (1104) 80–1; (1105) 85; (1106) 87, 88; on crusade 35–6, 260, 310; return 38, 52
   quarrels with father 21, 24, 119
   sexuality 308
   situation in Normandy 73, 78, 103
   and Tinchebray 89–94, 102
Robert abbot of Bury St Edmunds 49, 265
Robert Achard 23
   see also Achard
Robert bishop of Chester 62, 67, 68, 207
Robert bishop of St Andrews 272
Robert Bloet, bishop of Lincoln, chancellor 62, 79, 130, 242, 243, 262, 269
   assessment of 178
   death 177–8
   on Henry I 115, 312
Robert chaplain of the bishop of Lisieux 103
Robert I count of Flanders 197
Robert II count of Flanders 50, 61, 62, 74, 93, 120, 121, 124, 197
Robert count of Meulan 27, 59, 61, 62, 68, 97
   after 1087 37, 43
   assessment of 141, 187
   attacks Paris 122–3
   death 140
   fights at Hastings 123, 314
   granted earldom of Leicester 108
   and Henry I 61, 73, 80, 81, 83, 86, 134, 187, 292, 293, 308, 313, 314
   lands ravaged 119
   mealtimes 292
   and Tinchebray 89, 91
   see also Beaumont twins, Isabel daughter of Robert de Meulan, Robert earl of Leicester, Waleran count of Meulan
Robert count of Mortain 24, 90
Robert d'Arches 84
Robert de Beauchamp 122
Robert de Bellême 28, 29, 32, 37, 50; and Henry I 58, 62, 63, 64, 66, 68–72, 76, 80, 86, 89, 90, 96, 97, 99, 102, 107, 126, 130, 142, 145, 159, 174, 205, 217, 227, 231, 232, 233, 252, 268, 313, 317; allies with Duke Robert 78, 80
   arrested and imprisoned 125, 127, 156, 293, 317
   attacks Henry's men 81
   death 217
   destroys church 83
   dispute with Rotrou 80
   in Normandy 75
   loyal to Duke Robert 88
   opposed to Henry 124
   reconciled with Henry 99, 313
   and Tinchebray 92, 93
   visits England 86
Robert de Bolio 202
Robert de Brus 33, 108, 177, 227
Robert de Candos 107
   castellan of Gisors 184–5
Robert II de Courcy 70, 102, 103
Robert III de Courcy 153
Robert de Grandmesnil 70, 90, 205
Robert de Lacy 229
Robert de la Haye 102, 103
Robert de Montfort 49, 70, 90, 100, 108, 180
Robert de Mowbray 34
Robert de Neufbourg 143, 157
Robert de Semblençay 202
Robert de Sigillo 209, 212
Robert de Trivers 226
Robert d'Oilly 23, 243, 300, 302, 308
Robert de Rhuddlan 69
Robert de Stuteville 89, 90, 92
Robert earl of Gloucester 108, 151, 174, 182, 184, 192, 193, 194, 195, 203, 209, 218, 220, 222, 235, 292, 298, 309
Robert earl of Leicester 140, 180, 182, 187
   see also Beaumont twins
Robert FitzBaldwin 50
Robert FitzHaimon 38, 50, 61, 62, 64, 82, 83, 84, 108, 235, 313
Robert Giroie 149, 205
Robert Goel 180
Robert I 'the pious' king of France 258
Robert Malarteis 115
Robert Malet 49, 108

Robert Marmion 97
Robert Mauduit 167
Robert of Arbrissel 281
Robert of Béthune bishop of Hereford 264
Robert of Bonnebosc 93
Robert of Bostare 242
Robert of Cricklade 294
Robert of Evreux 103
Robert of Neuville 70
Robert of Saint-Rémy 84
Robert of Torigny 7, 166, 183, 217, 222, 234
Robert Pullen 265
Roche-Mabille, La 142
Rochester
  bishops of, *see* Gundulf bishop of Rochester, Ralph d'Escures, archbishop of Canterbury
  castle 195, 270
  cathedral 291
Rockingham 302
Rodley 216
Roger abbot of Mont-Saint-Michel 266
Roger Bigod 49, 61, 108
Roger Bishop of Chester 207
Roger bishop of Coutances 166, 291
Roger bishop of Coventry and Lichfield, *see* Roger bishop of Chester
Roger I count of Sicily 191
Roger II king of Sicily 191, 208, 209, 295
Roger d'Avranches, bishop of Salisbury 14–15, 33–4, 130, 169, 177, 213
  advises queen 79
  castles 270, 305
  chancellor 50
  family 275, 282
  influence 179, 214, 236, 245, 269, 314
  king 262
  and Malmesbury abbey 195, 265
  and moneyers 189
  presides at exchequer 107, 113, 117
  and royal ceremonies 140, 169, 194, 195, 290, 292
  and royal revenue 183, 207
  and St Frideswide's Oxford 301–2
  views on the oath to Matilda 212
  viceroy 182
Roger de Mandeville 33
Roger de Nonant 62, 142
Roger de Saint-Jean 142
Roger de Tosny 218
Roger earl of Hereford 288
Roger earl of Warwick 182, 207, 245
Roger FitzRichard 40
  at Brémule 151, 152
Roger Marmion 102
Roger of Gloucester 84

Roger of Howden 217
Roger of Montgomery 148, 174, 242
Roger of Wendover 9, 216
Roger son of Corbet 70
Roger son of Peter de Fontenay 102
Roger the Poitevin 50, 59, 68, 71, 72, 86, 99, 107, 128, 230
Rollo duke of Normandy 83, 217, 260
Rome 55, 67, 81, 86, 87, 131, 144, 179, 263, 269, 271, 276, 294
Romsey 53, 57, 280, 287
Roncevalles, battle of 6
Roscelin of Beaumont-sur-Sarthe 218
Rotrou count of Perche 80, 127, 154, 220, 230, 233, 281, 289
Rouen 24, 25, 29, 32, 36, 87, 88, 96, 102, 104, 143, 157, 161, 166, 170, 186, 199, 201, 206, 210, 211, 217, 219, 221, 222, 230, 248, 251, 270, 286, 290, 292
  abbey of Saint-Ouen 139, 267
  archbishop 105, 123, 263; *see also* Geoffrey the Breton, William Bonne Ame
  archbishop's chamber 6
  castle 22, 96, 183, 251, 303, 314
  cathedral church of St Mary 259
  chapter 256, 259
  councils at (1107) 98; (1118) 144; (1128) 205
  court at 99, 135, 277, 299
  hospital of Mont-aux-Malades 279
  mint 104
  nunnery of Saint-Amand 280
  vicomte of, *see* Anselm *vicomte* of Rouen
Rougemomtier 185
Roumare
  forest of 107
  see also William of Roumare
Rowner 303
Rualon d'Avranches 33, 153

St Albans
  abbey 62, 216, 229, 278, 302
  consecration of church 136, 291
Saint-Alveus 281
St Andrews, bishops of, *see* Eadmer, Robert bishop of St Andrews
Sainte-Barbe en Auge 295
Saint-Cénéri 142
Saint-Clair-sur-Epte 138
Saint-Denis 88, 105
  abbey 188, 221, 240, 260, 295
Saint-Denis, forest of Lyons 219
St Denys, Portswood priory 279
Sainte-Barbe-en-Auge 295
St Edmunds, *see under* Bury St Edmunds

Saint-Evroult abbey 3, 29, 126, 131, 149, 176, 205, 231, 265, 266, 268, 313, 317
    monks from 100
Saint-Georges de Boscherville 100, 235
Saint-Germer-de-Fly 229
Saint-Gervais, near Rouen 24, 25
Saint-James-de-Beuvron 33
Saint-Jean d'Angély 212
Saint-Jean-le-Thomas 89
    lords of, *see* John de Saint-Jean, Roger de Saint-Jean, Thomas de Saint-Jean
Saint-Léonard de Bellême 240
Saint-Malo, bishop of 263
Saint-Omer 198, 199
    church of Saint-Bertin 204
Saint-Pierre-sur-Dives 88, 89, 91
    abbey of 268
Saint-Saëns:
    castle 122
    see also Helias of Saint-Saëns
Saint-Sauveur, lord of, *see* Nigel of Saint-Sauveur
Salisbury 52
    bishops of, *see* Osmund bishop of Salisbury, Roger d'Avranches bishop of Salisbury
    castle 270, 305
    cathedral 305
    council at 141
    oathtaking ceremonies 135, 290
Samson bishop of Worcester 101, 270
San Silvestro, cardinal priest of 212
Sap, Le 149
Sarthe, river 108
Savigny 90, 124, 125, 170, 231, 280, 317
Sayles, G. O. 94
Scotland 225, 252, 269
    church in 272
seals, Henry I's 11, 287
Secqueville 82, 102
Sées 240
    abbey of Saint-Martin 130
    abbot *see* Ralph d'Escures, subsequently bishop of Rochester and archbishop of Canterbury
    archdeacon of, *see* John, bishop of Lisieux
    bishopric of 75
    bishops of 270; and *see also* John, Serlo
    castle 142, 222
    cathedral 190, 291
    chapter 279
    diocese 231, 240, 252, 283
    monk of 131
    region 219
Seffrid (Siegfried) d'Escures abbot of Glastonbury, bishop of Chichester 264
Seine, river 88, 100, 123, 138, 145, 186, 230

Selby abbey 20
Senlis 123, 161
    see also Simon de Senlis
Serlo abbot of St Peter's Gloucester 38
Serlo bishop of Sées 35, 76, 82, 83, 97, 100, 292
Serlo the deaf 103
Severn, river 58
Sharpe, Richard 9
Sherborne
    castle 270, 305
sheriffs 10, 116, 183, 237, 238, 243
Shrewsbury 70, 71, 174
Shropshire 35, 69, 133, 174, 195, 242
Sibyl daughter of Fulk of Anjou 181, 204, 276
Sibyl daughter of Geoffrey of Conversano 38, 52
Sibyl de Lacy 133, 174
Sibyl queen of Scots 176
Simon count of the Vexin 24
Simon dean of Lincoln 285
Simon de Moulins 108, 150
Simon de Senlis, earl of Northampton 49, 129
Sleaford castle 214
Somerset 214
Song of Roland 6
Sorel 124
Southampton 46, 211, 279, 298
Southern, Sir Richard 13, 14, 15, 52, 244, 246, 314
Southwark 134
Speyer 221
Stafford castle 70
Staffordshire 69, 245
Stephen abbot of St Mary's York 116
Stephen count of Aumale 72, 80, 142, 143, 157, 158, 162–3
Stephen count of Blois and Chartres 21, 191
Stephen count of Brittany 62
Stephen de Garlande 200, 207, 246
Stephen Harding 281
Stephen king of England 15, 55, 115, 128, 138, 144, 145, 147, 181, 193, 194, 200, 204, 213
    at Henry's funeral 222, 290
    does not board White Ship 165
    marriage 181
    receives lands 128, 142, 174, 230, 235, 245, 314, 317
    and the succession 191, 195, 220, 292, 320
Stephen of Rouen 6
Stephen the Steersman 164
Stigand archbishop of Canterbury 130, 263, 273
Strathclyde 226, 231
Stubbs, W. 16
Sturminster 97, 182
Stuteville family, *see* Robert de Stuteville
Suetonius, *Lives of the Twelve Caesars* 5

Index

Suffolk 108, 268, 270
  shrievalty of (with Norfolk) 108
Suger abbot of Saint-Denis 39, 104–5, 119, 120, 123, 127, 138, 143, 152, 179, 188, 192, 197, 210, 221, 223, 240, 295
  Life of Louis VI 7–8
  views on Henry 240, 261
Sussex 70, 122, 142, 170, 202
Sutton Courtenay 67
Symeon of Durham 163, 184, 206, 207

Tancarville, lords of, *see* Rabel de Tancarville, William de Tancarville
Tarragona, archbishop of 210
Templars 201, 278, 294, 312
Teviotdale 129
Textus Roffensis 269
Thames, river 56
Theobald count of Blois and Chartres 21, 120, 123, 127, 135, 142, 144, 146, 147, 154, 156, 159, 161, 162, 167, 168, 182, 188, 191, 200, 206, 209, 210, 213, 222, 230, 280, 281, 289, 295, 320; and the succession 168, 191, 211, 213, 222
Theobald Payn, lord of Gisors 119, 180, 185, 230
Theulf bishop of Worcester 129, 264
Thierry count of Alsace 197, 199, 203, 204, 205, 206
Thiron 281
Thomas I archbishop of York 44, 271
Thomas II archbishop of York 101, 263, 270, 271, 272
Thomas Becket archbishop of Canterbury 67, 120, 251; his shrine at Canterbury 291
Thomas de Coucy 197
Thomas de Saint-Jean 89, 239
Thomas, H. M. 16–17
Thomas son of Stephen 164, 165, 166
Thorney 130, 131
Thurstan archbishop of York 131, 155, 157, 159–60, 162, 163, 179, 195, 199, 263, 270, 276, 313
  refuses to make profession to Canterbury 131, 141, 155, 160, 175, 193, 271
  and York primacy 193, 214, 272, 273
Tickhill 70
Tilleul 78, 154
Tillières 154, 183, 230
Tilshead 210, 280
Tinchebray:
  battle of 76, 91, 93, 96, 98, 100, 101, 119, 122, 141, 142, 195, 235, 251, 265, 268, 271, 313
  castle 78, 89
Tirel of Mainières 188

Tiron 170
  see also Thiron
Tomen-y-Mur 132
Tonbridge 50
Torigny 82
Tosny, *see* Ralph de Tosny
Tottenham 140
Tournai-sur-Dive 83
tournaments 289
Tours 155
  archbishop of 161; *see also* Hildebert of Lavardin
  archdiocese of 124, 240
towns 19, 249
trade 19, 248, 251
Trawsfynydd 132
treaty, Anglo-Flemish 31, 61–2, 121, 158, 181
Tréport, Le 63
Trinité, La, abbey of, *see under* Caen
Trotton 202
Troyes 107
Truce of God 106, 156, 219, 241
Turgis bishop of Avranches 239
Turgis Brundos 226
Turold bishop of Bayeux 35, 101
Tweed, river 176
Tutbury priory 171
Tynemouth priory 176

Ulger the huntsman 70
Urban bishop of Llandaff 134, 209, 272
Urban II, pope 35, 51, 53, 156, 256
Urraca queen of Castile 191
Urse d'Abetot 115
Utrecht 121

Valognes 33
  see also Peter de Valognes
Varenne, river 32
Vatteville, castle 185, 187
Vaudreuil 280
Verneuces 149
Verneuil 106, 183, 234, 252, 270
Vernon 161, 183, 230, 252, 270
Vexin 24, 32, 37, 40, 65, 138, 184, 188, 196, 197, 229
  banner 188
  castles 119
  count of, *see* Simon count of the Vexin
  French 24, 36–7, 148, 150, 151, 196
  men of 152
  Norman 37, 151, 180, 196, 230, 234
vicomtes see Argentan, Arques, Bayeux, Falaise, Rouen
Vignats 70, 90, 100

Vincent, N. 291
Vire 82, 183
Vitalis, St 90, 124–5
Voyage of St Brendan, see Brendan

Wace, canon of Bayeux, *Roman de Rou* 8, 32, 64, 82, 83, 84, 307
Waldric the king's chancellor, bishop of Laon 92
Waleran count of Meulan 97, 141, 143, 179, 183, 235, 252, 298
  conspiracy of 179, 180, 182, 183, 184, 185, 186, 187, 268, 313, 316
  imprisoned 187, 192, 206
  see also Beaumont twins
Wales 35, 69, 108, 118, 122, 132, 133, 172–5, 219, 225, 226, 227, 228, 231, 309, 310
  church in 254, 272
  Marches of 133, 176
Wallingford 23, 192
Walo of Trie 148
Walter Espec 133, 176, 244, 317
Walter Giffard 49, 151
Walter Map 286, 293, 295
  Courtiers' Trifles 9
Walter of Gloucester 108, 174
Walter Tirel 38–9, 40–1, 50
Waltham abbey 301
Waltheof, earl 74, 90, 129, 227
Wareham 125
Warenne family, *see* Reginald de Warenne, William de Warenne
Wargrave 171
Warin sheriff of Shropshire 133
Wark 176
Warren, W. L. 15
Warter 243
Wartling 243, 303
Warwick, earls of, *see* Henry de Beaumont earl of Warwick, Roger earl of Warwick
Warwickshire 182
  sheriff of 207
Watling Street 177, 302
Waverley 211
Wayland the Smith 202
Wellow by Grimsby priory 279
Welsh Chronicler, *see* Brut
Welsh rising 35, 71
Westbourne 303
Westminster 23, 113, 136, 274, 278, 286, 299, 300
  abbey 11, 43, 56, 134, 140, 172, 173, 257, 278, 300
  court at 58, 86
  crown-wearing at 173, 289, 303
  exchequer at 300

hall 2, 193, 300, 303
palace 301
White Ship 1, 6, 138, 164–7, 172, 198, 235, 284, 286, 291, 293, 298, 311
Whithorn 273
Wigan the Marshal 103, 242, 287
William I Longsword, duke of Normandy 217, 260
William the Conqueror, duke of Normandy, king of England 20, 21, 22, 24, 65, 104, 119, 164, 218, 308
  coinage 47
  court 92
  creates New Forest 48
  crown-wearings 289
  death 24–5, 220, 260; funeral 25, 223, 259, 290
  frontiers 225
  and London 30, 249
  and papacy 255
  reform of church 255, 273
  regency in Normandy 107
  religious patronage 170, 240, 273
  Truce of God 219
William II Rufus king of England 64, 99, 100, 299
life:
  birth 21; youth 21; claim to succeed to throne 24, 191; as king 28, 29, 31, 34, 35, 36, 49, 99, 237, 244; and Anselm 51, 52, 72, 294; as guardian of Normandy 36–7; and Maine 37; death 38, 50, 287, 290, 316; funeral 25, 41, 52, 223, 259
character and personality:
  appearance 2; education 22; love of hunting 307; reputation for irreligion 274; reputation as warrior 94, 310; sexuality 308; taste in buildings 303, 306
other topics:
  Channel crossings 298; church 45; disorderly court 110; magnates 11; papacy 238; relations with Henry 27; relations with Scots 16, 36, 54, 92, 225; religious patronage 170, 210
William archdeacon of Evreux 101
William Baynard 121
  see also London, Baynard's Castle
William Bigod 167
William Bonne Ame, archbishop of Rouen 25, 101, 107, 137, 256
William Clito 143, 155, 163, 216
  assessment of 204–5
  his cause 118, 119, 121–2, 124, 126, 135, 137, 152–3, 155, 163, 168, 175, 179, 182, 188–9, 191, 192, 195–6, 228, 233, 320

at Falaise (1106) 96; betrothal to Sibyl of
    Anjou 181, 182, 204; annulled 190, 276,
    277
birth 73
death 203–4, 312, 320
and Flanders 8, 175, 197, 198, 199
granted the Vexin 196
guardianship of Count Helias 121, 159
offers terms 158
and revolt of 1123–4 184; aftermath 188
sheltered by Count Baldwin 134–5
tries to secure father's release 313
William count of Evreux 31, 73, 80, 89, 124, 126,
    139, 203, 204–5, 230, 233, 320
William count of Mortain 50, 59, 63, 64, 78, 81,
    86, 88, 89, 92, 93, 107, 110, 125, 216, 230,
    233, 278, 307, 313, 315, 316, 317
support for 125, 141, 153
William count of Nevers 135, 156, 159
William III Crispin 92, 101, 124, 126, 143, 152,
    154, 185, 230, 259
William I d'Aubigny 50, 62, 108, 244
William II d'Aubigny 170
William de Courcy 50, 62
William de Ferrers 90, 92, 96
William de Garlande 200
William de Mandeville 61
William de Pirou 164
William de Pont-de-l'Arche 207, 243,
    245
William de Tancarville 100, 102, 143, 147,
    151, 235, 295
William de Warenne 54, 63, 64, 66, 68,
    76, 90, 91, 108, 122, 151, 157, 158, 209,
    220
William FitzAnsger 251
William FitzOdo 103
William FitzOsbern 42, 73
William FitzOtto 250
William FitzStephen 67
William Giffard, bishop of Winchester 49, 73,
    134, 169, 182, 211
William Gouet 230
William Louvel (Lovel) 180, 186
William Malet 121, 230
William of Breteuil 30, 42, 73, 75, 147, 148, 230,
    316
William of Chaumont 154
William of Corbeil, archbishop of
    Canterbury 178, 179, 195, 263, 275, 276
at Henry's funeral 222–3
consecration 179
crowns Stephen 213, 222
granted Rochester castle 270
holds legatine council 199

and primacy 193, 195
St Martin's Dover 212
travels to Rome 272
William of Gael 73
William of Glastonbury 103
William of Grandcourt 288
William of Jumièges, *The Deeds of the Dukes of
    the Normans (Gesta Normannorum
    Ducum)* 7, 260
William of Malmesbury:
    and Bishop Roger 4, 195, 245
    comments on Henry I:
    appearance 2; education 3, 22; favourite
        oath 174, 307; hatred and friendships 313;
        and the magnates 231; and Normandy 253,
        320; meeting with pope (1119) 158;
        menagerie 5, 294; personality 3; love of
        peace 310
    History of the Kings of the English 2, 3, 5,
        30, 31, 32, 38, 39, 54, 60, 61, 66, 75, 93, 113,
        143, 162, 163, 164, 193, 194, 258, 289, 292,
        314
    History of Recent Events 193, 194, 208, 210,
        215
    other comments:
    Queen Matilda 2, 57, 58, 297; Robert of
        Meulan 292, 314; William Rufus 2
William of La Ferté-Fresnel 149
William of Newburgh 33
William of Pont-Authou 185
William of Rhuddlan 167, 288
William of Roumare 142, 180, 214, 229
William of Tyre 43
William of Ypres 197
William Pantulf 70, 71
William Peverel 35, 102
    of Dover 133
    of Nottingham 133
William son of Ansger 30
William son of Henry I 118, 291, 309
    at Brémule 152
    betrothal and marriage 126, 149, 182
    birth 58, 75, 317
    death 138, 165–7, 193
    pays homage 138, 162, 163, 228
    recognised as Henry's heir 134–5, 136, 137,
        290
William Talvas 125, 126, 142, 149, 162, 205, 217,
    218, 222, 233, 234, 317
William Trussebut 242, 243
William Warelwast, bishop of Exeter 51, 74,
    269, 275, 276
Wilton 54, 56, 57
Wiltshire 210, 280
    forests of 299

Winchester 20, 41, 42, 43, 63, 64, 67, 189, 249, 286, 287, 290, 299, 300
  bishop of 116
  bishops of, *see* Henry of Blois, William Giffard
  castle 42
  cathedral 131
  council (1141) 194
  crown-wearings 289, 303
  New Minster 265
  Old Minster, monk of 131
  treasury 203, 222, 298
Windsor 66, 128, 169, 171, 192, 193, 213, 299
  council at 130
  court 107
Wissant 52, 181, 298
Woodstock 5, 177, 179, 182, 212, 243, 308
  court at 207, 299, 301
  menagerie at 5, 294
Worcester:
  bishop of 115; *see also* Theulf
  chronicle composed at 7, 31, 92, 112, 209, 211, 213, 311
  monks of 311
  sheriff of 116; *see also* Urse d'Abetot
Wulfric of Haselbury 214, 297

York 20, 61, 86, 108, 131, 176, 265
  abbey of St Mary's 116, 130, 265
  abbot of, *see* Stephen abbot of York
  archbishops of 6, 116, 130, 131, 175, 225, 263, 270–1, 273; *see also* Gerard archbishop of York, Thomas I archbishop of York, Thomas II archbishop of York, Thurstan archbishop of York
  castles 244
  chronicler, *see* Hugh the Chanter
  hospital of St Leonard 21
Yorkshire 20, 70, 108, 211, 215, 252, 258, 279;
  sheriff of 116
Ypres 198
  see also William of Ypres